More praise for *Ancient Mysteries*

"COMPREHENSIVE . . . James and Thorpe view their subjects from a middle ground. They are not wide-eyed believers in every theory that comes to light, nor are they narrow-minded traditionalists. They seek to present explanations that are scientifically plausible, but in the end it is up to the reader to decide what he or she thinks."
—*Tampa Tribune & Times*

"COMPELLING . . . *Ancient Mysteries* will give you endless enjoyment. . . . A wide-ranging and richly detailed look at parts of our past that grab the imagination . . . The layout of this book is excellent; you can read it front to back or pick your way through its thoroughly cross-referenced pages, with one subject serendipitously leading to another. Sort of a 'Choose Your Own Adventure' book for adults."
—*BookPage*

And acclaim for *Ancient Inventions*

"FASCINATING . . . AMAZING . . . This book should be read by everyone interested in science or technology."
—*Nature*

"ENGROSSING . . . REWARDING . . . IMPRESSIVE . . . It is impossible not to be astonished."
—*New Scientist*

"IT'S CHOCKABLOCK WITH CURIOUS LORE. . . . [James and Thorpe] have amassed scores of persuasive testimonials of primeval ingenuity."
—*The Boston Globe*

"THOROUGHLY RESEARCHED . . . It is doubtful that anyone could examine [this book] without coming away enlightened in one of its broadly ranging areas."
—*Library Journal*

621

ANCIENT MYSTERIES

PETER JAMES
&
NICK THORPE

Ballantine Books · New York

A Ballantine Book
Published by The Random House Publishing Group

Copyright © 1999 by Peter James and Nick Thorpe

www.ballantinebooks.com

Library of Congress Card Number: 2001094426

ISBN-13: 978-0-307-29060-1
ISBN-10: 0-307-29060-3

Cover design by Christine Kell
Akivi Ahu Statues, Easter Island, Chile (Richard T. Nowitz/Corbis), Theseus slaying the Minotaur (Bettmann/Corbis), Stonehenge (Corbis), The Pyramids and Sphinx of Giza (Charles & Josette Lenars/Corbis), Pyramid (Corbis)

Printed in the United States of America

First Hardcover Edition: November 1999
First Trade Paperback Edition: November 2001

This edition printed in 2006

For Catherine (James), Louise (James), and Freya (Thorpe)

CONTENTS

ACKNOWLEDGMENTS

It would have been impossible to write a book of this scope without help from many friends and colleagues. To them we extend our warm thanks, as well as to those experts we contacted who were kind enough to respond to questions out of the blue:

Philip Attwood—medallist
Ruth Baker—linguist
Andrij Cholij—film buff
Dr. Victor Clube—astronomer
Dr. Garmon Harbottle—archaeological scientist
Bob Forrest—mathematician
Dr. Nikos Kokkinos—ancient historian/archaeologist
Brian Moore—librarian
Dr. Robert Morkot—Egyptologist
Dr. Bernard Ortiz de Montellano—anthropologist
Dr. Dino Politis—archaeologist
Bob Porter—engineer/archaeologist
Andrew Rosenbaum—journalist
Robert Temple—historian of science
Allison Thorpe—environmentalist
Dick Vigers—TV producer

Special thanks have to go to Peter Koenig for his painstaking work on the new illustrations; Leslie Primo and Nikos Kokkinos for taking photographs on research trips (England and the Aegean, respectively); Richard Dean for his usual and amazingly generous help in troubleshooting computer problems; Phil Marter and Geoff Couling for their timely production of two maps; Dr. Birgitta Wallace for her kindness in providing a selection of Viking illustrations; author Francis Hitching for permission to reproduce some of Ken Smith's drawings from the *World Atlas of Mysteries* (1978), as well as for setting Peter off (as researcher) in the mysteries field all those years ago; Rosemary Burnard for her drawing of Quetzalcoatl; Haydar Aksakal and the Alpinists club of Manisa for their extraordinary hospitality and help in Turkey, especially in getting Peter and Nikos to the throne of Pelops; Julie Clements of the Ashmolean for her kind help in finding photographs; Sue Hutchinson of the Griffith Institute for finding us photographs even when the institute was officially shut; the authorities of Glastonbury Abbey for allowing us to spend hours photographing it from every possible angle; and the Goulds for giving us access to Chalice Hill, a great vantage point for Glastonbury Tor.

At Ballantine we have to thank a succession of patient editors: Phebe Kirkham, Andrea Schulz, but most of all Elizabeth Zack. Last, but by no means least, thanks to our wonderful agent, Leslie Gardner, for looking after us so well.

Peter James and Nick Thorpe
London and Chichester, March 1999

Rather than attempting perfect consistency in our spelling of non-European names, we have used those forms which we feel will be most familiar to out readers. While we have expressed serious doubts about the conventional dates for the Egyptian New Kingdom (c. 1550–1070 B.C.) and the Late Bronze Age in the Old World (see our book *Centuries of Darkness*, 1991), we have kept to generally accepted chronology for this book.

After the publication of *Ancient Inventions*—which we're pleased to say was a great success—we were discussing another project when the idea was suggested to us of writing a book on "Ancient Mysteries"—the unsolved puzzles of lost civilizations and knowledge; the inexplicable monuments and earthworks built by the ancients; the strange messages conveyed by the world's great legends; the riddles of early exploration; and even apparent evidence of extraterrestrial and paranormal phenomena in ancient times. There were scores of compelling subjects, yet our initial reaction to the idea was mixed. The stores are already crammed with books on ancient mysteries, even some with that very title, so why add to the agony?

On reflection, we decided that there was actually an urgent need for a new book on the subject. Interest is burgeoning, but most books on ancient mysteries are written by authors with little, if any, background in the fields involved—which range from ancient history and archaeology to geology and astronomy. Many of these titles, full of amazing claims about lost civilizations, Atlanteans, extraterrestrial visitors, and the "secret wisdom" of the ancients, are frankly very badly researched and can be completely misleading. The authors do not treat the evidence critically, and deliberately overmystify subjects in order to convince readers that they are being told some awesome secret about the past.

On the other side of the coin are the ancient mysteries books written by professional historians and archaeologists. Unfortunately, these are usually sterile exercises in debunking, written with a closed rather than an inquiring mind. Their authors easily fall into a lecturing mode, telling their readers loudly and slowly that such and such is merely nonsense—a style particularly common in America. Perhaps here the dividing lines between conventional and unconventional views of the past have been drawn so sharply because of the battle between evolutionists and "creation scientists" over what should be taught in schools. Archaeologists have felt themselves under attack, and have sometimes responded by trying to claim a monopoly on the past. Those adopting this approach often belittle the interested but "ignorant" layperson, arguing that discussion should be left to the professionals. Theories developed by amateurs—or even academics from different fields—are often rejected wholesale as "fringe" or "cult" archaeology.

Professional archaeologists have also been concerned by the level of belief in such cult archaeology topics among their own students. To assess this, two surveys were carried out at Central Connecticut University in 1984 and 1994, with students asked their opinions on a variety of topics, including religion, the paranormal and controversial fringe theories in archaeology. The surveys showed that 27 percent accepted that Earth had been visited by extraterrestrials, rising to 31 percent by 1994; the reality of the curse of Tutankhamun was supported by 12 percent, doubling to 24 percent a decade later, and the existence of the lost continent of Atlantis was accepted by 29 percent in both surveys. (These figures compare closely to the answers provided by the general public.) Archaeologists have agonized over the gullibility and "ignorance" that they perceive these figures as showing. This is a rather arrogant attitude. For example, believing that extraterrestrials have visited the world is hardly a sign of ignorance! It all depends on how one reads the question. Astronomers are increasingly finding evidence that the raw materials necessary for life— such as water—are to be found in abundance elsewhere in the universe, and with every discovery the statistical likelihood increases that other technological civilizations exist—even some advanced enough to make the long trip to our solar system. The real question is whether there is any sound archaeological evidence for extraterrestrial visitations in the past. We do not feel there is, but would not call anyone who believed in them "ignorant"—nor, for that matter, people who have a belief in the efficacy of curses, which is as much a cultural judgment as a scientific one.

Books debunking "cult archaeology" also strongly imply that there are no ancient mysteries left, the professionals having sorted everything out nicely. Pat, rather than realistic, answers are freely offered. Discussions of the controversial Vinland Map, for example, are often limited to the bald statement that examination of the map with a light microscope in 1974 showed conclusively that it is a fake. This blithely ignores other scientific examinations carried out subsequently that do not agree with the original findings, ruining the neat story of the honest professionals triumphing over the rascally hoaxer. The real story of the Vinland Map is far more complex. Similarly, the immediate response to the seemingly outrageous claim that the Dogon tribe of Mali have inherited accurate knowledge of the movements of the stars in the Sirius system, brought thousands of years ago by space-traveling amphibians, was that the Dogon must have picked up such knowledge from western missionaries. The possibility that such supposedly "primitive" groups could have actually taken a detailed interest in the heavens was barely discussed, although there are indeed other nonwestern observers who appear to have made remarkable discoveries without the aid of telescopes. Again, the Dogon question is far more complicated than the skeptics understand, part of the problem lying with the research methods of the anthropologist who reported the Dogon beliefs about Sirius.

It is actually completely unreasonable to claim that archaeologists and historians are agreed on the solutions to most ancient mysteries. Nothing could be farther from the truth. The drive behind the ancient desire to sculpt and pattern the landscape—producing wonders like the Nazca lines—still eludes the understanding of archaeologists. Even major events such as the dramatic collapse of the Maya civilization of Central America remain completely unexplained despite a century of investigation. As different explanatory trends come and go, solutions ranging from natural catastrophe to warfare have been offered—with no sign of a consensus emerging. The recent breakthrough in deciphering the Maya language has laid to rest many long-established misconceptions about Maya society, but we are still no nearer to agreeing on the cause of its sudden fall.

On the historical side, the very existence, for example, of King Arthur, famed in British legend, is still hotly disputed, with opinions ranging from the simple assumption that he must have existed to the equally unfounded assertion that he could not have. Exactly the same is true of almost all legendary or semi-legendary people, events and even places, from the Trojan War to the biblical cities of Sodom and Gomorrah. Disputes rage even over events in well-documented historical times—the identity of Robin Hood, the greatest hero of medieval England, remains a complete mystery, further confused by the existence of several possible candidates.

In many cases, continuing inability to produce a convincing solution to a given ancient mystery can derive from a narrowness of approach. Many historians and archaeologists stick rigidly within their fields of study and are blissfully unaware of anything happening outside them; for example, they take little, if any interest in astronomy. Part of the problem is that most academics live and work in crowded cities where the objects in the night sky are barely visible. Many ancient historians and classicists lack even a basic grounding in astronomy, and treat the subject with the same aversion as they do astrology or UFOs. However, one would expect them to keep abreast of current developments in the field, which have made it quite clear just how crowded our skies actually are with potentially menacing objects, from comets to asteroids. These mean that ancient legends of destruction from the sky, such as the devastation of Sodom and Gomorrah, will have to be reexamined with a completely open mind.

While we would ask the professionals to be more open-minded and self-critical, that is not to say that amateurs in history and archaeology always get it right. Graham Hancock became world famous for his book *Fingerprints of the Gods*, which presents a case for a lost civilization in Antarctica having built many of the world's ancient architectural wonders, including the Sphinx in Egypt and the city of Tiahuanaco in Bolivia, some 11,000 years ago. Although Hancock is a professional journalist, he presents a remarkably one-sided and often outdated view of the human past, which, in our opinion, denies the true builders the credit for building these impressive monuments.

In this book we have tried to chart a middle course between the uncritical enthusiasts and the professional skeptics. Each of the topics covered steers the reader through the main lines of evidence and most frequently offered explanations, although these cannot, of course, be exhaustive. We present our opinions not as fact but as an attempt at a reasoned conclusion from the material, rather than starting from a position of acceptance or rejection. We have tried to condense and present enough evidence on each mystery for readers to judge for themselves and, we hope, have fun devising their own solutions.

Finally, we have tried to make the scope of this book as wide as possible. Our definition of "ancient" is very broad and follows that used in *Ancient Inventions*, with a cutoff point at A.D. 1492. With Columbus's voyage to America and the Renaissance in Europe in full swing, the ancient world can then truly be said to have come to a close. But we apologize to those readers who find that some of their favorite ancient mysteries are not covered here, owing to lack of space. Our choice was a personal one, made from those subjects we saw as the most significant, intractable, or remarkable of the mysteries presented by the ancient world.

CHAPTER ONE

LOST LANDS
AND
CATASTROPHES

INTRODUCTION

On July 16, 1994, a small fragmenting comet known as Shoemaker-Levy began ripping through the atmosphere of the planet Jupiter, causing explosions of almost unimaginable intensity. As the second fragment fell there was a blast equivalent to 250 million tons of TNT—several times more powerful than all the world's nuclear arsenals put together. When the third chunk of the comet struck it created a hole in Jupiter's atmosphere the size of the Earth. The full extent of the damage that Shoemaker-Levy inflicted on Jupiter is still being assessed, though one thing is already

Noah sacrificing after the Flood. From an early-19th-century family Bible.

perfectly clear: the long-cherished scientific belief that comets are harmless and cannot crash into planets has been dispelled forever.

The question immediately arises—could a comet, or cometary fragment, crash into the Earth? Or has it already done so? In the seventeenth and eighteenth centuries, in the days before Darwin, scientists freely speculated about such matters, wondering whether a comet might have been responsible for the Great Flood described in the Bible. While theologians were happy to accept that the Flood was caused by God directly, scientists were busy researching possible physical mechanisms. Some, including the great Edmond Halley (who gave his name to the famous comet), looked beyond the Earth for a trigger. In 1694 he proposed, in a paper to the Royal Society, that Noah's Flood was caused by the collision between the Earth and a comet, which landed in the Caspian Sea and drenched the surrounding lands with water. Others speculated that a watery comet was responsible.

From the standpoint of pre-Darwinian science, belief in a Great Flood was entirely reasonable, as such an event seemed to explain many of the world's greatest historical enigmas. The rocks that scientists were beginning to examine were full of the fossilized remains of millions of extinct plants and creatures, and a catastrophic flood could account for why these life-forms no longer existed and why their remains had been trapped and preserved in sedimentary rock. It seemed natural, then, to borrow an explanation from the Bible, which told of the deluge in the time of Noah. Assuming that there had been a real Flood also provided an economical explanation for why there are so many similar legends around the world.

Such quaint ideas went completely out of fashion in the early nineteenth century. The relatively new science of geology was maturing, and the naive view that all the world's rock strata had been laid down in a single event was seen to be unworkable. It was becoming clear that there was a whole sequence of layers from different ages, laid one upon the other, each containing its own life-forms. The question now was what had created these strata and how long they took to form. One school of geology was the catastrophists, who expanded the idea of a Great Flood into a whole series of cataclysms—sometimes of water, sometimes of fire (from volcanic activity). Their opponents represented a new school of thought—the uniformitarians. Founded in the 1830s by lawyer Charles Lyell, they set new ground rules for the debate. Geologists generally agreed that special causes—such as direct divine intervention—should be excluded from scientific discussion, and Lyell now introduced his principles of "uniformity," which attempted to rule out special events as well.

The law of uniformity states that the "present is the key to the past": only the same forces that are visible today were responsible for shaping the world. On a general level this makes perfect sense. There is no point assuming that the laws of physics were once different and, for example, that gravity had no effect a million years ago. On the other hand, Lyell and his followers excluded the possibility of anything happening in the past that is not observable now: there were no great deluges, global conflagrations, impacts by comets, or other major catastrophes for the simple reason that such things do not happen today. (Had they witnessed something like the Shoemaker-Levy event, they might have thought very differently about comets.) Instead, the uniformitarians argued, the Earth's strata had been laid down gradually over millions of years.

It was easy for Lyell and his followers to characterize catastrophism as smacking of old-time religion, and to present themselves as progressive and scientific. Catastrophist geologists—most of whom were just as secular in outlook as their opponents—were forced into retreat, and the triumph of Charles Darwin sealed their fate. When Darwin published his controversial *Origin of Species* in 1859, he chose to fit his theory of evolution into a uniformitarian, gradualist mold. Evolution as such does not require a gradual path—in fact, the fossil record suggests that all major changes have been very rapid. Yet Darwin, despite his own observations in South America of the sudden and catastrophic demise of its prehistoric fauna, elected for gradualism. Part of the reason must have been to be on the "winning side." The other was that the uniformitarians, like Darwin, inevitably challenged the literal truth of the Bible.

By this stage, catastrophism, antievolutionism, and biblical fundamentalism had become nicely muddled—at least in the minds of Darwinians. When Darwinism won the debate, catastrophism was thought to have been debunked, along with the stories of Adam and Eve and Noah's Flood. Here there was another force at work besides the desire to develop a rationalist view of the Earth's history free from biblical influence. This was the straightforward desire—shared by scientists with the rest of us—to view the Earth as a safe place to live. This desire was the root cause of a fierce and protracted philosophical debate that had been raging for over two thousand years. On the one side was Plato, who used the evidence of myth and legend (as well as his own gleanings from geology and archaeology) to argue that the

Charles Darwin (1809–1882), as lampooned in a contemporary cartoon.

Earth had been subject to periodic catastrophes brought about by causes outside our world. On the other side was his pupil Aristotle, who insisted that as the heavens were made of perfect matter they could present no dangers to the Earth.

Aristotle's cozy worldview had been steadily eroded since the Middle Ages, but in the eighteenth century it managed to sneak back into scientific thinking through the work of Sir Isaac Newton. His hidden agenda was to restore an Aristotelian worldview, in which the world was protected from catastrophe by Divine Providence. In 1708, when his star pupil, mathematician William Whiston, published a book arguing that a comet had caused Noah's Flood, Newton turned on him and started a campaign to wreck his career.

Newton, Lyell and Darwin made a formidable combination. From the late nineteenth century onward, catastrophist theories were sidelined, at least in Britain, then the leader of the world's scientific trends.

Matters were not helped by the stream of books on lost lands and catastrophes that began to pour from the pens of writers on the wilder fringe of archaeology. The idea of a lost continent in the Atlantic, first written about by Plato, became a favorite topic, particularly among those who claimed they had psychic sources of information about the supercivilization of "Atlantis" (see **Edgar Cayce on Atlantis** in **Archaeology and the Supernatural**). Not content with one lost continent, some of these writers invented a partner for Atlantis called Mu or Lemuria, which began its literary career in the Indian Ocean but later expanded into the Pacific. Despite numerous claims to the contrary, absolutely nothing about it is based in genuine myth or legend.

The name Mu comes from that of "Queen Moo" of Atlantis, which Augustus le Plongeon (1826–1908), an eccentric pioneer of Central American archaeology, mistakenly believed he could read in the texts of the ancient Maya of Central America. (According to le Plongeon, the Maya came from Atlantis.) The alternative name Lemuria came about in the late nineteenth century when the great German naturalist Ernst Haeckel suggested that a land-bridge stretching across the Indian Ocean from Madagascar to India might explain the widespread distribution of the small tree-dwelling mammals called lemurs. An English naturalist, Philip Sclater, soon afterward coined the name "Lemuria." There was never any solid evidence for such a land-bridge—an idea that became redundant after the discovery of continental drift—yet this did not stop occult theorists from developing Lemuria into the "real" homeland of the human race.

Lemuria was taken to its greatest heights in the writings of Madame

Helena Blavatsky, the eccentric Russian émigré who founded the Theosophical Society in London in 1875. Theosophy blended the teachings of Christianity and Buddhism with mystical revelations that Blavatsky claimed to have received personally from "Secret Masters," mysterious guardians of an ancient tradition who lived in hidden cities in Tibet. The Masters revealed to her the true history of the Earth, including a succession of strange "races" that had inhabited the world before our own species emerged. The Third Race, which had lived on Lemuria, were egg-laying hermaphrodites, sometimes with four arms and an eye in the back of their heads. According to some Theosophist writers, these Lemurians evolved into a Fourth Race, strapping giants up to 15 feet tall who led around pet dinosaurs on leashes. Lemuria/Mu, like Atlantis, was thought to have been destroyed by earthquakes and sunk beneath the waves.

With enthusiasts like the occultists, catastrophism had little need for enemies. By the middle of this century the idea of past global upheavals was treated by scientists with abhorrence. It was extremely unfortunate timing for Immanuel Velikovsky, who produced an extreme catastrophist model for solar system history in 1950 (see **The Day the Sun Stood Still?** in **Watching the Skies**).

Yet catastrophism is now making a serious comeback—because of the sheer weight of hard evidence in its favor. The geological evidence is, in fact, perfectly clear: all the great epochs in Earth's history ended with the complete extermination of vast numbers of lifeforms. During the 1960s a trickle, then a steady stream, of scientific studies began to appear correlating the great extinctions with other upheavals of nature—including massive changes in climate, dramatic fluctuations in sea level, peaks of volcanic activity, and even reversals of the Earth's magnetic field. Far from being quiet, it now seems that Earth's history has been shaped by massive catastrophes, sometimes of global proportions. Of course gradual processes—of the kind we see today—have always played their part. The uniformitarians were right to stress these, but utterly wrong in excluding catastrophes. As put by Derek Ager, Professor of Geology at the University of Bristol, England, and a pioneer in the renaissance of catastrophist thinking, "the history of any one part of the earth, like the life of a soldier, consists of long periods of boredom and short periods of terror."

So what was behind the great upheavals that had punctuated the Earth's history? In some cases, such as the massive catastrophe that ended the Cretaceous period and wiped out the dinosaurs, some 65 million years ago, the answer is quite clear. It is now beyond reasonable doubt that at the end of the Cretaceous the world was struck with devastating effect by an asteroid.

The first hard evidence came in 1980, when Walter Alvarez, a geologist from the University of California at Berkeley, found anomalous levels of the rare element iridium in the last Cretaceous layers at Gubbio in northern Italy. Iridium is not found in the Earth's crust but occurs in abundance in asteroids, meteorites, and comets. By 1984 the number of Cretaceous sites with similar levels of iridium had already risen to as many as sixty-six. The search was on for traces of an impact crater that would clinch the asteroid case. Amazingly a candidate was soon identified near the Gulf of Mexico, at Chicxulub on the Yucatán Peninsula. The original size of this crater is hard to determine, but even at the minimum estimate of 110 miles in diameter, Chicxulub is the biggest impact crater on Earth yet discovered. The projectile that formed it must have been between 6.5 and 9.5 miles in size, about the same size as the nucleus of Halley's comet. When it hit, the asteroid would have thrown up millions of tons of debris, which would have rained down over the entire globe. Everything near the point of impact would have been killed by the shock waves, while the enormous clouds of dust raised would block out the sun and introduce a sudden and prolonged "winter," like that which would follow a nuclear holocaust.

Whether the Chicxulub impact was the *sole* cause of the death of the dinosaurs is a moot point. Another, smaller crater has also been identified at Manson, Iowa, and it may well be that the Cretaceous period ended with a whole series of bombardments, as well as a choking of the Earth's atmosphere by cometary dust. Yet the evidence for an extraterrestrial cause is now so strong that there is simply no point looking for gradualist explanations anymore.

The impact that killed the dinosaurs was certainly not a unique event. Evidence has been steadily coming to light that *all* the great extinctions were brought about by outside causes. Anomalous amounts of iridium have been found in the final layers of other geological epochs, and have now come into play in the controversy over one of the greatest of geological mysteries—the Ice Ages. There were several Ice Ages, but the best investigated was the last, when glacial sheets covered huge tracts of North America and Europe (110,000–9000 B.C.). On the fringes of this icy world lived our Stone Age ancestors, hunter-gatherers who competed for existence with a variety of gigantic mammals—including the mammoths, mastodons, saber-toothed tigers, and giant sloths.

Despite many confident pronouncements in the past, the real cause of the Ice Ages is still unknown, but recent core drillings into the ancient ice of Greenland have provided dramatic new evidence that may lead to an answer. It has been shown that the amount of extraterrestrial dust settling on the Earth between 20,000 and 14,000 years ago was a hundred times the present-day quantity. This dust is especially rich in iridium, as well as nickel, another element abundant in comets. In fact, it shows the same exotic chemistry as that left by the

Maximum extent of the ice sheet over Europe during the last Ice Age (c. 60,000–10,000 B.C.).

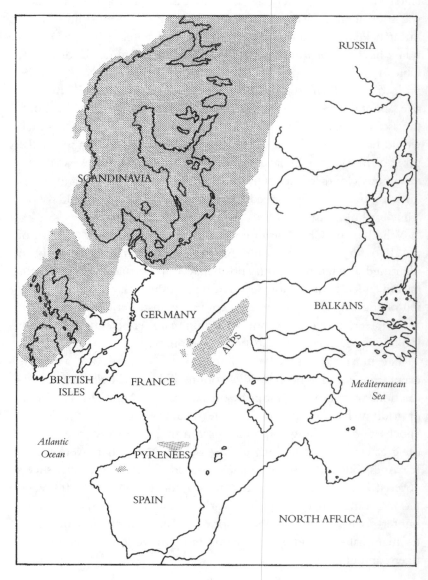

cometary fragment that exploded over Tunguska in 1908 (see **The Day the Sun Stood Still?** in **Watching the Skies**).

This huge amount of dust was the very cause of the Ice Ages, in the opinion of two senior British astronomers, Dr. Victor Clube of Oxford University and Dr. Bill Napier of the Armagh Observatory (Northern Ireland). They have spent years tracking the asteroids, comets, meteor streams, and other cosmic debris that surround our planet. Much of this material seems to be fragments from much larger "parent" bodies; one in particular has been on an Earth-crossing orbit for thousands of years as it disintegrated, and now survives partly as the small body known as Encke's comet. Clube and Napier are now developing their theory that the last Ice Age was caused by an early phase in the breakup of its ancestor, a giant comet they refer to as "Proto-Encke." Material from it formed a stream on an earth-crossing orbit, liberally dusting our planet with the extraterrestrial material that has been found in the ice cores. The dust would have formed a screen blocking out the Sun's rays, and the global drop in temperature would have caused the Ice Age.

Clube and Napier's modeling of this "gradual" catastrophe is still in progress and cannot be properly tested until the iridium levels in ice layers throughout the Ice Age have been thoroughly examined. The high levels of iridium from 20,000 to 14,000 years ago correspond to the time of the last Glacial Maximum, when the ice sheets were at their greatest extent. So does this mean that the extraterrestrial dust caused, or merely aggravated, Ice Age conditions?

And what of the amazing suddenness with which the last Ice Age ended? In 1998 scientists working on ice cores from Greenland announced that just over 11,000 years ago the temperature shot up by 9 to 18 degrees Fahrenheit—at least a third of the total recovery to today's warmth—in possibly less than a single decade. "That amount of heating, coming so quickly, is astounding," remarked one of the investigators, Dr. Richard Alley of Pennsylvania State University. With the change in climate the ice sheets melted and sea levels rose rapidly. At the same time, the giant animals that flourished during the Ice Age were all wiped out—by a cause or causes unknown. Was the rise in temperature itself responsible? This seems unlikely, as it would have been easy enough for tough, successful animals like mammoths and saber-toothed tigers simply to migrate to cooler regions. Or were the giant fauna of the Ice Age hunted to extinction by our Stone Age people? Again, while hunting might have contributed in a small way, it seems too far-fetched to imagine that our ancestors were so short of

Engraving of mammoth
from Ice Age Europe.

food or so genocidal that this forms a sensible explanation (see **The First Americans** in **Voyagers and Discoveries**).

There is also evidence that the Earth's magnetic field was upset near the end of the last Ice Age, and the theory has been recently revived that the North and South Poles themselves moved their positions—caused by the Earth's crust slipping over its interior (see **Poleshift** in this chapter). Every volcano around the globe would have blown at the same time, raising immense clouds of dust. Yet this would have tended to reduce global temperature, perpetuating the Ice Age rather than concluding it. Clube and Napier feel that the close of the Ice Age came about when the source of the extraterrestrial dusting of the atmosphere expired, as Proto-Encke finished one stage of its long disintegration. Again, this cannot be the whole answer—the *ending* of a long period during which the Earth was bombarded with extraterrestrial material can hardly explain the sheer violence of the events that happened about 11,000 years ago. The end, like the beginning, of the last Ice Age still remains one of the Earth's great mysteries. As in so many scientific areas, the more we learn, the more we realize we do not yet understand.

Evidence is now accumulating to show that global catastrophes continued to occur beyond the remote epochs of the dinosaurs and mammoths—and well into the times of the earliest civilizations when our ancestors began to keep written records and compose the first epics and religious literature. Reconstructing the history of the super comet Proto-Encke, Clube and Napier arrived at the startling conclusion that some of its major periods of fragmentation occurred during the Bronze Ages, when the first civilizations of Egypt and Mesopotamia (Iraq) were flourishing. While they are not talking about catastrophes on the scale of that which finished the dinosaurs, their model predicts that there would have been frequent impacts from the stream of debris created by Proto-Encke. At certain dates—for example, about 2000 B.C.—the risk would have been the greatest.

Though historians and archaeologists are tending to drag their feet on the question of extraterrestrial impacts in ancient times, there is no shortage of evidence that Clube and Napier's model is realistic. Bronze Age texts are chock-full of references to the frightening prodigies seen in the sky, of "gods" who rained stones, fire, and poison on the lands.

There is also solid archaeological evidence for almost global upheavals over the same period of time. As long ago as 1948, the eminent French archaeologist Claude Schaeffer detected a pattern in the destructions of ancient Near Eastern sites. At every ancient city he examined he found three main breaks in culture—at the ends of the Early, Middle, and Late Bronze Ages, about 2300, 1500, and 1200 B.C. respectively. Schaeffer had some doubts about what caused the last upheaval, but was convinced that the Early and Middle Bronze Age civilizations of the Near East had been literally shaken to the ground by earthquakes. At the time Schaeffer published, geologists doubted that such widespread tectonic upheavals were possible, so archaeologists could safely ignore his theory. Yet knowledge has moved on. In the opinion of geologist Amos Nur, Professor of Geophysics and Earth Sciences at Stanford University, upheavals of the scale that Schaeffer envisaged were not only possible but *likely* to have happened.

The perplexing thing is that the breaks in civilization that Schaeffer highlighted were also accompanied by dramatic changes in climate. There is now ample evidence that, at the end of the Late Bronze Age in the Mediterranean, cities suffered both earthquakes and drought, due to a sudden shift to a hotter, drier climate. Even more devastating was the climate change that occurred about 2300 B.C., at the end of the Early Bronze Age. In Egypt, the level of the Nile dropped dramatically, bringing to an end the age of the great pyramid builders. (See **How Were the Pyramids Built?** in **Architectural Wonders**). To the west of Egypt the effects were even worse. Though it is still little known, the Saharan region of North Africa was once home to peoples who for thousands of years lived, raised cattle, and grew crops in a comparatively lush, green environment. Today we know them mainly through the unique rock paintings they left, such as those at Tassili (800 miles south of Algiers), which were accidentally discovered by a French soldier in 1933. In a landscape where barely a plant or an insect now survives, there are hundreds upon hundreds of such paintings—depicting elephants, hippopotami, rhinoceroses, ostriches, giraffes, antelopes, cows, and sheep as well as people working, hunting and worshiping—silent witnesses to an irretrievably lost world. About 2300 B.C. the catastrophe struck, rivers and inland lakes dried up, and with it the culture of the rock painters shriveled and eventually died. The Sahara Desert as we know it was largely formed from this event.

An extraterrestrial cause—such as meteorite impacts—could explain both the earthquakes and the climate change at the end of the Early Bronze Age. This extraordinary possibility means that a new look at some of the ancient legends of sky-borne disasters—such as those preserved in the Bible—is timely. Is there any truth, after all, in the much-derided story of the lost cities of Sodom and Gomorrah?

The "Martian god" from Tassili. Not an alien, but someone wearing a tribal mask, as similar scenes show.

From a time when the Sahara was green—rock painting from Tin Tazarift near Tassili showing people herding cattle.

And what of the greatest catastrophe legend of all, the worldwide story of a Great Flood? The Flood story still remains one of the most baffling, unsolved mysteries of our distant past. Only biblical fundamentalists accept the story in the completely literal sense that the entire world was covered by a single deluge, from which Noah and his family were the sole survivors. Despite the best efforts of creationist scientists, they have never been able to agree among themselves on a model that can explain the Earth's strata in terms of the Flood, let alone produce one that is convincing to secular scientists.

Atlantologists, of course, have tried to explain the origin of the Flood legends by the sinking of Atlantis—survivors fled to different parts of the globe, bringing with them similar versions of the same events. But the theory is only credible if we accept the existence of a lost Atlantic continent.

The longest-standing explanation of the Flood legends is that the story spread from the ancient Near East, having grown from a real but localized event, which struck some of the earliest cities of southern Mesopotamia. In 1928 British archaeologist Sir Leonard Woolley was excavating the Sumerian city of Ur when, underneath a city dating to c. 3500 B.C., he came across a thick layer of "clean water-laid mud." Somewhat puzzled, he continued digging and eight feet farther down he found flint implements and pottery again—remains of an earlier phase of the city *before* the mud was laid down. It was Woolley's wife who voiced their suspicions about the cause of the mysterious sediment layer: "Well, of course, it's the Flood."

It seemed easy enough to deduce that a great flood had swept across southern Mesopotamia, and that from there the story had spread, giving rise to different but closely related versions around the Near East and Eastern Mediterranean. Small details changed, such as the name of the hero who survived the Flood, known in Mesopotamia as Utnapishtim—the Hebrews called him Noah, while the Greeks remembered the Flood of Deucalion. Woolley's "Flood level" at Ur is still frequently cited as if the mystery were completely solved. Yet matters are not quite so simple. The flood discovered by Woolley doesn't seem to have been that important, as it caused no real break in culture at Ur. Nor was it that extensive. There is no trace of the same mud level at other cities, even at Ubaid, a mere twenty miles away. Other cities have evidence of equally great floods. For example, another British archaeologist, Sir Max Mallowan (the husband of Agatha Christie), identified a slightly later sediment layer at another Sumerian city, Kish, as traces of the Flood. Yet Mallowan's candidate suffers from the same problems as Woolley's—it was extremely localized and not that disastrous. In fact, flood levels are common at Mesopotamian sites. The twin rivers, Tigris and Euphrates, around which Mesopotamian civilization grew, were an ever-present danger, as well as a blessing, and there are many textual references to massive local floods. Yet the ancient Mesopotamians, rather like the people who live today in the tornado belt of Texas, Oklahoma, Kansas and Nebraska, seem to have taken such disasters in their stride. It is hard to believe that such local floods could have inspired the myth of a universal deluge.

Unconvinced by the Mesopotamian theory, biblical scholar John Bright argued in 1942 that the Flood legend must date much earlier than the fourth millennium B.C., possibly reflecting a real catastrophe of much greater dimensions "taking place far back in the Stone Age." In the last couple of years a fascinating new theory proposed by two

American geologists would seem to fit the bill. Ever since the end of the Ice Age the world's sea levels have been rising, usually gradually, but sometimes in fits and starts. Bill Ryan and Walt Pitman, marine geologists at the Lamont-Doherty Earth Observatory in New York, have proposed that a catastrophic episode around 7000 B.C. completely transformed the Black Sea. During the Ice Age it seems that sea levels were so low that the Black Sea, surrounded as it is by the Balkans, southern Russia, and Turkey, was like a gigantic freshwater lake, unconnected with the salty Mediterranean. Separating the two seas was a plug of sediment where the Bosphorus Straits now lie. Ryan and Pitman argue that as the level of the Mediterranean rose, the pressure of the water on this plug would have reached a critical point, with the sea bursting through about 7000 B.C. With this sudden onrush, all the coasts of the Black Sea would have been swamped and their inhabitants driven farther afield. If some migrated southward to Mesopotamia, they could have preserved memories of this catastrophe as the legend of the Great Flood.

Ryan and Pitman's new theory has much to recommend it. Both the biblical and Babylonian traditions locate the place of refuge of the Flood survivors in the mountains to the north of Mesopotamia (Ararat), the high ground just to the south of the Black Sea coast. But while it is intriguing, their theory doesn't quite reach to the heart of the Flood problem—which is why there are so many similarities to the Flood legends *globally*. (Only Africa seems to lack many examples.)

One of John Bright's reasons for challenging the old Mesopotamian theory was that native Americans have flood legends strikingly similar to those of the Bible and the Sumerians. He felt that these could have spread only by diffusion, at the time that the Amerindians were thought to have crossed the Bering Strait from Asia into the New World—a migration now dated to at least 10,000 B.C., or possibly several thousand years before that (see **The First Americans** in **Voyagers and Discoveries**). Pushing the date for a common origin of the world's Flood legends so many thousands of years back begins to feel uncomfortable, yet brings us, strangely enough, to a time when there *was* widespread flooding. The rapid melting of the ice sheets and dramatic rise in sea levels at the end of the Ice Age, about 9000 B.C., might have inspired legends of a global Flood.

But matters are complicated further by the kind of similarities that exist between Old and New World Flood legends. Many of the common elements—such as the hero building an "ark" in which he rescues his family and animals—might be explained as "logical" developments. If two peoples shared a belief that the whole world was once flooded, they might deduce that the survivors had been saved by building an enormous boat. Much more difficult to explain are curious similarities of small detail. Just as the first act of Noah after the deluge was to plant vines, make wine, and become leglessly drunk (Genesis 9:20–21), so did the Maya of Central America believe that the "four hundred" sons who survived the Flood (in their case by turning into fish) set about brewing *pulque*: they became so drunk that they ascended to heaven to become the constellation Pleiades. Strangely enough the Pleiades crop up again in an extrabiblical Hebrew tradition: a medieval rabbinical text states that the deluge was caused when God removed two stars from the Pleiades, forming holes through which the waters of the firmament rushed. Conceivably the recurrence of the Pleiades in both Old and New World Flood traditions might have its roots in astronomical reality—if, for example, floods had been caused in both areas by a comet or meteorite seen to have approached the Earth from the direction of that constellation. Yet no such natural explanation could explain why the culture heroes who survived the Mayan and biblical floods were both associated with alcohol. A possible solution—the spread of stories by diffusion in pre-Columbian times—seems unlikely given the lack of other evidence for such contacts (see **Introduction** to **Voyagers and Discoveries**). Or were these tales brought by the Amerindians when they arrived in the New World? In this case, their diffusion would predate the end of the Ice Age and we no longer have a natural event that could plausibly explain their origin.

So at present the conundrum of the world's Flood stories remains unsolved, even in catastrophist terms. In other respects the new school of catastrophism has gone from strength to strength. Clube and Napier have been joined by other British astronomers and scientists in developing a new school of thought known as "coherent catastrophism," which can tie in a vast range of data from the death of the dinosaurs to the mysterious explosion that took place over Tunguska, Siberia, in 1908. (See **The Day the Sun Stood Still?** in **Watching the Skies**). The new catastrophism that is emerging is quite different from all earlier approaches. It invokes only agents and forces that can be detected—the meteorites, asteroids and cometary fragments are there for all to see. It doesn't need to rearrange the solar system, as proposed in the bold model of planetary catastrophism expounded by Immanuel Velikovsky in the 1950s. And while it is fully accepted that whole civilizations—such as that which was once developing in a green Sahara—can be wiped out by catastrophes, the idea of losing whole continents is no longer thought plausible. Even the most speculative writers, these days, shy away from the task of plunging a whole continent beneath the waves—though by identifying Antarctica as the homeland of a lost civilization, some have recently introduced a novel way of making a continent "disappear," by putting one under ice.

Catastrophism has clearly won the day, yet it shouldn't be turned into a catchall explanation for every puzzling change in history. The Mayan civilization of Central America mysteriously disappeared in the ninth century A.D. and many archaeologists have readily suggested catastrophic causes, such as massive floods and hurricanes. The Maya themselves strongly believed in a system of World Ages, each ended by fire or flood. Yet their own demise seems to have been due to a catastrophe of a different sort. Ironically enough, a major factor in their downfall was their own paranoid fears of cosmic disaster.

The Maya may have been wrong in dreading a natural catastrophe, but we would do well to follow their lead in being cautious. Reversing Lyell's dogma that the "present is the key to the past," we should now begin to see the past as the key to the present—and future. The collapse of so many ancient civilizations and cultures from natural disasters should surely give us pause for thought.

Two decades ago some scientists were arrogantly predicting the impending arrival of a new Ice Age—despite global warming. (One British scientist, with fantastic carelessness, predicted both effects in consecutive radio interviews within two days.) Researching the causes of the last Ice Age is not an academic exercise of interest only to geologists; it is research that will provide vital evidence for our continued existence. Until we know what causes ice ages, we cannot honestly understand the history of our planet's climate. Sea levels and global temperature seem to have been steadily rising since the last Ice Age. Why? It would be best to arm ourselves with some answers to these questions so that we can assess how seriously our own misbehavior is contributing to the problems.

ATLANTIS—LOST AND FOUND?

The very name Atlantis has a romantic, magical ring to it. It conjures an indelible image of a continent, once home to a high civilization of unimaginable antiquity, but now lost beneath the waves of the Atlantic. As an icon, Atlantis is as potent and as lasting as any in western civilization—from the Holy Grail to the idea of a Superman—and it has inspired mystics, philosophers, and writers for well over two thousand years.

The most familiar images of Atlantis are those from science fiction, developed by dozens of authors since the time of Jules Verne. In *Twenty Thousand Leagues under the Sea* (1869), Verne's hero Pierre Arronax is taken on an undersea walk by Captain Nemo, who shows him crumbling ruins and rows of mighty columns like Greek temples, festooned with a thick mantle of seaweed. Arronax is agog at the signs of this high civilization, older than any known to history. The scene, naturally, is the bottom of the Atlantic, traditional resting place of the lost continent.

It is a strangely poignant image. The idea that there were people like us, almost another human race, who developed a civilization before time began, has a strong romantic appeal. Moreover, millions have accepted the reality of Atlantis almost as an article of faith. The claims of supposed nonfiction writers are no less fantastic than those of Verne and his successors. Literally hundreds of books have been written claiming to reconstruct Atlantean civilization from scraps of information drawn from mythology, archaeology, and geology. The general line is that Atlantis was completely destroyed in a massive catastrophe about 12,000 years ago, at the time the mammoths died and the last great Ice Age ended. It is argued to have been the grandmother of all civilizations, with the apparently ancient cultures of Egypt, Mesopotamia, and Central America as mere offshoots. Its civilization is thought to have been as advanced as, or even more advanced than, our own. The Atlanteans were either wiped out by a natural upheaval—such as an asteroid impact or massive shift in the Earth's crust—or even destroyed themselves by madcap experiments with "cosmic" energies.

It has often been argued, or assumed, that the Atlanteans had an awesome, though rather occult, grasp of technology. Using the mysterious properties of crystals, they dabbled with forces best left alone and succeeded in wiping themselves out in a nuclear holocaust. These ideas have been seriously suggested in a number of works, mainly by those who claim to be able to derive information on Atlantis by psychic means (see **Edgar Cayce on Atlantis** in **Archaeology and the Supernatural**).

Plato's Atlantis

Before examining the many and varied theories about Atlantis, we need to go back to the beginning and see where the idea of this lost supercontinent came from in the first place.

Most people have an idea that Atlantis has something to do with Greek myth and legend, but that is only partly correct. The origin of the Atlantis story lies in the ancient Greek world, but it is not strictly speaking a myth or legend like the stories of Jason and the Argonauts, of Theseus and the Minotaur or of the Trojan War (see **Introduction** to **Legendary History**). Such tales were the common property of the ancient Greek people, related and shaped over the centuries by poets, playwrights and storytellers. People disagreed on details, but the stories were generally agreed on, part of a shared heritage going back to the Bronze Age. The Atlantis story is a different case entirely, as we basically have the word of only *one* person, the Athenian philosopher Plato (429–347 B.C.). Other Greek authors later discussed Atlantis, but their ideas are clearly derivative.

When Plato described Atlantis, in two of his short dialogues, he was not relying on the usual Greek traditions. He claimed to have a special source—his distant relative, the politician and poet Solon (c. 615–535 B.C.). Solon had traveled widely throughout the Mediterranean, and one of his ports of call was Egypt. Already famous as a wise man, Solon was able to interview the priests of the city of Sais in the Egyptian Delta. According to Plato, Solon asked them about "old things," the most ancient matters that their records included, and the priests replied with a quite incredible tale.

First they laughed at the stories Solon presented as the oldest memories of the Greeks, chiding him: "Solon, Solon, all you Greeks are children." The priests boasted that Egyptian history went back thousands of years before that of the present Greek civilization: their institutions had begun no less than eight thousand years ago, and they had memories of events that took place even earlier. Nine thousand years ago (i.e., 9570 B.C.), they claimed, there was already a great city at Athens that the present Greeks barely remembered—if at all—because of intervening catastrophes. At that remote period Athens was ruled by an ideal society of warriors who had no love of riches, but lived a simple, communal lifestyle. The Athenians had successfully led the resistance of the peoples of Europe against the invasion of a tyrannical regime—the combined forces of the empire of Atlantis.

Atlantis was an island continent that lay westward beyond the Pil-

Plato (c. 429–347 B.C.), the creator of Atlantis. A Roman portrait following a Greek original.

lars of Heracles (the Straits of Gibraltar). It was ruled by a coalition of kings descended from the sea god Poseidon. The chief king was descended from Poseidon's oldest son, Atlas, who gave his name both to the island and the surrounding Atlantic Ocean. Once the Atlanteans had been almost godlike in their purity of heart, but as the divine blood in them faded they became corrupt and greedy. They already ruled a vast empire, stretching as far as central Italy in Europe and to the borders of Egypt in Africa, but now they decided to enslave the rest of the Mediterranean world as well. They invaded, but the Athenians, though deserted by their allies, managed to defeat them.

Just as the war was ending, the gods held a council and decided to punish the Atlanteans for their overweening pride. "There were earthquakes and floods of extraordinary violence," wrote Plato, "and in a single dreadful day and night . . . the island of Atlantis disappeared into the depths of the sea." During the same catastrophe. the Athenian army, which was still on campaign, was swallowed up by the earth.

Plato's account in the *Critias* includes a detailed description of Atlantean society. The island was a paradise blessed with every natural resource: plenty of fresh water, an abundance of metal ores, luxuriant vegetation producing everything from food to perfumes, and herds of animals including elephants. Anything the island might lack was drawn from its overseas empire. As a result, the kings of Atlantis "had such an amount of wealth as was never before possessed by kings and potentates, and is not likely ever to be seen again."

Each of the kings had his own royal city, but the grandest, the capital of Atlantis, was the royal metropolis ruled over by the descendants of Atlas. Poseidon himself had founded it, carving out a series of concentric rings of water to surround and protect the site. Successive kings embellished the city, digging a great subterranean channel through the rings of land to join the circular canals and connect them to the nearby sea. They built huge bridges over the canals and defensive walls around each of the rings of land, encasing them in metal: the outermost glittered with bronze, the next with tin, and the innermost with *orichalcum*, an unknown metal "which sparkled like fire." In the outer sections of the city they built a harbor, warehouses, barracks, racetracks, groves, and temples, and on the central island a palace complex that was a wonderland. The main temple (to Poseidon and his wife, the nymph Cleito) was coated with silver and pinnacles of gold; its roof was made of solid ivory decorated with precious metals. It was three times the size of the Parthenon in Athens. Inside were images of the first kings and queens of Atlantis and a solid gold statue

Plan of the Royal Metropolis of Athens, following Plato's description. (Bottom right) The wider setting of the city—the outskirts were surrounded by an enormous circuit wall enclosing houses and a harbor on the coast of the Atlantic Ocean.

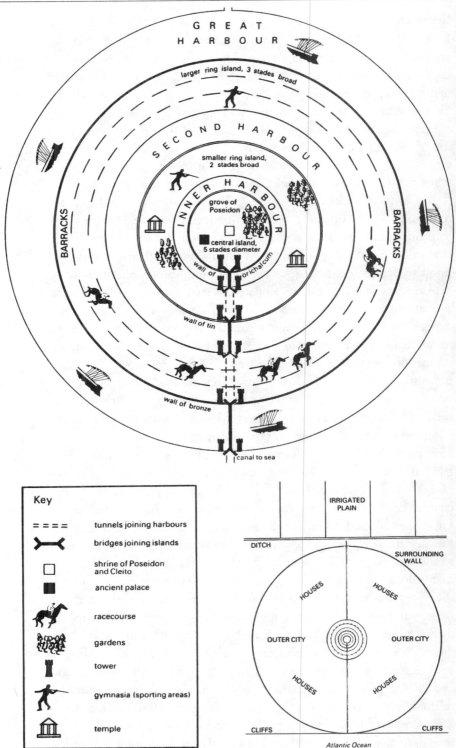

GREAT HARBOUR

larger ring island, 3 stades broad

SECOND HARBOUR

smaller ring island, 2 stades broad

INNER HARBOUR

grove of Poseidon

central island, 5 stades diameter

wall of orichalcum

wall of tin

wall of bronze

canal to sea

BARRACKS

BARRACKS

Key

==== tunnels joining harbours

bridges joining islands

☐ shrine of Poseidon and Cleito

■ ancient palace

racecourse

gardens

tower

gymnasia (sporting areas)

temple

IRRIGATED PLAIN

DITCH

SURROUNDING WALL

HOUSES   HOUSES

OUTER CITY   OUTER CITY

HOUSES   HOUSES

CLIFFS   CLIFFS

Atlantic Ocean

of Poseidon, which nearly touched the roof, itself some 300 feet high. (For comparison, New York's Statue of Liberty is 151 feet high, standing on a 155-foot pedestal.)

There is nothing in Plato's account to support the worst excesses of some popular books about Atlantis—no trace of flying machines and ray-guns, no priests with weird psychic powers, nor any dark hints that the Atlanteans were dabbling with dangerous cosmic forces. All the same, much of what Plato describes—such as the advanced engineering achievements and an unsurpassable level of material wealth—must have read like science fiction at the time his dialogues were written (about 360–350 B.C.). The sheer scale of everything he said about Atlantis is staggering, from the size of the continent and the grandeur of its buildings to the enormous timescale involved. Egyptian civilization claimed to be the oldest in the Mediterranean world, and the Greeks respected it for its hoary antiquity. Yet Atlantis was supposed to have been even older than Egypt.

Plato's account seemed so far-fetched that the philosopher Aristotle (384–322 B.C.), an ex-pupil, simply dismissed it out of hand as sheer invention. Against this we have the repeated assertion, put by Plato in the mouth of Critias (who relates the Atlantis tale in the *Timaeus* and *Critias*), that the story is "literally true." Critias was a relative of Plato, in fact his great-grandfather. The story was supposed to have been handed down through the family from their distant relative Solon, who was said to have been composing an epic about Atlantis before his death. For Plato to lie he would have had to implicate two of his eminent relatives in the forgery, which, even though they were safely out of the way, seems unlikely.

We are therefore left with a riddle that has baffled scholars ever since Plato wrote: could his story really have been a complete fabrication, or did some historical reality lie behind it?

An Atlantic Continent?

The most obvious test is to look for remains of Atlantis where Plato says they should be. If we are to take him literally, we should find evidence of Atlantean civilization around the fringes of the Atlantic Ocean, including the Americas, which he implies were connected to Atlantis by a chain of islands.

That this evidence is there, for all to see, was the argument of Ignatius Donnelly (1832–1901), an eccentric American politician and writer who, with his book on Atlantis published in 1882, single-

The Atlantean continent, as reconstructed by Ignatius Donnelly (1882) from deep-sea soundings. He implies it was once connected to South America by a ridge of land.

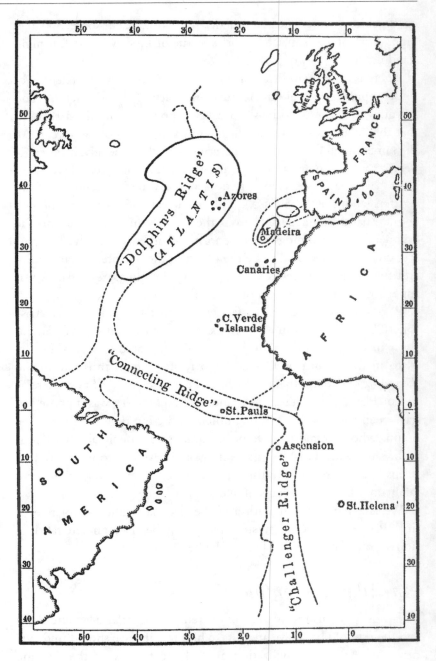

handedly resurrected the subject from the doldrums, where it had languished since Renaissance times. Donnelly listed dozens of parallels between the pre-Columbian civilizations of the Old and New Worlds, ranging from the construction of pyramids and mummification to similarities in myth and shared symbols such as the cross. These, he argued, needed an explanation, and Atlantis provided it. In Donnelly's view all ancient civilization was an "inheritance": "as 'all roads lead to Rome,' " so all the "converging lines of civilisation lead to Atlantis."

An uncritical scholar, Donnelly threw into the pot every conceivable parallel he could find, tending to rely on their cumulative effect. Some of his parallels are extremely weak: to note, for example, that the art of painting "was known on both sides of the Atlantic" says absolutely nothing. Nor does one need an Atlantic continent to explain why the Sun was worshiped in both Peru and Egypt. Other parallels are more intriguing, such as the practice of mummification, though the methods used in South America and Egypt were very different.

Others, such as the supposed similarity between the Old and New World pyramids, are simply unworkable. The Egyptian examples are true pyramids, coming to a point at the top. Those in Central America are not really pyramids at all, as they are flat-topped, to support temple buildings in which worshipers would be raised nearer the heavens. Egyptian pyramid building began about 2700 B.C. and continued in Egypt and Sudan into Roman times. Most Mesoamerican "pyramids" are almost modern by contrast. The great temple at Tenochtitlan was completed as recently as A.D. 1487. The earliest known Mesoamerican "pyramids," those at Teotihuacan and nearby Cuicuilco, compare well in size to the Great Pyramid of Cheops at Giza, and can be dated by radiocarbon to the last few centuries B.C. So while there is some overlap in the pyramid-building ages of Mesoamerica and Africa, their dates hardly suggest a common origin in Atlantis more than eleven thousand years ago.

Such problems are merrily glossed over in dozens of books by traditional "Atlantologists" who follow Donnelly in linking the pyramids with Atlantis. A moment's reflection on geography is enough to show another major weakness in their case. If the art of pyramid building originated in Atlantis, we might expect to find the earliest examples in western Europe and northwest Africa, where, of course, there are no pyramids or pyramidlike structures at all. The earliest stone buildings of Europe are the chambered tombs and other stone monuments (including stone circles) of the megalith builders (see **Megalithic Astronomers** in **Watching the Skies**). The megalithic civilization of prehistoric Europe was definitely an Atlantic seaboard culture, and its blossoming, about 4500 B.C., is indeed something of a mystery. Not surprisingly, Atlantologists have drawn on the megaliths as evidence for their case, but the problem is that there is nothing to match them on the other side of the Atlantic. Despite claims that there are megalithic buildings in North America, none has been shown to be genuinely prehistoric, and it should be manifestly obvious that there are no American equivalents of the chambered tombs or of the stone rings at Stonehenge, Avebury, and Carnac. Loose claims have been repeatedly made about the discovery of mysterious "megalithic" ruins in the waters of Bimini in the Bahamas, but they always fall through under close inspection (see **Edgar Cayce on Atlantis** in **Archaeology and the Supernatural**).

Even if we were to reduce Plato's date for Atlantis to match the age of megalith building (4500 B.C. onward) or pyramid building (2700 B.C. onward), the existence of these monuments in themselves says nothing about an Atlantic continent. In short, there is simply no archaeological evidence of such a transatlantic connection. If civilization had really been diffused from a center in the Atlantic, then we would expect at least to find similar pottery and tool types on both sides of the ocean. We do not.

This is not to sweep aside all similarities between the ancient civilizations of the Old and New Worlds. Donnelly, for example, was right to stress that pre-Columbian cultures on both sides of the Atlantic have strikingly similar myths about a Great Flood. Yet there are many explanations possible other than the sinking of an Atlantic continent (see **Introduction** to this chapter). And if any of the transatlantic parallels were genuine, which is highly doubtful, it would be far more economical to imagine that they came about through early sea voyages than to invoke the existence of an unknown continent. That there are undiscovered centers of civilization, missing pieces in the jigsaw of prehistory, seems a certainty. Yet nothing in the pattern of archaeological evidence points to one of these "missing pieces" being in the Atlantic.

From the standpoint of geology, the case for a lost continent of Atlantis is just as weak. Until the early twentieth century many geologists were happy to countenance the idea that a sizable land-bridge had once existed between Europe and North America, partly to account for similarities in the prehistoric flora and fauna on both sides of the Atlantic. Though they usually dated its disappearance hundreds of thousands of years before the sinking of Plato's continent (c. 9600 B.C.), some geologists speculated that it endured much later and gave rise to the Atlantis legend. This was the opinion of the eminent French geologist Louis de Launay, as published in 1921. Yet a massive revolution in geological thinking was already under way that would completely scotch the possibility of a real Atlantis.

In 1915 the German meteorologist Alfred Wegener published his theory of "continental drift." Wegener had noticed that if you cut out the continents from a map, the pieces can be roughly fitted together like a jigsaw puzzle. He concluded that all the world's continents had once been joined in a single landmass, which had fragmented and then slowly drifted apart. At first Wegener was laughed at, but by 1950 his theory was being treated seriously. In the 1960s, through the sheer weight of evidence, the theory of continental drift (now better known as the plate tectonics theory) became geological orthodoxy. By then scientists had discovered that the Earth's crust is not of uniform thickness and composition, as was hitherto believed. The crust at the bottom of the oceans is about 4 miles in thickness. The continental crust effectively sits on top of this, and on average is about 20 miles thick. The two kinds of crust are different—for example, the oceanic crust lacks the layer of granite beneath the continents. So the formation of continents could no longer be seen in terms of landmasses simply moving up or down, but was now explained by the continental crust shifting over the oceanic.

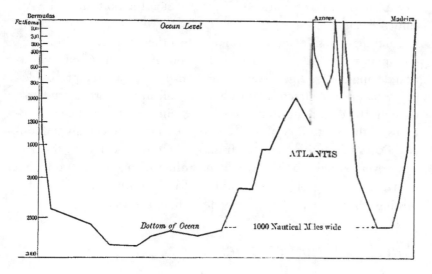

Profile of the Mid-Atlantic Ridge, as revealed by the deep-sea soundings of H.M.S. *Challenger* and the U.S. ship *Dolphin* in the 1870s. As presented by Donnelly (1882), the findings seemed to be clear evidence of a sunken Atlantic continent.

Key evidence in support of continental drift comes from the mid-Atlantic, where a long swath of undersea volcanoes runs down the center of the ocean. This Mid-Atlantic Ridge, as it is known, was seen by Atlantologists, from Donnelly onward, as the remains of the central mountains of Atlantis. Geologists now recognize this unstable ridge not as the remains of an old continent but as much younger material, formed by magma welling up through faults in the crust. As this magma spreads outward from the ridge, it pushes away the plates on either side, moving the Americas and Europe/Africa ever farther apart. This picture has been confirmed by study of the old magnetism (palaeomagnetism) trapped in the rocks either side of the Ridge. Every few million years the polarity of the Earth's magnetic field has changed, magnetic north becoming south and vice versa. When molten rocks cool down they preserve a "signature" of the Earth's magnetism at the time. Significantly, the same sequence of magnetic signatures is found in the rocks on both sides of the Mid-Atlantic Ridge. This is convincing evidence for sea-floor spreading, continental drift, and the relative youth of the Atlantic ocean bed. Finally, if the plate tectonics theory is correct, when we join together the American and European/African landmasses as they once would have been, there is no space left in the middle for another continent.

Strictly speaking plate tectonics is still only a theoretical model. Yet it is one supported by hundreds of individual pieces of research and evidence, and the traditional Atlantologists have yet to propose an equally good model that can explain them. Nor have they been able to explain the lack of continental-type crust at the bottom of the Atlantic Ocean.

All things considered, the possibility that there was ever a "missing" continent in the Atlantic, capable of supporting an advanced civilization during the Ice Age, is vanishingly small. Recent attempts to relocate Atlantis in Antarctica—involving a shift in the Earth's crust that brought the continent from a temperate climate into the freezing regions of the South Pole about 10,000 years ago—are equally dubious (see **Poleshift** in this chapter). In short there is no evidence that Atlantis ever existed as a "lost continent," other than a literal and highly uncritical reading of Plato. Without Plato's writings the idea of a missing continent would probably never have been suggested.

The Explosion of Thera

The shift in geological thinking in the 1960s finally turned scholars off Atlantis as a subject for serious research. Plato's reputation itself had taken a nosedive in the years preceding the Second World War. Unfortunately some of his political pronouncements were adopted by the National Socialist party in Germany, and the reaction from the West, even more unfortunately, was to denounce Plato as an enemy of democracy. The mid–twentieth century was also a notoriously conservative period in the history of science. Any ideas that smacked of catastrophism were unwelcome. In the *Timaeus* and *Critias*, our sources for the Atlantis story, Plato expounded his theory of how the world had been periodically decimated by cataclysms of fire and water. These writings of Plato, along with much of his other work, began to be blithely ignored by scholars.

The subject of Atlantis was relegated to the cranks and kooks. There was one notable exception, however, during the 1950s and '60s, when a number of geologists and archaeologists attempted to find an academically "respectable" answer to the Atlantis problem. Feeling it unlikely that Plato was a complete fraud, they revived a theory originally suggested in 1909 by K. T. Frost, a young classical scholar from Belfast University. At that time the great Bronze Age palace of Knossos on the Aegean island of Crete was being uncovered by Sir Arthur Evans, and the western world was agog with his discoveries (see **Theseus and the Minotaur** in **Legendary History**). Was the story of Atlantis, Frost asked in a letter to the London *Times*, an echo of the great Minoan civilization that had once thrived on Crete? The island was, from an Egyptian perspective, far to the west, while Plato's description of the ritual slaughter of bulls by the Atlantean kings would fit with the prominent role played by bulls in Minoan religion. Egyptian tomb paintings depicting visitors in Minoan-style costume showed that the Egyptians were aware of this civilization, while its sudden disappearance about 1400 B.C., Frost suggested, might have given them the impression that "the whole kingdom had sunk in the sea."

Tribute-bearer wearing Aegean costume from an Egyptian relief of the mid–15th century B.C.

Frost's intriguing argument seemed to lack only a grand enough catastrophe. This was supplied in 1939 by Greek archaeologist Spyridon Marinatos. From his excavations at the Minoan villa of Amnisos on the north coast of Crete, Marinatos concluded that Minoan civilization had been destroyed by an explosion of the nearby volcanic island of Thera (Santorini). Pumice had been found at Amnisos, while Marinatos speculated that the villa walls had been collapsed by a massive tidal wave, or tsunami, caused by the exploding volcano. That Thera exploded in Bronze Age times there was no doubt—Minoan pottery had already been discovered under the volcanic debris on the island. By 1950 Marinatos had developed his thesis further, arguing, from the size of the crater left by the explosion on Thera, that the event had been four times as violent as the well-documented eruption of Krakatoa in 1883. The Krakatoa explosion released 100 to 150 megatons of energy, a staggering 60,000 to 90,000 times greater than the power of the earliest nuclear bombs tested in the Nevada desert. That there would have been pandemonium on the island of Crete when Thera exploded in the Bronze Age there can be little doubt.

Marinatos drew into his case Frost's identification of Atlantis with Crete and suggested that the eruption of Thera (which he dated to 1500 B.C.) had given rise to the story of Atlantis' destruction. When he began excavations on Thera in 1967, he discovered a veritable Minoan Pompeii. His spade uncovered, beneath a thick protective layer of volcanic ash and tephra, street after street of Minoan houses, some with beautifully colored frescoes and intact pottery.

The romantic appeal of this once prosperous town, devastated by a volcano, inspired a rash of books in 1969, all arguing that Thera had been the "real" Atlantis. Foremost was that by Greek geologist Professor Angelos Galanopoulos, who produced detailed arguments to explain how Thera and Minoan civilization could have given rise to the Atlantis legend. His key argument was that many factors in the story had become multiplied by a factor of 10 in the retelling. Galanopoulos argued that the Egyptians could have originally said to Solon that Atlantis sank beneath the waves 900, rather than 9,000, years before their time. This would mean a date of c. 1500 B.C. (c. 600 B.C. + 900 years), the very period when Thera is thought to have erupted. Likewise, Plato said that the huge plain that lay behind the Atlantean metropolis measured 3,000 by 2,000 Greek *stades*, so Galanopoulos scaled the figures down to 300 by 200 *stades*, approximately 34 by 23 miles—and roughly the size of the central plain (Mesara) on the island of Crete. As for the metropolis itself, Galanopoulos separated it from the plain, and argued that at the size Plato gave (with no reduction by 10) it made a fair match with the original extent of the island of Thera before its explosion. Though he did not apply his method consistently, Galanopoulos triumphantly announced that dividing Plato's figures by 10 was *the* solution to the riddle of Atlantis.

With the dates and dimensions of Atlantis apparently resolved, the proponents of the Thera hypothesis went on to produce a stream of comparisons between Atlantean and Minoan civilizations. Almost everything about Thera could be seen to fit—or be made to fit—Plato's Atlantis narrative. The rational, academic answer to the problem seemed to have arrived at last.

Yet does the attractive Minoan theory of Atlantis bear up under close scrutiny? After all, Plato described a catastrophe involving earthquake and flood, but the Thera event was a volcanic explosion. Most

Scenes of bull-catching from a beautiful Bronze Age cup found at Vapheio, near Sparta.

of the other comparisons of Atlantis and Crete/Thera are equally generalized and unconvincing. Plato, for example, said that the defensive ring walls that surrounded the metropolis were built of red, white, and black stone. This has been compared to the colors of the volcanic rocks that can be found on Thera; yet red, white and black rocks can be found in dozens of places, including those with no volcanoes. He also said that the bulls that the kings of Atlantis sacrificed in an elaborate ritual were caught without the aid of metal weapons, by using wooden clubs and nooses. The Thera supporters point, not only to the Minoan bull games, but also to a beautiful silver cup of Minoan design (the Vapheio Cup) that shows bulls being captured with ropes and nets. Yet bull cults were widespread throughout the ancient Mediterranean world from at least 6,000 B.C. onward, and it was the common custom to trap all sacrificial animals without the use of weapons that might injure them—only perfect specimens could be sacrificed to the gods. Nothing in Plato's story remotely suggests the bull-leaping games that the excavations on Crete have revealed. The distinctive element of the Atlantean bull sacrifices was that the animals were suspended from pillars before their throats were slit. It was pointed out as long ago as 1927 that the only evidence for this custom in the ancient Aegean comes, not from Crete, but from Troy in northwestern Anatolia (modern Turkey). Many of the other "parallels" argued between Atlantean and Minoan civilization, such as the comparison of the massive public baths of Atlantis (including special baths for horses) with the Minoan hip baths discovered at Knossos, are too weak to merit discussion.

When it comes to the dating and dimensions of the Atlantean city, the heart of the Minoan/Thera case collapses completely. The method of division by 10 seems plausible but is really a bit of modern number juggling. The ancient Egyptians *did* exaggerate things, including dates, but not by simply multiplying things by 10! In various accounts they gave to the Greeks they claimed that their civilization was anything up to 12,000 years old. In the *Timaeus*, Plato cites the Egyptians as saying that their civilization was founded 8,000 years before the time of Solon, and that Atlantis was destroyed a thousand years before that. If we were to scale down both figures together, we would have to accept that the priests who spoke to Solon dated the origin of Egyptian civilization to 1400 B.C. (600 B.C. + 800 years), which would be plainly ridiculous. Equally absurd is the other explanation offered as to how the figures in Plato's narrative came to be exaggerated by 10—that Solon simply misunderstood the numbers given him by the priests. Solon was a shipowner and financed his overseas travels by trading. He would have conducted some rather hopeless business if he could not distinguish between the Egyptian words for "one hundred" and "a thousand."

Moreover, the Greeks were quite well informed about ancient Cretan civilization, as echoed in the stories of Minos, Theseus, and the Minotaur in the Labyrinth (see **Theseus and the Minotaur** in **Legendary History**). Plato himself was intimately acquainted with the history, geography, and customs of Crete. It seems highly unlikely that the Greeks would have, first, learned a story about ancient Crete from the Egyptians and, second, not recognized what their source was supposedly describing.

Finally, the whole idea of linking Thera with Atlantis was rocked to its foundations when it became clear, during the late 1980s, that the explosion of Thera did *not* destroy the Minoan civilization of Crete. Thera exploded anything up to a hundred and fifty years before the destruction of Knossos and the other great Cretan palaces—as shown, for example, by the discovery of Theran ash in deposits *beneath* those of the last heyday of the palaces c. 1500 B.C. The explosion may have dealt some long-term damage to the morale and economy of the Minoan civilization, but it was *not* responsible for its demise. The visitors in Minoan dress with which Frost began his argument continued to appear in Egyptian tomb paintings long after the eruption of Thera. The archaeological record shows that trade between Egypt and the Aegean world carried on much as normal after the eruption. There is nothing suggesting a massive break in communications that the Egyptians might have interpreted as the "sinking" of a western island owned by their trading partners.

In short, a Minoan Atlantis—whether it be Crete or Thera—explains nothing. It is clearly time for a new approach to the whole problem.

Atlas, King of Atlantis

Most theories about Atlantis have been constructed by believers. Their method has been to take a few perceived resemblances from the culture, archaeology, or geography of a given area, pile on the circumstantial detail, and then announce that the "real" Atlantis has been found. This methodology has resulted in myriad identifications. To date Atlantis has been "discovered" in North America, Ceylon, Palestine, Mongolia, Carthage, Spain, Malta, central France, Nigeria, Brazil, Peru, the Caucasus Mountains, Morocco, the Sahara Desert, the Arctic, the Antarctic, the Netherlands, East Prussia and the Baltic, Greenland, the South Pacific, Mexico, Iran, Iraq, the Crimea, the West Indies, Sweden, the British Isles, and, of course, Minoan Crete and Thera. None of these theories—with the possible exception of the Minoan hypothesis—really tackles the question of how Plato could have come by genuine knowledge of these locations. They simply work on the idea that somehow Plato was telling the truth. On the other side from the believers are the skeptics, who simply dismiss the search for Atlantis as futile—Plato was just fantasizing.

The only real way out of this impasse is to suspend any naive hope of finding a real Atlantis and to concentrate instead on the key question: can we identify a source for Plato's story?

While Plato always added his own slant to traditional material, he has never been shown to be guilty of wholesale fabrication. It is worth giving him the benefit of the doubt and, for the sake of argument, investigating his claim that he got the Atlantis story from his ancestor Solon, who was composing an epic on the subject. Yet was Plato right in understanding that Solon was originally told the story by Egyptian priests?

The supposed Egyptian connection is the crux of the problem. The ancient Egyptians took an extremely dim view of foreigners, so the idea that they preserved a detailed tradition describing two remote civilizations—Atlantis and its rival Athens—seems highly improbable, to say the least. (The only descriptions we have from ancient Egypt of foreign countries are of immediate neighbors, with whom they had had direct political or economic dealings, and whom they regarded as massively inferior.) Even more implausible is the idea that the Egyptians, who took pride in being the "oldest" culture in the world, would have happily described a civilization such as Atlantis, which was far senior, and hence superior, to their own. Besides, how could the Egyptians have possibly recorded events that supposedly took place a thousand years *before* their own culture started?

The role of Athens in the story provides a further complication. The Athenians were supposed to have repulsed the invasion of the Atlanteans. Yet, far from having existed a thousand years before Egyptian civilization, Athenian society lagged far, far behind it. In the third millennium B.C., the age of the pyramid builders, the Athenian country of Attica had been settled, but at the level of simple farming communities. As a town Athens did not really exist until about 1400 B.C. (There is not a single shred of evidence for a great Athenian civilization having existed long before this.) We can turn the elements Egypt, Atlantis, and Athens around continuously like a Rubik's Cube, but in terms of dates they refuse to fit into an intelligible pattern. As long as we accept the Egyptian connection in the transmission of the Atlantis story, nothing seems to make any sense.

Alternatively, is it possible that Plato was right that Solon gathered the story on his travels, but was mistaken in assuming that this was during his famous visit to Egypt? Solon traveled elsewhere, notably to the kingdom of Lydia, on the Aegean coast of Anatolia (Turkey) opposite Greece. There, at the court of King Croesus (560–547 B.C.)—proverbial for his riches, but historical nonetheless—Solon is said to have swapped stories not only with the king but also with the great fable writer, Aesop himself.

It is to Anatolia that many other clues lead, beginning with Atlas, the famous giant of Greek myth who was believed to support the sky. Atlas, Plato tells us, was the first king—and eponym—of Atlantis. He is thus the key mythological character in the Atlantis tale, and the best clue to its origin. The Greeks believed that when the older race of gods, the Titans, were defeated by Zeus and the Olympians, the Titan leader Atlas was condemned to the far western edge of the world, where he was made to shoulder the enormous weight of the sky for all eternity. He was eventually transformed into a mountain—the Atlas Mountains of Morocco—and also gave his name to the Atlantic Ocean. Yet before his banishment, Atlas and his family had domains much farther to the east. Atlas's daughters were the ancestors of a number of royal dynasties, the most important being that of Troy in northwestern Anatolia (Turkey), while another ruled the island of Lesbos off its Aegean coast. Atlas's sister was thought to have founded cities in Cilicia in southwestern Anatolia, while his mother was said to be the nymph Asia. Her name, now applied to the whole vast continent east of the Mediterranean, meant Anatolia (Asia Minor) in Roman times, and before that was a term for the specific area of Lydia on the western coast.

The repeated Anatolian connections in the myths about Atlas suggest that the Greeks may have learned the idea of the sky-supporting giant from that quarter. (By comparison, although Crete is littered with mythological associations, absolutely none of them concerns Atlas—another weakness of the Minoan hypothesis.) Pictorial representations of Atlas-style figures go back to about 1500 B.C. in Anatolia, a thousand years before the earliest Greek depictions. These come mainly from the great civilization of the Hittites, whose empire ruled from central Anatolia in the second millennium B.C. Numerous carvings, from rock sculptures to sealstones, show human or half-human figures (very often mountain gods) raising their hands to hold the heavens. A Hittite text described the enormous giant Ubelleris, whose feet stood in the underworld and whose shoulders supported the earth and sky. When the Greeks said that Atlas's family came from Anatolia, there is every reason to believe them.

The punishment of Atlas, condemned to hold up the sky forever; from a Greek vase of the 6th century B.C. On the right his Titan brother Prometheus is chained to a rock as a bird pecks out his liver.

The Lost City of Tantalis

There would have been many tales told in ancient Anatolia about the giants or mountain gods who held up the skies. Fortunately, preserved in the writings of classical authors, we have the story of one of these mythological characters. His name was Tantalus, and he was a legendary king of Lydia (where Croesus later ruled) and nearby Phrygia.

Classical scholars have long accepted that Tantalus is essentially a Lydian version of Atlas. Tantalus had so many family connections with the Titans, the race of Atlas, that he probably counted as a Titan himself; he was even said to have been Atlas's son-in-law. Both names (Tantalus and Atlas) were derived from the same Greek word *tlao*, meaning "to carry," or "endure," a reflection of the sufferings that myth says were inflicted on them. For Tantalus, like Atlas, overstepped himself and defied the Olympian gods. The gods had honored him as their friend and confidant, even accepting his invitation to dinner, when he made the fatal mistake of serving up his son in a stew. Others said that Tantalus stole ambrosia, the food of the gods, and shared it with mortals. Whatever his crime, Zeus struck down Tantalus with a thunderbolt and condemned him to an eternal torment, which gave us the word *tantalize*. In the version given by Homer, Tantalus' punishment was everlasting hunger and thirst, but the more common tale was of a rock that perpetually teetered over his head, threatening to fall. Other versions say he was attached to the rock, that he was condemned to support it and that the "rock" was the sky itself—these leave no doubt that Tantalus was the Lydian Atlas.

The punishment of Tantalus in the underworld; after a Greek painting, c. 450 B.C.

Similarities between the two figures do not end there. Tantalus, like Atlas, was once thought to have ruled an earthly kingdom. Its center was the city he founded at Mount Sipylus, in the gold-rich country of Lydia. Like the historical king Croesus, Tantalus became a byword for riches. When Tantalus fell from favor, his city was shattered and swallowed by a massive earthquake, then drowned beneath a lake. The name of the lost city was Tantalis.

The resemblances between Tantalis and the incredibly similar-sounding Atlantis are inescapable—a fabulously rich city, once favored by the gods, falls from grace and is destroyed by earthquake and flood. The fact that the respective kings of these cities, Tantalus and Atlas, were two versions of the same mythological figure means that the two stories must be genetically related.

As the story of Tantalis was a Lydian one, it seems reasonable to suppose that it was known at the court of the Lydian king Croesus, whom Solon visited about 570 B.C. At the famous meeting, as described by the Greek historian Herodotus, the two swapped stories illustrating the vicissitudes of fate. The Lydian story of Tantalus and his city, with its moral of how even the mighty can fall, would have fit the agenda perfectly. At the very least, the often repeated claim that Atlantis was a complete invention of Plato's can now be countered. His source, Solon, could have picked up in Lydia the story of Tantalis that had all the key elements for its later exaggeration into Atlantis, from its fabulous wealth to its catastrophic transformation into a "sunken kingdom."

Yet how could the story of a sunken city in Lydia have been transformed into the tale of a continent that was destroyed about 9600 B.C.? Its geographical relocation is easy to explain. If Solon or Plato "translated" Tantalus into his better-known version, Atlas, the scene of the catastrophe could have been mistakenly transferred to the far west, the location of Atlas after his downfall, but not his original home. And once set in the Atlantic, the story of the "sunken kingdom" could grow uncontrollably during its retelling through the generations from Solon to Plato.

As for the date, it is far more natural to assume that a *non*-Egyptian source—used by Solon and then Plato—was talking about a kingdom that existed a thousand years before the beginning of Egyptian civilization. In the ancient world there was great competition among the Near Eastern neighbors of the Greeks as to which was the oldest race. About 440 B.C., Herodotus said that the two leading contenders were the Egyptians and the Phrygians. (The Phrygians lived next door to their cousins the Lydians and had been part of Tantalus' kingdom.) It was believed by many people in the ancient world that the first people in the world spontaneously sprang from the soil of Phrygia like plants. Herodotus reports an anthropological experiment carried out by an Egyptian Pharaoh in the seventh century B.C. to resolve the matter. He isolated two children, one Phrygian, one Egyptian, and had them fed by a dumb goatherd in order to determine which was the "real," "original" language of the human race. The first word uttered by the children was *bek*, the Phrygian word for "bread." (The joke is that the children would more likely have been mimicking the sound of the goats!) Whether the story is true or not doesn't matter. The result was that the Phrygians "won" the case, and that their seniority over the Egyptians was "proven" and even accepted by the Pharaoh. Tantalus was as much a Phrygian king as he was a Lydian one. At the court of King Croesus (6th century B.C.) it may have been said with some confidence that the great city built by Tantalus existed long before the Egyptians. It would not have been true, but that was what people believed. As Plato himself dated the origin of the Egyptians to eight or ten thousand years before his time, it would have been a simple deduction to place Atlantis (i.e., Tantalis) a thousand years even earlier.

The Legend Behind the Legend

One could stop here, with the conclusion that Plato *did* have a source for his Atlantis story, albeit one that was completely recast and exaggerated by Solon and Plato, who turned it into a global epic.

Yet we can go further and ask: can the site of legendary Tantalis be located? Ancient accounts, such as that by the Greek travel-writer Pausanias (2nd century A.D.), make it clear that Tantalus' lost city was believed to lie at Mount Sipylus, modern Manisa Dagh, twenty or so miles inland from the modern port of Izmir (Smyrna) on the Aegean coast.

Classical writers describe Tantalis/Sipylus not only as the original capital of Lydia but also as the ancestral seat of the Mycenaean kings. Agamemnon, king of Mycenae and the leader of the Greek forces against Troy (see **Introduction** to **Legendary History** and **Schliemann's Treasure** in **Hoax?**), was reckoned to be the greatgrandson of Pelops, a son of Tantalus who migrated westward from Sipylus to Greece, where he founded a new dynasty and gave his name to the Peloponnese ("island of Pelops"). Could Mount Sipylus really have been the seat of a Bronze Age kingdom?

In Bronze Age terms, Sipylus lay within the Arzawa lands, a loose conglomeration of states along the western coast of Anatolia that acted as a buffer zone between two major power blocs—the Mycenaean kings of Greece and the Hittite emperors ruling from Boghazköy in central Anatolia. In the fifteenth century B.C., the Arzawan kings were nominally vassals of the Hittites. Then came some momentous developments, related in a fragmentary text from the Boghazköy archive dating to about 1420 B.C. It describes the rising power of one Arzawan vassal, who was in league with the Mycenaean enemies of the Hittites. His name was Madduwattas, and his power base was known as "the mountain land of Zippasla." For a number of reasons this area can be located in the general vicinity of Lydia, making Mount Sipylus an ideal identification for Zippasla. Step by step, Madduwattas conquered all the Arzawan states, and then invaded southern Anatolia, challenging Hittite authority directly. The crucial tablet relating these events breaks off just as he was raiding the island of Cyprus in conjunction with his Mycenaean allies. To have gotten that far, Madduwattas would effectively have had to destroy the Hittite Empire. This he apparently did. How much farther the Zippaslan forces went is hard to say, but it took fifty years for the Hittite Empire to resurface as a major power in the Near East. No records, unfortunately, exist to complete the story of Zippasla, with its ephemeral empire. In fact, it never appears again in Hittite records. Was it perhaps destroyed, like the Tantalis/Sipylus of legend, by a massive earthquake?

Answers will come if we can locate the city of Tantalis, the prototype of Atlantis, in its original setting. Here history, archaeology and legend seem to converge neatly. When one of the authors went to Turkey in 1994 to investigate, it was possible to locate all the monuments that Pausanias associated with Tantalus and his family, although most of them are neglected by archaeologists.

On the north face of Mount Sipylus, a huge effigy of a Mother Goddess, some 30 feet high, is carved into the side of the mountain, about 300 feet above the plain below. Pausanias describes it as the first sculpture of the Mother Goddess Cybele ever made, and says it was carved by Tantalus' son Broteas. Following Pausanias the sculpture is referred to locally as Cybele. Hittite hieroglyphic inscriptions show that this unique monument was made in Bronze Age times, probably about 1400 B.C. or earlier.

Nearby, said Pausanias, lay "the by-no-means inglorious grave" of King Tantalus. Sure enough, a few miles eastward of Cybele there is an extraordinary tomb, with an approaching flight of steps, entirely cut from the rock. It is certainly from preclassical times, but exactly how old is hard to say as its design is unique and there are no remains inside. It could well be of Bronze Age date.

On a mountain crag between Cybele and the tomb of Tantalus are the remains of a Greek sanctuary, leading up to a feature known to Pausanias as "the throne of Pelops." It is a giant-size seat, carved out of the stone at the top of the crag. Sitting or standing in it gives a commanding view of the plain below. As rock-cut "seats" like this are known from Hittite Boghazköy, Pelops' "throne" could be another curious relic of the Bronze Age settlers of Sipylus.

Finally, just below the crag is Yarikkaya, a deep ravine that makes the mountain look "cleft as if by some terrible convulsion of nature," in the words of a nineteenth-century explorer. Classical writers told how Mount Sipylus was shattered by the earthquake that destroyed

"Cybele"—rock carving of the Mother Goddess on Mount Sipylus, near modern Manisa, Turkey.

Tantalis. Yarikkaya is almost certainly the crack in the mountain from which Pausanias said that the waters flowed to drown the city.

Then what of Tantalis itself and the lake that was said to cover it? Until about forty years ago there was a small lake on the plain—as shown on old maps—just below the image of Cybele. The reports of early travelers show that a hundred and fifty years ago this lake was much bigger. It is also in precisely the right location to be the lake

The "tomb of Tantalus" near Manisa.

called Saloe, in which Pausanias said the ruins of the lost city could once be seen before mud had obscured them. Nineteenth-century classicists such as Sir William Ramsay and Sir James Frazer had already identified it as the spot where the ancients believed Tantalis lay submerged underwater. During this century Lake Saloe, the last resting place of Tantalis, was unceremoniously pumped out to make more room for farmland.

The "throne of Pelops" on a pinnacle of Mount Sipylus.

As the location for a real city, this spot would be hard to improve: it lies on a fertile plain between the ancient caravan route skirting the mountain and the river Gediz, the main artery of Lydia. Standing on the dry land where the lake once was, one realizes that the huge sculpture of Cybele, the Mother Goddess, gazes out over this very spot. A 30-foot carving 300 feet up the mountainside is not the sort of thing that will be made by passing shepherds. It was made by a highly organized Bronze Age community, and it is only natural to suppose that its makers lived directly on the plain below, where the Great Mother could watch over them every day.

More than likely the settlement responsible for Cybele—and the other curious monuments nearby—was the center of the kingdom of Zippasla known from Hittite documents. Almost certainly it was the Sipylus or Tantalis of classical legend. It is a prime site for archaeological excavation. The traditions suggest that Sipylus would have been a major interface between the Hittite and Mycenaean civilizations, and may have been the ancestral seat of the dynasty of Agamemnon, lord of Mycenae. It is reasonable to expect that under the plain in front of Cybele lie the remains of a Bronze Age city. We should not expect the center of a supercivilization, like Plato's Atlantis, but a major city nonetheless—probably similar to the great city of Troy, its contemporary to the north, with its massive circuit wall of stone.

For its fate we have only the traditions to go on, but the belief that Tantalis was totally devastated by an earthquake is not at all far-fetched. The Izmir region, as travelers to Turkey will know, lies in one of the worst earthquake zones of the world, while the appalling damage suffered by the cities of Lydia during the great earthquake of A.D. 17 is well documented. Contemporaries reported that twelve cities were devastated in one night. There were reports of holes opening in the ground, of mountains subsiding and of flat ground rising high in the air. The second-worst casualty of the twelve cities was Magnesia at Sipylus, a Greek settlement not far from the old site of Tantalis. Cities cannot exactly be "swallowed up by the earth," as classical writers stated of Tantalis. Yet during violent earthquakes large pieces of land can slump well below the water table. During the New Madrid earthquake of 1811 a huge tract of land in northeastern Tennessee sank many feet and filled with water, creating Reelfoot Lake, which is nine miles long and two miles across. Areas of land adjacent to mountains are particularly susceptible to such slumping, with the added hazard of avalanche. In 1970 the towns of Yungay and Ranrajirca in Peru, together with tens of thousands of inhabitants, were completely buried in four minutes by the debris thrown down from Mount Huascaran during an earthquake.

The fate of Tantalis near Mount Sipylus, as described by classical legend, is perfectly plausible. It is hoped that excavation will one day determine whether a Bronze Age city at Mount Sipylus—like the Atlantis of legend—was really destroyed by an earthquake and consigned to a watery grave.

SODOM AND GOMORRAH

Somewhat hijacked by tub-thumping preachers in their efforts to warn the ungodly, the biblical story of Sodom and Gomorrah may be all too easily dismissed as fable. The idea of two cities being destroyed by "fire and brimstone" from heaven because of the sinful behavior of their inhabitants seems a little too pat. Yet archaeological evidence has not only shown that these cities existed but it may even provide confirmation of the biblical description of their catastrophic destruction.

The story of Sodom and Gomorrah takes us back to the very earliest days of Hebrew history, long before the Israelites had settled in their Promised Land and even before they existed as a nation. Their ancestors still lived a seminomadic lifestyle, moving from region to region through the Near East to trade and find grazing land for their flocks and herds. Their leader, at the time of the Sodom and Gomorrah catastrophe, was the patriarch Abraham, revered as the founding father and ancestor, through his son Isaac, of all the Jews, and through another son, Ishmael, of the Arabs. So Abraham figures prominently in both the Old Testament and the Koran, which give essentially the same stories. The time was about 2100 B.C., according to a fairly literal interpretation of biblical chronology.

Abraham was born in "Ur of the Chaldees," usually thought to be the Sumerian city of Ur in southern Mesopotamia (Iraq). His family moved from there to Harran in northern Mesopotamia, where his father died. It was then, the Book of Genesis (12:1–5) relates, that God revealed his fate to him. He was to leave Mesopotamia and settle in Canaan (Palestine): "And I will make of thee a great nation, and I will bless thee, and make thy name great." Taking his wife and his nephew Lot, together with their retainers, Abraham went down into Canaan. After a brief spell in Egypt (while there was a famine in Canaan), Abraham and Lot settled in the south of the land to raise their animals.

A dispute arose between the herdsmen of Abraham and Lot over grazing rights, so Abraham suggested that they go their separate ways. Lot and his party moved farther east, to the plain on the other side of the Dead Sea (in the modern country of Jordan), pitching their tents near the city of Sodom. He found the plain "well-watered everywhere," a veritable "garden of the Lord" as fertile as Egypt (Genesis 13:10). Now—as in later biblical times—the region is a wasteland, with an oppressively hot climate and a desperate shortage of water. Yet when Lot arrived, there were five thriving cities on the plain—Sodom, Gomorrah, Admah, Zeboiim, and Zoar. Ruled by five kings, they were rich and powerful enough to take on a coalition of Mesopotamian rulers and defeat them.

All this was to be changed, according to Genesis, by the events of a single day. The Bible constantly stresses the "wickedness" of the inhabitants of the five cities, particularly those of Sodom and Gomorrah. The exact nature of their "wickedness," popularly assumed to be of a sexual kind, is not clear. But among the sins of the Sodomites inhospitality ranks high, and their downfall was only hastened by their treatment of two angels whom Lot had taken as guests into his house in the city. The

As Lot and his daughters take refuge in a cave, one daughter points to the smoking ruins of Sodom. Drawing by French artist N. Lemit (1794).

men of Sodom demanded that Lot bring them out of his house, either to interrogate them or possibly rape them. (See **Box: The Sin of Sodom**.) Those breaking down the door were blinded by the angels, who announced to Lot that they had been sent by God to destroy the city; he should gather his family immediately and run to the mountains for shelter, making sure they did not look behind them as they fled.

Lot took his wife and daughters and left the city, which was shortly turned into a smoking ruin. His wife, as everyone knows, disobeyed the angel's instructions, turned to look behind her, and was transformed into a "pillar of salt." Lot's daughters took shelter with their father in a cave in the mountains, where they feared that they were the last people alive in the world. In one of those colorful touches that the Old Testament so often adds, they get their father drunk—so drunk that he sleeps with them unawares and impregnates them with sons. The sons were to become the ancestors of the Moab and Ammon, Jordanian tribes who were to become archenemies of the Israelites. After that we hear no more of Lot. As for Abraham, he viewed the catastrophe from a safe distance in southern Palestine. When he looked in the direction of Sodom and Gomorrah, "lo, the smoke of the country went up as the smoke of a furnace." All the cities of the plain had been "overthrown" by an angry God.

THE SIN OF SODOM

In passing, it is worth clarifying exactly what the "sin of Sodom" was. Since Roman times it has often been assumed that their sin was indulgence in homosexuality. When the two angels took up lodgings in Lot's home, Genesis says that the men of Sodom, "both old and young," surrounded the house and demanded of Lot: "Where are the men which came in to thee this night? Bring them out that we may know them." As the Hebrew word for "know" *(yadha)* used in this context sometimes implies knowing sexually, as in "Adam knew Eve his wife," this passage has been freely interpreted by right-wing Christians as meaning that the town of Sodom was entirely populated by raving homosexuals who wanted to have sex with the angels. Therefore the sin of Sodom was homosexuality, and all homosexuals deserve the same fate as the "Sodomites," to be burned by righteous fire from heaven.

Translations of the Bible have not helped the press of the ancient Sodomites. The King James version contains a few passages in which "sodomites" are condemned for their lascivious behavior. Yet despite the apparent similarity in name, these have nothing to do with the citizens of Sodom. The "sodomites" *(qadeshim)* in question were male temple prostitutes. In many ancient Near Eastern societies, ritual prostitution was a regular part of temple life. Sexual activity was deemed to be sacred in certain contexts as it imitated the mating of the gods. In ancient Mesopotamia there is also good evidence that temple prostitutes, both male and female, were consciously accepted as a means of population control. It was believed that the Great Flood had been caused by overpopulation—the racket caused by the ever-growing numbers of the human race was keeping the gods awake at nights. After the Flood new social groups were introduced, including nuns and various kinds of temple prostitutes. The female prostitutes offered types of nonprocreative sexual activity. Male prostitutes, such as the *qadeshim* mentioned in the Old Testament, provided similar services.

As for the Sodomites (with a capital *S*), Genesis leaves the nature of their sin extremely vague. Other passages in the Old and New Testaments referring to them list a variety of crimes: negligence of the poor, inhospitality, idolatry, and arrogance frequently crop up. The sins listed might best be summed up as "lack of charity." Sodom and its four sister cities housed rich urban societies that lived on a fertile plain and were apparently the dominant economic and military power in Palestine—a modern view might interpret them as greedy capitalists who had no compassion for the poor or respect for the rights of more transient communities (such as the Hebrews) living on the margins of their society. The customs of the ancient Near East required that hospitality be given to strangers. And indeed, when Lot settled with his flocks near

Sodom he was received into the city with no trouble. Presumably he had gone through the right formalities.

But when Lot suddenly introduced other people—the angels who appeared from nowhere—he transgressed the time-honored customs of host and guest. Lot was a guest resident himself, and it would naturally have been assumed that his own visitors, who had never been formally welcomed into the city, must have had something to hide. Were they spies? It is against this background that we should consider the story of the citizens of Sodom, both young and old, crowding around Lot's house so that they might "know" the strangers.

This is the interpretation often put forward by liberal theologians and biblical scholars. It would also be the end of the story were it not for the obvious sexual content suggested by the fact that Lot offered his two daughters, "which have not known [yadha] man" in place of the angels, inviting the Sodomites to do with the girls whatever they pleased. A parallel story occurs in the Book of Judges (19:16–30), where a stranger arriving in the city of Gibeah is given shelter for the night by an old man. Certain "sons of Belial" (a pagan god) crowd around the old man's house demanding to "know" the stranger. The old man refuses, but gives them instead the stranger's concubine to do with as they wish. The worshipers of Belial "knew her, and abused her all the night until morning"; the unfortunate woman dies shortly after her night of torment. In this case the sexual content is even more explicit than in the Sodom and Gomorrah story. If we assume that the citizens of Gibeah and Sodom had the same intentions, then the men demanding to "know" the angels did have rape in mind. Almost the ultimate form of inhospitality, humiliating strangers by threatening rape fits into the more general descriptions of the "sins of Sodom." If we take this as the meaning of the story, the Old Testament was not condemning homosexuality as such, but rather attempted homosexual rape, which is an utterly different matter. (Still, it is hard to see the moral value in an ethical system that considered the rape of young girls and "concubines" as somehow preferable to that of men, guests or otherwise.)

In any case, if Sodom was a historical city destroyed by a natural catastrophe, the story of the attempted homosexual rape was presumably added to the account to "explain" just how bad the inhospitable Sodomites had become and why their downfall was necessary. The Bible provides no evidence that homosexuality per se was the "sin of Sodom," and it was only about the first century A.D. that the extra crime of "unnatural fornication" began to appear in Jewish writings. By then there was a backlash among the Jews against the "Hellenization" of their society, as Greek influence was threatening to destroy their traditional lifestyle. The Greeks were well known for their acceptance of homosexuality, and this, along with other things such as naked athletics, was rejected by the Jews as a corrupt, foreign custom.

Folktale, Folk Memory?

So runs the story in Genesis. By any reckoning, it is riddled with fanciful detail. The story of Lot and his daughters in the cave is clearly an Israelite "just so" story, invented with almost comical relish to explain just what bastards their Moabite and Ammonite enemies really were. Nor is it difficult to imagine how the idea that Lot's wife was transformed into a pillar of salt came about. The Dead Sea is so thick with salt that fish cannot live in it, and it is dotted with columns of crystallized salt that take any number of shapes—a chance resemblance between one of these and a human figure could easily have sparked off a story explaining the origin of the column. The area is also rich in sulfur, sometimes found in small balls that have formed naturally in the soil. Could these have given rise to another aspect of the story, the belief that God once rained "brimstone [sulfur]" on the land?

Many other motifs are familiar from folklore. The warning that looking back would be fatal, ignored by Lot's wife, can be found, for example, in the Greek story of the musician Orpheus. He managed to rescue his wife Eurydice from death, but only on condition that she did not look back as she left the underworld; she turned around and was lost to him forever. Turning around to look back was taboo in rituals performed by ancient societies from Rome to India. For example, when the Romans made offerings at the graves of their dead, they were careful not to look backward as they walked away.

The story of the visit of the two angels sounds very like another story from classical legend, recorded by the poet Ovid. He tells how the gods Jupiter and Mercury, disguised as mortals, visited a city in Phrygia (now central Turkey) and were appalled by the lack of hospitality they found there. In return for their ill-treatment, the gods destroyed the entire city, sparing only the poverty-stricken old couple who had taken them in and offered them food.

Indeed, the very motif of a city being destroyed for its sins is extremely common. The annals of folklore are crowded with examples. So the temptation to interpret the Sodom and Gomorrah story purely as folklore is strong. Yet a folkloric content is not evidence enough in itself to dismiss the story. In A.D. 79 there were doubtless soothsayers and moralists who muttered in retrospect that they had "seen it coming" and that the citizens of Pompeii had "asked for it" when they were engulfed by the ashes of Vesuvius. That *some* real events lie behind the widespread motif of rich and "sinful" cities destroyed by natural catastrophes seems more than likely.

Cave in Mount Sodom. As the mountain is entirely made of salt, caves like this are easily worn by water erosion.

The ancient tale of Tantalis in western Turkey, smashed by an earthquake and sunk beneath a lake because of the sins of its king, fits the pattern of the folklore motif perfectly. Yet the legend can be assessed without having to accept that King Tantalus really existed, or that he cooked his son into a stew and served him to the gods. There are good reasons for thinking that the story was based on a real Bronze Age city that disappeared during a seismic upheaval. Its site was remembered in classical times, where tourists still came to view some of its outlying remains. (See **Atlantis—Lost and Found?** in this chapter.)

In the case of Sodom and Gomorrah we have similar testimony. The destruction of Sodom was discussed by many classical writers, including the Greek geographer Strabo and the Roman historian Tacitus (both 1st century A.D.), who stated that the story was widely believed, for the simple reason that people could still go and see the remains of the destroyed cities for themselves (providing they could brave the hostile climate of the "land of Sodom").

The best description of what could still be seen near the Dead Sea in the first century A.D. comes from the Jewish historian Josephus, who wrote the history of his people for a Graeco-Roman audience. Josephus appears to have been to see for himself:

> The country of Sodom borders upon it [the Dead Sea]. It was of old a most happy land, both for the crops it bore and the wealth of its cities, but now it is all burnt up. It is related how, owing to the impiety of its inhabitants, it was burnt up by thunderbolts; indeed there are still marks of that Divine Fire, and the traces [or shadows] of the five cities are still to be seen, as well as the ashes of their growing fruits; these fruits have a color as if they were fit to be eaten, but if you pluck them with your hands, they dissolve into smoke and ashes. So what is told about the land of Sodom is confirmed by the evidence of our eyes.

In early modern times it was easy enough to imagine that Josephus was making all this up. While wishing to give him the benefit of the doubt, William Whiston, whose translation of Josephus appeared in 1737, despaired of the lack of reliable reports:

> Its remote situation, at the most southern point of the Sea of Sodom, in the wild and dangerous deserts of Arabia, makes it exceeding difficult for inquisitive travelers to examine the place; and for common reports of country people, at a distance, they are not very satisfactory.

The situation was no better in 1894, when George Adam Smith wrote his benchmark work on the geography of the Holy Land. Exploration of the erstwhile "land of Sodom," which he described as "hell with the sun shining on it," was little more advanced, and Smith assumed that the ruins of the catastrophe had simply disappeared. Other scholars were beginning to insist that there had never been any in the first place. After the triumph of Darwinism, rejecting the importance of catastrophes and denying the value of the Bible as a historical record became the established academic fashion.

Even biblical scholars had little to say in favor of the reality of Sodom and Gomorrah. Writing in the prestigious *Encyclopædia Biblica* in 1903, the Reverend T. K. Cheyne (Oriel Professor of the Interpretation of Holy Scripture at Oxford University) explained the story as a variation of the familiar deluge myth, in which sin is punished by a Great Flood. The righteous Lot, who survived with his daughters, was the equivalent of Noah, who survived the deluge with his family. Cheyne was not deterred by the fact that there is no trace of a flood in the biblical account of Sodom and Gomorrah. While he could not quite agree with a German colleague who claimed that it was a "dry-deluge story" (whatever that may be), Cheyne satisfied himself by asserting that the original story must have had water in it—and that was that. Skeptics must have been delighted by his spirited defense of Scripture.

View from the plain of the site of "Lot's Cave," at Deir 'Ain-'Abata, Jordan. The cave was inhabited during the Early and Middle Bronze Ages and in early Christian times was incorporated into a Byzantine church dedicated to Lot.

The Cities of the Plain

In 1924 a team led by the young William Foxwell Albright—later to become the greatest biblical archaeologist of this century—braved the punishing heat of the arid wastelands to the southeast of the Dead Sea, to perform the first archaeological survey of the area. At a place called Bab edh-Dhra they came across a Bronze Age site. They collected some potsherds and Bab edh-Dhra was added to the archaeological map of Jordan.

Some excavations were carried out in the 1960s, but it was not until the more extensive campaigns of 1975 onward that archaeologists began to appreciate the real nature of the site. Beneath the dust of a desert region that can now barely support life was a large settlement dating to the Early Bronze Age (roughly 3100 to 2300 B.C.).

Bab edh-Dhra is now known to be one of the earliest towns in Palestine. Though its excavation is far from complete, work has already uncovered a temple, other cultic centers, and remains of a massive defensive wall running around the city, some 23 feet thick and made of stone and mud-brick. But the greatest surprise so far has been the nearby cemetery, one of the largest found in the entire Near East. There are an estimated twenty thousand tombs, containing the burials of half a million people (together with some three million pots as grave-goods).

Even before excavation, evidence of the fiery catastrophe that engulfed Bab edh-Dhra was visible—lumps of spongy charcoal are scattered everywhere over the site. Ancient cities that have been destroyed by fire are not particularly significant in themselves. A considerable percentage of the archaeological sites in the Near East were burnt to the ground—a fate that strangely enough then preserves them. But Bab edh-Dhra differs in other respects. Most other prime sites in Palestine were continually destroyed and then resettled over the ages. After the catastrophe that destroyed Bab edh-Dhra at the end of the Early Bronze Age III period, a "new" style of pottery appears and may be due to a brief reoccupation (though it has sometimes been argued that this "Early Bronze IV" pottery was a contemporary, nomadic style). Otherwise, Bab edh-Dhra remained *completely deserted* for two thousand years—until the Hellenistic era of the third century onward.

Bab edh-Dhra was not the only city to suffer this fate. Shortly before they began work in 1975, the excavators, Walter Rast and Thomas Schaub, discovered another Early Bronze Age site seven miles to the south, at Numeira—also smothered with "spongy charcoal," which can be scooped up by the handful from the surface. Destroyed by fire at the same time as Bab edh-Dhra, Numeira was similarly abandoned for two

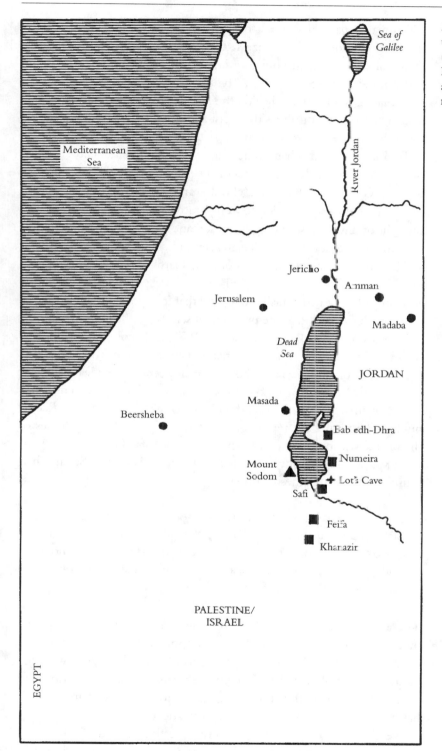

Map showing the location of the five Early Bronze Age cities (■) at the southern end of the Dead Sea—most likely these are the "five cities of the plain" mentioned in the Bible.

millennia. A pattern seemed to be emerging. Exploring further, they found three more Early Bronze settlements, each at the head of a *wadi* (seasonal stream), strung out in a line southward from Bab edh-Dhra and Numeira. These have yet to be excavated, though at least one of them, Feifa, is reported as having the familiar covering of spongy charcoal. The important thing is that Rast and Schaub's survey revealed five major Early Bronze Age settlements in the region, and five only.

By 1980 Rast and Schaub were ready to present their tentative conclusion that these were the "five cities of the plain" mentioned in Genesis— Sodom, Gomorrah, Admah, Zeboiim, and Zoar. Yet they needed to proceed cautiously; academic temperatures can run high at the thought of anything sounding like a sensational claim. The question of Sodom and Gomorrah is particularly sensitive. As it happens, what Rast and Schaub were suggesting was not particularly new. In 1944, when he published his report on the Early Bronze pottery from Bab edh-Dhra, William Albright had casually suggested that it might be the biblical city of Zoar. But Albright, as the preeminent scholar in the field, was free to express his opinions. After his death in 1971, archaeologists working in the Holy Land began to make a concerted effort to dispel the image that they were "doing biblical archaeology" in any sense. The idea that excavation could "confirm" the Bible was shunned as strictly unscientific.

Unfortunately for Rast and Schaub, *Biblical Archaeology Review* published a premature report on their identification of the "cities of the plain," without fully consulting the excavators. The article stressed what was already beginning to seem obvious—Rast and Schaub had found the biblical "cities of the plain":

> That there are five and five only cities located in the Dead Sea area— each located near a flowing spring; that all five date to the same archaeological period—the Early Bronze Age; and that there is no other evidence of occupation in the area until the Roman period over 2000 years is not without significance.

There were howls of anguish from some quarters. One academic immediately threatened to withdraw support for Rast and Schaub's funding if they really were proposing to identify these sites with the biblical "cities of the plain." Fortunately this hysterical reaction had no serious effect on the continuing excavations, and Rast and Schaub have confidently reasserted their identification.

Nearly twenty years later the dust is settling on the Sodom and Gomorrah controversy, and many archaeologists now calmly accept it as a commonplace that Bab edh-Dhra was one of the "cities of the plain."

Perhaps the only real surprise is that it took so long for the cities to be discovered in the first place. Earlier attempts had sought them in vain along the northern reaches of the Dead Sea. Other theories claimed that the cities now lay under its waters. Yet the evidence of the Old Testament, Josephus, and other classical writers makes it quite clear that the cities lay near the southern end of the sea, and

Detail from the Byzantine mosaic map at Medaba (6th–7th century A.D.) showing the location of the city of Zoar (surrounded by date palms).

that they were not drowned but abandoned. As long ago as 1884 a mosaic map was discovered in the ruins of a Byzantine church at Medeba, about thirty miles to the north of Bab edh-Dhra, which shows the position of the resettled city of Zoar about A.D. 550—at the southeastern corner of the Dead Sea, not far from the archaeological sites of Numeira. And given remaining uncertainties in the overall chronology, an archaeological date around 2350 B.C. for the destruction of a group of cities contemporary with the patriarch Abraham is quite acceptable.

Outstanding disputes concern the precise identification of the archaeological cities with the biblical ones. Fine tuning, like the discovery of Sodom itself, may take much longer. In the meantime, there is little reason to doubt that some, if not all, of the once great "five cities" have been found.

Fire from Heaven?

So what was it that devastated this cluster of thriving Bronze Age cities about 2300 B.C.? Do archaeology and tradition agree?

The Bible, of course, says that God rained down "brimstone [sulfur] and fire" on Sodom and its sister cities. Lightning strikes are often accompanied by a sulfurous smell, and some of the ancient writers, including Tacitus, seem to have assumed that lightning struck the cities. Josephus wrote about "thunderbolts" or, in a second description, simply a "bolt." Then was a lightning storm the cause?

As geologist Dorothy Vitaliano remarked, "It does not seem likely that a bolt of lightning alone could have produced a fire so uncontrollable that it devoured four separate cities." (Vitaliano said four, as some have argued that the city of Zoar survived the catastrophe.) Yet there is another important factor to consider. It has always been known that the Dead Sea area is extremely rich in oil. Even the account in Genesis refers to the "slime pits" of Siddim that lay near Sodom, and in Josephus' day the Dead Sea was known as "Lake Asphaltites," after the masses of solidified hydrocarbon, or bitumen, sometimes seen floating in it. After earthquakes these are particularly noticeable, with chunks as large as houses being reported.

Sodom and Gomorrah were practically sitting on a powder keg. To make things worse they were built on a major fault in the Earth's crust—the valley of the River Jordan and the Dead Sea are a continuation of the Great Rift Valley of Africa, one of the world's major earthquake zones. And earthquakes, of course, can start fires. Today the cause may be electrical cables snapping; in the distant past it was oil lamps being upset or furnishings falling into hearths.

Vitaliano blended together the suggestions of earlier geologists:

> A disastrous earthquake shook the Vale of Siddim in about 2000 B.C., releasing large quantities of natural gases and bitumens which were ignited by scattered hearth fires. . . . If some of the highly bituminous rock had been used in the construction of walls or buildings, it would have added fuel to the flames.

Interestingly, she wrote these words in 1973, before Rast and Schaub's discoveries were published. Research at the sites has now confirmed that earthquakes did play a key role in destroying the cities.

In 1995 two eminent specialists, David Neev of the Geological Survey of Israel and K. O. Emery of the Woods Hole Oceanographic Institution (Massachusetts), devoted a whole book to the destruction of Sodom and Gomorrah. Seen through geologists' eyes, they argue, the idea that the story is a memory of a massive seismic upheaval at the end of the Bronze Age seems perfectly natural. The Bible itself speaks not only of "fire from heaven" but also of how all the cities of the plain were "overthrown," which as they note is as nice a way as any to describe an earthquake.

The whole area to the south and east of the Dead Sea bears the scars of past earthquakes, and, from their study of the evidence on the ground, Neev and Emery are convinced that a major disaster occurred near the end of the third millennium B.C. At the sites themselves, Bab edh-Dhra and Numeira, huge towers had been thrown to the ground, while three skeletons have been discovered buried beneath the fallen walls. On the other side of the River Jordan the city of Jericho was destroyed—again with telltale signs of earthquake.

Neev and Emery agree that any fires would have been fed as hydrocarbons streamed from fractures in the ground. As for the biblical "brimstone," the bitumens in the region are rich in sulfur. Hot salty water released by the earthquake may have produced a deadly mixture of hydrocarbon gas, rich in sulfur and hydrogen sulfide:

> This mixture when burned probably would emit large volumes of thick black smoke capable of being seen from great distances as from Hebron, about 60 km from Sodom Plain. Sulfur dioxide could generate a fallout of concentrated acidic rain resulting in mass mortality of animals—including people—and vegetation near the bitumen seeps.

The Sodom and Gomorrah mystery would thus seem to be an open-and-shut case, except for one last question.

Geologists and environmental archaeologists have complicated the matter a step further by demonstrating that at the same time as the earthquakes, the region southeast of the Dead Sea underwent a massive climatic change. An area that had once been well-watered arable land, fertile enough to support five thriving cities, quite suddenly became much hotter and drier—at the same time as the cities fell. This explains why they were not resettled for so long. An acutely arid spell followed, lasting for some three hundred years, during which time the desiccated wasteland that is now visible was formed. The land never recovered, despite some later phases of cooler, moister weather.

What had happened? Some explanations have been offered—for example, that the level of the Dead Sea dropped dramatically and that the water table of the land nearby drained and lowered, leaving the soil dry. Neev and Emery's thorough study disputes such models. So they are left, rather awkwardly, with the conclusion that the earthquake and the climate change just happened to occur at the same time, but with no link between them.

But it is now becoming increasingly clear that the demise of Sodom and Gomorrah is merely one small piece in a much bigger puzzle. About 2300 B.C. the whole of the Near East underwent a climatic and geological upheaval. Excavation of Tell Leilan in Syria, for example, showed not only that the once thriving city there was abandoned, but that the very soil changed radically—from rich farmland to a layer of windblown dust. Tell Leilan remained abandoned for three centuries. Some extraordinary evidence that this drought was not a localized phenomenon came to light in 1998, from study of the sediments that lay on the ocean bed in the Gulf of Oman (southern Arabia). Around 2200 B.C. there was a sudden leap (up to six times the normal amount) in the quantities of dolomite particles being deposited. The windblown dolomite particles proved to have come from the mountains of eastern Turkey and northern Iraq and provide conclusive evidence of a period of extreme dustiness in the Near East, which peaked about 2200 B.C. and continued for at least two centuries. In fact, the Oman sediments show that this was the worst dry spell in the Near East over the last 10,000 years.

At the same time as this drastic downturn in climate, practically all of the great urban centers of the Levant were destroyed, many through earthquake. Throughout Turkey no fewer than three hundred cities were burned or deserted. (Among them was the city of

Troy thought by Schliemann to be Homer's—see **Schliemann's Treasure** in **Hoax?**) At the same time the Early Bronze Age civilization of Greece fell. In Egypt the Old Kingdom, the age of the great pyramid builders, came to a close and the country slipped into anarchy (see **How Were the Pyramids Built?** in **Architectural Wonders**). The level of the Nile dropped dramatically, and to the west the Sahara Desert made massive encroachments into areas that had once been well watered and fertile.

What can have caused these massive upheavals? There is evidence that there were some massive volcanic eruptions in eastern Turkey at the same time, which spewed out ash far over Mesopotamia. At Tell Leilan a layer of volcanic ash about half an inch thick was found immediately underneath the arid dust layer. By raising clouds of dust into the atmosphere volcanoes can block out the sun's rays and cause rapid changes in climate. So were the upheavals around 2300 B.C. caused by a chain of volcanic eruptions? This seems plausible up to a point, until one remembers that, aside from local tremors, volcanoes do not cause earthquakes. So what is it that can cause a sudden change in climate *and* a peak in volcanic and earthquake activity?

Moreover, there is now increasing evidence that the catastrophe in the Near East toward the end of the third millennium was part of a global upheaval. (See **Introduction** to this chapter.) The evidence has now accumulated to the point that scientists are beginning to look beyond the Earth for an explanation. There is one cause that could explain the widespread seismic activity quite easily, as well as lending a hand in altering the climate by throwing up dust veils: the impact of large meteorites and cometary fragments. The relatively small cometary fragment that exploded above Tunguska in Siberia in 1908 caused earth tremors, and burned and devastated an enormous expanse of forest. (See **The Day the Sun Stood Still?** in **Watching the Skies**.) A larger body actually impacting near a fault in the crust such as the Great Rift Valley could trigger off both earthquakes and volcanoes.

Which brings one back, of course, to the biblical account. What exactly was the "fire from heaven" that, according to Genesis, destroyed Sodom and Gomorrah? Arab tradition, as recorded in the Koran, describes it as "a stone-charged whirlwind" or a rain of "stone-bricks," which sounds remarkably like a meteorite shower. Josephus' "thunderbolt" is not quite the innocent lightning that it might appear at first glance. Of the Greek words he used, *keraunos* (thunderbolt) and *bolos* (missile), he never uses either again in the

Painted juglet from "Lot's Cave" of the Early Bronze Age I period (c. 3000 B.C.)— a typical example of the Early Bronze Age ceramics from the southern Dead Sea area.

context of describing ordinary thunderstorms. *Keraunos* in particular was a word used for the sacred and most deadly weapon of the Greek god Zeus, which he used only on special occasions. In the Hellenistic world, Zeus of the "thunderbolt" was associated with a number of meteorite cults, where "samples from heaven" were preserved and worshiped for centuries after they fell.

It would seem impossibly fortuitous that Sodom and Gomorrah, lying as they did on a geological fault line packed with flammable hydrocarbons, were *also* struck by a meteorite. (Though it has been argued.) But if the disaster was remembered as happening at a time when a shower of meteorites fell, the two could easily have been confused in terms of cause and effect. A fragment landing elsewhere could have caused the seismic upheaval while its companions lit up the night sky. The scenario is speculative, but if the "cities of the plain" have been correctly linked with the cataclysm that overthrew the Early Bronze Age of the ancient Mediterranean world, then it is one that will have to be considered.

The much-derided story of Sodom and Gomorrah, destroyed by "fire from heaven," may then be a unique record of humanity's response, in one small corner of the world, to a catastrophe of global dimensions.

POLESHIFT

Fifteen thousand years ago Antarctica was not the icy wasteland it is today, but a continent with flowing rivers, lush pastures, and a rich and varied fauna. It was also inhabited by people. The world's first great civilization was founded there, by an ancient race who excelled in civil engineering, astronomy, and seafaring. They explored the globe, planting colonies in South America, Egypt, and southern Iraq.

Then came the catastrophe. About 10,000 B.C. the whole outer crust of the Earth slipped in one piece, moving the continents thousands of miles into new geographical positions. Northeastern America, once covered by an enormous ice sheet, shifted to a more southerly, warm climate, ending the Ice Age that had held it in its grip for millennia. The polar region now moved northward to its present position in the Arctic Ocean, extending its grasp to Siberia and Alaska. In the opposite hemisphere the once balmy continent of Antarctica slid southward toward the pole. Its great civilization, snuffed out by cataclysmic earthquakes and floods, was laid to rest under a thick sheet of ice and snow as the continent froze over.

The people of Antarctica died out, but not before leaving markers for a future civilization to discover. So great was their scientific understanding that they had predicted the catastrophe that destroyed them. They constructed the Sphinx and great pyramids of Egypt and the Sun Temple of Tiahuanaco in Bolivia, using precise astronomical alignments, in the hope that when human civilization had once again developed to the required level their meaning could be decoded. This was one of the ways in which the wise men of Antarctica passed on their knowledge. In the colonies where there were enough survivors, priests transmitted the ancient Antarctican wisdom from generation to generation, by encoding it in myths, legends, and calendars. As well as myths describing the great catastrophe, they prepared specific indicators about the periodic destructions of the world. The ancient calendar of the Maya of Central America, for example, contains a grave warning—the present World Age is predicted to end in the year A.D. 2012 (see **Box: The Maya Calendar** in this chapter). If this is true, another catastrophic poleshift will happen and our own civilization—like that of Ice Age Antarctica—could disappear almost without trace.

Though it may sound like one, this extraordinary scenario is not supposed to be a science fiction story. It has been seriously proposed by British journalist Graham Hancock, in his best-selling *Fingerprints of the Gods* (1995), and has been developed further in spin-off books by Hancock and others. Their ideas have been given such massive publicity that it is becoming difficult to find anyone who has not heard of them.

Geologists have rejected the theory out of hand, simply ignoring it. Conventional geology, of course, does not accept the idea that the Earth's crust shifted about 10,000 B.C. or that the poles were in different geographical locations so recently. (The effect of tens of millions of years of continental drift is a different matter.) Archaeologists have been equally silent about Hancock's general thesis, perhaps feeling that it is so preposterous it will just fade away. Yet there is little sign of that. Instead it seems to be forming the core of an alternative view of prehistory, embraced by Hancock's readers as more meaningful than the version offered by academics. At one stroke, it seems, Hancock has explained the cause of the Ice Ages, the meaning of the world's Flood legends, the mysteries of the Sphinx and Tiahuanaco, the origins of Egyptian and other civilizations, and much else. As an added attraction his theory agrees very neatly with the claims of many psychics, including the great Edgar Cayce (see **Edgar Cayce on Atlantis** in **Archaeology and the Supernatural**).

The proofs offered by Hancock seem impressive. First, and central to his case, are some ancient maps that are claimed to give accurate depictions of an ice-free Antarctica. Hancock insists there can be only one explanation. Seeming evidence of the impossible, the maps are extraordinary relics from a civilization that existed *before* Antarctica was iced over.

Maps of the Ancient Sea Kings

The existence of these anomalous maps has long been known. As Antarctica was only officially discovered by the British in 1819, maps from before that date charting its coastline with any accuracy should simply not exist. Maps showing Antarctica as it is *underneath* the ice would be an even greater embarrassment to the history of science. Their existence would prove that the currently accepted understanding of prehistory is completely wrong.

The maps in question were first brought to a wide audience in the 1960s by Professor Charles Hapgood, who taught history of science at Keene College, New Hampshire. Hapgood was a brilliant theorist and a good enough scholar to throw down serious challenges to academic dogma. He first came across the problem of the maps when he was researching a related question—what caused the Ice Ages? As long ago as 1848 the great Swiss naturalist Louis Agassiz had demonstrated that there had been several periods in the Earth's history when glacial sheets had covered vast areas of the globe that are now temperate. Ever since his time scientists have speculated on the cause of these Ice Ages. Most theories have tended to involve an overall reduction in global temperature, brought about by gradual changes in the Earth's orbit and the direction of its axis. Hapgood felt that such explanations failed to account for the violent upheavals that accompanied the end of the best-documented and last Ice Age.

Hapgood wondered whether the weight of the polar caps themselves might have periodically unbalanced the Earth and caused the Ice Ages. Together with his collaborator, engineer James Campbell, he explored the idea that the Earth's crust rests upon a very weak, virtually liquid layer. They argued that when the ice on the polar caps reaches a critical mass, its weight will cause the outer crust to slip over the globe until equilibrium is reached. So while the Earth's axis stays fixed—with the North and South Poles remaining the coldest parts of the planet—the continental crust shifts. If, for example, Europe were to move some two thousand miles northward, then it would enter the polar region and start to ice over.

This simple mechanism, Hapgood argued, explains the phenomenon we know as the Ice Ages. There was no global change in temperature; rather, the ice was redistributed as different parts of the globe took their turns at entering the Arctic and Antarctic circles. During the last "Ice Age" the North Pole was located in Hudson Bay, with the result that northern America was in the grip of a glacial sheet (see **The First Americans** in **Voyagers and Discoveries**). The end of the Ice Age, according to Hapgood, came about when the Earth's crust started shifting its position about 18,000 years ago. America gradually moved southward, the ice cap melting away within ten thousand years. Floods, earthquakes, and volcanoes decimated the flora and fauna of northern America and Eurasia. Volcanoes belched out dust over Siberia, shielding it from the sun and drastically reducing the temperature. The upheavals and the climate change wiped out the giant mammoths of Siberia. They never recovered, as Siberia was slipping within the polar circle and becoming an inhospitable land of snow and permafrost. In the Southern Hemisphere, Antarctica, having been largely ice-free during the Ice Age of America, was suffering a similar fate. By 6000 B.C. it was completely within the polar circle and was iced over within two thousand years.

Hapgood's model was first published in 1958 in *The Earth's Shifting Crust* and, radical though it seemed, was fairly well received by the scientific community. A foreword to the British edition of his book was written by Kirtley F. Mather, Emeritus Professor of Geology at Harvard University and former President of the American Association for the Advancement of Science, while James C. Brice, Professor of Geology at Washington University, added a firm endorsement: "The assembled geological and geophysical evidence for crustal shifting is convincing." Even Albert Einstein was impressed. Intrigued by their case, he met Hapgood and Campbell to discuss and refine the mathematical aspects of their model, and wrote the original foreword to the book, urging its serious discussion. Hapgood seemed to be onto something big.

It was when he was writing *The Earth's Shifting Crust* that Hapgood first came across the riddle of the early maps of Antarctica. The most famous is that drawn by the Turkish navigator Piri Reis (Captain Piri) in 1513. Given its date, only twenty-one years after the official

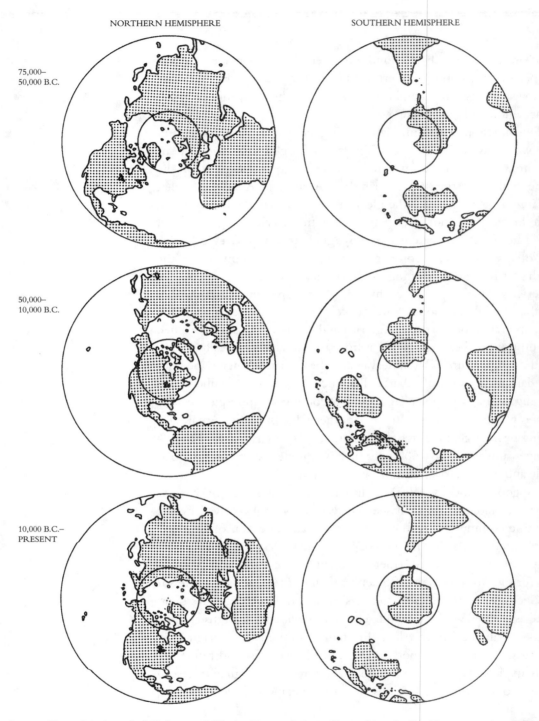

NORTHERN HEMISPHERE   SOUTHERN HEMISPHERE

75,000–
50,000 B.C.

50,000–
10,000 B.C.

10,000 B.C.–
PRESENT

Sketch maps illustrating the poleshift theory of Charles Hapgood. According to him, the Earth's crust was in a different position between 75,000 and 50,000 years B.C.—northern Europe would have been within the Arctic circle, causing the last Ice Age there. After a crustal shift c. 50,000 B.C. most of North America was brought under the ice sheets. Another shift c. 10,000 B.C. brought the polar regions into their present position. Under the previous regimes large parts of Antarctica would have been ice-free. After Flem-Ath and Flem-Ath 1995.

discovery of the New World by Christopher Columbus, it shows the Atlantic coast of South America in remarkable detail. Yet the coastline running south of Brazil is depicted with a strange extension that appears to tail off eastward in the direction of Africa. This section was thought to be fanciful until a modern navigator, Captain Arlington Mallery, studied the map and discovered that it had been drawn according to a projection centered on Cairo. Once this was solved the map could be redrawn using a familiar modern projection, and looked at afresh. The strange extension of South America, according to Mallery, was actually part of the Antarctican coast as it would have appeared before the continent was covered with ice.

Hapgood was thrilled by Mallery's claims, as they seemed to provide unexpected support for his own view that Antarctica had become glaciated in fairly recent times. Determined to get to the bottom of the mystery, he used the subject as a wonderfully interdisciplinary problem for his students at Keene College. Hapgood and his team were surprised to learn that other maps from Renaissance times went much further than the Piri Reis chart and gave *complete* depictions of a southern polar continent. (We have only a portion of the original Piri Reis map.) Theoretically, none could have been drawn before the official discovery of Antarctica in 1819, while the pack ice that surrounds the continent would have prevented any serious investigation of the coastline until the development of ironclad ships. Yet Mercator, the famous sixteenth-century cartographer, drew in fine detail a massive southern continent within the Antarctic circle. His source for this turned out to be the "Terra Australis" (southern land) depicted by the French geographer Oronteus Finaeus in 1531. Hapgood and his students redrew this map on a modern projection and were startled by its general similarity to the shape of Antarctica as it is beneath the ice. In particular, Oronteus Finaeus shows a distinct triangular "bite" into the coastline of his roughly circular southern continent. This appears to correspond with the Ross Sea, an arrow-shaped body of water that penetrates far into Antarctica. The resemblance is intriguing, to say the least.

Hapgood published his conclusions in 1966 in *Maps of the Ancient Sea Kings*. Piri Reis declared that his chart had been compiled from many sources, including Greek maps drawn in the time of Alexander the Great (336–323 B.C.). Could the Greeks themselves have had access to even older maps, reaching back into the mists of antiquity? Hapgood made a daring guess. Perhaps there were earlier civilizations whose seafaring abilities had long been forgotten. They may have explored and mapped the coasts of Antarctica, perhaps as early as 4000

The southern continent shown on the Oronteus Finaeus World Map of 1532.

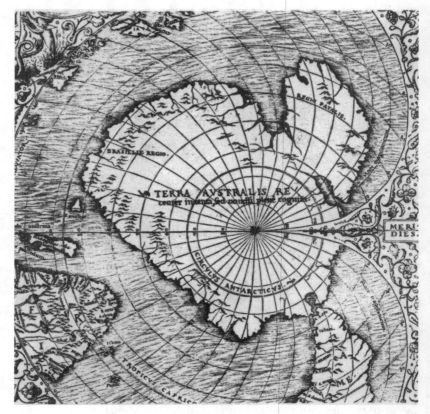

B.C., just before the final stages of its glaciation were completed (according to his Ice Age model). Exactly who these prehistoric mariners and cartographers were, he could not guess. Hapgood devoted much of the rest of his life, before his death in 1982, looking for vestiges of the "ancient sea kings."

The Atlantis Connection

Hapgood's theory of an advanced maritime civilization in prehistoric times was so shocking that professional archaeologists and historians could not bring themselves to discuss it. As for his poleshift theory, it was sidelined during the 1960s, when continental drift rapidly became geological orthodoxy (see **Atlantis—Lost and Found?** in this chapter). Much of the background evidence for crustal shift used by Hapgood—such as the fossilized remains of tropical palm trees found in Greenland—now had another explanation. It was the continents, rather than the crust as a whole, that had shifted.

Hapgood's work was largely forgotten outside of catastrophist circles. Hapgood himself had increasing doubts about the validity of the mechanism he had proposed. Professors Einstein and Mather had both queried whether the weight of the ice caps themselves was really sufficient to bring about a crustal shift. By 1970 Hapgood admitted that the mechanism was inadequate, wondering instead whether the cause of the displacements lay much deeper in the Earth's crust. Yet, undeterred by the lack of an explanation, he felt confident that his basic model was stronger than ever—it was shifts in the position of the Earth's pole that had caused the Ice Ages. Hapgood now had at his disposal dozens of results from the relatively new radiocarbon method, giving dates for geological deposits from the end of the Ice Age. These seemed to confirm that its close had been both rapid and catastrophic, and Hapgood refined his chronology, shortening his time scale for the upheavals that brought the North Pole from Hudson Bay to its present position. He now believed the end of the Ice Age of North America had taken five thousand years (15,000–10,000 B.C.) rather than ten.

Then, in the late 1970s, two Canadian librarians, Rand and Rose Flem-Ath, became interested in Hapgood's work. Hapgood had never identified the mysterious culture responsible for his "Ice Age maps," but the Flem-Aths felt they could solve the problem. In the mid–seventeenth century the visionary scientist Athanasius Kircher drew the first map of the lost continent of Atlantis, following the information given by the Greek philosopher Plato (see **Atlantis—Lost and**

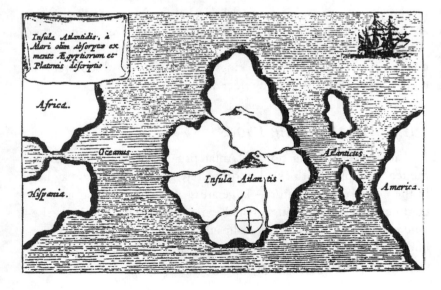

The island-continent of Atlantis as conceived by the visionary scientist Athanasius Kircher (1644)—north is at the bottom of the map.

Found? in this chapter). But he also claimed he had an extra source: a map drawn by the ancient Egyptians and stolen by the Romans, who preserved it. Though the story seems far-fetched, the Flem-Aths believe that his map gives a genuine representation of the shape of Atlantis. When looked at in the right way, the Flem-Aths argue, "we can immediately see that the Egyptian map of Atlantis represents in size, shape, scale, and position, an ice-free Antarctica." If Atlantis was Antarctica, then the mystery of the "ancient sea kings" was solved—they were the Atlanteans.

While the Flem-Aths were writing their findings, Graham Hancock was working on his own blockbuster. Hancock had been on an extended round-the-world tour searching for the "fingerprints" of the lost civilization responsible for Hapgood's maps. At an early stage in the work a crisis had been reached with his researcher. For the kind of civilization that Hancock was envisaging, the researcher insisted, a realistic homeland was needed, preferably one several thousand miles across, with mountain ranges, large rivers, and a stable, congenial climate in which a major culture could develop and flourish over at least ten thousand years. Insisting that there was no such place, the researcher decided the project was hopeless and resigned. Hancock himself agreed that it was a geophysical impossibility for a continent-size landmass to disappear—in the way that people used to believe Atlantis had sunk beneath the waves.

So when he heard from the Flem-Aths in the summer of 1993, Hancock was delighted. By suggesting that Antarctica itself was homeland to the lost civilization, they had supplied "the missing piece of the jigsaw puzzle." It seemed logical that if Hapgood's theories about the maps and the cause of the Ice Ages were correct, then Antarctica had been largely ice-free for thousands of years. The super-civilization of the ancient sea kings had never been discovered because its cities now lie buried under an enormous ice cap.

Fingerprints of the Gods

Archaeological investigation of Antarctica is practically impossible: the ice is simply too thick. (Unfortunately global warming may help in the not too distant future—large areas of the ice sheet around the continent are now melting.) For the moment we have to look elsewhere. Remarkably, Hancock claims that at many of the world's best-known archaeological sites the "fingerprints" of the lost Antarctic civilization can indeed be detected.

Many ancient peoples have stories of culture-bringers of mysterious origin who brought with them the seeds of their civilization. The traditions of the Babylonians of southern Iraq talked of a strange fish-like being called Oannes, who along with others of his kind had taught them writing, agriculture, mathematics, and laws. The Egyptians believed that the gods had taught them every art and science. We find similar culture-bringers in the traditions of the Americas. The Mexicans worshiped the memory of a godlike being called Quetzalcoatl, who "came from across the sea in a boat that moved by itself without paddles," and taught the people how to make fire, build houses, and "live in peace." Different versions, or aliases, of this figure are known from across Central and South America. The Maya of Guatemala called him Kukulkan, "the great organiser, the founder of cities, the former of laws and the teacher of the calendar." Among the Inca peoples of Peru, this revered civilizer was known as Viracocha, and his followers the Viracochas.

Following the trail of these culture-bringers, Hancock looked at Tiahuanaco in Bolivia, believed by the Incas to be the very spot where Viracocha had appeared to order the world. Then, his work complete, Viracocha disappeared like all the mysterious culture-bringers, sailing away with his followers across the Pacific Ocean. The imposing ruins of Tiahuanaco (see **Architectural Wonders**) have inspired many strange theories, one of which provided Hancock with a major lead. Earlier this century Austrian engineer Arthur Posnansky had argued that the main monuments at Tiahuanaco had been built at the breathtakingly early date of 15,000 B.C. Around 10,000 B.C. the city was destroyed by an enormous flood and its surviving inhabitants dispersed through the American continent, spreading civilization as they went. Were then, Hancock wondered, the builders of Tiahuanaco, the legendary Viracochas, and the ancient sea kings of Antarctica one and the same?

Hancock found other fingerprints of the lost civilization throughout the Americas. The extraordinary feats of Mayan, Olmec, Mexican, and Inca civilizations—and in particular their sophisticated calendars and the mastery they showed in carving and building with huge stone blocks—Hancock sees as a legacy from the Viracocha people of Antarctica. He claims that their faces can still be seen on the colossal sculpted heads at San Lorenzo, La Venta, and other Olmec sites near the Gulf coast of Mexico, generally dated to between 1200 and 400 B.C. It has frequently been suggested that the carved faces, with broad noses and thick lips, show that the models must have been

Colossal Olmec head, about 80 tons in weight.

Ceremonial Olmec axe made of jade.

of African origin. This is a startling conclusion, completely at variance with the conventional understanding of history, which sees no contacts between Africa and the Americas before Columbus. It would be less of a mystery, Hancock argues, if we see the heads as relics of a far earlier age, long before the Olmecs, when the Viracochas sailed the world's oceans planting colonies.

The Negroid heads led Hancock to Africa, where he feels there is even clearer evidence of the Viracochas. Ancient historians have noted with surprise that Egyptian civilization arose quite suddenly, apparently appearing fully fledged about 3400 B.C.—with writing, monumental architecture, "and the arts and crafts developed to an astonishing degree," to use the words of Walter Emery, Professor of Egyptology at the University of London. Where were its predecessors? Had Egyptian civilization been founded by outsiders? Hancock believes so. He also argues that the earliest trace of these founders— the Sphinx, whose features he compares to those of the Olmec heads—was made long before the conventional dates for the origins of Egyptian civilization. In 1991 a Boston geologist, Professor Robert Schoch, argued from the erosion on the Sphinx that it must date thousands of years earlier than 2500 B.C., when it is usually thought to have been carved (see **The Riddle of the Sphinx** in **Architectural Wonders**). Hancock himself, with his colleague Adrian Gilbert, has argued that the Sphinx can be redated by using astronomical calculations—to the staggeringly early date of 10,500 B.C.

Do the Great Pyramids also belong to this age? Hancock's colleague Robert Bauval has argued that they were planned to reflect the position of the stars in the constellation Orion over twelve thousand years ago (see **The Orion Mystery** in **Watching the Skies**). If the Pyramids were not actually constructed then, Hancock and Bauval argue that they must have been planned during the eleventh millennium B.C., before the close of the last Ice Age. In their view the Sphinx and the Pyramids were designed specifically by the Viracochas as markers; their astronomical alignments are coded messages that reveal the existence and real dates of the lost civilization.

Never-Never Land

As Hancock presents it, this wide-ranging case, drawing on evidence from archaeology, astronomy, and geology, may seem very persuasive. Yet when we break it down into its constituent parts and examine them in more detail, the edifice he has built soon begins to look shaky.

The dates that Hancock advocates for the relics of his Antarctican civilization are all highly dubious. He takes Posnansky's incredible dates for Tiahuanaco—based on supposed astronomical alignments—simply on trust and completely ignores the years of work put in by archaeologists at the site over recent decades. That work makes it clear that Posnansky was gloriously wrong, and that the city of Tiahuanaco, far from being a relic of the Ice Age, was really built around A.D. 100, as we can see from both pottery and radiocarbon evidence (see **Tiahuanaco** in **Architectural Wonders**).

There is equally no good reason to doubt that the giant sculpted heads from the Gulf of Mexico were made by the Olmecs, the beginnings of whose civilization can be dated by radiocarbon to about 1200 B.C. Hancock's method here is to challenge the assumption that the heads are associated with nearby Olmec remains, but in doing so he leaves them in a complete vacuum. When there is no trace at all of anything dating from the eleventh millennium in the area, and when the sculptures are surrounded by other remains of the Olmecs, the obvious and natural conclusion is that they are Olmec. Similar faces appear on numerous Olmec carvings such as jade ornaments. As for the race depicted, the case for their being African is vigorously disputed by specialists in Mexican archaeology (see **Introduction** to **Voyagers and Discoveries**).

Hancock's claim that the Sphinx has been redated by scientific means—through geological estimates and astronomical calculations—is immensely overblown. There are many other ways of reading the evidence, and at present the conventional date for the Sphinx, around 2500 B.C., is still the best. Likewise the case for backdating the Pyramids is hopelessly weak (see **The Riddle of the Sphinx** in **Architectural Wonders** and **The Orion Mystery** in **Watching the Skies**).

The idea that the Pyramids, even though they were constructed in the third millennium B.C., were designed to match the skies of the eleventh, is merely fantastic. How the organizers of such a grand scheme, concocted about 10,500 B.C., could impose their will on the Egyptians living eight thousand years later is something that Hancock never fully explains—he would be hard-pressed to. Like his claims that "secret knowledge" from his Ice Age civilization was preserved over the millennia by priests, it begs the question of how the information was transmitted.

As Hancock himself admits, his model leaves a huge gulf between his Sphinx builders in the eleventh millennium and the Egyptians, whose civilization appeared around 3400 B.C. By the eleventh millennium there were settlers in the Nile Valley, hunters and gatherers who used stone tools, and by the late sixth millennium simple farming communities were flourishing. So there were Egyptians during Hancock's gulf. Yet before about 3400 B.C., shortly before the First Dynasty, there were no towns, temples, pyramids, obelisks, statues, inscriptions, or indeed any of the other things that we think of as characterizing Egyptian civilization. So if the Egyptians learned their arts and sciences from the Viracochas, how did they remember them over all those thousands of years?

John Anthony West, a colleague of Hancock's and the main proponent of backdating the Sphinx, admitted that this is a serious difficulty, to say the least:

> The big problem with all this, from my point of view, is the transmission process: how exactly the knowledge does get handed on during the thousands and thousands of years between the construction of the Sphinx and the flowering of dynastic Egypt. Theoretically you're sort of stuck—aren't you?—with this vast period in which the knowledge has to be transmitted. This is not easy to slough off.

Quite. All West could come up with is the weak suggestion that the "knowledge" was transmitted orally, passed down through hundreds of generations in the form of myths and legends. This might work well for religious or esoteric information. One could even imagine mathematical or astronomical knowledge being handed down this way. But how on earth could knowledge—"secret" or otherwise—about highly practical matters such as working and moving large stones be preserved without people actually building things? And if they already possessed the skills to construct pyramids and other great monuments in the eleventh millennium B.C., why did the Egyptians wait so long before they chose to benefit from such knowledge? Why indeed do the earliest pyramids of Egypt reveal trial-and-error experimentation, showing that their builders were not working from an existing blueprint, but clearly working things out as they went along? (See **How Were the Pyramids Built?** in **Architectural Wonders**.)

Exactly the same problems apply to Hancock's model for the rise of ancient American civilizations. While he argues that the Olmecs, Incas, and others were merely inheritors of a great legacy from the Viracochas, an immense gulf exists between his hypothetical Ice Age colonists who arrived before 10,000 B.C. and the first glimmerings of urban civilizations in the third millennium. Even the idea that the Americas were inhabited at all before about 9500 B.C. is highly controversial (see **The First Americans** in **Voyagers and Discoveries**).

In short, Hancock's explanation of the origin of ancient civilizations doesn't do much explaining. All his theory really does is set up a pattern of problems, composed of vast gaps between the imagined and real beginnings of ancient societies.

Lost Antarctica

So who, then, drew the Ice Age maps? Or perhaps we should be asking a different question. Is the evidence that the maps show an ice-free Antarctica really that strong?

Of the cases presented, that of the Flem-Aths regarding Athanasius Kircher's map is by far the weakest. Kircher's drawing clearly shows that he believed Atlantis was plumb in the middle of the Atlantic, and not at the South Pole. The Flem-Aths claim that if we look at the map "differently," then Kircher's Atlantis can be identified as Antarctica— but in order to perform the trick they have to ignore Kircher's own captions. Even after this subterfuge, Kircher's Atlantis is still not in the right place for Antarctica, while the resemblance between the shapes of the two continents is hardly compelling.

Mallery and Hapgood's bold claims about the Piri Reis maps are more intriguing, but highly questionable. They were certainly right about the map's projection. A sixteenth-century Turkish navigator could have very likely centered a chart on a point within Egypt. Yet, given that, what do modern reconstructions of such a projection show? As graphically confirmed by space photos taken almost due overhead from Egypt, this projection shows South America with a curiously elongated shape curving out southeastward into the Atlantic. In that sense the veracity of the Piri Reis map *is* confirmed. But there is no reason to see the "tail" of South America as being anything other than that elongation.

Hapgood had to make some extraordinary assumptions in order to make the map show Antarctica instead. If the elongated coastline really included Antarctica as well, he had to assume that some two thousand miles of the South American continent had been omitted (which would hardly say much for the map's accuracy), and that the Drake Passage, the sea route between the two continents, was omitted by Piri Reis. This fact, that the "two" continents are joined together on the map, is an important clue; if we read the map the most obvious

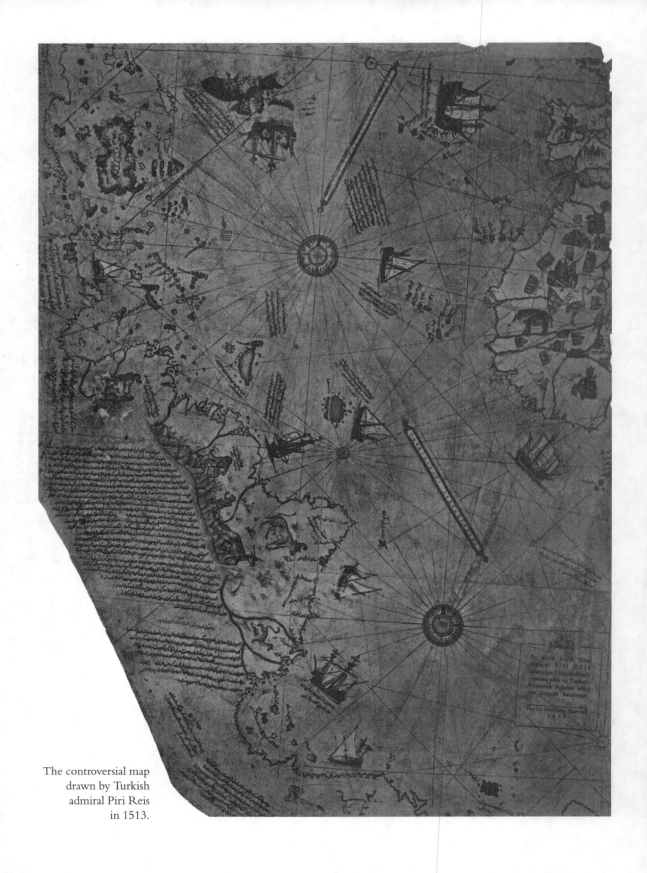

The controversial map
drawn by Turkish
admiral Piri Reis
in 1513.

way and assume that only *one* continent is shown, then the "missing" two thousand miles of South American coastline reappear.

The captions on the map clearly support this "normal" reading. When the map was drawn (1513) the Portuguese were exploring and laying claim to large areas of South America, and it is to the Portuguese that the captions specifically refer. One says that a Portuguese ship arrived on the coast from India ("Hind"), to be shot at with arrows by aggressive natives. These locals were "all of them naked"—feasible for South America but hardly likely for Antarctica! The next captions, farther along the supposed Antarctican coast, refer to Portuguese reports of "white-haired monsters," "six-horned oxen," "large snakes," and hot weather—again, this cannot be Antarctica. Referring to the monsters, Piri states: "The Portuguese infidels have written it in their maps." Clearly Piri was using maps and descriptions made by *contemporary Portuguese* navigators.

Hapgood might have saved himself a lot of trouble if he had paid closer attention to the captions on the Piri Reis map. Its creator said that his most ancient sources (from the time of Alexander the Great) showed "the inhabited quarter of the world"—this is obviously the Mediterranean and surroundings (the Graeco-Roman world). There is not a hint in Piri Reis's captions that he had used extremely ancient maps for the coastlines of southern America. Instead Piri makes explicit statements about the Portuguese.

Finally, what of Mallery and Hapgood's belief that their interpretation of Piri Reis is supported by modern findings about the shape of Antarctica beneath the ice? In 1949 a seismic survey, carried out by a joint Norwegian-British-Swedish team of scientists, suggested that a group of islands, now hidden by ice, lies off the mountainous coast of Antarctica near the tip of South America. Hapgood saw here a good match with the southernmost section of the Piri Reis map, showing (in his interpretation) a group of islands off a coast with mountains.

Unfortunately for Hapgood, information from more recent scientific research goes against his interpretation. The real shape of Antarctica's geography under glaciation is not revealed by simply taking the ice off. The millions of tons of ice depress the continental crust by hundreds of feet. If we were to compensate for that distortion, then the coastline would look very different from its present shape beneath the ice. The islands off the coast that Hapgood compared to those on the Piri Reis map would disappear. Taking the map at face value—as showing only one continent—then the islands that intrigued

When the Oronteus Finaeus map is redrawn on a modern projection, it appears to show a surprising match with the sub-ice coastline of Antarctica. However, if the weight of the ice sheet were actually removed from the continent, the coastline would change considerably—for example, the western arm of the continent (to left) would be largely submerged by water and broken into islands, unlike the Finaeus map.

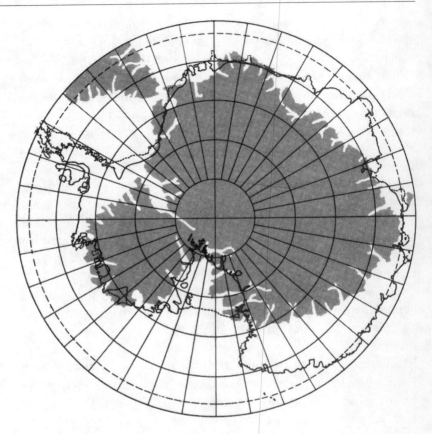

Hapgood match quite happily with the Falklands, famous as the scene of the war between Britain and Argentina in 1982.

The same problem affects Hapgood's most convincing exhibit, the Oronteus Finaeus map of 1531. If we removed the ice cover, then the shape of Antarctica would change dramatically, ruining Hapgood's comparison. Yet how could Oronteus Finaeus have shown an Antarctic continent at all, when there should be none in terms of sixteenth-century geographical knowledge? As Hapgood admits himself, it was a custom of Renaissance cartographers to draw a huge continent at the South Pole simply to balance out the landmasses around the North Pole. Dozens of attempts were inked out to describe the shape of a hypothetical *Terra Australis* (the "Southern Land"), as it was known. Oronteus Finaeus's map might be seen as the best, or luckiest guess, perhaps including some information from mariners who had glimpsed the extent of the southern continent before its official discovery in 1819.

As for Hapgood's more general model of poleshifting, the scientific results coming from Antarctica did, at one time, seem to show that there was something odd about its climatic history At a meeting with Hapgood in 1955, Einstein was particularly impressed with some recent and surprising evidence, the cores taken from the bed of Antarctica's Ross Sea by the Byrd Expedition of 1947–48 and dated by using the new ionium radioactive method. The cores showed that between 13,000 and 4,000 B.C. fine-grained sediments—like those laid down by rivers—were being deposited at the bottom of the Ross Sea. The conclusion of the expedition was that Antarctica must have had a temperate climate, and been unglaciated, between those dates. In Einstein's view the data "virtually compel the conclusion that a shift of the earth's entire crust must have taken place."

The evidence of more recent years leads to quite a different conclusion. Hapgood himself may have realized he was in trouble in 1970, when he reissued his original book. Using the latest radiocarbon dates, he had shifted his estimate for the end of the Ice Age back to 10,000 B.C., with the shift of the poles to their present positions starting in 15,000 B.C. According to this model Antarctica should have been ice-free before 15,000 B.C., after which it would have gradually frozen over. Yet the evidence from the Ross Sea cores, once Hapgood's star witness, appeared to show completely the *opposite* pattern—Antarctica was glaciated before 13,000 B.C. and *then* gradually lost its ice cover. Hapgood was unable to provide a clear or convincing answer to this problem. Worse still for his model, it is now known that glaciers can deposit fine-grained sediments like rivers, so there is no need to deduce that Antarctica was ice-free at any time in the recent geological past. Other well-dated and more direct evidence of ice deposits themselves seems to show quite clearly that Antarctica has been covered by its ice sheet for at least 100,000 years.

The most recent evidence tends to show that North America, Europe, and Antarctica all suffered at much the same time from the maximum extension of the ice sheets (about 21,000 to 18,000 years ago) during the last major glaciation. The ice sheets began to retreat *globally*, rather than regionally, about 12,000 years ago. So it seems that something else, not poleshifting, was causing their movement.

You will find none of these problems in the books of Graham Hancock or the Flem-Aths, who still present the old evidence seized on by Hapgood as if it were meaningful today. Einstein's endorsement of Hapgood's theory is proudly displayed as if he had never expressed doubts about the mechanisms behind Hapgood's crustal-shift model and as if the "proof" (from the 1940s) about Antarctica's recent ice-free history had not fallen through. Einstein was no idiot—he would have kept in touch with the current scientific literature and reassessed things accordingly. The same is true of Hapgood. Though they were sometimes embarrassing for his model, he reported the new scientific data on the Ice Ages and did his best to explain them. Hancock and the Flem-Aths merely ignore the problems and repeat Hapgood's research as if it were as fresh as today's news.

We still do not know what caused the Ice Ages, so in that sense the theory of poleshifting has not been *completely* ruled out. But to present it the way that Hancock does, as a theory supported not only by Einstein but also by scientific dating methods, is misleading. One can search in vain through Hancock's bibliography for *any* mention of contemporary research on the Ice Age and Antarctica, such as the 680-page multiauthored work on the geology of Antarctica published in Oxford (on behalf of the Australian government) in 1991. This is distressing. What is even more sad is that a (typical) review of *Fingerprints of the Gods*, in the *Literary Review*, can describe Hancock's work as "impressive and scholarly . . . one of the intellectual landmarks of the decade." That, for sure, it is not.

All things considered, it is fairly safe to say that Hancock's prediction of another poleshift in the year A.D. 2012 is a complete fantasy. There are serious things to worry about in the near future, including environmental disasters and the chance impact from asteroids and other space debris. And if we are going to be realistic—and properly learn from the messages of the past—then we will do well to dispense with the fiction of an Antarctic super-civilization.

THE RISE AND FALL OF MAYA CIVILIZATION

In October 1839, American traveler John Stephens and English artist Frederick Catherwood arrived by ship from New York at the port of Belize. This tiny outpost of the British Empire lay on the coast of the Yucatán Peninsula of Mexico. Stephens and Catherwood headed inland, in search of the mysterious, overgrown cities glimpsed by the sixteenth-century Spanish *conquistadores* in the depths of the rain forest. Only recently had historians rescued their accounts, which had long moldered in Spanish archives, and begun to speculate about lost civilizations in the jungles of Central America. Some brief reports from local explorers, especially the account by one Captain del Rio of a visit to the ruined city of Palenque made in 1737, eventually published in England in 1822, appeared to back up the Spanish chroniclers. Rather than debate the reliability of the claims from the safety of their libraries, Stephens and Catherwood were inspired to follow up these extraordinary accounts firsthand.

After a difficult journey through bandit-infested country, they penetrated the dense rain forest of Honduras to reach the ancient city of Copán. They were awed by the scale and magnificence of the ruins, which included houses, statues, plazas, and pyramids. Although Stephens and Catherwood guessed from the Spanish chroniclers that this was the work of a people called the Maya, they were frustratingly unable to discover anything further about its ancient builders from the local inhabitants. Stephens confessed himself entirely baffled:

There were no associations connected with this place. But architecture, sculpture, and painting, all arts which embellish life, had flourished in this overgrown forest; orators, warriors, and statesmen,

The Stephens and Catherwood expedition reaches Labná.

beauty, ambition, and glory had lived and passed away, and none knew that such things had been, or could tell of their past existence.

The City was desolate. No remnant of this race hangs round the ruins, with traditions handed down from father to son and from generation to generation. It lay before us like a shattered bark [ship] in the midst of the ocean, her masts gone, her name effaced, her crew perished, and none to tell whence she came. . . . The place where we were sitting, was it a citadel from which an unknown people had sounded the trumpet of war? Or a temple for the worship of the God of peace? Or did the inhabitants worship idols made with their own hands and offer sacrifices on the stones before them? All was mystery, dark, impenetrable mystery, and every circumstance increased it.

The Rise of the Maya

A hundred and fifty years of painstaking archaeological inquiry allows us today to understand how the Maya emerged to transform the rain forest of Central America into a scene of urban civilization. By 1000 B.C. the Maya were settled agriculturalists growing a variety of crops in clearings in the forest, which they turned into villages. They appear to have lived in a society of equals, without clear rulers or ceremonial centers. Then between 800 and 500 B.C. signs of a ruling elite within Maya society start to emerge in the form of elaborate burial monuments. At Los Mangales in the Salama Valley of highland Mexico, a chief was buried on a special mortuary platform accompanied by human sacrifices and rich grave goods of jade and shell. Slightly later the ceremonial center at El Portón was built, involving the construction of earth terraces and platforms, on which were erected altars and standing stones, one with a brief written inscription, alas too damaged to be read today.

In the lowlands of Guatemala and the Yucatán Peninsula of Mexico, vast ceremonial centers appeared quite suddenly after 600 B.C. At Nakbé in northern Guatemala, the site was swiftly transformed from a modest village into a city with a major monumental structure at its heart. A massive platform was constructed on the ruins of the original settlement, on top of which were a series of terraced buildings up to 60 feet tall. Without any doubt we can see here the development of a more complex society.

From 400 B.C. to A.D. 250 major ceremonial centers developed in all parts of the Maya area, many carved out of the tropical rain forest that covered the southern lowlands of Guatemala, Belize, and

Mexico. These cities were dominated by enormous terraced platforms, some forming giant temple-pyramids. Vast palaces of limestone masonry with vaulted rooms were constructed, set within architectural layouts that emphasized the most important buildings of a city, arranged around plazas with rows of standing stones lined up in front of them. A highly sophisticated art style emerged, seen in bas-reliefs, wall paintings, and beautiful pottery with multicolored fired decoration. Hieroglyphic writing became widespread, and inscriptions can be dated by using the Maya Long Count, an elaborate but incredibly accurate calendrical system (see **Box: The Maya Calendar**).

The most impressive surviving example of an early center is that at El Mirador in Guatemala, which was abandoned and never built over later on. This great city has a central built-up area covering some one and a half miles from east to west. At the heart of El Mirador was a series of enormous temple-pyramids that reach heights of over 200 feet above the jungle floor. There are two sets of pyramids and platforms, connected by a stone causeway.

The East group is dominated by the Danta pyramid and its associated platforms, which cover an area of some two million square feet. This vast pyramid and the structure on which it sits have a combined height of 230 feet, with smaller superstructures on top of that, forming what is probably the largest single monument in the Americas. (The Great Pyramid of Cheops in Egypt is twice as tall.) In the West group the Tigre pyramid is 180 feet high, with an estimated volume of over 13,000,000 cubic feet. It was not only the buildings at El Mirador that were larger than life; gigantic plaster masks of deities flanked the stairways leading to the major temples, ensuring that worshipers were doubly overawed. Below the pyramids lie other structures, probably lavish royal tombs, unfortunately now virtually all looted.

Such impressive monuments are a clear sign that the Maya had by now successfully carved a civilization out of the rain forest, but who was in charge? Earlier generations of archaeologists considered the great Maya cities to be purely ceremonial centers, occupied only by their peace-loving priestly rulers and their retinues except at great festivals. The British Mayanist Sir Eric Thompson, working at the Field Museum of Chicago, suggested that the Maya character encouraged the development of religious authority: "devoutness, discipline, and respect for authority would have facilitated the emergence of a theocracy."

This was not, however, an age of peace ruled over by unworldly priests living in solitude among the temples. In the last twenty-five years a succession of remarkable breakthroughs have enabled us to read the Maya's hieroglyphic language. Whereas Thompson and others assumed that inscriptions outside temples concerned abstruse matters of astronomy and calendrics that fascinated the priests, the translations now available show beyond any doubt that the cities were ruled by an aristocracy that was firmly secular and indeed warlike in outlook. Hieroglyphic writing on monuments was mainly used to record the achievements of Maya rulers, especially in war. Victory stones were erected outside the temples, bearing the names of famous captives. Great monuments were liberally marked with the names and faces of the rulers who commissioned them. Rule by peaceful priests is out, but it is also clear that the aristocracy was intensely superstitious, especially where lucky days and years in the calendar were concerned (see **Box: The Maya Calendar**).

Professor Michael Coe of Yale University, leading scholar of Maya culture, sums up the extraordinary shift that has taken place:

> From a picture of the Maya that emphasized peaceful theocracies led by priest-astronomers, ruling over relatively empty "ceremonial centers," we now have highly warlike city-states led by grim dynasts obsessed with human sacrifice and the ritual letting of their own blood.

Excavation has also played its part in overturning the established picture of Maya cities. Vital evidence that the cities were not just ceremonial centers has now been found at many lowland sites. On the outskirts of cities such as El Mirador are groups of low rectangular mounds of earth and stone long ignored, but which archaeological investigations have now shown were occupied by small wooden houses, raised above the level of the summer flooding. These humble dwellings housed the ordinary inhabitants who served the aristocrats living it up in the palaces at the heart of the city.

The Classic Maya

Once the form of Maya civilization was set, it went on to new heights of extravagance and sophistication. Archaeologists investigating the ancient Maya have become enormously impressed with their achievements, showering them with praise. Thus Michael Coe sees the period known as the Classic as the high point of Central American history:

During a span of six centuries, from about A.D. 250 to 900, the Maya, particularly those of the Central Area, reached intellectual and artistic heights which no others in the New World, and few in the Old, could match at that time. The Classic period was a kind of Golden Age.

There was a huge population settled in the major cities, smaller towns, and surrounding countryside. Trade both in everyday items such as food and in precious minerals, especially jade, flourished among the Maya centers. Jade carving reached considerable heights. Superb murals decorated the palaces of the rulers, the best surviving examples being those at Bonampak in the southern lowlands, dating to A.D. 792. They depict a successful campaign led by Chan-muan, king of Bonampak, and the sacrifice of his noble prisoners. Artistic ability was highly prized, for many of the magnificent painted pots are signed by the artist himself, who in some cases turns out to be a member of the aristocracy. Presumably writing the difficult hieroglyphic script was a skill mastered only by the elite of Maya society, so a scribe would necessarily be of noble birth. It still seems extraordinary, however, that the Maya aristocracy sometimes personally decorated their own pottery.

The intellectual achievements of the Classic Maya period were also impressive, especially in the fields of astronomy and mathematics. At Chichén Itzá in the Yucatán Peninsula an observatory was constructed to watch the movements of the sun and the planet Venus. The Maya carried out detailed observations of the Sun, the Moon, Venus, Mars, and Jupiter, working out their movements with such precision that they were able to predict eclipses. Such complex records required a sound mathematical system, and here too the Maya achieved great successes. Their invention of a symbol for zero gave the system (which used 20, rather than 10, as a base) such flexibility that numbers in the millions could be expressed with only three symbols: a bar for 5, a dot for 1, and a stylized shell for zero.

Most thoroughly mapped of the great cities of the Classic Maya is Tikal in the southern lowlands, where an area of six square miles contains some 3,000 structures, ranging from towering temple-pyramids (one 230 feet high) containing up to 150,000 tons of stone and rubble, and vast palaces with hundreds of rooms, to tiny platforms on which there once stood thatch-roofed wooden huts. The size of these ordinary buildings increases the closer one approaches the ceremonial heart of Tikal, suggesting that a good town center address was important to the Maya middle class. Tikal's population is thought to have

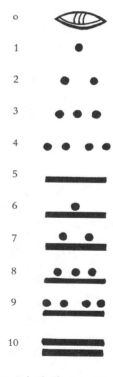

Mayan glyphs for 0 to 10.

Monument from Copán, as
depicted by Catherwood.

F. Catherwood.

S. H. Gimber

The Temple of the
Inscriptions, Palenque.

been something like 90,000 people, the vast majority of this multitude being peasants and workers supporting the rulers.

Dozens of Maya cities existed in this period, a few of which dominated many others, with rivalries between overlords and their subjects being intense. Violent conflicts between major centers and smaller cities can be seen clearly in Mayan Honduras. Here the massive city of Copán is impressively well preserved, with its ball court for playing the sacred game being justly famous for its superb sculptures of macaws. The thirteenth king in the ruling dynasty of Copán (which took power around A.D. 400) was "Gopher-Provider," who ascended to the throne on July 9 in A.D. 695. On May 3 of A.D. 738, shortly after dedicating the final version of the ball court, he led a raid on the smaller city of Quiriguá some thirty miles away, a center that was probably under the control of Copán for much of the time and frequently used to show off its power. Only this time everything went wrong—Gopher-Provider was humiliatingly captured and beheaded by "Cauac Sky" of Quiriguá. These rivalries between neighboring cities must have been a constant source of tension and a major drain on resources.

Most famous of all the Maya rulers is undoubtedly "Sun Lord Pacal" of the city of Palenque on the western edge of the Maya world in central Mexico. In the late 1940s Mexican archaeologist Alberto Ruz Lhuillier was investigating the site of the Temple of the Inscriptions, which rests on a 65-foot-high stepped pyramid. He was intrigued by a stone in the floor of the temple that had drilled into it a double row of holes filled with removable stone stoppers. Lifting this slab revealed a hidden stairway, leading down below the temple. This secret passage, which proved to reach down some 70 feet into the pyramid, was choked with rubble, which took two years to clear. Eventually Ruz and his team came up against a huge triangular slab, in front of which was a stone box containing pottery and precious jade, shell, and pearl items. Nearby were the bodies of half a dozen youths, perhaps sacrificed as an offering together with the contents of the stone box.

On June 15, 1952, the massive slab was removed and archaeologists entered a vault. In the middle of the room was a massive sarcophagus carved from a single block of limestone and covered with intricate reliefs. Attached to the wall were nine over-life-size figures made of plaster, presumably representing gods or earlier rulers of Palenque. Pottery vessels and plates littered the floor of the tomb, placed there as accompaniments for the ruler in the splendid afterlife that was guaranteed him. Along with these were two plaster heads that had been removed from life-size statues elsewhere at Palenque. Archaeologists speculated that they were portraits of the dead ruler. Laid on top of the sarcophagus were several stone axes, perhaps symbolizing success in battle.

When the stone coffin was opened it revealed the body of a man, with a jade bead in each of his hands and another in his mouth, two jade figurines next to the body, a jade diadem, earplugs and rings, a belt with jade masks suspended from it, and a hip cloth decorated with jade beads. Most spectacular of the contents of the tomb was a life-size jade mosaic mask with eyes made from shell and obsidian that had been set over the corpse's face. This superb mask bore a remarkable resemblance to the two plaster heads, confirming Ruz's suspicions.

Archaeologists had to wait until the 1970s and the extraordinary breakthrough in deciphering Maya hieroglyphic writing to learn the identity of this jade-bedecked ruler of Palenque. Up until that time he was taken to be a high priest, but when the texts lining the walls of the Temple of the Inscriptions could be read, they revealed in amazing detail the life story of "Sun Lord Pacal (Hand-shield)." Born on

The cover of Sun Lord Pacal's tomb inside the Temple of the Inscriptions.

March 26 in A.D. 603, he ascended the throne at the tender age of twelve in the year 615. Pacal then ruled for sixty-nine years, dying at the age of eighty on August 31, A.D. 683. Construction of the Temple of the Inscriptions was Pacal's own project, for work began in 675. He did not live to see it finished, and it was left to his son, "Jaguar Serpent," to complete the pyramid's façade and the temple on top, which he did by A.D. 692. The sixty-nine steps (one for each year of his reign) that front the Temple are a lasting tribute to Pacal's extraordinary reign.

Pacal's tomb at Palenque has been made somewhat notorious by the writings of "ancient astronaut" theorist Erich Von Däniken (see **Introduction** to **Architectural Wonders**), who claims that the carvings on the sarcophagus show an astronaut in his spaceship:

> There sits a human being, with the upper part of his body bent forward like a racing motorcyclist; today any child would identify his vehicle as a rocket. It is pointed at the front, then changes to strangely grooved indentations like inlet ports, widens out, and terminates at the tail in a darting flame. . . . Our space traveler—he is clearly depicted as one—is not only bent forward tensely; he is also looking intently at an apparatus hanging in front of his face.

Von Däniken himself clearly finds his evidence compelling, concluding that "a genuinely unprejudiced look at this picture would make even the most die-hard skeptic stop and think." In fact, anyone familiar with Mayan art can identify Von Däniken's astronaut as a typical Mayan aristocrat, dressed as Pacal was in his coffin and in murals elsewhere at Palenque, and his supposed rocket as a series of perfectly standard decorative motifs. Two things about the carving completely give the game away. At the pointed top of the rocket is a quetzal, the national bird of Guatemala, which would be a fatally unaerodynamic ornament for any spaceship. Even more of a problem for the astronaut is that his head is sticking out of the rocket without a helmet. If all extraterrestrials were as incompetent as this, it is no wonder that the Maya decided to build their civilization without help from another planet.

The Fall of the Maya

The collapse of Maya society was just as dramatic as its achievements. It began shortly after A.D. 800 at a few locations, then spread rapidly throughout the southern tropical forest lowlands of Guatemala, Belize, and Mexico. The hallmarks of Mayan high culture were abandoned, populations shrank dramatically (probably by millions), and within just over a century huge tracts of the lowlands were abandoned, never to be reoccupied. One clear indication of the disaster that had struck the southern lowlands is the disappearance, around A.D. 830, of the boastful inscriptions erected by Maya rulers. In itself, this is not enough to say that the Maya as a whole were in serious trouble, but their rulers certainly were—no new monuments were built and aristocratic burials became rarer and less elaborate, while the major cities went into inexorable decline.

The fate of Tikal is typical of the great Mayan cities. Tikal's rulers stopped constructing monuments by A.D. 800 and the inscriptions recording their lives and times become rarer and are full of gaps after this date. By A.D. 830 no new buildings at all were being started and the inscriptions fade out. The population fell by two-thirds, judging by the abandoned house platforms. Tikal's remaining occupants huddled in the surviving stone structures, the roofs constantly in danger of falling in, strewing their rubbish in rooms and across once carefully swept courtyards. The survivors tried to keep up ceremonial traditions, but this amounted to little more than hauling around fragments of ancient inscribed stones and setting them up in a haphazard manner, even upside down. After a century of this twilight living, Tikal was abandoned for good. The rain forest soon returned to swallow it up, and so it remained until its rediscovery at the end of the nineteenth century.

Some centers were not so immediately affected. Indeed, for a brief time their rulers became more powerful, reflecting this higher status in the erection of inscribed stones, as their overlords in other cities vanished. So at Seibal in the southern lowlands a series of monuments were constructed after A.D. 830, but this short period of importance ended by 889, and Seibal was abandoned.

Events were rather different in the Yucatán Peninsula to the north, where the upheavals were delayed by a century. In the Puuc Hills bordering the lowlands, the city of Uxmal emerged around A.D. 850 as the capital of a large territory. Uxmal is dominated by two enormous temple-pyramids, but is better known for its inappropriately named Nunnery, actually a palace complex of four buildings around a courtyard, and the Palace of the Governors built on artificial terracing made from some 500,000 tons of rubble. The palace has an extraordinarily elaborate stone mosaic frieze, 300 feet long, on its eastern façade. Although it was once believed that refugees from the collapse of lowland Maya civilization flooded into the Puuc area after 830, there is little archaeological evidence to support this. In any case, Uxmal itself seems to have declined around 925.

Much the most important center in Yucatán to survive and indeed flourish after the abandonment of the southern lowland cities was Chichén Itzá, taken over in A.D. 987, according to Mayan oral histories (written down after the Spanish conquest), by a group of Mexican Toltecs. They brought about a renaissance at Chichén Itzá, creating hybrid artistic and architectural styles and embarking on a major building program of temples, sacrificial platforms, and a ballcourt. Spectacular though Chichén Itzá was, the flourishing of this one city, under foreign domination, was hardly a revival of Classic Maya civilization.

Collapsing Theories

Ever since the rediscovery of the Mayan cities in the rain forest, explorers and archaeologists have debated the reason for their abandonment. Not surprisingly, given the way that the jungle had swallowed

Temple at Chichén Itzá, as depicted by Catherwood.

up once-great cities, many Europeans and North Americans at first found the idea of a civilization flourishing in the rain forest impossible to accept. They concluded that the downfall of the Mayan cities was inevitable in such an inhospitable environment, and that civilization could never have arisen there. The Maya must have been colonists from elsewhere, and possible origins were proposed, ranging from Mexico to locations as remote as Egypt and China. Today archaeologists are not inclined to take such a dim view of the rain forest, and have no problem accepting that the Maya were of local origin.

Another explanation popular in early writings on the Maya collapse was a sudden natural catastrophe. The silent cities reclaimed by the rain forest certainly had the look of being hurriedly abandoned, their populations fleeing disaster never to return. Earthquakes undoubtedly hit a number of Maya cities, including Quiriguá, and at Xunantunich major damage inflicted on a palace went unrepaired. However, most large Maya centers (which were located well away from fault lines) show no signs of earthquake damage.

Epidemic diseases such as the Black Death of medieval Europe have undoubtedly led to massive casualties and enormous social upheaval. Yellow fever has been put forward as a cause for the abandonment of the Maya lowlands, although it does not seem to have been a major killer in the New World before 1492. Although not impossible, no direct evidence exists to support this theory either from the skeletons of the lowland Maya themselves (despite the best efforts of physical anthropologists) or in the form of mass burials of the victims of an epidemic.

Caribbean hurricanes frequently sweep over the Maya lowlands, destroying large areas of agricultural land. Hurricanes and disease have been combined in a variation on the theme of catastrophe in the suggestion that the destructive maize mosaic virus reached the lowlands from the eastern Caribbean borne on the winds of a hurricane, wiping out the crop on which the Maya depended. As leading Mayanist Professor Robert Sharer of the University of Pennsylvania points out:

> The idea that the transient and relatively localized effects of hurricanes could trigger the failure of a whole civilization is difficult to swallow. The destruction of a forest in a hurricane's path might even prove to be beneficial, for a major effect of the destruction is likely to be the clearing of new lands for agricultural exploitation.

A different kind of catastrophe is involved in the suggestion that an invasion of more warlike peoples from Mexico brought about the

Mayan emblem for the city of
Seibal.

downfall of the Maya. Professors Jeremy Sabloff and Gordon Willey of Harvard University suggested that invaders armed with superior weapons arrived from the Gulf coast of Mexico and swept through the Maya heartland. At the cities of Seibal and Altar de Sacrificios there are abrupt changes in pottery, architecture, and sculpture, leading to the idea that these centers had been captured and new ways introduced by the conquerors. A foreign presence at these specific sites is clearly indicated, seen at Seibal with the introduction of Mexican gods and the depiction of an obvious outsider with pageboy haircut and clipped mustache called "Ah Bolon Tun" on a sculpture dated to A.D. 849. However, most archaeologists agree that the obvious candidates for this takeover are the Putún Maya, Mexicanized trader-warriors who controlled the coastal trade routes. What would the greatest merchants of ancient Central America possibly hope to gain from destroying their main customers? Perhaps the invaders were more a symptom than a cause of the problems; maybe the Putún Maya simply moved in to protect their valuable trade routes as lowland Maya civilization collapsed around them.

Mexicans are also implicated in a more peaceful conflict that some believe brought about the downfall of the Maya. They argue that the lowlands were dependent on trade relations with Mexico to support the ambitious programs of building indulged in by the city rulers. Everything was fine so long as trade routes were channeled through Tikal, but in the ninth century A.D. a quicker sea route around the Yucatán Peninsula was opened up. Deprived of their main source of wealth, the Maya rulers and their cities soon collapsed. Archaeological evidence from island trading centers does show that they were on the rise at this time, so there is some support for this theory. However, the Putún Maya occupation of Seibal hardly fits comfortably within this model. In any case, most Mayanists do not believe that external trade was essential to the rise of lowland civilization, so even its complete disappearance would not lead the cities to fall.

Too Many Mouths, Too Little Food

The discovery that common people lived in the major cities of the Maya has revolutionized archaeological thinking in more ways than just overthrowing old ideas of empty ceremonial centers. Finding a vast number of house mounds, and recently even more humble dwellings between them, has raised the specter of overpopulation having brought about the Maya collapse.

According to this theory, supported by most Mayanists, including

Michael Coe and Robert Sharer, an ever-increasing population proved difficult to feed without taking areas of poorer land under cultivation. Less productive ground had to be worked even harder than fields on better soils to come up with a worthwhile return on the investment of time and effort. No longer could Maya farmers allow land to recover by lying fallow. As greater efforts were made to squeeze the last grain from unhelpful soil, plant diseases and insect pests increased while grasses began to invade the fields.

There may also have been droughts, fatal to a society on the edge. Local crop failures were dealt with by importing food, but this could only be a short-term solution. As food shortages started to bite, malnutrition lessened resistance to diseases, reducing the workforce significantly. Fewer peasants meant less agricultural production. Perhaps southern lowland Maya civilization would have survived, but this combination of overpopulation and overexploitation of the environment coincided with a peak of monument building that stretched resources beyond their limit. Maya aristocrats reacted to the crisis in the only way they knew how—carry on as before, but this time guarantee the gods' favor by building even bigger monuments. A complete collapse was unavoidable.

How can we test whether this theory is correct? It is notoriously difficult both to determine the population at any given moment in the past and to estimate the number of people that a particular area could support. Even if answers to these questions could be conjured up, we have no idea how the Maya divided up their crops, except a shrewd suspicion that it wasn't exactly a matter of even shares. What can be documented is a trend in Maya agriculture toward increasingly intensive exploitation of the environment. The lakes of the southern lowlands contain vital evidence of both increased soil erosion, as they steadily filled up with sediments washed down the slopes, and deforestation, as the same sediments contain less tree pollen through time. Michael Coe finds this a persuasive scenario:

One can only conclude that by the end of the eighth century, the Classic Maya population of the southern lowlands had probably increased beyond the carrying capacity of the land, no matter what system of agriculture was in use. There is mounting evidence for massive deforestation and erosion throughout the Central Area, only alleviated in a few favourable zones by dry slope terracing. In short, overpopulation and environmental degradation had advanced to a degree only matched by what is happening in many of the poorest tropical countries today. The Maya apocalypse, for such it was, surely had ecological roots.

Yet is the Mayan collapse quite such an open-and-shut case? Agricultural intensification there undoubtedly was, but was it such a complete disaster? After all, soil erosion and deforestation have not automatically led to widespread malnutrition and disease in the modern world; when famine strikes today, most observers attribute it to political causes, not an absolute lack of food. Perhaps a fall in population might even have benefited the Maya, bringing about a new balance between people and the land.

For direct evidence of the human effects of agricultural intensification, archaeologists have turned to physical anatomists. They have examined the actual skeletons of Maya from Classic times. From these bones they are able to assess both the diet and general health of the population. The work of physical anatomists has been used to uphold the overpopulation model, leading to its becoming by far the most popular explanation of the Maya collapse. Robert Sharer sums up the archaeological perception of the anatomical studies as follows:

> That the ancient Maya were vulnerable to epidemic disease is indicated by skeletal studies at Tikal, Altar de Sacrificios, and Copán. These studies demonstrate progressive nutritional deficiencies and increasing disease potentials in lowland populations towards the end of the Classic period, owing probably to food shortages, crowding, and overpopulation.

Mayan emblem for the city of Tikal.

However, recent reassessment of the skeletal material suggests that Sharer and others have taken the evidence far beyond what the anatomists intended. In a 1996 study Dr. Lori Wright of the Department of Anthropology, Texas A & M University, and Dr. Christine White of the Department of Anthropology, University of Western Ontario, have argued from their work at Seibal, Altar de Sacrificios, Dos Pilas, Aguateca, and Lamantai that a drastic rethink is needed. Anemia, caused by a lack of iron in the diet, and scurvy, which develops when vitamin C levels are deficient, had previously been identified among Classic Maya skeletons; but Wright and White find no sign of scurvy and they consider the case for anemia shaky. A fall in the height of adult Maya through time is claimed for both Altar de Sacrificios and Tikal, but is based on a meager total of only eleven skeletons over a massive 1,500-year time span at Altar, and at Tikal mainly on estimates of body size from drawings of burials. What can be said with certainty is that the present-day Maya are some two inches shorter on average than their prehistoric ancestors, yet they are not starving to death. Fairly poor childhood health among the ancient Maya can be identified from the high frequency of bands of defective enamel on their teeth, but levels are no higher than other prehistoric societies. Moreover, as Wright and White stress:

> Although Classic Maya children suffered a severe health burden, there is no indication that health deteriorated over time or with increasing population density and postulated demographic pressure.

Wright and White "expect that some of our colleagues will be surprised by the conclusion that the Lowland Maya did not suffer an anomalous health burden and that health was largely stable over the Classic Period." Their review of the evidence certainly gives cause to question the overpopulation bandwagon.

A Peasant Revolt?

Perhaps it is time to reconsider an alternative political theory of the collapse. First suggested almost half a century ago, its strongest advocate was Eric Thompson, who summed up his views on a television program for the BBC in 1972:

> The theory that I myself like best of all is that it was due to a revolt of the peasants against their rulers, because the rulers were losing that old attitude of co-operation—"we'll supply the rain provided you build the pyramids." In Old Testament terms they went whoring after other gods, gods like the planet Venus and war gods, which didn't help the peasant at all. So, I think, the peasants threw out the ruling group.

Thompson also argued that the collapse of population was limited to the cities, and that the peasantry, freed from the oppressions of its rulers, carried on living there quite contentedly, although at a lower population level:

> I think the fundamental mistake has been to assume that the whole area was abandoned because activities ceased in the great ceremonial centers. As a matter of fact, we know that there was a considerable population in the region in the sixteenth century. . . . Clearly the population of the Central area at the time of the Spanish Conquest was considerably smaller than it had been eight hundred years earlier, but it is incorrect to suppose that this vast area had been a vacuum for hundreds of years.

One factor not considered by Thompson was warfare between the Maya states, as he was wedded to the notion of the Maya rulers as peaceful astronomer-priests: the decipherment of Maya hieroglyphs has put that idea to rest. Late in the Classic period real warfare began in the Maya heartland, with cities such as Dos Pilas embarking on campaigns of conquest, commemorated on statues depicting aristocratic captives. Eventually Dos Pilas itself was besieged and sacked, leading to its abandonment. Increasing warfare between cities resulted in the diversion of labor into constructing fortifications around the cities. No attempt was made to protect the peasantry except those who moved into the cities.

Insecurity in the countryside and a greater proportion of people being forced into the cities would undoubtedly have caused great disruption to agricultural production. Aristocrats were ultimately responsible for these man-made problems, and it may be they who got the blame.

Significantly, it is the region around Dos Pilas that seems to have suffered a total collapse of population. Elsewhere, continuing archaeological work suggests that the hinterland of the cities was by no means completely abandoned, as Thompson proposed. Intensive survey work around Copán showed that occupation of the Copán Valley continued possibly as late as A.D. 1200, some three hundred years after the aristocracy disappeared. Similarly, at Altar de Sacrificios a considerable population remained in the area after the rulers vanished from the scene. Belize had a high population long after the cities collapsed. Although there was a clear fall in numbers, enough evidence certainly exists to doubt the blanket assertion that the whole lowland rain forest was immediately abandoned when people started leaving the cities.

Mayan emblem for the city of Copán.

Population continuity is a strong argument against the overpopulation and environmental disaster theory. If the land really had been exhausted by overexploitation, then how did the peasants manage to carry on living off it after the fall of the cities? The difference between the territories ravaged by warfare and those not affected also points to the importance of human factors in the collapse. Ever-increasing burdens on the peasantry and failure on the part of the aristocracy must have been a powerful catalyst for change. Earthquakes and crop shortages would only have aggravated matters.

Working against any attempt to rescue the situation was a peculiar factor inherent to the Classic Maya worldview. This was the aristocrats' strong belief in the predictive power of their intricate calendrical system. In particular they thought that the end of a calendrical cycle in A.D. 790 predestined political upheaval. Warfare, social unrest, and invasions were therefore inevitable, and should not be stopped because they were ingrained in the very fabric of the universe. Indeed, wars became more bloody as the rulers of neighboring cities fought during this ordained time of war, sacrificing their captives to feed the demands of the gods. Tired of watching their world fall apart as the aristocrats did nothing but fight among themselves, the peasants took matters into their own hands.

THE MAYA CALENDAR

Possibly the greatest intellectual achievement of the Maya was their complex calendar system. They operated two calendars at once: one of 260 days, the other 360 days. The Maya inherited the shorter of the two from the Zapotec civilization of the Oaxaca Valley in Mexico, who began to record dates in this way around 600 B.C. There were twenty named days in this calendar, each repeated thirteen times, making a short "year" of 260 days called a *tzolkin*.

This was not only a way of keeping time but also a guide to the future, as leading Mayanist Professor Michael Coe makes clear:

> Every single day had its own omens and associations, and the inexorable march of the twenty days acted as a kind of perpetual fortune-telling machine guiding the destinies of the Maya and of all the peoples of Mexico.

In the Guatemalan highlands today there are still calendar priests who can name the right day in the 260-day count.

How did this short year tie in with the real year? After seventy-three 260-day periods (18,980 days) fifty-two actual years have passed, at which point the two calendars have synchronized again. So a Calendar Round that began again every fifty-two years was developed.

A calendrical cycle that repeated itself after only some fifty years seems very short for a culture with such mathematical ability as the Maya. Here we may have the spur to their creation of the Long Count calendar in the first century B.C. The everyday Maya calendar was made up of eighteen months of twenty days each, with a greatly feared extra five unlucky days added on at the end, to round up to 365 days to match the solar year. Presumably because these didn't fit neatly in their counting system based on twenties, the Maya ignored the five additional days and stuck to a 360-day period (a *tun*) for their Long Count.

The Long Count was made up of a series of increasingly large quantities counting upward from one day (a *kin*):

20 *kins*	=	1 *uinal*	(20 days)	
18 *uinals*	=	1 *tun*	(360 days)	
20 *tuns*	=	1 *katun*	(7,200 days)	= 19.7 modern years
20 *katuns*	=	1 *baktun*	(144,000 days)	= 394.3 modern years

There were then thought to be thirteen *baktuns* within a Great Cycle of 1,872,000 days (or some 5,130 years). All dates were expressed relative to a date in August 3114 B.C. when the present Great Cycle or World Age was said to have begun. This has been thought to represent the creation of the world, or the gods, but it is more likely to be a mythical date for the creation of the Maya themselves, as there are inscriptions referring to events among the gods in times even before this.

The end of the current Great Cycle is scheduled for December 23, 2012, when Mayan prophecy says that the world as we know it will come to an end with an overwhelming flood. This is not the only element of prophecy involved in the Great Cycle, however, for as with the Calendar Round, events were thought to repeat themselves. Each *katun* was named from the day it ended, and owing to the way the calendar was constructed, only thirteen different days could fall at the end of a *katun*. So after each period of 260 *tuns* (93,600 days, or slightly over 256 years), a *katun* of the same name would begin, lasting just under twenty years. As time passed, each of the thirteen *katuns* acquired a reputation, ten of them bad, suggesting rather a gloomy outlook on the part of the Maya. One of the worst was *katun* 8 Ahau, which signaled fighting and political change.

During the *katun* 8 Ahau, which lasted from 1441 to 1461, disaster overtook the Mayan Itzá tribe that ruled over Chichén Itzá in the northern Yucatán peninsula. They were driven from their homes, just as they had been in the previous *katun* 8 Ahau, when they wandered through the rain forest before eventually chancing on the abandoned city that they named Chichén Itzá. This time they retraced their steps southward until they reached Lake Petén Itzá in northern Guatemala, where they founded a new capital, Tah Itzá, on an island. Hernán Cortés visited Tayasal, as the Spanish named it, in 1524, but did not stay long. Even after the Spanish had secured the whole of Central America the Itzá remained untouched in Tayasal.

Only in the seventeenth century did the Spanish decide that an independent Tayasal was an affront. The church led the way, sending missionaries to convert the Itzá without success. The last group to try was led by the Franciscan monk Fray Andres de Avendaño, who visited Tayasal in January 1696. Avendaño warned the Itzá that *katun* 8 Ahau was about to return, bringing massive upheavals with it, and that the time to convert to Christianity had therefore come. The Itzá did not submit immediately, but the same year the nephew of the king of Tayasal is recorded as presenting his uncle's feather headdress to the governor of Yucatán as a sign of their willingness to accept Spanish authority. The Itzá were not quick enough, however, or perhaps the governor saw a chance for some looting, as Spanish troops attacked Tayasal in March 1697, four months before the end of the *katun*. Despite their reputation as feared warriors, the Itzá put up only a brief struggle—perhaps they already knew they had lost before the fighting began.

Earlier *katun* cycles also seem to have marked major upheavals. Around A.D. 278 there was a decisive shift in power as the southern Maya declined, after the catastrophic eruption of the Ilopango volcano in El Salvador, while lowland Maya cities gained the upper hand. Two hundred and fifty-six years later (A.D. 534), at the corresponding point in the next cycle, the great city of Tikal, among others in the lowlands, declined dramatically. There was internal dissension, possibly a peasant revolt, with the widespread and deliberate damaging of public monuments. In the case of Tikal this seems to have been sparked off by a disastrous defeat at the hands of its aggressive neighbor, Caracol in Belize. (Only at the beginning of the seventh century did the lowlands recover.) Finally, A.D. 790 saw the last of the standing stones erected at Tikal, marking the beginning of the equivalent point in the following cycle. Given the disasters that had happened at previous intervals of 256 years, a crisis was surely expected. Indeed it did come, this time bringing an end to lowland Maya civilization.

CHAPTER TWO

WATCHING THE SKIES

INTRODUCTION

For modern city folk, it can be difficult to appreciate why the sky, particularly the night sky, was so important to ancient peoples. Streetlighting and pollution mean that the sheer splendor of sights such as the Milky Way is a pleasure that urban dwellers can now only rarely—if at all—enjoy. In the ancient world, watching the skies was not just a leisure activity; the heavens bristled with meaning and were alive with gods.

Indeed, in many ancient religions the gods and stars were thought to be one and the same thing. The oldest deciphered writing in the world comes from the Sumerian civilization of Babylonia (southern Iraq) and dates to about 3500 B.C. It has hieroglyphic-like symbols, and the sign for a "god," is very telling. It was a simple drawing of a star, which stood for the words *dingir*, "god," and Anu, their name for the god of Heaven. The classical Greeks and Romans were also aware of this idea. Their philosophers whiled away endless hours pondering the question: what were the gods? The deities they worshiped seem to represent so many different things, from aspects of nature to human qualities, that it is not surprising that they themselves were baffled. But an answer that they often came back to was that the gods had originally been planets. As Aristotle (384–322 B.C.) noted:

> A tradition has been handed down by the ancient thinkers of very early times to the effect that these heavenly bodies [the planets] are gods. The rest of their tradition has been added later in a mythological form to influence the common people.

As the heavenly bodies were believed to be divine they were studied intently, as to understand them was to penetrate the mysteries of the gods. Many of the urban civilizations of the ancient world had an organized system of astronomical observations carried out by specialists. From the mid–second millennium onward the priests of Babylonia recorded the movements of Venus and the Moon on clay tablets, trying to use their notes to predict lunar eclipses. The Maya of Central America constructed observatories to meet their obsession with the heavens (see **The Rise and Fall of Maya Civilization** in **Lost Lands and Catastrophes**). They were motivated by a powerful belief that the skies mirrored or brought about dramatic events here on

(Top) The first known writing of the word for "heaven" or "god"; from earliest Sumerian texts, c. 3500 B.C. Over the centuries it became gradually more stylized. (Bottom) The symbol as it was written in Babylonia, c. 700 B.C.

the Earth, such as the birth or death of kings or religious leaders or the overthrow of great powers. Observations of the heavens could lead to predictions of heavenly phenomena, which could in turn reveal the future course of political events. It is no wonder that some ancient societies have been seen as dominated by the calendar.

Calendars—which are all ultimately based on the movements of the Sun and Moon, and the rising and setting of the planets and stars—also had more practical aspects. Regulating a calendar by the heavens was vital for organizing every event from public festivals to the agricultural year. While it may not have been essential for farmers to know that the year was 365 days long, they needed to know precisely when to begin their annual tasks, such as plowing, sowing, and pruning. In the eighth century B.C., Hesiod, the oldest known Greek poet aside from Homer, wrote a poetical farmer's almanac, full of such advice: "When Orion and Sirius are come into mid-heaven, and Arcturus rises at dawn, then cut off all the grape-clusters and bring them home." The Incas of Peru set up a series of stone pillars on the hillside overlooking their capital at Cuzco, and one in the town square. Observations taken from the city stone of the Sun's movements relative to the hillside pillars were used to determine agricultural activities in this tightly controlled empire.

The earliest possible calendars (from Stone Age Europe) date back more than twenty thousand years, and show special interest in recording the lunar months. Given the extreme antiquity of calendar making, there may be an element of truth in a curious statement made by the Greek philosopher Plato. He claimed that the heavens had "taught us numbers," arguing that mathematics began when people started reckoning the phases of the Moon. Complex tasks like building a lunar calendar, as opposed to simple counting, might well have been the beginnings of calculation and hence mathematics, as Plato believed.

Given the strong connection between observing the heavenly bodies and religion, which shows itself in the fact that ancient astronomers were generally also priests, it is not surprising that the results of their work were often built into religious monuments. Five thousand years ago the entrance passage of the megalithic tomb of Newgrange in Ireland was specially constructed so that the Sun shines down it into the heart of the tomb at the midwinter solstice. Many other megalithic monuments, including Stonehenge, have solar alignments (see **Stonehenge** in **Architectural Wonders**). In the 1960s, however, there was a trend toward interpreting these stone circles as

One of the hillside stone markers at Cuzco used by the Incas to regulate their calendar.

incredibly sophisticated astronomical "computers" for making fine adjustments to the lunar calendar and even for predicting eclipses of the Moon. How far the megalith builders of northwestern Europe went in designing their monuments as astronomical markers is still a highly controversial issue. Even more controversial is the recently proposed idea that the Great Pyramids of Egypt were positioned to reflect the layout of the stars in the constellation Orion.

Yet there were far more reasons for watching the skies than simply monitoring the heavenly bodies. More than anything else the ancients regarded the heavens with an awe that did not just spring from the intrinsic beauty of the night sky. The gods of heaven made their presence forcefully known by periodically hurling very real reminders of their existence at their earthly subjects. A surprising number of ancient religious cults were based around meteorites, fragments of heaven that had fallen to the Earth.

Best known of the ancient meteorite cults is that of the Great Goddess Diana, which flourished at Ephesus (on the Aegean coast of present-day Turkey) in classical times. When the missionary Saint Paul went to Ephesus in A.D. 54 a riot nearly started when he condemned the worship of Diana, whose "image fell down from Jupiter" (Acts of the Apostles 19:35). Classical sources indicate that rather than the whole statue being carved from a meteorite, the holy stone was kept in a hollow inside the image. By an extraordinary stroke of luck, an ancient text from the Hittite empire that once ruled Turkey preserves an account of this meteorite actually landing. About 1300 B.C. the Hittite emperor recorded how his foe, the king of "Apasas" (clearly Ephesus), was struck down by a thunderbolt thrown by the god Teshub (the Hittite equivalent of Jupiter).

In Egypt, Amun, king of the gods, was closely associated with meteorites, and one was preserved as a sacred object in the temple complex at the Egyptian religious capital Thebes. According to rabbinical tradition, the site where King Solomon built his temple (in the 10th century B.C.) was determined by the fall of the *Eben Shetiya* ("Fire Stone"), which landed during the reign of Solomon's father David.

The most enduring meteorite cult of all is that of the Black Stone of Mecca, set into the wall of the Ka'bah, a small stone building that is Islam's holiest shrine. The Black Stone is literally shrouded in mystery, for it is normally covered by a thick black cloth, and photography at the Ka'bah is not generally allowed, so even its overall size and shape is uncertain. What we can say is that it is set in a silver mount fixed into the corner of the building.

Traditions concerning the Black Stone state that the Hebrew patri-

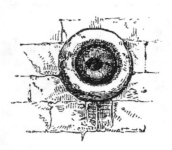

(Above) The holy Ka'bah at Mecca. (Below) Detail of corner, through which the Ka'bah stone can be seen.

arch Abraham, together with his son Ishmael, father of the Arabs, had constructed a building of similar black rocks under direct heavenly instruction. Much later the prophet Mohammed cleansed the shrine of idols and rededicated it to its original true God. Having suffered from numerous floods, the Black Stone was by this time the only piece of the original building left, hence the measures since taken to protect it. The Black Stone seems to have been important even before Abraham's time, however, for Muslim tradition holds that it originally fell from the skies (or was delivered to Earth by the angel Gabriel). At this time it was white in color, turning black as a result of absorbing the sins of the pilgrims to Mecca.

There are so many well-attested records of meteorite falls in ancient times that one suspects—though it is hard to quantify—that they were once more frequent than they are at present. The same is true of comets. In the early days of the Roman Empire hardly any important political event seemed to pass without a comet appearing on the scene, such as the one that made a timely appearance on the first day of Julius Caesar's funeral ceremonies in 44 B.C. The comet was widely believed to be his soul, winging its way toward heaven. A few decades later, another portent in the sky, most likely a comet, led the Magi to the birthplace of a great leader of a very different kind.

No fewer than four comets were reported in the reign of the notorious Nero (A.D. 54–68). The first arrived shortly before the death of his predecessor Claudius, and continued to shine "with a terrible glare" into Nero's principate. When the next arrived in A.D. 60 word went around that it signified a change of emperor. Nero promptly exiled one Rubellius, the favorite tipped for succession. The comet of A.D. 64 provoked a more serious crisis. According to the Roman writer Suetonius, Nero consulted his astrologer, who advised him that

> monarchs usually avoid portents of this kind by executing their most prominent subjects and thus directing the wrath of heaven elsewhere. So Nero resolved on a wholesale massacre of the nobility.

The slaughter was horrible; even the children of the victims were starved to death or poisoned. Nero appeared to take no notice of Halley's comet when it appeared in A.D. 66, but by that date his reign had degenerated into such a bloodbath that he no longer needed comets as an excuse.

Excessive reactions like Nero's to the appearance of comets merely reinforced the traditional fear that they usually engendered in people (and often still do). It was not, however, a completely irrational fear, as

ISTIMIRANT STELLA

Halley's comet as shown on the Bayeux tapestry, which records the Norman conquest of England in A.D. 1066. The appearance of the comet in that year was thought to herald the Norman victory.

scientists were fond of telling us until very recently—till, that is, July 1994, when astounded astronomers witnessed comet Shoemaker-Levy smash into Jupiter.

Scientists are now increasingly accepting the fact that small comets and cometary fragments have impacted with the Earth, while even the larger ones that do not hit pose other dangers. Material constantly streams off comets, forming trails that sometimes intersect with the Earth's orbit. These streams of dust and small bodies are the cause of meteor showers. Again, there is increasing evidence that in the not-too-distant past meteor showers were far more spectacular events, with streams of fireballs large enough to be threatening. At present we are fortunate enough to be living in a very quiet period of cometary activity. Not so the ancient world. There is now a mass of evidence to suggest that during Bronze Age times a large disintegrating comet on an Earth-crossing orbit was causing actual catastrophes (see **Introduction** to **Lost Lands and Catastrophes**).

There was not only one threatening comet in Bronze Age times. A few thousand years ago Halley's comet would have been much larger (comets are constantly shrinking as they lose material), and calculations of its past orbit by Donald K. Yeomans of the Jet Propulsion Laboratory, Pasadena, the world's leading expert on the motions of Halley's comet, produced a very striking result. Yeomans found he could retrocalculate the orbit of Halley to 1404 B.C. but no farther, as it came so close to our world that its motion would have been altered by the Earth's gravity. Given the immense length of Halley's tail (presently still about 100 million miles), it is more than possible that the Earth passed through it and that gases, dust, and debris entered the atmosphere. Halley's comet may have even been the very body responsible for the strange phenomena experienced by the ancient Israelites under Joshua on the "day the sun stood still." (Alternatively, and perhaps more likely from a chronological perspective, the tail of Halley may have been the cause of the airborne "Plagues of Egypt" at the time of the Israelite Exodus, said to have been forty years before Joshua's time.)

In many ways modern science is catching up with the truths of ancient knowledge about the skies. The ancients stated that comets were dangerous, and knew that meteorites fell from the sky. Quite amazingly, the reality of meteorites was not accepted by western science until the mid–nineteenth century. When two Yale University scholars reported that over 300 pounds of meteorites had fallen at Weston, Connecticut, in December 1807, President Thomas Jefferson exclaimed: "It is easier to believe that two Yankee professors would lie, than that stones would fall from heaven." Unfortunately Jefferson was in agreement with the majority of western scientific opinion, still under the stranglehold of Aristotle, who had categorically insisted that stones could not fall from the sky. He also dismissed meteors and comets as merely atmospheric phenomena.

It would be difficult to overestimate the crippling influence that Aristotle has had on western science. As well as pronouncing that everything beyond the Moon was made of "ether," and therefore was not really solid, he insisted that the Earth was fixed in space and did not move. The medieval Church elevated Aristotle's teachings to the status of dogma and the clock was effectively turned back on scientific progress by almost two thousand years. Staggeringly enough, Europeans in the year 1500 knew far less than the ancient Greeks did around 200 B.C.

The surprising breadth of astronomical knowledge of the ancient Greeks can be judged from some of their discoveries:

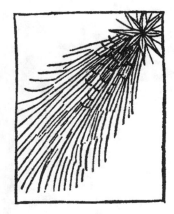

Halley's comet, as depicted in a chronicle from Nuremberg, Germany (A.D. 1483)

- The Earth is a sphere. The great sage Pythagoras (c. 525 B.C.) taught that the world was spherical rather than flat.
- The Earth moves. The first recorded suggestion of this was made by the philosopher Philolaus around 450 B.C.
- The Earth rotates on its axis. Described by Herakleides in the late fourth century B.C. He also suggested that the inner planets Venus and Mercury moved in circular orbits around the Sun, and may even have taken the next step of applying the same logic to the Earth.
- The Earth moves around the Sun. A full heliocentric (sun-centered) system was developed by Aristarchus around 280 B.C. The greatest of the ancient Greek astronomers, he recognized that the Earth revolves on its axis and that it moves around the Sun on a circular orbit along with the other planets. No improvements were made on Aristarchus' system, which was perfectly correct, until the time of Galileo in the seventeenth century. Aristarchus also recognized that the stars were an almost infinite distance away.
- The size of the Earth. The geographer Eratosthenes (c. 273–192 B.C.) calculated the Earth's diameter as 7,850 miles, with an error of only half a percent.
- The distance of the Moon. Hipparchus (c. 125 B.C.) calculated the distance of the Moon from the Earth as being thirty and a quarter Earth diameters, with startling accuracy—the error was only 0.3 percent. He also discovered the precession of the equinoxes, the slow wobble of the Earth's axis over the centuries, which alters the position of the "fixed" stars.
- Comets return periodically. The Roman writer Seneca, tutor of emperor Nero, c. A.D. 60, referred to the periodic return of comets as a fact, well over 1,600 years before Sir Edmund Halley proved the idea mathematically.

The truth is that the discoveries made during the sixteenth and seventeenth centuries were *re*discoveries of knowledge. Renaissance means "rebirth," and the great Renaissance of arts and sciences was precisely that.

Yet how did the classical world come to possess such a vast body of advanced astronomical knowledge? Part was due to the debt they owed to earlier cultures, whose systematic recording of astronomical phenomena, while it may not have been carried out for scientific ends (as we see them), was nonetheless invaluable. When the Greeks came into regular contact with the ancient Babylonian civilization, from about 600 B.C. onward, they gained access to a vast corpus of observations, which the Greek philosophers were able to use as a database.

The rest was due to the sheer brilliance of the ancient Greek philosophers and mathematicians. Some are still strangely undervalued by modern writers. Plato, for example, is still widely referred to as being a "poor astronomer." He most certainly was not. One cannot fail to be amazed when one reads his calm statement that "the Sun is larger than the whole of the Earth, and all the planets are of amazing size." Or that the Earth is a sphere that stands unsuspended in space and that it has existed for millions of years. Or that the stars as well as the planets rotate on their own axes. For him to have known all these things in the fourth century B.C. almost seems preternatural.

The same slightly eerie feeling arises on encountering the apparently anomalous knowledge of the solar system possessed by some so-called primitive tribal cultures. Remarkably, they appear to know of the existence of features of the outer planets that were only officially discovered after the invention of the telescope at the beginning of the seventeenth century.

The first westerner to take the traditions of the African Pygmies with any seriousness was Belgian sociologist Jean-Pierre Hallet, who, during the 1950s, spent eighteen months living with the Efé tribe of the Ituri Forest in Central Africa. They told him that they call the planet Saturn "the star of the nine moons." If this was a guess, it is a pretty good one, as Saturn actually has ten satellites, the smallest of which is fairly insignificant as it is only about 200 kilometers in diameter.

The Pygmies are not alone in possessing such apparently supernatural knowledge. According to one tradition of the Maori of New Zealand, an old name for Saturn was *Parearu*, meaning "caught in a band," as it had a circlet or band around it. By the time this was recorded by anthropologist Elsdon Best in the 1920s, there was some uncertainty about the identity of *Parearu*, but its other title of "puller of the Milky Way" seems to confirm it was Saturn. Saturn was the outermost planet known to the ancients and was seen as the interface between our solar system and the galaxy.

But the most striking case of anomalous astronomical knowledge concerns the Dogon tribe of Mali in West Africa. In the 1930s, French anthropologist Marcel Griaule went to live with the Dogon, and became so well acquainted with them that he was accepted as one of their own; after a special conference, some of the tribal priests

Dogon drawings of Saturn's rings (above) and Jupiter's moons (below).

decided to make him the first outsider to whom they would reveal their secret traditions, known only to an initiated few. What Griaule learned was nothing short of extraordinary. Their detailed cosmology contained much astronomical lore, of an amazingly advanced nature for a people who had no telescopes and who had barely had any contact with the western world. The Dogon priests state that the planet Saturn has a permanent halo around it and their drawings show it clearly surrounded by a ring. They also say that Jupiter has four little "stars" that turn around it. As it happens Jupiter has over a dozen moons, but only four major ones; the others are mere moonlets and pieces of space debris.

How are we to explain all this? Not surprisingly, an amazing variety of theories have been put forward. The easiest explanation, that usually put forward by skeptics, is that the Pygmies, Maori, and Dogon simply acquired their information about Saturn and Jupiter from western visitors such as missionaries. As an answer this is completely ad hoc, and no one has ever produced any concrete evidence to explain when, how, or why such visitors would have passed on such specific astronomical details.

Others have suggested that an early invention of the telescope might be the answer. Lenses—usually ground from rock crystal—were being made in the ancient world as long ago as 2300 B.C., and it *is* theoretically possible that if someone put two convex lenses together (not a difficult step), they could have invented the telescope. If the Egyptians, for example, had had such devices, they could have observed the moons of Jupiter and the rings of Saturn and passed their knowledge on to the Pygmies and Dogon. Yet there is not a single description or drawing from ancient times to back up this idea, so the ancient telescope remains completely hypothetical.

Simple sighting tubes, however, are known to have been used by Roman surveyors. Looking through a tube narrows the field of vision and can clarify distant objects even without the aid of lenses. This brings us to the most likely explanation: that the moons of Jupiter and the rings of Saturn might have been observed basically with the naked eye. In 1981 researchers from the Chinese Institute for the History of Natural Science uncovered a remarkable record of observation from pre-telescope times. Gan Dej, a pioneer of ancient Chinese astronomy, stated that in 364 B.C. he had seen with the naked eye a moon near Jupiter. Inspired by this ancient record, the researchers set up an experiment to see whether they could repeat Gan Dej's feat. Seven observers were able to see Ganymede, Jupiter's largest moon, with three of them able to see Europa as well. Other reports, from the nineteenth century, also claim that Jupiter's moons, as well as the rings of Saturn, can indeed be made out by the keen-sighted, given ideal conditions.

Naked-eye observation might well explain how pre-telescope astronomers saw Saturn's rings and Jupiter's moons, but the Dogon's most mind-blowing piece of astronomical lore concerns stars that could never have been seen with the naked eye. Their initiates told Griaule that Sirius *(sigu tolo)* has two star companions that circle it, and drew him a diagram showing their relative positions. Griaule and his colleague Germaine Dieterlen published an article on the Dogon's Sirius system theory in 1950, in which they explained that the focal point of the major Dogon initiation ceremony called Sigui was the first of these mysterious extra stars, which they called *to polo* (after a kind of wild grain). The Dogon priests stated that *to polo* circles around Sirius once every fifty years and though it is "the smallest thing there is," it is "the heaviest star." Griaule and Dieterlen published all this without comment, yet the extraordinary thing is that Sirius *does* have a star companion, Sirius B, discovered by astronomers in 1863 and first photographed through powerful telescopes in 1970. This partner of Sirius is a white dwarf star, hence immensely dense and heavy, and it orbits its companion once every fifty years.

How could the Dogon have known all this about a star that is totally invisible to the naked eye? Intrigued by this riddle, American writer and historian of science Robert Temple spent ten years researching

(Left) According to anthropologist Marcel Griaule, the Dogon depict the orbit of the invisible star Sirius B ("Digitaria") in their sand drawings. (Right) The orbit of Sirius B through the decades of the 20th century, as calculated by modern astronomers.

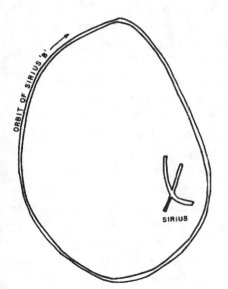

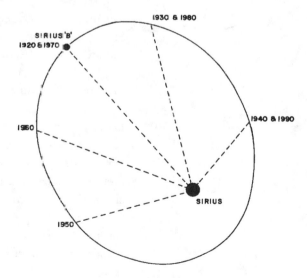

the question. The answer he came up with in *The Sirius Mystery* (1976) was startling. Temple concluded that the only way the Dogon could have learned about Sirius B was if they had been told. He ruled out the possibility of learned missionaries—as usual thrown in by skeptics—which Dieterlen herself rejects as "absurd." She insists that Dogon artifacts hundreds of years old already depict the three stars of the Sirius system. The Dogon themselves talk of culture heroes called the Nommo, also known as the "instructors" and "masters of the water," fishlike visitors whose home they locate in the Sirius star system. As Temple notes, these beings sound uncannily like the fish-tailed creatures from whom the Babylonians said they had learned the arts and sciences (see **Poleshift** in **Lost Lands and Catastrophes**). He drew the bold conclusion that the Sirius system may be inhabited by amphibious beings, who had traveled to our solar system several thousand years ago and visited the Earth. Temple developed his case by arguing that the secrets of the Sirius system were also known in ancient Egypt, and that it was from there that the ancestors of the Dogon had obtained their knowledge.

Temple seemed to have found the first and only piece of plausible evidence for extraterrestrial contact in ancient times. Yet the Sirius mystery remains far from being clear-cut. While Temple, following Griaule, assumes that *to polo* is the invisible star Sirius B, the Dogon themselves, as reported by Griaule, say something quite different: "When Digitaria *[to polo]* is close to Sirius, the latter becomes brighter; when it is at its most distant from Sirius, Digitaria gives off a twinkling effect, suggesting several stars to the observer."

One wonders, then, whether *to polo* is actually an ordinary star near Sirius. That would leave the other information given by the Dogon initiates about the orbit and extreme weight of *to polo* unaccounted for, but here we reach a stumbling block—the idea of a secret tradition in itself. As anthropologist Professor Walter Van Beek points out, "a secret not shared is not cultural." It is difficult to see how, as Dieterlen insisted, the Dogon had been making artifacts for public ceremonies showing the Sirius system for hundreds of years if the very existence of Sirius's companions had been a closely guarded secret. This means that the historical proof that the Dogon have known about the Sirius mystery for centuries rests entirely on Griaule and Dieterlen's interpretation of Dogon art. As it happens, no other anthropologist supports their opinion. With this key point in doubt, the possibility is reopened that the Dogon may have heard of modern astronomical research on the Sirius system by one means or another.

Further doubts set in when we consider the results of more recent anthropological research. In 1991 Van Beek, along with other anthropologists who have worked with the Dogon, declared that they could find absolutely no trace of the detailed Sirius lore reported by Griaule and Dieterlen. This is very worrying. Although Griaule claimed that the knowledge about Sirius he was passed was a secret tradition known only to initiates, he also estimated that 15 percent of the Dogon shared these insights. Surely, then, contemporary anthropologists like Van Beek, after over a decade's fieldwork among the Dogon, would have found some evidence for Griaule's claims. Van Beek was initially keen to find such confirmation, but had to admit, after quizzing numerous Dogon, that there may simply have been a problem with Griaule's methods of collecting data. Griaule's circle of informants was very limited, and it is a classic problem with anthropological fieldwork that one's informants (who reasonably expect some gifts in return) will often try to come up with material that fulfills the expectations of their questioner. In the case of Griaule, he was especially interested in astronomy, having studied it in Paris, and he took star maps along with him on his field trips as a way of prompting his informants to divulge their knowledge of the stars. As Griaule himself was well aware of the discovery of Sirius B, it is always possible that he overinterpreted the Dogon responses to his questions and was simply being "told" what he wanted to hear. Deeply troubled by this possibility, Van Beek interviewed some of the original informants about *sigu tolo*, which Griaule presented as being the Dogon name for Sirius:

> Though they do speak about *sigu tolo*, they disagree completely with each other as to which star is meant; for some, it is an invisible star that should rise to announce the *sigu* [festival], for another it is Venus that through a different position appears as *sigu tolo*. All agree, however, that they learned about the star from Griaule.

Van Beek found that the Dogon are, of course, well aware of Sirius, but that they know it under the different name of *dana tolo*. As for Sirius B, only Griaule's informants had ever heard of it. In the second edition of his work *The Sirius Mystery* (1998), Temple was pleased to note that the existence of a third star in the system, Sirius C, had been officially confirmed in 1995. This discovery of this small dwarf star seemed to confirm Griaule's report that the Dogon initiates talk of a second companion to Sirius called *emme ya tolo*. Unfortunately Temple did not know about the recent criticisms of Griaule's fieldwork aired by Van Beek and others, which somewhat spoil the impact of this discovery. Given his interest in astronomy, Griaule is likely to have heard of both the discovery of Sirius B and the possible existence of Sirius C, unconfirmed sightings of which were reported by several astronomers in the 1920s. Both stars, and discussion of their amazingly dense nature, were much in the news at the time. The unfortunate truth may be that Griaule, having extracted some vague traditions about Sirius and neighboring stars from his Dogon informants, inadvertently imposed order on their responses by trying to make sense of them in terms of the latest astronomical thinking.

With the Sirius mystery left in such doubt, there is very little else to say in favor of extraterrestrial contact in ancient times. Most of the arguments used by other authors are based on the supposed inability of past cultures to have built their own greatest monuments and are simply untenable (see **Introduction** to **Architectural Wonders**). If the case for extraterrestrial involvement on Earth is something of a letdown, is there any other reason to imagine the existence of intelligent life on other planets, other than the abstract notion that this must have happened in a large enough universe?

There have been many attempts to show that at least one other planet within our own solar system was once home to a civilization even more developed than our own. Back in the nineteenth century, astronomers began to detect faint lines on the surface of Mars. Alerted by this unusual observation, astronomers started to study the red planet more intently, and further markings were seen. Eventually a whole network of straight lines crisscrossing Mars had been mapped. The geometrical regularity of the lines seemed to prove that they had to be of intelligent origin, and they were identified as canals. Oddly, however, they could not be detected on photographs, and this eventually led skeptics to suggest that even the most eminent of astronomers could make mistakes when operating at the bounds of the technology of the day.

The first of the other worlds in the solar system to be seen close up was, of course, the Moon—from the early 1960s onward. Astronauts took hundreds of photographs from their tiny spaceships, which were then pored over back on Earth. Extraterrestrial enthusiasts reported giant numbers inscribed on the Moon's surface, roads, bridges, and pyramids. None of these claims survived the test of further photographs of the same area.

That appeared to be it for extraterrestrial civilizations within our own backyard—until 1976. In July of that year, NASA's *Viking Orbiter I* went into orbit around Mars and started to take thousands of photographs to check for a safe site for its Lander to come to ground. Eventually a spot was chosen and the Lander set down. After the Lander took photographs and analyzed soil samples, NASA came to the disappointing conclusion that there was no evidence for life on Mars. Little did they know.

One of the photographs taken from a thousand miles above the Martian surface appeared to show half a giant humanoid face with a slightly open mouth and eyes that look straight up into the sky. The other side of this strange feature lay in shadow. An off-the-cuff reaction by a NASA scientist quizzed by curious reporters was that the supposed face was simply an effect of shadows on a single print. This turned out to be a major error, for several other prints showing the same feature were located by enthusiasts outside NASA. Advocates of the extraterrestrial hypothesis, among them some well-qualified scientists (such as astronomer Tom Van Flandern), now had two new guns in their arsenal—a remarkable image and an apparent cover-up.

Forced to backtrack, NASA scientists turned their attention to what became known as "the Mars Face." If this was indeed an artifact rather than a natural feature, it was enormous, a mile long from the chin to the top of its head. The implications, if this were actually a monument, were equally awe-inspiring. Computer enhancement of the photographs has produced further details, but these have not convinced NASA. Neither have the claims by some more enthusiastic researchers that pyramids, cities, and fields, all equally gigantic, can be seen elsewhere in the Cydonia region of Mars. Instead, the preferred NASA explanation is that the face is a natural geological feature. They rightly point to the long history of overinterpreted lunar photographs and the well-established tendency of human beings to read meanings into natural features both here on Earth and in the heavens.

(Left) The "Face on Mars" as it looked in the original photograph taken by *Viking Orbiter I* on July 25, 1976. (Center) The second, more detailed photograph taken by Mars Global Surveyor, April 5, 1998. (Right) NASA computer-enhanced image, with reversed contrast.

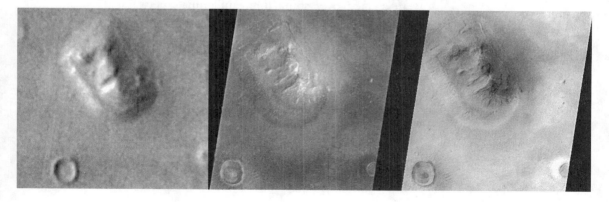

The NASA view seems the most prudent, but even they have bowed to pressure and have included the Cydonia region in the schedule of the 1998–1999 Mars Global Surveyor project. New photographs taken in the first year of the project produced diametrically opposed reactions from the pro- and anti- lobbies. At first glance the skeptics seem to have won, in that the "face" in the new photos—taken from a different angle—is nowhere near as convincing as it was in the originals. On the other hand, the enthusiasts quite rightly point out that the new photographs show that the "platform" on which the "face" rests has a perfectly geometrical shape like a shield. In the opinion of Van Flandern, "nothing yet seen on our Moon or any other solar system surface besides Earth suggests artificiality to a comparable degree." The dispute over the "Mars Face" seems set to run until a manned landing actually investigates the Cydonia area firsthand.

A second Mars controversy started in 1996, when NASA scientists reported the discovery of possible traces of fossil microscopic organisms in a meteorite found in Antarctica that appeared, from the composition of its rocks, to have come from Mars. The question of life on Mars, never properly answered, has now been reopened. How much the putative discovery influenced NASA's decision to reinvestigate the notorious face is anybody's guess. So is the question of whether we will ever see the beginnings of a new field of alien archaeology.

MEGALITHIC ASTRONOMERS

Scattered across the British Isles and northern France are some of the world's most enigmatic monuments, stone ruins of both mysterious beauty and breathtaking antiquity. Massive tombs and huge standing stones set in circles and rows, these wonders of the prehistoric world were erected over some three millennia—between 4500 and 1500 B.C. These megaliths (from the Greek for "large stones") are justly famous for their size, showing that the ancient peoples of western Europe were capable of considerable feats of engineering as well as organization (see **Stonehenge** in **Architectural Wonders**). Yet do they tell us something even more surprising about these prehistoric societies? Over the last hundred years debate has raged over the possibility that rather than being religious monuments these sites demonstrate the existence thousands of years ago of astronomer-priests at the apex of society, laying out observatories using standard units of measurement to point to the heavens with incredible accuracy.

If this theory were true, it would decisively overturn many traditional notions of such communities as "primitive," revolutionizing our understanding of the prehistoric past. Many archaeologists have shied away from considering the possibilities, but some have grasped the nettle firmly, and advocated a radical change in our interpretation of the capabilities of our distant ancestors. Thus Dr. Euan MacKie of the Hunterian Museum in Glasgow proposed in 1981 that the enormous circular "henge" enclosures of Britain served as a network of astronomical universities:

> [Henges were] the living and training places of learned orders of astronomer priests and wise men, the activities of which are everywhere to be seen in the standing stones and stone circles.

The massive henge of Avebury, comprising a stone circle inside a ditch and bank enclosure.

Yet there have been false dawns in megalithic astronomy before, and these claims need to be assessed to see if the evidence is more compelling this time around.

The Dawn of Astronomy

Sir Norman Lockyer, director of the Solar Physics Observatory in London, and founder and editor for half a century of the leading science journal *Nature*, was one of the great figures of experimental science a hundred years ago. In 1890 and 1891 he visited Greece and Egypt, and became intrigued by the orientation of temples in both countries. Knowing that in the Christian world churches were traditionally oriented toward sunrise on the feast day of their patron saint, he wondered if some similar tradition had held in the ancient world. His initial researches convinced him that Egyptian temples had been laid out to incorporate both solar (specifically midsummer solstice) and stellar alignments. Moreover, owing to the movements of the heavens relative to the Earth, these alignments could also be used to date the construction of monuments. Lockyer published his Egyptian results in a book titled *The Dawn of Astronomy* in 1894 to a skeptical reception from the Egyptological world.

When he turned his attention to prehistoric Britain, however, Lockyer was to receive a rather better hearing. For the next few years he devoted his holidays to systematically examining possible alignments to heavenly bodies along stone rows, down the entrance passages of megalithic tombs, and from the center of stone circles. From a series of highly accurate measurements he concluded that the primary function of many of these monuments was not burial or ceremonial but rather calendrical observations. According to Lockyer, monuments such as Stonehenge were constructed to incorporate sight lines to sunrise or sunset, or to the rising of stars, on important days in the calendar later used by the Celts, which divided the year into eight parts.

Lockyer thought that the same calendar had been used at all his sites, from one end of Britain to the other. This led him to conclude that a class of astronomer-priests must have existed "on whom the early peoples depended for guidance in all things, not only of economic, but of religious, medicinal and superstitious value." Within the scientific community Lockyer found supporters, but archaeologists were generally hostile or at best lukewarm. They simply found the whole idea implausible, for it did not fit with their view of "barbarian" prehistory.

Moreover, they suspected that the alignments were being presented in a highly selective way. As Dr. Douglas Heggie, mathematician at Edinburgh University and author of the main critical study on megalithic astronomy in modern times, sees it, Lockyer's problem was one of statistical proof:

> Despite Lockyer's expressed diffidence . . . he had no doubt about the essential correctness of the astronomical theories. Unfortunately, what he never really concerned himself with . . . was the problem of showing that the supposed alignments could not reasonably be attributed to chance. After all, many [potential] lines [of sight] are defined by a site if it is not too simple, and there are a considerable number of astronomical phenomena with which each might be associated. One might therefore expect some alignments to occur quite by accident.

Only with the development of the computer after World War II did it become possible to perform the large number of calculations required to assess all the potential alignments given by a circle of, say, a dozen stones. One of the most involved sites from this point of view is Stonehenge in southern England, where there are two circles and two horseshoes of stones together with several single standing stones and a vast number of burial mounds and the sites of prehistoric timber rings, lines, and single uprights that would have been visible at and from the monument (see **Stonehenge** in **Architectural Wonders**). Perhaps tens of thousands of possible alignments exist in the Stonehenge complex.

This was the problem archaeologists had in accepting the theories of Dr. Gerald Hawkins, an astronomer from Boston University, when he published them in *Nature* in 1963. Hawkins claimed that there was a less than one in ten million possibility of the alignments he had detected using his computer occurring by chance, concluding that "there can be no doubt that Stonehenge was an observatory." However, alternative calculations using Hawkins's data came up with quite different figures: of 240 lines studied, thirty-two matched astronomically significant lunar or solar alignments (and some of these were pretty broad bands rather than thin lines, so not suitable for accurate astronomy), but forty-eight would be expected by chance. Moreover, some of the alignments included elements of widely differing dates or possibly natural features, so archaeologists remained unimpressed (see **Stonehenge** in **Architectural Wonders**). As we have come to realize, computers are wholly dependent on the quality of information fed into them, and garbage in = garbage out.

Megalithic Universities

Shortly after Hawkins's much-publicized but ultimately unsupported claims, a far more sober piece of archaeological astronomy appeared. This was a study of some 500 stone circles, rows, and single stones by Alexander Thom, Professor of Engineering at Oxford University, who like Lockyer had devoted his summer holidays to surveying obscure megalithic monuments, in his case for decades.

In a series of books, Thom set out the detailed evidence he believed should prompt a rethinking of archaeologists' views of the abilities of prehistoric Europeans in surveying, geometry, and astronomy. He argued that his surveys proved that megalithic sites had been laid out using the same measurement of length, with a value of 2.72 feet, which he called the "megalithic yard." Yet how could this degree of accuracy be maintained across the whole country? If we imagine that an original standard rod of 2.72 feet was copied, and further copies made from this replica, then there would inevitably be an increasing level of inaccuracy as time went on. Thom realized the problem this posed and suggested that "there must have been a headquarters from which standard rods were sent out."

This impression of precision engineering was confirmed by the actual layouts of stone rings. Thom noted that while some rings were true circles, others seemed to be more elaborate geometrical arrangements, including egg shapes and ellipses. A few "circles" were even formed by joining together a whole series of arcs. Thom believed that their builders had originally developed an advanced understanding of theoretical geometry, including Pythagorean or right-angle triangles, some two thousand years before the time of the Greek mathematician. Wishing to express these elaborate patterns in a permanent form, they then "mastered elementary geometrical construction" in the building of megalithic monuments.

Not only did the megaliths reveal an advanced understanding of geometry, they also showed consistent alignments to solar and lunar phenomena. Thom revived Lockyer's suggestion of an eightfold solar calendar, but thought that it had actually been twice as complex, with sixteen divisions in the year. More far-reaching was his conclusion that monuments along the Atlantic from Shetland off the northern coast of Scotland down to Brittany in northern France had been set up to allow accurate observations of the movements of the moon over hundreds of years—all with the aim of predicting eclipses. The sheer number of sites devoted to this purpose led him to argue that new observatories were built as the movements of the heavens rendered existing ones inaccurate. There were, however, Thom believed, mixed motives for this immense effort. Pure scientific curiosity was the dominant one, with Thom seeing his megalithic astronomer as a potential scientist:

> He did not know where this was leading him any more than today's scientist really knows what the outcome of his work will be, but the earlier people were motivated by the same urge to study phenomena that drives the scientists of today.

There was also a less disinterested motive behind this intellectual achievement—the desire to impress on the ordinary members of society the powerful knowledge of the heavens held by the astronomical priesthood.

Archaeologist Euan MacKie took the logical step of trying to identify

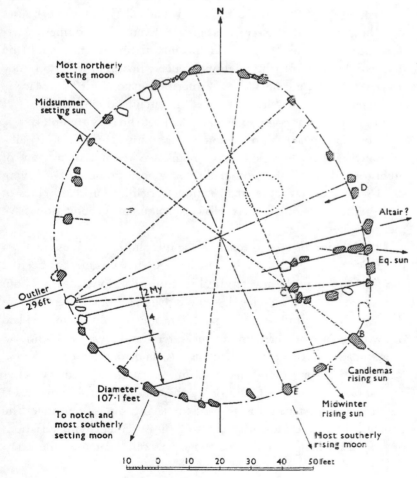

Professor Alexander Thom's interpretation of the astronomical alignments of the stone circle at Castlerigg, Cumbria, northern England.

the headquarters of Thom's astronomer-priests. He turned to the Maya of central America for a possible analogy (see **The Rise and Fall of Maya Civilization** in **Lost Lands and Catastrophes**), following the interpretation of Maya cities as ceremonial centers occupied only by the elite group of astronomer-priests. Casting around for something similar in prehistoric Britain, he examined the henge enclosures of the Neolithic (around 2800–2200 B.C.). Although Stonehenge is the best known of these, there are other, far larger examples, including Durrington Walls, only two miles away. In the 1960s archaeological investigations inside several examples in southern England uncovered timber circles, interpreted by the excavators as the remains of substantial buildings, and large quantities of a flat-bottomed type of pottery known as Grooved Ware.

MacKie seized on these mega-henges as the expected astronomical training centers—the timber circles were their living quarters, with Grooved Ware seen as pottery for the social elite. In parts of the country lacking giant henges, he suggested that villages of stone houses were built to house these early scientists. Even where domestic evidence for the priestly elite was missing, their presence could be detected by the megalithic monuments whose construction they oversaw. Developing his Central American analogy further, MacKie wondered if stone circles might be "the architecturally cruder—yet ceremonially just as complex—equivalents of the Maya temples."

Thom and MacKie made some important claims that, if substantiated, should have led archaeologists to rethink their view of prehistoric Britain, which has traditionally been thought of as having small-scale societies rather than national organizations, and elites of chiefs rather than astronomers. However, all their interpretations have met fierce resistance.

The question of the existence of the megalithic yard is essentially a matter of statistics, and mathematician Douglas Heggie has been at the forefront here. Using statistical methods developed since Thom considered the question, Heggie showed that there was strong evidence that stone circles and other megalithic monuments were indeed laid out with the use of a base unit of measurement. However, Thom had overestimated the degree to which this was standardized. Heggie "found little evidence for a highly accurate unit . . . with an accuracy better than about 1 per cent." Questioning the feasibility of Thom's headquarters issuing standard-issue rods for laying out stone circles, he concluded that the most likely unit of measurement with variations of several percent around the average was one related to the body, perhaps the pace. If that were the case, then there is simply no need for Thom's central control.

The results of Heggie's investigation of the layout of megalithic monuments were less clear-cut. It became apparent that no statistical check could show one way or the other whether advanced geometrical concepts had been employed. However, experimental work by Dr. Ian Angell of London University showed that all the patterns seen in the layout of stone circles could have been achieved by the use of wooden stakes and ropes, and need not have involved any abstract mathematical thinking. One flaw of the Thom approach was that it tended to study megalithic sites as ground plans rather than as monuments constructed in specific places. When the setting of stone circles is considered, it becomes clear that in many cases the builders were working on uneven ground, and that in order to achieve the effect of a ring that looked circular to people when they stood inside it, they had to bend the outline slightly. So perhaps visual effects were more important than geometry.

In the end, however, it is the astronomical and archaeological arguments that are at the heart of Thom and MacKie's theories. Was there really a network of megalithic solar and lunar observatories throughout Britain and Brittany staffed by astronomer-priests living in relative luxury, supported by a grateful peasantry?

Heggie's reanalysis of Thom's data did support the idea of solar alignments, with much the most convincing case, in statistical terms, being made out for stone circles and rows incorporating alignments to the solstices. There was far less sign of the equinoxes being marked and little to back up the notion of a year divided into eight equal parts. When he came to lunar observations Thom's theory fared less well:

> Though there is some evidence in Thom's first book for relatively inaccurate lunar lines, there is little of this which suggests that the orientations were set up so as to discriminate the fine details in the motion of the moon. . . . We find a little evidence for rough lunar orientations but none of any statistical significance for very accurate ones.

So while there are good grounds to believe that prehistoric Europeans did take an interest in the movements of the Sun and Moon, the evidence for a scientific community of highly skilled astronomers has not stood up to the statistical challenge.

Does MacKie's archaeological case fare any better? It has certainly not been helped by dramatic changes in archaeologists' knowledge of the Maya that made it clear that, although astronomy had been important to them, they had not been ruled by scientist-priests. Their society was a highly urbanized and literate one, completely unlike prehistoric Britain (see **The Rise and Fall of Maya Civilization** in **Lost Lands and Catastrophes**).

When it comes to the mega-henges, most archaeologists think that the timber circles they contain were not luxury housing but the wooden equivalent of megalithic monuments, constructed for holding ceremonies. Many more settlements occupied by the makers of Grooved Ware pottery have now been found, and there is nothing about them that points to a priesthood. Even Mackie's favorite site, the stone-built village of Skara Brae on Orkney, is now known to be just one of several—either all these were occupied by astronomer-priests, or none of them were.

So is there anything left of the Thom model? While there is little left of the idea of an international network of scientists, that need not in itself mean that individual monuments were not the site of high-precision astronomy. Discussion has focused on two Scottish examples, at Kintraw and Ballochroy on the west coast, both claimed to be highly accurate solar observatories.

Kintraw consists of a single standing stone some 12 feet tall near a pair of burial mounds. Some thirty miles away to the southwest are the mountains on the island of Jura. Looking along the line from the larger of the burial mounds above the top of the stone to Jura, an observer would see the midwinter solstice sunset. Moreover, because the alignment is so long, the Sun would set in a clearly different place each day around the solstice, so a highly accurate watch could be kept on the Sun's movements and the date of midwinter calculated precisely. Two difficulties stood in the way of this theory, however. One was a low ridge of hills, which meant that Jura is out of sight from the mound, so how did the observatory work? The other problem is that there is nothing about the standing stone itself that says that it must be pointing toward Jura, or indeed anything.

Excavations by MacKie in 1970 seemed to provide an answer to both issues. Thom had spotted an apparent platform on the hillside behind the mound from which Jura could just be made out. MacKie's investigation of this produced no ancient objects, but did seem to show that it was a deliberately laid surface—if so, then what other motive could there be for its construction besides astronomical? Unfortunately, archaeologists were unconvinced. When they tried to see Jura from the platform, several claimed it was either impossible or only feasible on rare occasions, owing to atmospheric conditions affecting visibility. It is actually much easier to see Jura from higher up the slope, but no traces of human activity can be seen there. Geologists were divided on the question of the platform being man-made. Kintraw remains unproved.

Just down the coast from Kintraw, Ballochroy incorporates two alignments. A row of three stones points toward a stone box (a cist) set in the ground that would originally have held a cremated body. If one

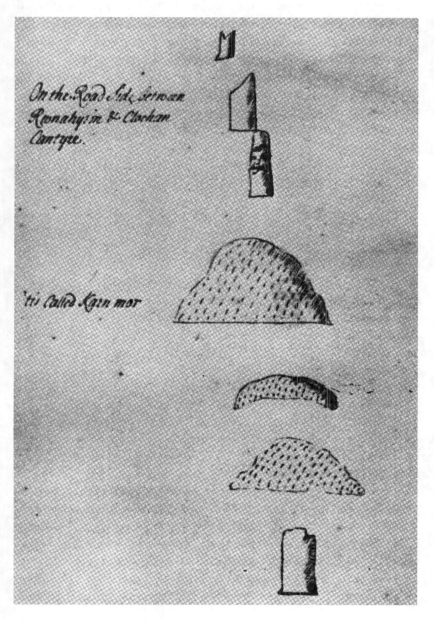

Seventeenth-century engraving of the site of Ballochroy, Scotland, showing the stone mound that would have blocked the alignment to the midsummer sunset.

were looking along a line from the stones, the midwinter sunset would have occurred behind the cist. The central one of the three stones has a rectangular shape, and looking along the long flat face, the observer can see the Sun set at midsummer behind the same mountains on Jura as seen from Kintraw. Once again, things are not as clear as Thom would wish. The cist was once covered by a massive mound of stones, which would have blocked any view of the midwinter sunset. Another of the three stones in the row has its flat faces pointing toward Jura but not the sunset, while the tallest cannot be said to indicate any particular direction—the only difference between the stones is that one seems to have astronomical significance while the other ones do not, so to elevate one to the status of an observation point and ignore the others seems completely arbitrary. A critical examination of Ballochroy gives no real support to claims of accurate solar observations.

The overall conclusion on Thom's astronomer-priests must be that they were largely a product of the wishful thinking of a dedicated scientist. As Dr. Evan Hadingham, archaeologist and science writer, concluded after going to Brittany in 1983 to assess the evidence for himself:

> The result, in the case of Professor Thom's research, is a kind of science fiction in which the prehistoric Bretons operate their lunar observatory with a passion for precision suspiciously like that of modern engineers and astronomers. While the megaliths were indeed connected with beliefs about the sun and moon, it is clear that these were only aspects of a complicated mass of ideas and practices involving [religious beliefs].
>
> We must be grateful to Thom and his colleagues for awakening interest in the intellectual skills of prehistoric Europeans. Yet many of the claims for a Stone Age science are now proving to be little more than an unconscious projection of our contemporary technical world onto the silent ruins of four thousand years ago. There is little "hard" evidence to support the theory that accurate eclipse predictions were undertaken by the megalith builders, who would have found their task extraordinarily difficult in the absence of written recording aids.

Festive Astronomy

With the extreme theories of Thom and MacKie out of the way, is there anything left of prehistoric astronomy? Indeed there is. As at Ballochroy, there are many burial sites that incorporate astronomical alignments, presumably because the cycle of movements of the Sun and the Moon were thought to relate to the cycles of human experience from birth to life to death, and perhaps rebirth if there was a belief in reincarnation.

The most famous of these is Newgrange in the Boyne Valley of Ireland, a massive stone chambered tomb constructed around 3500 B.C. From the central burial chambers a long passage runs to the

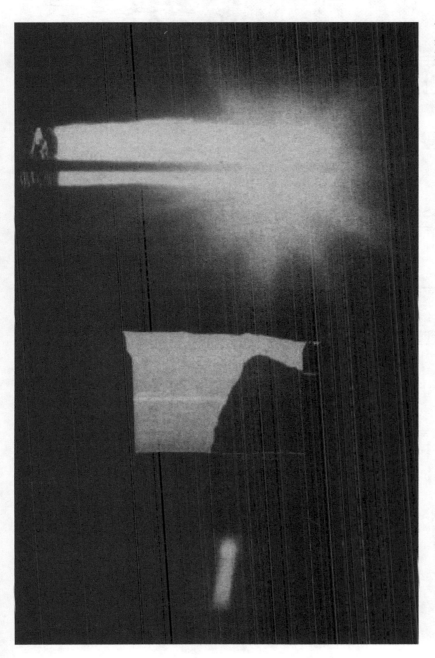

The midwinter sunrise seen from inside the tomb of Newgrange, Ireland.

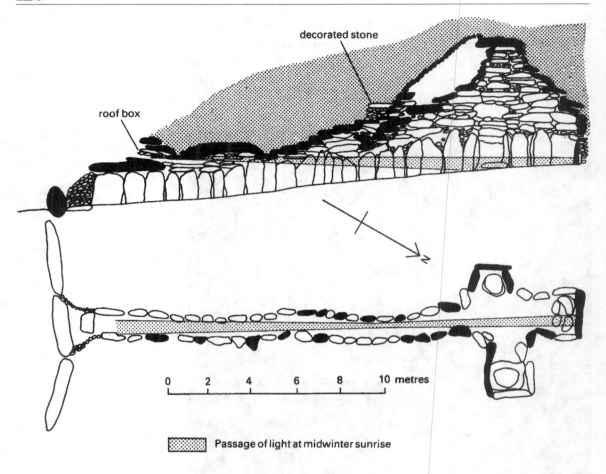

decorated stone

roof box

0   2   4   6   8   10 metres

▨ Passage of light at midwinter sunrise

Diagram showing how the midwinter sunrise enters the tomb at Newgrange through the roof-box to light up the central chamber.

outside of the mound and a doorway to the outside world, marked by a large boulder covered with carvings of spirals. Above this entrance is an unusual feature, the "roof-box." This is a narrow opening revealed only during the long excavations by Michael and Claire O'Kelly of Cork University. It was blocked with large pieces of quartz, but these could be removed. Following restoration of the entrance it was noted that the midwinter Sun entered through the roof-box, shining along the passage and illuminating the chamber at the center of the mound. Claire O'Kelly was greatly impressed by the phenomenon:

It is difficult to remain sceptical once one has actually seen. as I have, the thin thread of sunlight striking in along the passage at this most dismal of all times of the year until the dark of the chamber begins to disperse and more and more of it becomes visible as the sun rises and the light strengthens. Upon looking outwards towards the entrance, one sees the ball of the sun framed dramatically in the slit of the roof-box and one realizes that in the whole course of the year this brief spell is the only period when daylight has sway over the darkness of the tomb.

Other chambered tombs of this period have similar alignments and arrangements for letting in the Sun. Striking though this is, it should not be confused with scientific astronomy. The width of the passages means that, for example, the Sun shines into Newgrange for several days either side of the winter solstice. In any case, the only observers would have been the dead. Instead this seems to be a kind of ritual astronomy, with important points in the Sun's annual cycle, perhaps festivals, being connected to the dead.

Lunar observations of a kind can be seen at a group of stone circles in Scotland, which share the unusual feature that one of the stones in the ring was deliberately laid on its side, with uprights flanking it, forming the lower half of a "window." These recumbent stones are always on the southern side of the circle, between southwest and

Some of the massive uncut stones making up the great circle at Avebury.

south-southeast, and were placed to command a good view of the horizon. With this orientation the Moon would pass over the recumbent, and every eighteen and a half years its cycle of movement meant that it appeared to swoop down to be framed within the stone window. Again this has nothing to do with accurate observations or predicting eclipses, but it links the heavens to the dead, for the cremated bones of human burials are often found within the circles, as are chunks of milky-colored quartz, a very appropriate material to symbolize ethereal moonlight.

Dr. Clive Ruggles of Leicester University, the current expert on prehistoric British astronomy, is quite clear on the implications of these widely accepted cases:

> The use of monumental stone architecture to express astronomical alignments is itself a strong argument that such alignments were symbolic, rather than intended for any use that would seem to us "practical."

Stone is hardly a suitable material for marking astronomical observations, and most societies have found wood a much more sensible choice. Unlike stone it can easily be shifted as the heavens themselves move relative to the Earth.

The prehistoric people of Europe were keen watchers of the skies over 5,000 years ago, but their astronomy made sense in their terms, not those of twentieth-century scientists.

THE ORION MYSTERY

Were the great pyramids of Egypt laid out to form a map of the stars? This is the revolutionary thesis proposed in 1994 by Robert Bauval and Adrian Gilbert in *The Orion Mystery*.

The inspiration came to Bauval, a construction engineer born in Egypt, when he was gazing at the stars one night through the clear skies of the Arabian Desert. For many years he had pondered the engineering problems involved in building the Pyramids, as well as their orientation and layout, particularly that of the three Great Pyramids on the Giza plateau (see **How Were the Pyramids Built?** in **Architectural Wonders**). Though built by three different Pharaohs, they seem to form a harmonious arrangement—yet why were they not placed in the "ideal" layout of a simple straight line? The third pyramid, that built by Mycerinus, is not only much smaller than those of

Cheops and Chephren but is also conspicuously offset from the axis running through them. A chance remark made by a friend that night in the desert seemed to provide Bauval with an answer. His friend noted that the three stars forming the "belt" of the well-known constellation Orion (named after a hunter and giant of Greek myth) were not in a straight line, but that the top right and smallest star, as we see it, is offset. Bauval was immediately reminded of the Pyramids, and the seeds of the "Orion mystery" were sown.

Bauval followed up his hunch by studying a plan of the Pyramid complex around Giza. Two other Fourth Dynasty Pyramids seemed to fit the Orion pattern. To the north of Giza, the Pyramid of Djedefra at Abu Ruwash matched the bright star forming the "left foot" of the Orion constellation. To the south, the Pyramid of Nebka at Zawyat al Aryan matches the star that marks Orion's "right shoulder." The last two Pyramids needed to complete the standard figure of Orion could not be found, and Bauval "could only conclude that these had never been built or that they had long since been demolished and disappeared under the sand of the western desert." Still, five out of seven of the bright stars of Orion could be accounted for. So Bauval argued that the Fourth Dynasty Egyptians had deliberately positioned their pyramids to mark out the figure of the constellation Orion, which would have looked almost exactly the same five thousand years ago as it does today.

Layout of the three great pyramids at Giza compared to the stars of Orion's belt.

Yet is there any reason to imagine that the Egyptians would have been interested in such an undertaking—an attempt to model the heavens on Earth? The answer is yes, and at this general level Bauval's Orion theory makes good sense. Greek writers of classical times tell us that the Egyptians saw the Milky Way, the sinuous band of distant stars that cuts through the sky, as a heavenly counterpart to the River Nile. As they were always highly chauvinistic about the importance of their river in cosmogony, it seems likely that the Egyptians had long held the belief that the Milky Way was the celestial reflection of the Nile, and vice versa. So the motivation may well have been there to add other "stars" to the terrestrial pattern.

The Pyramid Texts

As Bauval rightly points out, the writings that survive describing the ritual significance of the Pyramids are positively littered with references to the stars. They were inscribed on the chamber walls of Pyramids from the Fifth and Sixth Dynasties (c. 2450–2250 B.C.), later

The night sky seen through the Grand Gallery of the Great Pyramid of Cheops. Before the Pyramid was sealed, the Gallery would have made a perfect vantage point for astronomical observation.

than the time of Cheops and the other Fourth Dynasty builders of the Giza complex—yet there is no reason to assume that slightly earlier Pharaohs did not hold similar views. These Pyramid Texts contain numerous references to buried Pharaohs going to the stars or becoming stars, and particular importance is given to the constellation *Sahu*, the Egyptian name for Orion—believed to be the home of Osiris, the great god of the dead. In a typical passage, one Pyramid Text states "behold he [the Pharaoh] has come as Orion, behold Osiris has come as Orion." It seems that it was believed that the soul of the dead Pharaoh would travel to Orion and then unite with Osiris: "May you ascend to the sky, may the sky give birth to you like Orion." As for the Pyramids where the kings were buried, one of the texts explicitly identifies them with Orion: "these kings are Orion-Osiris, these pyramids of theirs are Orion-Osiris, these constructions of theirs are Orion-Osiris."

Egyptologists, on the whole, have neglected the astronomical content of such passages, sometimes glossing over them as mumbo jumbo. Yet the texts show indisputably that there was a link between the Pyramid cults and those of the constellation Orion (the god Osiris), as well as the Pole Star and the star Sirius (thought to be Osiris' wife Isis). There may even be specific features built into the Great Pyramid of Cheops that point at certain stars. Inside the Pyramid are two narrow shafts (too small for a person to enter) that lead outward from the King's Chamber. As they have no openings on the outside of the Pyramid, the original idea that they were ventilation shafts was long ago abandoned, with theories concentrating instead on some ritual purpose such as passages through which the Pharaoh's soul could escape to make journeys.

In 1964, Egyptologist Alexander Badawy developed the idea further, arguing from the Pyramid Texts that the shafts acted as channels through which the Pharaoh could journey to the stars—the northern shaft leading to the Polar Stars, the southern one to Orion. His theory was backed with calculations made by astronomer Virginia Trimble. The northern shaft (inclined at 31 degrees to the horizontal) points directly at Alpha Draconis, which was the Pole Star between about 3000 and 2500 B.C. As for the southern shaft (inclined at 44.5 degrees), it lines up with the position of Orion at culmination between 2840 to 2480 B.C.; every twenty-four hours the "belt" of stars in the middle of this constellation would have passed directly over the shaft.

Bauval and Gilbert use Badawy and Trimble's work to good effect, but perhaps the most striking piece of evidence that they bring to bear are the names that the Egyptians themselves gave to the Pyramids. Two of the Pyramids involved in the Orion layout actually have stellar names. That of Nebka (Orion's "right shoulder") was called "Nebka Is a Star," while the Pyramid of Djedefra (Orion's "left foot") was known as "Djedefra Is a Sehetu Star." The name of the Great Pyramid itself, "the Horizon of Khufu," is suggestive. If the Egyptians conceived of the Pyramids as stars, then maybe they positioned them to mirror the heavens.

Reactions to the Orion theory from Egyptologists—who generally know nothing of astronomy and have a habit of ignoring new ideas— have been noticeably cool, but with a few important exceptions. Professor I. E. S. Edwards, the grand old man of pyramidology, made some quite encouraging noises and, at the very least, accepted that the southern shaft of Cheops' Pyramid was aligned with the belt of Orion. Professor Jaromir Malek, Director of the Griffith Institite for Egyptology at Oxford University, was also receptive. In a letter to Bauval in 1985, he stated that he "would be prepared to consider seriously the observation that the Giza Pyramids were positioned or sited in a manner as to represent the three stars of Orion."

It is true to say that the importance of astronomy in Egyptian religion has definitely been underplayed, and it is to Bauval's credit that he has given the subject a much-needed airing. And some of the evidence he has presented linking the Pyramids and the stars is extremely persuasive. Yet it is in the fine detail that the Orion theory is difficult to support. The match between Orion and the Giza Pyramids is intriguing but unsatisfying. Two important stars from the constellation cannot be matched at all on the ground, and Bauval has to fall back on the possibility that they were never built, or may yet be found. Even the two extra stars that he did manage to identify (apart from the "belt") fit rather awkwardly. The distances and angles involved are actually wrong. If we were to take the three Giza Pyramids and superimpose on them Orion's belt (see diagram, page 132), then the other features of Orion at the same scale, including the points of his shoulders and feet, completely miss the pyramids of Djedefra and Nebka, which are much too far to the north and south respectively.

Similar problems arise wherever Bauval and Gilbert tried to extend their model beyond the original three stars of Orion's belt. Professor Malek recommended that they develop the theory by looking for constellation patterns in the distribution of other Pyramids from the same period. This was attempted, but the exercise can only be

Star chart superimposed on a map of the main Pyramids of Old Kingdom Egypt. Though the belt of Orion matches well with the three Great Pyramids at Giza, the other Pyramids (Zawyat al Aryan and Abu Ruwash) argued by Bauval and Gilbert to match the constellation pattern are well off the mark. None of the stars in the Hyades or Taurus fit with the Pyramids at Abusir, as they claim. NB: South is at the top of the map.

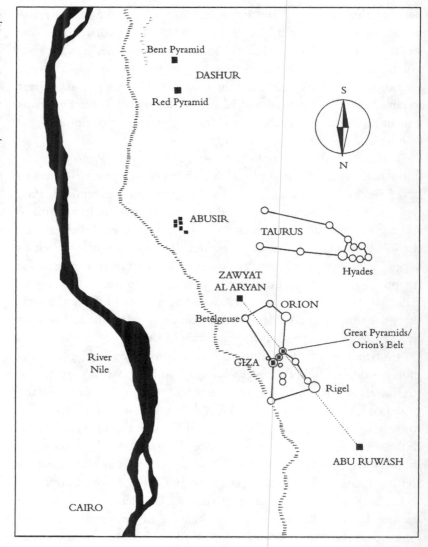

described as a miserable failure. For the Fourth Dynasty, the best that Bauval and Gilbert could come up with was to match two of the Pyramids in the Dashur region, north of Giza, with stars in the constellation Hyades, which appears above Orion in the sky. Yet there are another five conspicuous stars in the Hyades that cannot be matched at all on the ground. Besides, *two* points hardly provide a pattern of any kind. Two adjacent Pyramids could be matched with *any* two stars. The only other match they came up with was to compare the group of Fifth Dynasty Pyramids at Abusir with the cluster of stars above Orion and thought to mark his "head"—again, there is no pattern as such here.

Dr. Robert Chadwick, an ancient Near Eastern historian, has taken Bauval to task on other matters. He has shown that the orientation of the putative Orion Pyramids and those of the Hyades simply does not work for any given moment in the night sky. Bauval has used their positions for *different* times of the night: "Taurus [of which the Hyades are the "head"] only matches the layout of the Dashur pyramids when it is rising in the east, and Orion only matches the Giza pyramids when it is on the meridian, ninety degrees away. What kind of 'correlation' is that?"

The other side of the coin is that there are, of course, many other Pyramids that appear to fit no recognizable star pattern at all. Bauval and Gilbert claim that it was only really the Fourth Dynasty builders who followed the astronomical master plan. On the other hand, they do include the Fifth Dynasty Pyramids at Abusir, claimed to represent Orion's "head"; and they freely draw on texts from Sixth Dynasty Pyramids, which while they clearly link Pyramids with Orion-Osiris, do not fall within the Orion pattern at all.

Looked at from a statistical point of view, the Orion theory makes a pretty poor showing, as Chadwick has scathingly remarked:

> Robert Bauval and Adrian Gilbert never succeed in matching more than three pyramids to three stars at any one time. Since there are nearly thirty pyramids in the region between Abu Ruwash and Dashur, this supposed match-up is serendipitous and may be attributed to chance rather than some kind of master plan devised by the ancient Egyptians of the Fourth Dynasty. Matching ten percent of pyramids in that area to thousands of visible stars in the firmament does not constitute any viable pyramid-star correlation. Knowing the practical nature of the ancient Egyptians, had they really wanted to create a pyramid-star matching scheme, it is certain that they would have done a much better job.

Despite the single rough-and-ready correlation they have produced between the stars and the constellation Orion, Bauval and his new colleague Graham Hancock (see **Poleshift** in **Lost Lands and Catastrophes**) claim that the pyramids were positioned and oriented with unerring precision—so much so that they claim to be able to determine from the configuration of the three Pyramids at Giza exactly when the blueprint for building them was drawn up. They base this on a comparison of the angle formed by the line of the three Great Pyramids and the Nile, with the angle of the belt of Orion with respect to the Milky Way. The constellation has rotated slightly over the millennia, and by using computer simulations of the sky as it would have appeared over Giza, Bauval and Hancock claim to have found an exact "meridian for meridian" match at 10,500 B.C. Their method is abstruse, and not helped by the fact that the diagrams they give for the angle of Orion's belt at various dates differ from one book to another. The whole idea that the angle of the three Great Pyramids "precisely and surgically" marks a particular astronomical epoch is hopelessly far-fetched, considering that the Egyptians were not even able to complete the standard Orion figure with any accuracy.

So, interesting speculation though it is, Bauval's Orion theory is far from proven and there remain some conspicuous problems—not the least being the lack of Pyramids to complete the figures of Orion and the Hyades. Even so, Bauval's general approach may yet be worth further study. The idea that the Egyptians might have been attempting to reflect the heavens on earth is not outside their way of thinking. Finds of extra Pyramids (though unlikely at this stage) *might* yet help to confirm the basic thesis.

Or perhaps there are other ways of looking at the correlations involved. In fairness to Bauval and Gilbert, the Egyptians tended to focus very much on the three stars of Orion's belt, rather than the outlying ones forming his shoulders and feet. On the tomb of the Eighteenth Dynasty vizier Senmut (about 1450 B.C.) the constellation Sahu (Orion) is represented simply by a line of three stars, *not* by seven. (Compare the ancient Chinese name for Orion—*Shen*, meaning a "union of three.") In fact, until clear evidence is produced that the Egyptians *did* recognize Orion as a seven-starred constellation, perhaps there is no need at all to try to find the shape that we are familiar with on the ground.

Looking at it this way, we might think in terms of a much more limited Orion correlation. The Egyptians may have been aware that the three Giza Pyramids resembled Orion's belt—and that might have influenced the design of their layout. But they might simply have left it at that.

In the meantime, Bauval and Hancock have unwisely taken the case further and reached some extravagant conclusions. With the basic theory so uncertain, to pile on even greater claims—such as backdating the pyramids to 10,500 B.C.—is merely wishful thinking.

THE DAY THE SUN STOOD STILL?

In what has fairly been described as the most incredible story in the entire Bible, God made the Sun itself stand still in the sky to help the Israelites, his chosen people. Led by Joshua, they were continuing their march into the Promised Land (Canaan) after the fall of Jericho. Adoni-zedek, king of Jerusalem, called up his Amorite allies to halt the Israelite advance and the two armies met in battle at Gibeon. The Israelites won the day and chased their enemies to the pass of Beth Horon. Here the miracle began. God appeared to intercede on behalf of the Israelites, slaughtering the Amorites as they tried to escape:

> And it came to pass, as they fled from before Israel, and were in the going down to Beth-horon, that the Lord cast down great stones from heaven upon them . . . and they died; they were more which died with hailstones than they whom the children of Israel slew with the sword.

Intent on destroying his enemies utterly, Joshua called on God to lengthen the day:

> "Sun, stand thou still upon Gibeon; and thou, Moon, in the valley of Aijalon."
> And the sun stood still, and the moon stayed, until the people had avenged themselves upon their enemies. . . . So the sun stood still in the midst of heaven, and hasted not to go down about a whole day.
> And there was no day like that before it or after it, that the Lord hearkened unto the voice of a man. . . . (Joshua 10:11–14)

The biblical description is alarmingly brief for an event of such staggering implications. The story of "Joshua's long day" stands in a quite different class from most biblical miracles. Many people, for example, believe in the miraculous cures attributed to Jesus and others, perhaps seeing them as acts of faith healing. Others accept that Daniel somehow managed to survive a night in the lions' den unscathed, or that God spoke to Moses from a burning bush. Yet even the most devout Jews and Christians find it difficult to swallow the idea that the Sun once stood still, simply to satisfy the blood lust of Joshua and his invading Israelites.

Obviously, for the Sun to appear to stop moving across the sky, the motion of the Earth would have to be interrupted. Even the faithful are curious enough to ask what mechanism the Almighty could have used to perform such a miracle. As a result, there can be few passages in the Old Testament that have exercised the minds of academics, from biblical scholars to astronomers, so vigorously.

The Old Testament has a reasonable track record in terms of its miracles having natural explanations. In particular, many of the other momentous events described in the Book of Joshua can no longer be treated as mere folktales, devoid of scientific context or historical content. When the Israelites began their conquest of Canaan (most probably sometime between 1450 and 1300 B.C.), Jericho was said to have been the first city they captured. This city most certainly existed, and the walls that "came tumbling down" when Joshua's army marched around it can be identified as those of Middle Bronze Age Jericho. Geological evidence also shows that the River Jordan can be crossed "on dry land," a feat achieved by Joshua and the Israelites just before they attacked Jericho. Jericho lies on a major geological fault line prone to sudden and violent earthquakes. In ten out of thirty recorded earthquakes, including one as recently as 1927, mud slides blocked the River Jordan and stopped it flowing for one or two days. The damming of the river and the fall of the walls of Jericho could easily have resulted from the same earthquake episode.

With this background in mind, it is worth looking at the explanations that have been offered for the most outrageous of biblical miracles—the day the Sun stood still.

The walls of Jericho tumble down as Joshua's army invades. From an early-19th-century family Bible.

Omens and Eclipses

Solving the mystery of Joshua's long day seemed to become a favorite pastime of biblical scholars around the middle of this century. Professor John Bright, one of the leading authorities on the Bible of the mid–twentieth century, suggested that the story might have arisen as a misunderstanding of the prayer uttered by Joshua. Bright assumed that the Israelites were planning a surprise attack under cover of a thick, early-morning mist and that Joshua was praying for the Sun not to appear quickly and dissolve the mist. Bright's theory does not so much explain the story as deny it. Neither a mist nor a surprise attack is mentioned in the Bible—in fact, Joshua utters his prayer in the middle of a battle; if Joshua was just praying for a mist to linger, one wonders how the story became so memorable in the first place.

Another suggestion, made by biblical scholar R. C. Fuller, interprets the fall of "great stones" as a severe hailstorm. Fuller suggested the storm may have lasted for a whole day, blocking out the light of the Sun and Moon. Like Bright's theory, Fuller's seems to deny the clear meaning of the biblical text—far from suggesting that the light of the Sun and Moon was obscured, the Book of Joshua says that it was unnaturally prolonged.

A more probable approach was taken in 1968 by Near Eastern archaeologist John S. Holladay, in an article provocatively titled "The Day(s) the *Moon* Stood Still." Whereas most commentators had concentrated on the Sun's behavior in the story, Holladay focused on the fact that the Moon also was invoked by Joshua. So Holladay argued that the key to the meaning of this cryptic verse may be that the Sun and Moon were requested to be there *together* on the day of the battle with the Amorites.

Holladay then searched through the extensive writings on omens and astrology that survive from ancient Babylonia (southern Iraq). Ancient Near Eastern calendars—like our own—were based on the movements of both the Sun and Moon. With the calendar adjusted correctly, the full Moon would first appear with the Sun in the middle of a twenty-nine-day month, that is, on the 14th. If it did so, the Babylonians considered it to be a healthy sign for the nation: "the land will be satisfied . . . joy is in the heart of the people," runs one of their omen tablets. However, if the Sun and new Moon were in the sky together on the 13th or 15th of the month, it was thought to presage disaster, and defeat at the hands of enemies.

Read in the light of these texts, Holladay claimed, 'the meaning of

Joshua 10:12–13 could hardly be more clear": it was a prayer for a favorable omen, for the Sun and Moon to be in the sky together ("in opposition") throughout the day of the battle. Quite possibly the ancient Hebrews shared the same belief as the Babylonians: that disaster would have struck had the Moon left its partner early in the day. When the text says "stand," in Holladay's interpretation, it doesn't mean "cease moving" but rather "be there in place."

Yet Holladay's apparently neat explanation accounts only for Joshua's prayer, and not for the verse that immediately follows it. This makes it very clear that the Sun, rather than the Moon, was the more important partner in the story: "So the sun stood still in the midst of heaven, and hasted not to go down about a whole day." Holladay has to assume that this was a later commentary, added by a scribe who misunderstood the original meaning of Joshua's prayer. So while Holladay has cleverly squeezed a new meaning out of the text, it is, by his own argument, one that the ancient Hebrews themselves did not accept. The Jewish scholar Josephus, who in the first century A.D. rewrote and presented biblical history for a Graeco-Roman audience, would certainly have disagreed with Holladay. For him the text clearly concerned an unnaturally prolonged day:

> It happened that the day was lengthened, that the night might not come too soon and be an obstruction to the zeal of the Hebrews in pursuing their enemies. . . . Now, that the day was lengthened at this time, and was longer than ordinary, is expressed in the books laid up in the temple.

Holladay's argument also breaks down when we consider that the Hebrews must have fought and won many battles on the 14th of the month. What made this occasion so special that they thought "never before or since has there been such a day"?

A study published in 1972, by historian John Sawyer, took the more promising approach that the Israelites *did* witness some prodigious heavenly event affecting the Sun—namely, a total solar eclipse. Sawyer began with the interesting observation that total eclipses can give the impression of lasting far longer than they actually do. For example, an eclipse in 1927 "seemed like half an hour" to observers in northern England, though it actually lasted a mere twenty-five seconds. That seen from Dongola in the Sudan in 1860, just one minute and fifty seconds in duration, was reported by observers as taking more like two hours. Sawyer believes that this well-attested illusory effect, of a prolongation of time followed by the reappearance of the Sun in the same part of the sky, could have prompted the story of the Sun "standing still" for an unnatural length of time. The Hebrew verb "to stand still" in this instance, *daman,* is interpreted by Sawyer as meaning "to be still, inactive," in other words "to stop shining."

Sawyer tested this idea by investigating the eclipses that may have been visible in southern Palestine between 1500 and 1050 B.C., a broad range of dates around the time of the Israelite conquest of Canaan. Mathematical retrocalculations (which assume that the motion of the Earth and the Moon has not changed since the time of Joshua) throw up two such possible eclipses, one in August 1157 B.C. and a later one in September 1131 B.C. Of the two candidates Sawyer preferred the second, mainly because it occurred at 12:40 P.M., around noon as the biblical account suggests—"so the Sun stayed in mid-heaven." This spectacular eclipse is calculated to have lasted over four minutes and may well have given the illusion of the Sun standing still for much longer before continuing its normal course, remembering the 1860 Dongola report of an eclipse under two minutes seeming like two hours.

Sawyer's theory is ingenious, but it faces some serious objections. A major stumbling block is the dates of the eclipses. Both of them (1157 and 1131 B.C.) are far too recent for the time of Joshua, on any possible model. On the conventional dating scheme it is clear from Egyptian records that the people of Israel were *already* in Palestine by about 1200 B.C. To get around this chronological problem, Sawyer argued either that the "long day" was a later event erroneously attached to the cycles of stories about Joshua, or that Joshua himself lived much later than the other events (such as the crossing of the Jordan and the fall of Jericho) usually associated with him. These ad hoc explanations weaken Sawyer's case considerably.

Further, it seems doubtful that the text could really be referring to an eclipse. Several eclipses have been identified in the Old Testament. None of these passages uses the verb *daman,* "to stand still." Instead they have their own terminology that quite clearly refers to the Sun becoming darkened. For example, the eighth-century B.C. prophet Amos described how God "turneth the shadow of death into the morning and maketh the day dark with night"—most probably an echo of the major solar eclipse of June 763 B.C. The later prophet Joel (2:31) foretold that on the "day of the Lord" "the sun shall be turned to darkness." If such terminology was available to describe eclipses, why didn't the writers of the Book of Joshua employ it? In fact, the "long day" story seems to be referring to exactly the opposite of a darkened Sun—the whole point was that the daylight continued for a prolonged period so Joshua was able to mop up his enemies.

Stones from Heaven

None of these worthy attempts to explain Joshua's long day by re-interpreting the text is convincing. But before relegating the whole story to the scrap heap of history, there are a number of more radical possibilities that need to be explored.

While devout nineteenth-century readers of the Bible may simply have assumed that God somehow stopped the Earth turning to make the Sun "stand still," what does twentieth-century science have to say about the possibility, and plausibility, of a slowing down of the Earth's rotation? At first glance the idea of an interruption in the Earth's speed of rotation seems unacceptable, as well as downright unnerving. Day and night succeed each other with unnerving precision, and each day is 23 hours, 56 minutes, and 4.1 seconds long. If it weren't, we would be perpetually resetting our watches. So we tend to think that the regularity of the day's length is beyond question. But is it?

As it happens, one of the most curious, though little-publicized, discoveries of the last few decades is that the length of the day *can* vary. In 1960 Anton Danjon, Director of the Paris Observatory, reported that the length of the day temporarily increased by 0.85 milliseconds following an intense solar flare. For a while Danjon's claim was treated lightly, but his work was followed up and confirmed. Since the 1970s scientists have seriously entertained the idea that severe solar storms can produce temporary accelerations and decelerations of the Earth's rotation, known as "glitches." It has also become clear that the Earth's speed of rotation is steadily decreasing, at a minuscule rate detectable only with the most sophisticated of instruments.

Yet while it has been shown that the speed of the Earth's rotation can change, this provides the possibility of variations of the order of only a few milliseconds—hardly comparable to the extended day reported in the Book of Joshua. A solar flare has immense power, but its effects on Earth are, of course, diluted by the vast distance involved. For a solar storm great enough to work a "miracle" of several hours' duration, the Sun would probably have to have exploded—and nobody would be alive to tell the tale.

Is there anything that could possibly provide the energy necessary to alter the Earth's rotation without actually destroying it? A force

much nearer than the Sun would do the job, but there seems to be only one way of providing it—a body almost as large as Earth itself must pass close enough to affect it with its gravitational pull. In astronomical terms such an event would be extraordinary, to say the very least. Yet a detail of the incident at Beth Horon does suggest that the Book of Joshua was describing an extraordinary astronomical event.

The omen and eclipse interpretations of Joshua's long day (provided by Holladay and Sawyer) completely overlooked what was said to have happened just before the Sun "stood still." A rain of stones was supposed to have fallen on the Amorites and decimated them before Joshua's army chased them through the Beth Horon pass to finish them off. What kind of stones were they? In some modern translations of the Old Testament, such as the often far from literal *New English Bible*, the impression is given that hailstones—the familiar blobs of ice that are frozen from rain as it falls—were involved. However, the Hebrew text describes the deadly rain as "great stones," or

The Israelites cross the River Jordan on dry land—a "miracle" believed to have preceded the conquest of Jericho.

"stones of *barad*." *Barad* were also said to have fallen as one of the Ten Plagues of Egypt, which forced the Pharaoh to release the Israelites from bondage. Rabbinical tradition is clear in noting that *barad* were not mere hailstones. At the time of the Exodus, *barad* fell mingled with fire, and the stones themselves were said to be hot, which would rule out ice and leave only one possibility—meteorites. (Volcanic ejecta are unlikely—there are no volcanoes near enough to have actually rained rocks on Palestine.)

These apparent meteorites are the most tangible part of the "long day story," and they may provide the clue to understanding the rest. The most realistic explanation of the biblical story would be one that accounts for *both* the extraordinary phenomena at the battle of Beth Horon: a devastating rain of stones, followed by the Sun's standing still in an extended day. Can a reasonable explanation be found to connect the two?

Worlds in Collision

A large enough comet (or some other rogue body) moving close to the Earth might cause both the interruption to the Earth's rotation and the fall of stones at the Beth Horon pass. This was realized as long ago as 1883 by the maverick American theorist Ignatius Donnelly (see **Atlantis—Lost and Found?** in **Lost Lands and Catastrophes**). It also formed the mainspring of the argument presented by the great catastrophist Immanuel Velikovsky in his first book, *Worlds in Collision* (1950), which his British publishers promoted rather sensationally as "The Book about the Day the Sun Stood Still." The coincidence of a fall of stones and an apparent disturbance in the Earth's motion formed Velikovsky's logical starting point:

> The author of the Book of Joshua was surely ignorant of any connection between the two phenomena. He could not be expected to have had any knowledge about the nature of aerolites [meteorites], about the forces of attraction between celestial bodies, and the like. As these phenomena were recorded to have occurred together, it is improbable that the records were invented.

Moreover, it seemed that the story of Joshua's long day could be matched in legends from other Old World cultures. For example, the Chinese relate that in the time of the Emperor Yahou, "the miracle is said to have happened that the Sun during a span of ten days did not set, the forests were ignited, and a multitude of vermin were brought forth." A prolonged day in one hemisphere, Velikovsky reasoned, should be matched by a prolonged night in the other. He found an apparent mythological corollary to the long-day story in Native American traditions of a night of unnatural length, when the world was visited by disasters. The Aztecs of Mexico preserved the curious story of a morning when the Sun hovered on the horizon and took many hours to actually rise.

The cause of this worldwide disturbance, Velikovsky suggested, was a giant comet passing extremely close to the Earth, which rained down meteoritic debris from its tail and upset the rotation of the Earth by its gravitational or electromagnetic pull. The comet responsible was on an elliptical Earth-crossing path, but later, Velikovsky argued, settled into a circular orbit out of harm's way and became the planet Venus.

The virulence of the academic reaction to Velikovsky's theory was extraordinary. Many scientists were just as rankled by the suggestion that the Earth's rotation could have been abruptly altered as they were by the notion that Venus had once been a comet. Scientists, like any of us, are subject to irrational fears, and scientific "laws" have often been engraved in stone as comforters. In 1825 the great French astronomer Laplace laid down this dictum, which became almost a scientific law in itself: "The whole of astronomy is based on the invariability of the position of the axis of rotation of the Earth. . . ." The point was never proved, yet the idea that our planet's axis could have suffered any change—in either its direction or speed—became scientific taboo. It became common knowledge that such a thing was "scientifically impossible." When biblical fundamentalism and the theory of evolution faced each other in court, at the famous Scopes Trial at Dayton, Tennessee, in 1925 (see **Introduction** to **Hoax?**), the problem of Joshua's long day was raised. Clarence Darrow, the lawyer defending the teaching of evolution in schools, demanded to know of his opposite number William Jennings Bryan, "Have you ever pondered what would have happened to the Earth if it had stood still?" Bryan's reply was that "the God I believe in could have taken care of that." Darrow hurled back a question: "Don't you know that it would have converted into a molten mass of matter?" Darrow's claim was complete nonsense, yet was symptomatic of popular "scientific" belief earlier this century—that certain things were scientifically impossible simply because scientists said they were.

Little seemed to have changed by the middle of the century, a notoriously conservative era. *Worlds in Collision* was greeted by a flurry of reviews by outraged academics, many focusing on Velikovsky's treatment of the long-day question. Frank Edmondson, Director of the Goethe Link Observatory (University of Indiana), was one of several to raise this objection:

> Velikovsky is not bothered by the elementary fact that if the Earth were stopped, inertia would cause Joshua and his companions to fly off into space with a speed of nine hundred miles an hour.

Edmondson's remark shows an extraordinary lapse from common sense for a professional astronomer. He seemed to have forgotten the small matter of gravity, generally assumed to be the force that keeps us, and everything else, attached to the planet. If the Earth did suddenly come to a dead halt, its inhabitants would be hurled across the ground violently, and subjected to earthquakes and floods on an unprecedented scale, but they would not be sent into orbit. Even Professor Carl Sagan, the famous astronomer who became Velikovsky's greatest critic in the 1970s, conceded this.

Yet the real point missed by Edmondson and other early detractors of Velikovsky is that he never actually claimed that the Earth had stopped rotating. In fact he suggested two ways in which the illusion of the long day may have come about: either the Earth's rotation was temporarily slowed, or its axis was tilted, possibly by as much as 180 degrees. Carl Sagan calculated that a gradual deceleration of the Earth (even to zero speed) could theoretically take place within less than a day without hurling off any of its passengers; nor would the Earth have melted, though there would have been a sharp increase in global temperature. What Sagan had more difficulty with was the problem of how, once it had slowed down, the Earth could have speeded up again, rotating at about the same rate of spin.

Velikovsky, too, had problems answering this question. He gave a number of possible answers, though they were necessarily sketchy as they concerned the electromagnetic interaction between two planets in close proximity—something that has not been observed and we hope will never be, at least from the standpoint of this planet. It was part of Velikovsky's more general theory that electromagnetic forces are equally important as, if not more important than, gravity in celestial mechanics, an argument that most astronomers tended to dismiss as special pleading.

Topsy-Turvy World

For a short while, beginning in 1978, it seemed that the day might have been saved for Velikovsky's model. An innovative British scientist called Peter Warlow published a paper in the highly respected *Journal of Physics* proposing a new model for Earth inversions. While Warlow's main concern was to explain geomagnetic reversals—events in the remote past when the Earth's magnetic poles had swapped places (see **Atlantis—Lost and Found?** in **Lost Lands and Catastrophes**)—his article made several nods in Velikovsky's direction.

Warlow's ingenious theory of geomagnetic reversals argued that while the Earth's spin is fixed (with respect to space), the planet can move through its own axis of spin. In other words, if pushed by a great enough force, the Earth would not act like a familiar gyroscope in which the spin and the axis are rigidly tied. Warlow showed that the Earth would probably react more like a kind of spinning top known as the tippe-top, sometimes included as a novelty in British Christmas crackers. While a toy, it illustrates perfectly a curious property of many spinning bodies. With a minimal amount of outside force (provided by the surface it is spinning on), a tippe-top will turn completely upside down *through* the direction of its spin. It is hard to imagine the effect without seeing it, but the surface of a tippe-top, once it has gone through its motions, actually ends up spinning in the opposite direction.

Warlow argued that the Earth, if subject to an outside force, would act like a tippe-top. The direction of the Earth's spin, which apparently generates the geomagnetic field, would remain the same, while the Earth's geographical axis would turn through it. If the outside force were great enough the Earth would effectively turn upside down. So, instead of talking about "geomagnetic reversals," Warlow argued that we should be thinking in terms of the Earth itself having reversed.

Warlow's model would explain the phenomenon of geomagnetic reversals without having to assume that the Earth's magnetism had periodically run out and regenerated itself. It has, of course, much wider consequences. After a tippe-top-style reversal it would also appear to an observer on the Earth that the Sun was rising on the opposite horizon—East and West would have changed places. Warlow followed Velikovsky in citing myths and traditions about extraordinary changes in the Sun's behavior. Easily the most direct—and baffling—is the claim of Egyptian priests, as reported by the Greek historian Herodotus (c. 450 B.C.), that the Sun had changed its direction of rising no fewer

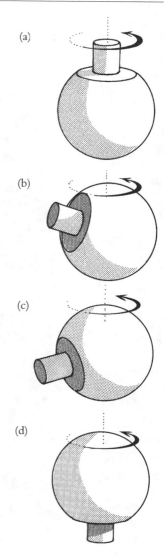

(a)

(b)

(c)

(d)

Motion of a "tippe-top" (a) in its initial state with a spin applied via the handle; (b) and (c) "fast precession" introduces a secondary rotation and results in the top inverting (d). Even though upside down, the top is still spinning in the original direction.

than four times within their recorded history. Joshua's long day falls into the same category. A tippe-top reversal, or partial reversal, of the Earth would have given the effect of the Sun "standing still."

So far so good. Yet only three years after the appearance of Warlow's paper, the *Journal of Physics* published a critique by astronomer Victor Slabinski revealing some serious oversights in Warlow's calculations. Slabinski showed that a tippe-top reversal of the Earth could not be achieved in a day by a planetary body about the size of Venus. In fact, the passing body would need to be 417 times the mass of the Earth, which is even greater than Jupiter, our largest planet (at 318 Earth masses). We would be talking about a massive disruption by a colossal unknown body, which would have undoubtedly involved a considerable shift in the Earth's orbit at the same time. It seems unlikely that anyone would have survived to tell the tale of Joshua's long day. Warlow never provided an answer to Slabinski's criticisms of his mathematics.

A further problem for Warlow's model—not touched on by Slabinski—is the record of the Earth's magnetism. Geologists believe that there have been some 120 geomagnetic reversals since the age of the dinosaurs, 65 million years ago. If Warlow's explanation of such events is correct, then the Earth would have to have been toppled over as many times by close encounters with Jupiter-size bodies. One such encounter seems improbable enough, so the idea that there were as many as 120 seems vanishingly small, even given the huge time scale involved. And if Warlow is right that Earth reversals cause geomagnetic reversals, then we should expect that rocks and pottery from before the time of Joshua (between 1450 and 1200 B.C.) would show the opposite polarity to material from later centuries. There is no evidence that they do. Geologists generally agree that the last geomagnetic reversal took place about 700,000 years ago, though there was a possible event about 12,500 years ago, toward the end of the last Ice Age (see **Poleshift** in **Lost Lands and Catastrophes**). Dozens of pots and bricks from the Near East from between about 2000 B.C. and 1000 B.C. have been analyzed for magnetic traces, yet they show no trace of a geomagnetic reversal.

The bad news for Warlow was bad news for Velikovsky as well. There was still no plausible mechanism for his idea of a massive shift in the Earth's axis or rotation in the fifteenth century B.C. There were many other problems with Velikovsky's wide-ranging model of planetary catastrophism. Much of the criticism carelessly thrown at him over the previous thirty years had indeed been little more than invective. As Archie Roy, Professor of Astronomy at Glasgow University and one of the world's leading experts in celestial dynamics, once remarked, it was only "uninformed" views of celestial mechanics that insisted that the orbits of the planets had remained stable since the solar system formed. Many physicists went further and insisted that Velikovsky's apparently outrageous model did not flout any known physical laws, and was therefore possible. But possibility is not the same as plausibility, and as Carl Sagan remarked, extraordinary claims require extraordinary evidence.

During the early 1980s, the Velikovskian bubble finally burst, or rather began to sag to the point of deflation. Venus is indeed an odd planet in many respects, and much of the ancient mythology about it is equally strange. Yet, as post-Velikovskian researchers dissected the case he built from folklore and myth, they came to question the very basis for his reconstruction of the catastrophic events that accompanied the Israelite Exodus and Conquest. The links between such events and the planet Venus were extremely weak.

It was also during the early 1980s that the research of British astronomers Victor Clube and Bill Napier (see **Introduction** to **Lost Lands and Catastrophes**) demonstrated that there was at least one giant comet on an Earth-crossing orbit during the Bronze Age. As it fragmented by stages into smaller bodies, this supercomet would have provided not only spectacular sights in the sky but also a major hazard to human society—streams of meteoritic debris would have been left in its path.

With the advent of this model, produced by professional astronomers, Velikovsky's extreme model became redundant. He had amassed considerable evidence that the memory of comet-spawned catastrophes was enshrined in ancient myth and folklore, but this was much more satisfactorily explained by Clube and Napier's comet—the remains of which are still observable—than by a hypothetical history of Venus as a comet.

A Bronze Age Tunguska?

On June 30, 1908, about 7:17 A.M., something exploded over Tunguska in central Siberia with ferocious intensity. Eyewitnesses a long distance away saw a fireball "brighter than the sun" hurtling toward the ground, followed by a deafening explosion that could be heard at a distance of two hundred miles. Earth tremors were felt over five hundred miles away. Over Tunguska a flame or "pillar of fire" shot up to a height of twelve miles, followed by a giant mushroom cloud of smoke from the burning forest.

Fortunately, Tunguska, in one of the most remote parts of Siberia, was sparsely inhabited—only a few reindeer herdsmen lived in the region. No one near the center of the blast would have stood a chance. A herd of 1,500 reindeer, last seen about six miles from the impact point, was exterminated; only a few roasted carcasses were found, the rest having been reduced to ashes. As for the forest itself, an area of about 4,000 square miles was devastated. Thousands of trees were smashed down, left lying on the ground pointing away from the center of the blast like the spokes on a wheel. Those trees left standing were snapped in half or completely stripped of foliage.

What on earth had happened? The remoteness of the site and the onset of the First World War meant that the whole matter was left largely ignored until a Russian meteorite worker, Leonard Kulik, located the site of the explosion in 1927. He could barely believe the scene of destruction that confronted him: "the results of even a cursory examination exceeded all the tales of the eye witnesses and my wildest expectations." Kulik's only disappointment was that he could not find a crater or other debris to support his theory that a meteorite was responsible.

In the years after Kulik's expedition, a range of bizarre speculations were offered to explain the Tunguska event. The absence of a crater stimulated theories that the explosion had been caused by an atom-size "black hole," a piece of antimatter, or even a malfunction in a nuclear-powered UFO. Some Russian scientists were so intrigued by the idea of a crashed alien spaceship that they made further expeditions to Tunguska to search for evidence of anomalous radioactivity. Like those searching for a crater, they drew a blank.

Speculations were more restrained in the West, where calculations eventually convinced most astronomers that the lack of a crater was not really so mysterious. Coming in at the right speed and trajectory, a small comet or fragment of a comet would have exploded before it hit the ground, its material completely vaporizing without apparent trace. Virtual proof that the Tunguska fireball was composed of "ordinary" extraterrestrial material has now come from the work of Menotti Galli, of the University of Bologna, Italy. In 1991 he went to Tunguska and drilled samples from many of the trees that survived the blast, and examined them for microparticles. In tree rings from the period of the disaster Galli found ten times more copper, gold, and nickel than in the rings from periods before and after. These elements, particularly nickel and gold, are well known to be abundant in bodies such as meteorites.

The Tunguska fireball has now been incorporated as a showpiece event into the Clube and Napier model. The very date of the explosion, June 30, coincides with the peak of the annual meteor shower from the Beta Taurid stream—itself associated with comet Encke, which Clube and Napier see as the main remnant of the giant comet that once loomed in the skies during the Bronze Age. According to their estimate, the stream of debris formed by the comet's breakup still contains something like 10,000 bodies of the size that caused the Tunguska event. It is a frightening statistic for our own future. And it is one that should also make us seriously reflect on the meaning of ancient tales such as the "rain of stones" that fell on Joshua's enemies at the battle of Beth Horon. The stream of debris from Clube and Napier's disintegrating comet is not evenly spread, but occurs in clumps surrounding a core or cores of the original body. At certain points in the past, events such as a devastating shower of meteorites would not be unlikely—in fact, according to Clube and Napier's model we should expect them to have happened.

So was Joshua's long day itself caused by a comet, or a fragment that fell like the Tunguska fireball? It seems unlikely that a comet itself, however bright, could have provided a "sun" to light the way for Joshua's battle. Surely such a body would have been seen for more than one day, and in the daytime sky as well—so it would have been quite easy to distinguish from the familiar Sun. Nor could a fireball as such have been the "sun" in the story—the Tunguska object was visible for only a few seconds before it exploded. Yet a comet *does* seem to have been around in the time of Joshua. As he laid siege to Jericho, Joshua was said to have seen an apparition in the sky:

> he lifted up his eyes and looked, and behold, there stood a man over against him with his sword drawn in his hand: and Joshua went unto him, and said unto him, Art thou for us, or for our adversaries?
> And he said, Nay; but as captain of the host of the Lord am I now come. And Joshua fell on his face to the earth, and did worship. . . . (Joshua 5:13–14)

The shape of comets lends them toward imagery connected with swords. In the tenth century B.C., King David "lifted up his eyes, and saw the angel of the Lord stand between the earth and the heaven, having a drawn sword in his hand stretched out over Jerusalem"

THE "MISSING DAY"

Answers to the problem of Joshua's long day periodically hit the headlines. Unfortunately, one of the most heavily featured "solutions" has only been an impediment to serious discussion of the subject.

In the 1970s, the story was widely circulated in the tabloid press that a "missing day" had been discovered by NASA scientists who were running computer calculations of the past and future movements of the planets. Supposedly the computer stopped at a given (but unspecified) date around the time of Joshua, apparently showing that a day was missing from its calculations. The amazed boffins checked their equipment and reran the program, yet found the glitch again at the same date. One of the scientists eventually remembered the story of Joshua, in which the Sun had been stopped for about (or almost) a day. When NASA checked more closely, they supposedly discovered that the "missing" time was 23 hours and 20 minutes, just short of a day.

The story is as spurious as it is ridiculous. No computer on earth could calculate that a day, or even a minute, was missing from history. Today it is recognized as a piece of modern mythology or urban folklore (like the periodically repeated space-fillers about dizzy old ladies microwaving their poodles in order to dry them). Usually the origin of such stories is difficult to track, but in this case researchers have pinned down the source of the "missing day" story as one Harold Hill, who claimed that he was present at NASA's Goddard Space Flight Center when the alleged events took place. Hill was a past president of the Curtis Engine Company of Baltimore, which was involved in diesel engine operations at Goddard. Yet he had no connection with its computer operations and the entire episode has been denied by NASA.

What led Hill to promulgate the story is anybody's guess. He eventually admitted that he had "misplaced details regarding names and places," in other words, that he had fabricated the NASA connection, yet still insisted that the "missing day" claim was essentially true. It appears that Hill's real source, as it was the only thing he could mention, was not baffled NASA scientists but a nineteenth-century writer named Charles Totten. In 1890 Totten published a book called *Joshua's Long Day and the Dial of Ahaz: A Scientific Vindication*, in which he claimed to have found the "missing day" through calculations based on the records of past eclipses. Of course, the kind of result produced by Totten is completely impossible. To demonstrate a massive upset to the Earth's rotation through calculations, astronomers would have to have a complete and exact record of calendars and eclipses from before and after Joshua's time. Unfortunately we possess no such thing. Totten himself did not care to publish either his data or his calculations, stating laconically, and with little respect for the intelligence of his readers: "The mere figures are of no interest save to the verifier."

(1 Chronicles 21:16). Such an apparition could easily be a comet, and is matched by the imagery used by the ancient Jewish author Josephus, who described the return of Halley's comet in A.D. 66 as a celestial sword hanging over Jerusalem (see **The Star of Bethlehem**, this chapter). It is easy to imagine why a comet, seen by Joshua, was conceived as an angel by the Old Testament compilers: to avoid the ghastly admission that one of the founding fathers of their nation had fallen on his face to worship it. (The same reason may account for the fact that Velikovsky, a devout Jew, never drew attention to this passage in Joshua.)

So if we seek a reference to a comet at the time of Joshua, there is one available. Yet the apparition occurred some time—days or weeks—before the rain of stones at Beth Horon. Is there still a way to connect all these threads and explain Joshua's long day?

The key to the puzzle was actually provided as long ago as 1946 by a British archaeologist named John Phythian-Adams. When the Tunguska fireball fell on June 30, 1908, he was still a young man. In fact, that very night he was with a friend on a cycling holiday in southwest England. He later recorded the extraordinary phenomenon he saw, and could never forget:

> The weather was very fine and hot, and feeling disinclined for sleep, we strolled for a considerable time about the town. It was then that we noticed that the night was strangely light. It was near midsummer, but this fact could not account for the illumination. At 11.30 P.M. one was able to read the print of a newspaper by it without any difficulty; and it was clear to both of us that the situation was abnormal. We thought at first, naturally, that it must be due to an aurora but there was no sign of the flickering which is a feature of the Northern Lights. There was, rather, one steady diffused radiance suggestive of a sunset afterglow or the light from an invisible full-moon.

Phythian-Adams was not exaggerating what he saw. Thousands of reports were made that night (in diaries, newspapers, and police records) of the incredibly bright sky. In England, people not only read (indoors!) but played cricket until after midnight. In Scotland and Sweden, photographs were taken at midnight, or later, with exposures of only a minute. It was as if the whole of Europe had become suddenly floodlit on the evening of June 30, 1908. It was, in effect, a prolonged day. Why this happened is still not certain. It has been suggested that dust hurled into the upper atmosphere by the Tunguska explosion reflected sunlight across the globe. Yet, as astronomer Duncan Steel, an expert on such impacts, frankly admitted, we still don't know exactly how the fireball explosion lit the sky up for a such a prolonged period. But what we can say with certainty is that it happened.

It was not until 1945 that Phythian-Adams, by then a seasoned excavator in Palestine, read a scientific account of what had happened in Siberia the night he had been on that memorable cycling holiday. Having been an eyewitness to the effects of Tunguska, he could immediately—and confidently—draw a parallel with the "miraculous" lengthening of daylight described in the book of Joshua. He also drew attention to the logical link between a Tunguska-like explosion and the shower of stones that fell over Beth Horon.

Phythian-Adams's brilliant suggestion had been almost completely overlooked for fifty years. Ancient historians are notoriously conservative about "extraterrestrial" matters, especially catastrophism. And despite Kulik's reports from his expedition in 1927, the real nature of the Tunguska event remained quite obscure until the late 1970s, when interest in the West was reawoken by an article in the British scientific journal *Nature*. Without the sanction of astronomers—and in view of the "Velikovsky affair" and the more bizarre suggestions about Tunguska—it is hardly surprising that biblical scholars took no heed of the strange event that had happened in Siberia in 1908. Phythian-Adams's theory, at the time he produced it, might have seemed like a weak attempt to explain one mystery with another.

It is only now that Phythian-Adams's suggestion can come into its own. Coupled with the mounting evidence for the existence of Earth-threatening comets in ancient times, his theory can explain at a stroke all the strange phenomena that surround Joshua's story: the apparition of the angel with a sword, the rain of stones, and the long day. The work of Clube, Napier, and other astronomers now allows us to provide a coherent explanation for these phenomena.

It should also be remembered that the Book of Joshua appears to refer to earthquakes severe enough to flatten the walls of Jericho and dam the River Jordan. Meteorites can, of course, set off earthquakes. That the writers of the Old Testament were able to string together so many phenomena that could have a single physical cause seems to be due to far more than coincidence. As the Earth passed through a stream of cometary debris, some impacts may have caused widespread earth tremors; a "rain" of smaller stones could have fallen over southern Palestine; the impact of a larger, Tunguska-size object, wherever it fell (perhaps on the central Asian landmass again), would have lit up the sky and produced the effect of an unnaturally long day. The Sun and Moon did not actually "stand still" in the sky, but it may well have seemed to Joshua's army that they did.

THE STAR OF BETHLEHEM

Toward the end of the first century B.C. a portent was seen in the skies over the Near East that marked the beginning of a new era in world history. The story, as told in the New Testament, is familiar to everyone. Palestine, then, as now, a seething political cauldron, was under Roman domination, and the puppet ruler of Judaea, the ambitious despot Herod, maintained a precarious hold over his kingdom. The Jews, refusing to conform to the Graeco-Roman culture that King Herod was subtly imposing, confidently expected a Messiah who would deliver them and impatiently awaited the signs that would announce his arrival. Such was the political mood when, according to the Gospels, Jesus was born in Bethlehem and some mysterious travelers arrived in Judaea: "There came wise men from the east to Jerusalem, saying, Where is he that is born King of the Jews? for we have seen his star in the east, and are come to worship him" (Matthew 2:1-2).

King Herod was clearly terrified by the implications of their prediction about a *new* king. Summoning a conference of the leading Jewish priests and scholars, he ordered them to pinpoint the birthplace of the promised Messiah or "King of the Jews." The Old Testament prophet Micah (5:2) had foretold that the small town of Bethlehem would one day produce a new leader for Israel. Learning this, Herod interviewed the visiting wise men about the star and sent them to Bethlehem to find the new king—on the flimsy pretext that he wanted to pay homage himself. The wise men—or "Magi" in the New Testament Greek—approached Bethlehem, and saw the star again: "Lo, the star, which they saw in the east, went before them, till it came and stood over where the young child was" (Matthew 2:9). After presenting gifts to Jesus, the Magi were inspired by a dream—though common sense alone would have sufficed—to "return to their own country another way" without reporting back to Herod. Realizing that he was "mocked of the wise men," Herod flew into a rage. Having missed his chance of identifying the young Messiah, he ordered the slaughter of every child under two years of age in the vicinity of Bethlehem. Joseph and Mary had meanwhile fled with Jesus to Egypt.

Gospel Truth?

Such is the colorful tale of the Magi and the star, now an integral feature of Christmas folklore throughout the world—but how valid is it? The story is found in only one of the four Gospels, that of St. Matthew. With only one source to substantiate it, the historian is naturally wary. Setting aside the wider arguments about the authenticity of the Gospels as a whole, Matthew is considered to be one of the oldest accounts of Christ's life, and therefore one of the most trustworthy. Yet it has to be said that the earlier parts of Matthew's Gospel often read like a pastiche of fact and fancy. Supposed prophecies from the Old Testament are cited by Matthew on four occasions, coupled with the observation that they were fulfilled when such and such happened. For example, Matthew related the Holy Family's flight into Egypt and subsequent return to a statement made by the Old Testament prophet Hosea (11:1): "When Israel was a child, then I loved him and called my son out of Egypt."

It would be easy to make the inference that Matthew fabricated the whole Nativity story, basing it entirely on scraps of old prophecy in order to give Jesus the necessary birth credentials of a Jewish Messiah. Historian Michael Grant, for example, has argued that Christ was really born in Nazareth, Galilee (where he spent his childhood), and that Matthew amended Christ's biography to conform to Micah's prophecy that the little town of Bethlehem would one day produce a great leader of Israel.

Such "improvements" to the narrative by a zealous apostle are more than possible, but careful analysis of the text stands firmly against such an interpretation of Matthew's Nativity story. The supposed prophecies cited by Matthew match the events of the Nativity very clumsily. To take the quotation he used about God bringing his child up from Egypt, the original passage in Hosea shows that it was not a prophecy at all. Hosea was actually referring to the Exodus, Jehovah's deliverance of the Israelites from their slavery in Egypt at least 1,200 years before Christ. Hosea goes on to say that the "child" (i.e., the nation of Israel) brought out from Egypt later fell into idolatry, hardly an idea applicable to Christ! Hosea's words, taken out of context by Matthew, have nothing to do with messianic prophecy.

So, ironically enough, the weakest parts of Matthew's account, the "prophecies," don't prove that he was not working from genuine oral traditions about Christ's birth. Had Matthew merely been concocting events from old prophecies, one feels he could have picked some more appropriate ones and made a better job of it. In any case, the idea that Matthew could have invented the entire story of the Star of Bethlehem seems in itself far-fetched. With most of Christ's miracles, such as the "feeding of the five thousand," we naturally run up against the problem of the subjective interpretation of events, with each eyewitness coming away with a different version of what "really" happened. The case of Christ's early life is very different, as we are dealing with basic biographical material that should have been common knowledge. Matthew's Gospel is thought to have been written around A.D. 70–80, little more than a generation after Christ's death. Would he really have fabricated details such as the flight into Egypt or the story of the star, when there must have been many of Christ's contemporaries still living? There would have been old people around who would have heard from their parents whether or not there had been a notable portent in the sky at the time of Christ's birth.

It might be more reasonable to see the prophecies in Matthew as extraneous elements awkwardly pressed into service as window dressing for the narrative, rather than the bare bones from which a story was invented. Still, the acid test is, of course, the star itself. If it can be shown that something matching Matthew's description *was* seen in the skies over Palestine at the time when Christ was thought to have been born, then we have to take his narrative more seriously.

Who Were the Wise Men?

To begin with the intriguing tale of the "wise men" who followed the Star, there are no grounds for dismissing such characters as purely fictitious. In fact, the story could fit very neatly into the pattern of evidence regarding the religious beliefs and political intrigues of the time.

Classical sources describe the Magi as an aristocratic priestly caste in ancient Persia, comparable in many ways to the Brahmins of Indian society today. The Magi were the successors of the Chaldaean wise men of ancient Babylonia, whose obsessive study of the skies had developed a surprisingly advanced astronomical science (see **Introduction** to this chapter). As astrological consultants to the Persian Emperors (c. 550–323 B.C.), the Magi became feared and respected as wise men and wonder workers from the Mediterranean to the Indus Valley. They later formed one of the two Councils of the Parthian Kingdom, which in 247 B.C. resurrected the Persian Empire and began a long struggle with Rome for control over the smaller states of the Near East.

Judaea, strategically placed on the trade routes between east and west, was an area of particular interest to both Parthia and Rome. In 39 B.C. a Parthian army succeeded in sacking Jerusalem and expelling the ambitious young Herod. Reinstalled three years later with the help of a large Roman army, Herod reopened diplomatic relations with the Parthian empire, which continued to watch with jealous eyes the gradual entrenchment of Roman power in Palestine and Syria. A tense stalemate set in, punctuated by phases of border conflict. Each superpower attempted to foment rebellion against the puppet rulers set up by the other in the border kingdoms.

Viewed against this background, the quaint story of the three wise men related by Matthew makes perfect historical sense. The Magi would have made excellent spies or *agents provocateurs* for the Parthian Empire. The monotheistic religion of the Magi, Zoroastrianism, was held in some degree of respect by the Jews, so Magian priests, unlike those of most other religions, would have been fairly welcome in Judaea. The Magi traveled into the heart of Herod's kingdom, presumably at a time of truce between Rome and Parthia, and publicly announced that they were seeking the new King of the Jews. Their request was politically sensitive, to say the least, but the Magi, in their defense, could have insisted that they were on a purely scientific mission, to verify the astrological portents they had observed. Herod might well have taken them seriously enough to assemble his own wise men to find out the birthplace of the predicted king.

Astronomical Problems

The Magi and King Herod were real enough, leaving the star itself as the missing factor in the story. Here the problems of interpretation are more difficult. What kind of star is it that could have led the Magi from the east (Parthia) and then reappeared to stand over Bethlehem, indicating the place where Christ lay? Suggestions have included practically anything that can appear in the heavens: from fireballs (meteors and meteorites), comets, novae, and supernovae to planetary conjunctions, the star Mira and the planet Venus, and even ball lightning and UFOs.

Are any of these theories correct? In fact, can we deduce any concrete solution from the fairly skimpy narrative in Matthew? Dr. David Hughes, a lecturer in astronomy at Sheffield University in the U.K., has made the most extensive modern study of the problem, and he argues that we can. Sifting through the clues in Matthew, Hughes listed a number of criteria for determining the nature of the star, including the following:

1. The "Star" seems to have appeared twice; first as a sign to the Magi in their own country, then as an indicator over Bethlehem on the last stage of their journey.
2. The star must have had an explicit astrological meaning for the Magi.
3. The star was first seen "in the east." The Greek phrase *ex en anatole* used by St. Matthew is considered by some scholars to be a technical term for an "acronychal rising"—i.e., the appearance of a star or planet in the east just as the Sun sets in the west.
4. The star was able to "stand over" Bethlehem in such a way that it indicated the whereabouts of Jesus.

We should add to Hughes's analysis a fifth, equally important, criterion:

5. The star was seen to move (it "went before them").

As acknowledged by many writers over the centuries, only a comet can fulfill all these conditions. Comets often appear twice, once before their passage behind the Sun, and then again after passing perihelion (the nearest point that an orbiting body reaches the Sun). They can rise at many points in the sky, the east included, and travel across the heavens at a rate of as much as 10 degrees a day, moving from one constellation to the next every three or four days. They can also "stand" over particular sites, their tails pointing ominously. The contemporary Jewish historian Josephus records how a sword-shaped comet (which must have been Halley's) "stood" over Jerusalem in A.D. 66 as a harbinger of doom. In fact, the Greek word for "stand" is identical in both the St. Matthew and Josephus narratives.

In the Roman world, comets were generally thought to predict momentous events of state, usually disasters such as the deaths of rulers. Their appearance often created panic, particularly on the part of paranoid emperors such as Nero, who decided to avert the evil influence of comets by executing as many of the Roman nobility as he could lay his hands on (see **Introduction** to this chapter). So wouldn't this reputation of comets as harbingers of doom make one a rather unlikely candidate for the birth star of a new Messiah? David Hughes, among others, has raised this objection against the comet theory. Yet the Romans were also capable of seeing the brighter side of such omens—the comet that appeared on the death of Julius Caesar in 44 B.C. was generally believed to be the great man's soul ascending to heaven to take its place among the gods. More significantly, the Magi seem to have taken a very positive view of comets. Pontus was a state on the Black Sea coast of Turkey ruled by a dynasty of Persian descent, and its religious affairs were in the hands of the Magi. One of the Pontian kings, Mithridates VI, was believed to have a special relationship with comets. As recorded by the Roman historian Justin, Mithridates' future greatness was predicted by celestial portents: "For both in the year in which he was begotten and in that in which he first began to reign, the star Cometes shone for seventy days on each occasion with such luster that the whole sky seemed to be on fire." The spectacular comets seen at the time of his conception (134 B.C.) and accession (120 B.C.) have been successfully identified in ancient Chinese records by the astronomer J. K. Fotheringham. Far from being portents of disaster, they were taken by Mithridates as good omens and he frequently decorated his coins with the emblem of a comet. The Magi would have had good reason, with the precedent of Mithridates, to see a later comet as the sign of a new king's birth. Once again we find support for the idea that the "star" seen at Christ's birth was a comet.

Comet depicted on coin of Mithridates VI (120–63 B.C.), king of Pontus in northern Turkey.

A cometary solution to the Star of Bethlehem mystery was recognized as long ago as the third century A.D., by the early Christian writer Origen:

> We think that the star which appeared in the east was a new star and not like any of the ordinary ones, neither of those in the fixed sphere [the stars proper], nor of those in the lower sphere [planets], but it is to be classed with the comets which occasionally occur, or meteors, or bearded or jar-shaped stars, or any other such name by which the Greeks may like to describe their different forms.

He added that he had read

> in the *Treatise on Comets* by Chaeremon the Stoic that on some occasions when *good* was to happen, comets made their appearance . . . If then, at the commencement of new dynasties there arises a comet . . . why should it be a matter of wonder that at the birth of

Him who was to introduce a new doctrine to the human race . . . a star should have arisen?

Origen's theory stands at the beginning of a long tradition that the Star of Bethlehem was a comet. The idea was especially popular during the Middle Ages and was taken up by several artists, including the

Giotto's painting *The Adoration of the Magi*, with Halley's comet overhead.

great painter Giotto di Bondone (1267–1337), who, between 1301 and 1305, produced a remarkable series of beautiful frescoes on the walls of the Arena Chapel in Padua, northern Italy. The year 1301 saw one of comet Halley's most spectacular visits, described in detail by Giotto's contemporaries and almost certainly seen by the artist himself. The Nativity scene from the chapel includes a strikingly naturalistic painting of a comet, hovering above the stable as the Holy Family receives the three Wise Men. The European space probe sent to rendezvous with Halley's comet in 1986 was fittingly named *Giotto*, in honor of the artist.

The Great Conjunction Myth

Which comet, then, could have been seen to "stand" over Bethlehem at Christ's birth? Here the comet explanation appears to run into an insuperable problem—the date of Christ's birth.

It may come as a surprise that the generally accepted view does *not* place Christ's birth on December 25, in the year 1 B.C. Almost without exception, biblical scholars agree that Christ's birth took place no later than 4 B.C., for the simple reason that the death of King Herod, in whose reign he was born, can be dated by a number of methods to that year. According to the Gospel of St. Luke (2:2), Jesus' parents had traveled to their ancestral town of Bethlehem to register in a census being drawn up for Roman taxation purposes, and it is generally believed that such a census could have taken place in 8 B.C. Thus, the years 7 to 4 B.C. are the traditionally favored date for the Nativity. Yet, unfortunately for the comet theory, while Chinese records mention a couple of minor comets during these years, none of the Greek, Roman, or Babylonian records between 7 and 4 B.C. mention any— not what we would expect for the kind of magnificent spectacle suggested by Matthew.

Because chronology seemed to have ruled out a comet, numerous other ways have been sought to pin down the Star of Bethlehem astronomically. Meteors ("fireballs") and novae have been suggested but are poor candidates, as they are totally unexpected events. Meteors, the streaks of light formed by a meteoroid entering the atmosphere, are brilliant phenomena but are visible for only a matter of seconds at the most—hardly enough time for the Magi to pack their bags, let alone follow one on a protracted journey. Novae are a special enough phenomenon, occurring only every few hundred years, when the light from a stellar explosion light-years away eventually hits the

Earth and creates the illusion of a "new" star. Within the time range usually allowed for Christ's birth there does seem to have been a brilliant nova in 5 B.C., as we know from Chinese astronomical records, but it did not attract the attention of the Roman world. And while novae can be seen in the skies for weeks, they lack the features we would expect in order for the Magi to make complex predictions; they simply appear and then disappear, and they do not move or point, like the Star of Bethlehem.

So the favored approach has been to find some significant arrangement of the planets from which the Magian astrologers could have read their "signs." One phenomenon astrologers have always been interested in is planetary "conjunctions," which happen when two planets appear (from our viewpoint) to come very close together, sometimes even blending together to give the appearance of one "star." Could the "star" have been a planetary conjunction?

A link between the Star of Bethlehem and a planetary conjunction was first suggested by Johannes Kepler (1571–1630), the great mathematician and mystic whose study of planetary orbits made him the founding father of modern astronomy. On the night of December 17, 1603, Kepler used his rudimentary telescope to make detailed observations of the movements of Jupiter and Saturn as they approached conjunction, with Mars moving into the vicinity shortly afterward. Over the next two years a supernova was visible in the constellation Ophiuchus, also observed by Kepler. Remembering an old rabbinical commentary on the biblical Book of Daniel to the effect that a conjunction of Jupiter and Saturn in the constellation of Pisces was of special importance to Israel, Kepler wondered whether a similar event had been witnessed by the Magi. He was intrigued by the idea that there might have been a causal relationship between a planetary conjunction and the "new star" that subsequently appeared. There was no connection, of course, but these were the early days of scientific astronomy. Still, Kepler's supposition was that, after being guided to Judaea by the conjunction, the Magi may have witnessed another supernova shining in the skies when they reached Bethlehem.

Kepler's calculations showed that a conjunction of this type had occurred in 7 B.C. He concluded that this was the date of Mary's conception and that the Nativity followed in 6 B.C. It all seemed to make good astrological sense—Jupiter was traditionally the planet of kingship and, according to the Roman writers, Saturn was the planetary deity that the Jews worshiped under the name of Jehovah.

At the same time, far too much has been made of Kepler's astrological

Kepler's drawing of the conjunction of Mercury, Jupiter, and Saturn in December A.D. 1603.

speculation, which has been frequently misreported. A modern myth grew that Kepler saw the *conjunction* itself as the Star of Bethlehem. It has been propagated in a number of books, such as the influential *The Bible as History* by the German writer Werner Keller, which has, for better or worse, been a best-seller since it first appeared in 1956. Keller omits any reference to the supernova and claims that during the twentieth century "scientific proof" of the conjunction theory appeared. This came, apparently, from the work of the German scholar Schnabel, who in 1925 deciphered some cuneiform tablets prepared by the astrologers of Babylonia:

> Among endless series of prosaic dates of observation he came across a note about the position of the planets in the constellation of Pisces. Jupiter and Saturn are carefully marked in over a period of five months. Reckoned in our calendar the year was 7 B.C.!

It took nearly sixty years for the myth of Kepler's Nativity "conjunction" to be dispelled. Detective work by Dr. Christopher Walker of the British Museum, in collaboration with Professor Abraham Sachs, an American scholar specializing in Babylonian astronomical texts, revealed a very different story. Their work underscored the fact that the texts are actually *predictions* rather than observations. Even so, the Babylonian astrologers of this period were more than capable of predicting such conjunctions within a few years of their happening. Yet, as Walker and Sachs have shown, while the texts predict the movements of Jupiter and Saturn in some detail, there is no reference to a conjunction.

Modern research has confirmed the accuracy of the ancient Babylonian predictions. Astronomer David Hughes still favors a modified version of the Kepler conjunction theory. Yet, after applying modern techniques to retrocalculate the movements of Jupiter and Saturn during 7–6 B.C., even Hughes had to admit:

> Although Saturn and Jupiter and their triple conjunction fit most of the requisites of the "star of Bethlehem" and are in my opinion at the top of the list of likely candidates, the fact that they could never have been seen as "one star" leaves a feeling of uncertainty. . . . Their closest approach was 0.98 degrees, which astronomically speaking is not close at all.

Other specialists in ancient astronomy, less generous than Hughes, have rejected out of hand the 7 B.C. "conjunction" theory. Different theories have been put forward to replace that supposedly started by Kepler, including an ingenious hypothesis by Roger Sinnot that re-dates the death of Herod to 1 B.C. (allowing a later date for Christ's birth) and identifies a spectacular display of planetary conjunctions during 3–2 B.C. as the star. Apart from the impossibility of redating Herod's death in this way, Sinnot's theory falls on the same points as the other conjunction theories: a cluster of stars, however closely in conjunction, is not a single "star"; conjunctions do not move; and they cannot "point" in a particular direction. Time and again, all manner of attractive hypotheses have foundered on these same diffi-culties, while the most obvious solution, suggested by Origen sixteen hundred years ago, remained quietly in the background waiting to be dusted off and reexamined.

The Real Star of Bethlehem

Strangely enough, while scholars had been prepared to juggle with the dates of planetary conjunctions—and even with the year of Herod's death—in order to help the biblical evidence fit with the as-tronomical, no one had made a serious reexamination of the tradi-tional arguments for dating Christ's birth. That has now been achieved, over the last twenty years, by Dr. Nikos Kokkinos, a scholar from Athens now living in England. Trained in theology, Roman archaeology, and ancient history, Kokkinos is one of the few researchers polymathic enough to tackle the vast range of evidence bearing on this important question. As long ago as 1980 he proposed a radically different chronol-ogy for Jesus. Detailed study of the Roman and New Testament evi-dence shows that Christ would have been crucified in A.D 36 (rather than the traditional A.D. 33). This date, now widely accepted by other New Testament scholars, provides the first step toward dating Christ's birth.

The next step, of course, is to work out how old Christ was when he was crucified. The most common view accepts that Christ was quite a young man, in his thirties. As Kokkinos points out, this does not ring true. To be considered a rabbi (religious teacher) in ancient Jewish society, one normally had to have reached the age of fifty. A mass of other evidence draws us to the same conclusion. For example, Bishop Irenaeus stated in the second century A.D. that Jesus was about fifty years of age when he taught. (Irenaeus was a pupil of Polycarp, who knew people who claimed to have actually seen Christ.) Most intriguing of all are the precise indications offered by the Gospel of

St. John, which states at one point (8:57) that Christ was "not yet fifty." Another passage in John (2:20) relates a curious story in which Christ compares his body—indeed his life—to the temple in Jerusalem, which was "forty and six years in building." None of Jerusalem's three successive temples took forty-six years to build, and the best interpretation of this riddling anecdote is that argued by Kokkinos: that Christ was saying that he was the same age as the temple—i.e., forty-six years. The temple that stood in Jerusalem during Christ's lifetime was that completed by King Herod in 12 B.C. Forty-six years brings us to A.D. 34, the first year of Christ's ministry, according to Kokkinos. It would follow that Christ was forty-eight when he was crucified in A.D. 36, agreeing with all the other indications that he was nearly fifty.

The other fallout is that Jesus would have been born in 12 B.C. The cutoff point of 8 B.C. accepted by many scholars as the earliest date for Jesus' birth has been shown by Kokkinos to rest on very weak grounds. There is no good evidence of a Roman taxation census in that year—the earliest Roman census in Judaea was actually in A.D. 6, too late for any Nativity chronology. More likely Joseph and Mary went to Bethlehem in 12 B.C. to be registered for a local tax census organized by King Herod. If Kokkinos is correct, then all the conjunction theories about the Star of Bethlehem can at last be discarded. It was only after arguing the 12 B.C. date on other grounds that Kokkinos noticed the coincidence with the appearance of Halley's comet in 12–11 B.C.

With Kokkinos' revised dating for Christ's life, Halley's comet falls into place as *the* ideal candidate for the "star." It was a conspicuous portent that appeared twice and steadily moved across the sky to guide the Magi. Its tail could well have been thought to point to Bethlehem, just as in A.D. 66 (on its next visit during its seventy-six-year cycle) when it was envisaged as a giant "sword" in the sky, hanging ominously over Jerusalem.

Further, unlike the various planetary conjunctions offered as the "star," the appearance of Halley's comet in 12 B.C. *was* noted with awe in the Mediterranean region. At the time of its arrival the Roman world was buzzing with rumors and prophecies that a new world ruler was about to appear. Some said he would come from the East. Many thought the prophecies had already been fulfilled in the person of the Emperor Augustus (31 B.C.–A.D. 14), who seemed to have ushered in a golden age of Roman peace and prosperity. Others thought that the prophecies applied to his son-in-law and heir apparent, Marcus Agrippa. Agrippa, a capable man of humble origins, had been appointed by

Augustus as his deputy in the troubled eastern provinces of the empire. But after a successful partnership with Augustus lasting many years, Agrippa died of fever in 12 B.C. As he lay dying in Rome, Halley's comet appeared. The accounts say that it appeared to "hang" over Rome, just as the star seemed to "stand" over Bethlehem.

This adds another dimension to the Star of Bethlehem story. King Herod's patron was Agrippa, and he depended very much on the continued favor of a man he could count as a close personal friend. News of Agrippa's death must have come as a great shock to the tyrant of Judaea, and it would surely have been accompanied by a report of the deadly portent seen in the skies above Rome. What was in Herod's mind when he interviewed the Magi and "enquired of them diligently what time the star appeared" (Matthew 2:7)? It would not have been difficult for him to connect the Magi's star with the death-comet of Agrippa. We can now fully understand Herod's terror at the news the Magi brought. Agrippa had been the ruler of the eastern empire. If the comet had foretold his death, perhaps it could also foretell the birth of a new ruler in the East, just as the Magi hinted.

A detailed computer simulation of the exact movements and appearance of the comet, as seen from Rome, Parthia, and Jerusalem in 12–11 B.C., would be a final test of the idea. After nearly seven centuries it would be gratifying to know whether Giotto, in his famous painting, was uncannily correct when he placed the image of Halley's comet over the stable in Bethlehem.

CHAPTER THREE

ARCHITECTURAL WONDERS

INTRODUCTION

The sheer size of some of the ancient world's stone monuments takes our breath away. So does their age. Our forebears in classical and medieval days marveled at huge structures built in times so distant from their own that no knowledge of them had been preserved, and wondered who, or what, had built them.

Cyclopean masonry at the Lion Gate of Mycenae, built about 1300 B.C.

The classical Greeks, themselves no mean builders, were so impressed by the size of the stones in the walls of Bronze Age Mycenae and Tiryns that they thought they had been built by Cyclopes, the one-eyed giants of mythology. (Archaeologists still use the term "cyclopean" to describe the style of masonry, composed of large rough-hewn blocks fitted together.) Similar tales were told across Europe to account for prehistoric standing stones and tombs. Some connected them with fairies or dwarves, but giants were always the most popular explanation. In Holland, the megalithic passage tombs, some of them up to 60 feet in length, are traditionally known as "Giants' Beds" *(Hunebedden)*. In Germany, dolmens, the huge tablelike structures formed from a huge slab of stone placed on two or three uprights, were called "Giant's Graves" *(Hunengraben)*.

The thirteenth-century historian Saxo Grammaticus was particularly impressed by the evidence of the dolmens in his Danish homeland:

> The fact that the land of Denmark was once inhabited by a race of giants is attested by the huge boulders found next to ancient burial mounds and caves. If anyone doubts whether or not this was carried out by superhuman power, let him ponder the heights of certain mounds and then say, if he can, who carried such huge rocks to their tops. Anyone considering this wonder must reckon it unthinkable that ordinary human strength could lift such bulk to that height.

The scholars of medieval England had a similar theory, believing that the British Isles had been inhabited by a race of giants before the first British arrived. According to Geoffrey of Monmouth (writing about A.D. 1136), Stonehenge was originally built in Ireland by the giants. They had brought the stones, which had magical healing properties and were so "enormous that there is no one alive strong enough to move them," from the remotest confines of Africa and arranged them in a circle known as the Giant's Round. Only the mighty wizard Merlin was able, through his awesome powers, to transport and reerect them on their present site on Salisbury Plain.

When European travelers encountered the great stone monuments built by the native cultures of the Americas, they fell back on the idea of a lost race of giants to explain what they saw. In the minds of the Spanish *conquistadores*, the mysterious ruins they found at Tiahuanaco, on a desolate plain thousands of feet high in the Bolivian mountains, had to have been built by giants. The Inca fortress of Sacsayhuamán, perched on a mountaintop above Cuzco, is composed of huge blocks weighing up to a hundred tons. The construction is so sophisticated, and the blocks fitted together so perfectly, that about A.D. 1600 Garcilaso de la Vega, himself part Inca, was prompted to describe Sacsayhuamán as:

> the greatest and most splendid building erected to show the power and majesty of the Incas . . . the grandeur of which would be incredible to anyone who had seen it. And even those who have seen it and considered it with attention imagine, and even believe, that it was made by enchantment, the handiwork of demons, rather than of men.

The idea that superhuman beings had to have lent a hand to build the great stone monuments of antiquity resurfaced again in the 1960s in a slightly different guise. Swiss hotelier-turned-writer Erich von Däniken burst upon the world of archaeology in 1968, when he published the famous *Chariots of the Gods?* Although this was not the first book to propose that extraterrestrials had played an active role in Earth's past, von Däniken caught the mood of the times, with the world enthralled by the first Apollo Moon landing in 1969. His book was an instant best-seller in Germany, then, translated into English, it appeared in Britain and America. Sales were considerable, but what turned von Däniken into a publishing phenomenon was the NBC-TV documentary *In Search of Ancient Astronauts* shown on January 5, 1973. In the following two days, over a quarter of a million copies of *Chariots of the Gods?* were sold. The ancient astronaut bandwagon was well and truly rolling.

Since that time von Däniken and a host of others have produced a stream of books all proposing essentially the same hypothesis: that not only was Earth visited in the past by extraterrestrials, but that they played a crucial part in forming ancient societies. What evidence do they produce to back up this remarkable claim? The vast bulk of their attention has been focused on the stone monuments of the ancient world, such as the Pyramids of Egypt, the statues of Easter Island, the Bolivian city of Tiahuanaco, and the prehistoric temples of Malta and Stonehenge; but they have naturally seized upon anything that could be said to provide evidence of ancient flying, such as the Piri Reis map and the Nazca Lines. The Piri Reis map is often claimed to depict Antarctica and claimed by von Däniken to do so with incredible accuracy, thus revealing its origin in an aerial survey. Yet it may not show Antarctica at all, and is certainly not a remarkably accurate feat of mapping (see **Poleshift** in **Lost Lands and Catastrophes**). The Nazca Lines show von Däniken at his worst, attempting to interpret them as some kind of alien aerodrome (see **The Nazca Lines** in **Earth Patterns**). His interpretation of the figure of the Mayan ruler Pacal carved on his tomb at Palenque as an astronaut in a rocket was equally risible (see **The Rise and Fall of Maya Civilization** in **Lost Lands and Catastrophes**).

In the case of the great stone constructions, von Däniken's case was, in a nutshell, that ancient peoples simply did not have the technical ability or the tools to construct them. Yet a combination of experimental work, textual and pictorial evidence, and archaeological finds can provide in each instance, from the Easter Island statues to the pyramids, a reasonable picture of both how the monuments were constructed or moved and who carried out the work. Every time it is undeniable that local people had the ability and know-how to do the job without needing to call in experts from another world.

Von Däniken's extraterrestrials thus become more elusive the closer we examine the evidence. What emerges from his work is a pattern of denying the ability of non-Europeans to construct their own monuments. Archaeologist Professor Ken Feder of Central Connecticut State University analyzed the geography of von Däniken's *Chariots of the Gods?* and found that of fifty-one examples of extraterrestrial intervention only two came from Europe. Von Däniken has subsequently dealt with some prehistoric European sites, but the emphasis is still very much on nonwesterners needing outside help. The whole ancient astronauts case is actually a kind of racism through time.

Unfortunately we find archaeologists and anthropologists themselves have been guilty in the past of applying similar logic. The architectural wonders of prehistory have, for some reason, prompted the worst excesses of diffusionism, the school of thought that argues that independent invention is unlikely (or impossible) and that culture has always diffused from one area to another, by means either peaceful or warlike. Diffusionist thinking on the megaliths began with the work of Scottish antiquarian James Fergusson. In 1872 he published the results of his investigations as *Rude Stone Monuments in All Countries*, recording the presence of megaliths across Europe, North Africa, western Asia, and the Middle East. Fergusson deduced that megalith building had originated in India, from whence it spread across the world. As he had his own bizarre dating scheme for the British megaliths—believing them to have been built in the Arthurian period after the Romans left in A.D. 410 (see **King Arthur** in **Legendary**

History)—his theory made little sense and did not catch on. It was already becoming clear that the megaliths of Europe were at least pre-Roman in date.

Further workers found megaliths to be even more widespread, discovering them in East Asia, throughout the Pacific, and in the Americas. Could such far-flung monuments really be connected, and, if so, where was the center from which megalith building spread? By the 1880s archaeologists, overawed at the discoveries being made in Egypt, generally believed that it was Egyptian and Near Eastern influence that had "civilized" prehistoric Europe.

It was a natural—if extreme—step for someone to argue that Egypt had also provided the inspiration for megalith building not only across Europe but throughout the world. This was the belief of the hyper-diffusionist Grafton Elliot Smith and his disciple W. J. Perry. Elliot Smith was a brilliant physician, Professor of Anatomy at Cairo in Egypt and then Manchester in England, and a leading pioneer in the study of mummies, while Perry was a Reader in Cultural Anthropology at London University. Elliot Smith was convinced that the ancient techniques of embalming were so complicated that they could not possibly have been invented independently in two different areas. Therefore, wherever there was mummification, the influence of Egypt was proved, even if it was as far away as Peru (now known in fact to have even earlier mummies than Egypt). Perry took Elliot Smith's work to its logical conclusion, developing his theory in a series of books published in the 1920s into the story of the "Children of the Sun." Merchant venturers from Archaic Egypt (4th millennium B.C.), they had sailed the world founding colonies and spreading civilization with its three essential elements—Sun worship, mummification, and, of course, megalith building. That the chambered tombs and stone rings of prehistoric Europe do not bear the faintest resemblance to the pyramids and temples of Egypt did not seem to bother Elliot Smith and Perry, whose ideas became crazier with every publication. Elliot Smith seriously suggested that the motive of the Egyptian colonists in exploring the globe had been to search for an "elixir of life."

In fairness to Elliot Smith and Perry, at the time they wrote practically every other archaeologist believed that the techniques of stone architecture had come to prehistoric Europe from Egypt and the Near East, via the Mycenaean civilization of Bronze Age Greece and the island of Malta. All that changed with the advent of radiocarbon dating, discovered in 1952. Radiocarbon dates (especially when corrected by tree-ring chronologies) show that most of the traditional dates used by the diffusionist arguments were simply wrong. The cultures of Neolithic (New Stone Age) and Early Bronze Age Europe responsible for the great chambered tombs, dolmens, and stone circles were pushed back in time by a good thousand years. The upheaval has left an indelible mark on European prehistory. Speculations that Stonehenge was built by a Mycenaean prince or itinerant Egyptian priests are simply no longer permissible. The major developments in prehistoric Europe did not depend on a simple chain of diffusion from the Near East.

The most recent radiocarbon dates show that the world's oldest megalithic constructions are the tombs of Brittany in northwest France and the Atlantic coast of Spain and Portugal around 4700 B.C. They were built some two thousand years before the first Egyptian Pyramids. Even so, while it is crystal clear that the development of prehistoric stone architecture in western Europe was independent of the Near East, archaeologists still remain divided about the amount of diffusion that took place among the different areas of megalithic culture. And hyperdiffusionism is still alive and well outside the mainstream of archaeological thinking. The "children of the sun" have

West Kennet near Avebury, southern England, a stone chambered tomb constructed before 3500 B.C.

been recently revived in a new guise by Graeme Hancock and his colleagues, who argue that the seeds of ancient civilization were planted in areas as far afield as Bolivia and Egypt by an advanced civilization that once thrived on the continent of Antarctica (see **Poleshift** in **Lost Lands and Catastrophes**).

Hyperdiffusionism, like the ancient astronaut theories, is inherently racist—albeit unconsciously—as it denigrates the abilities of some ancient peoples and explains their achievements in terms of a superior "master race." Some interpretations, however, are not so subtle. In the case of the imposing ruins of the huge architectural complex at Great Zimbabwe in Zimbabwe (the former Rhodesia), the intentions of most of the theorists interpreting them have been absolutely blatant.

The Portuguese in the sixteenth century were the first Europeans to hear of the gold-rich city of Zimbabwe, probably through Arab traders. Stories of its fabulous wealth continued to grow, and Zimbabwe (before a single westerner had actually seen it) became a magnet for speculative theories. The Bible refers to the distant land of Ophir, from which King Solomon of Israel (10th century B.C.) imported the vast amounts of gold with which he decorated his temple in Jerusalem. From this grew the idea of "King Solomon's mines," awaiting discovery and further exploitation, and the rumors of Zimbabwe prompted many to connect the two.

The first eyewitness account of Great Zimbabwe was published in 1871 by one Karl Mauch, a German explorer. After a hurried investigation of the abandoned city, Mauch announced that this must have been the Zimbabwe of Portuguese reports and named the site accordingly. He was certain that the impressive walls, skillfully constructed from thousands of granite blocks, could not have been the handiwork of Africans. Rather, they had been designed and constructed by the Phoenicians, King Solomon's commercial partners (see **Phoenicians Around Africa** in **Voyagers and Discoveries**). He confidently identified one building as a copy of King Solomon's temple and another as the palace of the Queen of Sheba. For Mauch, final confirmation came from a sample of wood from a doorway; it smelled like his cedarwood pencil and so must be imported cedarwood from Lebanon, homeland of the Phoenicians.

British archaeologist James Bent was the first to dig at Zimbabwe, in 1891. His conclusion was that the city had been built by a "bastard" race fathered on local African women by white invaders from the north. Next to investigate the site was W. G. Neil of the Ancient Ruins Company, who was granted a franchise in 1895 to exploit all

One of the beautifully constructed towers of Great Zimbabwe.

ancient sites in Rhodesia. Among the forty-odd sites that they systematically looted, Neil's workmen concentrated on Great Zimbabwe, tearing down walls and ripping up floors to recover a few hundred ounces of gold, throwing away everything else that seemed to them to have no monetary value. In 1902, not surprisingly, the franchise of Neil's company was revoked. The site was put in the charge of a journalist, Richard Hall, who cowrote with Neil a report arguing that the architecture was clearly Phoenician or Arabian.

A completely different story emerged in 1905 when Egyptologist

David Randall–MacIver started proper excavations at Great Zimbabwe. Unlike previous investigators, he did not simply discard the everyday objects found among the ruins. Among these were large amounts of imported objects, including Arab and Persian beads, Syrian glass, and Chinese ceramics. All these foreign items could be dated to the fourteenth and fifteenth centuries A.D. Pottery fragments found by Randall-MacIver were clearly related to the vessels being used by the Shona tribes who lived near the site, the word *dzimbabwe* in their language meaning "houses of stone." So Randall-MacIver's meticulous work showed not only that Great Zimbabwe belonged to a time two and a half thousand years after King Solomon and the Phoenicians but that it was almost certainly built by the local African population. Radiocarbon tests subsequently confirmed his dates, suggesting that construction began around 1100 A.D., with the city reaching its height in the fourteenth century. Archaeologists agreed that the question of the builders of Great Zimbabwe was now firmly settled.

It was therefore all the more a shock when the Rhodesian government began, after 1965 and the breakaway from British rule to prevent Africans being given the vote, to promote an interpretation of Zimbabwe that flew in the face of agreed archaeological opinion to revive racist theories of Phoenician inspiration. Archaeologist Peter Garlake, who objected vociferously to this utterly misleading policy, was jailed and eventually deported, while several others were fired. Only with the advent of black majority rule in 1980 did reason return to Great Zimbabwe.

Unfortunately, similar theories, such as the insistence of explorer Thor Heyerdahl that the Easter Islanders could not have built the great stone heads that decorate the island, carry much the same implications as the old notions about Zimbabwe.

Even ruling out outside help to explain the ancient world's architectural wonders, there is no shortage of theories about *how* they were achieved. It has been repeated so many times in so many books that monuments like the Pyramids of Egypt could not even be built today that the idea is widely believed. So the belief has arisen that the ancients possessed technological secrets that have been long forgotten. The idea that some kind of esoteric knowledge was involved goes right back to the speculations that Merlin built Stonehenge. One medieval painting shows Merlin, having transformed himself into a giant, building it with his bare hands. But Geoffrey of Monmouth refers to superior machinery that he used: having laughed at the efforts of others to move Stonehenge from its original site in Ireland,

Merlin placed a minimal amount of gear in place and "dismantled the stones more easily than you could ever believe." He then easily re-erected them in England, "proving that his artistry was worth more than any brute strength."

The quest for Merlin's secret has preoccupied many researchers in modern times. Earlier this century one of its most eccentric characters, Edward Leedskalnin, claimed that he had indeed rediscovered the lost secrets of ancient stoneworking and moving, as used in the construction of the pyramids and Stonehenge.

Leedskalnin had emigrated from his home country of Latvia in the 1920s to get over being jilted by his girlfriend on the eve of their marriage. After odd-jobbing around America he eventually settled on the southern coast of Florida. Here he began his bizarre solo career of megalithic building by making himself a house from the local rock, a very hard form of coral, interspersed with timber. Working in secret, behind an 8-foot-high wall of coral that he threw around the site, Leedskalnin created a private wonderland of stone. Using tools and devices made from wood and scrap metal, he beavered away, quarrying blocks of stone up to thirty tons (greater than the average weight of the sarsen stones at Stonehenge). He erected a 25-foot obelisk, markers for observing the stars, a grotto depicting the story of Goldilocks and the Three Bears, a huge Florida-shaped stone table surrounded by rocking chairs, and an elaborate boudoir with two carved beds and a cradle and smaller beds for children—just in case his sweetheart changed her mind and decided to marry him one day. All this, and much, much more—1,100 tons' worth in all—was painstakingly carved out of coral. The pièce de résistance was the entrance door to the complex, a nine-ton slab delicately pivoted on its center of gravity that swung open at the lightest touch.

After many years of solitude Leedskalnin decided to move, so, having chosen a site near the main highway south of Miami, he hired a tractor and, working mainly at night, dismantled, moved, and re-assembled everything in its new location, now known as Coral Castle and the center of a small tourist industry. In 1951 Leedskalnin died, and his secrets went with him. How he managed to perform all these amazing feats, apparently without help, was, and still is, a mystery. He was slight of build, a hundred pounds in weight and barely five feet tall. His neighbors have been interviewed many times by the press and TV, but no one actually ever saw him working. Attempts to spy on him failed—he seemed to have a sixth sense about being watched. There were, of course, rumors. The most absurd was that he "sang to

Edward Leedskalnin seated in the splendor of his bizarre personal creation— Coral Castle.

the stones," which somehow made them lighter. Rather more reasonable is the idea that he had a series of chains and pulleys, powered by the motor from an old Ford car. Yet, even so, it still seems incredible that he could have performed so much working alone. The car motor would have provided only the equivalent of some extra manpower.

Leedskalnin left no real clues to his work other than saying that he had rediscovered the ancient techniques of leverage and balance. He also wrote a series of pamphlets on the universal importance of magnetism. They seem to make little sense (from the standpoint of conventional physics), but have naturally provoked speculations that he invented some magnetic method of antigravity. In the 1960s, the golden age of "alternative archaeology" (and bizarre speculations generally), antigravity or levitation was frequently proposed as a way that the great stones were lifted and placed by prehistoric builders. Numerous books and articles argued that there are unknown energies running through the Earth's surface (see **Introduction** to **Earth Patterns**), which the ancients could harness to levitate and transport huge masses of stone. Others argued that sound could do the trick. (Acoustic levitation is, in fact, possible, using large enough loudspeakers and small enough objects.) But despite all the theorizing, no practical experiments were ever carried out to demonstrate that any of these methods could shift small—let alone large—stone blocks.

How the tightly fitting stones of ancient buildings were shaped has attracted as much speculation as the means by which they were raised into place. Ivan Watkins, who teaches geoscience at St. Cloud State University in Minnesota, refuses to believe that the building blocks of Inca cities were cut and shaped with crude hammer stones, so he has developed his own novel theory. According to him, the Inca builders used solar energy focused to laserlike strength by means of large parabolic mirrors to cut and shape rocks. Watkins admits that no records of this extraordinary technology survive, but explains this by claiming that the secrets of the burning mirrors died with the last Inca emperor. In 1996 the BBC gave him a chance to test his theory publicly during the filming of a more conventional experiment at replicating Inca masonry techniques. Wearing protective goggles and asbestos gloves, Watkins tried to split a stone using the Sun's heat but failed miserably to even mark it. The best he could manage was to scorch a lollipop stick. The other team succeeded much better. Using stone hammers, ropes, and wooden levers, they cut and fitted a few stones in the same style of the masonry at Cuzco and Sacsayhuamán. With a little more practice, they could confidently state, they should be able to produce results as polished as those of the Incas.

The truth is that the sheer sweat of massed labor is the basic answer to the mystery of how the ancient world's great monuments were built. In the sixteenth century the Spanish *conquistador* Pedro de Cieza de León recorded the numbers of Inca workers employed to build the fortress of Sacsayhuamán, still under construction when the Spanish arrived:

Inca walls at Cuzo, Peru, surviving despite the Spanish conquest.

Four thousand of them quarried and cut the stones; six thousand hauled them with great cables of leather and hemp; the others dug the ditch and laid the foundations, while still others cut the poles and beams for the timbers.

Other Spanish sources at the time say that the Inca emperor employed four master masons and thirty thousand laborers to carry out his building projects.

Likewise there is little mystery as to how the ancient Egyptians transported and raised their giant obelisks and the statues and columns of their temples. An Egyptian tomb painting shows 172 men dragging along a giant statue of a nobleman on a large wooden sled. This particular statue—an estimated 60 tons in weight—was a relatively small one by Egyptian standards (see illustration, p. 203). The biggest surviving freestanding stone sculptures from the ancient world are the two "colossi of Memnon," set up under Pharaoh Amenhotep III about 1375 B.C. on the plain of Thebes. These massive figures weigh about 1,000 tons each.

While it seems that the Egyptians made do with simple sleds, ropes, pulleys, and levers, the Romans "cheated" by developing cranes. These were in common use at great public works, such as the Temple of Jupiter Heliopolis at Baalbek in Lebanon, built around A.D. 60 under Emperor Nero. The platform of the Temple includes stones over 30 feet long and weighing some 350 tons. On top of this are three stones about 60 feet long, 14 feet high, and 12 feet deep, the largest weighing 970 tons.

The "Colossi of Memnon."

If there is any doubt that stone blocks this big can be moved without paranormal means, or help from spacemen, we need only turn to recent history. A prime example comes from Russia, where, in the reign of Empress Catherine II (A.D. 1762–1796), a colossal stone block weighing 1,250 tons was transported several miles to St. Petersburg on a wooden sledge to form the base of an equestrian statue of her famous predecessor, Peter the Great (1682–1725).

This is not to say that the secrets of the ancient master masons are all known. Constant work in experimental archaeology is steadily revealing, step by step, exactly how each culture built its great monuments. We have to face the fact that our modern western civilization is nowhere near as good at masonry as those of thousands of years past. But that should not be so surprising. The ancients did not have the vast array of materials that we have at our disposal, from steel to plastics, to manufacture building components and tools. Instead stone, more often than not, was the material that had to be used, and the ancients acquired an intimate knowledge of its practical potential that may never again be surpassed. Flint, the favorite stone of the ancient toolmaker, could be turned into hefty axes to chop down trees, barbed arrowheads for hunting, or even razors keen enough to shave with. In order to understand such tools better, archaeologists began, in the 1960s, to replicate flint tools by knapping their own. It was soon appreciated, after fumbling attempts, that what at first sight appear to be crude stone tools are in fact extremely sophisticated and very difficult to make. One has to learn a great deal about the properties of flint, and then practice for years in order to make tools as good as those from the Stone Age.

On a larger scale, archaeologists are now, through trial-and-error experimentation, rediscovering the techniques used by the ancients to quarry, shape, handle, and transport massive stones using only simple technology. Our remote ancestors certainly did have secrets, but these were more like tricks of the trade—like those used in flint knapping—rather than esoteric skills. Perhaps there was some sense in Leedskalnin's claim that he had reinvented the ancient skills of leverage and balance. In the twenty years of his hermitlike existence building Coral Castle, he could well have spotted a few simple tricks that still evade the efforts of today's zealous experimental archaeologists.

Finally, why were so many stone structures built on so massive a scale in ancient times? A large part of the answer is that they were built by elites to cow, even bamboozle, the people they ruled. One of the clearest examples of this comes from the prehistoric temples on the island of Malta in the Mediterranean. The temples of Malta were constructed in the period 3600–2500 B.C. Built from the local limestone, they are still impressive monuments today. Approaching one of these temples, an observer would see a blank exterior wall broken by a monumental doorway opening into a courtyard; beyond this was another narrow doorway, behind which was a further courtyard. Although today the observer can see quite clearly into the heart of the temples from outside, this would not have been possible when they were roofed, as we know they were from ancient models and carvings. Rather than the sunlit sites seen by tourists today, the temples would have been more like caves five thousand years ago. The temples were dimly lit by smoky torches or lamps of fat, so only those allowed inside the monument would have had any view of the shrines recessed around the courtyards. In some cases the view of these inner sanctums was restricted still further by requiring the worshiper to gain access to the shrine by climbing through a stone porthole. Indeed, two underground temple and burial complexes from this time have been explored. The better preserved, known as the Hypogeum, is a maze of rooms and niches carved out of the rock on three levels. The uninitiated would have found moving around this artificial cave a confusing and disorienting experience.

The impressive façade of the Maltese temple at Hagar Qim, dating from around 2800 B.C.

At several Maltese temples the builders created small spaces within the walls, reached from passages running to the outside. The only features of these tiny rooms are holes cut through the inner wall of the temple to the courtyard: their most likely function was to act as speaking holes through which those hidden inside the hollow walls could communicate with worshipers in the courtyard. Were their words thought to be oracles, or the gods themselves passing on their wisdom to the people? A similar illusion was created by some of the statues and statuettes of obese goddesses that had detachable heads fitted into sockets, with holes cut from the neck of the figures to meet the socket holes. Most likely these holes held strings, used to move the statues' heads in response to the questions or prayers of the worshipers.

Professor John Evans of London University, who has studied the monuments of Malta for over thirty years, sums up his impression of the temples:

Both the buildings and their contents seem to point unequivocally to the existence of a privileged minority which was using them to overawe and control the larger part of the population. The façades themselves must certainly have made a powerful impression on all who

Stone figurine of possible "mother goddess" with holes for attaching a movable head and a string to manipulate it. From the Maltese temple at Hagar Qim.

entered the forecourts, but I think this was reinforced by what those admitted to the interior encountered inside. . . . Such features as the inter-mural rooms and the moveable heads of the statues smack to me rather of priestly transactions with the uninitiated.

The Maltese temples appear strange and awesome, as that was the desired effect of their builders. The same is true of Stonehenge, deliberately positioned so that it appeared suddenly on the horizon to surprise approaching worshipers. The Sphinx was such an imposing monument that even the Pharaohs of Egypt were moved to worship it as a god and were baffled as to its age. The architectural wonders of ancient and prehistoric times can appear mysterious (to us) because they were deliberately designed to be so. It is a tribute to the architects who built them that their power can reach over centuries and millennia and still sway us today.

STONEHENGE

Standing, apparently in splendid isolation, on the grassy Salisbury Plain in southern England, is Stonehenge—the most well known prehistoric monument in the world. Visited annually by hundreds of thousands of people and puzzled over by generations of antiquarians and archaeologists, Stonehenge is a byword for ancient mystery. Massive blocks of gray sarsen—a tough sandstone—painstakingly carved into upright stones some 13 feet tall, and topped by horizontal slabs to create a continuous circle with narrow openings, are the first thing to strike the visitor. Approaching the site from the northeast takes one along an avenue marked on either side by a shallow ditch.

Entering the monument past the Heel Stone (a standing sarsen), you cross the line of the slight ditch and bank, which form a round enclosure, within which is the megalithic (large stone) circle. Inside this is another ring of stones, but these are much smaller and made of a different material—bluestone. Enclosed by the bluestone circle is a horseshoe arrangement of stones open to the northeast. Sarsen trilithons (pairs of stones with a third horizontal lintel joining them at the top) tower above the tourist at over 20 feet high. Matching this is an inner horseshoe of small bluestones.

Being made largely of stone, the monument has always been highly visible, and this is reflected in the long history of its study. The first record of Stonehenge comes in the work of the cleric Henry of

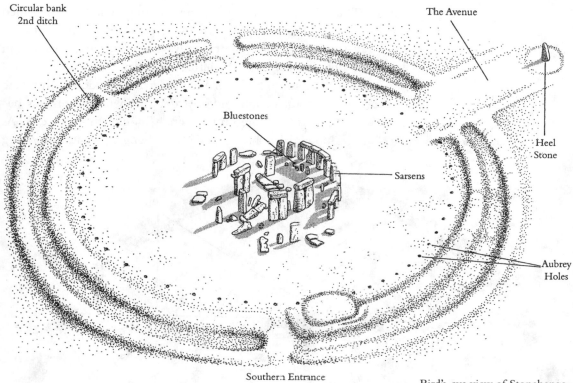

Circular bank
2nd ditch

The Avenue

Bluestones

Heel
Stone

Sarsens

Aubrey
Holes

Southern Entrance

Bird's-eye view of Stonehenge, showing the location of the sarsens, bluestones, and the Heel Stone in the Avenue.

Huntingdon, who wrote a history of England around A.D. 1130. It was the only ancient monument he thought worthy of including:

> Stanenges, where stones of wonderful size have been erected after the manner of doorways, so that doorway appears to have been raised upon doorway; and no one can conceive how such great stones have been so raised aloft, or why they were built there.

Even before Henry's time, however, there must have been a degree of interest in the site, for its name—made from "stan," a stone, and "hencg," hinge—comes from Old English, the language of the Saxon conquerors of Britain hundreds of years before. Stonehenge is the only stone circle in Britain whose name can be traced back so far.

Henry's cautious avoidance of speculation did not impress his contemporaries, who much preferred the vigorous account presented by Geoffrey of Monmouth a few years later. Geoffrey attributed the building of Stonehenge to Merlin the magician, acting at the command of Aurelius Ambrosius (according to legend, King Arthur's uncle). The monument was erected in commemoration of unarmed British nobles massacred by the treacherous Saxons. Interestingly, Geoffrey argued that the stone circle was already standing in Ireland but was brought to England by Merlin's wizardry.

Geoffrey's history, full of convincing detail, provided both a date for the circle's construction and an explanation of the reasons behind it, and it was therefore unsurprisingly an enormous success. As Dr. Chris Chippindale, chronicler of Stonehenge, puts it, a satisfying

Stonehenge as a Roman temple, as conceived by the 17th-century architect Inigo Jones.

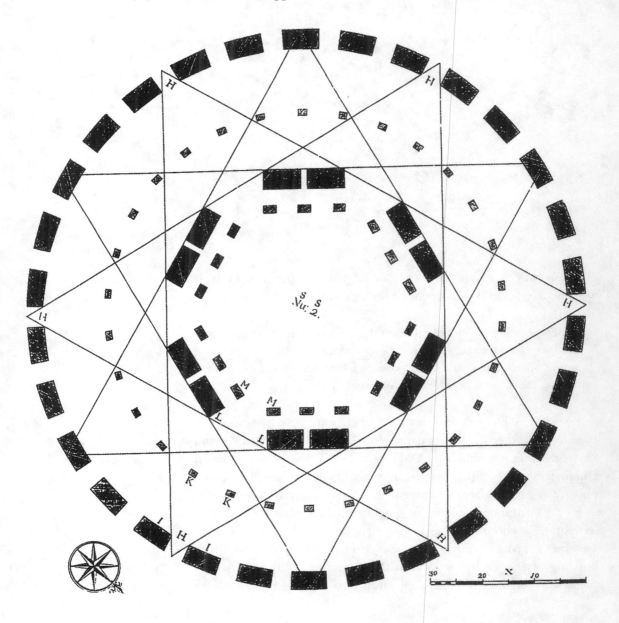

narrative was "what English audiences wanted to hear: adventures of suspense, valor and chivalry on a resoundingly patriotic theme." Geoffrey's account dominated the understanding of Stonehenge throughout medieval times.

How Grand! How Wonderful! How Incomprehensible!

By the seventeenth century the new spirit of inquiry demanded more evidence in support of Geoffrey's theory than the claim that he had used "a certain very ancient book written in the British language." The first excavations at Stonehenge were carried out with the encouragement of King James I, who visited the monument in 1620. His host that day, the Duke of Buckingham, offered the owner, Robert Newdyk, a considerable sum to sell the site, but he was turned down. Buckingham was, however, given permission to dig a hole at the center of the monument. No account of his work exists, and the pioneer antiquarian John Aubrey, who quizzed the locals about it in 1666, found that they could remember only the finding of "Stagges-hornes and Bull's hornes and Charcoales." Infuriatingly, there were hints of more important lost discoveries: "something was found, but Mrs. Mary Trotman [one of his informants] hath forgot."

The king asked leading architect Inigo Jones to make a record of the remarkable monument. From his observations, Jones concluded that Roman rules of layout had been followed at Stonehenge and Tuscan columns employed, but he died before he could publish his ideas. Using notes left behind by Jones at his death in 1652, his assistant and loyal disciple John Webb produced a volume titled *The Most Notable Antiquity of Great Britain Vulgarly Called Stone-heng on Salisbury Plain. Restored.* For Jones and Webb, the architectural sophistication of Stonehenge was a match for anything produced by the Romans in Italy. The quality of the construction ruled out the ancient British, seen as "a savage and barbarous People," incapable of clothing themselves, let alone building "such remarkable works as Stone-heng." Instead it belonged to the first to fourth centuries A.D., an age of peace and plenty, when England was part of Imperial Rome's domains.

Critics were quick to pounce on the evidence thought to support the theory, pointing out gleefully that the Roman proportions of the plan worked only by turning the horseshoe shape of the inner sarsen setting into a hexagon. The uprights are not even columns at all, let alone Tuscan ones, as they lack both bases and capitals. Moreover, scholarly contemporaries found it hard to believe that the Romans would have completed such a grand building project without covering it liberally with inscriptions.

A few years later Dr. Walter Charleton, personal physician to King Charles II, proposed a radically different date after seeking continental parallels. Charleton's correspondence with the Danish antiquary Olaus Worm convinced him that Stonehenge was a monument of the ninth century A.D., when the Norse overran much of England. He argued that it served as a place of inauguration for the Danish kings and that the monument was laid out in the form of a crown. This was a topical suggestion, given that Charles II had only just been restored to the throne, but had little else to recommend it. The lack of any references to Stonehenge's construction in early medieval texts made this theory highly implausible, while growing familiarity with the megaliths of Scandinavia showed that they were much smaller than Stonehenge.

The first to propose that the prehistoric British were the builders of Stonehenge was Aubrey in 1666. Aubrey himself sketched a plan of the site, and noticed a circle of depressions just inside the bank, now known as the Aubrey Holes. He took a quite different approach from previous commentators—not starting from the assumption that he should be looking abroad for Stonehenge's origin, but instead connecting it to the many other stone circles of Britain. Having found that neither the Romans, the Saxons, nor the Danes had built any

Engraving by antiquarian William Stukeley (1740) showing the dilapidated state of the monument.

such monuments, Aubrey concluded that they must be a native invention. Stonehenge was but the finest of these circles, and needed no foreign inspiration. Instead, Aubrey attributed it to the Druids, known from Roman writings (see **Box: The Druids**).

William Stukeley popularized the prehistoric theory of Stonehenge's creation in 1740 with the publication of his book *Stonehenge: a Temple Restor'd to the British Druids*. Unfortunately his excavations at the center of the horseshoe produced nothing to confirm this. The first discovery of any datable objects at the monument—a group of Roman coins thrown up by rabbits—did cause him some concern, but he decided that these must have been left behind by visitors to the site. Stukeley also discovered the avenue running away from the northeast entrance.

By Stukeley's day there was already a growing tourist industry. Not only were fires set among the stones, but many visitors also wanted to take home a souvenir. Stukeley railed against the "detestable practice" of "breaking pieces off with large hammers." The sarsens were the main sufferers from this vandalism, as the bluestones were harder. Continued neglect of the monument had its price, and in January 1797 one of the trilithons fell to the ground.

This disaster was the spur for further excavations. These were carried out by William Cunnington, who dug into some two hundred burial mounds, known as barrows, around Stonehenge on Salisbury Plain. In 1802 he investigated the central area, with no great success, except that he did find prehistoric pottery:

> I have this summer dug in several places in the Area and neighbourhood of Stonehenge (taking care not to go too near the Stones) & particularly at the front of the Altar [a fallen sandstone upright], where I dug to the depth of 5 feet or more & found charred Wood, Animal Bones, & Pottery, of the latter there were several pieces similar to the rude Urns found in the Barrows—also some pieces of Roman Pottery.

Cunnington's diggings were published by his wealthy patron, Sir Richard Colt Hoare, who commented at length on the long-dead inhabitants of the Salisbury Plain barrows, but fell back on expressions of awe when he tried to cope with Stonehenge: "HOW GRAND! HOW WONDERFUL! HOW INCOMPREHENSIBLE!"

In the spring of 1810 Cunnington dug at Stonehenge once more, establishing that the "Slaughter Stone" (its lurid name deriving from a misunderstanding of the red stain produced by rainwater bringing out the natural iron content of the rock) had originally stood upright. This was the barrow digger's swan song, as he died at the end of the year. Fieldwork at Stonehenge virtually ceased.

Beyond All Historical Recall

While Cunnington's excavations seemed to confirm that Stonehenge was prehistoric, he could say nothing more about its date. This seems to have been welcomed by contemporaries, who were rather keen on the idea of Stonehenge as an unsolved conundrum. The great painter John Constable captioned his 1835 watercolor of the stones with a flamboyant expression of this romantic view:

> The mysterious monument of Stonehenge, standing remote on a bare and boundless heath, as much unconnected with the events of past ages as it is with the uses of the present, carries you back beyond all historical recall into the obscurity of a totally unknown period.

Serious study of the monument resumed with Flinders Petrie, later to become famous as the pioneer of systematic archaeological excavation in Egypt. In 1877 he carried out a painstaking survey of the surviving stones, plotting their positions to within a tenth of an inch. He called for renewed excavations, coming up with an ingenious solution to the problem of looking below the stones:

> By having a timber frame to carry the weight of a stone, clamped by its middle, it would be possible to remove the whole of the disturbed layer from underneath each of the still erect stones, leaving the stone suspended; the earth being replaced and rammed, the stone would undergo no perceptible change, and could not be upset during the operations.

Fortunately, no one took up Petrie's idea, which would almost certainly have been disastrous in practice.

Petrie also had a unique approach to dating Stonehenge. He assumed that the monument had been laid out on the basis of one particular solar alignment. Looking through the Great Trilithon over the Heel Stone to view the midsummer sunrise, he was able to produce a date of A.D. 730 for the construction of the sarsen horseshoe by calculating when these points would all have been precisely in line. This would have made the Saxons its builders. Petrie's theory was almost universally dismissed, partly because he could not justify why this single alignment should be taken as the key to the whole monument, but mainly because he seemed to have deliberately ignored what little archaeological evidence was available at the time.

In 1918 Stonehenge passed into state ownership, making it possible for the first time to undertake a major excavation campaign. Colonel William Hawley, an experienced archaeologist, was placed in charge and embarked on a seven-year project. Unfortunately it was a massive undertaking on a shoestring budget, with Hawley often working alone. Nevertheless, Hawley eventually dug half the site, uncovering some important features, such as the circle of Aubrey Holes just inside the bank and a mass of pits, in which wooden uprights had once stood, at the center of the monument.

Unfortunately, Hawley was clearly not the man for the job. He tried to limit himself to being "an excavator and recorder of facts." But hard facts were few and far between on this complex and badly disturbed site, and Hawley himself confessed in 1923 that he wished he could stop. Quizzed by reporters, he admitted that "the more we dig, the more the mystery seems to deepen." In his final report he could only hope that "future excavators will be able to throw more light on it than I have done."

Chris Chippindale sums up the despairing modern verdict on Hawley's work:

The Hawley years, 1919 to 1926, were a disaster. The excavation, rightly said at its beginning to have been "the most important yet undertaken" in England, was managed on absurdly inadequate resources. Once it was in train, those who saw how badly wrong it was going were too shy or embarrassed to intervene effectively.

Archaeologists were naturally dissatisfied with the confusing end to Hawley's work. After a lengthy delay it was agreed that Professor Richard Atkinson of Cardiff University would attempt the awkward task of producing a final report from Hawley's notes and undertake small-scale excavations where necessary. Although the fairly minor excavations were efficiently conducted, publication of the work, and of Hawley's, was a different matter. Atkinson did present his interpretation of Stonehenge, pushing its date back to before 1500 B.C., in the Bronze Age, but no full account appeared.

It was not until 1995 that a team led by Dr. Ros Cleal of Avebury Museum finally produced the definitive record of Hawley's and Atkinson's excavations. One of their main achievements was to produce a sound chronology of Stonehenge's development. The bank and ditch were constructed around 3000 B.C., enclosing a circle of timbers set in the Aubrey Holes; from 2900 to 2500 B.C. one or more small wooden structures were erected at the center, with lines of posts running from them to the southern entrance, while cremation burials were placed in the Aubrey Holes; then over the next thousand years (about 2500–1600 B.C.) the bluestones and sarsens arrived, to be formed into various circles, culminating in the present arrangement of circles and horseshoes. The avenue was created as a formal access route before 2000 B.C. Stonehenge was largely abandoned after 1600 B.C., with only occasional visitors and a single burial.

Along the Greasy Track

Knowing when Stonehenge was built is only part of the picture. Like other megalithic sites, much discussion has focused on the question of how it was built. Geoffrey of Monmouth had a ready answer to this, for Merlin advised Ambrosius to help himself to a circle already standing in Ireland:

> Send for the Giants' Round which is on Mount Killarus in Ireland. For there stands a stone construction which no man of this age could ever erect, unless he combined great cunning and artistry. The stones are enormous. . . . If they are placed round this site, in the way they are put up over there, they will stand here for ever. . . . Many years ago the Giants transported them from the furthest ends of Africa and set them up in Ireland at a time when they lived in that country.

As time went on Geoffrey's account began to be regarded as a mere fairy tale, and by the nineteenth century it was clear to geologists that the source of the sarsen stones (his "enormous" stones) was the hills some twenty miles to the north. The bluestones were more of a mystery, however. Only in 1923 did Dr. D. H. Thomas of the Geological Survey succeed in tracking down their origin, which turned out to be the Preseli Mountains in southwest Wales, near a possible source for the sandstone Altar Stone. This brought back memories of Geoffrey. As Atkinson put it, his story "contains a most surprising suggestion of the persistence right up to the twelfth century A.D. of a genuine folk memory of the actual building of Stonehenge." This hint of a distorted recollection (for Geoffrey's stones were the sarsens, not the bluestones, and came from Africa via Ireland, rather than Wales) is intriguing, but can take us little farther.

In an alternative geological view, the bluestones arrived on Salisbury Plain through an entirely natural mechanism—glacial transport. The strength and weakness of this theory is Stonehenge's uniqueness. It is certainly the case that no other megalithic monument in western Europe involved moving stones more than a few miles. However, it is also true that no fragments of bluestones can be found on the plain today. Even the glaciation of the Stonehenge area is not firmly established, without which the idea of natural movement is impossible. Archaeological opinion has therefore come down firmly on the side of human movement, a decision that seems to be confirmed by the recent discovery of a small piece of bluestone on the island of Steep Holm in the Bristol Channel, right on the line of the shortest sea route from South Wales to Salisbury Plain.

Experiments in the 1950s demonstrated that it was perfectly feasible to float the bluestones along rivers to within a couple of miles of Stonehenge and then drag them on sleds to the site. But the sarsens are a rather different proposition; although the total distance they traveled was much shorter, they still had to cross hills and valleys, and the stones are vastly bigger—up to 40 tons in weight.

In 1995 the BBC decided to tackle this problem, bringing together civil engineer Mark Whitby and archaeologist Julian Richards and an enormous concrete replica of one of the sarsens from the Great Trilithon. Whitby was not happy with the usual idea that the builders had used wooden rollers, which he thought would snag on each other when supporting a weight over 10 tons, even though this is the preferred theory of researchers investigating the giant statues of Polynesia (see **The Mystery of Easter Island** in this chapter). He also thought the method of "walking" stones tried by Thor Heyerdahl on Easter Island was too dangerous on a twenty-mile journey. So Whitby came up with the idea of the stone being tied to a sled and then pulled along a greased track. With some 135 people heaving on ropes attached to the 40-ton slab they found it easy enough to move the block downhill, but much more difficult to achieve any movement upslope. The problem was, ironically enough, the grease itself, which had glued the sled to the track, and no amount of levering seemed to be able to free it. Cynthia Page of the BBC takes up the story:

Eventually, though, the people on the levers and the teams of pullers made one last supreme effort and the stone started to inch forward up the hill. And then something quite amazing happened. Everyone had assumed that if this small number of pullers did manage to move the stone it would be a slow and laborious process. What was surprising was that, once it did start moving, instead of inching its way up the slope, it moved quite quickly, starting slowly and gathering momentum—in fact it moved at a decent walking pace.

Although no one can say for sure whether this was the method used by the builders of Stonehenge, it was certainly within their technological capacity.

Erecting the giant slab was rather easier. A stone hole was dug and the block dragged up to and slightly over it. A small sled of stones was then placed on the top of the concrete slab. This was slowly pulled along toward the hole, until the weight made the large block swing down and into its hole. Hauling it upright was more of a job, but this was eventually achieved with the use of a timber A-frame and a team of willing rope pullers.

The final operation, placing the lintel stone on top of the two uprights to create the finished trilithon, was carried out using a ramp. Engineers and archaeologists agreed, however, that a more likely method was to inch it up to the required height using levers and a timber crib, with levers lifting up the stone and timbers quickly pushed under it to gain the height. This more likely method was ruled out on the basis of time, but a small experiment did show it to be an eminently practical solution.

Mycenaeans, Britons, and Bretons

We now know how old Stonehenge is, where the stones came from, and how it was constructed, but none of this tells us who built it.

Older theories involving Saxons, Danes, Romans, Phoenicians, and even the Druids (see **Box: The Druids**) are obviously ruled out by the date of the monument. None of these groups was around in the Neolithic or Bronze Age of Britain.

A more plausible candidate appeared in July 1953. Richard Atkinson was photographing a seventeenth-century graffito on one of the sarsens in the horseshoe when he noticed the faintly carved outline of a dagger. Atkinson became even more excited by his discovery after he examined it closely. For to him the carving did not look like a prehistoric British dagger, but one from the Mycenaean civilization of Greece, of a kind made around 1500 B.C. He went on to speculate that Stonehenge itself might have been built under Mycenaean influence, as the techniques used in its construction were beyond the capacity he expected of prehistoric Britons:

[It is] surely more fitting to see them as the product of the relatively sophisticated civilization of Mycenae, rather than of the essentially barbarous, even if commercially successful, aristocracy of our native [land].

Other archaeologists poured scorn on the notion, pointing out that the Mycenaeans themselves had not built anything remotely resembling Stonehenge, while the eye of faith was needed to be so sure about the precise identification of the type of dagger from a badly weathered carving. Apart from the sheer implausibility of the theory, the recent program of radiocarbon dating shows that the sarsen on which the dagger is carved was probably erected before 2000 B.C. The Mycenaeans could not have built Stonehenge.

"Mycenaean" daggers carved on a sarsen stone.

The most recent claim of continental influences has been put forward by Aubrey Burl, the main authority on British stone circles. He has argued that the horseshoe arrangement of stones found at Stonehenge is extremely rare in Britain, but less so in Brittany, northwest France. Links between Britons and Bretons in the Bronze Age are well established, with similar developments in pottery, goldwork, and flintwork. As Burl admits, these are later than Stonehenge, but there is another possible direct connection that would take us back to the Neolithic. On one of the stones a rectangular area has been outlined, which Atkinson and others compared to carvings found in the megalithic tombs of Brittany. This evidence is not entirely clear-cut, for the Cleal team suggested that the carving might have been carried out after the stone fell in 1797, as a panel in which the perpetrator hoped to later add his name. Burl pooh-poohs their argument on the basis that hammering out the panel would have taken weeks.

Reaction from the archaeological community to Burl's theory has not been favorable. Once again the stumbling block is the date of Stonehenge, although this time it is not too early, but too late. Both the Breton horseshoe stone settings and the carvings are well over a thousand years older than this phase of Stonehenge, so we are left to wonder why Burl's "intrusive and powerful leaders from Brittany" were so out-of-date. There seems no real need to question the deduction first made by John Aubrey in 1666 that the builders of Stonehenge were British.

Why Was It Built?

Not surprisingly, much of the ink spilled over Stonehenge in centuries of debate has been concerning its purpose. Early antiquarians tended to see Stonehenge as a "monument" without any specific use, although they did usually believe that it commemorated a particular event, such as Geoffrey of Monmouth's theory that it was built in memory of the Britons slaughtered by the Saxons.

From Aubrey and Stukeley's time the idea of Stonehenge as a Druid temple dominated the literature, but as the Druids slipped from the scene so did the identification as a temple. It did, however, fit in quite well with ideas emerging at the end of the nineteenth century of astronomical activities among the ancient Britons. The axis of Stonehenge is clearly on the midsummer sunrise/midwinter sunset line, with the sunrise occurring over the avenue, leading to the conclusion that this was probably the more important astronomical feature. However, this simple observation soon became lost in over-elaboration, as astronomers sought out precise alignments to the Sun and stars in the belief that "scientific" astronomy had been practiced in prehistory (see **Megalithic Astronomers** in **Watching the Skies**). Trying to avoid wild speculation, early-twentieth-century archaeologists such as Hawley went to the opposite extreme and refused to theorize at all.

It took an American astronomer, Dr. Gerald Hawkins of Boston University, to break the silence. He surveyed the possible alignments presented by the monument, then fed the results into a computer to

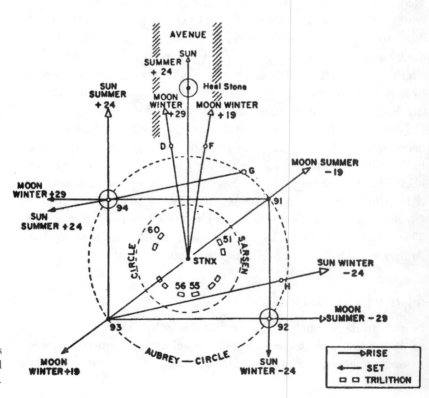

Professor Gerald Hawkins's theory of astronomical alignments at Stonehenge.

see if they had any astronomical significance. If the number of astronomically meaningful alignments this produced was greater than would result from a random series of lines drawn through the site, then the astronomical hypothesis would be proved, Hawkins thought. Setting the computer to cross-check the lines against a map of the heavens set at a date of 1500 B.C., he came up with a whole pattern of solar and lunar alignments (but none for the planets or stars) that he decided could not possibly be the result of chance. He went on to argue in his 1965 book *Stonehenge Decoded* that the Aubrey Holes had been used as a "Neolithic computer": markers had been set in the fifty-six pits, and moved around the circle as an aid to predicting lunar eclipses. These occur every 18.61 years, and fifty-six is three times that, to the nearest whole number.

Despite the authority of the computer, archaeologists were not impressed, and the excavator Richard Atkinson hit back in an article titled "Moonshine on Stonehenge," in which he described Hawkins's work as "slipshod and unconvincing." Most of the alignments involved joining together features from different periods of Stonehenge's long history, while some used pits and hollows that could not even be shown to be man-made. We now know that the date chosen, 1500 B.C., was too late. The "Neolithic computer" is equally unconvincing; it could only predict an eclipse to the nearest year, which hardly makes it a valuable astronomical tool. Besides this, the Aubrey Holes were filled in by 2500 B.C., so any markers would have to be even earlier than this, from a time before any of the stones were set up.

Archaeologists today have returned to ideas of Stonehenge as a ceremonial center. The early wooden phase seems to have involved

View along the line of the Avenue to Stonehenge at the point where it stands out proud against the skyline.

circles of timbers at the middle of the monument, with access tightly controlled by a wooden passageway and fencing. Even the entrances through the ditch had a forest of posts set into them, making it difficult just to walk in.

The later stone circles and horseshoe continue in the same vein, with access restricted by the stones themselves, and visibility of events at the center of the monument obscured for those outside. The avenue seems quite clearly to be a processional way, when its course is followed. This runs in an arc around Stonehenge, going down into a dip. Only after continuing for some time out of sight of the monument does its course begin to climb again, at which point visitors saw the stone circle standing out proud against the skyline. Inside the circular sacred area defined by the bank and ditch they would have seen a crowd of worshipers, and occasional glimpses of those directing ceremonies from the center of the stones. For those privileged few looking out from the heart of the monument, the high point of the year must have been the moment when the Sun rose over the avenue on midsummer morning. So perhaps it is not too wide of the mark to see Stonehenge as a Sun temple.

THE DRUIDS

Celtic society in western Europe in the last centuries B.C. was apparently dominated by the remarkable Druid priesthood, although most of what we know about them comes from Greek and Roman writers. The most substantial account of the Druids comes from Julius Caesar, conqueror of Gaul (modern France) and unsuccessful invader of Britain in 55 B.C. Although military affairs were his prime concern, he did take an interest in Gaulish customs, including their religion:

> The Druids are concerned with the worship of the gods, look after public and private sacrifice, and expound religious matters. A large number of young men flock to them for training and hold them in high honour. . . . It is thought that Druidism originated in Britain and was taken over from there to Gaul, and at the present time diligent students of the subject mostly travel there to study it. . . . It is said that they commit to memory vast amounts of poetry. And so some of them continue their studies for twenty years. They consider it wrong to entrust their studies to writing. . . . They also have much knowledge of the stars and their motion, of the size of the world and of the earth, of natural philosophy,

and of the powers and spheres of action of the immortal gods, which they discuss and hand down to their young students.

More information can be gleaned from passing remarks of other classical writers. There were male and female Druids, both involved in prophesying the future from the outcome of ceremonial sacrifices, which could include animals and humans. Elsewhere Caesar refers to the "wicker man," a huge wickerwork figure filled with living people and then set on fire. Calendars were also under Druid control.

The question of when an actual Druid priesthood originated is difficult to answer. Although archaeologists have claimed particular burials to be those of Druids or that specific objects show elements of Druidic thinking, none of these identifications are very convincing, with the exception of the calendar from Coligny in eastern Gaul, found by chance in 1897. This was an enormous bronze sheet, some 5 by 3½ feet in size, engraved with lunar months and marking lucky and unlucky days. The numbering, however, is Roman, so the calendar may have been influenced by Roman thinking.

The earliest writer known to have discussed the Druids is the Greek geographer Poseidonius, who lived around 100 B.C.; later authors refer to him frequently. Beyond that, the early history of the Druids lies in the realms of speculation. Even if the origin of the Druids goes back several hundred years before Poseidonius, there is still a massive gap of at least a thousand years between their appearance and the last building phase at Stonehenge. This lack of connection is confirmed by the archaeological record from the time of the Druids at both Stonehenge itself and elsewhere in Britain. From Stonehenge there are few traces of activity after the final arrangement of sarsens and bluestones was constructed, and only a few stray scraps of pottery from Druid times. Stone circles played no part in Druid religion, which was centered on the use of wooden temples or groves of trees—indeed, the term Druid may well derive from the word *dru* for "oak."

What happened to the Druids? Most modern accounts end with the fateful massacre carried out by the Romans on the island of Anglesey off the northwest coast of Wales. In A.D. 61 the Romans were completing the conquest of Wales, when they arrived at the Menai Straits to be confronted by a terrible enemy. The scene was recorded by the Roman historian Tacitus:

William Stukeley's romantic conception of himself as an "arch-Druid."

> Drawn up on the seashore [of Anglesey] was a dense mass of armed warriors. Among them, bearing flaming torches, ran women with funereal robes and dishevelled hair like Furies, and all around stood Druids, raising their hands to heaven and calling down dreadful curses.

The Roman general Paulinus persuaded his troops to press on regardless, and they crossed over to Anglesey, inflicting a horrific slaughter on the British.

Druidism was outlawed by the Roman emperors, who appear to have taken exception both to the practice of human sacrifice and to the use made of religion by anti-Roman noble Druids. Yet this was not the end of the Druids. Even in Gaul there are occasional later references to Druid priestesses, although Druidry must have been finished as an organized priesthood.

The situation was different in Scotland and Ireland, beyond the empire. Both the Irish tales and Irish and Scottish (and some Welsh) saints' lives mention Druids. The Druids generally receive a negative press, hardly surprising in Christian literature. But there are some surprising exceptions. The sixth-century Welsh Saint Bueno is supposed to have been met at the Gates of Heaven by Saint Peter, the Apostles, and some Druids. In Ireland, Saint Brigit, who traditionally lived at the same time as Saint Bueno, was brought up in a Druid's household.

Yet the thread of Druidry ran out as Christianity spread, with Druids presented first as evil and then as ludicrous figures—presumably after they were no longer seen as a threat to the progress of the church.

The eighteenth-century Druid revival by antiquarians such as William Stukeley and among Welsh nationalists keen to restore their nation's pride therefore took place only after a long gap in Druid history. The London *Morning Chronicle* recorded a striking assembly of individuals calling themselves "Welsh bards," which occurred on September 23 (the autumn equinox), 1792, on Primrose Hill:

> The wonted ceremonies were observed. A circle of stones formed, in the middle of which was the *Maen Gorsedd* (throne stone), or altar, on which a naked sword being placed, all the Bards assisted to sheath it.

Unfortunately, this dramatic ceremony was almost entirely the product of vivid imaginations. The Welsh bardic tradition of poets, singers, and harpists was real enough, and its modern strength owes much to the Druid revival, but it had nothing to do with altar stones and sacrifices, swords or stone circles. Present-day Druids claim a religious right of access to Stonehenge, but while they may wish that they were the heirs to an unbroken religious tradition, they are actually descendants of romantic fantasists.

HOW WERE THE PYRAMIDS BUILT?

Up to this century the Great Pyramid at Giza in Egypt was the largest monument ever built, and without a doubt it still remains the world's most spectacular construction. Given that it is generally agreed to have been built around 2500 B.C., by Pharaoh Cheops, it is only natural that people have asked the question: How could this be possible? How could so ancient a race perform an architectural feat that was bested only in our modern industrial age?

In one sense it *is* true to say that the Great Pyramids of the Egyptians could not be built today. The simple reason is that, unless we changed to some bizarre kind of fundamentalist state ruled by high priests believing in pyramid power, no one would want to. The building of the Great Pyramids of Egypt must have consumed a massive slice of their gross national product—a far larger percentage, say, than the space program is of the United States' total revenues. To build a pyramid of the size of the three colossi on the Giza plateau—those built by Pharaohs Cheops (Khufu), Chephren (Khafre), and Menkaure (Mycerinus)—almost the entire country would have been mobilized into the workforce. There would not only have been expert

The Great Pyramid at Giza, built by Pharaoh Cheops c. 2500 B.C.

stonemasons and engineers. Thousands of laborers would have been drafted to provide the muscle power to drag the stones into position, sailors would have transported stone from quarries elsewhere in the Nile Valley, and farmers would be working overtime to provide the food for the builders. Hordes of architects and scribes would be needed to organize and supervise the work in every detail, from the quarrying of the stone to the supplies of food and water. As part of the massive effort to construct the Giza Pyramids, the world's first known dam, the Sadd al-Kafara (Arabic for "Dam of the Pagans"), was built near Helwan, twenty miles south of Cairo. Made of imported stone, and seventy-eight feet thick at the base, the dam created a huge reservoir to provide water for the workers quarrying the blocks for the Pyramids.

Refusal to accept the obvious—that the Egyptians were masters of organization, as well as stoneworking—has led to many bizarre speculations. Most frequent is the insistence that the Egyptians were simply not capable of building the Pyramids without some kind of outside help. Theories that the Great Pyramids were really built by aliens started in the 1960s, when the notorious Swiss writer Erich von Däniken penned *Chariots of the Gods?* (see **Introduction** to this chapter).

Von Däniken based his theory on a whole range of claims concerning the Pyramids. He argued that they appeared suddenly, without any architectural precursors; that more people would be needed to construct the Pyramids using the methods suggested by archaeologists than could be sustained by Egyptian agriculture; that there was no wood, except for a few palm trees, in Egypt to make the rollers and sleds supposedly used to shift the massive pyramid blocks, nor did the Egyptians have any ropes to help drag them along; that the stone blocks could not have been quarried with the available technology; that the ancient Egyptians could not have leveled the ground on which the Pyramid of Khufu stands with such incredible precision. The perimeter of the Great Pyramid divided by twice its height happens to be 3.14159, the same as the ratio π *(pi)* used to calculate the circumference of a circle from its radius. Von Däniken argued that this was no coincidence, implying that the Egyptian knowledge of this advanced mathematical formula is anomalous.

The answers to von Däniken's claims are quite simple. As the outer surface and top of the Great Pyramid are missing, we cannot know the exact ratio between its height and perimeter. It is roughly the same as *pi*, that is, 22 units divided by 7. That the Egyptians knew of *pi* as a ratio is not quite the same as assuming, for example, that they knew its true value to several decimal places. As to whether they were aware of *pi* at all, the question remains a moot point. They probably did know it. The ancient Greeks had great respect for Egyptian mathematics and freely admitted how much mathematical knowledge had been borrowed from this older civilization. Yet if the Egyptians *did* know of *pi* and incorporated it into the building of the Pyramids, how or why does this point to extraterrestrial involvement? *Pi* is indeed a special formula, central to much of modern science and engineering. But is it so extraordinary that we cannot imagine the Egyptians, highly skilled at mathematics, discovering it for themselves?

Regarding his claim that there were not enough people in Egypt to build the pyramids, von Däniken provided no figures to back the assertion. On the other hand, as we shall see, archaeologists have made plenty of reasonable calculations regarding the manpower needed to build a Great Pyramid. As for the lack of trees in Egypt, this is simply gross exaggeration. Egypt may be relatively treeless now—except for the date palms that grow along the banks of the Nile—but there have been significant climate changes since the time of the pyramid builders. Since the last Ice Age the climate of the Near East has become steadily drier, and conditions were much wetter during the great age of pyramid building. At that time Egypt was home to a variety of trees, including oak and pine. When they needed more timber, the Egyptians simply imported it from neighboring countries, such as Lebanon, which is rich in pine and cedar.

Von Däniken's claim that the Egyptians did not have ropes barely needs answering—but Egyptian reliefs frequently depict builders using ropes to drag obelisks and statues into place. As to the cutting of

Egyptian workmen drag a gigantic statue of a nobleman, using a sled and ropes.

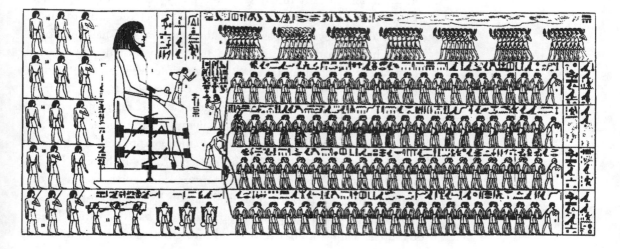

the blocks, the Pyramids are made of limestone, a fairly soft rock, which is easy enough to cut with copper chisels. Von Däniken was right in saying that the area of the Great Pyramid must have been made absolutely level before it was built, but the Egyptians could have achieved this simply by using water. Water will find its own level when poured into a hole and will provide a perfectly accurate guide for leveling off a piece of ground.

The Rise and Fall of Pyramids

Perhaps more serious is the claim of von Däniken that the Great Pyramids of Egypt appeared with no trace of architectural precursors. This argument has been repeated by many authors and has almost become a commonplace in fringe archaeological writing. Egyptian civilization as a whole did indeed arise with remarkable suddenness, probably under the influence of the nearby cultures of the Levant and Mesopotamia (see **Poleshift** in **Lost Lands and Catastrophes**). The appearance of the Pyramids is often confused with the origins of Egyptian civilization itself but is really a very different matter.

There is actually a clear sequence of trial-and-error development of the Pyramids from the early structures, called *mastabas*, through the step pyramid and the bent pyramid to the final form. In the earliest days of Egyptian civilization, about 3200 B.C., kings and nobles decided to protect their burials from the elements by building over them large mud-brick platforms, known today as *mastabas* (after the Arabic word for a bench). Some of these were quite complex structures, including a grid of square-shaped rooms for storing wine jars, food vessels, weapons, and anything else—even boats—that a king might need in the afterlife. (Corridors were not needed between the rooms, as spirits were believed to pass easily through walls.) These platform-shaped houses for the dead would have been roofed over, though none of the original roofing survives. As time went on, the *mastabas* became increasingly elaborate, with two or three levels, and fine limestone began to be used instead of mud-brick to create more permanent structures. The evolution of the pyramid had begun.

The first pyramid as such was built in the royal burial ground at Saqqara around 2700 B.C., by the great architect Imhotep. (He was so admired for his knowledge that he was later worshiped as a god.) As the resting place for his master, Pharaoh Djoser (Third Dynasty), Imhotep constructed a giant stepped mound based on the old idea of the *mastaba* tomb, but developed into a far grander monument as if several *mastabas* had been piled one on top of another. This step pyramid was built completely from limestone. Some fifty years later, Pharaoh Sneferu began an eight-stepped pyramid, but it was abandoned when the idea arose of building a pyramid with smooth sides. Construction work started on this structure, but the enormous mass of stone caused it to sag in the middle before it was half-built. The architects reduced the angle of slope drastically, from 60 degrees to 43 degrees, to cope with this problem, resulting in the bent pyramid. Cracks in the structure can still be seen today, so their dramatic change of plan was clearly too late. Undaunted, Sneferu ordered work to begin on a third pyramid (just a few hundred yards from the bent pyramid), with a more manageable angle of 43 degrees. Having finally succeeded in finishing a pyramid, Sneferu set to work on his step pyramid once again, transforming it into a smooth-sided pyramid with an angle of 51 degrees. This was the shape used by his son Cheops (Khufu) for the greatest pyramid of all.

So there clearly was an evolution in pyramid construction. The claim of von Däniken and others that pyramids suddenly appear with no predecessors is quite ridiculous. On the other hand, it does seem remarkable that the golden age of pyramid building in Egypt came so early on. After the massive examples built during the Fourth Dynasty, pyramid building went into decline and even stopped for a while. The next series of pyramids, built under the Twelfth Dynasty, are grand, but nowhere near the scale of the Giza Pyramids.

To many people this seems odd. Why were the best and largest pyramids built first? Surely, it has been argued, one would expect the small pyramids to come earliest and the greatest later, as the techniques to build them were slowly perfected. This argument, echoing von Däniken's claim that there was no evolution in pyramid building, has been used frequently by the ancient astronaut lobby—perhaps the Egyptians *did* have "outside" help at an early period, but the helpers went away and the Egyptians were never able to build anything as magnificent as the Great Pyramid again.

Part of the answer to this question lies in our own attitude toward the Egyptians and to the history of ancient technology generally. Since the triumph of Darwinism in the nineteenth century, the theory of evolution has been woefully misinterpreted by many people as meaning that everything is constantly progressing, including human intelligence and technical ingenuity. This simply isn't true. As we showed in our *Ancient Inventions*, many amazing technological discoveries in the past were simply forgotten, sometimes waiting centuries before they were rediscovered (if ever). Yet we have gotten so hung up on the idea of progress that the idea of a straight line of evolution from ancient civilizations through to our own still keeps its stranglehold on people's imaginations. And even today it is used to provide specious arguments about the Egyptians not being clever enough to have built the Great Pyramids on their own.

Egyptian civilization took a far from steady course. From the perspective of pyramid building, there *was* a steady progression in the development of techniques during the first four dynasties, and along with them the size that could be created. Yet, obviously, there had to be a limit. Pyramids could not continue to become bigger *ad infinitum*. The sheer effort involved in building these monstrosities must have begun to become a strain on the economy, and though the pyramids of the Sixth Dynasty are masterpieces of construction, they are dwarfs in comparison with the Pyramid of Cheops.

Then, at the end of the Sixth Dynasty, Egyptian civilization itself suffered a complete collapse. There were massive environmental changes as the level of the Nile dropped and the western desert began to encroach further. Central authority broke down completely. Foreigners from Syria crossed the border and invaded the Delta. There was famine and widespread anarchy, as grandees in separate parts of Egypt set up authority and warred with each other for control. The kings of the Seventh, Eighth, Ninth, and Tenth Dynasties were largely nonentities who simply did not have the power to control the country or organize the building of large monuments. As stressed by Dr. I. E. S. Edwards, Britain's foremost authority on the Pyramids:

> Not only was no attention paid to the development of arts and crafts but most of the temples and tombs of the Pyramid Age, with their artistic masterpieces and untold treasures, were systematically pillaged and destroyed.

It is hardly surprising, then, that the art of pyramid building declined. In fact it is amazing that it survived at all. Most probably the techniques necessary had to be resurrected and redeveloped when peace was restored. It was only by the Eleventh Dynasty (about 2000 B.C.) that central authority was properly reimposed and the colossal effort of constructing a pyramid could be undertaken again.

So the decline in pyramid building at the end of the Sixth Dynasty was the result of a social collapse, most probably sparked by an environmental upheaval about 2300 B.C. While the cause of this catastrophe may have been extraterrestrial (see **Sodom and Gomorrah** in **Lost Lands and Catastrophes**), the rise and fall of great pyramid building had nothing to do with aliens landing and going away again.

Rebuilding the Pyramids

Rather than wondering about the possible "outside" help needed by the Egyptians to build the Pyramids, we should marvel at the sheer scope of their achievement. Without a doubt, the Great Pyramid of Cheops still remains the greatest architectural wonder of the world. It comprises some 2.3 million blocks of stone, weighing an average of 2½ tons each, making a total of 6 million tons of rock shifted. It was originally 481 feet high, and covers an area of 13 acres at the base. Its base is leveled to within an inch and a half of mathematical perfection. The sides are oriented to the cardinal points (geographical north, south, east, and west) to within a margin of error of less than four feet. How, then, did the Egyptians manage this degree of precision?

To answer some of the practical questions about pyramid building, the American NOVA Channel teamed up Egyptologist Professor Mark Lehner of the University of Chicago and American stonemason Roger Hopkins—to build a small pyramid on the Giza plateau without the help of modern technology. Recruiting a team of masons and willing laborers, Lehner and Hopkins started from scratch, spending three weeks quarrying the blocks they would need for the project. Due to budget constraints, limiting time and manpower, they allowed themselves to cheat slightly at this stage by using iron hammers, chisels, and levers; the ancient Egyptians would have had much softer copper tools.

While the quarrying was in progress, the layout of the pyramid was planned. An important preliminary was to establish true north, which they did with the aid of a vertical post to mark the shadow of the Sun, which rises and sets at equal and opposite angles to true north each day. Repeating this at intervals across the ground would give the Egyptian surveyors a series of north-south lines, which they could improve and check as the line was extended till it was hundreds of feet long. The straight lines of holes found next to the Cheops and Chephren Pyramids are probably remnants of this procedure.

The quarrying complete, Lehner and Hopkins had another three weeks to build their mini-pyramid. They found that stones of the size of those making up the pyramids were not that hard to handle, provided that they weren't allowed to settle into the sand. Blocks weighing as much as 2.5 tons could be moved simply by tumbling them. Experiments showed that larger stones could be shifted by a team of twenty men pulling them with an attached rope, with another two men levering the blocks from behind. So getting the blocks to the site was fairly straightforward. To speed things up, the blocks were shifted onto wooden sleds and pulled along a clay roadbed with wooden sleepers embedded into it to give a firm foundation. Similar tracks have been discovered near the Pyramids.

Earthen ramps that survive near some of the Pyramids indicate how the blocks were raised above ground level. After laying the first course of stones, the team built a ramp around the growing pyramid, enabling blocks to be shifted into position from any side. Maneuvering them up the ramp was achieved by using the same kind of equipment shown in Egyptian tomb paintings—such as wooden sleds and rollers of hard wood, together with round balls of dolerite (a hard black stone), like those that have sometimes been found underneath massive stone coffins.

Easing the blocks into place was difficult and sometimes dangerous work, but the crew soon began to pick up skills in handling the blocks, showing how important experience in dealing with massive stone blocks was and how difficult it is to appreciate the abilities of a trained workforce applying even the simplest tools.

At the very top of the pyramid, a ramp would become almost unworkable, the slope becoming ever steeper and the faces of the pyramid too narrow to support the ramp from one corner to the next. So the topmost stones of the Lehner-Hopkins pyramid had to be placed in position by levering, jacking them up slowly from one level to the next on piles of timber. An alternative method suggested by British engineer-archaeologist Bob Porter is much simpler. According to his calculations, the most energy-efficient way to raise the blocks for the upper courses would be simply to drag them up with ropes. Using a papyrus rope of 2.5-inch diameter (like those found at an ancient Egyptian quarry), a hundred men could raise a 2.5-ton block. To stop the rope from scraping on the stone and fraying, Porter suggests that a greased copper plate may have been used, shaped with ridges to guide the rope. A better solution to the fraying problem might come from some mushroom-shaped stone objects that have been found near the Great Pyramid. As Lehner has noted, these mystery objects look very much like simple pulleys. The holes at the base of the objects suggest that they were mounted into the top of a wooden pole. An arrangement like this could have been used to haul blocks to the top by rope.

Porter has no suggestion, however, for how the capstone (pyramid-ion) was placed on the top of a pyramid. This was the trickiest part of the entire operation—as the Lehner-Hopkins experiment clearly demonstrated. Fortunately, the capstone for their mini-pyramid was small enough for the workmen to be able to carry it on a wooden frame. However, it was still heavy enough that there was no hope of a rest halfway, so they fairly charged up the ramp and the unfinished courses above. A heart-stopping moment came when the men hoisting one side of the frame got too far ahead of the others and the capstone started to slide off, threatening disaster if the capstone tumbled down onto the spectators below. Some quick corrections saved the day, and the capstone was lifted into place with a sigh of relief. Recently discovered carvings that show dancing and singing following a successful setting of a capstone (for the Pyramid of the Fifth Dynasty king Sahure at Abusir) suggest that nasty moments were common in the past too.

Lehner's conclusion was that practical knowledge rather than any mysterious lost wisdom lay behind the remarkable engineering achievement represented by the pyramids:

> Our aim was to test some of the current theories of armchair pyramid builders and try out ancient techniques as authentically as possible. We knew that to fully replicate pyramid building would require nothing less than replicating ancient Egyptian society. Although we failed to match the best efforts of the ancient builders, it was abundantly clear that their expertise was the result not of some mysterious technology or mysterious sophistication, but of generations of practice and experiment.

(Top) Mystery object of a kind frequently found near the Great Pyramids. It is most likely a simple pulley, as reconstructed here (bottom).

Hidden Chambers

This is not to say that the Pyramids have revealed all their secrets. Far from it. We still understand little of the motives behind the building of such incredibly complex and costly monuments. The standard Egyptological answer to the purpose of the Pyramids is "of course" they were royal tombs. This seems to be clear from the fact that, architecturally speaking, they evolved from *mastabas* (which were definitely tombs). There are also literary references to royalty being buried in pyramids, while many of them contain obvious evidence of funerary activity, such as stone coffins (sarcophagi). At the center of the King's Chamber, deep within the Great Pyramid of Cheops, lies a massive granite coffin that was clearly designed to receive the burial of a very important person.

Still, the apparently obvious conclusion that the Pyramids were built as royal burial chambers can be nicely countered by the fact that archaeologists have not found a single burial in any of the Pyramids! This point has been constantly stressed by fringe archaeology writers and used to argue that the Pyramids had some completely different, more arcane purpose. So how does one explain the mystery of tombs with no burials?

The answer lies in the very ancient and completely unmysterious custom of tomb robbing. Under the Eighteenth Dynasty (c. 1520–1300 B.C.) it had become such a problem that a special police force had to be formed to patrol the Valleys of the Kings and Queens at Thebes. But such forces could be effective only at times when the government was strong. By the Twenty-first Dynasty (c. 1070–945 B.C.), when the Pharaohs were mere shadows of their former selves, a less costly expedient was used. The coffins and mummies of the great Eighteenth and Nineteenth Dynasty rulers were simply collected up and reburied, with little ceremony, in a secret cache in the cliff face near the Valley of the Kings. This single act in itself explains why the

Plan of the chambers, passages, and shafts inside the Great Pyramid.

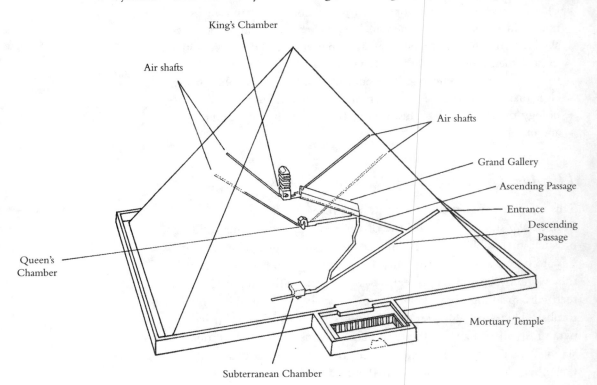

King's Chamber

Air shafts

Air shafts

Grand Gallery

Ascending Passage

Entrance

Descending Passage

Queen's Chamber

Mortuary Temple

Subterranean Chamber

tombs of the great Pharaohs such as Thutmose III and Rameses II were found empty. The prevalence of tomb robbing is the reason the burial of Tutankhamun was unique—for the first time archaeologists discovered an intact royal burial, complete with mummy and lavish grave-goods (see **The Curse of Tutankhamun** in **Archaeology and the Supernatural**).

Pyramid robbing is specifically mentioned in a papyrus known as the "Admonitions of Ipuwer," which laments the terrible state into which Egypt fell after the collapse of the Sixth Dynasty (late 3rd millennium B.C.). Ipuwer complained that the sanctity of the Pyramids was no longer respected and that royal mummies were being stolen from their resting places by vagabonds:

Behold now, something has been done which never happened for a long time: the king has been taken away by poor men. . . . What the pyramid hid has become empty.

Whether Ipuwer was referring to a specific pyramid, such as the titanic structure built by Cheops, or to pyramids generally we cannot tell. But all things considered, it seems very likely that the Great Pyramid was robbed of its contents like most other Egyptian tombs.

Yet can we be so certain? It is always assumed that Cheops was buried in the massive coffin that lies in the center of the King's Chamber, but is that merely what we are supposed to think? Some of the tombs of the Eighteenth Dynasty were craftily designed to deceive anyone who penetrated them, leading them into imposing but empty chambers to convince them that other tomb robbers had beat them to it. The real burial chamber lay much better hidden, with its doorway plastered and painted over so that it blended invisibly into the wall. Could the same thing apply to the Pyramids, particularly the Great Pyramid of Cheops?

There is in fact an intriguing possibility that the real burial place of Cheops has not yet been found. The Great Pyramid is a highly complex structure containing a baffling system of chambers and tunnels. There are also some enigmatic shafts running from the main chambers outward into the thick casing of the Pyramid—two from the King's Chamber and two from the Queen's Chamber. They do not reach as far as the outside of the structure, and they are too small for a person to enter. Archaeologists once thought these were ventilation shafts, though it is more likely that they served some ritual purpose—such as channels for the king's soul to journey to the heavens. Indeed, it seems clear that the two shafts that run outward from the King's Chamber point at specific stars that were very important in Egyptian cosmology (see **The Orion Mystery** in **Watching the Skies**).

The shafts in the King's Chamber were visible when Egyptologists first examined the Great Pyramid. Not so those in the Queen's Chamber. These were originally completely hidden by masonry and were discovered in 1872 by an English engineer named Waynman Dixon. As the Queen's Chamber mirrored that of the king in most respects, Dixon suspected that it would have similar shafts. Tapping around the walls, he located two hollow spaces, and his workmen opened one shaft by smashing through the stonework with hammer and chisel. This brutal technique revealed

> a rectangular, horizontal, tubular channel, about 9 inches by 8 inches in traverse breadth and height, going back seven feet into the wall, and then rising at an angle into an unknown, dark distance.

Though these shafts—which show in themselves that the Pyramid contained deliberately hidden features—were never properly explored, Egyptologists have confidently repeated over the years their belief that there are no unknown chambers within the Great Pyramid.

Yet a recent development shows how little we still know about the interior of this enormous mass of stone. German robotics engineer Rudolf Gantenbrink has made a staggering discovery with the aid of

The hidden door inside the Great Pyramid, photographed by the purpose-built robot Upuaut in March 1993.

a small purpose-built robot called Upuaut (an Egyptian word meaning "opener of the ways"). Costing a quarter of a million dollars to build, Upuaut has tractor wheels, carries a light and a tiny video camera, and is operated by remote control.

In March 1993 Gantenbrink sent Upuaut to explore the mysterious shaft running from the Queen's Chamber that Dixon had discovered. The robot crawled up the shaft for a distance of 213 feet, until it came to a small limestone plug or door. Attached to the plug are two copper pins, presumably handles, and in front of a tiny gap at one corner was a patch of black dust, possibly organic material seeping through from the other side.

So what, then, lies beyond this tiny door? Theories are legion, but nothing can be certain until further investigation is carried out. Gantenbrink modified his robot to carry a small fiber-optic camera that might be able to slide under the gap in the door and peep into the chamber beyond, but he is still awaiting permission to continue his work. Due to massive bureaucratic entanglements, of a kind that seem to be unique to Egyptian archaeology, aggravated by the internal politics and jealousies within the Department of Antiquities, Gantenbrink's pioneering work has come to an unfortunate halt.

However, Upuaut's first foray into the shaft has already established an important principle. It seems very likely that behind the little door there lies another, completely unknown chamber, even though it may be very small. And if there is one hidden chamber, perhaps there are others. Is it possible that the King's Chamber is, after all, merely a bluff to throw us off the scent and that Cheops is buried somewhere else, even behind the tiny door with copper handles?

Far from having learned all its secrets, we are now only beginning to appreciate the full complexity of Cheops's extraordinary monument. It is becoming increasingly clear that when the Egyptians built the Great Pyramid they *intended* it to be a mystery. They certainly succeeded.

THE RIDDLE OF THE SPHINX

Close to the Great Pyramid, on the edge of the Giza plateau in northern Egypt, sits the world's most enigmatic sculpture—the Sphinx. Worn by the ravages of time and scarred by the hand of man, this colossal figure of a human-headed lion, 240 feet long and 56 feet high, is the largest surviving statue from the ancient world.

The Sphinx—one of the most
baffling monuments of the
ancient world.

How the Sphinx was carved is not a great mystery in itself. It is a freestanding statue in one sense, though it was not carved and then placed in position. The Sphinx was chiseled from living rock, a stony outcrop protruding from the limestone plateau. By the digging of a huge, rectangular trench around it, this outcrop was enlarged into the raw material for the Sphinx's body. It was then sculpted into the image of a lion with a man's head.

Additional pieces of limestone were used to add finishing touches, including a beard. This fell off long ago, but can be reconstructed from the fragments that survive (three in Cairo and one in the basement of the British Museum). Its long curling shape was typical of the beards worn by the gods in Egyptian art. The Sphinx, it seems, was a god; we know from texts that the Egyptians paid it divine honors.

Huge though the Sphinx is, it has never been suggested that the ancient Egyptians needed any special techniques beyond sheer hard work and organization to build it. Stone hammers and copper chisels would have been enough to break up the limestone (which is quite soft), dig the enclosure around the Sphinx, and sculpt its details. What does remain a mystery, however, is why it was built, by whom, and when.

Modern Egyptology textbooks confidently claim to give the answers to all three questions. According to them the Sphinx was made about 2500 B.C. on the orders of Pharaoh Chephren (or Khafre) of the Egyptian Fourth Dynasty. The same Pharaoh built, and was buried in, the second largest of the three Great Pyramids at Giza. The Sphinx was a statue of the god Harmachis (god of the rising Sun), and, as the Pharaoh was considered to be a god manifest on Earth, its sculptors modeled its face on that of the Pharaoh himself. The resemblance of the Sphinx's face to Chephren's confirms that he built the monument.

Redating the Sphinx

The Egyptological consensus, arrived at early this century, remained basically unchallenged until recently, when three new pieces of research apparently hit like bombshells. The conventional case is now, in the view of many, in complete ruins.

The first surprise came in 1991 from Professor Robert Schoch, a Boston geologist. After studying the erosion patterns on the Sphinx, he announced that it must be *several thousand* years older than Egyptologists think—conceivably dating from 7,000 B.C. or possibly even older.

The second bombshell came from a police artist, Lieutenant Frank Domingo of the New York City Police Department. After performing a detailed comparison of the face of the Sphinx and the face of Pharaoh Chephren (as depicted on a statue in the Cairo Museum), Domingo concluded that the features of the Sphinx were *not* modeled on those of Chephren after all.

The final piece of research came from Adrian Gilbert, coauthor of *The Orion Mystery* (see **The Orion Mystery** in **Watching the Skies**). By "using sophisticated computer techniques," Bauval claims to have demonstrated that about 10,500 B.C., on the morning of the spring equinox, the constellation Leo (the Lion) would have risen on the eastern horizon directly in front of the Sphinx. He concludes that the lion-shaped Sphinx was therefore built around that date as a marker of this astronomical event. Bauval has now joined forces with Graham Hancock, author of the best-selling *Fingerprints of the Gods* (see **Poleshift** in **Lost Lands and Catastrophes**), and they have developed the argument about this new astronomical dating of the Sphinx in *Keeper of Genesis* (1996).

These sensational claims have been well publicized, in TV programs, magazine articles, and Internet discussions, but most of all through the books of Graham Hancock, which have become something of a publishing phenomenon worldwide. A good percentage of Hancock's millions of readers are now doubtless convinced that the Sphinx was really carved about 10,500 B.C., before the end of the last Ice Age, and not, as conventionally taught, in about 2500 B.C.

Were such a drastic redating of the Sphinx correct, then the field of Egyptology would be turned on its head and the textbook versions of the ancient past would have to be totally rewritten.

Conventional wisdom holds that Egyptian civilization—as we know it—arose quite suddenly about 3200 B.C., when towns, temples, hieroglyphic writing, and monumental art first began to appear in Egypt. Who, then, made the Sphinx, if it was carved as long ago as 7,000 B.C. (Schoch) or even 10,500 B.C. (Hancock)? The prospects are quite hair-raising. In either case it would mean that thousands of years before Egypt's first written records there was another, *unknown*, civilization, well organized and wealthy enough to build monuments as great as those of pharaonic times. The idea of another civilization, so ancient that it has been completely forgotten, has great romantic appeal, echoing the tales of fabled Atlantis. In fact the redating of the Sphinx has been used by Hancock and others to argue that an Atlantis-like civilization really did exist during Ice Age times and was based on the continent of Antarctica (see **Atlantis—Lost and Found?** and **Poleshift** in **Lost Lands and Catastrophes**).

It requires an enormous intellectual leap to assume that such an unknown civilization might have existed. For some, taking a ringside seat, such a leap seems plausible, even attractive. It is always fun to see "the experts" contradicted, and the strong impression has been given in the writings of Hancock and others that new, *scientific* evidence for dating the Sphinx has caught Egyptology with its trousers down. Yet massive shifts in scientific understanding require first-class proof. Is there really any truth in the claims that the Sphinx has been redated by a combination of geological, forensic, and astronomical evidence? We need to take a closer look at each of the arguments involved.

Mistaken Identity?

Credit—or blame, depending on one's point of view—for the present controversy about the Sphinx largely goes to one man, John Anthony West, an amateur Egyptologist and guidebook writer who has spent many years exploring the mysteries of ancient Egypt. West has written enthusiastically about astrology, argued for the reality of the lost continent of Atlantis, and believes that a past civilization on Mars influenced the development of our own ancient civilizations. The famous "face" on Mars, for example, he interprets as an alien counterpart to the Sphinx (see **Introduction** to **Watching the Skies**). None of these ideas, of course, endears him to professional Egyptologists, who dismiss West as a complete crank. Crank or not, West scores full marks for persistence. For some twenty years now he has doggedly pursued the idea that the Sphinx is far older than normally allowed.

The inspiration for West's theory came in the late 1970s, when he was studying the work of French mathematician and occultist Schwaller de Lubicz. De Lubicz argued that Egyptian art and architecture encoded symbols that were both mathematical and mystical at the same time, and that by deciphering these symbols we can gain insights into their culture unfathomed by ordinary Egyptological methods. As a corollary he held that the ancient Egyptians were far more advanced scientifically than is normally thought, and he occasionally let out hints that the Egyptians had obtained their knowledge from another, even earlier, civilization. This must have disappeared in the cataclysmic floods that de Lubicz believed had swept Egypt in prehistoric times:

A great civilization must have preceded the vast movements of water that passed over Egypt, which leads us to assume that the Sphinx already existed, sculptured in the rock of the west cliff at Giza—that Sphinx whose leonine body, except for the head, shows indisputable signs of aquatic erosion.

It was this brief aside that was to start the whole discussion about the redating of the Sphinx. West picked up on it and wondered whether the heavy weathering on the body of the Sphinx had really been due to torrents of water rather than the buffeting of wind and sand, as Egyptologists had generally assumed. To West's eye it was obvious that the Sphinx *had* been eroded by water, and given that Egypt, during all its recorded history, has never been noted for heavy rainfall, this posed something of a puzzle. So initially West agreed with de Lubicz—the Sphinx must have been built before an incredibly deep flood (possibly *the* Great Flood, of Noah) that had swamped the whole of Egypt. Such a massive flood, West reasoned, could only have happened when the massive ice caps melted at the end of the Ice Age, about 9000 B.C. The single, commonsense observation that the Sphinx was eroded by water could thus bring about a major scientific revolution:

> If the single fact of the water erosion of the Sphinx could be confirmed, it would in itself overthrow all accepted chronologies of the history of civilization; it would force a drastic re-evaluation of the assumption of "progress"—the assumption upon which the whole of modern education is based. It would be difficult to find a single, simple question with graver implications.

West eventually managed to persuade a Boston University geologist, Professor Robert Schoch, to examine the Sphinx and give an expert opinion on its weathering. Schoch made two trips to Egypt with West, and after the second, in 1991, concluded that heavy rain over a prolonged period of time had been the primary cause of the Sphinx's erosion. In his view the Sphinx showed an undulating and deeply weathered profile characteristic of rain-eroded rock. Channels in the ditch around the Sphinx also looked like they had been worn by rain. Other monuments on the Giza plateau known to date to the period about 2500 B.C. showed, in Schoch's opinion, a different angular pattern of weathering. Schoch concluded that the deep erosion visible on the Sphinx could not have happened during the last dry phase of Egypt's climatological history. Before the time of the Pharaohs archaeologists have identified a lengthy period when a much wetter regime prevailed in Egypt—known as the Nabtian Pluvial, it lasted

Diorite statue of Pharaoh
Chephren, found in the Valley
Temple not far from the
Sphinx.

from about 10,000 to 3000 B.C. It was during this period, Schoch argued, that the Sphinx was weathered by rain. Allowing a lengthy period for the erosion, he arrived at a guesstimate of 7000 to 5000 B.C. for its construction.

What, then, of Pharaoh Chephren, thought to have built the Sphinx? Schoch accepted that the Sphinx's head, including the headdress, was in the classic Egyptian style of pharaonic times, so he argued that it had been remodeled in the reign of Chephren. This would explain, in his view, why the head is disproportionately small compared to the body and why it shows far fewer signs of erosion.

In answer to the question of who built the Sphinx, Schoch offered a radically different scenario from that usually accepted. Farming, it is agreed, had started in the Near East by the seventh millennium B.C., and the world's first towns were already springing up. The extraordinarily precocious Çatal Hüyük in Turkey, where rows of houses with painted murals were neatly arranged around streets, was founded about 6700 B.C. Jericho in Palestine is even earlier. By 7000 B.C. it already boasted defensive walls and a colossal stone tower with a winding staircase. Well-organized Neolithic societies like these, Schoch reasoned, would have been capable of constructing large-scale monuments such as the Sphinx. Perhaps, he argued, an equivalent of these proto-urban cultures flourished in Egypt, and the Sphinx was their greatest surviving monument. It was not long after 7000 B.C. that agriculture and settled communities began in Egypt itself. So Schoch's model is archaeologically plausible (to the open-minded), and he means it to be so—to keep within the known parameters of early agriculture he limits his backdating to about 7000 B.C., though he allows the possibility of an earlier date.

West, of course, was delighted with Schoch's geological conclusions and was happy to substitute heavy rainfall for his earlier model of flooding. On the question of the date, however, the two begin to part company. West links the creation of the Sphinx to the legendary Atlantean civilization that, according to Plato, sank about 9600 B.C. (see **Atlantis—Lost and Found?** in **Lost Lands and Catastrophes**). He also feels that the traces of Egyptian civilization in the time frame that Schoch focused on are too slight. Rather than the known Neolithic cultures discussed by Schoch, West still prefers to think in terms of a *truly* lost civilization, dating back as far as 15,000 B.C.; its other remains, he argues, are now buried under deep sediments laid down by the annual Nile floods over the millennia.

Yet whatever the date, West feels that, at a single stroke, Schoch's work has vindicated him and overturned conventional Egyptology.

Chephren, however, still remained to be fully dealt with. In 1993 West encouraged police artist Lieutenant Frank Domingo to go to Egypt and compare the Sphinx and a diorite statue of Chephren in the Cairo Museum. (The statue was found in the Valley Temple, adjacent to the Sphinx Temple.) Domingo used the standard police tests for determining the identity of two individuals and, with the help of computer graphics, he produced a point-by-point comparison of the distinctive features of each face. His conclusion was emphatic:

> After reviewing my various drawings, schematics and measurements, my final conclusion concurs with my initial reaction, i.e that the two works represent two separate individuals. The proportions in the frontal view, and expecially the angles and facial proportions in the lateral views convinced me that the Sphinx is not Khafre [Chephren].

Domingo's results, especially when represented graphically, are hard to dispute.

Whatever one may make of West's own theories about the Sphinx, he has succeeded, by recruiting Domingo's help, in reopening a question about which Egyptology has been too complacent. The widespread belief that the Sphinx's face is a portrait of Pharaoh Chephren is really no more than an assumption, and a rather weak one at that.

In 1992 Mark Lehner, an Egyptologist at the Oriental Institute of the University of Chicago, published a detailed computer reconstruction

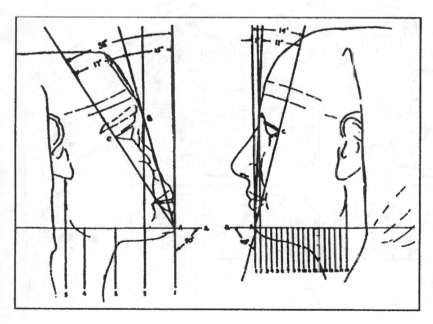

Comparison by police artist Frank Domingo of the proportions of the Sphinx's face with those of Pharaoh Chephren known from his diorite statue.

of the Sphinx. The face was made by superimposing that of Chephren, but in order to do so Lehner had to use not only the head on the diorite statue but also features (eyes, eyebrows, headband, and mouth) from a second sculpture, an alabaster face of Chephren in the Boston Museum of Fine Arts. The very fact that features from two portraits were needed shows that they differ somewhat. In one sense this weakens Domingo's conclusions. He would have done better if he had analyzed both known artworks of Chephren. And if, as it seems, there were variant depictions of Chephren, then it becomes very hard to *prove* that the Sphinx is not one of them. On the other hand, it now seems clear that we do not really know what Chephren looked like. Any perceived resemblance between his statues and the Sphinx proves nothing.

How, then, did Chephren come into the picture at all? Near the end of the last century Sir Ernest Wallis Budge, Keeper of Egyptian and Assyrian Antiquities at the British Museum, summarized the arguments for linking Chephren and the Sphinx that were being proposed in his day. Excavation between the huge paws of the Sphinx uncovered a chapel containing dozens of inscribed stelae placed there by the Pharaohs to honor Harmachis, the Sphinx god. According to one of these stelae, Thutmose IV (c. 1415 B.C.) was having an after-dinner

The Sphinx stela of Pharaoh
Thutmose IV (c. 1400 B.C.).

nap when Harmachis (the Sphinx) appeared to him and promised to bestow upon him the crown of Egypt if he would dig the Sphinx out of the sand. Budge notes that "at the end of the inscription part of the name of Cha-f-Ra or Chephren appears, and hence some have thought that this king was the maker of the Sphinx; and as the statue of Chephren was subsequently found in the temple close by this theory was generally adopted." The part of the name that survives on the stela is simply the syllable *Khaf* (without the oval line or "cartouche" that usually surrounds royal names), and it appears in a frustratingly broken context, where the words "the image made for Atum-Harmakhis" also appear. No proof here that Chephren built the Sphinx—the text could just as easily be referring to restoration work carried out by that Pharaoh (if it mentions him at all).

Budge remained unconvinced by the inscription. He was also able to cite evidence that flatly contradicted the belief that the Sphinx was built by Chephren. An inscription found in a temple near the Great Pyramid of Cheops (Khufu) states that this Pharaoh carried out repairs to the Sphinx's tail and headdress. As Cheops was Chephren's older brother and predecessor, the logical conclusion is that the Sphinx had already existed long *before* the time of Chephren. Admittedly the inscription in question is very late—possibly dating to about 600 B.C., nearly two thousand years after Chephren. It may reflect an Egyptian desire to make their own ancient monuments even more ancient. At any rate, it seems clear that in later pharaonic times the Egyptians *themselves* thought that the Sphinx had been built before Chephren!

Budge concluded: "The age of the Sphinx is unknown . . . it was in existence in the time of, and was probably repaired by, Cheops and Chephren." His own feeling, shared by some of his contemporaries, was that the Sphinx belonged to the Archaic period, just before the unification of Egypt by the First Dynasty (about 3100 B.C.). So in one sense West's case that the Sphinx predates Chephren is a return to a position held by the earliest Egyptologists.

Schoch Treatment

With no direct evidence that Chephren made the Sphinx, the possibility does arise that it was built before his time. Should we, then, simply turn to geology as a means of dating it?

The response of archaeologists working in Egypt has been a resounding no. While there may be no *direct* evidence that Chephren created the Sphinx, they are able to bring in an impressive mass of circumstantial evidence.

The Sphinx is perfectly integrated into the wider landscape of monuments built on the Giza plateau under the Fourth Dynasty Pharaohs. Behind the Sphinx lie the three Great Pyramids built by the Fourth Dynasty rulers Cheops, Chephren, and Mycerinus, while to the front the paws of the Sphinx stretch out to the "Sphinx Temple," also built during the Fourth Dynasty. Immediately in front of Chephren's pyramid there is his mortuary temple, from which a limestone causeway leads down to one corner of the Sphinx enclosure. A drainage channel or gutter opens into the pit around the Sphinx. It seems very likely, then, that Chephren's causeway and the Sphinx enclosure were planned and built together.

All over the plateau there are traces of Fourth Dynasty activity. In pits—including one at the very side of the Sphinx enclosure—stone hammers, pottery, and other artifacts of the Fourth Dynasty have been found. There is *nothing* substantial from any earlier periods—and not a trace of the Neolithic builders suggested by Schoch. (Even less, if that were possible, of West's hypothetical Ice Age civilization.) Thus, Egyptologists argue, though there is no inscription stating that Chephren built the Sphinx, it belongs to the Fourth Dynasty and must date very closely to his time. Of the Fourth Dynasty builders, Chephren, whose causeway led to the Sphinx and whose image was discovered in the nearby Valley Temple, is the most likely candidate for its creator.

In the opinion of Egyptologists, West, Schoch, and their followers have literally taken the Sphinx out of context. So closely linked are the monuments on the plateau that if one of them—that is, the Sphinx—is backdated by thousands of years, then they would all have to go along with it, pyramids and all. This, of course, is a conclusion that is not unpalatable to West, Hancock, and others.

Yet how can archaeologists dismiss the findings of a respected scientist like Robert Schoch so easily? Both he and his supporters constantly remind us that there is no alternative explanation for the particular patterns of weathering he has documented on the Sphinx. In no uncertain terms he has accused some of his Egyptological opponents of simply being unable to think in the same way as scientists and that they are inherently biased (implying that as a scientist he cannot suffer from this fault). He ends a 1995 defense of his views by suggesting that "perhaps it is time to inject a little more science into Egyptology."

In a general sense Schoch's point is fair. As a discipline Egyptology is renowned for being insular and in many respects it has lagged behind other archaeological fields—sometimes disgracefully—in the adoption of new techniques. Yet the impression that Schoch and his followers have given, of a straightforward conflict between an Egyptological date for the Sphinx and a geological one, is completely misleading—to a quite worrying degree.

Writers like West and Hancock frequently state that geologists as a whole agree with Schoch's work and can find no fault with it. Their pronouncements sometimes involve a fair degree of exaggeration. Bauval and Hancock, for example, state that when West and Schoch presented a summary of their work at a meeting of the Geological Society of America in October 1992, "several hundred geologists agreed with the logic of their contentions and dozens offered practical help and advice to further the investigation." Their only reference for this is West's own (hardly unbiased) account, which states that he and Schoch presented a poster display on their fieldwork at the meeting: "Geologists from all over the world thronged our booth, much intrigued. Dozens of experts in fields relevant to our research offered help and advice." Where, then, do Bauval and Hancock's "several hundred geologists" in agreement come from? In some respects academic meetings are not dissimilar to business conventions. Dozens of people may well visit your stand and offer interested, helpful comments. But the fact that they popped in for a chat does not mean that they have bought, or even intend to buy, your product. The "dozens" and "hundreds" of geologists who we are led to believe endorse Schoch's theory are, of course, never named.

The misleading impression—that somehow there is unanimity in the geological camp—has unfortunately been helped along by Schoch himself. In his 1995 article discussing the "unscientific" reactions to his work, Schoch mentions the disagreement of Professor K. Lal Gauri, referring to him as a "prominent Egyptologist." One would not conclude from this that Dr. Gauri, of the University of Louisville, Kentucky, is actually a geologist and an expert in the erosion of rock. He was actually responsible for the initial observations of the limestone from the Sphinx and its neighboring monuments that were later used by Professor Schoch.

Gauri was not the first geologist to disagree with Schoch. When Schoch published his arguments (the only detailed version so far) in the Egyptological journal *KMT* in 1992, a reply was soon forthcoming from Dr. James Harrell, Professor of Geology at the University of Toledo. As the director of a six-year-long project studying the ancient quarries of Egypt, Harrell is no stranger to conditions there. Harrell argued that the weathering that Schoch insisted came from rainfall could have been produced by other mechanisms. During recent excavations of the Sphinx the sand that had accumulated in the enclosure "was completely soaked a few inches below the surface." As we know that the Sphinx was covered with sand throughout much of history—Thutmose IV, for example, had to dig it out from the accumulation of centuries of neglect—it is very likely that for much of its existence the Sphinx lay in a bog of wet sand. The moisture in the sand would have accelerated chemical weathering. Why, Harrell argued, had Schoch not considered such possibilities? He rejected Schoch's case as "poorly supported" and "outlandish."

Schoch replied to Harrell's paper, dismissing his arguments as *ad hoc* theorizing. The minutiae of their argument are not important, as Harrell's main point, about chemical weathering, had already been developed fully by Gauri at a 1992 meeting of the American Association for the Advancement of Science. His paper, published in 1995, makes short shrift of Schoch's theory. Gauri and his team stress that the real cause of the erosion of the Sphinx can still be observed today. Almost every day slivers of limestone the size of potato chips drop from the sides of the Sphinx, and urgent debates are taking place as to how to repair and conserve it before the whole monument simply withers away. Modern pollution, of course, has aggravated the problem, but it is not the primary cause, which lies in the limestone itself. In the cool of the night, dew condenses on the stone surface and is drawn into the pores of the limestone, forming a solution with the salts in the rock. When the Sun rises and the moisture evaporates, the salt solution crystallizes and puts pressure on the walls of the pores. The surface cracks and small pieces of limestone are popped off the surface by the pressure of the crystals. As Gauri rightly insists, this process, visible every dawn, cannot be ignored when discussing the weathering of the Sphinx.

As for the undulating sides of the Sphinx, which Schoch attributes to cascading rain, Gauri (in agreement with Harrell and other geologists) merely stresses the facts—the rock from which the Sphinx was carved is composed of at least three distinct bands of slightly different limestone. The softer layers of limestone have larger pores and will weather more quickly through salt crystallization. The undulating profile is simply the result of these different bands of limestone of varying hardness weathering at different rates. Similar rolling profiles can be seen on other limestone monuments of later date. As for the deep channels in the walls of the Sphinx enclosure, which Schoch sees as further evidence of heavy rainfall, Gauri notes that they are actually small caves formed by underground water at a geological epoch millions of years before the Sphinx was carved—when the ditch around it was dug they were uncovered, so they are completely irrelevant to the date of the sculpture.

Gauri's paper has been overlooked by supporters of Schoch as if it had never been written. Schoch in the meantime has yet to publish his promised reply. This is not to prejudge the outcome. Whether every argument of Gauri or Harrell is correct is not the issue. The point is that while no geologist has gone on record as supporting Schoch, two senior geologists, with years of experience in Egypt, have produced alternative explanations of the erosion on the Sphinx. As Egyptologist Mark Lehner has frequently tried to stress, this is not a case of "geologists against archaeologists. This is archaeologists and geologists against one geologist—Robert Schoch."

If geologists cannot agree on what caused the erosion of the Sphinx, how can any estimate be made of the length of time the process took? Since apparently reasonable explanations of the erosion patterns of the Sphinx, which do not require several thousands of

The Sphinx and the Great Pyramid as drawn by the artists of Napoleon during his Egyptian campaign of 1798–1799.

years of extra history for the monument, have been offered by professional geologists, the claim that "geology" has backdated the Sphinx is clearly fallacious.

Stargazer

The geological jury is still out on the dating of the Sphinx. Indeed, it may be out indefinitely.

There is still the apparently weighty claim of Bauval and Hancock that yet another scientific method, astronomical retrocalculations, can date the Sphinx to 10,500 B.C. If someone, as Bauval and Hancock do, says that they have discovered a particular alignment using sophisticated computer techniques, the impression can easily be given that the result is not only precise but also somehow scientifically proven.

A computer, of course, can give a correct answer only if the correct question—in all its parts—has been asked in the first place. This is acutely so in the field of archaeoastronomy (see **Stonehenge** in this chapter). Hundreds of computer studies have been performed that showed to the satisfaction of the experimenter that a given ancient monument was aligned to such and such a star or was positioned to mark certain phases of the Moon or rising of the Sun. Unfortunately the whole area of study is a minefield. The main hazard is the assumption that if a result is found, then it must be significant. More often than not it will not be, for the simple reason that finding results is just all too easy.

Throw a pen down on the table and, as sure as you threw it, the pen will be pointing toward a star or a rising point of the Sun or Moon. Yet this will hardly be a significant or meaningful result. The same applies to archaeological monuments. There are an infinite number of stars in the sky, and because of that practically every building ever constructed could be shown to be aligned with one or another of them. The most hideous complications arise, of course, when we are uncertain about the date of a given structure, as the pattern of the heavens slowly but constantly shifts through time. A monument with an unknown date *and* astronomical purpose poses a perfectly insoluble problem. Astronomy can be used to help date ancient monuments, but this is clearly something that must be done with the utmost care to avoid arriving at spurious and completely misleading results.

It is only by understanding the nature of a monument that we can hope to filter out significant alignments from chance ones. The monument under study has to be clearly "special" in terms of its construction. Obviously the alignments of religious and sacred structures are far more likely to have astronomical significance than those of mundane buildings like houses. The Sphinx eminently satisfies this criterion. But before jumping to any conclusions based on the astronomical alignments a computer might offer us, we need to consider the context further and make sure we are asking the right questions.

As Bauval and Hancock rightly point out, the fact that the Sphinx faces due east surely indicates some astronomical significance. This seems unquestionable, especially since the Sphinx was identified by the Egyptians with various solar deities. Among its Egyptian names were Hor-em-Akhet (Harmachis), "Horus in the Horizon," and Sheshep-ankh Atum, "the living image of Atum." (The Greek word *sphinx* seems to be a contraction of Shesep-ankh.) As Horus and Atum were both Sun gods, a solar alignment for the east-facing Sphinx is almost manifestly obvious. Bauval and Hancock note that due (geographical) east is the direction of the rising Sun at the spring (vernal) equinox (March 21), one of two points in Earth's orbit around the Sun when night and day are of equal length. They go on to assume that the Sphinx was built as a marker of the spring equinox—and this remains the key factor in their computer retrocalculations.

Prompted by their belief that the pyramid complex at Giza represents the constellation Orion as it was seen around 10,500 B.C. (see **The Orion Mystery** in **Watching the Skies**), Bauval and Hancock set their computer simulation of the skies to that date and found that at the spring equinox, shortly before dawn, the Sphinx would have gazed across the Giza plateau directly at the constellation we call Leo (the Lion). Owing to the slow wobble of the Earth's axis over the ages (known as precession), constellations not only rise in different positions but their angle also changes considerably. Thus, according to Bauval and Hancock's computations, just before dawn on the spring equinox in 2500 B.C. (approximate conventional date for the building of the Sphinx), the constellation Leo would have not risen in the east, but 28 degrees toward the north. Moreover, the constellation would be at a sharp angle, the front part of the lion's body being much higher than its rear. Yet in 10,500 B.C., at predawn on the spring equinox, Leo would not only rise *directly* in front of the east-facing Sphinx but also be lying flat with respect to the horizon. They illustrate their point with diagrams comparing the situation in 2500 B.C. with that in 10,500 B.C. The match at the latter date seems perfect.

Bauval and Hancock take this impressive correlation even further.

Lion constellation from Egyptian star ceiling.

The precession of the Earth through the millennia means that every 2,160 years the Sun rises at the spring equinox in front of a different constellation. Presently that constellation is Pisces, and, as everyone knows from the famous 1960s song, we will shortly be entering the Age of the star sign Aquarius. Progressing backward in time through the star signs from the present Age of Pisces, which began about 160 B.C., and assuming that the Earth's motion has not radically altered, the Sun's rising at the spring equinox would have passed through the "houses" of Aries (the Ram), Taurus (the Bull), Gemini (the Twins), and Cancer (the Crab), until we reach about 10,960 to 8800 B.C., when the Sun's rising on the spring equinox would have been in the "house" of Leo. Having already dated the construction of the leonine Sphinx to c. 10,500 B.C., Bauval and Hancock now seemed to find further confirmation—what could be more natural than that the Sphinx was erected during the Age of Leo?

Zodiac Time

The astronomical calculations of Bauval and Hancock present such a neat case that it is easy to understand its attraction. Yet what they have not properly considered is that the "amazing" correlations they claim to have found may be purely accidental.

First, there is no evidence at all that the Egyptians had any interest in the twelve signs of the zodiac, as we know them, before about 200 B.C. Without informing their readers of this, Bauval and Hancock proceed as if the zodiac was as familiar to the ancient Egyptians as it is to us today. Our arrangement of twelve constellations into a zodiac comes from ancient Babylonia (southern Iraq), where it seems to have been conceived no earlier than about 1500 B.C. After that date, though we have thousands of Babylonian astronomical records written on clay tablets, the concept of the twelve signs as a group does not seem to have been of any great importance until the Hellenistic period (323 B.C. onward), when Greek culture dominated the Near East. It was during this period that the idea of the twelve signs of the zodiac became commonplace, and first spread to Egypt, probably via Greek astrologers. The earliest Egyptian representation of the zodiac appears on the ceiling of the Temple of Denderah, carved about 200 B.C., over ten thousand years later than Bauval and Hancock would have us believe that the idea was already central to Egyptian philosophy, religion, and science.

Prior to the Hellenistic period—when the discovery of Earth's precessional wandering must have hit with a force akin to Einstein's Law of

"Leo" from the Denderah zodiac.

Relativity—there is no evidence of any awareness of the Sun's slow progress through a different zodiacal sign every two thousand years. Astrologically minded writers today are fond of noting that during the last two millennia B.C.—roughly the Age of Aries—the chief god of the Egyptians was Amun-Ra, whose sacred animal was the ram. Another match can be offered for the preceding Age of Taurus (c. 4480–2320 B.C.), when bull worship was undoubtedly popular. Yet when we consider how common bull worship was at all periods of prehistory, the "match" pales into insignificance. Bull and cow cults flourished long before and well after the putative Age of Taurus. At Çatal Hüyük bull worship was already preeminent by 6500 B.C., while the dramatic bull rituals of Minoan Crete, perhaps the most elaborate to be developed in the entire ancient world, flourished at their peak around 1500 B.C. (see **Theseus and the Minotaur** in **Legendary History**).

Before the supposed Age of Taurus the tenuous connections that can be drawn between religious developments and the zodiac become ever fainter. Where is the evidence for a cult of heavenly twins beginning about 6640 B.C. (for the constellation Gemini)? Or, for that matter, a golden age of crab worship to match the "Age of Cancer," starting about 8800 B.C.! Bauval and Hancock expect us to accept that before these completely unattested ages, springing out of the blue, there was an age of respect for the constellation Leo—of which the leonine Sphinx was constructed as an eternal symbol about 10,500 B.C. For Leo's importance to be appreciated at this remote period, before the end of the Ice Age, prehistoric sky watchers would already have to have developed a keen interest in the spring equinox and the star "house" into which the Sun rose. It is not impossible that they did, but given that no one showed any great interest in the matter until Hellenistic times, ten thousand years later, it seems vanishingly unlikely.

Bauval and Hancock go a stage further and argue that the precession of the equinoxes, usually thought to have been discovered by the Greek astronomer Hipparchus in the second century B.C., was already known about in 10,500 B.C. Yet in order for prehistoric people to discover the precession of the equinoxes they would have needed to keep detailed astronomical records going back for centuries, if not thousands of years. (Hipparchus had access to Babylonian records going back at least five hundred years.) Despite the undoubted brilliance of prehistoric calendar makers, who in Europe were notching their efforts on stone perhaps as early as 20,000 B.C., there is simply no trace of such records detailing the positions of the stars

For Hancock the answer to this lack of records is easily supplied, as he believes the veneration of Leo to be part of the legacy from a technologically advanced civilization that flourished on the continent of Antarctica during the Ice Age. There is not a shred of evidence that it ever existed (see **Poleshift** in **Lost Lands and Catastrophes**), and in fact Hancock's far-fetched theory directly conflicts with his arguments for redating the Sphinx. To explain why Antarctica was free of ice during the last glacial period, Hancock subscribes to the theory that the Ice Age was ended by a massive shift in Earth's crust. Yet what he seems to have overlooked here is that such an upheaval would immediately throw out of the window any computer retrocalculations based on the gentle precessional wobble of Earth's axis over the last 12,000 years. The crustal shift Hancock envisages would mean that Egypt, and every other part of the globe, was on a different latitude, and hence in a completely different relationship to the rising and setting positions of the Sun, equinoxes, and positions of the constellations. One cannot, as Hancock tries to, have it both ways.

Astronomical Claims

On closer examination the new, "scientific" evidence for the dating of the Sphinx simply melts away. The astronomical arguments are extremely weak, and the geological case highly dubious. Putting them together, as many writers are presently doing, is merely building a house of cards.

All the same, the Sphinx resolutely keeps its secrets. We still don't really know why it was built, or exactly when. So the efforts of West and those who have followed him are not entirely in vain. Old assumptions have been challenged, Egyptologists have had to lay their cards on the table, and evidence that was last looked at with any real seriousness at the beginning of this century has now been subjected to a more critical, modern gaze. New methods and new approaches are always welcome, though some, inevitably, may not come up with the right answers.

Further scientific examination of the Sphinx may one day produce a concrete explanation of its curious erosion. Unconfirmed rumors have recently circulated about the discovery of hollows in the rock beneath the Sphinx. Are they man-made? Could they even be, as the followers of Edgar Cayce believe, secret chambers, containing a Hall of Records hidden since time immemorial? (See **Edgar Cayce on Atlantis** in **Archaeology and the Supernatural**.) Or are they natural caves in the limestone, of the kind that Gauri feels misled Schoch in the first place? Time will, we hope, tell.

Meanwhile, it is safe to say that relegating the Sphinx to a time period thousands of years earlier than the pyramids is not a realistic or necessary answer. A combination of factors—but mainly chemical erosion—was most likely responsible for its heavily weathered appearance. Heavy rainfall, as Schoch argues, could also have played its part. Though he does not stress the point himself, the period of heavy rainfall to which he has redated the Sphinx carried on, in the view of many climatologists, to at least 2300 B.C. It may well have ended quite abruptly, at a time when the climatic regime of the entire Mediterranean and Near East saw a dramatic change (see **Sodom and Gomorrah** in **Lost Lands and Catastrophes**).

And for the benefit of those to whom it is still "obvious" that the Sphinx was eroded by water, a highly novel suggestion was made in 1998 by historian Robert Temple. Noting that the Egyptians were fond of artificial lakes and pools, Temple has thrown out the suggestion that the Sphinx itself was *intended* to be largely submerged by water. The enclosure around the Sphinx would simply have to be filled. Temple's almost mischievous speculation has yet to be discussed, yet it is worth noting a possible supporting point. The drainage channel from Chephren's causeway emptied into the ditch around the Sphinx; whether water was deliberately poured down it or not, it would have meant that the enclosure was periodically topped up with water. When full, only the head and shoulders of the Sphinx—the least eroded parts of the whole figure—would have been visible above water.

Many other questions remain unanswered. Was the Sphinx really modeled on the likeness of Pharaoh Chephren or not? Did he, or another king, build it? The possibility that the Sphinx *may* be older than his time still presents a major challenge to Egyptology. If so, how much older? We can safely rule out the idea that the Sphinx was a Stone Age monument refurbished by the Pharaohs. Placed back into its context, the Sphinx is too much an integral part of the mysterious landscape so meticulously prepared by the builders of the Fourth Dynasty. The age of the Great Pyramids, which it still guards, is the logical setting of the Sphinx.

TIAHUANACO

Lake Titicaca is a remarkable salty body of water in the middle of the Andean *altiplano* (high plain) straddling the border of Peru and Bolivia some 12,500 feet above sea level. At this height signs of human activity, past or present, are few and far between, and, when spotted, pretty unimpressive compared with the scenery. That is, until you reach the site of Tiahuanaco in Bolivia, a dozen miles from, and a hundred feet above, the current shoreline of the lake. Here there are enormous artificial mounds, massive carved rocks forming enormous walls, large gateways fashioned from single stone blocks, vast sunken courtyards, and giant brooding statues of forgotten gods. All this makes up the highest major city the world has ever known, set against the spectacular backdrop of the snow-shrouded Andes.

"The Oldest Antiquity in All of Peru"

In 1549, Pedro de Cieza de León, a Spanish *conquistador* and the first historian of Peru, headed inland from the new city of Lima up into the Andean mountains. He came in search of Tiahuanaco, rumors of which had reached the Spanish conquerors. Cieza de León was not disappointed:

Elaborate stone gateway at Tiahuanaco.

Tihuanaca . . . is famous for its great buildings, which, without question, are a remarkable thing to behold. . . . [One is] a man-made hill, built on great stone foundations. Beyond this hill are two stone idols of human size and shape, with the features beautifully carved, so much so that they seem the work of great artists or masters. They are so large that they seem small giants. . . .

There is no knowledge of who the people that built these great foundations and strongholds were, or how much time has gone by since then, for at present all one sees is a finely built wall which must have been constructed many ages ago. Some of these stones are very worn and wasted, and there are others so large that one wonders how human hands could have brought them to where they now stand. . . . I would say that I consider this to be the oldest antiquity in all of Peru. . . . I asked the natives . . . if these buildings had been built in the time of the Incas, and they laughed at the question, repeating what I have said, that they were built before they reigned, but that they could not state or affirm who built them.

Later Spanish visitors had no more luck than Cieza de León in discovering who the builders might have been, so that Jesuit Father Bernabé Cobo, writing in the early seventeenth century, came to the conclusion that they had been a vanished race of giants.

By the mid–nineteenth century, Tiahuanaco had become a place of pilgrimage for rich European visitors, who found it impossible to believe local traditions that the ancestors of the Aymara Indians, whom they saw scratching a living from the hostile plain, could have built anything so magnificent. French count Francis de Castelnau was adamant on this point:

They say these monuments [Tiahuanaco] were constructed by the Aymara Indians, whose civilisation must then have been far more advanced than that even of the Incas. However, the buildings of Tiahuanacu do not seem to have been finished; they probably belong to a civilisation which has left no traces and disappeared suddenly as a result of some great event whose memory has not been retained in the imbecilic race that inhabits the country today.

Shortly after de Castelnau's visit, archaeological work to record and excavate the ruins began. The first accurate drawings of the site were made by the American Ephraim Squier, who had excavated vast numbers of burial mounds across the Mississippi Valley in his youth (see **Introduction** to **Earth Patterns**) and was now a diplomat in

The "Gateway of the Sun," drawn by pioneer American archaeologist Ephraim Squier in 1877.

Central America. He visited Tiahuanaco in 1877, making a plan of the main monuments in its central area.

The largest structure was the artificial hill noted by Cieza de León and called The Fortress in Squier's time, some 650 by 600 feet at the base and over 50 feet high; cut down into the center of this mound was a vast sunken courtyard. Around The Fortress (today known as the Akapana) were a series of further temples, smaller mounds, and courtyards. All the buildings were made of enormous stones held together with copper clamps.

Squier also produced the first detailed drawing of the broken monumental Gateway of the Sun, hewn from a single stone block weighing some 10 tons. Above the entrance was carved a central figure, probably the god Viracocha, known from Inca traditions, flanked by small human and animal running figures.

More accurate plans and photographs of the site were published by

German archaeologists in 1892. Their work attracted the Austrian naval engineer Arthur Posnansky, who reached Bolivia in 1903 after trying his hand at running a rubber plantation in the Amazon jungle. Beginning the following year, Posnansky embarked on a campaign of detailed mapping of the major monuments of Tiahuanaco, accompanied by some small excavations. He continued to work there until the 1940s. Meanwhile, American archaeologist Wendell Bennett carried out larger-scale excavations among the monuments. In 1932, Bennett located the largest single statue ever discovered at Tiahuanaco, in the Semi-subterranean Temple—a truly monolithic block of stone covered with the highly intricate carving of an elegant figure, either a god or a ruler, which stands over 24 feet tall.

These early investigators of Tiahuanaco agreed on one essential feature of the site—that it was not a true city but a ceremonial center with only a small number of permanent residents. As Squier concluded back in 1877:

> This is not . . . a region for nurturing or sustaining a large population and certainly not one wherein we should expect a capital. Tiahuanaco may have been a sacred spot or shrine, the position of which was determined by accident, an augury, or a dream, but I can hardly believe that it was a seat of dominion.

"The Cradle of American Man"

While there may have been a consensus on the nature of Tiahuanaco, estimates of its date varied dramatically. Making comparisons with other Andean cultures, Bennett came up with a rough placement in the later first millennium A.D. Posnansky, however, had a radically different view; he argued that the Tiahuanaco monuments were, as Cieza de León had suggested back in 1549, the oldest in Peru. He went even farther, as the title of his main work, *Tihuanacu: The Cradle of American Man,* published in 1945, demonstrates.

Posnansky's theory depended on astronomical dating. He argued that the platform temple known as the Kalasasaya (at the northwest corner of which stands the Gateway of the Sun) had originally pointed precisely to the Sun's solstices (the longest and shortest days of the year) and equinoxes (the spring and autumn days when night and day are equal), although this was no longer true. Extremely slow changes in Earth's axis over thousands of years mean that any alignment with the Sun will gradually become inaccurate over time.

Because this shift is very regular it was possible for Posnansky to work out when the Kalasasaya would have been exactly in alignment with the Sun: the last time was around 15,000 B.C. A group of eminent German astronomers checked Posnansky's figures in the 1920s and found them correct. This would mean that Tiahuanaco was actually constructed during the last Ice Age.

Confirmation of this remarkably early date came from an unexpected source: the study of extinct animals. On the Gateway of the Sun are several carvings of a strange creature unlike any to be seen today. The same bizarre animal was to be seen painted on pottery and crafted in fine metalwork. It looks from the depictions to be a mix between a rhinoceros and a hippopotamus. Biologists in the 1930s identified it as a toxodont, belonging to a species that died out at the end of the last Ice Age, some eleven thousand years ago.

For Posnansky, Tiahuanaco was both the oldest and the most important city in the Americas. Here a superior race ruled during a golden age before 10,000 B.C. in which moral codes were promulgated, influencing areas as far distant as Argentina and the southwestern United States. Tiahuanaco's authority was, Posnansky theorized, due to its vast antiquity compared with other American civilizations.

Seventeen thousand years ago, Posnansky believed, was also a golden age in terms of the climate of the Lake Titicaca basin. While today the arid *altiplano* surrounds Tiahuanaco up to a hundred feet above the lakeshore, Posnansky thought that at the time of the city's prosperity this *altiplano* had been below water. He therefore identified a mound and sunken courtyard seen by Squier some distance from the main group of monuments as the remains of a port. Most remarkable was his claim to have discovered "a true and magnificent pier or wharf . . . where hundreds of ships could at the same time take on and unload their heavy burdens." Further evidence of the former extent of the Lake was seen by Posnansky in the "extensive series of canals and hydraulic works, dry at present, but which are all in communication with the former lake bed." This also seemed to confirm that Tiahuanaco belonged in the dim and distant past, before the lake shrunk to its present extent.

The lakeside location of Tiahuanaco, crucial to its prosperity, was also central to its downfall. Posnansky argued that an appalling natural disaster had overwhelmed the city around 10,000 B.C.:

This catastrophe was caused by seismic movements which resulted in an overflow of the waters of Lake Titicaca and in volcanic eruptions . . . releasing the waters which descended . . . in onrushing and unrestrainable torrents.

Evidence of the disastrous flood could be seen at Tiahuanaco in dramatic scenes of destruction, with animal and human corpses strewn among the ruins, and shells, sand, and gravel heaped up among the monuments. At the Gateway of the Sun Posnansky thought the carver had been "putting the final touches to his work" at the very moment the flood struck. The sculptor abandoned his work, "to drop his chisel for ever."

Posnansky's theories were largely ignored by professional archaeologists, who preferred the more sober-sounding later dates favored by Bennett. Yet they found an eager audience among influential Bolivians, and indeed South Americans as a whole. The outside world had heard little of Posnansky, however, until his work was featured in the global reinterpretation of human history currently being proposed by journalist Graham Hancock and his collaborators (see **Poleshift** in **Lost Lands and Catastrophes**). Posnansky's Tiahuanaco fits perfectly with Hancock's idea of a lost high civilization that flourished during the last Ice Age.

Although one would not realize it from reading Hancock, a great deal of further research has been undertaken at Tiahuanaco and related sites over the half-century since Posnansky's day. Excavations have been carried out at Tiahuanaco itself by a Bolivian and American team from the 1960s onward, and for nearly the last twenty years under the leadership of Dr. Oswaldo Rivera of the National Institute of Archaeology and Dr. Alan Kolata of the University of Chicago. Kolata and his collaborators have also carried out extensive work in the countryside surrounding Tiahuanaco, looking at the towns of Lukurmata and Iwawe, villages and farms, and the extensive areas of fields and water channels (Posnansky's canals).

So how well does Posnansky's theory of an Ice Age date stand up to contemporary archaeological knowledge? A combination of old-fashioned pottery sequences and scientific radiocarbon dating provide the archaeological chronology. Bennett's excavations established a clear picture of the way that pottery at Tiahuanaco changed through time; this was then tied in with the ceramics from other Andean sites to see where the Tiahuanaco material fitted. Outside Tiahuanaco one or two other styles of pottery were developed after Tiahuanaco-type ceramics were no longer made, before the appearance of Inca pottery in the area. We know from Spanish records that the Inca empire conquered the Lake Titicaca basin around A.D. 1450. So working back from that known point, Bennett allowed about a thousand years for the changes in pottery he had detected. After Bennett's time, radiocarbon dating on material found preserved below the mounds and courtyards has pushed back the date for the beginning of Tiahuanaco's life as a city by a few hundred years, but has essentially confirmed his work.

Current thinking is that the village of Tiahuanaco was founded around 400 B.C.; in the period A.D. 100–300 it became a city, and by the end of that time it had come to dominate the other towns of the Lake Titicaca basin. This had all happened long before the Inca, just as the local Aymara Indians had told Cieza de León back in A.D. 1549. From then on until the downfall of the city around A.D. 1000 Tiahuanaco itself saw ever more grandiose building projects, while it came to control an ever-expanding trading empire, dictating events five hundred miles to the south in Chile. So archaeologists do at least agree with Posnansky that Tiahuanaco was a major power, even if they can't accept his dates.

Yet what of Posnansky's own scientific chronology—the astronomical alignments of the major monuments of Tiahuanaco? After all, his calculations received the approval of several eminent astronomers. The problem here is not with his figures as such, but with their relevance to the dating question. Posnansky's astronomical age estimates depend entirely on one basic assumption—that the Kalasasaya temple was originally laid out so that it could be used as an incredibly precise solar observatory. But there is nothing about the Kalasasaya that points to it being the headquarters of astronomical science. Kolata and other archaeologists do see the major monuments of Tiahuanaco as incorporating astronomical alignments, but not of an exact kind. As he notes, "The major structures within the civic-ceremonial core of Tiwanaku are aligned generally to the cardinal directions, as a whole 4.5 degrees west of true north."

This also means that they are oriented to the rising and setting Sun. Cieza de León was the first to notice this in 1549, writing that the two artificial hills, which he termed "sepulchral towers of the native lords of Tihuanaca," had their "doorways [facing toward] the rising sun." People in the Tiahuanaco Valley today still think of the Sun as rising at the ice-covered peaks of Mount Illimani to the east, and setting in Lake Titicaca to the west. Kolata suggests that this natural phenomenon was of central importance to the inhabitants of ancient Tiahuanaco:

The great snow-capped peaks and the lake are readily visible from the flanks of the mountains that enclose the valley, but both can be glimpsed simultaneously from the city of Tiwanaku on the valley floor *only* from the summit of the Akapana, Tiwanaku's tallest terraced platform mound. . . . From this summit alone could one track the entire celestial path of the sun from its twin anchors in the mountains and the lake.

As Kolata notes, the Kalasasaya platform temple itself shares a solar alignment with the neighboring Semi-subterranean Temple. This ties the two monuments together at the time of the spring and autumn equinoxes, vital points in the agricultural year: "Specifically, on the morning of the equinoxes, the sun bisects the Semi-subterranean Temple and appears in the center of Kalasasaya's monumental staircase." So the solar alignments of the Kalasasaya seem to work perfectly well *today*, making Posnansky's astronomical dating plausible only if one accepts the tenuous theory that the temple was actually an observatory and chooses to set aside the radiocarbon dates that now exist.

His confirmatory evidence—the supposed depictions of extinct animals and the lakeside location of Tiahuanaco—held up no better against current knowledge. Deciding which specific animal is being shown by a particular piece of religious art is a notoriously uncertain business. After all, in many cases there was no intention to produce a photographic image, but instead convey something of the essence of the creature. Certainly, Posnansky never argued that the men with wings shown on the Gateway of the Sun demonstrated that angels existed at the time of Tiahuanaco. In fact, archaeologists have always quite happily seen Posnansky's toxodont as a stylized puma. (Completely ignoring this, Hancock baldly states that the toxodont has been "convincingly identified" at Tiahuanaco.)

As for the port of Tiahuanaco, more recent archaeological work has produced crucial evidence. Earlier excavators such as Bennett and Posnansky had focused almost entirely on the ceremonial center of Tiahuanaco, ignoring the less spectacular remains of houses and rubbish dumps. These houses and heaps of debris are filled with pottery of exactly the same date as is found within the monuments at the heart of the city. Tiahuanaco is now thought to have been a normal city with a large resident population, of some 40,000–80,000, spread over an area of some five to six miles. So a port would be a quite reasonable discovery. Unfortunately for Posnansky, these humble dwellings are in the very area he thought lay covered by Lake Titicaca. So is the large town of Lukurmata, contemporary with Tiahuanaco. These new discoveries are conclusive evidence that Tiahuanaco was not a port. Indeed, at Iwawe, on the present shore of Lake Titicaca, excavations have uncovered

Frieze of angels from the "Gateway of the Sun."

remains of a Tiahuanaco-period port, showing that the lake level was much the same at the time of Tiahuanaco as it is today.

Posnansky can be forgiven for his overenthusiasm and mistaken identification of a sunken courtyard as a dock; less understandable is that Hancock entirely fails to mention this new evidence, simply repeating Posnansky's views as if nothing further had been discovered.

What of the other element in Posnansky's picture of Tiahuanaco— its dramatic end in a massive flood? Anatomical examinations suggest that Posnansky's flood casualties were actually the victims of human sacrifices carried out to appease the gods, while the layer of green water-rolled pebbles detected by Posnansky on the summit of the Akapana (Squier's Fortress), largest of the Tiahuanaco mounds, was not brought there by a great flood, but by human sweat. The upper levels of the Akapana are in fact made up of layers of thick clay, interspersed with thin spreads of this gravel. Kolata argues that these distinctive pebbles were brought to Tiahuanaco from the Quimsachata Mountains as building materials for the construction of the Akapana as a symbolic mountain. So Posnansky's dramatic flood also trickles away into the dry soil of Tiahuanaco.

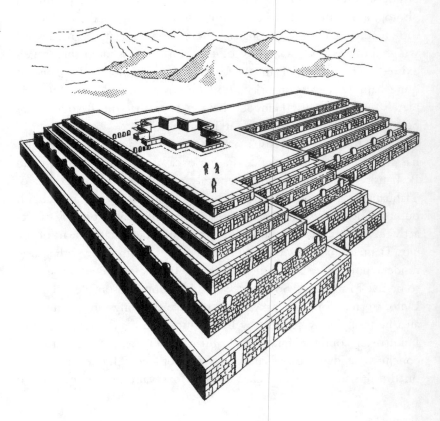

Reconstruction of the artificial hill known as the Akapana.

The Viracochas

Even if we can dismiss Posnansky's Ice Age Tiahuanaco as the product of wishful thinking, one major question remains unanswered. Who were the builders of this magnificent city?

From the time of Francis de Castelnau (who visited Tiahuanaco in 1850) onward, a constant refrain was that the Aymara, whom observers saw scratching a bare living from the *altiplano*, were incapable of such a complex undertaking. Pablo Chalon, writing a generation later than de Castelnau, was certain that the ancestors of the Aymara had nothing to do with Tiahuanaco:

> We must suppose that the builders [of Tiahuanaco] arrived suddenly in that place from some region that was already civilised by the influence of the Old World, only to disappear after a short residence without leaving descendants and without having transmitted to their successors the secret of their prodigious capabilities . . . traditions tell us little of these people other than that they were white men and bearded, and that having been expelled from the land, were forced to take refuge on the islands of the lake where they were exterminated.

His account draws heavily on a story recorded by Cieza de León of a "white man of tall stature" called Ticciviracocha.

Posnansky was less definite in his identification of the builders of Tiahuanaco, but he was equally sure that they were not related to the "wretched" Aymara, concluding that "the Andean Altiplano was not always . . . inhabited in part by groups of apparently inferior races, possessing scant civilization." Unlike Chalon, who thought that the master builders had been destroyed, Posnansky believed that some of them escaped the disaster that overwhelmed Tiahuanaco, to spread out across the Americas, bringing civilization to the continent.

Thor Heyerdahl, the famous Norwegian explorer, combined Chalon's and Posnansky's ideas to argue that a white race had built Tiahuanaco and then moved on. Local myths recorded by the Spanish said that the world had been created at Tiahuanaco by Kon-Tiki Viracocha, who emerged from Lake Titicaca and called forth people from caves, rivers, and springs. The creation legends end with Kon Tiki Viracocha and his followers setting out to sea into the Pacific Ocean. Heyerdahl thought that there was a germ of truth in these myths, and that they reflected a voyage of discovery by the white builders of Tiahuanaco under the leadership of Kon-Tiki Viracocha (see **The Mystery of Easter Island** in this chapter).

Statue, probably of a deity, with massive staring eyes, from the Kalasasaya platform temple.

The creation myths are probably a broadly accurate record of the beliefs of certain Andean peoples, but were the Viracochas white and bearded as Chalon and Heyerdahl believed? The idea has not fared well at the hands of later commentators. Dr. Evan Hadingham, archaeologist and science writer, was less than complimentary about Heyerdahl's white Viracochas:

His theory . . . was more or less pure fantasy. Heyerdahl relied heavily on the accounts of certain Spanish priests who were clearly attempting to assimilate native beliefs into the Catholic faith. Such sources portray Kon-Tiki as a bearded individual clad in white robes. In fact, some descriptions of this benevolent personality, who wanders through the Andes performing miracles, quite obviously echo the stories of Catholic saints.

There seems little doubt that some of the Spanish accounts were deliberately setting out to find in native beliefs echoes of Jesus that they could use to make Christianity more acceptable in Andean terms. Indeed, the chronicler Juan de Santa Cruz Pachacuti suggested that Viracocha might have been Saint Thomas.

A statue of Viracocha was to be seen at the town of Cacha, but only Cieza de León reported the figure as being both bearded and white. However, after viewing the statue for himself he admitted that only a blind man could imagine that it bore any similarity to one of Jesus' apostles. The weakness of the white Viracochas theory is laid bare by Cieza de León himself; he says that the Amerindians themselves did not call the Spanish Viracochas until the invaders told local leaders, whose support they needed, that they had been sent by Viracocha and his sons.

But why did the local inhabitants questioned by the Spanish not appear to know who *had* built Tiahuanaco? Maybe they simply gave the answer they thought the Spanish wanted, at a time when theories of vanished races were becoming popular. Or perhaps the memory genuinely had been lost. Kolata reminds us of the impact of Inca and Spanish conquests on the people of the Lake Titicaca basin. The Inca absorbed the area around A.D. 1450, and followed their standard method of uprooting and resettling a large part of the population to try to break down local resistance to their rule. Spanish rule was even more disruptive. Their own records show that in some provinces of *Alto Peru* (their name for the *altiplano*) 90 percent of the population perished within fifty years. Some fled the country, others were murdered, many were sent to labor to death in the silver mines, but above all, vast numbers died in wave after wave of disease introduced by the foreigners. It is a wonder that anyone at all was left to be quizzed by curious Spanish visitors.

Eventually, the Aymara did recover, only to find themselves a downtrodden and misunderstood minority in their own country. It is no surprise that Posnansky's theories proved so popular among the European elite that ran Bolivia. As Kolata puts it:

> Reading Posnansky's weighty volumes permitted the Europeanized upper and middle classes to feel a romantic sense of national pride in the heroism, nobility, and splendor of the ancients without the messy inconvenience of attributing those past glories to the direct ancestors of the Indians whose repression was an essential cog in the economic machine of modern Bolivian society.

Europeans also found it hard to understand how anybody could have assembled such massive blocks in the rarefied atmosphere of Tiahuanaco. Yet the Aymara today live and work quite happily at even higher altitudes, while Europeans can only gasp for breath. The reason is quite simple. Over time the Aymara have adapted to their mountainous environment, developing much larger lungs than other Peruvians.

Recent archaeological investigations have also made it clear that the ancient Aymara had a far more developed agricultural economy than that imposed by the Spanish. The mainstay of agriculture before, during, and after the heyday of Tiahuanaco had been raised fields. On the plain around Lake Titicaca the inhabitants built up artificial mounds of soil, watered by canals between the fields. Experimental work to re-create such a system has shown that crops such as potatoes grow far better in the raised fields than when they are simply planted in dry fields on the plain. At this altitude the main enemy of farmers is frost damage to their crops. This was minimized in the raised fields as the canal water around them trapped the heat of the day, keeping them warmer than the surrounding plain. Using this unique technology, local Amerindians, ancestors of the Aymara, could easily have supported a thriving city at Tiahuanaco. Only under Spanish rule did the *altiplano* become a desert, later visitors assuming that this had always been the case.

Why, then, did Tiahuanaco fall, given the sound economic base on which it was founded? Kolata believes that it was brought low by "a natural catastrophe of unprecedented proportions," but not Posnansky's flood. In fact, exactly the opposite—records of the past environment preserved in the snows of the Andes and the sediments at the bottom of Lake Titicaca reveal a lengthy drought that began by A.D. 1000 and lasted until beyond 1300. As the water table steadily fell, the raised fields lost their immunity to frost and crop yields began to plummet. The population servicing the massive monuments of Tiahuanaco depended on a stable agricultural economy, and crop failure meant that the whole costly edifice of imperial power began to crumble. Unable to maintain the impressive city any longer, the people deserted Tiahuanaco, never to return.

THE MYSTERY OF EASTER ISLAND

On Easter Sunday, 1722, the Dutch Admiral Jacob Roggeveen led his tiny fleet of three sailing ships into the shelter of a small and unknown island deep in the southern Pacific Ocean. The Dutch christened this new land Easter Island, though it soon became obvious that they were not the first people to arrive there. The island was clearly inhabited, as fires had been lit along the shore seemingly to welcome the visitors. When the Dutch drew closer to land, they were amazed to see people bowing down at the feet of gigantic stone figures surmounted with crowns. Vast numbers of the islanders came out on tiny reed rafts to meet their visitors, and the Dutch had no qualms about going ashore.

The Dutch left accounts of what they saw on Easter Island. They described the inhabitants as very mixed in appearance, with people of brown, white, and red skin color living in houses made of reeds in a shape like an upturned boat. Roggeveen and his men encountered individuals they believed to be priests and chiefs, including a group with fairer skin who wore large disks in pierced ears. Above all, however, the Dutch explorers were struck by the statues, as this note in Admiral Roggeveen's journal shows:

> These stone images at first caused us to be struck with astonishment, because we could not comprehend how it was possible that these people, who are devoid of any heavy thick timber for making any machines, as well as strong ropes, nevertheless had been able to erect such images, which were fully thirty feet high and thick in proportion.

However, for Roggeveen the mystery was a short-lived one. He hacked off part of a statue and convinced himself that it was a clever counterfeit made from clay with a surfacing of pebbles.

The Dutch stayed only for a few hours, but as Roggeveen recorded in his journal, it was a sad day indeed for the islanders: one was shot by accident and a dozen others killed in a brawl when the sailors caught two of them stealing.

The Destruction of the Easter Islanders

Easter Island was left in peace for nearly another half-century, but once its existence was widely known it became a magnet for European and American explorers. In October 1770, the Spanish viceroy of Peru sent out a fleet to find Easter Island. After two weeks at sea the Spanish fleet succeeded in their search, remaining anchored off the island for six days. They eventually went ashore to the Poike Peninsula, raised three crosses, and had the islanders sign the papers that made their home a part of Spanish Peru. The Spaniards were completely unable to understand the Easter Islanders' speech or their signatures, and it is doubtful whether the islanders realized what they had agreed to. Like the Dutch, the Spaniards thought that different races were present on Easter Island. But they did refute Roggeveen's claim that the statues were made of clay. Francisco Antonio de Agüera, one of the fleet's pilots, carried out a practical test on a statue: "The material of the statue is very hard stone and therefore weighty; having tried it myself with a hoe it struck fire: a proof of its density."

Easter Island had visitors from even more distant lands a few years later. The famous English navigator Captain James Cook arrived in March 1774. A small group landed, including Mahine, a Polynesian from Tahiti, who was able to converse with the islanders to a limited degree, although much of their speech proved unintelligible. These new explorers found circumstances on the island very different from those encountered by the Dutch and Spanish. For one thing, the islanders now carried wooden weapons, food seemed in short supply, and the natives appeared ill-nourished and few in number. There was also no trace of the white-skinned natives apparently seen by the Dutch and Spanish.

Most dramatically of all, many of the statues had been toppled from their stone platforms and broken. Cook and his companions noted abandoned plantations, and recognizing that the island's only mountain was a volcano, speculated that an eruption had devastated the population, reducing it to a mere 700 islanders. Of one thing Cook was certain. The islanders he encountered had nothing to do with the impressive statues:

They must have been a work of immense time, and sufficiently show the ingenuity and perseverance of the islanders in the age in which they were built; for the present inhabitants have most certainly had no hand in them, as they do not even repair the foundations of those which are going to decay.

The statue platforms now seemed to be used as burial sites. Mahine the interpreter was apparently able to extract the information from the islanders that some of the statues were named after kings, concluding that they were therefore memorials to past rulers.

Only twelve years later a French expedition reached Easter Island to find yet another complete transformation. The explorers encountered large numbers of islanders, estimating the population to be at least 2,000 people. There was no trace of famine either. The French concluded that the islanders must have hidden in caves during Cook's visit. La Pérouse also noted that only three or four men carried wooden clubs, and that these in any case might be symbols of office rather than weapons. The French did, however, confirm the destruction wreaked on the statues and the use of the platforms for burial. Bernizet, the expedition's geographer, drew several accurate plans of both ceremonial centers and settlements. Although the French did not describe the islanders as fair-skinned, the expedition artist showed both the islanders and the statues with distinctly European features. La Pérouse speculated that the decline in monument construction came about from previously extensive forests being cut down and springs drying up, although he did not observe any traces of woodland.

The Easter Islanders' caution regarding visitors unfortunately proved to be well founded, for from 1805 onward American and then Peruvian ships raided Easter Island for slaves. Slave-ship depredations were abetted by the introduction of smallpox. So crushing were these blows that by 1877 only 111 people were left alive on Easter Island.

Extraterrestrials and Experiments

By the time scientific investigation into the mystery of Easter Island began in earnest, its inhabitants were actually outnumbered by the giant stone statues. In 1886 a team from the American ship USS *Mohican* carried out a general survey of the island that located 555 statues. Further archaeological expeditions have found even more. There are between 900 and 1,000 statues, or *moai* (meaning "images"), surviving today, with others recorded but now washed into the sea, which continually erodes the coasts.

Easter Island statues.

The statues range from 6 to almost 33 feet high but there is a standard style and shape: a long human head and torso with prominent chin and stretched earlobes, arms held tightly at the sides and hands resting on the stomach. To some of the statues were added eyes of red and white stone and coral and red stone *pukao* (topknots) on top of the head, which could represent hair or the red feather headdresses seen by early visitors. Some 230 of the statues were once set upright on platforms, one to fifteen of them in a row. About 250 to 300 platforms once existed, nearly all around the coast, only some of them surmounted by statues. The statues were all mounted to face toward the interior of the island, like giant sentinels watching over the inhabitants.

There has been much discussion of the technology needed to construct and move the statues ever since Admiral Roggeveen's puzzled remarks back in 1722. Not surprisingly, ancient astronaut theorist Erich von Däniken (see **Introduction** to this chapter) argued that the statues could not have been carved using locally available tools. "Nobody could ever have freed such gigantic lumps of lava with small primitive stone tools. . . . The men who could execute such perfect work must have possessed ultra-modern tools." Von Däniken proposed a scenario in which a small group of "intelligent beings" from another world was stranded on the island for a time, taking the opportunity to teach the natives some of their skills, fashioning the statues (von Däniken stressing their "robot-like appearance") to kill time before their rescue. After these godlike beings left, the islanders tried to complete the statues with stone tools, but had to admit failure.

Unfortunately for von Däniken, archaeologists have constructed a very different picture of the development of Easter Island society and its monuments. The first inhabitants arrived sometime in the fourth to seventh centuries A.D. Platforms were being constructed from an early date, and the statues began to be carved after A.D. 1000. After A.D. 1680 there was a general social collapse resulting in warfare and the end of statue carving. Easter Island statues were therefore being carved, moved, and placed in position for a period of some 500 years, so Von Däniken's stranded spacemen would have had a very long wait before their rescue.

This still leaves the questions of how the statues were carved, how they were moved, and how they were put in place. Here we have three guides: archaeological evidence, the results of experiments, and the islanders' traditions.

Locating the source of the stone used to make nearly all the statues is no great achievement, for it forms an impressive monument in itself. The quarry inside the old volcano at Rano Raraku is an extraordinary sight, with hundreds of niches left behind when the finished statues were transported and nearly 400 mostly uncompleted examples. Unfinished statues include *El Gigante*, the largest carving at 65 feet high and 270 tons in weight.

As for carving the stone, de Agüera was certainly right about the hardness that the surface of the yellow-brown volcanic tuff rock found at Rano Raraku can achieve when it is weathered. Yet once this surface crust has been broken through, the rock beneath is only a little harder than chalk and can easily be shaped, helped along by softening it with water. It was this difference between the surface and the inside of the rock that led Admiral Roggeveen to conclude mistakenly that the statues had a hard pebble coating and a soft interior of clay.

The tools used to carve and free the statues from the ground were undoubtedly the pointed picks of hard stone discarded in vast numbers at the quarry. In a well-known experiment, Thor Heyerdahl, leader of the 1955 Norwegian archaeological expedition that first studied Easter Island in detail, arranged with the native mayor to carve the outline of a statue at Rano Raraku. Six men hammered away with stone picks for three days, wetting the rock as they worked, at the end of which they had produced the outline of a statue some 16 feet long. From this Heyerdahl estimated that six men could have carved the whole statue in about a year.

Once the giant statues had been freed from the rock, some of them were transported to their eventual resting places on platforms up to six miles away, along the tracks that radiate out from Rano Raraku, although the larger the statue, the shorter the distance it was moved. This was not necessarily because of their weight, but more likely because of the fragility of the carved statues. The largest statue to be transported is that known as Paro, a giant 32 feet tall and over 80 tons in weight, which was shifted some four miles across rough country.

The early explorers who assumed that the island had always been treeless were completely baffled as to how the statues could have been transported without the help of wooden levers and rollers. However, archaeologists have been able to show that the landscape of Easter Island was once very different. By analyzing the pollen deposited by vegetation in the three lake beds on the island they have drawn up a picture of the changing environment, confirming La Pérouse's hunch of 1786 that the island was once forested, with palm pollen being the dominant type. (Recent work suggests that this is probably the Chilean palm tree, which grows up to 65 feet tall with a trunk 3 feet in diameter.)

There is, therefore, no objection to methods of moving the statues that use trees or ropes. The first experiment was directed by Thor Heyerdahl in 1955, who organized a group of 180 men, women, and children to pull a 13-foot-tall statue a short distance while it was tied onto a Y-shaped sled made from a forked tree.

During the Norwegian expedition of 1955, islanders told Heyerdahl of stories that the statues moved themselves by wriggling along on their bases. A Czech engineer, Dr. Pavel Pavel, read this and performed a successful test on a concrete replica, so Heyerdahl invited him to join his 1986 expedition. By attaching ropes to the head and base of a 13-foot-high statue, a fifteen-man crew was able to inch it forward by swiveling it on the base when it was tilted forward, just as one would move a refrigerator. Again only a few yards were traveled by the statue. Reports of the success of this experiment vary wildly: Thor Heyerdahl saw the method as "incredibly effective," while American archaeologist Dr. Jo Anne Van Tilburg states that the method "visibly damaged the base in the process and raised a cry of protest in the community and among scholars." American geologist Dr. Charles Love carried out a similar experiment using a concrete replica that also suffered clear damage to the base. He therefore switched over to placing his statue on a small wooden platform and running it across wooden rollers. Using this method twenty-five men managed to move the statue 150 feet in only two minutes, but misspacing the rollers caused Love's statue to come crashing down. Although suitable for flat terrain, the small bases of the statues would make it difficult to control them on even gentle slopes, while some had to be transported across steep gradients.

Van Tilburg tested another method by computer simulation, in which the statues were lain on their backs on a wooden frame and moved on wooden rollers. Hers certainly seems the most likely method for moving statues across rough ground, while upright transport on rollers would be fine on even terrain. The tilt-and-swivel technique could have been used for short distances at either end of the journey.

Dr. Charles Love's successful experiment moving a concrete replica of a statue on wooden rollers.

There are only two main theories of how the statues were raised into place. In 1955 the team of islanders raised a 25-ton statue into place by levering it up and slipping stones underneath, a slow but steady process that took eighteen days. Alternatively, now that we know that timber was not in short supply, it is possible that a wooden framework was used to support the levers as they pushed the statue into place.

Von Däniken's questions can therefore be seen to have been answered in full by archaeologists. Yet these experiments do not explain the purpose of these giant statues. Mahine the Tahitian did record that some islanders claimed the statues represented past rulers. Archaeologists have wondered if this was the whole story, however. Current thinking holds that they were not portraits of individuals, but had a dual role of representing the ideal chief and being a suitable stone body into which the gods could be called by human ceremonies. They could then be asked for good weather, help in constructing statues, or support against rival groups. For, of course, one very human purpose of the statues was as monuments designed to impress others with the power and organization of those responsible for carving and moving these giants.

The Norwegian Expedition's 1955 experiment, with a team of islanders levering a statue into place.

Their work leaves us with feelings of admiration for the achievements of the ancient Easter Islanders. Yet who were they? Where did they come from?

The Kon-Tiki Man

The origin of the Easter Islanders has intrigued visitors ever since Roggeveen's day. Early archaeological expeditions to Easter Island considered the issue at length, concluding that the islanders were of Polynesian stock, based mainly on the linguistic evidence. This fitted well with the general understanding of the time that the Polynesians as a whole had spread eastward across the Pacific Ocean from an origin in Melanesia, the island group that lies to the north of Australia.

A challenge to this conventional picture was thrown down by Thor Heyerdahl, who, while he has done much to encourage the study of Easter Island, has been a gadfly to archaeology. An honorary Polynesian—he settled on the lonely island of Fatu-Hiva in 1937—Heyerdahl began his career as a biologist, and it was from this perspective that he first came to doubt the accepted view of the colonization of the Pacific. Starting from the distribution of crops, he began to argue that Polynesia had been settled from the East, from the Americas, specifically Peru. To his theory, however, the archaeological authorities he approached had one simple objection: the ancient Peruvians did not possess seacraft, for the balsa-wood vessels of ancient South America were utterly incapable of traveling far before becoming waterlogged and sinking.

Such flat dismissals of his ideas led Heyerdahl to set up the famous *Kon-Tiki* expedition of 1947. He organized the construction of a raft of balsa logs lashed together with hemp rope following the design of traditional Peruvian vessels, and named it after an Inca Sun god. In a justly celebrated feat of daring, Heyerdahl and his companions (five men and a parrot), having been towed out from the shore of Peru, sailed the *Kon-Tiki* for 101 days and 4,300 miles across the open sea. They eventually landed on the uninhabited atoll of Raroia in the Tuamotu Islands, east of Tahiti, from which they were rescued a week later. The *Kon-Tiki* is now preserved in a museum in Oslo. Having demonstrated that contact between the Americas and Polynesia was possible, Heyerdahl went on to develop his theory of South American colonization of the Pacific. He argued that Polynesia was first settled by a white race from Tiahuanaco in Bolivia (see **Tiahuanaco** in this

chapter) around A.D. 800, then by people from British Columbia between 1100 and 1300, who gradually replaced the earlier population.

Archaeological work in the half-century since the *Kon-Tiki* expedition has shown Heyerdahl's scenario to be completely wrong. For
example, radiocarbon dating shows that Tonga was first settled around
1300 B.C., by people from Fiji in Melanesia who used the Lapita type
of pottery found throughout Melanesia. Samoa was reached around
1000 B.C., again by makers of Lapita pottery, while Hawaii, Tahiti,

Thor Heyerdahl's balsa-log raft,
Kon-Tiki, encounters rough
seas during its 1947
Pacific voyage.

and the Marquesas were settled between 200 B.C. and A.D. 700. The settlement of Polynesia, including Easter Island, was thus over before Heyerdahl's hypothetical waves of American voyagers would even have set out.

Although his grand theory of the American colonization of Polynesia has been definitively ruled out (and quietly been dropped by him), Heyerdahl has stuck to the view that the primary settlement of Easter Island was from the coast of South America before A.D. 1000, and that the Polynesians arrived there only later, between 1450 and 1500. He draws upon a variety of evidence to bolster this conviction, including oral history, botany, archaeology, linguistics, and physical anthropology. His vigorously promoted views have undoubtedly had far more of an impact than the archaeological literature.

Beginning his case with the islanders' own traditions, Heyerdahl found two of particular significance. One is the tale of Hotu Matua ("Great Parent"), the ruler who sailed westward from his desert land and landed on Easter Island to claim it as his new kingdom. The other is an account, first recorded in 1911, of a dual origin for the present islanders. According to this, there were two groups on Easter Island, the Long-ears, who had arrived first, carved the earliest statues, and created the *rongorongo* script (see **Box: Rongorongo**), and the Short-ears who came much later. The Short-ears acted as the servants of the established islanders for 200 years before rebelling, toppling the statues, and killing their masters. Only a few Long-ears survived the holocaust. Bereft of their leaders, the Short-ears descended into a spiral of civil war.

Heyerdahl has woven these two traditions together into a seamless racial narrative of an initial settlement from the coast of South America by white-skinned ancestors of the Long-ears, led by Hotu Matua, to be joined later by dark-skinned Polynesians (the Short-ears) from the Pacific islands. Heyerdahl, writing in 1989, is crystal clear on the lowly role he believes the Polynesians had on Easter Island:

> Ethnographic evidence thus indicates that the Polynesians were indeed brought to Easter Island, either with their consent or against their will, by navigators from a more culturally developed area of ancient Peru, using either force or cunning. Maybe the nineteenth-century Europeans were not the first to sail from Peru into the Pacific as slave raiders.

Heyerdahl backs up his case with botanical evidence. Some of the staple items in the Easter Island diet undoubtedly came from Polyne-

Reconstruction of Easter Island house with stone base and thatch roof, looking like an upturned boat.

sia, such as bananas and sugarcane (along with the chicken), but the sweet potato and the bottle gourd are definitely South American, while the Spanish in 1770 thought they saw manioc (another South American crop) being cultivated. Other plants of apparent South American origin are found on Easter Island, including the once ubiquitous palm tree, the totora reed, which flourished in the island lakes and was harvested to roof houses and make small boats, clothing, and ropes, and *tavai*, a medicinal plant that Heyerdahl notes is also found around Lake Titicaca in Bolivia, along with totora reeds.

From the archaeological standpoint, Heyerdahl concentrates on the statues, and the resemblance between these and examples from South America. He argues that colossal standing stones carved into human form are characteristic of pre-Inca (before the twelfth century A.D.) societies to the west of the Andes. More specifically, a unique kneeling statue found on the edge of the Rano Raraku quarry and a broken small female figure are thought to be paralleled only at Tiahuanaco in Bolivia. In recent times Heyerdahl has compared the inlaid eyes of Easter Island statues to those found in the Bronze Age Hittite statuary of Turkey. His current suspicion is that the custom spread from the Hittites via the Phoenicians across the Atlantic to Mexico and Peru and then to Easter Island.

Enormous statues are not the only impressive monuments on Easter Island, for there are also the platforms on which statues were erected. The megalithic walls of the platforms, constructed using blocks several tons in weight, have long been compared to the Inca walls of Peru. Parallels can also be seen at Tiahuanaco, where the inhabitants were making equally fine walls before A.D. 1000. Heyerdahl sees this as conclusive proof of American settlement on Easter Island:

> Nothing like [the wall at the Naunau platform] has been found on a single island in the whole of Polynesia, but it is typical of the megalithic

walls of South America. No Polynesian fisherman would have been capable of conceiving, much less building, such a wall, and as it was built in an early period of the settlement of the island, the probability is overwhelming that the inspiration came from [South America].

The platforms themselves were often built as stepped pyramids, and there are many examples from Peru and Bolivia of this sort of architecture.

More mundane archaeological evidence also has a story to tell. Stone-walled houses of the kind found on Easter Island are, according to Heyerdahl, unknown in Polynesia. The largest buildings seen by the early explorers were boat-shaped structures 300 feet long. Some round houses had arched (corbeled) roofs, and other dwellings were semisubterranean. Heyerdahl states firmly that none of these types of house or building techniques are Polynesian, but were widely used in South America.

Heyerdahl admits that one area of clear Polynesian influence on Easter Island is language. The Easter Island language used today is undeniably Polynesian, but, of course, we must allow that modern contacts and settlers may have led to non-Polynesian words disappearing from the original island vocabulary. Heyerdahl therefore concentrates on the earliest accounts of the language, such as those of the Spanish expedition of 1770. The words they recorded for the numbers 1 to 10, for example, do not appear to be Polynesian. Neither are they from any existing South American language. Still, as Heyerdahl stresses, the original coastal tongues of Peru and Ecuador were replaced by Quechua when the Incas conquered the area around A.D. 1450. Despite this, there are a few linguistic clues pointing to South American connections, such as the name *kumara* for the sweet potato, remarkably similar to the Quechua word *cumar*.

Finally, the blood and bones of Easter Islanders themselves can provide us with vital evidence. The Norwegian expedition in 1955 sampled the blood of islanders. Comparisons with samples from both America and Polynesia resulted in the conclusion that Easter Island had close connections with South America. Apparently confirming this is the work of American anthropologist Professor George Gill, which, according to Heyerdahl, "found traits that deviated from the Polynesian norm; many of the crania, for example, had curved 'rocking-chair' jawbones, an un-Polynesian feature known from the aboriginal population of America."

Polynesian Origins

Heyerdahl has certainly amassed an impressive list of similarities, yet all the individual points he makes have been challenged by archaeologists. His critics start with the *Kon-Tiki* expedition. Although this was an extraordinary feat of bravery and endurance, it may not be all that useful a guide to ancient South American seafaring. *Kon-Tiki* herself was modeled on a particular vessel developed after the Spanish introduced the sail in the sixteenth century A.D. Moreover, *Kon-Tiki* had to be towed 50 miles out to sea in order to avoid the strong offshore currents—these swept many later explorers, trying to emulate Heyerdahl, north to Panama rather than west into the Pacific. Even those few modern voyagers who did head out into the Pacific all ended up reaching the islands of the Marquesas or the Tuamotus, not Easter Island, thousands of miles away to the south. Why, then, are there no traces of South American influence on these islands?

Heyerdahl's reconstruction of the Easter Islanders' oral history has come under heavy fire for its selectivity. His opponents point to myths recorded in the nineteenth and early twentieth century in which the founding king Hotu Matua came from an island, reaching Easter Island by sailing toward the sunrise. When he was close to death, Hotu Matua went to the westernmost part of the island to look out toward the land of his birth. This would obviously place Hotu Matua's original home in Polynesia. Heyerdahl has replied to this by arguing that he is relying on the original traditions, which were altered to fit with the prejudices of later visitors. It seems surprising, however, that Katherine Routledge, who spent sixteen months on Easter Island during the First World War collecting traditions, heard only the version in which Hotu Matua came from the west.

Theories of two races, one light-skinned with long ears and the other dark-skinned with short ears, can also be seen in a different light. Early explorers do talk about white islanders, but similar remarks were made about many other Polynesian groups, which also appear to have a wide variety of skin coloring. The way in which the La Pérouse expedition's artist depicted both the statues and the islanders with European features suggests a tendency to try to make them whiter than they really were. Certainly Captain Cook had no doubt about their general similarity to people in Polynesia, describing the inhabitants of Easter Island and New Zealand as coming from "the same Nation."

As far as Heyerdahl's interpretation of the people with long ears and the people with short ears as two separate racial groups is concerned, it

Rongorongo symbols thought to stand for the Easter Island palm tree.

relies strongly on a single oral tradition recorded in 1911. The listeners may well have been influenced by the notions of superior and inferior races in which they were accustomed to think. Stories of two groups on the island could equally well be interpreted in terms of social classes.

Botanical evidence for Heyerdahl's argument ought to be less open to question, but a closer look does not back him up. The giant palm tree that once grew on Easter Island is probably the same as that known in Chile, while both the totora reed and the medicinal plant *tavai* definitely originate in South America. However, they could have been brought to Easter Island by the wind, by the ocean, or on the feet of birds. One or more of these natural methods was certainly responsible for the arrival of both the giant palm and the totora reed on Easter Island, for pollen analysis has shown that both have flourished there for the last 30,000 years—long before the settlement of Polynesia even began. No human intervention is needed to explain the presence of the bottle gourd, for it is known to spread by itself through drifting on the world's oceans.

That leaves only the food crops of manioc and sweet potato. The situation regarding manioc is highly uncertain, for the Spanish who identified it in 1770 were presumably not botanists, while only four years later Captain Cook's botanist, Johann Forster, did not report it. Manioc was only officially recorded in 1911, after several introductions of people and crops from South America. By far the best candidate for a botanical transfer is the sweet potato, which is normally propagated by taking cuttings. Although seeds are rarely produced, they do occur, so there is a possibility that birds carried seeds to the Marquesas, from which it could have been introduced to Easter Island and the rest of Polynesia.

So Heyerdahl's botanical evidence can all be explained without any need for early colonists from South America. Indeed, the botanical record seems to argue strongly against his theory. If Easter Island was settled by an organized party from South America, why did the colonists not bring with them maize, beans, or squash, by far the most important of their food crops?

As for the archaeological record, there certainly are resemblances between the statues and megalithic platforms of Easter Island and those found in Peru or at Tiahuanaco in Bolivia. But Heyerdahl overstates his case when he claims that there is nothing at all comparable in Polynesia. There *are* stone statues in Polynesia, including a kneeling figure from the island of Ra'ivavae near Tahiti some 6 feet tall. The general plan of the platforms is reminiscent of Polynesian *marae* (shrines to ancestral gods), with the closest parallels being between the oldest platforms of Easter Island and an example on Timoe Island near Mangareva. Most intriguing of all are the links that may have existed with the nearest inhabited land, Pitcairn Island, some 1,400 miles to the west: when the famous mutineers from the *Bounty* reached here in 1790 they found traces of past inhabitants, including large stone statues on a platform, which they unfortunately pushed into the sea.

Much the most persuasive architectural evidence for South American contact is the massive walling of fitted stones with which some of the platforms are faced, which certainly looks very like Inca masonry. Even here, however, the evidence is not conclusive. South American walls were built of solid stone, while the Easter Island examples were constructed using a core of rubble to which an impressive surface facing was added. Again, megalithic architecture can be seen in Polynesia, most famously the 16-foot-tall trilithon (two uprights joined at the top by a horizontal stone) of cut and fitted coral made around A.D. 1200 on Tonga. Archaeologist Dr. Peter Bellwood of the Australian National University sees megalithic architecture as Heyerdahl's strongest point:

> The *ahu* [platform] number 1 at Vinapu was probably constructed sometime . . . prior to A.D. 1520, and its superb face of precisely fitted blocks is so similar to contemporary Peruvian Inca masonry that I feel some limited contact did take place about this time. However, it should be pointed out that Vinapu I is the only *ahu* of this type out of some 300 on the island, and it may represent no more than the chance arrival of a raft-load of Peruvian Indians acquainted with Inca techniques of construction.

Bellwood's modest suggestion would, of course, make Peruvians late contributors to Easter Island culture, not its founders.

There are also clear Polynesian parallels for the houses of Easter Island, contrary to Heyerdahl. The boat-shaped type resembles structures from Mangareva, Rapa, and the Tuamotus, while buildings with low stone walls supporting wickerwork roofs and walls are known from Mangareva and the Society Islands. Even arched roofs created using the corbeling technique can be seen on Hawaii.

The area of evidence given most weight by Heyerdahl's archaeological critics is the distinctively South American cultural features that are *not* found on Easter Island (or, indeed, elsewhere in Polynesia). Most obvious of these are ceramics and cotton textiles, which were produced by every South American society mentioned by Heyerdahl, yet are completely missing from Easter Island. We should also note the use on Easter Island of a completely different and less effective stone tool technology to that found in South America. Indeed, this was the point that left William Mulloy, chief archaeologist on the Norwegian expedition of 1955, "unconvinced an American Indian had ever set foot on the island." These unexplained absences were certainly not for any want of raw materials, for cotton grows well on Easter Island, good-quality potting clay was found by the Norwegian expedition, and the island's obsidian is perfectly suitable for South American methods of producing stone tools.

Not surprisingly, anthropologists have agreed with Heyerdahl on the presence of Polynesian vocabulary in the Easter Island language, but not with his speculations concerning lost South American languages and connections with Easter Island. The Spanish who claimed Easter Island in 1770 were entirely unfamiliar with Polynesian languages, so it was only to be expected that the conquerors were completely unable to understand the islanders' speech. Spanish records of Easter Island vocabulary, central to Heyerdahl's case that the islanders spoke a non-Polynesian language, can hardly be relied on. Only four years later Captain Cook noted that the first Easter Islander to board one of his ships counted in a language that the Tahitian interpreter Mahine could recognize. However, as Heyerdahl has stressed, Cook added that the visitor's "language was, in a manner, wholly unintelligible to all of us," and despite his best efforts at communication, Cook actually published a list of only seventeen Polynesian words used by the islanders. At first sight this appears to support Heyerdahl's theory of a South American contribution to Easter Island vocabulary; it would certainly explain the use of words unfamiliar to a Tahitian. Against this, linguists have discovered that populations that have been isolated for long periods, such as the Easter Islanders, commonly develop their own local vocabulary.

What about the case of the sweet potato, called *kumara* on Easter Island and *cumar* by the Quechua of Peru, descendants of the Incas? Even here we can find no agreement, for the normal Quechua name for the sweet potato was *apichu*, and nowhere on the coast of South America was the term *cumar* used. Instead the Quechua borrowed the word from an inland group. Another difficulty for the Heyerdahl view is that the sweet potato had spread right across Polynesia, as far as New Zealand, under a similar name, probably long before Inca times.

The most important potential source of evidence on the origins of the Easter Islanders is the ancient inhabitants themselves. Heyerdahl claimed that Gill's examination of the skeletons of Easter Islanders showed that they had a peculiarity of the jaw, curved "rocking-chair" jawbones, which is paralleled in South America but unknown in Polynesia. In fact, Gill's conclusion was exactly the opposite, as "rocking-chair" jaws show Polynesian rather than South American contact, for Amerindians typically have a flat jaw. However, most of the skeletons examined by Gill are quite recent, leaving open the possibility of earlier South American settlers.

More recently, DNA analysis has been brought to bear on the origin of the Easter Islanders. A dozen adult bones dating from A.D. 1100 up to 1868 were sampled. The analyses were clear-cut, showing DNA types also known from Hawaii and the Chatham Islands near New Zealand. As Dr. Erika Hagelberg, of Cambridge University, England, the leader of the team, noted: "Our results confirm the Polynesian affinities of the original settlers." They certainly do show that Polynesians were on the island long before Heyerdahl believes they arrived. This isn't quite the end of the story, however, as the DNA analyses do not prove that *all* the original settlers came from Polynesia. For it is possible that there were different genetic groups on Easter Island, one with a South American origin, who married only within their own communities, and that the DNA testing has so far only identified the Polynesian part of the population.

So what conclusion can we draw from these two remarkably different views of the evidence? The Polynesian presence on Easter Island is undeniable. South American influences are certainly possible, but if anything, very late. There is no compelling reason to explain them by immigration from the continent, and there is certainly no convincing backing for the Heyerdahl theory that Easter Island was originally settled by a fleet of balsa rafts sailing from the coast of Peru.

Disaster in Paradise

Whether the occupants of Easter Island were purely Polynesian or not, they seem to have been responsible for a major ecological disaster. We know from pollen analyses that the landscape of the island was dominated by lowland forest before the settlers arrived. Yet by the time of the Dutch contact there was barely a tree to be seen. What had happened?

The tree cover on the island started to decline from about A.D. 750, with fairly complete deforestation of the lowlands by 1150. Tree pollen

Birdman carving from the Orongo religious center, which grew in importance as statue making ground to a halt.

fell to its lowest recorded level around 1450. Thus an almost treeless landscape had been created centuries before the time of the Dutch visit. With the disappearance of the trees came considerable soil erosion, which made it far more difficult to grow food crops.

Here, almost certainly, are the causes underlying the social collapse after A.D. 1680 that resulted in warfare and the end of statue carving. It was this society, torn apart by conflict, which the European explorers stumbled upon in 1722. Quite reasonably, they concluded that the islanders could never have been capable of creating the spectacular monumental landscape in which they lived.

Why did the forests of Easter Island vanish? A surprising clue came from the small indentations that appear on most of the ancient palm nuts discovered by archaeologists. These turned out to be toothmarks of the small Polynesian rat, introduced across the Pacific as a source of food (in the same way that Peruvians use the guinea pig). By eating the nuts, the rats badly affected the propagation of the palm trees, already under assault from the human inhabitants of the island. Its forests were steadily depleted by canoe building—the islanders needed boats to make regular visits, for example, to the small reef of Sala-y-Gómez some 260 miles to the northeast, probably to catch nesting seabirds. By the time of the European visits there were almost no trees left, so Captain Cook was probably justified in describing Easter Island canoes as the worst in the Pacific. Finally, religious activity stripped most of the island of woodland. Thousands of large trees were chopped down to turn them into the rollers, levers, and other wooden tools needed to move and erect the giant statues. Ironically enough, as they built the colossal guardians that gave spritual protection to the homeland, the islanders were inadvertently helping to destroy it. Once the trees disappeared the statues had to be left where they stood, many of them condemned never to complete their journey from the quarry to the seaside platforms.

We may never know quite what led the Easter Islanders to behave in the way that they did, apparently preferring to allow the trees to vanish until none were left rather than abandon their religious ways and call a halt to the statue-building cult. As the trees disappeared, the rats made sure that they could not grow back. By this time it was too late to think of setting sail in search of a new homeland, for contact with the rest of Polynesia had long been lost, as were the trees the Easter Islanders would have needed to build a rescue fleet of canoes.

RONGORONGO

Rongorongo (meaning chants or recitations), the Easter Islanders' own form of writing, was first recorded by Father Joseph Eyraud, the earliest nonislander to become a resident. His religious mission of 1864 was a failure, but the report he produced for his order provides valuable glimpses into the last days of Easter Island society before slavery, disease, and Christianity took their toll. He stated that "one finds in all the houses wooden tablets or staffs covered with sorts of hieroglyphic characters." Unfortunately he was unable to find anyone willing to translate one of these inscriptions. When the missionaries returned in force the following year, they pressed the islanders to accept Christianity, and to make a clean break with the past they destroyed all possible religious objects including *rongorongo* inscriptions. The result was to make this unique form of picture writing, with symbols resembling birds, fish, the Sun, and trees, among others, a mystery that still defies solution.

What is the source of this extraordinary form of writing, now known only from twenty-five surviving inscriptions? Thor Heyerdahl, the Norwegian explorer, has suggested, in line with his thinking on the origin of the Easter Islanders, that it has a source in the Americas. No Polynesians possessed the art of writing, but it might have existed in Peru, for the Spanish conquerors said they burned boards on which the Incas had painted their history. Somewhat farther away, the Cuna Indians of Panama and Colombia apparently incised religious texts on wooden tablets.

Anthropologists agree with Heyerdahl that writing is unique in Polynesia to Easter Island. However, they have a completely different view of its origin, arguing that it was inspired by the signing ceremony at which the Spanish claimed ownership of the island in 1770. No *rongorongo* inscriptions have been found in an archaeological excavation, while surviving examples are all from the late eighteenth or early nineteenth century. The script used is also remarkably uniform, showing no signs of change through time.

Still, even if it did have a late beginning, if *rongorongo* writing were deciphered, it should throw new light on Easter Island religion and possibly the statues. Unfortunately, despite a century of study, no convincing translation has yet been made of a single tablet, although there has been no shortage of self-proclaimed translators.

There were several false starts in the nineteenth century. Bishop Jaussen of Tahiti found a young Easter Islander named Metoro who claimed to be able to translate the tablets in the bishop's possession. After Metoro chanted for fifteen days the bishop reluctantly concluded that he was a fraud, for he gave the same symbol different meanings on occasion and identified the same word with several alternative signs.

The most convincing translation was that obtained by Paymaster William Thomson of the American ship USS *Mohican*, which landed on Easter Island in 1886. Among the objects he collected on his mission for the National Museum in Washington were two wooden tablets covered with *rongorongo*. Desperate to procure a translation, Thomson sought out the eighty-three-year-old islander Ure Va'e Iko, who admitted to knowing *rongorongo* but was reluctant to break the Catholic commands to have nothing to do with it. Thomson resorted to bribery, and although Ure Va'e Iko would not touch the tablets Thomson had collected, he did look at photographs of Bishop Jaussen's tablets, his resolve weakened by alcohol. Looking at the photographs, Ure Va'e Iko began to sing a fertility chant while Thomson's companions hurriedly scribbled down his words. But with no confirmation from other informants, this was always an uncertain guide, and Thomson still found himself unable to read any other inscription.

The first linguist to study *rongorongo* in modern times was the German scholar Thomas Barthel. He identified some 120 basic elements that combined to form 1,500 to 2,000 different signs. He argued that *rongorongo* was a system of picture symbols that expressed both objects and ideas, so that an individual sign or glyph could represent a whole phrase, making it much harder to produce a translation. He was able to make the most progress with the Mamari tablet, which seems to be a lunar calendar.

The most recent research is that of American linguist Steven Fischer, who has carried out an examination of nearly all the surviving *rongorongo* inscriptions. He gives particular attention to the Santiago staff, a 4-foot-long scepter that once belonged to an Easter Island chief and is covered with 2,300 symbols. Uniquely, this text is divided up by a series of vertical lines drawn between signs at irregular intervals. Within each section, almost every third symbol has attached to it another sign that Fischer describes as "phallus-like." This attached sign never occurs with the last or next-to-last symbol before a dividing line, and no section between lines has fewer than three symbols. All this leads Fischer to argue that the texts have a structure based on counts of three; in other words, that they are "triads."

Next Fischer turned to Ure Va'e Iko's fertility chant recorded by Thomson. This involved forty-one mythical matings that produced the flora and fauna of Easter Island. For Fischer, the most significant thing about the chant was that the god who initiated the mating was always named first, his goddess mate second, and the offspring third. So we have here a triad structure with a male figure named first. The similarity with Fischer's understanding of the Santiago staff is clear.

He has gone on to show that two other texts have the same phallus-like addition to glyphs and a triad structure. He therefore believes that these texts all relate to Easter Island creation myths. Fischer has, however, proposed a translation for only a single sentence, which has three symbols in the order "bird" (with phallus), "fish," "sun."

Lines of *rongorongo* script from the Santiago staff, with possible word-divider lines and symbols with a "phallus-like" attachment.

His reading is "All the birds copulated with fish: there issued forth the sun." While this is possible, it hardly provides an exact match to Ure Va'e Iko's matings of gods and goddesses.

Far less convincing is Fischer's suggestion that another dozen of the tablets also deal with creation chants. His evidence here is limited to the repetition of the bird, fish, Sun symbol sequence, and a general triad structure, as these other texts lack the phallus-like figure. While there may well be an underlying three-step structure to the *rongorongo* inscriptions, this in itself is hardly strong enough evidence to conclude that all the texts relate to creation myths. The verdict of most scholars is that Fischer's work is important, but not a crucial breakthrough in understanding *rongorongo*. There are still some Easter Island mysteries.

CHAPTER FOUR

EARTH PATTERNS

INTRODUCTION

In a remote corner of the English countryside lies the largest artificial mound in Europe. Silbury Hill in Wiltshire is located at the heart of an extraordinary concentration of prehistoric monuments, ranging from massive chambered tombs to the stone circle at Avebury, the biggest in the British Isles. Yet the hill itself, of all these monuments, remains the most enigmatic. Silbury is a huge flat-topped cone, 130 feet high and 500 feet in diameter, mainly made of chalk dug from the massive ditch, 125 feet wide, that surrounds it. The volume of chalk and soil piled up was a staggering 12.5 million cubic feet. Estimates of the labor needed to build it vary considerably, but it was something on the order of 15 million hours. Yet what was the purpose behind this massive expenditure of effort?

Because of its scale, Silbury Hill has always invited comparison with the Egyptian Pyramids, and the earliest theory was that, like them, this huge structure was a tomb. About 1660, the great English antiquarian John Aubrey recorded a local tradition that a King Sil was buried here on horseback, perhaps covered with gold. A later pioneer of prehistoric archaeology, William Stukeley, suggested in 1723 that Silbury was "the most magnificent Mausoleum in the world, without excepting the Egyptian pyramids." Other antiquarians, hoping to find a splendid burial, dug tunnels into the hill in 1776 and 1849, but revealed nothing of interest—except that at the center of the chalk hill lay another mound of soil and turf, about 100 feet in diameter and 17 feet high.

The vast artificial mound of Silbury Hill, constructed around 2500 B.C.

Many questions, not least the date of this baffling monument, remained unanswered, and in 1968 the BBC sponsored new excavations under the leadership of Professor Richard Atkinson of Cardiff University, well known for his work at Stonehenge (see **Stonehenge** in **Architectural Wonders**). The television executives confidently expected that enough interest would be generated to justify the considerable expense. Plans were made for live broadcasts from the site in the event of dramatic discoveries. These were never needed.

Atkinson brought in Welsh coal miners to reopen the tunnel begun in 1849 and the team burrowed on through the very heart of the mound, where they found . . . nothing. The BBC cut its losses and the plans to examine the ditches were abandoned.

Though there were no spectacular revelations, Atkinson's work did throw light on how the hill had been constructed. Careful recording of the layers of soil and chalk making up the mound showed that it had been built in three stages (the first being that identified in 1849), around about 2500 B.C. Yet, especially as no trace of a burial had been found, the purpose of the mound was now even more of a mystery than ever. Silbury is clearly part of the Avebury complex, but it is hard to imagine how it could have played any part in the ceremonies held there. The hill was constructed in a depression, and all the furious effort of excavating and piling up thousands of tons of chalk and earth merely raised the level of the spot to that of the surrounding hills. It can barely be seen from neighboring monuments, and provides no vantage point, for example, for astronomical observations.

So Silbury Hill seems to have been built for no practical purpose at all—at least one that we can understand. Dr. Alasdair Whittle, who took over publication of the Silbury excavations in the 1990s, argues that for the ancient inhabitants of Wiltshire, constructing the great artificial hill or "sacred mound" was a labor of love, with the builders inspired by a common religious belief to contribute their work voluntarily. What exactly this religious motivation was is hard to guess. But there was undeniably an urge, common among our ancestors, to reshape the landscape for reasons that to us seem quite irrational. About fifty miles southeast of Silbury in Somerset lies Glastonbury Tor, which according to one theory is another example of the handiwork of prehistoric landscape artists. Though the Tor (hill) is basically natural, it has been argued that its curious spiral shape comes from its having been sculpted by prehistoric engineers into a gigantic labyrinth.

Whittle has compared Silbury Hill to the artificial mounds that have been found by the hundreds in the southeastern United States, ranging from tall cones to the mysterious effigy mounds molded into the shapes of various animals and birds. The mounds first came to the attention of European settlers after the end of the Anglo-French war in 1756. A vast area between the existing colonies and the Mississippi was opened up for settlement. When pioneers started to flood into the Ohio River Valley, they found the fertile plains dotted with mounds and many more concealed in woodlands. In all some ten thousand mounds have been recorded within the Valley. As further lands were settled reports of mounds eventually came from an enormous territory: the shores of the great rivers of the American heartland, the Ohio, Illinois, Indiana, and Missouri, were lined with mounds.

Colonists were so struck with this spectacular array of earthworks that theories arose of a mysterious race of "Moundbuilders." Unfortunately there was little hope of establishing the identity of these builders by interrogating the local inhabitants, who had been dispersed far and wide or killed by warfare and the new diseases introduced by the settlers. Incredulous that Indians could have had the engineering skills to build the mounds, antiquarians assumed that the "Moundbuilders" must have been a "superior" race who had migrated from the Old World: Egyptians, Mongols, Vikings, Hindu colonists from India, and lost tribes from ancient Israel. The simple truth that the mounds had been built by the American Indians was studiously avoided until it was proved by a U.S. government report on the mounds prepared by Cyrus Thomas in 1894. Thomas demonstrated beyond doubt that the finds that had been excavated from the mounds were basically Amerindian. Continuity with the "Moundbuilders" could be traced through Indian traditions, and even a rare account from early French explorers who in 1720 witnessed the burial, in a mound, of a chief of the Natchez tribe of Louisiana.

Natchez burial ceremony as recorded by French explorers in 1720.

This does not mean that mound building as a whole was a recent phenomenon. The oldest known mound complex is the recently investigated site of Watson Brake in Louisiana, with radiocarbon dates of around 3400 B.C., a good three thousand years older than the majority of sites in the eastern United States. Yet Watson Brake was not a simple site: it has eleven mounds connected by an earthen bank enclosing an area nearly a thousand feet in diameter.

Later mound complexes were vast. The largest settlement in North America before the early nineteenth century was the town at Cahokia, on the banks of the Mississippi near the modern city of St. Louis, Missouri. It covered an area of some six miles, containing about a hundred

Nineteenth-century depictions of the North American mounds, such as these in the Mississippi Valley, fostered romantic notions of a vanished race of moundbuilders.

and twenty mounds in and around a series of open spaces. The largest mound, Monks Mound (named after a monastery built on top of it last century), rose a hundred feet above the central plaza. One thousand by 770 feet at the base, it is the greatest prehistoric earthen structure in the New World, containing an estimated 22 million cubic feet of soil and a recently discovered layer of stone brought to Cahokia from ten to fifteen miles away. On the summit, the outline of a wooden structure over a hundred feet long has been traced. Around the mounds were small wooden buildings that held most of the population of perhaps 40,000 at Cahokia's peak, which was from A.D. 1050 to 1150. Other substantial contemporary communities existed at sites such as Aztalan in Wisconsin, where a twenty-acre fortified town stood next to a whole menagerie of mounds in the shapes of animals and birds sculpted hundreds of years before by even earlier settlers.

Some fifty groups of effigy mounds are known to have existed. The most spectacular example of all is the Serpent Mound of Ohio, constructed out of clay on a natural promontory sometime around A.D. 1000. It is more than 1250 feet long, 20 feet wide, and 4 feet high. It looks like a snake holding (eating?) an egg in its mouth, while uncoiling ready to slither away, with seven coils of its body extended and another three still in the tail. A small circle of burned stones was found on the egg, the trace of fires lit for some ceremonial purpose.

Many mounds, of course, have been found to contain burials, but is that true of all mounds? There was considerable variety in the use of mounds even within a single site, as at Cahokia. Here there were platform mounds, conical mounds, and ridge-top mounds. Platform mounds are monuments such as Monks Mound, with flat tops on which there are traces of substantial wooden buildings. These have been variously interpreted as temples or the homes of rulers or religious leaders. The distinction between these need not, of course, have been so clear-cut as it would be today. The rarer conical mounds were for wealthy burials, while the small number of ridge-top mounds were communal burial places, mostly for poorer individuals.

Other mounds have been less willing to give up their secrets; the Serpent Mound has long been thought to be a snake god, and there is a serpent deity recorded in various Amerindian traditions that is a guardian of life from the earth, especially water. The site overlooks a substantial water catchment, and the fire on the egg may have been lit to act as a sign that the serpent was watching over the waters. So much is understood, but why was it thought necessary to sculpt the Serpent Mound on such a vast scale?

Was there something important in the act of mound building itself? This seems to be the case from the very beginning. Puzzled by the almost complete lack of artifacts from the Watson Brake site, and the extremely scanty evidence for activity on the site after construction finished, the excavator, Joe Saunders of Northeast Louisiana University, was forced to suggest that "maybe the answer is that building them was the purpose."

The full extent of ancient mound building in the United States will never be known, as thousands of mounds were unfortunately destroyed by the earliest European settlers, to make way for towns, villages, and farmland, despite the attempts of early antiquarians to preserve or record them. Later activity may have masked or destroyed similar monuments, of course, in other parts of the world. It has been argued that the

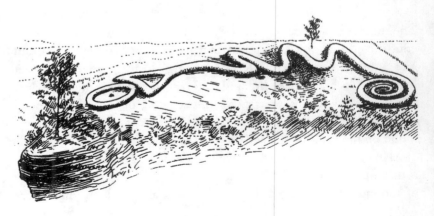

The Great Serpent Mound of Ohio, constructed around A.D. 1000, as mapped at the time of its excavation by Frederic Putnam in 1890.

discerning eye can detect, under the present countryside around Glastonbury in Somerset, the shapes of a vast complex of gigantic figures rather like the effigy mounds of North America. They are believed to represent a primitive zodiac, forming a "temple of the stars."

While the Somerset zodiac is highly controversial, the existence of giant figures in the landscape of Britain is a fact. These are the mysterious chalk-cut figures of southern England. Pictures can be "drawn" on hillsides by removing the green turf that has long covered them to reveal the white chalk below. Such carvings will soon grass over again, so for a figure to remain visible it is necessary to scour the chalk to keep it gleaming white. This means that though many chalk carvings are known to have once existed, few survive today. In any case, the survival of some chalk figures, thought to be prehistoric, shows a remarkable continuity in local customs, stretching back possibly thousands of years.

Of the chalk figures that do still exist, the best known are the White Horse at Uffington in Berkshire, the Cerne Abbas Giant of Dorset, and the Long Man of Wilmington in Sussex. The White Horse is on a hillside overlooking a major valley and can be seen only

Illustration from *The Scouring of the White Horse* by Victorian novelist Thomas Hughes, who argued that the Uffington White Horse was created to commemorate a victory by King Alfred the Great (A.D. 849–899).

obliquely from the bottom of the hill; to view its whole outline the observer actually needs to be several miles away. The White Horse is some 360 feet long and 130 feet tall, although its exact form is a matter of some debate. Nineteenth-century authorities differ in depicting it either as an emaciated beast or a round-bodied animal. In either case, the most distinctive features are the dragonlike head with its beak (two lines protruding from the mouth) and the detached legs.

The earliest record of the White Horse at Uffington comes from a monastic document written before A.D. 1100, which talks about a monk inheriting some land near "White Horse Hill." For a long time the idea held that the horse was only a couple of centuries earlier than its first mention, carved as a victory monument by King Alfred the Great, the Saxon king who liberated southern England from its Viking conquerors in the late ninth century A.D. But in 1931 archaeologist Stuart Piggott came forward with a detailed argument for assigning the White Horse to the last century B.C. or first century A.D., by using comparisons between the Uffington carving and horses depicted on coins and elaborately decorated bronze buckets of that date.

Iron Age coin from southern England of the 1st century B.C. It shows a stylized horse similar to the Uffington White Horse.

Piggott's interpretation won the day, and virtually all debate on the date of the White Horse ceased—though some archaeologists argued that the close proximity of a nearby hillfort from about 650 B.C. suggested that the horse had been cut by its Iron Age builders as a tribal symbol. Then in the 1990s new work by Oxford archaeologists David Miles and Simon Palmer brought about a dramatic breakthrough: a trench cut right into the chalk marking the outline of the horse enabled a new dating method to be tried out. This is optical dating, which determines the last time a buried deposit of soil was exposed to sunlight. The dates this produced were remarkable, ranging between 1400 and 600 B.C. So the Uffington White Horse now seems to be a relic of the Bronze or Iron Age, perhaps the earliest evidence from Britain of the development of a tribal identity.

Sir Flinders Petrie's 1920 survey of the Cerne Abbas Giant.

The Cerne Abbas Giant of Dorset would certainly make a powerful tribal deity, as he stands 180 feet high, is 40 feet wide at the waist, carries a club over 100 feet long in his right hand, and has an erect penis 25 feet long (although it is probably rather more impressive than the original, as the present version seems to have incorporated his navel). The notorious giant is certainly older than 1694, for in that year the village church's accounts record a payment "for repaireing of ye Giant 3s. 0d." Unfortunately there are grave doubts about the real antiquity of the giant, the most entertaining of English chalk figures and a constant annoyance to local prudes. While Piggott argued

The Long Man of Wilmington.

that the Giant depicts the hero Hercules and was carved during the Roman period (1st–5th centuries A.D.), there are grounds for suspicion that it is actually much later. The first to propose a date and explanation for the Cerne Abbas figure was John Hutchins in his *History and Antiquities of the County of Dorset* of 1774, who stated that the figure was said to have been cut in the mid–seventeenth century as a jest. Such a date is always possible, and a number of historians have argued that nude figures were produced in this time of political ferment, when the monarchy was overthrown and civil wars racked the land. Another major argument for a late date is the clear lack of earlier references. However, other hill figures that do appear to be genuinely old, including the White Horse, are not mentioned in early records either, so the case of the Cerne Abbas Giant is not yet closed.

The most mysterious of the great chalk carvings—and one that is definitely ancient—is the Long Man of Wilmington. Although archaeological excavations have provided important clues to the date of the figure, its purpose is far harder to judge. The Long Man (given it is a man) is the tallest of the chalk giants, at 231 feet in height; he holds in each hand a wand or staff, giving him the appearance of standing in a doorway on the steep hillside. Our first record is even later than that for the Cerne Abbas Giant—a drawing on a 1710 land survey—and no very convincing date for the Long Man was put forward until 1964, when a bronze belt buckle was found in an Anglo-Saxon burial at Finglesham, in the neighboring county of Kent, decorated with a small nude figure holding a spear in each hand.

The sixth- to seventh-century date suggested by this Saxon parallel appears to be ruled out, however, by finds made during the 1969 restoration of the figure. Excavations into the shoulder and one of the staffs produced pieces of what seem to be Roman floor tile, though the excavators were by no means certain. Even so, most archaeologists agree that a prehistoric date is likely for the Long Man, but just when cannot be determined. Far less clear is his purpose. He does not seem a likely tribal symbol or recognizable Celtic god, and nothing resembling him is known from prehistoric Britain. When, and if, optical dating can be applied to the Long Man we will be on more certain ground.

One of the most intriguing suggestions made about the Long Man was that offered early this century by antiquarian Alfred Watkins. He proposed that the figure was nothing less than a prehistoric surveyor, holding a sighting staff in each hand. Given that laying out the well-proportioned figure would have involved some careful surveying, the idea has a pleasing irony to it.

Yet Watkins's suggestion was part of a much wider theory. While the chalk figures on the English hillsides are gigantic designs in themselves, Watkins saw them as merely small elements in a much grander scheme. He believed that practically every ancient monument in Britain—from prehistoric chalk figures and stone circles to medieval churches—had been deliberately positioned on a vast network of straight lines. Watkins argued that these "ley lines," as they are known, were originally built as tracks, but that the points along them gradually acquired religious significance. Many of his followers argue that the lines in themselves had a sacred purpose. No resolution has come about, as the very existence of ley lines in themselves is still hotly disputed.

Yet Watkins's disciples can draw great strength from the fact that huge systems of mysterious straight lines have now been identified in a number of regions in the Americas. Most famous, of course, are the Nazca lines of Peru, a system of lines and giant figures inscribed on the desert floor in much the same way that the chalk figures were drawn in England. There are also the enigmatic "roads" of the Anasazi people of the U.S. Southwest. These share with Silbury Hill the initial impression of having had a normal purpose—even more clear-cut than Silbury's appearing to be a tomb—that does not prove to be the case on closer examination.

The Anasazi, an unfortunate name as it means "ancient enemies" in the Navajo language, are called "The Old Ones" by their Pueblo descendants. They flourished in the dry country of Arizona, New Mexico, Utah, and Colorado from about A.D. 850 until 1300, when many settlements were abruptly abandoned. Anasazi archaeology is best known for its remarkable Great Houses, communal multistory buildings almost like modern apartment blocks, with up to 650 rooms holding perhaps thousands of people. The heart of Anasazi civilization seems to have been the densely settled Chaco Canyon of New Mexico, containing a series of nine Great Houses built between A.D. 950 and 1130, made from superbly crafted sandstone walls with floors and roofs constructed out of over 20,000 trees, some of the timber being imported from up to eighty miles away.

An extraordinary discovery of recent years has been that Chaco Canyon also lies at the center of a network of roads, hundreds of miles of which have now been plotted from aerial photographs. The most far-flung road connection so far known connects the canyon with a settlement sixty-two miles away. Anasazi roads are straight paths 13 to 40 feet wide, mostly made by simply clearing the ground of stones, the same technique used to create the Nazca Lines of Peru, but nearer to the canyon are more substantial roads cut into the rock with masonry or mud-brick curbs.

In the 1970s, as the road network began to appear on aerial photographs, it seemed that it had served straightforward economic ends. There are many sites of Anasazi date outside Chaco Canyon that share architectural features with the Great Houses in the valley, including isolated Great Houses and Great Kivas (large subterranean religious structures), together with smaller settlements. The Chacoan phenomenon, as archaeologists have dubbed it, covers some one hundred and fifty villages spread across northern New Mexico and Arizona Given these known connections, archaeologists naturally assumed that the road system served to integrate the scattered communities. Timber would be brought into Chaco Canyon along with exotic goods such as turquoise from central New Mexico and macaw feathers from Mexico. In times of drought, food could flow out from the prime agricultural land within Chaco Canyon to relieve isolated communities.

However, as the road network was plotted further, this obvious economic explanation became more difficult to sustain. Not only do the roads run dead straight, refusing to follow the bottoms or sides of valleys or skirt around intervening hills, they do not even follow the most direct route between settlements. Then there are neighboring sections of road that run parallel to each other; in the case of the Great North Road, which runs almost due north from the edge of Chaco Canyon, there are two to four parallel roadways. This can hardly reflect an economic decision based on the volume of traffic. Moreover, when the roads enter the canyon they often turn into stairways, cut into the cliff faces using stone hammers and an awful lot of sweat. At the steepest sections they even had to construct scaffolds to clamber up virtually sheer faces. Although these stairways do lead to Great Houses, they are so difficult to climb that anyone carrying much of a load would have run a real risk of plummeting into the bottom of the canyon if they put a foot wrong. Finally, some of the roads appear to end in the middle of nowhere rather than at a settlement of any kind. Although some stretches of road may have been eroded or washed away, these lonely terminuses occur so often that they cannot simply be explained away.

Producing an alternative interpretation has largely been the work of the Solstice Project, based in Washington. Project workers have argued that a far more productive way to understand the Chacoan roads is as religious constructions. As well as the nonfunctional features of the roads, they point to the location alongside several of the roads of small buildings that closely resemble the shrines of historical Pueblo peoples. The idea of a straight road running to the north is central to Pueblo religion, in which spirits move along it, to and from our world, with the word *road* being translated as "channel for the life's breath." This is a clear indication that the Great North Road, at least, had a symbolic meaning above the everyday.

But can this religious interpretation make sense of the wider phenomenon of Anasazi road building? Stephen Lekson of the University of Colorado certainly believes that it can. He has recently argued that the roads are the visible aspect of a remarkable system of connections that tied the Anasazi world together. Extending the line of the Great North Road running from Chaco Canyon would, he suggests, eventually lead to Aztec Ruins, a major concentration of Great Houses some fifty-five miles to the north. Although this extension cannot be traced at present, it is possible that the road may eventually be discovered to have joined the two centers. More incredible is Lekson's suggestion that, if the Great North Road had a long-distance companion running due south, it would eventually reach Casas Grande 390 miles away in Mexico. Casas Grande is a huge site showing a remarkable mixture of Mexican and Anasazi architectural traits, combining small mounds like central Mexican pyramids with five-story mud-brick houses very similar to those of Chaco Canyon.

Lekson's "Great South Road" can so far be traced only some twenty miles before it forks, but he is not deterred and instead stresses the idea of an important north-south alignment of power. In any case, these three great centers of power at Chaco Canyon, Aztec Ruins, and Casas Grande were not at their height together, for Aztec Ruins came to prominence only shortly before Chaco Canyon was deserted, while Casas Grande arose about A.D. 1250, just before Aztec Ruins, along with the rest of the Anasazi area, was suddenly abandoned. So a road connecting them would serve no practical purpose, but instead would be a kind of "road through time" making a physical connection between these three centers otherwise presumably linked by powerful traditions.

Proponents of ley lines in prehistoric Britain, which are believed to cut straight across the landscape, have naturally seen the Anasazi roads as a parallel development. However, the Great North Road is not quite as straight as Lekson and others have sometimes implied. Although it does run due north from Chaco Canyon for over thirty miles to the Great House at Twin Angels Pueblo, the road then turns slightly to the northwest to head toward Salmon Ruin. Aztec Ruins lies due north of there. So the Anasazi were not entirely slavish in following a north-south alignment; perhaps it was just as important to them to join up major sites. Anasazi roads are not therefore quite so similar to claimed ley lines. There is another crucial difference between the Chacoan North-South alignment and ley lines: the Anasazi example connects a group of similar sites built by the same cultural group within a period of just two hundred years, while the vast majority of claimed ley lines link sites of quite different kinds spread over thousands of years.

Whether the Anasazi roads form a parallel to European ley lines or not, we are still left with the question of *why* straight lines generally appear to have played such an important role in the siting of ancient monuments. In the case of the Nazca lines it has often been suggested that they were constructed to aim at the rising and setting points of important stars. Yet recent work at Nazca has come up with a very different interpretation, involving the rituals of shamans or tribal "witch doctors." Shamans claim to take magical journeys (often in

animal or bird form) in which their spirits fly across the earth to remote locations. Such journeys have been linked to both the lines in
the Nazca desert and the supposed ley lines of Britain, though it remains a moot point as to how straight a shaman's spiritual "flight
path" may or may not be.

The interest in shamanic practices recently taken by ley hunters in
shamanic beliefs has evolved quite naturally from their earlier research
into other possibilities that touch on the paranormal. Many writers on
ley lines have argued that ancient peoples had senses far more highly
tuned than our own and that they were aware of mysterious forces in
the Earth itself that we are only beginning to discover. Watkins himself shied away from this topic, but in the work of later writers the
subject of ley lines became inextricably intertwined with the quest for
hidden "earth energies."

Leading the way were a number of British dowsers, individuals
who claim, with the aid of divining rods and other instruments, to be
able to detect the location of underground water (see **Introduction
to Archaeology and the Supernatural**). With the explosion of
New Age research in the 1960s, dowsers went far beyond their normal brief and many became dedicated ley hunters. At Stonehenge,
Avebury, and all the other great megalithic sites of Britain, dowsers
were reporting strange effects. They could detect the confluence of
underground springs beneath these monuments, creating eddies of
some intangible force, possibly electromagnetic in origin. Dowsing is
certainly an ancient art (though how old nobody knows), so dowsers
followed up with the suggestion that their predecessors in prehistoric
times were aware of the same energies. Many dowsers also claimed to
be able to trace such energies from one site to another, and Watkins's
idea of the "old straight track" was reborn in a 1960s mold in the
concept of lines of mysterious power. The ancients, it was argued,
had deliberately built their great monuments of stone and earth over
the confluence points of this energy, where it could be most easily
harnessed—for purposes unknown. While this kind of research was
largely restricted to Britain, had teams of dowsers reached Nazca,
Ohio, or the Anazasi lands, they would doubtless have come up with
similar conclusions.

The whole subject of earth energies remained very vague until
some researchers decided to apply practical tests. In the mid-1970s,
Francis Hitching, an author interested in prehistoric mysteries, set up
an experiment to test the claims made about megalithic monuments
by Bill Lewis, a Welsh farmer rated as one of the best dowsers in

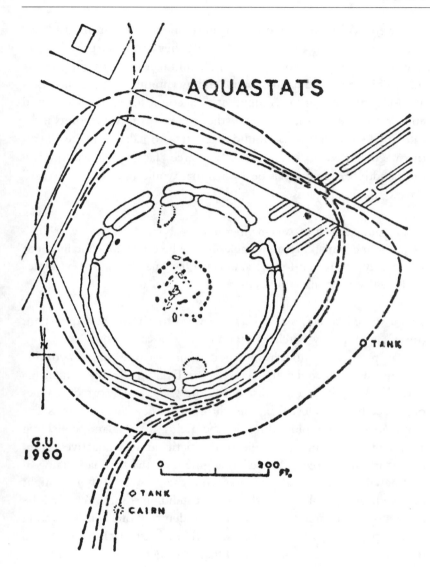

AQUASTATS

G.U.
1960

0 ——— 200 FT.

0 TANK

0 TANK
CAIRN

Spiraling "energy lines" as detected underneath Stonehenge by dowser Guy Underwood.

Britain. Lewis said that he could detect an energy that seemed to run in a spiral path up and down standing stones. Given the evident fascination of prehistoric people with the spiral pattern, the idea could apparently tie together a number of loose ends at once. Hitching contacted John Taylor, Professor of Mathematics at Kings College, London, who at the time was intrigued by the possible relationship between apparently paranormal abilities (such as spoon bending) and electromagnetic forces.

Taylor oversaw the project and supplied an open-minded physicist, Dr. Eduardo Balanovski, equipped with a portable magnetometer, who went with Hitching to investigate a lone standing stone at Llang-ynidr in Wales near Lewis's home. What they found surprised them. Lewis indicated with chalk where he could feel—as a tingling sensation in his fingers—a band of spiral energy running up the stone; Balanovski, after setting his equipment to account for local background energy, then tested the surface of the stone. At the very points indicated by Lewis, Balanovski found magnetic anomalies. The needle on the magnetometer's dial shot up to a degree "far greater than the few thousandths or hundredths of a gauss that would have been normal." Balanovski was impressed:

> The point is that a water-diviner told us about it, and we went there and found something measurable. It may be the stone contains, geologically, the reason for the anomaly. Or it may be caused by something that we don't yet understand.

Taylor joined Balanovski shortly afterward to repeat the experiment (this time filmed by Hitching), with much the same results.

This promising, though unorthodox, line of research was continued in the 1980s under the aegis of the Dragon Project, which involved a group of interested scientists, dowsers, and assorted pyschics organized by Paul Devereux, the editor of the *Ley Hunter*. They spent many seasons tramping through the fields of England collecting anomalous readings—both electromagnetic and radioactive—from prehistoric monuments, as well as augmenting the familiar catalog of traditional and anecdotal evidence about the "power" (often thought to have healing qualities) of the ancient standing stones. Yet, alas, the Dragon Project came to naught. The golden rule of scientific testing is the repeatability of experiments. Partly owing to lack of funds and strict academic organization, the Dragon Project succeeded in coming up with what can only be described as scrappy results. Potentially interesting readings were not replicated using different equipment or monitors. Controls, in terms of background readings of radioactivity and magnetism, were lax or not properly recorded, and it is fair to say that the book produced by Devereux in 1990 *(Places of Power)* does not contain a single instance that would convince a skeptic. Nothing was produced that bettered the original Hitching-Taylor experiments at Llangynidr, and even those were not followed up rigorously. All Devereux had to report was a comment from Professor Taylor that further tests on the Llangynidr stone had "proved a little contradictory."

Some of the curious results obtained from megaliths could be significant—though for very different reasons from those imagined by "earth mysteries" enthusiasts. Many of the stones selected by prehistoric builders may well have strange properties. Granite with heavy inclusions of quartz was often chosen as a building material, probably because of the shine and shades of color—from white to pink—that quartz crystals can lend to otherwise dull stone. Quartz also has extraordinary piezo-electric properties. (Electric cigarette lighters work by stressing a quartz so that it shoots out a stream of electrons.) So it is perhaps not so surprising that "anomalous" electromagnetic readings can be obtained from some ancient standing stones. Whether ancient people appreciated the electrical properties of quartz is a different matter entirely.

With the lack of serious testing and publication, enthusiasm for the existence of anomalous energies at prehistoric sites has quietly bottomed out over the last decade. Along with it has gone the desire to join up groups of ancient monuments with lines of mysterious energies. By 1990 even dowser Tom Graves, who twenty years earlier had been one of the main proponents of an earth energies/ley lines connection, was beginning to carefully distance himself from the subject. Dowsing, unfortunately, is an intuitive skill that doesn't lend itself well to scientific testing or repeatability (see **Introduction** to **Archaeology and the Supernatural**). Of the numerous diagrams drawn by dowsers of the underground streams to be found underneath Stonehenge and other monuments, no two versions agree.

As a motive to explain the ancient desire to resculpt and pattern the landscape, the idea of mysterious earth energies fails to convince—and is really only using one unknown to explain another.

But if the driving force was not something in the Earth, could it have been something above it? Were the ancients attempting to mirror the heavens on Earth by building huge effigies or models of the stars and constellations? (See **The Orion Mystery** in **Watching the Skies.**) This is what proponents of the Somerset Zodiac would argue, while the Nazca lines have often been interpreted as a gigantic picture of the heavens. These and similar theories remain highly controversial, to say the least, yet the possibility that the ancients were following such grand schemes is certainly worth examining. So many of their monuments have been destroyed—or are no longer visible—that there may well have been patterns in their distribution now hard to discern. Given that we still know so little about motives of the ancient builders of earthworks and megaliths, there is every reason to continue the search, even if some of the avenues explored may seem rather surprising.

THE GLASTONBURY SPIRAL

Spiral labyrinth on rock carving near Tintagel, Cornwall.

Coin of classical period from the Greek island of Crete. Struck at Knossos, the coin bears the abbreviation "KNO" in Greek letters.

In 1944, an Irish businessman named Geoffrey Russell had a dream of such vividness that, when he awoke, he immediately committed to paper the image still drifting in front of his eyes. It was a spiral shape formed from a single line wrapped into seven coils. Somewhat bemused, he filed the drawing and thought little more about it.

Eighteen years later he was browsing through *Country Life* magazine when he saw a photograph of a rock carving that had recently been discovered near Tintagel, a famous Arthurian site in Cornwall (see **King Arthur** in **Legendary History**). Much to his amazement, he recognized in the Tintagel carving the image from his dream—what he had drawn was, in fact, the archetypal form of the ancient maze or labyrinth. He soon found the same shape again, on a coin from classical Crete, where legend said that the Minotaur had once lived in a gigantic labyrinth (see **Theseus and the Minotaur** in **Legendary History**).

After this strange experience, a search for the enigmatic labyrinth pattern and its meaning became Russell's personal quest. On a trip to Glastonbury in 1966 he claimed to have found another example, which, if it is genuine, would be one of the most spectacular archaeological discoveries ever made.

The town of Glastonbury, in the county of Somerset in western England, must have more strange legends—and bizarre New Age theories—attached to it than any other site in Britain (see **The Somerset Zodiac** in this chapter, **King Arthur's Grave** in **Hoax?** and **The Company of Avalon** in **Archaeology and the Supernatural**). In the Middle Ages it attracted so many pilgrims that it was hailed as "a second Rome." In modern times it has attracted mystics like a magnet, among them occultist Dion Fortune (1891–1946), who in the 1920s settled in Glastonbury in a house on the lower slopes of the Tor, the focal point of the Glastonbury legends. The Tor is an imposing hill, formed from an outcrop of rock some 500 feet high, and visible up to twenty-five miles away. The remains of a medieval chapel, dedicated to Saint Michael, stand on the top, but the most striking feature of the Tor is its very shape. Fortune described it in 1934:

> Seen from a distance, the Tor is a perfect pyramid; but as we draw nearer . . . we see that it is shaped like a couchant lion bearing a tower

on its crest. . . . Its pyramidal form, set in the center of a great plain, is almost too good to be true—too appropriate to be the unaided work of Nature. Viewed from near at hand, a terraced track can clearly be seen winding in three tiers round the core of the Tor, and this is indisputably the work of man.

A Sevenfold Path

At the time Fortune made this inspired claim, it was usually assumed that the terraces of the Tor were either completely natural or that they had been shaped by medieval farming. When Geoffrey Russell arrived at Glastonbury he conceived a very different picture, going much further than Fortune in his interpretation. It is odd that she had perceived only three "tiers" on the Tor—several others are clearly visible from most angles. Russell saw something much more complex. In fact, he recognized at Glastonbury the same seven-coiled spiral shape that had haunted him for so many years. His theory was that the whole Tor had been sculpted in prehistoric times into an enormous three-dimensional maze.

Russell's suggestion was eagerly adopted by Glastonbury enthusiasts and has been incorporated into its modern folklore. Yet was Russell's "discovery" real or merely a will-o'-the-wisp like some of the other claims made about the Glastonbury terrain (see **The Somerset Zodiac** in this chapter)?

Russell pursued the testing of his theory vigorously. After making

The eastern end of Glastonbury Tor. The tower of the ruined St. Michael's church stands on the top.

a series of sand models of the Tor to illustrate its relationship to the classic labyrinth pattern, he commissioned an aerial photographic survey that allowed the contours of the Tor to be plotted in detail. The research seemed to confirm his original hunch that it had a spiral shape.

The case was later taken up by Geoffrey Ashe, the grand old man of Arthurian studies (see **King Arthur** in **Legendary History**), who, like so many other writers, was drawn by the magic of Glastonbury to set up home there. Ashe bought the house where Dion Fortune once lived and, after years of strolling around the Tor, he probably knows its terrain better than anyone. Intrigued by the spiral-maze theory, Ashe noted that Russell "had never attempted to prove his maze by the

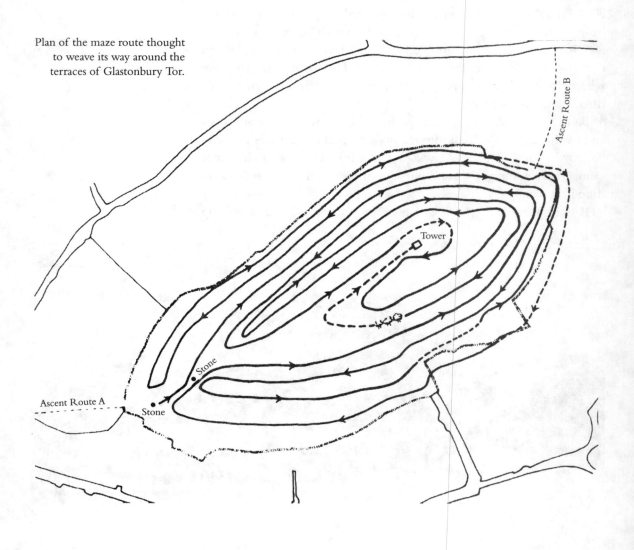

Plan of the maze route thought to weave its way around the terraces of Glastonbury Tor.

most elementary method of all," the simple practical test of "threading" or walking the supposed spiral pathway. Ashe himself took on the task in the summer of 1979; succeeding in working out a spiral route, Ashe published his findings the same year.

The path he traced begins at the lowest (southwestern) end of the Tor, the natural place to ascend. As one climbs up, the route is marked by a large stone, argued by Ashe to be a deliberate marker, showing the "entrance." From there the route progresses inward and outward in a series of looping curves that eventually take one to the center of the labyrinth—the peak of the Tor. One or two parts of the route are a little hazy, but, in Ashe's defense, these are at points where erosion or later activity may have masked it. The seven-coiled spiral shape suggested by Russell, and plotted in detail by Ashe, is perfectly feasible.

The possibility that the Tor has been sculpted into an enormous labyrinth raises momentous questions. As there is no record of such a vast undertaking in historical times, Russell and Ashe assume that the Glastonbury labyrinth was a prehistoric construction. The effort and manpower needed to build it would have been colossal, possibly rivaling that needed for the construction of the great prehistoric monuments such as Stonehenge. (See **Stonehenge** in **Architectural Wonders**.)

Overall, it is fair to say that Ashe has proved his point—that the terracing around the Tor *does* work as a seven-spiraled labyrinth. Ashe himself admits that this falls short of proof that the entire Tor *was* deliberately sculpted in this way—only archaeology can prove or disprove that point.

Unfortunately excavation work here has been limited, partly owing to the difficult conditions on the Tor. When Philip Rahtz of Birmingham University investigated the exposed peak of the Tor in the 1960s (funded partly by a trust that Russell founded), the work was "arduous." After carrying equipment up and down the steep sides every day, the team faced whipping winds on bad days, while on fine days "it was like an oven." Finds from Roman, Dark Age, and medieval times were made, all of great interest (see **King Arthur** in **Legendary History**). Activity from earlier periods was harder to detect. Medieval building work and heavy erosion, aggravated by the occasional earthquake, would have removed most traces of earlier activity. Still, Rahtz and his team were able to show that the Tor was known and visited during the Stone Age. Among the earliest finds were flints from the Palaeolithic and Neolithic, dating to c. 10,000–2000 B.C., and a Neolithic polished axe made of greenish stone.

Rahtz did not have the time or resources for the much broader undertaking needed to check Russell's idea—excavating the terraces themselves—tempted though he may have been. Theories like Russell's are often dismissed by archaeologists with a wave of the hand. Not so in the case of the Glastonbury spiral. Basing his judgment on the surface features, Rahtz takes the theory quite seriously. If Russell was right, Rahtz believes that the spiral could only have been built in Neolithic or Bronze Age times (the fourth to second millennia B.C.). The engineering skills of that time are more than evident from the great earth-moving operation required to construct the artificial mound at Silbury Hill (see **Introduction** to this chapter). Rahtz also thinks that Russell's theory might help explain Glastonbury's role as a major spiritual center: "The maze would have been a major cultural and religious focus for the area, initiating the fame of Glastonbury in later times."

The arguments in favor of the labyrinth theory are certainly attractive, and those against it unconvincing. As Geoffrey Ashe puts it, the "main opposition . . . does not come from any counter-argument but from the dogma that the whole system has an obvious commonsense explanation." Yet, Ashe stresses, depending on whom you speak to, that "obvious explanation" varies considerably. Geologists have argued that the terraces formed through erosion. On the other hand, as Ronald Hutton, Professor of History at Bristol University, notes, "To archaeologists, the terraces upon the hill look like perfectly normal medieval or Iron Age hillside field systems." But both opinions cannot be correct. Which, if either, is?

The erosion idea suggested by geologists is plausible, but only up to a point. The Tor is composed of four different layers of rock, beginning with the cap of sandstone that forms the peak. One can imagine the layers weathering in such a way that "steps" might form between them. But no one has actually produced a model of how this could have come about, or result in the intricate sevenfold pathway that Russell and Ashe have discovered.

With no satisfactory geological model, Rahtz and others have given greater weight to theories of a man-made origin for the terracing. Of the possible human activities responsible, defensive works can be immediately ruled out, as the terraces look nothing like the huge earthworks that were thrown up around Iron Age (Celtic) forts. Instead, the favored explanation, as adopted by the Tor's custodians, the National Trust, is that the terraces were made for farming—in the same way that one sees hillsides leveled into steps in France and Germany for growing grapes, or in the Philippines for cultivating rice.

From prehistoric times onward, farmers in England have sculpted south-facing slopes along the sides of valleys into long, narrow "strip" fields.

Before it was drained in the eighteenth and nineteenth centuries (see **The Somerset Zodiac** in this chapter), the Glastonbury area was largely marshland, so there would have been a need to maximize the value of every piece of possible agricultural land. In that case, perhaps the terraces were built by medieval monks, or even pre-Roman farmers. The idea sounds feasible at first. The ancient farmers of Britain often found it easier to work the lighter, well-drained soils of hillsides rather than the heavy soils of the lowlands. Indeed, a map of 1844 marks some of the lower terraces on the southern and eastern flanks of the hill as "Tor Linches," a linch or lynchet being a terrace of land wide enough to plow. (Some linches were deliberately fashioned; others came about as the land flattened into platforms through being worked.) As it is clear that this part of the terracing was, at least in the nineteenth century, used as agricultural land, it has been argued that the entire system was originally created for this purpose.

Yet of all the terracing systems known from prehistoric, ancient, and medieval Britain, there seems to be nothing precisely comparable to Glastonbury Tor. (Of course, isolated hills like the Tor are rare in themselves.) While the agricultural theory is confidently cited as "the obvious" archaeological explanation, no one has examined the evidence critically. The theory is merely assumed, and is not without problems.

Many English hillsides have strips of linches, but none have them going all the way around, or in such an exposed situation. Most known linches, for obvious reasons, are horizontal. By contrast, the terraces on the Tor are far from level, at points forming steep slopes that would hardly have been suitable for plowing—rainfall would have swept plowed soil down them helter-skelter. Alternatively, it has been suggested that the terraces were used by medieval monks to cultivate grapevines, which need hoeing rather than deep plowing. Yet it is hard to imagine how grapes could have been grown on the north-facing slopes. For any kind of cultivation, the top and upper terraces on the Tor seem too exposed to the winds and extremes of temperature. As anyone climbing the Tor will realize, seedlings planted on the upper terraces would be whisked away by the wind and rain in a matter of days, if not hours. When Rahtz and his team were excavating, the wind threw the soil back in their faces as soon as they dug it. Perhaps it was this practical realization that led Rahtz to the conclusion that Russell's spiral theory was well worth consideration.

So the agricultural explanation is not as secure as some might believe. Without backing from archaeological evidence it cannot be used to brush aside Russell's maze theory, especially as it seems to face problems itself—at the very least, if the terrace system of Glastonbury Tor *was* built for farming, it is unique, even anomalous. Indeed, the National Trust, while it officially prefers the agricultural theory, is, like the excavator Rahtz, respectful of Russell's idea. The trust has to make occasional repairs to the sides of the Tor, and in 1980 its Tor Committee resolved that "nothing should be done which would interfere with the maze features."

Russell's theory remains as viable as the agricultural one, and some, like Ashe, would argue that it is better. Yet if the Tor really was sculpted as a prehistoric religious center, what was it for?

Spiral Castle

Visitors to Glastonbury today are immediately struck by the shape of the Tor. If the labyrinth theory is correct, it would have been a much more imposing sight in ancient times—an island spiraling up from the mists of the surrounding waters like a spectral castle. Surely if the Tor were once a labyrinthine temple of some kind it would have left some mark on local myths and traditions?

A possible lead comes from a sixteenth-century manuscript recording the *Life of Saint Collen*, agreed by historians to be a genuine copy of an early medieval text. Saint Collen was a Welsh saint of the seventh century A.D. After retiring as abbot of Glastonbury, he lived as a hermit near the foot of the Tor, where he once overheard two peasants talking about the castle of Gwyn son of Nudd that was concealed within it. Gwyn was the king of the fairies and the ruler of Annwm, the Celtic underworld. Collen dismissed such talk as superstitious nonsense, but that night a spectral messenger called at his hermitage and invited him to the castle. The invitation was repeated night after night, and eventually Collen accepted, having armed himself with a bottle of holy water. Mounting the Tor, he was conducted through a secret entrance to the underworld and found himself in Gwyn's shining castle, where finely dressed fairies were feasting and drinking to music. Saint Collen refused the food offered him, which would have been deadly to eat, and responded to Gwyn's blandishments by hurling holy water all around. The castle disappeared, fairies and all, and Collen was left standing on the lonely Tor.

Gwyn, whose name means "the White One," is well known from Welsh folklore and was almost certainly a pre-Christian Celtic deity

An English "fairy hill" with a door to the underworld. Glastonbury Tor seems to have been conceived in this way, at least in early Welsh tradition.

like his father "Nudd," or Nodens, known to have been worshiped in southwest Britain in Roman times. The story of Gwyn's fairy castle, hidden within the Tor, provides an intriguing link with the spiral theory. Clues from a number of different cultures suggest that the labyrinth shape was widely used in ancient times as an icon of the underworld, with its paths spiraling in and out to represent death and rebirth. The medieval belief that there was an entrance to Annwm, the Celtic underworld, at the top of the Tor, certainly fits with the labyrinth theory.

The story of Saint Collen ties in with another medieval legend. Russell argued that the Glastonbury spiral is specifically mentioned in a cryptic medieval Welsh poem called *The Spoils of Annwm*. Dating from the tenth century A.D., it contains some of the earliest known verses about King Arthur, presented here as trying to steal the treasures of the underworld with the aid of a shipload of warriors. Each refrain mentions the name of an otherworldly castle that was impossible to assault. The castle names—which may all be variants for the same place, an entrance to Annwm—are indeed suggestive of Glastonbury. Caer Pedryvan, described as "forever revolving," means the "four-cornered" castle—Glastonbury Tor is roughly lozenge-shaped. Caer Wydyr means the castle of "glass," a word that the Welsh, rightly or wrongly, associated with the name of Glastonbury. Caer Veddwit, the castle of "carousal," recalls the feasting hall of Gwyn supposed to be hidden in the Tor. Caer Sidi, which means the "turning" or "spiral" castle, was taken by Russell to be a specific reference to the Glastonbury labyrinth. (The alternative reading, "Caer Siddi," would mean the "fairy castle.") The magic number 7 also occurs repeatedly in the poem, as the number of Arthur's men who survived the attack on each castle.

The image of an entrance to the underworld, found through a spiral castle surrounded by water and connected with the number 7, is common to both the castles in the poem and Glastonbury Tor. Another medieval legend, which claims that King Arthur laid siege to Glastonbury, seems to confirm the link. His wife Guinevere had been abducted by one Melwas, whose stronghold was the Tor (see **King Arthur** in **Legendary History**). Melwas is otherwise known as another name for the ruler of the underworld, a version of Gwyn himself.

So the description of the "spiral castle" in *The Spoils of Annwm* could well fit Glastonbury. Yet was the Caer Sidi of legend really inspired by Glastonbury Tor? Other aspects of the poem fit less well, such as references to a sea surrounding the magical castle—although the marshes and lakes surrounding Glastonbury could have been seen as an inland sea. Welsh traditions finger other, more obvious islands as candidates for the otherworld castles mentioned in the *Spoils*, including the Isle of Wight (which is definitely "four-cornered") and the tiny island of Lundy off the coast of Wales.

Overall, it seems unlikely that Glastonbury inspired *all* the imagery of the Celtic underworld contained in the *Spoils*. More likely the Celts believed that there were several entrances to Annwm, and that Glastonbury Tor was one of them, albeit an important one. So was Glastonbury Tor sculpted into a physical representation of a spiral-shaped entrance to the underworld, where worshipers presumably came to be introduced to the mysteries of death and rebirth? We know that the spiral, as a symbol of afterlife, was used in the British Isles long before Celtic times—in fact, the earliest examples go back to the Neolithic. For example, the tomb of Newgrange in Ireland, built around 3500 B.C. (see **Megalithic Astronomers** in **Watching the Skies**), is decorated with dozens of spiral motifs. If Glastonbury Tor was really made into a spiral labyrinth in the third or second millennium B.C., the imagery later associated with it by the Celts could open a new window on the religion of prehistoric Britain.

A final text that might throw some light on the mystery of the Tor

Spiral carvings from the spectacular Neolithic tomb at Newgrange in Ireland.

was offered by Geoffrey Ashe. It is a passage in the writings of the Greek encyclopedist Diodorus (1st century B.C.), which appears to contain a startling description of some of the religious monuments of ancient Britain. Taking his evidence from the geographer Hecataeus, who lived in the fourth century B.C., Diodorus described the land of the Hyperboreans, whose name means "those who live beyond the North Wind." They lived on an island in the sea beyond the land of the Celts (i.e., Gaul, or France) that was bigger than Sicily. Britain is clearly the subject:

> Apollo is honoured among them above all other gods. . . . And there is also on the island both a magnificent precinct of Apollo and a notable temple which is adorned with many votive offerings and is spherical in shape. Furthermore, a city is there which is sacred to this god, and the majority of its inhabitants are players on the cithara [an ancient lute or guitar]; and they continually play on this instrument in the temple and sing hymns of praise to the god, glorifying his deeds.

The reference to a "spherical" temple has naturally inspired most historians to see here a reference to Stonehenge. Apollo was a Greek god of the Sun, and the solar associations of Stonehenge—out of all the proposed astronomical alignments—are unquestioned (see **Stonehenge** in **Architectural Wonders**). Geoffrey Ashe used to accept this interpretation, until he pondered more closely on the words. Strictly speaking, Stonehenge is circular, not spherical. Yet the precise meaning of the Greek word used by Diodorus is "globular, ball-shaped." It is hard to imagine any temple actually being spherical in shape, so as it stands the text sounds slightly absurd. So Ashe wondered whether a copyist's error in the transmission of the Greek manuscript may have misled us. The Greek for "spherical" is *sphairoeidês*. The very similar Greek word *speiroeidês* means "coiled" or "spiral-shaped." (The Greek consonants *phi* and *pi* were very close in their sound.)

So was Diodorus actually referring to a famous *spiral* temple in Britain? If that were the case, the temple referred to could only be Glastonbury. (The "magnificent precinct" of Apollo might then be Avebury, a huge megalithic complex some forty miles away.) Unfortunately, unless we find an earlier manuscript of Diodorus, or the original of his source Hecataeus, this tantalizing possibility can only be added to the list of "maybes" in the ever-growing Glastonbury mystery.

A Sun Temple?

With the suggestion that Glastonbury Tor was once a temple of the Sun god, famous throughout the ancient world for its extraordinary spiral shape—or indeed that it was any kind of temple at all—we have entered the realms of speculation upon speculation.

Yet there is some further evidence that may help cut through the theorizing. Glastonbury Tor has a peculiar geographical characteristic: its lozenge shape gives it an orientation running roughly southwest to northeast, with an axis passing through the crest of the Tor where the chapel to Saint Michael was built. The line takes in the large stone that Ashe sees as the marker for the entrance to the Tor labyrinth. What is noteworthy is that this axis is at 63 degrees to the east of North, the direction of the sunrise on the first of May. (Now on May 6, because of the change from the Julian to Gregorian calendars.) In later Celtic cultures, from the Middle Ages to modern times, May Day, or Beltane, was the most important festival of the year, respected as marking the rebirth of the Sun after winter and the advent of summer.

That is not all. If one extends the axis of the Tor as an imaginary line in both directions, it crosses other significant points. Ten miles away in a southwesterly direction is Burrowbridge Mump, an unusual conical hill that looks like a miniature version of Glastonbury Tor. It lies precisely on the Tor axis—viewed from Burrowbridge Mump, the

Glastonbury Tor as seen from the north.

Sun rises over Glastonbury Tor on May Day morning. It may be coincidence, but if one continues the line in a northeasterly direction it cuts through the southern entrance of the huge stone circle of Avebury, center of the largest complex of prehistoric structures in the whole of the British Isles. Ley line enthusiasts have extended the line even farther in both directions, taking in a huge swath of prehistoric and sacred sites running right across southern Britain (see **Ley Lines** in this chapter).

Wider speculation aside, it is enough to note the simple fact that three entirely natural features—the top of Burrowbridge Mump, the axis running through the Tor, and the direction of the May Day sunrise—fall perfectly in line. Skeptics have generally failed to comment on the question of the May Day sunrise at Glastonbury, concentrating their fire on the weaknesses of the suggested ley line. Yet the Glastonbury problem is different. A frequent criticism of ley lines is that they do not include enough points showing hard evidence of prehistoric activity. With the May Day sunrise at Glastonbury this question does not arise. It is the natural shape of the Tor itself that forms the alignment. With the addition of Burrowbridge Mump, it is hard to believe that the prehistoric Britons, given their keen interest in the heavens, and particularly the behavior of the Sun (see **Megalithic Astronomers** in **Watching the Skies**), would have missed such a striking natural coincidence.

Here Celtic myth and folklore come into play again, offering an explanation of the apparently incongruous link between the Tor as a model of the underworld and the part it might have played in ancient Sun worship. Surviving May Day festivals in the Celtic fringe of the British Isles show that a ritual enacting the conquest of the Winter Sun by the Summer Sun was at the heart of the celebrations, with the May Queen as prize. A mock combat was staged between armies supporting Winter and Summer and, after a great deal of horseplay, Summer would gain mastery. The Summer captain would then nominate a May King, who "marries" the May Queen and parades with her through the village. The same May Day ritual can be seen in another story about the fairy king Gwyn. Gwythyr, son of Greidawl, was betrothed to the maiden Creiddylad (who appears as Cordelia in Shakespeare's *King Lear*), but before he could marry her Gwyn came and carried her away by force. Gwythyr raised an army and made war on Gwyn, but King Arthur intervened and forced a peace on them, with these terms:

> The maiden should remain in her father's house, without advantage to either of them, and that Gwyn son of Nudd and Gwythyr the son of Greidawl should fight for her every first of May, from thenceforth until the day of doom, and that whichever of them should be conqueror should have the maiden.

It is easy to recognize this never-ending combat as a parallel version of the war between King Arthur and King Melwas. In the Welsh legend Melwas abducts Guinevere, Arthur's wife, and takes her to his stronghold on Glastonbury Tor. Arthur searches for her for a year, then raises an army and besieges Melwas, until the abbot of Glastonbury intercedes and makes peace between the two kings. The story became a favorite of medieval romancers, who stressed that Queen Guinevere was abducted by the evil Sir Mellygaunce (clearly Melwas) when she was out "maying," collecting spring flowers on May Day.

Gwyn and Melwas were both located at Glastonbury. At the very least these pieces of medieval folklore show that the connection between the May Day sunrise and Glastonbury was not first discovered by modern ley line hunters. Given the importance of May Day in the Celtic calendar, the associations may be very ancient indeed. Glastonbury could once have been the focal point for a spring festival, where a struggle between the Winter and Summer Suns over a May Queen was believed to take place.

These traditions could tie together a number of strands, from the possible labyrinth to the alignment of the Tor toward the May Day sunrise. If Glastonbury were an ancient cult with an annual ceremony, the spiral terracing theory takes on new strength. The labyrinth may have been built as the symbolic domain of the old Sun (Gwyn or Melwas), seen as ruler of the underworld.

The intriguing possibilities offered by Glastonbury Tor remain dotted with large question marks; only archaeological evidence, excavated from the terraces, can truly decide the case. Yet surprising as it may seem, the idea that the Tor was deliberately resculpted as a ritual center is not out of step with current archaeological thinking about the Neolithic and early Bronze Age in Britain. Over the last few decades archaeologists have come to appreciate how large areas were gradually organized into "ritual landscapes" of interrelated monuments. There were not only circles of gigantic stones but also huge burial mounds and linear ditches, some several miles long (see **Ley Lines** in this chapter). Avebury, the largest stone ring in Britain, was built in an area crowded with great earthworks, one of which, the huge enclosure of Windmill Hill, is three-quarters of a mile round— some 13,000 tons of chalk were removed to dig the ditch that surrounds it. As if this spectacular complex, begun about 3500 B.C., were not enough, a mile away from the stone circle the enormous chalk and earth mound of Silbury Hill was erected. (See **Introduction** to this chapter). Things were being done on a decidedly grand scale.

The creation of a labyrinth on Glastonbury Tor, while unique, would have been well in keeping with what we know of the aspirations of these remarkable builders. It also seems unlikely that they would have passed up a chance of incorporating such a distinctive feature as Glastonbury Tor into their system. Though there is now little trace of prehistoric activity on the Tor, evidence of the engineering skills of Neolithic and Bronze Age settlers abounds in the Glastonbury region. Attracted by the supply of fish and game, prehistoric pioneers created a network of wooden trackways over the surrounding marshes. The "Abbott's Way," built between two islands near Glastonbury about 2500 B.C., was made from over ten thousand trees split into planks, then placed on piles of brush and wickerwork held in place with long pegs driven into the marsh. The Sweet Track was constructed even earlier, in precisely 3807 B.C. according to tree-ring dating, making it the oldest trackway in the world. In the Somerset marshes it would have been impossible to build earthworks or raise stone monuments as a religious center. So did the attractive site of Glastonbury Tor, with its natural alignment to an important point in the calendar, fulfill that role?

Here, however, Glastonbury raises yet another question. If the Tor really was selected as a ritual site because of its alignment with the May Day sunrise, prehistorians will have to tackle the problem of its relationship with Avebury. The line of the May Day sunrise, as observed from Glastonbury, passes through Avebury. Does this mean that Avebury was positioned where it is because of the Tor, and that the Tor is even older than Avebury as a prehistoric religious site? It would imply that Glastonbury was the very heart of religious worship in the British Isles.

A well-aimed archaeological trench or two, dug into the terraces, it is hoped will one day be enough to test Geoffrey Russell's inspiration about Glastonbury Tor and confirm or refute the idea that it is the hidden key to the ritual landscape of prehistoric Britain.

THE SOMERSET ZODIAC

Imagine an entire landscape, from its hills to its riverbeds, being sculpted into gigantic figures of star gods. This is precisely what many researchers claim happened to the county of Somerset in western England, in one of the most stupendous theories ever presented by fringe archaeology. Made up of these huge star symbols, the Somerset Zodiac is some ten miles across and thirty miles around. It is literally too big to see, becoming visible only through the study of maps and aerial photographs.

The focus of this extraordinary theory is Glastonbury, a sleepy English market town that has attracted pilgrims and mystics since the Middle Ages because of its reputation as the birthplace of British Christianity, and is now a mecca for New Age travelers and fringe archaeology believers. Many amazing claims have been made about the history of this town (see **The Company of Avalon** in **Archaeology and the Supernatural** and **The Glastonbury Spiral** in this chapter), but the giant zodiac that supposedly surrounds it, by its very scale, offers the most far-reaching implications for our understanding of prehistory.

Local sculptor and mystic Katherine Maltwood (1878–1961) discovered the Somerset Zodiac (with massive figures of the zodiac signs in the form of objects, birds, and animals) in the 1920s. She was deeply interested in the symbolism contained within the Holy Grail romances—in particular she was intrigued by the French medieval story known as the *High History of the Holy Grail* (or *Perlesvaus*). Its author claimed he had copied it from a Latin book kept in the "holy house of religion" on the island of Avalon, where King Arthur and Queen Guinevere were buried. This had to mean Glastonbury, as it was here in A.D. 1190 that the monks claimed to have uncovered Arthur's and Guinevere's bones (see **King Arthur's Grave** in **Hoax?**). If Avalon were Glastonbury, Maltwood wondered, could the adventures of Arthur's knights on the quest for the Holy Grail be traced through the hills and marshes of the Somerset countryside?

One foe encountered by the Grail-questing knights was a ferocious lion, so Maltwood was intrigued to notice on a modern map of the area that the twisting course of the Cary River (south of Glastonbury, near her summer home) resembled the underside of a lion seen in outline, from its ribs to the front part of the hind leg and foot. Smaller streams running into the Cary River seemed to supply more of the lion's shape, such as nose, mane, and tail, with the details of the face being suggested by ancient trackways and earthworks. Looking at the map with new eyes, she was soon able to see a whole series of figures in the courses of rivers and streams, tracks, and field boundaries.

After further study of both maps and aerial photographs, Mrs. Maltwood was able to make out a dozen giant zodiacal figures up to 6,000 feet in length (with some extra symbols) laid out in the hills, rivers, and fields to the south and east of Glastonbury. These she compared in terms of their scale to the giant effigy mounds of the United States (see **Introduction** to this chapter). There was even a pattern in the layout of the figures—the cold winter signs fell in the northern half of the layout and the warm summer signs in the southern half, with ten of the signs in the correct zodiacal order. It has been argued by Maltwood's followers that the likelihood of this arrangement arising by chance is an impressive 1 in 149 million, or even an incredible 1 in 479 million.

Beyond the circle of zodiacal figures itself was an additional figure that Mrs. Maltwood dubbed the "Great Dog of Langport" and interpreted as a guardian effigy for the whole vast undertaking. Here, as with other figures, place-names provided a measure of support for the identifications. For example, a number of places around the Great Dog contain the word *cur*, including the Curry River, North Curry, and Curland.

The scale of the work involved in creating the figures seems even more remarkable given the early date that Maltwood arrived at for the Somerset Zodiac. She used astronomical alignments apparently incorporated in the figures to date her "Temple of the Stars" to either 2700 or 2000 B.C., back in the Neolithic (New Stone Age). On linguistic grounds she identified its builders as metal prospectors from the great urban civilization of Sumer in southern Mesopotamia (Iraq), who named their new country Somerset in memory of their homeland. Thousands of years later, Maltwood believed, the Somerset Zodiac

The head of a lion, representing the constellation "Leo," which Katherine Maltwood believed she could detect in the features of the Somerset landscape.

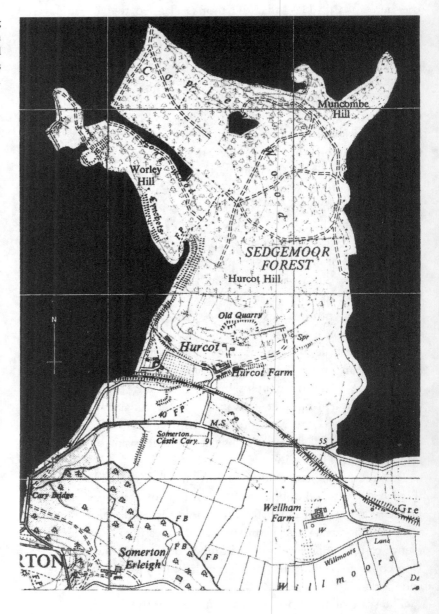

became known as "King Arthur's Round Table." This link comes from another medieval French Grail romance, the *Queste de Saint Graal*, written around A.D. 1200, which says that Merlin created the Round Table to symbolize the stars and planets.

Katherine Maltwood's insights concerning this lost history of the Somerset landscape were not widely believed outside esoteric circles, even though she published several short books on the subject. After she emigrated with her husband, a wealthy businessman, to Vancouver Island, British Columbia, in Canada, her theory was largely forgotten.

Then, in the 1960s, Maltwood's zodiac was revived along with many other alternative archaeological ideas. *Gandalf's Garden,* a magazine named after the wizard in Tolkien's *Lord of the Rings,* contained an article by Mary Caine that brought the Somerset figures to the attention of a wider public, and one more receptive to unconventional thinking. Since then the Somerset Zodiac has become firmly established in alternative archaeological circles as a topic worthy of discussion. Indeed, other giant zodiacs have subsequently been identified at some twenty sites in Britain, including Winchester and Kingston-

The Somerset Zodiac.

upon-Thames in England, Prescelly in Wales, and Glasgow and Edinburgh in Scotland, but none has seized the imagination like that
around Glastonbury.

Nevertheless, conventional archaeology has not hailed the Somerset
Zodiac as a great discovery. Why is this? First, the resemblance between
the standard heavenly zodiac and that at Glastonbury is by no means
perfect, with Libra being represented by a dove rather than the usual
scales, Cancer by a boat instead of a crab, and Aquarius by a phoenix,
not a water jug, while Cetus ("The Whale") puts in an appearance just
outside Glastonbury itself, even though it doesn't feature in the zodiac.
Admittedly, this is not a fatal objection, as the zodiacal symbols could
have changed through time or varied locally, and extra figures could
have been added as the landscape was further transformed.

More surprising is that there is no account, or even clear tradition,
of the construction of the Somerset Zodiac in any ancient written
source. (Several zodiac enthusiasts have claimed that it was referred to
by the occult scholar John Dee at the time of Elizabeth I, but the
source cannot be traced.) The Somerset Zodiac would therefore have
to date back to prehistoric times, as Maltwood indeed argued.

It is here that the Somerset Zodiac runs into some major problems.
Archaeologists are used to examining aerial photographs, maps, and
the remains of ancient earthworks such as banks and ditches in an attempt to trace the development of the present-day landscape. In 1983
two independent studies—one by Ian Burrow, the other by Tom
Williamson and Liz Bellamy—reexamined many of the features of
the landscape that make up the figures within the Somerset Zodiac to
check their validity. They followed the standard method used in landscape historical research; first rule out those features produced by
modern farming, then attempt to tie down the age of the individual
elements forming parts of the figures and, by extension, date the zodiac itself.

Their results have been conclusive. Some elements making up the
figures are indeed ancient, such as streams, rivers, and hills. Yet the actual courses of streams and rivers have in some cases changed significantly between prehistoric and modern times. In any case these are
natural features, and there is no good reason to see a human hand at
work in them. To archaeologists used to interpreting aerial photographs it was clear other supposed elements were simply mistakes
produced by unfamiliarity with a farming landscape seen from above.
For example, the eye of Pisces identified by Maltwood was probably
just the mess made by cattle cutting up the ground near the gate into a

field, while the eye of Capricorn was simply a haystack. This explains why these features later disappeared from view. Occasional elements making up the Somerset Zodiac figures seem to exist only at certain times of the year, such as the shadow made by the hill of Glastonbury Tor in the depths of winter, which shows up very clearly on aerial photographs and has been incorporated within the zodiac as the throat of the Aquarius "phoenix."

More worrying are the many lines in the figures that are formed by field boundaries, drainage ditches, and roads dated to the last few hundred years. While followers of the zodiac theory argue that these features all perpetuate significant points in the landscape, this seems hard to believe in many cases: the western wing of the Aquarius phoenix was created from a new road laid after 1782 to run around the town of Glastonbury (older maps dating back as far as the 1620s showing that this road had no predecessors); the front leg of Leo is formed by a road diverted during the construction of a new railway line in 1905; the Cancer boat is made up of a network of straight paths and drainage ditches created in the late eighteenth century after a large area of wetland was drained.

Looking at the general landscape of this area in the Neolithic, to which the Somerset Zodiac has been dated, we know from the remains of plants and animals preserved in local peat deposits that the environment of this largely low-lying area was, from 3000 B.C. onward, dominated by a treeless bog of stagnant pools separated by areas of moss, cotton grass, and heather. There were occasional wooden trackways, fragments of which miraculously still survive in the peat, snaking through the bog, avoiding the pools, but none of the known Neolithic tracks match up with the lines of the zodiac figures. Had the deep, straight drainage ditches marking the figures existed back in the Stone Age, then there would have been no bog or trackways. Nor could there have been an Isle of Avalon at Glastonbury set among the wetland, as it was in medieval times. The landscape was completely transformed by the drainage ditches dug in the late eighteenth and early nineteenth century.

Ironically, it was Mary Caine's own work in reviving the Somerset Zodiac in 1969 that most clearly showed the fundamental weakness of the whole theory. In her improvements to the zodiac she turned Scorpio upside down, added a monk into Gemini and altered the outlines of Capricorn, Libra, and Leo. While these were sincere efforts at refining a scheme she felt to be basically correct, it shows how little there is to prevent wholesale changes to Maltwood's original vision.

The Somerset Zodiac thus appears to be a classic product of wishful thinking. Certain lines on the landscape have been joined together to make figures not because there is anything special about those lines, but because they fit into a pattern that the interpreter sees there. Rather like the inkblot tests once so popular among psychiatrists, anything can be read into the lines on a map, the result depending on the observer rather than on the landscape itself.

LEY LINES

It is now over seventy-five years since Alfred Watkins, in a flash of inspiration, hit upon the idea of "ley lines." An amateur archaeologist, photographer, and devotee of the English countryside, Watkins was visiting the village of Blackwardine, in his native Herefordshire, one summer's day in 1921, when he stopped to look at his map. He was amazed to note that several hilltops with ancient ruins appeared to fall in a straight line.

A strange impression overwhelmed him, and his imagination allowed him to see a vast network of straight lines connecting together the traditional landmarks of the countryside. Hilltops, churches, standing stones, crossroads, castles, burial mounds, holy wells, and other time-honored spots appeared to him to be connected by these lines, forming a crisscrossing system like a spider's web. A few years later he wrote these words, most likely echoing his revelation on that summer's day:

> Imagine a fairy chain stretched from mountain peak to mountain peak, as far as the eye could reach, and paid out until it touched the "high places" of the earth at a number of ridges, banks and knowls. Then visualize a mound, circular earthwork, or clump of trees, planted on these high points, and in low points in the valley other mounds ringed with water to be seen from a distance. Then great standing stones brought to mark the way at intervals, and on a bank leading up to a mountain ridge or down to a ford the track cut deep so as to form a guiding notch on the skyline as you come up.

For Watkins this concept of a system of straight lines joining the points on the ancient landscape was more than something to be seen with just the mind's eye. A feverish period of work with Ordnance Survey maps and field observation convinced him that the special places of ancient Britain had indeed been sited along straight lines.

Alfred Watkins, the discoverer of ley lines.

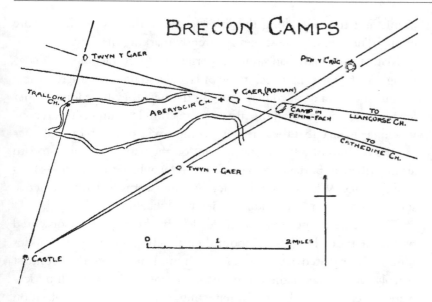

BRECON CAMPS

Sketch map by Watkins of the ley lines he detected near Brecon in Wales. He was particularly impressed by the fact that alignments could be drawn from a large mound known as the "Castle" that exactly touch the northern and southern edges of three Iron Age camps (Twyn-y-Gaer, Fenni-Fach, and Pen-y-Crug).

Watkins's work on "leys," as he called them, caused a minor sensation when it appeared as a book, titled *The Old Straight Track*, in 1925. Archaeologists vehemently denied the "preposterous" notion that ancient man was capable of laying out a vast grid of lines running across the country. When the leading British archaeological journal *Antiquity* was founded in 1927, its editor refused to take an advertisement for Watkins's book. A similar antipathy still exists today. All the same, Watkins has hundreds of dedicated followers, the ley hunters, who while away many pleasant hours tracing alignments between ancient mounds and monuments through the British countryside.

What Is a Ley Line?

Ley hunting draws its adherents from a broad range of backgrounds and interests, from wide-eyed mystics of the New Age variety to converted skeptics like Dr. Don Robins, a research chemist at the Institute of Archaeology, London University. Robins had read Watkins's book out of general interest, and when he found himself holidaying in Herefordshire, he decided to try following some of the proposed leys, just for amusement. Much to his surprise, he found that the alignments not only existed but also were "incredibly precise, depending upon sitings accurate to several yards either way." Robins followed this up with his own fieldwork on the Welsh border. From the basic leys already identified in that area he predicted the presence of further ley points and tramped along the lines to see if they were there. Sure enough, he found more stones apparently marking the way.

Many people have had similar experiences. After tracking or discovering a ley by the simple technique of laying a straight edge across three or four sites on a detailed map, once in the field they have found other ley points not marked on the map. For practical ley hunters this is convincing evidence that they are not chasing a will-o'-the-wisp, but tracing the remains of a systematic attempt on the part of our ancestors to arrange their important and sacred sites—for whatever reasons—along straight lines. Why, then, when ley hunting seems to have predictive success, is the idea of leys still scorned by archaeologists?

The debate about the existence of leys has been horribly obscured by the welter of hypotheses about their function and nature. Watkins himself interpreted ley lines in very mundane terms that contrast sharply with some of the claims made by later authors. For him, leys were purely practical, simply reflecting mankind's early realization that the quickest way between two points is a straight line. Watkins thought that leys originated as prehistoric trade routes for transporting salt, flint, and pottery and that it was only later that they acquired a religious significance.

Many of Watkins's successors in the ley-hunting game have not been so restrained. Rather than seeing ley lines as man-made, many theorists (from the 1960s onward) have perceived them in terms of "cosmic lines" of force, paths of an unknown energy that runs through the terrain. The idea is that people throughout prehistoric and ancient times were attracted by the energy in these lines and sited their monuments accordingly. Many claim to have used dowsing (see **Introduction** to this chapter) to detect this mysterious "earth energy." A UFO connection has been frequently suggested, with leys acting like ethereal tram lines, providing power for the alien craft that travel up and down them.

Such talk from New Age theorists does not delight archaeologists, who, for better or worse, try to limit their research to demonstrable facts. Nor does the apparent practical success of ley hunting in the field cut much ice with the skeptic. Though one test for a scientific theory is its ability to predict the results of further experiments—as in Robins's discovery of the four markstones—a few such cases are not enough to prove the existence of ley lines. The skeptic can rightly argue that if one has a pet theory it is all too easy to accumulate further data that appears to support it—and point to dozens of cases in scientific history where the wrong model has successfully "predicted" results. Indeed, the real mark of whether we are dealing with a scientific hypothesis in the first place is not its ability to attract evidence that "proves" it but if there exists a way to falsify it. If it is proposed that a straight line joining several ancient sites is not due to coincidence, how can one falsify such a claim?

Elusive Proof

Watkins himself tried to tackle this very problem:

> What really matters is whether it is a humanly designed fact, an accidental coincidence, or a "mare's nest" that mounds, moats, beacons and mark stones fall into straight lines throughout Britain.

That the whole thing might be a gigantic fluke worried him enough to try a rudimentary statistical check. Taking a map of the area around Andover (a town in Hampshire, southern England), he counted fifty-one churches and looked for leys between them. He found thirty-eight lines connecting three churches, eight lines that joined four churches, and one line that linked five churches. As a rough control, he randomly dotted a sheet of paper the same size as the map with fifty-one points; in this case there were thirty-four coincidences of three points, but only one with four and none at all with five.

Watkins was satisfied with the result. He concluded that lines that connected only three points could be due to chance, but that "four-point alignment is exceedingly strong evidence that such is design, not accident." Five, of course, would make an even stronger case.

Archaeologists were, however, not convinced. After all, if ley lines are supposed to be the remnants of a prehistoric system, then the patterns formed by medieval churches—however well they might align—hardly seem relevant. This leads on to a wider problem. Watkins's study of churches in the Andover district is rare, among the hundreds of cases he presented, in that *all* the points involved are the same kind of monument. As churches they are all of medieval or postmedieval date. Yet the typical ley line, as presented by Watkins and other ley hunters, is usually composed of a highly questionable mixture of features dating to widely differing periods: Neolithic and Bronze Age standing stones (raised between about 3000 and 1000 B.C.) are drawn uncomfortably into the same patterns as Iron Age hillforts (built during the last few centuries B.C.) or medieval churches.

Watkins countered this criticism by arguing that ancient sacred sites

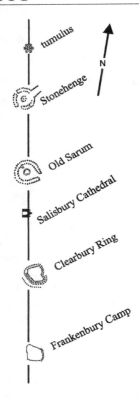

tumulus

Stonehenge

Old Sarum

Salisbury Cathedral

Clearbury Ring

Frankenbury Camp

Ley line running through Old Sarum (after Paul Devereux and Ian Thomson). The points on the line are of very mixed date, ranging from the prehistoric monument of Stonehenge, through the Iron Age camp at Old Sarum, to the medieval cathedral of Salisbury.

were often reused across the ages, even by followers of quite different religions. Jerusalem, crowded with the remains of synagogues, mosques, and churches built over the last two millennia, is a classic example, while the ability of the early Christian church to incorporate the customs, festivals, and sacred sites of earlier religions is well known. In A.D. 601 Pope Gregory sent an envoy to Britain with these instructions for Augustine (the first Archbishop of Canterbury), who was then struggling to convert the pagan Anglo-Saxons:

> We have been giving careful thought to the affairs of the English, and have come to the conclusion that the temples of the idols in that country should on no account be destroyed. Augustine is to destroy the idols, but the temples themselves are to be sprinkled with holy water, altars set up, and relics enclosed within them. . . . In this way, we hope that the people, seeing that their temples are not destroyed, may abandon idolatry and resort to these places as before, and may come to know and adore the true God.

Assuming that Augustine followed the pope's instructions, some of England's earliest churches must have been built on the sites of pagan temples.

The Augustine example would take us back, of course, only to the time of Anglo-Saxon settlers of Britain, who arrived in the early fifth century A.D. (see **King Arthur** in **Legendary History**), but it does provide a good illustration of how continuity in the use of sacred places can come about. Some Christian churches are known to be built directly on megalithic sites. A spectacular example comes from Arrichinaga in Spain, where the hermitage of Saint Michael houses *inside* it an enormous megalith. In northern England, a churchyard at Rudston in Yorkshire encloses the tallest standing stone (25 feet high) in the British Isles. There are many similar examples known, suggesting that the memory of their sacred character might have been preserved by local peoples, despite many changes in religion. As the late Glyn Daniel, Professor of Archaeology at Cambridge University, wrote:

> This may be too blunt a way of putting it, but I find it difficult to envisage why there should be a Christian occupation of some megalithic sites, unless a real tradition of their importance as special and sacred places was carried through the period of the Bronze Age and Early Iron of barbarian Europe into historic times.

The massive stones in the church of Arrichinaga, northern Spain. The stones are natural, so it is hard to tell whether they were once part of a megalithic tomb—but they were obviously important enough to be incorporated into a church in this way.

So far, so good, for those who argue that ley lines belong to a system originally laid out in remote prehistoric times. Yet the weakness of this argument is that it cannot be turned into a general rule. Short of tearing down hundreds of churches to dig beneath them, it is impossible to test the idea that they were built over sites already sacred in prehistoric times. And the religious continuity argument cannot be used for many of the sites offered as ley points by Watkins and others. Some hillforts built during the Iron Age included cult centers, but it would be begging the question to assume that they all did so. And what of the medieval castles and other purely secular features included in lines by ley hunters? Or even worse, vague items such as ponds and "marker stones" (which could simply be posts to mark field boundaries)? Some of these might be as recent as the nineteenth or twentieth century.

This problem, of ley points belonging to so many different periods and having so many different functions, has always put the ley hunters on the spot. How can one demonstrate that a particular feature incorporated into an alignment—such as a natural hill converted into a stronghold—was anything more than that *except* by arguing that it was so because it falls on a ley line?

Here we really enter the "mare's nest," as Watkins rightly called it, a tangled argument of horrible circularity. Since no one could show what ley lines really are, and few ley hunters agree, how can one possibly prove or disprove them? If they were man-made, the "evidence" for their existence is scattered over a good five thousand years of history—and begins, as we have seen, to seem very unconvincing. If they are not man-made, and the ley points were positioned to follow the paths of a mysterious and unknown earth force, the "evidence" for them looks much the same—an equally unconvincing jumble of monuments constructed over millennia by people attracted to these spots. It seems fair for the skeptic to state that in an area like the British Isles, crowded with archaeological remains, one is bound to find many things falling into apparent straight lines—through sheer chance.

Modern Ley Hunting

These were just some of the problems that confronted the ley line researchers of the 1970s. On the other hand, they had one distinct advantage over Watkins himself. By then a radically different view of the abilities of prehistoric people was hoving into view. Radiocarbon dating was demonstrating that the cultures responsible for the great megalithic structures of the Atlantic seaboard were not dependent on the "more civilized" regions of the Aegean and Near East, as had long been imagined (see **Introduction** to **Architectural Wonders**). At the same time, the work of researchers like Professor Alexander Thom, while not confirmed in its detail, dispelled forever the myth that the stone circles dotted across Britain and Europe had been built by grunting savages (see **Megalithic Astronomers** in **Watching the Skies**). It was becoming increasingly clear that the building of such monuments required considerable engineering skill.

The real nature and extent of "megalithic science" remains a moot point. But at least nobody could seriously argue any longer that prehistoric Britons did *not* have the ability or organization to arrange monuments in straight lines, even over large distances, however irrational it might seem from the modern perspective. By the 1970s, ley hunters were also able to compare the kind of thing that Watkins had "seen" in the English countryside with features that were undeniably real, not in Europe, but in South America. The Nazca lines of Peru, which first came to the attention of western readers when they were used by the von Däniken "ancient astronaut" school, were the visible product of a vast undertaking by the inhabitants of the Nazca desert plain. Some of the markings, which are meticulously straight, go on for several miles (see **The Nazca Lines** in this chapter). Similar lines have now been discovered in western Bolivia, running up to sixteen miles in length.

Archaeology could no longer reject the mysterious, but had to start discussing and interpreting it. The increased use of aerial photography had also revealed that Britain, for example, was littered with traces of henges, burial mounds, and other prehistoric earthworks, in numbers far exceeding previous expectations. Prehistorians began to talk in terms of ancient "sacred landscapes," in which monuments over wide areas were deliberately arranged and juxtaposed, which would not have been taken seriously in Watkins's day. Ley hunters, of course, were delighted, as their apparently parochial concerns now seemed to be part of a much wider picture. All things considered, a fresh look at ley lines seemed justified.

The leading light in modern ley research is Paul Devereux, who took over editorship of the English periodical *The Ley Hunter* in 1976. In a determined effort to get to the bottom of the mystery, Devereux began cataloging all the suggested leys that had been published, and asked the readership of *The Ley Hunter* to send him details of unpublished lines they may have discovered. Devereux and his colleagues then began checking the hundreds of claimed leys, first using detailed maps to filter out the weakest ones. After months of work, "it turned out that most of these lines were either very inaccurate, or else used extremely questionable sites, like farms."

Some of the most famous leys fell by the wayside. Probably the grandest ever suggested was that discovered by English writer John Michell, whose visionary work *The View Over Atlantis*, published in 1969, was seminal in the resurgence of interest in ley lines. This was the Saint Michael ley line, discovered by Michell when he noticed the alignment between two hills in Somerset—Burrowbridge Mump and Glastonbury Tor—and the direction of the May Day sunrise (see **The Glastonbury Spiral** in this chapter). Noting that there were medieval churches of Saint Michael on top of both the Mump and the Tor, Michell extended the line in both directions and found that he could trace it through many other sites, associated either with Saint Michael or with local traditions of dragons. The full line ran from St. Michael's Mount at the tip of Cornwall in southwestern Britain, through Glastonbury, numerous other "Saint Michael" (and St. George) points, the entrance of the major prehistoric complex at Avebury, and finally through the great abbey at Bury St. Edmunds before leaving the eastern coast of the island near Lowestoft. At four hundred miles, the line covers the longest continuous stretch of land in southern Britain, an impressive datum in itself. Though Michell stated that the line was "remarkable for its length and accuracy," that wasn't quite the case. The central portion, running from Burrowbridge Mump

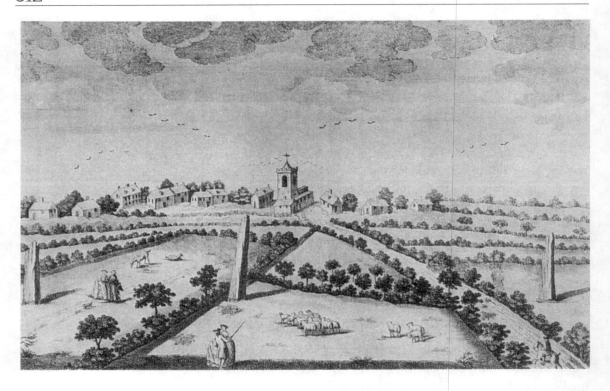

Engraving of the Devil's Arrows by the 18th-century antiquarian William Stukeley.

through Avebury to the church at Ogbourne St. George, is extremely accurate—within a margin of error of only a few yards at each point. However, its extensions to the southwest and northeast are much less accurate, some sites being as much as a mile and a half out of line. It was more like a ley "corridor" than a line, and, despite its attraction, the Saint Michael ley was gently dropped by the more rigorous ley hunters. (Another problem, not touched on by them, is the vast number of churches dedicated to Saint Michael in southern England; there are so many that lines could be drawn through them in almost any direction.)

Those lines that did make the grade on the map were checked in the field by Devereux and his colleagues. The forty-one ley lines deemed worthy of further investigation were published in 1979 in Devereux's book *The Ley Hunter's Companion*. The best potential leys, he concluded, were the shortest, and they should include at least five marker points (though four might be enough on a very short line).

At the same time, Devereux was initiating serious research into the thorny question of statistics. A formula had recently been devised by Cambridge University mathematician Michael Behrend that showed that sites will align by chance far more than one would expect. Using

Behrend's formula, ley-friendly mathematician Bob Forrest then analyzed the remaining "good" leys that Devereux had isolated through
research and fieldwork. Their general conclusions, as presented in
New Scientist in 1982, must have come as a shock to many dedicated
ley hunters:

> The old claim many enthusiasts made that Britain is criss-crossed with
> leys is almost certainly false . . . a great deal of ley hunting done over
> the past 50 years has been hunting chance alignments.

Nevertheless Devereux and Forrest felt there were a handful of
lines that did survive the statistical mill. Undoubtedly the best of these
are the two lines that run from the Devil's Arrows, a group of three
Bronze Age standing stones near Boroughbridge, Yorkshire, in the
north of England.

These gigantic monoliths, probably erected between about 1800
and 1200 B.C., are quite extraordinary in themselves. About 30 tons
each and ranging in height from 18 to 22 feet, they are the tallest
standing stones anywhere in the British Isles, except for the Rudston
monolith. Their name comes from a local legend that the Devil once
tried to destroy the nearby town of Aldborough, and that the stones
are his arrows, which fell short of the mark. The three stones are in
a rough, but not straight, line and provide the starting point for two
remarkable alignments. One line, stretching over five miles in a
northwesterly direction, runs through the edges of two of the stones,
crosses Cana Henge, a barrow (burial mound), and then another
henge, at Hutton Moor. The other line runs from the central Devil's
Arrow through Nunwick Henge and then the three Thornborough
Henges, altogether covering a distance of eleven miles. (Most henges,
unlike Stonehenge, were largely earthworks, though a few stones were
sometimes used to mark the entrances.)

The whole complex is extremely impressive. As Bob Forrest calculated, the alignments are most unlikely to be due to chance. Further,
unlike the very mixed leys that are often cited, the monuments on the
Devil's Arrows lines are *all* prehistoric—the henges are from the Late
Neolithic (c. 3000–2500 B.C.), the barrow and the arrows themselves
from the succeeding Bronze Age. (Monuments from these two periods are frequently related.) As Devereux put it, "To claim it as a coincidence would be the refuge of a knave."

Five other suggested ley lines proved to be statistically significant.
For Devereux the evidence came as a welcome shot in the arm for ley

Devil's Arrows ley line passing
through the Cana and Hutton
Moore henges (after Paul
Devereux and Ian Thomson).

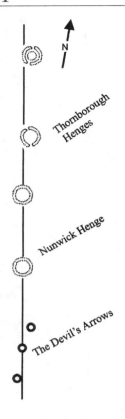

N

Thornborough Henges

Nunwick Henge

The Devil's Arrows

Devil's Arrows ley line passing through the Thornborough henges (after Paul Devereux and Ian Thomson).

hunting. While far from showing that most ley lines are "real," statistics did seem to establish, in principle, the existence of ley lines. Devereux was convinced that with enough resources he could go into the field and find many more lines that were not due to chance.

Shrinking Lines

Yet statistics did not prove to be the savior that Devereux hoped. The problem was that devising mathematical formulas to determine whether alignments have arisen by chance or not was a relatively new endeavor. It involved increasingly complex mathematical modeling, which had to take into account a wide range of factors. A major problem was variation in the size of the sites being aligned. Some sites were small targets like standing stones, others were bigger targets like churches, while others were very large targets indeed, such as earthworks. It is obviously one thing to calculate the odds of a number of objects a few yards across aligning by chance. But it is a very different matter to calculate the probability of chance "hits" on huge earthworks like Old Sarum hillfort (a favorite of ley hunters), which includes twenty-seven acres of land. (Stonehenge, another popular ley point, covers some two and a half acres, though it counts as a single monument.)

These were just some of the factors that Bob Forrest and Michael Behrend had to consider in the early 1980s, when they continued the herculean task of assessing ley lines statistically. Several methods were tried, including one they developed for a BBC documentary on "The Strange Affair of the Old Straight Track," screened in February 1986. This involved programing a computer to generate a simulated Ordnance Survey map with the same kind of sites and site distribution as an actual map. This proved to be very instructive as a control on "real" ley lines. Together with other techniques, it enabled them to conclude that earlier assumptions that short lines rarely occurred by chance "may well have been wildly inaccurate."

Thanks to this research, even some of the original six "statistically significant" ley lines began to look less convincing. These included those at Saintbury in the Cotswolds and Craigern near Aberdeen, which together with the Devil's Arrows alignments had formed the showcase examples for the *New Scientist* article. Within only three years both of these lines were again open to suspicion. Perhaps not surprisingly, having entered the field as an open-minded skeptic, Bob Forrest began to lose interest in the whole subject, as did Michael Behrend.

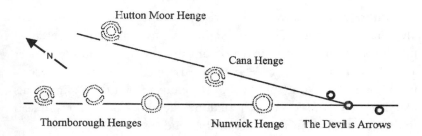

Hutton Moor Henge

Cana Henge

Thornborough Henges

Nunwick Henge

The Devil's Arrows

The combination of the ley lines passing through the Devil's Arrows increases their statistical significance (after Paul Devereux and Ian Thomson).

In 1994, Devereux published a revised edition of his ley gazetteer and noted, somewhat wistfully, the demise of Saintbury as a statistically proven example. By this time he had lost faith in the ability of statistics to prove the ley hunters' case and turned to other arguments in their defense. One was that a number of ley lines all running roughly north to south produced a similar pattern, in that they incorporated a set of features including "holy hills," churches, markers such as crosses, and one of the giant chalk figures carved into the English landscape (see **Introduction** to this chapter). The argument, involving markers from a mixture of periods, was, perhaps not surprisingly, completely lost on the skeptics.

Devereux argued, more powerfully, that the strict statistical approach might not, after all, be appropriate. By the time Forrest had finished wringing the best British ley lines through his statistical mangle there were really only two "significant" examples left: those starting at the Devil's Arrows. Yet as Forrest himself had already noted in 1981, we should be careful of both over- and underestimating the precision with which prehistoric people sited their monuments. Perhaps the rigid demands of the statistical approach were overshooting the target. Suppose, for argument's sake, that ley lines *were* constructed by prehistoric builders. To imply that they would construct alignments with the same precision that we can command today—with the advantages of modern surveying equipment, aerial photography, and detailed maps—and that they would meet the exacting standards of twentieth-century computer programs may be inappropriate.

Quite simply, the statistical school of ley research (encouraged by Devereux), while it performed vital tests, may have thrown the baby out with the bathwater.

Real "Ley Lines"

One way or another, the best ley researchers themselves have practically argued ley lines out of existence. Does the story simply end there? Perhaps not.

A more positive answer may arise if one just abandons the term "ley line" altogether. The Devil's Arrows "leys" are almost certainly not due to chance; for some reason or other a whole group of henges and standing stones were deliberately arranged along two interconnecting lines. And one should take Devereux's point that "alignments like this . . . did not occur in a vacuum." Ley hunting could well lead to the discovery of further lines of this kind.

Yet is there any need to call the Devil's Arrows examples "ley lines"? The eight-mile lineup of the three Thornborough henges with the one at Nunwick is clear enough. The four henges are even similar, each having two entrances, one facing northwest and another on the opposite side looking southeast. Archaeologists accept that they were built in a row, but assume this is because they all lie in the floor of a valley, roughly straight at this point. If the ley hunters are right, when the Devil's Arrows were erected a few hundred years after the henges, one was positioned so that it continued their alignment. Even if this is so, there is no good reason to call this a "ley line," with all the connotations that implies, from Watkins's straight tracks for salt trading to mystical lines of earth energy. "Prehistoric alignment (purpose unknown)" will do much better.

In terms of finding impressive prehistoric alignments, conventional archaeological work has now outstripped ley hunting. Almost ironically, while the serious ley hunters were concentrating their efforts on the analysis of an ever-diminishing number of short and rather unexciting lines, practical archaeological work was revealing massive linear structures running over the landscape that make most leys seem puny by comparison. These are the cursuses.

The first cursus was discovered in 1723 by the antiquarian William Stukeley, about half a mile north of Stonehenge. He thought it was a Romano-British track for horse racing and accordingly named it a "cursus" after the Latin for "racecourse." As they contain no structures, and are simply elongated rectangles formed by parallel lines of banks and ditches, cursuses are hard to trace at ground level. Most of the fifty or so now known were detected through aerial photography, carried out over the last few decades. Remains found in the ditches date them all to between about 3400 and 3000 B.C., the Neolithic period. While some are only a few hundred yards in length, others stretch for a mile or more. A fine example was discovered close to London's Heathrow Airport—two miles long, it makes the runways seem small.

Why Neolithic people went to all the trouble of building these vast

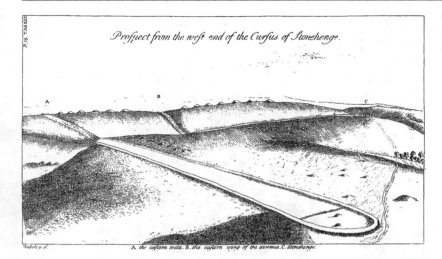

Prospect from the west end of the Cursus of Stonehenge.

A the eastern meta. B the eastern wing of the avenue. C. Stonehenge

The cursus at Stonehenge, as drawn by the 18th-century antiquarian William Stukeley.

structures remains a complete mystery, though their shape suggests that they may have been used for processions. Excavation of the colossal Dorset Cursus, which runs for six and a half miles, has provided some clues. The cursus was built so that it included two earlier burial mounds of the kind known as a "long barrow" (because of their shape); there are further long barrows just outside the ends of the cursus. Archaeologist Professor Richard Bradley of Reading University has suggested that the Dorset Cursus should be seen as a prehistoric "Avenue of the Dead." Presumably both spirits of the dead and those who wished to communicate with them would travel along these huge ritual walkways. Whether all cursuses had the same purpose is still debated.

Some cursuses are fairly straight, like that at Stonehenge. It has barrow burials at both ends, and if one draws an imaginary line eastward from the axis of its northern ditch it does indeed, in true ley fashion, pass through further monuments—a megalith known as the Cuckoo Stone and then Woodhenge, a smaller Neolithic henge enclosing a circle of upright timbers rather than stones. The alignment was first noted by archaeologist J. F. S. Stone in 1947. Whether this is significant is hard to say; the Stonehenge area is so littered with monuments that a continuation of a line from the cursus, whichever way it was oriented, would be almost bound to hit something else.

Other cursuses are far from straight. Many, like the Dorset Cursus, are giant crescents curving across the countryside to link older ritual sites. Some wobble this way and that, for reasons unknown. But among those that run a straight course, there are undoubtedly some, like the Stonehenge Cursus, that seem to "point" to other features like barrows and standing stones.

Cursuses are in one sense "real" ley lines discovered by archaeologists. Ironically, had they not survived in such tangible form, no amount of statistical research could have proved their existence, for the simple reason that they are rarely straight. Prehistoric people clearly

The standing stone in the churchyard at Rudston, Yorkshire. It lies at the center of a square defined by four cursuses.

did not share the modern ley hunters' passion for utterly precise linearity. An even greater irony is that, as ritual monuments for processions of the living and the dead, they are intrinsically far more mysterious than the dead-straight lines for the salt trade old Watkins envisaged when he invented ley lines.

Cursuses can also form patterns far more enigmatic than all the grids of lines once drawn by ley hunters through every ancient dot on the map. To judge from aerial photos, at Rudston in Yorkshire, four cursuses (none of them straight) almost converge at one point. Their ends appear to form a rough square, within which stands the giant megalith in the churchyard. Here we have something more tangible and thought-provoking than many of the hypothetical links offered by ley lines—medieval people were actually burying their dead near the confluence of four possible spirit walkways, constructed in Neolithic times. Were the builders of the medieval church aware of the significance of the monolith they incorporated into the churchyard?

Spirit Paths?

In a healthy development within ley research, Devereux, doyen of the British ley hunters, has now recommended dropping the all-encompassing term "ley line." He has been joined by Danny Sullivan, current editor of *The Ley Hunter*, who at a public lecture in April 1997 stated categorically "that there is no such thing as a ley." He particularly condemned the popular belief in the existence of leys as the paths taken by mysterious earth energies.

That is not to say that Devereux, Sullivan, and the "neo ley hunters" have denied straight-line building in the past. Eschewing Watkins's practice of lumping together every possible straight track into one system, they argue that a variety of alignments from different periods and with different purposes should be investigated.

One group are the real alignments that contain *just* prehistoric remains, such as those formed by cursuses or the Thornborough Henges. These offer further tempting possibilities. For the Stonehenge Cursus, for example, Devereux has suggested a hypothetical extension even farther east than Woodhenge, to meet a natural feature called Beacon Hill. Whether this is correct or not, the approach is a step in the right direction; with a cursus on board there is at least a solid starting point for such speculation.

Devereux has also suggested distinguishing and studying a class of medieval alignments. It makes better sense to assume that the alignment Watkins found in his study of the Andover churches was created in medieval times, rather than trying to link it with a hypothetical system of lines going back to the Neolithic. Devereux has made the observation that the "ley lines" that have been held to join so many churches may not be linking the places of worship as such, but their adjacent graveyards. In support of his idea he has amassed an impressive body of material, drawn from cultures all around the world, about the folklore of "spirit lines."

For example, in the Netherlands many perfectly straight trackways known as "dead roads" *(Doodwegen)* survive. They were built by the Dutch in the Middle Ages to connect villages with cemeteries, along which the deceased would be carried in procession. Not only was it the custom to carry corpses along straight paths to their burial but it was actually a legal requirement in medieval Holland. Local authorities were responsible for their upkeep, clearing them regularly to the statutory width of 6 feet. In Germany it was believed that one is most likely to meet ghosts on the straight paths along which they travel. Without veering one way or another, these spirit paths run over mountains, valleys, rivers, and marshes, passing straight through any houses en route, and they end (or begin) at a cemetery.

Similar concepts are found not only in Europe but also as far away as the Pacific and South America. In the Gilbert Islands of Polynesia, for example, it is thought that spirits leaving a body take an unerringly straight path to their next destination. In Costa Rica, NASA aerial imaging technology revealed a network of lines—not dissimilar to those on Peru's Nazca plain—thought to have been built between about A.D. 500 and 1200. They are generally straight, and sometimes continue in that fashion over even the most difficult terrain. One track runs straight over the top of a hill between a village and a burial ground (also started between A.D. 500 and 1200), and it is still occasionally used to carry corpses as well as building materials to the cemetery.

Devereux has used such material to reassess the traditional view of British church "leys." He argues that many could have been medieval "coffin" lines or spirit paths, vestiges of which might lie behind some of the "straight tracks" discovered by Watkins. Why spirits were thought to have moved in straight lines may be explained by other anthropological evidence. Devereux has stressed that shamans (the priests or witch doctors of many tribal peoples) claim to have "out of body" experiences during their trancelike states, often induced by ingesting hallucinogenic drugs. Some of their descriptions suggest that

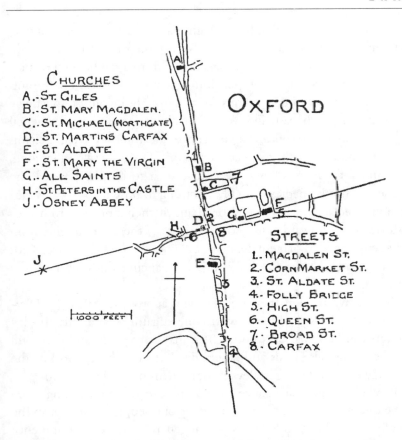

CHURCHES
A.- ST. GILES
B.- ST. MARY MAGDALEN.
C.- ST. MICHAEL (NORTHGATE)
D.- ST. MARTINS CARFAX
E.- ST ALDATE
F.- ST. MARY THE VIRGIN
G.- ALL SAINTS
H.- ST. PETERS IN THE CASTLE
J.- OSNEY ABBEY

OXFORD

1,000 FEET

STREETS
1.- MAGDALEN ST.
2.- CORNMARKET ST.
3.- ST. ALDATE ST.
4.- FOLLY BRIDGE
5.- HIGH ST.
6.- QUEEN ST.
7.- BROAD ST.
8.- CARFAX

Church ley lines in Oxford, as envisaged by Alfred Watkins.

they believe their souls "fly" along straight paths when traveling out of the body. So it may be the experience of shamans that gave rise to the popular belief that spirits—either of the dead or the living—travel in straight lines. Part of Devereux's theory has recently received confirmation from an independent study of the Nazca lines. Here a group of historians and archaeologists have suggested that the building of the lines was directed by shamans, whose spirits "flew" over the landscape to direct their construction. The lines were then used as processional walkways to invoke the gods to bring much-needed water (see **The Nazca Lines** in this chapter).

While he has collected some intriguing snippets of British folklore in support of his theory, Devereux has yet to prove his case about "spirit lines." It is easy to imagine that if people believed spirits moved in straight lines, then tracks might be marked out in order to guide ghosts safely from a given village to a graveyard. And one can see how that idea may have evolved into customs of carrying actual corpses along the same routes. But why should graveyards themselves be connected? To facilitate communication or gatherings between the dead?

German "ley hunter" Ulrich Magin has taken a completely different approach to church alignments. Researching those in his homeland, he argues that many may have arisen from a deliberate practice, in early medieval times, of positioning churches at cardinal points with respect to a cathedral. Thus churches might be built respectively to the north, south, east, and west of a cathedral, creating a "cathedral cross." As time went on the alignments might multiply. Magin claims to have found seven churches at Worms on a line only two miles long, one-third of which follows the course of a road. The practice, he stresses, is strictly medieval, and has nothing to do with Watkins's idea of how special sites "evolved" or changed their purpose from prehistoric times onward. He also distinguishes these alignments from Devereux's theory of cemetery lines: "These church lines were not for the dead, but for the holy spirit, enhancing the power of the cathedral."

Speculative though they are, the new approaches taken by Devereux and others are surely worth investigating—and this the ley hunters can be relied on to do. There may have been, and there still will be, many false leads and false trails, but intense fieldwork is the best way to include every relevant monument or local tradition.

It would be pure arrogance to imagine that there is nothing more to be discovered about the ways that ancient people—whether in the Neolithic or the Middle Ages—arranged their sacred monuments. Here old-fashioned ley hunting may still come into its own, as few people have so dedicatedly tramped through the muddy fields of Britain and continental Europe as the disciples of Watkins, or know every bump and stone on the landscape so intimately. Perhaps it is time for archaeologists and ley hunters to bury the hatchet and start pooling their resources and knowledge. The results may be interesting.

THE NAZCA LINES

In September 1936, archaeologists Alfred Kroeber, an American, and Toribio Mejía, a Peruvian, were excavating an ancient cemetery outside the town of Nazca in the foothills of the Peruvian Andes. Taking a break from their hot and dusty work late one afternoon, they wandered up a hill behind their campsite. The low Sun would make shadows cast by the walls of long-abandoned houses stand out clearly, and they hoped to spot settlement remains that might tie in with the burials they had been uncovering. Instead they saw something apparently much less exciting—some long straight furrows in the desert that they took to be surface channels for water, common in this high and dry *pampa*, or plain. Disappointed, they headed back to camp, where they made a few brief notes in the excavation diary.

The real nature of their discovery started to emerge only when flights across the desert began in the late 1930s and pilots reported a vast variety of lines inscribed on this natural canvas. Mejía revisited Nazca and drew a few of the groups of long straight lines, which he now thought might be some sort of religious roads. His main interest was always the remarkable underground water channels that ran for miles below the valley floor, tapping the groundwater to irrigate the *pampa*, so he contented himself with only the briefest of diversions to consider these desert markings.

Mejía presented his preliminary findings at an international gathering of archaeologists in Lima in 1939. Among the audience was historian Paul Kosok, of Long Island University in New York. Kosok was fascinated by the role of irrigation control in early civilizations, and in 1940 he took a year off from his teaching and returned to Peru to investigate further. Working in the area around Lima, he employed the German mathematician Maria Reiche as a translator, as she had already worked in that capacity for Mejía at the National Museum.

Kosok came to look at the Nazca lines for himself in June 1941, to decide if they might have had some connection with irrigation. With his wife Rose, Kosok began his investigations at a point where a desert road crossed one of the lines. From the road the line took off for a couple of miles in both directions, running straight as a die. One end led to a hilltop, the other to a range of hills. Reaching the single hill, the Kosoks climbed it to discover that it was at the center of a whole complex of lines, some very narrow, others over 10 feet wide. At the top, which had a fine view over the plain, they found heaps of stones marking the ends of lines and a roughly rectangular area cleared of stones. While tracing the outline of this clearing the Kosoks found a series of further lines; these were not straight and appeared to join together to make up a giant figure. What this might be could not be determined on the spot.

With time at a premium, Kosok decided that the key question was to see if any other complexes of lines existed. Aerial photographs soon established that his site was not alone. At least a dozen "radiating centers" were spotted, and he used the rest of his time at Nazca to produce a rough map of the centers to see if they had any common features.

Returning to Lima, Kosok enlisted the help of Reiche to try to make sense of his records. When plotted on paper, the confusing lines at one end of his original hill turned into the figure of an enormous bird, with a tail some 160 feet long. Kosok's brief investigation had produced a real discovery: not only was the desert covered with a network of straight lines running for miles to converge on central points but it also contained large areas cleared entirely of stones and, most extraordinary of all, giant pictures of animals. He offered to pay Reiche to continue mapping the Nazca lines after his year in Peru came to an end. Reiche was fascinated by the precision and scale of the lines and eagerly agreed to take on the task.

And what a job it proved to be! The lines spread over some 150 square miles, and Reiche's survey turned into a lifetime's labor of love, which occupied her until her death forty years later. As the scale of Reiche's task gradually became clear, archaeologists joined forces with her to document this unique survival from the ancient world. American expeditions in the 1960s and the 1980s have helped in the mammoth task of recording this vast canvas, and have also begun the work of archaeological investigations of the *pampa* and surrounding valleys.

The Lines and Their Makers

Half a century of work has given us a clear idea of how the lines were created. The plain is carpeted by rocks, the uppermost of which are covered by a brown-black layer of "desert varnish." To create the lines, these darkened stones were removed to reveal the white-yellow sandy soil beneath them. The lines became more difficult to spot with time, as dark rocks blew into them and the lighter soil was scoured away. Many of the animal figures proved impossible to see from the air (although the markings could be made out down on the ground) until Reiche had walked along them, brushing them clean once more.

Further important findings emerged from Reiche's careful observations. Most of the cleared areas are in the shape of a trapezoid—that is, a rectangle modified so that one end is wider than the other. Triangles are the next most common shape, with actual rectangles being rather rare. The forty or so animal and other figures found (which grew to include a monkey, a spider, a dog, killer whales, llamas, and several birds, as well as a few probable plants) were nearly all confined to a single corner of the *pampa* overlooking the Ingenio Valley, formed by one of the seasonal rivers that cut through the high plain. This is also the area where the densest concentration of lines and cleared

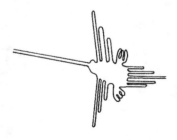

Nazca drawing of a
hummingbird.

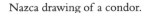

Nazca drawing of a condor.

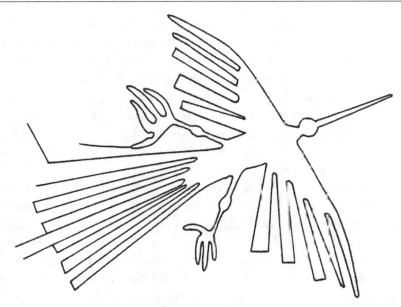

areas is to be found. Could this be the oldest and most important part of the line landscape?

Researchers also uncovered another group of markings: spiral patterns made from a single continuous line. An enormous double spiral in the Ingenio Valley concentration is some 300 feet in diameter. Near the center of this design Reiche found a small stone set upright in the ground, engraved with pictures of a severed head and a serpent, leading her to suggest that all spirals represent snakes.

As Reiche's work became better known outside Peru, it ironically led to the lines' being threatened by tourists. Her attempts to preserve the lines became more difficult after Erich von Däniken, the ancient astronaut theorist, published his bestseller *Chariots of the Gods?* The number of visitors increased dramatically, as well as the damage wrought to the fragile markings. Although the government declared the area a protected zone, monitoring was so inadequate that Reiche employed her own guards, paid for from sales of her book on the lines.

Von Däniken's interpretation of the lines and their makers was certainly original: "Seen from the air, the clear-cut impression that the 37-mile-long plain of Nazca made on *me* was that of an airfield." He also thought that the lines "could have been built according to instructions from an aircraft." In the aircraft were von Däniken's spacemen, responsible for constructing monuments around the world (see **Introduction** to **Architectural Wonders**).

There certainly is a striking resemblance between the large areas cleared of stones and airport runways, but what of the long lines and the animal figures? Von Däniken did not ignore the animal figures altogether, for a photograph in his book of some markings, captioned "Reminiscent of the aircraft parking bays on a modern airport," actually turned out to be a leg of a giant bird figure. The "parking bays" were only a small part of a much larger design, and in any case were far too small to receive airplanes. Von Däniken explained the bogus claim as an editor's mistake, although it went uncorrected in later editions of the book.

Is there any possible truth in von Däniken's idea? Those who have studied the Nazca lines are emphatic that there is not. It is hard to imagine that a civilization capable of crossing interstellar space would need landing strips. Even if spaceships had landed on von Däniken's landing strips and came to rest in his parking bays, it is highly likely they would have become stuck in the sand—only the smallest of light aircraft can land on the desert today, and the cleared areas are the softest of all, having had their surface stones removed.

So if von Däniken's spacemen can be found anywhere, it certainly isn't at Nazca. That doesn't rule out the possibility of the lines being seen from the air, however. A remarkable piece of experimental archaeology has demonstrated that the ancient Nascans could have constructed a hot-air balloon. Using cotton with a very tight weave, as found in local burials, a balloon was made by the International Explorers Society of Miami. On November 25, 1975, Jim Woodman of the Explorers and English balloonist Julian Nott ascended to 380 feet in a reed basket slung below their craft, stayed in the air for several minutes, and then safely descended. While this cannot in itself prove that the line builders did fly balloons, it did show that this was a real possibility.

Meanwhile, down on the ground, archaeologists have been plodding away at the more mundane but crucial tasks of trying to date the creation of the lines and attempting to find out more about their makers. Establishing a chronology for the lines has not been an easy task, as the cleared ground produces few helpful archaeological remains.

Three different approaches have been taken to this task: looking for situations where markings cut across each other, so providing evidence of which was created first; carrying out radiocarbon dating on wooden posts associated with some of the lines; and searching the surface of the desert for material left behind by builders or visitors. There are a number of cases in the Ingenio Valley concentration where the animal figures have later been partly obliterated by cleared areas, just as the first example spotted by the Kosoks had been. Radio-carbon dating has not really helped, for only in a couple of instances have posts set on the lines survived until today so that they may be dated; these have produced results in the middle of the first millennium A.D. This is clearly nowhere near an adequate sample to date the markings as a whole, and in any case there is no guarantee that the posts actually belong to the time of construction of the lines.

Researchers found the thought of a systematic hunt for items abandoned by the lines' makers so laborious that they put off beginning it until 1968, when American archaeologists finally collected artifacts from the Ingenio Valley complex; the pottery they picked up showed a clear concentration of activity in the period 100 B.C. to A.D. 100. But was this typical of the Nazca plain as a whole? Only in 1982 did work commence to test this assumption, when Persis Clarkson, a research student at Calgary University, started to walk the lines outside the Ingenio Valley area. In three seasons Clarkson followed the lines for hundreds of miles, noting every scrap of material. Her results were surprising, as they directly contradicted the earlier findings. The most common pottery was that dated to A.D. 900–1450, with the early pottery largely limited to sites right by the Nazca Valley, a dozen miles from the Ingenio Valley, in which there are several known settlements of the period. Clarkson concluded that the animal figures predated the vast majority of straight lines by a thousand years, raising the possibility that the two groups were made for different reasons.

Attention has not been focused solely on the archaeology of the Nazca *pampa*. The remarkable irrigation system first investigated by Mejía has now been traced over much of the *pampa*, feeding water into the seasonal rivers that cut through it. Much of the archaeology of the Nazca area is in the form of cemeteries containing burials with fine cotton textiles and brightly painted pots, decorated with animals (including killer whales, cats, and hummingbirds) or food plants such as beans and peppers. Some of these designs are very similar to the animal figures outlined on the *pampa*. The active collectors' market for these pots means that many of the burials have been and continue to be looted, so most of the cemeteries are pockmarked with craters and littered with the bones of violated burials. Less attention has been paid to the settlements of the ancient Nascans, far less rich in finds, but archaeologists have established that small villages of wooden huts sat in the bottoms of the valleys throughout the period of line building.

By far the largest archaeological site in the area is Cahauchi, down on the floodplain of the Nazca River. Cahauchi is a vast complex of buildings, pyramids, and squares, together with its cemeteries covering an area some two miles long and two-thirds of a mile wide. William Strong of Columbia University first excavated at Cahauchi in the early 1950s, and not surprisingly assumed he was dealing with a major town. Moreover, the large number of severed heads he recovered, and the frequency with which they are shown on painted pots, suggested to him that Cahauchi was the center of a particularly aggressive military empire. The ceremonial heart of Cahauchi contained a mud-brick pyramid some 70 feet high and associated buildings, constructed around a natural hill. At this monument, which Strong named the "Great Temple," he found sacrificial offerings, including bird feathers, llamas, and many broken pottery panpipes.

Strong's military-empire theory held sway until new excavations were undertaken in the 1980s by Helaine Silverman of the University of Texas. Although she confirmed Strong's findings concerning the severed heads, calculating that up to one in twenty of the Nascan population may have met their end in this gruesome fashion, she had a very different view of Cahauchi as a whole. Silverman found almost no sign of domestic occupation. Instead, the vast majority of the site was left empty, while the remainder was taken up by temples and pyramids based on natural hills. Silverman's conclusion is that Cahauchi was a ceremonial center, visited periodically by large numbers of pilgrims attending major religious festivals, just as many of Peru's Christian shrines are today.

Cahauchi itself seems to have been founded in the first century A.D., going out of use around A.D. 600, following an extended drought. Silverman wonders if the two may be connected:

> Perhaps the fundamental principles of Nasca religion were called into doubt, or the efficacy of the priests as intermediaries between this world and the other world became doubtful, if they were unable to bring rain, and maybe this accounts for the demise of the site.

A connection between Cahauchi and some of the Nazca lines emerged in 1985, when a group of long straight lines on the nearby Pampa de Atarco proved to point toward the hilltop shrines within Cahauchi. These were not the routes followed by early pilgrims, however, for the pottery collected by Silverman from these lines matched Clarkson's observations of pottery elsewhere on the desert, dating later than A.D. 800. Cahauchi clearly continued to be an important place even after it had been abandoned.

A demon holds a severed head, as depicted on a Nazca painted pot.

Killer whale holding a severed head, as depicted on a Nazca painted pot.

As Cahauchi was being abandoned, another ceremonial center was being constructed just two miles away at La Estaqueria (Spanish for "the place of stakes") on a terrace overlooking the Nazca River. A forest of tree trunks was set up here on a rectangular mud-brick platform. The 6-foot-tall posts were arranged in twelve rows of twenty, with a row of larger tree trunks extending to the west. La Estaqueria has been largely destroyed today by farmers removing the still-hard wood, leaving behind only a few stumps. Photographs from the time of its discovery do exist, however, and these show that nearly all the posts were originally forked at the top, perhaps to support the crossbeams of a low roof. Pottery of the seventh century A.D. and a large carved wooden face were recovered in excavations by Strong during the 1950s, but little more has been discovered about this enigmatic site in the years since.

"The Largest Astronomy Book in the World"

But no matter how much information archaeologists may gather on the nature of ancient Nascan society, we have to return to the Nazca lines themselves to seek an explanation of why they were constructed.

Ever since investigation of the Nazca lines began, back in the 1940s, most researchers have theorized that they have an astronomical significance. On the Kosoks' first visit to Nazca, they happened to be standing on a hilltop at the center of a group of lines just as the Sun began to set. Looking along one of the lines, they realized that the Sun was setting directly above it. They were greatly struck by this, for the date was June 21, the shortest day of the year in the Southern Hemisphere (the winter solstice). As Paul Kosok later reminisced:

> With a great thrill we realised at once that we had apparently found the key to the riddle! For undoubtedly the ancient Nazcans had constructed this line to mark the winter solstice. And if this were so, then the other markings might very likely be tied up in some way with astronomical and related activities. . . . What seemed to us "the largest astronomy book in the world" [lay] spread out in front of us.

Reiche first visited Nazca on December 21, 1941, and saw the Sun setting along certain lines, thus confirming Kosok's theory in her mind.

Reiche stuck to an astronomical interpretation of the lines for the rest of her life. She also argued that a number of the animal figures could represent constellations, such as the spider being a match for the

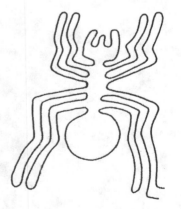

Nazca drawing of a spider.

shape of Orion in the sky. Unfortunately, neither Reiche nor Kosok ever published a full, detailed account of which lines they believed to have astronomically significant alignments.

But why would the ancient Nascans have gone to such trouble to connect their world with the heavens? Kosok argued that the Nazca Valley and *pampa* had seen "only demon-infested priest-dominated societies throughout their two-thousand or more years of history." He suggested that a corps of astronomer-priests had controlled ancient Nascan life, constructing the lines as a demonstration of their power. Yet no other archaeologist has seen any sign of astronomer-priests in Nascan remains, whether it be in architecture, pictorial pottery, or burials.

Reiche had a rather more down-to-earth view of the importance of astronomy to the inhabitants of this desperately dry country. Asked by BBC Television in 1963 why such incredibly time-consuming efforts had been expended by the ancient Nascans on alignments to the stars and the solstices, she was quite certain that they served entirely practical purposes:

Aerial photo of a condor, lines, and trapezoid.

For agricultural reasons. The people of the valley needed to know when the rivers, which are dry for much of the year, will fill with water. Before that happens they have to start and clean the irrigation ditches and get their seeds ready.

Nazca drawing of a monkey.

She also made a connection between one of the most famous of the figures—the giant monkey of the Ingenio Valley group—and a stellar calendar. Reiche thought that the monkey was identified by the ancient Nascans with the constellation we know today as the Big Dipper or the Great Bear. Below the figure of the monkey, and connected with it by a line running from the monkey's tail, was a long wide line that would have pointed to Benetasch, the star forming the tip of the Great Bear's tail, around A.D. 1000.

As Reiche's interpretations slowly came to the public eye, they caught the attention of the world's most well-known ancient astronomer, Dr. Gerald Hawkins of Boston University, famous for his work at Stonehenge (see **Megalithic Astronomers** in **Watching the Skies**). Hawkins flew into Nazca in December 1967, and over the following year his team ventured into the desert above the Ingenio Valley for five survey expeditions, mapping the lines and collecting ancient pottery found along them.

Hawkins's method was straightforward. Having accurately recorded the directions in which the hundred or so lines in his survey area pointed, the potential sight lines were fed into the computer to see if they consistently matched solar, lunar, or stellar alignments and if these matches would have happened at the same date. Unfortunately, the computer wasn't impressed: the news soon came back from Boston that only a minority of the lines seemed to have any astronomical significance. The best results were obtained for Sun and Moon lines, with 39 of the 186 possible alignments matching the major trajectory points of the Sun and Moon. While this is twice as good as pure chance would lead us to expect, several of the lines that were "hits" were on solar solstice alignments, and therefore counted twice—because a straight line pointing to the summer solstice in one direction must inevitably point to the winter solstice in the other. Hawkins himself was certain that the Nazca lines had failed the test— "the star-sun-moon calendar theory had been killed by the computer."

This was a severe setback for Reiche's astronomy theory, although she shrugged it off with the thought that these were early days and that a much more wide-ranging survey was necessary to assess her ideas properly. Neither she nor her supporters provided this survey, however, and astronomy tended to be used only to interpret specific sites and lines. But even her link between the monkey figure and the Great Bear constellation was subject to criticism following Hawkins's work, for his pottery collections from the area of the animal figures suggested that they belonged to a time a thousand years before Reiche's Benetasch alignment would have occurred.

Reiche's other theory of the lines—that they incorporated precise geometry and mathematics—ran into much the same problems. She suggested that the smallest details of the animal markings "must have had a hidden purpose—the basic elements used in these carefully executed geometric constructions could, for instance, represent numbers." Over time Reiche proposed several different standard units of measurement that she believed had been used in constructing the figures. These changes made it difficult for other investigators to test Reiche's claims, but intensive study of the geometry of a number of the figures did not bear out her theory that precise standard measurements were used.

In any case, experimental work in 1984 succeeded in clearing a rectangle and laying out two circular arcs without setting up a preceding grid of lines or the use of any technological aids beyond sticks and string. This method produced markings that were every bit as accurate as those that Reiche had claimed were designed with high geometrical and mathematical precision.

Astronomy returned to the Nazca lines with the 1981–84 expedition led by Professor Anthony Aveni of Colgate University in New York. His team surveyed a much larger area of the *pampa* than Hawkins's group had done, ending up with hundreds of lines whose direction could be studied. Like Hawkins, they did find some evidence of astronomical alignments, specifically to the Pleiades (locally called "the storehouse") and the solstices. Both astronomical features have been identified as important elements in the traditional Andean calendar by Colgate anthropologist Dr. Gary Urton.

Lines to the Mountain Gods

Urton's presence in the Colgate expedition marked the difference between it and previous work, for Aveni was determined to try to understand the Nazca lines in their South American context. Long straight lines are not unique to the Nazca plain, and have been reported from many parts of South America. The most interesting case is that of the Bolivian lines, originally discovered by French anthropologist Alfred Métraux. Climbing to 12,000 feet above sea level, he reached the remote village of Chipaya. The local Aymara Indians' religion was a version of nature worship overlain by a veneer of Christianity. In the countryside around Chipaya, there were many family chapels and shrines at which offerings were still made in the Andean tradition. There was every indication that the sites of these chapels and shrines had been sacred long before Christianity reached the area.

Remarkably, Métraux discovered that one group of chapels lay at the center of a network of tracks:

> Five- or six-meter wide roads that led in a straight line to every point on the horizon. These great, perfectly distinct avenues did not seem to have been used for a long time. I never found the opportunity to follow them to their ends . . . [nor did] the Indians ever volunteer any information on the purpose of these chapels. The priest of Huachacalla whom I interviewed told me they served "superstitious" ends, and that he wanted to know nothing of cults and pagan practices that were secretly held there.

The connection with the Nazca lines is obvious.

The key assumption underlying the Aveni project was that the Nazca lines "surely were intended to be walked upon." This marked a return to Mejía's original brief speculation that the straight lines might be some sort of religious roads. Inca records not considered by previous investigators speak of lines radiating from major centers that were supposed to be walked along, and this is how the Colgate team view the 762 straight lines that connect at sixty-two "line centers," as they have termed them—natural hills or mounds, often with stone heaps added to them, that lie at the meeting point of several long straight lines.

Given the relatively narrow width of these long straight lines, any group moving along them together would inevitably have taken on the character of a procession. The idea of a procession suggests ceremonies, and may connect with the fact that a number of lines were found to point to the old religious center at Cahuachi.

But can this notion of processional movement along the lines be applied to the other Nazca markings? There are some archaeologists who believe firmly that it can. When asked on a BBC Television program in 1997 how he thought the large cleared areas had been used, Peruvian government archaeologist David Browne was quite definite that these may also have been the scene of organized groups marching up and down:

> I think almost certainly what happened here was a procession. I found, in fact, on the low mound of this particular trapezoid, two small

Aerial photo showing converging lines and trapezoids.

pieces of actual Nasca panpipe. There's a lovely little modelled piece in the National Museum showing a procession with panpipes, so I think certainly you would have processions going up and down this particular trapezoid, and of course by implication other trapezoids, accompanied with panpipes, drums and flutes.

Even the animal figures have a processional feel to them, as they are made by clearing a single line that does not cross itself and that has separate start and end points. They could therefore have been walked. But who would walk along the outline of an animal or a plant? The most likely candidates would be shamans, who today act as healers in Andean communities, transforming themselves magically into animals to combat evil spirits. If shamans existed within Nascan society they might have walked along the animal tracks with the idea of putting themselves in touch with powerful animal spirits.

But why would processions have taken place upon this dry and dusty plain, where nobody actually lived? The Pleiades and solstice alignments accepted by the Colgate team provide a clue. As Reiche stated, the most obvious use for a calendar would be to know when the rains were coming. But what of the majority of the lines, which appear to have no calendrical purpose?

Anthropologist Johan Reinhard has shown the crucial importance of water in local Nascan belief, particularly in connection with the massive white sand dune of Cerro Blanco, visible from the lines, which has built up into a ridge some 7,000 feet high. Nascan farmers call Cerro Blanco the "Volcano of Water," and believe that it once erupted, spewing out water to create the underground irrigation canals that so fascinated Mejía. Reinhard has also recorded stories that a vast underground lake exists below the dune, and that this is the source of all water in the area. Might the lines relate to the vital role played by water in this desert?

The most important finding of the Colgate expedition was that a clear pattern existed in the location of the line centers:

> We find that with few exceptions, the centers are located *at the bases of hills that penetrate the pampa from the mountains and along the elevated rim of the pampa that border the two principal river valleys and their tributaries.*

When it rains on the Nazca hills, water comes off them into the rivers and streams and then feeds the communities living farther down the valleys. So the long straight lines head to locations that were highly suitable for contacting the gods who controlled the rainfall.

What about the cleared areas? Aveni's team showed that they are also connected to water, in that many of them lie beside watercourses and either run parallel to the direction of flow or at right angles to it, ending close to the river. As almost all the cleared areas are trapezoidal or triangular in shape, with actual rectangles being quite rare, they can reasonably be said to point in a particular direction. When the trapezoids are at right angles to the watercourse, their wider ends are located right at the edge of the steep river valleys.

So there is a clear link between watercourses and both the line centers and the trapezoidal clearings. The animal figures, the earliest of the markings, might then fit in as the first attempt to contact the gods, followed up by a more specific concentration on the gods as water makers.

Did a specific event spark the creation of the lines? Silverman has recently suggested that the beginning of the Nazca lines, specifically the animal figures (or geoglyphs) and the trapezoids, relates to the decades-long drought that she believes fatally undermined the authority of the Cahauchi priests, who proved incapable of intervening to put right this natural disaster:

> When Cahauchi declines there's an increase of geoglyph making on the Pampa, and maybe the making of trapezoids, especially trapezoids which point at sources of water, and the immense scale of these

geoglyphs—maybe this was a way of Nasca people without their priests trying to attract the attention of their gods so that rain would come.

The gods indeed did smile on the ancient Nascans, at least to the extent that the drought ended, but water shortages were always a harsh fact of life for the communities living in the valleys that cut through the desert. Perhaps individual clearings were designed to direct the water to a particular valley, away from others. Whether the lines in the end did gain the gods' attention, they have certainly succeeded in gripping the world's imagination ever since their rediscovery.

CHAPTER FIVE

VOYAGERS AND DISCOVERIES

INTRODUCTION

The first sailors to explore the world were our distant ancestors. Archaeology has gradually pushed back the beginnings of sea voyaging to an almost incredibly early period. The evidence comes from the most impressive feat of prehistoric navigation—the sea crossing from Southeast Asia to New Guinea and Australia. As these landmasses have been separated by water for millions of years, the first people to reach New Guinea and Australia, over 40,000 years ago, must have arrived by sea, crossing distances of fifty to sixty miles of open water.

How did they manage this? Current thinking is that they discovered that attaching a hollowed-out bamboo log to several wooden spars would produce a simple catamaran that was both stable and maneuverable enough to tackle the open seas. Developing such boats required both mental and carpentry skills, which are generally seen as lying within the capabilities of the earliest anatomically modern humans (people like us), who spread out of Africa some one hundred thousand years ago.

Although the sea level during the last Ice Age (60,000–10,000 B.C.) was lower than it is today, to travel from Asia to Australasia or the small island of Flores (just east of Java) always required a sea journey.

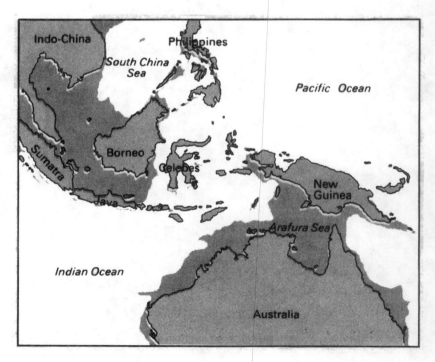

But a still-controversial discovery on the Indonesian island of Flores strongly implies that we were not the first humans capable of voyaging, and indeed the earliest navigators may not even have been fully human. Simple stone tools have been found together with the bones of stegodons (an extinct form of elephant), giant rats, and crocodiles in a deposit dated to about 800,000 B.C. Like Australia, Flores has always been an island, so again we are talking about seafaring colonists. This time, however, the date is vastly too early for modern people, and instead the voyagers would have to be *Homo erectus* (the first of our ancestors to walk upright). If the Flores dates prove to be right, then we must see the urge to explore the seas as among the most ancient of human traits.

These developments have implications for mankind's next major feat of exploration: the discovery of the New World by the ancestors of the Amerindians. They, too, are believed to have come from Asia, but did they reach their new home by land or by sea?

With the spread of hunter-gatherers throughout the world during the Stone Age, the first great age of discovery was complete. It is usually thought that the Americas and Australasia were then effectively isolated from contact with the Old World until the Renaissance Age of Discovery, beginning in the late fifteenth century. There have been many claims to the contrary, of course. For the possible achievements of pre-Columbian mariners we have not only the evidence of archaeology, but also historical documentation. These are the soundest things to rely on, but there are also traditions of incredible feats of early exploration that, tempting as they are, have to be handled with great care.

Unfortunately, many writers on voyagers and discoveries have fallen victim to wishful thinking, pushing often ambiguous sources to the limits to support a cherished theory. Some of the most ardent advocates of their countrymen's seaborne achievements have been national historians seeking to strengthen the pride of their downtrodden compatriots. Certainly the claims that Prince Madoc of Wales colonized America make sense when seen in that light.

The Irish priest Saint Brendan, who lived in the sixth century A.D., gained a great reputation in later traditions as a seafarer who had explored the Atlantic for seven years, beginning his voyages at the remarkably advanced age of seventy. His exploits were recorded some three centuries later in the *Navigatio Sanctii Brendani Abbatus* (The Voyage of Saint Brendan the Abbot), which became one of the most popular of medieval tales. In the *Navigatio*, Brendan encountered various fabulous beasts such as sea cats, pygmies, giant sheep, birds speaking Latin, and sea monsters. He saw many remarkable phenomena, including floating columns of crystal, a curdled sea, and smoking mountains. He named the islands he visited, far out in the ocean, after saints or their most prominent natural feature. The culmination of his voyaging was to reach the "Land Promised to the Saints," identified by many with America. This was a country full of trees bearing ripe apples, on which Brendan's crew lived quite happily during their forty days of exploration. They returned home laden with fruit and precious stones; shortly afterward Saint Brendan "departed to God."

Other sources, unchallenged by historians, show clearly that Irish monks were indeed daring navigators, pushing out into the northern Atlantic in search of places where they could worship God in peace. They discovered and settled the Orkney Islands as early as A.D. 579, moving north to the Shetland Islands, then the Faeroes, and finally reaching Iceland by A.D. 795, for the Vikings record their presence there when they "discovered" the island.

In 1976–77, explorer and experimental archaeologist Tim Severin sailed his boat, the *Brendan*, from Ireland north up to the Faeroes and Iceland, then west to Greenland and eventually to the island of Newfoundland off the coast of Canada, landing near the Viking site of L'Anse aux Meadows. Severin and his daring crew were able to show beyond doubt that it was possible to sail an ox-hide leather boat across the Atlantic.

But did Saint Brendan really reach America? Geoffrey Ashe, the great expert on King Arthur, has considered the *Navigatio* in considerable detail, reaching some significant conclusions. Ashe, together with authorities on ancient navigation such as Admiral Samuel Morison, scourge of exaggerated Viking claims, accepts that the majority of places named in the text were real. The "Island of Birds" can happily be identified with the Faeroes, the "Island of Sheep" as Soay in the Shetland Islands, and the volcanic "Island of Smiths" as Iceland. But, as Ashe stresses, the account in the *Navigatio* changes character significantly when the Land Promised to the Saints is reached. The description becomes vague and fantastic elements dominate completely. He concluded that at this point the tale switched styles from a dramatized version of real experiences to a vision of the promised world to come, especially welcome in the appalling time in which the *Navigatio* was written, with Irish Christianity beset by pagan Vikings and increasingly subject to the unwelcome authority of Rome. Despite the

St. Brendan and his monks hitch a ride from a friendly whale.

heartfelt desires of Irish writers and the bravery of Saint Brendan and Severin's crews, no real prospect can be held out that archaeologists will one day discover traces of Irish monks in the New World.

Sometimes, however, skepticism can go too far. For many years the ancient Greek historian Herodotus' mention of the claim made by the Phoenicians, the greatest explorers of the Mediterranean, to have circumnavigated Africa was dismissed as a mere fairy tale. But mounting archaeological evidence has shown that the Phoenicians did explore the Atlantic coast of Africa, leading to a reassessment of their navigational achievements.

We are on less secure ground when discussing one of the more surprising claims of discovery: that the Chinese reached Australia in the fifteenth century A.D., a hundred years before the Spanish probably landed there. Chinese traders had certainly reached Timor, four hundred miles north of Australia, by the thirteenth century, and records of both successful and disastrous voyages survive. There are also scattered references to foreigners with crooked knives (boomerangs?) living in a country also inhabited by an animal like a rat in front and a rabbit behind, which leaps around carrying its young—an attempt to describe a kangaroo? Several Chinese scholars have argued from these historical sources that Australians are meant, but there is hardly enough here to tie down the originals behind these stories.

Joseph Needham, the great historian of Chinese science, found Australian aboriginals' memories rather more convincing. These Australian traditions record visits to the northern coast by a light-skinned people possessing advanced technology whom they called the Baijini, which could be a version of the Chinese term *pei jen* (northerners). The only Chinese object from Australia also seems to fit Needham's picture. In 1879, a statuette of Shou Lao, the spirit of longevity, was discovered four feet below the ground in the roots of a two-hundred-year-old banyan tree (circumstances curiously reminiscent of the finding of the Kensington Rune Stone, a key piece of evidence for Vikings in America). The statuette is a genuine ancient object, perhaps of the fifteenth century, but the unanswerable question is when it was dropped. Unless a dramatic new discovery is made, the Chinese discovery of Australia will remain just a tantalizing possibility.

Archaeology can also throw up some real surprises on its own. The mystery of the "cocaine mummies" began in 1992, when curators at the Munich Museum decided to carry out scientific tests on an Egyptian mummy in their collections. Some three thousand years old, the mummy was that of the priestess Henttawy. As part of their investigations, museum officials called upon toxicologist Dr. Svetla Balabanova of the Institute of Forensic Medicine at the University of Ulm, an expert in the detection of drugs in the hair of corpses of present-day addicts. She was undertaking studies of pre-Columbian Peruvian mummies, in the hope of detecting the use of coca, which is known from archaeological evidence back to 2500 B.C. Balabanova didn't hold out much hope for Henttawy producing any great surprises, although opium was certainly known to the ancient Egyptians.

To the amazement of everyone concerned, Balabanova came up with positive results for both nicotine and cocaine from Henttawy's hair. Nicotine, in the form of tobacco, reached the Old World only after Columbus, becoming widespread as a result of Sir Walter Raleigh, the famous English sea captain, introducing the idea of smoking. Cocaine was also unknown in the Old World before Columbus, and really only became a popular drug there in the late nineteenth century. (Its users included Sigmund Freud, founder of psychoanalysis.)

Other Egyptian mummies in the Munich Museum collections produced the same incredible results. Balabanova was disturbed by these most unexpected findings. As she put it in a 1996 TV documentary, "The first positive results, of course, were a shock for me. I had not expected to find nicotine and cocaine but that's what happened. I was absolutely sure it must be a mistake." She went back to her laboratory and rechecked the equipment for evidence of contamination, but there was none.

Inspired by this remarkable discovery, Balabanova brought together a team of forensics experts that carried out further tests on Egyptian and Peruvian mummies and on skeletons from Sudan and southern Germany. To add to the mystery, these also showed traces of drugs. By the end of 1992, Balabanova and her colleagues had examined eleven Egyptian mummies, finding nicotine in all of them, cocaine in eight, and hashish in ten; of some seventy-two Peruvian mummies, at least twenty-six had traces of nicotine, sixteen of cocaine, and twenty of hashish; the two Sudanese skeletons both showed nicotine, but not cocaine or hashish, and of ten burials from Germany, eight had revealed the presence of nicotine, but none had any cocaine or hashish content.

Balabanova's results were bound to spark a furious controversy. Attention has focused on the cocaine mummies, seen by Egyptologists as an impossibility. They argue that there is no chance that a transatlantic drug trade could have been operating by 1000 B.C., for this would completely change our picture of the ancient world, and so there must be something wrong with Balabanova's method. Yet this is the same technique used by the police and private companies to determine whether people have been using drugs—the legal consequences of the method being flawed are considerable. Balabanova and her team stand by their work; they make no claims concerning ancient drug trading and simply present their results as a mystery that others will have to solve.

Is there any other evidence of ancient contacts between Africa and the Americas? According to one school of thought there is: the Olmec heads and later pyramids of Central America. Usually dated to around 1200 B.C. and later, the massive stone sculptures depict individuals with broad, fleshy round noses and thick lips. In 1920 Professor Leo Weiner of Harvard University (an expert on Slavic languages) was the first to suggest that the people shown in the Olmec heads were Negroes, and that the development of Mexican civilization had been strongly influenced by settlers from Africa. Archaeologists never took this idea seriously, but from the 1970s onward it has become an important element of Afrocentric thinking, which seeks to restore the crucial role of Africans in world development, arguing that it has consistently been downplayed in western scholarship.

Although racism undoubtedly has played a part in Africans' not being credited with their ancient achievements, archaeologists have wondered if claiming the Olmec heads as African merely denies Amerindians their past. In any case, what is meant here by African? The Olmec sculptures do not resemble Nubians (from Sudan) or Egyptians, but instead look more like West Africans. They live in a wet, tropical environment, similar to that of the Gulf coast of Mexico, so perhaps all that is involved here is parallel adaptations to climatic conditions. Certainly there are Amerindians with thick lips and round noses living in that part of Central America today. The newly available evidence for ancient DNA provides no support for theories of massive population movements from Africa to Central America.

Neither can any significant Egyptian influence be traced to Central American pyramid building. Despite the undeniable resemblance between them, chronology rules out any connection. The pyramids of Mexico are formed in a series of steps, and can be dated by radiocarbon and the objects they contain to no earlier than 1200 B.C., most being far later. The latest step pyramid in Egypt was constructed around 2600 B.C. (see **How Were the Pyramids Built?** in **Architectural Wonders**). The Pharaohs of 1200 B.C. were not using pyramids at all, but tunneled out secret burial chambers in the Valley of the Kings in the hope of escaping tomb robbers (see **The Curse of Tutankhamun** in **Archaeology and the Supernatural**); a pyramid would have been a complete giveaway. Only five hundred years later, in the Sudan, did classic pyramid building revive. Similarly, claims that the technique of mummification spread from Egypt to the Americas are misguided. Not only are the crucial details of the Egyptian ceremony concerning the removal of body organs missing from America, but it has also recently been established that mummification actually began earlier in Peru than in Egypt.

That there are no genuine traces of Egyptian influence on the ancient cultures of the New World should come as no surprise. While they were certainly competent at navigating inland waterways (such as the Nile and the canal system they build around it), the Egyptians were basically landlubbers. In fact, they seem to have been so ill at ease with the sea that their sole attested term for it was borrowed from another language, while the only Egyptian god to be associated with the sea, Seth, was both evil and foreign. Long sea trips were apparently so rare that the female Pharaoh Hatshepsut commemorated a visit to Punt along the coast of the Red Sea by having the feat painted on the walls of her temple at Deir el-Bahri. During this voyage the Egyptian fleet need never be out of sight of land, and for the shipbuilding and navigational skills necessary for a long voyage they almost certainly relied on their neighbors, the Phoenicians.

Of all the Old World candidates to have reached the Americas before the Vikings, the most likely are the Phoenicians, who had a wealth of exploration under their belts. Yet even with the Phoenicians, proof is entirely lacking in terms of artifacts from the area that is present-day Lebanon being discovered in the Americas or vice versa, although there has been no shortage of bogus or questionable Phoenician "finds" made since the nineteenth century.

What, then, of the cocaine mummies? Unfortunately, there is still no full publication of Balabanova's results, but her team has been busy. They have now sampled bodies as old as 8000 B.C. and as far away as China, consistently detecting nicotine. But no real answers have emerged from the archaeological community to explain these extraordinary findings. As the positive results continue to flood in, they also mount up to an increasing problem.

Further prehistoric Central European skeletons have tested positive for nicotine, so that the earliest evidence (before 2000 B.C.) for nicotine use now comes from the very part of Europe least likely to have connections with the Americas, and long before the Phoenicians. Indeed, no one has ever claimed that the prehistoric inhabitants of Germany and Austria were in touch with the ancient Egyptians, let alone forged transatlantic contacts. At the other end of the date range, a number of the Egyptian bodies examined are of the Roman period. Considering that vast numbers of original documents concerning trade have survived from Roman times, none of which mention transatlantic imports, it is no wonder that archaeologists have found the whole notion baffling.

Some answers came in a 1997 article, when further tests on a selection of bodies were published. Compared with modern smokers, nicotine levels in deliberately mummified ancient Egyptians were remarkably high. They were also far higher than in samples taken from bodies that had mummified naturally in the dry Egyptian climate. The most likely conclusion, Balabanova and her colleagues suggest, is that a nicotine-rich substance was applied to the bodies as part of the mummification process. A remarkable finding from the autopsy of the mummy of Ramses II (who died about 1200 B.C.), carried out in Paris in 1979, was that what appeared to be chopped tobacco leaves had been placed inside him along with many other plants as a stuffing. This was part of the mummification process, with the tobacco leaves presumably there because of their well-known use as an insecticide.

But this would not, of course, work for the naturally mummified

A Phoenician seagoing vessel, from an Assyrian relief sculpture of about 700 B.C.

bodies from Egypt or Europe. Here Balabanova and her team suggest a medicinal use for nicotine-rich plants. This may be true, but it still does not explain how tobacco, or indeed cocaine, reached prehistoric Europe. Maybe they did not. One alternative possibility is that another member of the nightshade family of plants (to which tobacco belongs) was used by the people of the Old World, this now having died out. Henbane, mandrake, and deadly nightshade also produce traces similar to cocaine, so again we cannot rule out the possibility of locally available plants being used. If this was the case, then the awkward necessity for a transatlantic connection would just disappear.

Yet if there was a drug trade in ancient times, we should not simply assume that it must have been organized by people from the Old World. After all, we do have some surprising evidence suggesting that some Americans may have discovered Europe. There are several accounts of Inuit (Eskimos) drifting across the Atlantic and fetching up on the coast of Scotland in their kayaks during the seventeenth and eighteenth centuries; one boat even survives in the museum at Aberdeen University. Whether they came all the way from America or from Greenland, we simply do not know. The earliest record of a transatlantic voyage comes, remarkably enough, from a note made by the great discoverer Christopher Columbus of his visit to Galway in Ireland in 1477. He says that "Men of Cathay have come from the west. We have seen many signs. And especially in Galway in Ireland, a man and a woman, of extraordinary appearance, have come to land on two tree trunks." Unfortunately, they had died at sea, so Columbus was unable to confirm this guess. Although historians usually suggest that they were Inuit in a kayak, the brief description sounds rather more like a dugout canoe, which would be the choice of Amerindians living on Newfoundland or farther south.

Although it is highly likely that Inuits or others from North America reached Britain before the official discovery of the Americas, their travels may have been entirely involuntary, just like those of the Roman legionaries who reached China in the first century A.D. In both cases, on the surface, at least, the travelers had no real effect on events. Apart from anything else, the Inuit may never have survived long enough to teach anyone in Britain enough of their language to explain where they came from.

However, this does raise one major question that would have some major implications for the history of exploration. Did Columbus already know about the Americas before he set out, making his expressed aim of reaching Asia a mere smoke screen? If so, how did he acquire that knowledge? While the Inuits are a possible source of that crucial piece of information, they are hardly likely, given the barriers of language and culture. Although the Viking Sagas did talk of their voyages of exploration to Vinland in the Americas, these seem to have been forgotten by Columbus's time, even though one controversial document suggests that they were still discussed (see **The Vinland Map** in **Hoax?**).

A much more persuasive case, championed by several eminent historians, is that sailors from Bristol (the greatest port of Western England in medieval times) had passed on knowledge gained during cod-fishing expeditions. That Bristol played a vital part in the exploration of North America has long been known, for it was the home port of the Italian navigator John Cabot, who sailed across to North America in May 1497, making his crew the first Europeans (since the Vikings) to land there. The exact spot is unknown, although rather vague records indicate that it was somewhere between New England and Newfoundland. Cabot claimed the territory he had discovered for the English crown. But this, of course, was five years after Columbus arrived in the Caribbean, and so can be seen simply as an outgrowth of the incredible Spanish discovery.

Is there any evidence to suggest that Cabot was not the originator of transatlantic voyages from Bristol, but was building on hard-won local knowledge? There is, at least indirectly. The Bristol fish industry was dominated by cod, which was salted and dried on land after being caught, then sold throughout Europe, turning the Bristolians who controlled the trade into wealthy men. In the fifteenth century the best fishing grounds for cod were in the North Atlantic off Iceland, and the Bristol boats headed there both to fish and to buy salted fish from the locals.

Unfortunately, their plans were thrown into confusion when the English and Danish crowns fell out in 1468. Denmark, which had taken over Iceland by this time, officially banned the English from the island, and passed over the trading rights to Baltic merchants. While the English continued to fish off Iceland and trade with its inhabitants, their position was now highly uncertain. Even if they could catch cod while running the risk of being intercepted by Danish pirates operating with official approval, they still had to land to salt the fish.

By 1480, it seems that some of the Bristol fish merchants had had enough, and a small group banded together. Three merchants, William Spencer, Robert Straunge, and William de la Fount, together with

Renaissance woodcut showing
King Ferdinand of Spain
sending Columbus to discover
the New World.

customs official Thomas Croft received a royal permit to trade with
three ships over a three-year period. One of the shipowners involved
in this venture is recorded as John Jay, a member of one of the families
controlling the Icelandic trade. Their destination was said to be the
Isle of Brazil in the "western part of Ireland," presumably meaning to
the west of Ireland.

The first expedition was a failure, with the tiny fleet driven back
to Ireland by storms, but undaunted they set out again in 1481. This
time two ships appear to have succeeded, although the actual aim of
the voyages is rather muddied by a government inquiry at the end of
1481. By taking part in trading expeditions, Croft would have broken
the rules governing his customs post, and he was hauled up in front of
a committee of inquiry to answer the charge. His version was that the
purpose of the voyage was "to serch and fynd a certaine Ile callid the
Isle of Brasile"; this appears to have satisfied the committee, largely

made up of prominent citizens of Bristol who would all have had dealings with Croft. They seem not to have conducted too searching an inquiry, however, for the recorded cargo of the ships when they left Bristol included a substantial quantity of salt—far greater than an ordinary voyage would require. It certainly seems possible that the real purpose of the expedition was to locate land near cod-fishing grounds where they might set up a fish-salting operation. No source survives, however, that lists the cargo of the ships on their return.

The records dry up after 1481, so we do not know whether official voyages continued, although these were probably only the tip of the iceberg. Fishing expeditions certainly could have carried on, probably on the quiet, for there would have been no advantage for the Bristolians to give away their hard-earned commercial secrets.

So a plausible case can be made for Bristol merchants heading out into the Atlantic in search of cod and finding Newfoundland—but can they be connected with Columbus? Two pieces of evidence say they can. On his 1477 visit to Britain, Columbus took ship to the seas around Iceland. By far the most likely means for him to do this was on a Bristol fishing vessel. Once contacts with Bristol were established they could easily have been maintained.

That connections were kept up is baldly stated in a remarkable document discovered in the Spanish government archives in 1955. This was a letter to Columbus in Spanish from John Day, a Bristol merchant with a substantial business with Spain, who seems to have been asked to provide up-to-date information on Cabot's 1497 voyage and other Bristolian activities. The bulk of his letter relates to a map of North America, which does not survive, but near the end Day touches on earlier voyages:

> It is considered to be certain that the cape [where Cabot landed] was found and discovered in past times by the men of Bristol who found Brasil as your Lordship knows. It was called the Island of Brasil, and it is presumed and believed to be the mainland that the men from Bristol found.

Here we seem to have proof positive, then, that Columbus knew of American landings by Bristolians before he reached the Caribbean.

Certainly this is the conclusion drawn by David Quinn, Professor of History at the University of Liverpool, who has conducted a near-forty-year campaign to have the achievements of the Bristol mariners recognized. Scandinavian historian Kirsten Seaver has recently weighed in strongly in support of Quinn, reexamining the Icelandic background to events and finding his theory a plausible reconstruction of events.

The majority of historians, however, remain unconvinced, although for Admiral Morison to dismiss Day's account as mere gossip is surely overconfident. The major stumbling block is the sheer number of assumptions involved. We do not know that Croft's 1481 expedition was successful in finding somewhere to process cod, or even if that was definitely the aim. The silence of later records can be read either way—that they gave up or that they wanted to keep the knowledge to themselves. In any case, why would Columbus have been let in on the secret? If he had visited Bristol in 1477 and sailed in a Bristolian ship to Iceland, then he might have kept up contacts with the navigators he met there. Quinn suggests that he was then asked to provide information on the Atlantic before Croft's voyages, and so became privy to the real purpose of the expedition. But no letters from Columbus to Bristol merchants survive. Day's report to Columbus is the most direct piece of evidence, but this could have been merely flattery. In any case, the Spanish phrase *en otros tiempos* could mean in "other," rather than past, "times," which renders it less than clear. Historians have noted from this linguistic confusion that a date only a short time in the past is not ruled out, so it could even be referring to a time shortly after 1492, robbing the claim of its main significance. The Bristol theory cannot show that Columbus was a fraud. One final intriguing possibility remains: if Columbus did know, or suspect, the existence of an American continent, it might explain why he took such a southerly route, when, as any competent navigator knows, the shape of the Earth dictates that the shortest route is that closest to the Poles. Was Columbus actually trying to avoid America and reach the fabulous Orient by circumventing what he thought was merely an inconvenient island?

THE FIRST AMERICANS

Early archaeologists had no real idea when people first stepped onto the American continent, although they suspected that it was a relatively recent event. Their suspicion was no more than that, however, for it was really based on lingering prejudices against the few surviving Amerindians who had fought so hard to repel the European invaders. Indeed, Amerindians were thought to have little to do with the ancient remains discovered and often destroyed by the pioneers. The existence of a lost race of Moundbuilders, colonists from the Old World rather than ancestors of Amerindians, became a popular explanation of the more impressive monuments in North America (see **Introduction** to **Earth Patterns**).

Although the worst racist excesses of archaeologists had subsided by the beginning of this century, there was still a strong feeling that Amerindians were themselves latecomers to the New World who therefore had no convincing claim to the land. But in 1927 at Folsom, New Mexico, stone spear points were found embedded in the rib cage of a kind of bison that had become extinct before the end of the last Ice Age. This seemed to show that the first Americans had actually arrived thousands of years ago. Shortly afterward, in 1932, Edgar Howard of the University of Pennsylvania uncovered spear points of a different, apparently earlier type along with a mammoth on an old lakeshore at Clovis in New Mexico, raising the possibility that the story of human activity in the Americas could be pushed back even further.

Traditionalist thinkers, wedded to the idea of Amerindians as recent colonists, did not give up easily. Anthropologist Dr. John Alsoszatai-Petheo of Central Washington University has described the consequences of this reactionary mind-set:

> For . . . decades, American archaeologists would labour under the view of man's relative recency in the New World, while the mere mention of the possibility of greater antiquity was tantamount to professional suicide. Given this orientation, it is not surprising that when the evidence of the antiquity of man in America was finally reported from Folsom, Clovis, and other High Plains sites, it was rejected out of hand by established authorities despite the clear nature of the evidence at multiple locations, uncovered by different researchers, and seen and attested to by a large variety of professional visitor/observers.

Only in 1949 did archaeologists return to Clovis, when they found that Folsom-type points were also present, in a higher and later level of the site. This confirmed Howard's suspicion that the Clovis hunters were even earlier in date than the makers of Folsom points. Since that time, many more sites of the Clovis culture have been located, leading to a universal acceptance of its reality, while scientific techniques (in particular the radiocarbon method) now allow them to be dated. The Clovis hunters appeared in North America sometime between

Clovis point (above) and Folsom point (below).

10,000 and 9200 B.C., a fairly broad range, with most archaeologists accepting a figure around 9500–9200 B.C.

Asian Origins

But where did the Clovis hunters come from, and how did they reach the Americas? There is certainly no good reason to think people crossed the Atlantic by boat at such an early date, although the possibility of later voyages is certainly worth considering (see **Introduction** to this chapter). Given the close physical resemblance between modern Amerindian and Asian peoples, the favored origin of the first Americans has always been Asia, specifically Siberia. Assuming an Asian origin, how were the settlers able to negotiate the Bering Strait, which today separates Alaska from Siberia? At the time of the Clovis hunters, the world was still in the grip of the last Ice Age, which had reached its coldest point around 16,000 B.C. Because so much water was locked into ice sheets, the sea level was up to 300 feet lower than today, resulting in large dry areas of the globe that are today below the oceans. One of these lost lands is Beringia, the name for a vast low-lying landmass that joined Asia and North America for tens of thousands of years.

During this time, therefore, Siberian hunters could have walked across Beringia, providing that they could survive the intense cold. Yet why would they bother? There are two quite different reconstructions of the Beringia environment: one view is that this was an arctic tundra landscape, with little to offer the hunter; the alternative is that it was a steppe landscape rich in mammoths and antelopes and therefore a magnet to Siberian hunters. The latest study of Beringian plant remains, by a team from the Institute of Arctic and Alpine Research at the University of Colorado, indicates that Beringia was not in general a steppe area, although some mammoths were undoubtedly present. On a more positive note, summer temperatures were higher than those of today, which may have attracted the hunters. The botanists have also shown that the land bridge existed until within Clovis times, around 9000 B.C.

A massive obstacle stood in the way of any Siberian hunters seeking to make their way into North America. During the last Ice Age much of Canada and the northern United States was covered by a vast ice sheet that spread from the Atlantic coast as far west as Alberta. On the coast of Alaska and British Columbia was another mass of ice extending as far south as Seattle. The big question is, of course, did these two inhospitable wildernesses meet in the Yukon? Geologists and climatologists have debated the issue for the last half-century without resolution.

Many scientists have argued that an ice-free corridor existed for over a thousand miles down through the Yukon and Alberta as far as Calgary, varying in width from fifteen to sixty miles. This would have been closed at the height of the Ice Age around 16,000 B.C., but was open both before and after that. At the opposite end of the spectrum are those, probably a majority, who believe that the corridor was sealed by ice from 23,000 to 11,000 or 10,500 B.C. Only when the icy block was released would the Clovis hunters have made the long trek through. At the moment there is no way to settle this question, although some proponents of the short ice blocking do admit that

Map showing claimed early archaeological sites in the Americas, the Beringia land bridge, and the probable extent of the American ice sheets during the last Ice Age.

the corridor may have been pretty unwelcoming terrain, with sparse vegetation and few game animals, so there was little incentive at this time for hunters to explore the American continent.

According to the model favored by most archaeologists, once the icy cork was out of the bottle, a tide of humanity swept south, encouraged by the improving climate. In 1967, biologist Paul Martin, of the University of Arizona, tied this supposed human tidal wave to another feature of the Americas after the Ice Age—the mass extinction of big-game animals. His theory is that mammoths, mastodons (distant cousins of the mammoth), ground sloths, and saber-toothed cats were wiped out in an unparalleled orgy of wasteful destruction. Martin thinks that the hunters caught their prey before they learned to avoid humans. So fast did the hunters spread out across the continent that they had reached the tip of South America within a thousand years, destroying all the large animals of the Americas on their way south. This seemed to provide a neat fit between the new dating evidence and the faunal record.

Not surprisingly, Amerindians have been indignant about their ancestors being blamed for massacring the original fauna of the Americas. They naturally favor alternative interpretations, most based on the dramatic shift in climate at the end of the last Ice Age, for the disappearance of so many important species (see **Introduction** to **Lost Lands and Catastrophes**). Amerindians have also been critical of the Bering Strait theory for the colonization of the Americas, as it does not match their own origin tales, many of which have them emerging from an underground world, and some involving crossing the ocean by boat. Only a few legends talk about a land of ice and snow, and even then they do not say that the tribes crossed this to reach their historical territories. Archaeologists have, of course, assumed that Amerindian oral histories could not possibly preserve memories stretching back thousands of years.

Although widely accepted, the Clovis hunters' colonization scenario has, nevertheless, been increasingly challenged in recent years even within the archaeological community itself. Elsewhere in the world new discoveries have radically altered perceptions of the colonizing abilities of early peoples. A generation ago, it was assumed that Australia and New Guinea were first settled at much the same time as the first Americans arrived. However, a steadily growing body of finds has now produced broad agreement that people first reached the shores of New Guinea 40,000 years ago, and Australia as early as 50,000 B.C. Recent, more controversial, discoveries could push the earliest seafar-

Spiral symbols said by the Hopi Indians to represent the migration routes taken to their present homelands.

ing as far back as 700,000 B.C. (see **Introduction** to this chapter). Archaeologists have become accustomed to backdating many inventions and cultural developments, yet the date for the first colonization of the Americas has remained stubbornly fixed at 9500–9200 B.C.

Before Clovis

There have long been claims of pre-Clovis finds and sites, but most of these have fallen by the wayside on closer consideration. Typical of such disputed sites are Old Crow River in the northern Yukon, where a stray bone tool, found in 1966, with a controversial radiocarbon date of c. 25,000 B.C., was argued to be a "flesher" for cleaning skins. Skeptics have suggested it was shaped by wolf gnawing rather than human hands, and in any case it has now been dated to A.D. 500 by a more sensitive radiocarbon method less prone to the effects of contamination.

Then there are sites such as Calico in California, once championed by the great fossil finder Louis Leakey as evidence of American colonization over 50,000 years ago. In one of the excavation pits, dug in the mid-1960s, Leakey recovered some 12,000 stones, of which he thought just three were possible "artifacts" made by humans. But the archaeological world thought even those three were solely of geological interest, probably rocks that had been struck together by water action. Even his wife, Mary, responsible for some remarkable archaeological discoveries in her own right, believed that all there was at Calico was geology, with stones having chips knocked off them through entirely natural processes. Despite this, a band of enthusiasts was still at work there in the 1980s.

There are also a large number of sites thought to contain early burials. One of them is Tepexpan "Man" (actually a woman), found on the edge of Lake Texcoco in Mexico by geologist Helmut de Terra while he was searching for mammoth skeletons in 1949. The Tepexpan woman was argued to be extremely ancient, from the geological context in which her body was resting. She is, however, now generally thought to lie in an unnoticed grave dug down from a later and higher level.

As a result of this mounting catalog of dashed hopes, two quite different feelings about the archaeological record have arisen. On one side there are many archaeologists who believe that the theory of an earlier colonization of the Americas has been given a fair run for its money and conspicuously failed to come up with the goods. In the other camp are those archaeologists who continue to put forward new sites with what they feel are good claims to crack the 9500 B.C. limit. They have become increasingly frustrated with what they see as an excessively critical approach toward any claims of pre-Clovis activity.

This atmosphere of distrust has undoubtedly colored the debates over a series of recently excavated sites. Strangely, most of these are in South America, rather than the Northern Hemisphere, which should have been occupied first according to the Bering Strait model.

Much the longest-standing debate concerns a more northerly site, Meadowcroft Rockshelter in Pennsylvania, excavated by James Adovasio of the University of Pennsylvania between 1973 and 1977. Archaeological remains in upper levels of the rock shelter, dating from after 9000 B.C., are uncontentious. Not so with the lower, earlier levels of the site. These levels, like those above them, have unquestioned stone artifacts buried within them, but this time with a series of radiocarbon dates that range from 12,500 to 12,000 B.C. Near the bottom are some less convincing stone artifacts and what appears to be a fragment of a basket with a far earlier radiocarbon date of 17,500 B.C. Even Adovasio admits this earliest indication of people visiting the rock shelter is uncertain. Yet he is convinced by the evidence that the site was occupied in the thirteenth millennium B.C., a good 3,000 years before Clovis.

A variety of questions have been raised concerning Meadowcroft. Why do the animal bones from the site's lower levels seem to show a warm climate rather than the icy conditions that existed before 11,000 B.C.? Were the radiocarbon samples contaminated by coal or old carbon in water seeping through the ground, or the lower levels disturbed by later pit digging? Adovasio and his team have replied fully to the scientific questions posed. For example, they stress that there are far too few animal bones (actually only eleven) from the lower levels to be sure what the climate was like. And to satisfy critics of the radiocarbon results, they had further tests made on materials that were carefully screened to avoid any contamination. Impressed by this exhaustive effort, many archaeologists are now convinced that Meadowcroft *is* a genuine contender for the title of a pre-Clovis site.

Controversy also dogs a similar site in the Southwest of the United States. In a cave at Pendejo in New Mexico, a team led by Dr. Richard MacNeish (of the Andover, Massachusetts, Foundation for Archaeological Research) recently excavated down to bedrock. As at Meadowcroft, no one doubts that there are genuine finds in the upper, later layers. But the claimed hearths and artifacts below this, with radiocarbon dates going as far back as 35,000 B.C., are hotly disputed. At this site, skeptics have not yet contested the dates in themselves, but whether humans actually created the remains discovered. As the excavators admit, the Pendejo Cave stone tools "have been criticized as being so crude they cannot be accepted as artifacts." On the other hand, they stress that the stones themselves are in some cases minerals not found in the cave itself, so who brought them there, if not people? More intriguing are the possible human hairs and the series of human fingerprints in burnt clay dated from 10,000 to 35,000 B.C.

As with many cave sites, Pendejo was occupied several times in its history, by both people and animals. One frequent visitor was the pack rat, which builds nests disturbing the ground surface. Dr. Dena Dincauze of the University of Massachusetts, who dug briefly on the site, suggested that later finds, including the fingerprinted clay (examples of which were also discovered in the upper levels of the cave), were dragged down by pack rats into earlier deposits. In any case, there have been questions raised about the identification of the marks on the clay as human fingerprints. While Pendejo Cave may one day take a place alongside Meadowcroft as an approved pre-Clovis site, that will not happen unless more normal and unarguable traces of human activity are found there.

Near the other end of the Americas is a site of a similar age to the confirmed levels at Meadowcroft Rockshelter but of a very different kind. This is Monte Verde in northern Chile, which is a low-lying site beside a river. Excavations took place here under Tom Dillehay of the University of Kentucky from 1977 to 1985. The waterlogged conditions have allowed many wooden items to survive, including spears. Although Monte Verde's wet location is hardly ideal for a campsite, the excavations uncovered what Dillehay identified as the foundations of a dozen wooden huts made from branches and traces of hearths. He also found very simple but definite wooden, bone, and stone artifacts, along with the bones and even some flesh of a variety of animals, including mastodons, llama, and small rodents and amphibians, and abundant plant remains, including wild potatoes, berries, nuts, and roots. Certainly there is little sign here of Clovis big-game hunters; hunting may not even have been the mainstay of the diet.

It is probably fair to say that if the Monte Verde site were several thousand years later in date it would hardly have generated much interest, but the glimpse it provides of an alternative to the Clovis hunters as the earliest Americans makes it a potentially crucial site. If Monte Verde is genuine evidence of early Americans with a

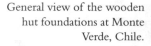

Simple stone tools from Monte Verde, Chile, used for cutting meat and making holes in hides.

completely different way of life to the Clovis hunters, then it suggests that we have to allow enough time for these two kinds of societies to emerge from a single parent culture.

The central question raised against Monte Verde has been the most fundamental: is it an archaeological site at all, or just a natural accumulation of objects swept down the river? Tom Dillehay has devoted much of his time over the last twenty years in trying to provide a definitive yes. He has gathered together a team of some eighty collaborators to produce a massive volume of over a thousand pages. Its publication in January 1997 was the occasion for a visit to Monte Verde by a dozen eminent archaeologists, including two prominent skeptics, who were converted by seeing a new area of the site that had been buried under peat for over 12,000 years. A majority of archaeologists now quite happily accept the reality of the Monte Verde findings, a scientific development compared by the *New York Times* to breaking the sound barrier.

Remarkable supporting evidence for early non-Clovis cultures has now emerged from the Amazon, until recently unknown archaeological territory. Anna Roosevelt (great-granddaughter of Theodore Roosevelt), Curator of Archaeology at the Field Museum, Chicago, and Professor of Anthropology at the University of Illinois, has been excavating a site at Monte Alegre on the bank of the lower Amazon in Brazil called Caverna da Pedra Pintada (Cave of the Painted Rock). The sandstone cave has long been known for its paintings of animals, humans, and symbols, but Roosevelt was the first to test it for evi-

General view of the wooden hut foundations at Monte Verde, Chile.

dence of ancient settlement. Tools of rock crystal, fruits, nuts and seeds, and small animal and fish bones were found throughout the early occupation layers within the cave. Most exciting among the finds were tiny pieces of red (iron oxide) pigment and two small fragments of the cave wall with remnants of paint that had fallen to the floor and been covered by the buildup of rubbish within the cave. At least some of the paintings were therefore made by Caverna da Pedra Pintada's earliest inhabitants. Roosevelt may well have uncovered the oldest art in the whole of the Americas.

The few radiocarbon dates from the lowest levels of the cave range from 9100 to 8500 B.C., while the remaining dates from all the other early levels of the site run from 8500 to 7800 B.C. The implications of these dates are profound. Not only were people living deep in South America when they were supposedly only just arriving in North America across the Bering Strait in the Clovis colonization model, but they had also adapted to a completely different environment of tropical rain forest in the Amazon. As at Monte Verde, there is no evidence for specialized big-game hunting here. Instead a much more wide-ranging economy was practiced, with smaller animals hunted and a wide variety of plants collected. Indeed, so comfortably were the occupants of Caverna da Pedra Pintada living that they had the leisure to paint the cave walls, thereby creating the earliest art in the Americas. All in all Caverna da Pedra Pintada is a major challenge to the Clovis first theory. As Roosevelt and her team put it:

> The existence of a distinct cultural tradition contemporary with the Clovis tradition but more than 5000 miles to the south does not fit the notion that the North American big-game hunters were the sole source of migration into South America. Clovis is evidently just one of several regional traditions.

Roosevelt's work has naturally had its critics. They do have a reasonable case in questioning the dating of the earliest occupation of the cave, in that the scientific methods available are probably not yet accurate enough to show a clear difference in time between the lowest levels of the site and those just above. If we adopt a conservative position on the chronology, placing the early occupation at Caverna da Pedra Pintada about 8500 B.C., then its importance would still be considerable—but not quite the final blow for the Clovis theory. If we allow a reasonable time lag for exploring the continent and developing new economic strategies to deal with the Amazon rain forests, then Pedra Pintada certainly strongly favors a pre-Clovis arrival in the Americas, but on its own can hardly be said to prove it.

The Hole in the Wall Gang

Even more radical claims than those made for the sites examined so far are put forward for the site of Pedra Furada ("Hole in the Wall") in the arid thorn forest landscape of northeastern Brazil. The deep rock shelter here was excavated by French archaeologist Nièide Guidon and Italian archaeologist Fabio Parenti over a decade from 1978 onward. They have dug down over 50 feet into the rock shelter, recovering some 600 quartzite stone tools along with charcoal in hearths dating back nearly 50,000 years.

Given the implications of accepting the extraordinary Pedra Furada dates, it is hardly surprising that a vigorous debate has broken out concerning their validity. Questions fall into two main groups: are the pieces of quartz found in large numbers on the site "artifacts" made by people or "geofacts" formed by entirely natural processes; are the spreads of charcoal that provide the radiocarbon dates for the proposed occupation the remains of hearths or natural brushfires? If the skeptical point of view is accepted on both counts, there is no archaeology to discuss. If the reality of the archaeology is admitted, it still may not be as old as Guidon and Parenti believe, if the verdict on the dating issue goes against them.

In an exercise similar to that at Monte Verde, a party of eminent archaeologists descended on Pedra Furada in December 1993. The result was very different here, however, for the visitors came away unconvinced. The most important criticisms were those voiced by David Meltzer of Southern Methodist University, Dallas; James Adovasio, excavator of Meadowcroft Rockshelter; and Tom Dillehay, discoverer of Monte Verde—experts in the excavation of rock shelters and experienced in dealing with controversial sites.

Meltzer and his colleagues noted that the source of the quartzite rocks found during the excavation was a band of cobbles some 300 feet up in the cliff face that towers over the rock shelter. Looking through the piles of stone that litter the surroundings of the site, they found many broken cobbles that were presumably of natural origin, yet seemed almost identical to the very simple human artifacts identified by Fabio Parenti. They wondered if the cobbles eroding out of the cliff face would hit others already on the ground with sufficient force to smash them apart, thereby mimicking the human action of striking two rocks together to produce one with a sharp cutting edge. So we are back with exactly the same problem as confronted Louis Leakey's Calico site in California.

The French archaeologist and expert stone worker Jacques Pelegrin argued at the Pedra Furada meeting that the kind of simple pieces found there can be produced by one stone falling on another at speed, but estimated the odds at less than one in a hundred. However, as Meltzer suggested, the piles of debris at Pedra Furada may add up to some 10 million cobbles, in which case vast numbers of pseudo-artifacts could have been created over the 50,000 years during which the rock shelter filled up.

When it comes to the age of Pedra Furada, Meltzer and his colleagues accept the validity of the scientific dates, in that they see no evidence for contamination. However, they argue that "in such a semi-arid region, brush fires are an obvious natural source of charcoal." One cannot be sure the hearths are not imaginary, the charcoal simply having been blown into the rock shelter during natural fires.

How have Guidon, Parenti, and their team responded to these questions? With a considerable degree of irritation in the case of theories proposing that their stone tools are actually naturally produced quartz geofacts, which they describe as "ridiculous." In particular, they point to a piece of quartz with chips removed from one edge on five successive occasions, resulting in an object with a very regular appearance. Other archaeologists have found the idea of pseudoartifacts being naturally produced by cobbles dropping onto other stones difficult to accept, but the essential difficulty remains. How can the excavators demonstrate to others' satisfaction that their artifacts are significantly different from those that natural processes could produce given enough time?

On the issue of the charcoal, Guidon, Parenti, and their team reply that the landscape of the Pedra Furada area in pre-Clovis times was not the arid thorn forest of today but a rain forest that would not burn naturally. If this dramatic environmental change could be demonstrated it would strengthen the Pedra Furada case, although it seems foolhardy to argue that there could never be any natural fires in a rain forest, or that the immediate surroundings of the site were always entirely covered by rain forest over this immense span of time.

What is the overall verdict on Pedra Furada? Given the remaining uncertainties concerning both the supposed artifacts and hearths, it has to be one of *not proven*.

Is there anything else that may back up the Pedra Furada claims? At

The rock shelter below the cliff
at Pedra Furada, Brazil.

the moment there isn't, although Tom Dillehay has located an earlier
level at Monte Verde, buried even deeper below the peat, which is
dated to before 30,000 B.C. He is not yet sure whether this represents
human occupation or just a natural collection of material, and plans
future excavations to investigate this new site.

Even on its own, however, the 10,500 B.C. Monte Verde site has opened up a whole new area of discussion in terms of when the Americas might first have been occupied. On the assumption that the Yukon-Alberta corridor was blocked by ice at the height of the last Ice Age, colonists must have reached North America before this. David Meltzer, for example, believes that "Monte Verde would imply an arrival in the New World before 20,000 years ago."

Siberian Silence

What light can the archaeology of Siberia throw on this debate? Logically, it would seem to provide the crucial background. After all, if Siberia is the origin of the first Americans, there should be traces of human activity there predating any American site. Unfortunately, Siberia has hardly been explored archaeologically, owing to the extraordinary severity of the conditions there, both now and in the past. What archaeology can be located in the wilderness is almost always badly affected by permafrost, which breaks up the ground and shifts any remains with it.

There are several prehistoric sites known in Siberia, although once again controversy surrounds those thought to be the oldest. By far the most ancient traces of humanity come from Diring Yuriakh on the Lena River in central Siberia. The site has been investigated since 1982 by Russian archaeologist Yuri Mochanov, who has used bulldozers to remove overlying gravels, opening up a massive area for examination. Of the vast number of stones on the site, Mochanov has identified some 4,000 chipped pebbles of quartz. As at Calico and Pedra Pintada, some experts accept the tools as genuine; others see them as the product of geological forces. The date of the site is even

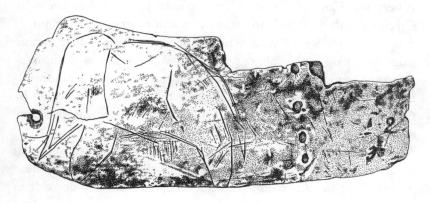

Engraving of mammoth on mammoth ivory. From Mal'ta, Siberia.

more uncertain, with estimates ranging from Mochanov's own of 1.8–3.2 million B.C. down to 15,000 years old.

Another major source of concern is the fact that an enormous gap would exist between Diring Yuriakh, if it were as old as Mochanov claims, and the next oldest traces of activity in Siberia, at around 25,000 B.C. At Mal'ta near Lake Baikal and elsewhere, hunters' villages with mammoth-bone houses and plentiful archaeological remains in the form of stone tools (with some similarity to Clovis finds), ivory carvings, and even burials have been known for over half a century. Leaving aside Diring Yuriakh, the Siberian mammoth-hunter sites still show the area was inhabited long before Monte Verde or Meadowcroft Rockshelter, so the idea of pre-Clovis colonization is a possibility. However, there is nothing very convincing as early as Pedra Furada in Siberia, so the potential for settlement of the Americas by 50,000 B.C. is lacking here.

Language and Genetic Origins

Given the desperate shortage of hard evidence, it is not surprising that archaeologists have turned to other possible sources of information. Linguistics entered the picture back in 1956, when Stanford University linguist Joseph Greenberg proposed that most North American and all Central and South American languages were part of a single "Amerind" family, with NaDene (spoken in Canada) and Aleut-Eskimo in the Arctic Circle as two later language arrivals, making three linguistic groups in total for the Americas. Greenberg went on to estimate dates for the arrival of these three groups by examining the degree to which the languages within these families differed from each other. His conclusion was that Amerinds arrived first around 9000 B.C., which would fit neatly with Clovis hunters as the first Americans. However, there is very little to confirm the validity of Greenberg's dates, which are based on a whole series of assumptions concerning the speed with which languages change. In addition, many linguists see Greenberg's three language families as a considerable oversimplification. They have come up with much older estimates of the first colonization, perhaps twice the time allowed by Greenberg, based on their belief that languages are actually very slow to change.

More recently, genetic evidence has been investigated to see what it can tell us of the earliest Americans. Blood samples of modern Amerindians and Siberians have been compared, coming up with an average difference of less than 1 percent between the DNA of the two populations. This extremely slight divergence is thought to show that the two groups separated relatively recently, perhaps between 41,000 and 21,000 years ago. A date either side of 30,000 B.C. for the first Americans would support the earlier estimates of the date of colonization derived from the degree of language development. Once again, however, the assumptions of the rate of genetic change that underlie this date have been challenged by some scientists.

A surprising feature of the genetic evidence was that one of the genetic groups identified for Amerindians was not found among Siberians. One possibility noted was that it represented a Polynesian contribution to Amerindian genetic makeup. This seems highly unlikely, as this group has now been found in an 8000-year-old skeleton in Colorado, which would predate the Polynesians by thousands of years (see **The Mystery of Easter Island** in **Architectural Wonders**).

By far the most substantial study undertaken as yet is that by geneticist Andrew Merriwether of the University of Michigan. He has recently examined the genetic makeup of some 1,800 genetic subjects, both living Amerindians and archaeological specimens. Merriwether identified nine genetic groups in all, with the main ones being present across the length and breadth of the Americas. He interprets this as showing that there was only one migration, although he can't say how long it took. He also believes that some of the genetic variation seen in his study occurred back in Asia before the Amerindians arrived in the Americas, which would mean that the Siberians are not their direct genetic ancestors. Instead, Merriwether finds the closest links with Mongolian populations, which do possess the genetic group missing among Siberians.

Hints of a non-Siberian genetic heritage are also given by recent finds of skeletons with a "Caucasoid" anatomy from the United States. Most famous and controversial of these is Kennewick Man, found by accident in Washington State in July 1996. He had died somewhere between the ages of forty and fifty-five, after a life, to judge by his injuries, full of incident. This had included being speared by a stone point, which X rays revealed embedded in the pelvis, covered over by later bone growth. First impressions were that he was a white pioneer, killed in some unrecorded frontier skirmish, but the stone point turned out to be of a type that went out of use around 2500 B.C. Then one of his finger bones was submitted for radiocarbon testing, producing a date around 6400 B.C. Kennewick Man, it seems, was a

Female figurine carved from mammoth ivory, found at Mal'ta, Siberia.

Skull and facial reconstruction of Kennewick Man.

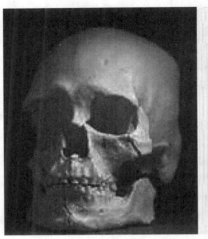

pioneer of a much earlier era. He is now the subject of rival claims under legislation designed to protect the rights of modern Amerindians over the remains of their ancestors. Conflict over Kennewick Man is sharpened by the belief of the Umatilla Indians (who have claimed the body) that they have always lived in Washington State, rejecting the idea that they are themselves immigrants. Similar arguments have embroiled another skeleton with Caucasoid anatomy—Spirit Cave Man from Nevada, a mummified body found in 1940 wearing leather moccasins and a woven mat shroud. He is now known to date from 7400 B.C.

Anatomists and archaeologists involved in the study of these skeletons are at pains to stress that Caucasoid anatomy does not mean "European." Indeed, there are Caucasoid groups in East Asia, most notably the Ainu of northern Japan. Could this prove to be the source of the Amerindians whose genetic ancestry cannot be traced back to Siberia? Is it possible that some of the original colonists bypassed the Bering Strait and the ice sheets of Canada to reach the Americas by sea across the northern Pacific? This might explain the anomaly of South America apparently being colonized as early as the north. It would also provide a surprising fit with the traditions of some Amerindian tribes that their ancestors arrived by sea.

This suggestion of oceanbound colonists would seem to tie in with some very recent discoveries on both coasts of North America that push back the dates for seafaring in both the east and west. At Cutler Ridge in Florida, local archaeologist Robert Carr has uncovered a rubbish dump containing the remains of sharks, barracuda, and tuna,

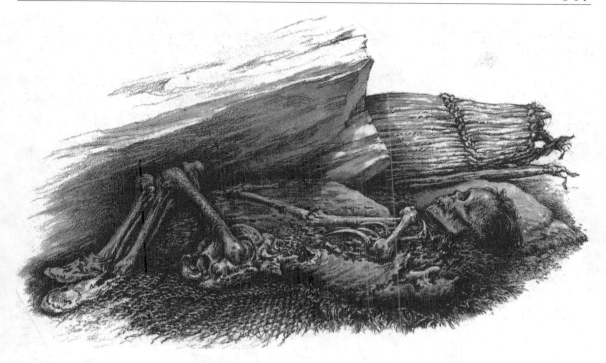

The Spirit Cave burial, as discovered.

which must have been caught from boats at sea. The site is dated to 7700 B.C. On the other side of North America, excavations by Jon Erlandson of the University of Oregon on San Miguel Island off California have located a campsite dated to 8500 B.C. As Erlandson notes, "they had to have seaworthy boats to make the crossing" as the seas there are so treacherous. Evidence is harder to come by farther to the north, but investigations by the Geological Survey of Canada off the coast of British Columbia have shown that there was a thin ice-free coastal strip on which voyagers could have landed after 11,500 B.C. So far there are no traces of activity along the coast at such an early date, but the coastline of that time now lies some 500 feet down in the Pacific. Occasional finds such as the recent discovery of a skeleton on Prince of Wales Island, British Columbia, dated to 7900 B.C., do, however, show the potential of this area for future surprises.

Putting this new evidence of early American sailing together with the global picture of extensive seafaring by 50,000 B.C., it seems highly unlikely that there were no Ice Age Asian sailors with a taste for adventure, brave enough to risk the perils of the icy Pacific. Will a coastal route prove to be the missing solution to the problem of the Yukon-Alberta ice corridor? Perhaps it was no barrier at all, if the first Americans arrived by sea.

PHOENICIANS AROUND AFRICA

Any textbook history will tell you that the first person to sail around Africa was the Portuguese explorer Vasco da Gama. In 1497 he succeeded in going beyond the Cape of Good Hope and pressed on to find a sea route to India, something the kings of Portugal had sought for decades. While their rivals the Spanish had claimed control of the Americas, the enterprising Portuguese now had a route to East Africa and the Indian Ocean. Da Gama's circumnavigation of Africa also settled a long-standing doubt about the nature of the "dark" continent. Those mapmakers who still showed it as joined to a vast southern continent were plainly wrong—the African continent is an island, except where it joins the Asian landmass near the Sinai.

Glorious though it may have been, there is a strong likelihood that da Gama's feat had already been performed two thousand years earlier, in the days of the Pharaohs.

Though it has been much debated, the evidence is actually quite straightforward. In his discussion of the shape of the continents, the Greek historian Herodotus (c. 440 B.C.) introduced the story of some Phoenician sailors in the service of Pharaoh Necho (610–595 B.C.), who had sailed around Africa and "proved that it is washed on all sides by sea except where it joins Asia." (Some Greek geographers, with whom Herodotus took issue, imagined that Africa was joined by a land bridge to India.)

The Phoenicians, a Semitic people closely related to the Hebrews, were the unsurpassed master sailors of the ancient world. The Phoe-

World map of the Greek geographer Ptolemy, 2nd century B.C. It joins Africa to eastern Asia by a land bridge, yet three centuries earlier Herodotus already knew that Africa could be sailed around.

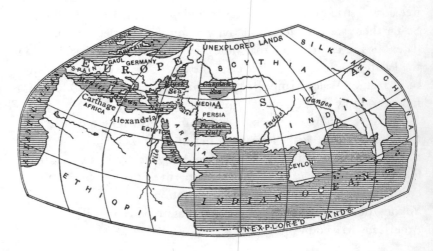

nician homeland, a few islands and a thin strip of land on the coast of the Lebanon, had few resources to offer, but the Phoenicians turned these to extraordinary effect. The mountains of the hinterland provided good timber, the coast was covered with silica-rich sand, and the sea was full of murex shells, which when crushed gave off a gorgeous purple color. From the murex the Phoenicians made dyes for coloring fabrics, from the sand they produced glass, and from the timber they constructed ships to carry their fancy goods to neighboring cities. So while they were never empire builders in the normal sense of the term, from their earliest days the Phoenicians thrived as experts at commerce and exploration. Their home cities, Tyre and Sidon, became centers of a commercial empire, connected by trading posts around the entire Mediterranean.

By 700 B.C. the Phoenicians had expanded considerably and built a permanent trading colony on the coast of North Africa, in present-day Tunisia. It grew into the mighty city of Carthage, Rome's greatest and deadliest rival in its early years of expansion. In the meantime Phoenician traders had begun to explore the Atlantic coasts of Spain and northwestern Africa. The world seemed to be their limit.

So it was Phoenician sailors that Pharaoh Necho chose to employ on the voyage of discovery around Africa he commissioned about 600 B.C. According to Herodotus, he sent a Phoenician fleet to sail south from the Arabian Gulf, work their way westward, and return home to the Mediterranean via the Straits of Gibraltar (the "Pillars of Heracles"). This colossal trip took over two years, during which time they stopped twice to sow grain and wait for the harvest. In the third year they returned home to Egypt and presented their report.

An Impossible Voyage

That, at least, is what Herodotus claimed. Herodotus, unfortunately, has been remembered both as the "Father of History" and the "Father of Lies," depending on one's opinion. Yet despite his reputation for telling tall stories, Herodotus has managed to flout the skeptics time and again. To take just one example, his description of the nomadic warrior women of southern Russia has been dramatically confirmed by recent archaeological finds (see **The Elusive Amazons** in **Legendary History**).

In the case of the Phoenician circumnavigation of Africa, the proof is already in the story itself, as related by Herodotus. He provides the clue, in a detail that he himself dismissed as fantastic:

These men [the Phoenicians] made a statement which I do not myself believe, though others may, to the effect that as they sailed on a westerly course round the southern end of Libya, they had the sun on their right—to northward of them.

Herodotus was a good geographer but had little grasp of the wider picture. He appears not to have known that the Earth is a sphere or, if he did, failed to appreciate its significance in geographical terms. From a Mediterranean perspective like his, if one sailed westward, then the Sun would *always* lie to the left, in the south. The Phoenician sailors of Necho must therefore have been romancing when they said that they saw the Sun to the north of them when they rounded Africa.

Ironically enough, the detail that Herodotus dismissed confirms the whole story. To reach the Cape of Africa the Phoenicians would have crossed the equator, where the Sun is effectively overhead from its rising to its setting. Past that point, in the Southern Hemisphere, the Sun does indeed appear to the right, in the north, if one is traveling westward. If they reached the Cape, as it seems they did, what

Reconstruction of the world drawn by the geographer Hecataeus about 500 B.C. Herodotus disputed this circular notion of geography.

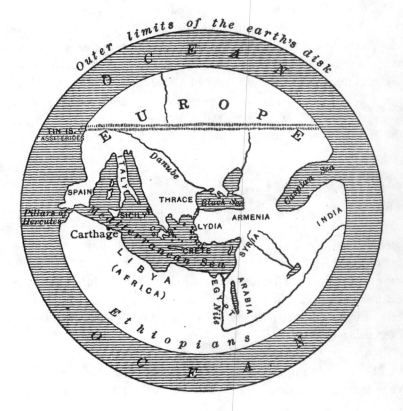

about the second half of their journey? In the view of Rhys Carpenter, Emeritus Professor of Classical Archaeology at Bryn Mawr college (Pennsylvania) and an authority on ancient exploration:

> If they succeeded in reaching the Cape, there is no good reason for refusing to believe that they kept on around it, to follow the retreating coast northward toward their now certain goal—especially as wind and ocean current alike would not merely have encouraged, but would practically have forced them on this course.

So, outrageous as the idea seems and though it took them three years to do it, the Phoenicians may well have beaten the Portuguese at rounding the Cape by a full two millennia.

Naturally there have been skeptics. Most recent to cast a critical eye over the whole story is Professor Alan Lloyd, an Egyptologist at the University of Swansea, Wales. He admits that the three-year length of the journey as described by Herodotus was about right in terms of the "average sailing speed in antiquity"; he also agrees that "winds and currents are favourable for an east-west circumnavigation."

Yet Lloyd disputes the crucial point—that the "information about the sun's position . . . could only have been obtained by experience." He states that the Greeks of Herodotus' time already had a "clearly defined concept of the earth's layout and the sun's course over it," and assumes that Herodotus was party to this knowledge. Therefore Herodotus would have known that any expedition, providing it traveled far south enough, would experience the phenomenon of Sun reversal. So why then did Herodotus seem so surprised? Lloyd: "It was not . . . the absolute feasibility of such an experience which he refused to accept, but simply the allegation that Africa extended far enough south for the phenomenon to be observed."

It is a shame that Herodotus is not around to answer Lloyd personally. Though some Greek philosophers had, almost a hundred years earlier, proposed that Earth is a sphere (see **Introduction to Watching the Skies**), Herodotus himself showed no awareness of the idea. His own concept of geography, though far better informed than that of most of his contemporaries, was conspicuously two-dimensional. As George Sarton, an acknowledged expert on the history of ancient science, remarked, "Herodotus was not a geographer in the scientific sense: for one thing his mathematical knowledge was insufficient for true geographic understanding . . . he was more interested in human than mathematical geography." Lloyd provides no evidence at all that

Trireme from a Greek vase of
the 6th century B.C.

Herodotus had sufficient knowledge of "the earth's layout and the sun's course over it" to deduce what the Phoenician sailors witnessed; he simply asserts it. As for his claim that Herodotus was surprised that Africa extended so far to the south that such a phenomenon could be seen, Lloyd again produces no evidence. On the contrary, Herodotus was at pains to stress that other geographers, obsessed with the idea that the continents formed a circular shape, were wrong and that Africa "covers a very large area."

The rest of Lloyd's case against the Phoenician voyage amounts to erudite nit-picking. He gives most space of all to a denunciation of the idea that a Pharaoh of the late seventh century B.C. could possibly have been interested in such an expedition in the first place:

> It is extremely unlikely that an Egyptian king would, or could, have acted as Necho is depicted as doing. Here we have an Egyptian ruler presented to us, like some philosopher-king, forming the notion of circumnavigating the continent of Africa and setting up an expedition for that purpose. This would surely have been a psychological impossibility for any Pharaoh, however able, for the simple reason that it would have involved a radical departure from basic Egyptian thought-processes. What possible end could an *Egyptian king* have thought an enterprise of this sort might have served? To anyone familiar with Pharaonic ways of doing things the reply immediately prompted is an emphatic "None at all!"

It is sheer arrogance for an Egyptologist to pretend that he can predict the behavior of the Pharaohs with such certainty, as if they were all characterless ciphers with a consistent mind-set. It is especially wrong when dealing with the 26th Egyptian Dynasty, of which Necho was one of the most prominent rulers. This period saw immense changes in Egypt, which was turning its back on the interior of Africa, now closed to it by the rival kingdom of Nubia (Meroe). Greek mercenaries and travelers were broadening Egypt's outlook and taking it into the wider Mediterranean world. As well as his fleet in the Mediterranean, Necho built a navy (undoubtedly with Greek and Phoenician help) to patrol the Red Sea. As Lloyd himself argues, Necho seems to have been interested in reestablishing trade with one of Egypt's traditional trading partners, the Land of Punt, an incense-rich region in Somalia on the Horn of Africa opposite Arabia. Necho was so convinced of the importance of Red Sea trade that he even attempted to build the ancient equivalent of the Suez Canal, to connect it with the Mediterranean. In any event, the effort proved too costly and the project was abandoned, though later completed by the Persians under Emperor Darius (522–486 B.C.).

So, far from being out of character, the idea of Pharaoh Necho sponsoring an expedition around Africa is entirely in keeping with his other policies. The motive for it, which Lloyd found so hard to fathom, was obviously commerce. As the Nubian empire of Meroe had shut Egypt out from the interior of Africa, the Egyptians needed to secure other routes to obtain the luxury goods of Africa. There was also the lure of the west. The Atlantic coast of Spain had already become legendary for its rich silver deposits, yet its trade was in the exclusive hands of the independent Phoenician state of Carthage. The circumnavigation of Africa might have provided Egypt with a back door to the riches of the Atlantic—had the journey not been so impractically long.

We might well imagine a Phoenician Columbus proposing the voyage at Pharaoh Necho's court; the expedition could explore all the coasts of Africa and find a new route to Spain at one go. Given the failure of his attempted Suez Canal, Necho could well have been tempted to fund such a venture. It would not have meant that he was a "philosopher-king" sponsoring disinterested research into global geography, as in Lloyd's caricature. Necho, personally, may have had no more faith in the scientific foundation for the voyage than Ferdinand and Isabella, monarchs of Spain, had in the proposals of Christopher Columbus. In both cases the investment seemed worth the risk.

A Journey Too Far?

The most valuable criticism raised by Lloyd—because it has wider implications—is the sheer difficulty of the journey. Would Necho's fleet have had the nerve to undertake such an incredible voyage, along thousands of miles of uncharted coast?

A century later the Phoenicians of Carthage began exploring the African coast from the opposite direction and did not seem to enjoy the experience. About 500 B.C., the Carthaginian fleet led by commander Hanno sailed westward through the Strait of Gibraltar and, after planting a string of colonies on the coast of Morocco, pressed on southward to see how far it could get. From their own account (preserved in a Greek translation), one can sense their growing fear as they sailed farther and farther from home. They passed a coastline that danced with flame (apparently a massive brushfire), had stones hurled at them by natives, were petrified by the sound of nocturnal drumming, and fled in terror from a volcano. (They did get the better, however, of a race of hairy, truculent "people" whom they called "gorillas"—the origin of the word.) Hanno's expedition might well have reached as far as Mount Cameroon, which is the only volcanic mountain visible from the coast of West Africa. Yet shortly afterward they turned back, recording that their provisions had run out. Two decades later a Persian noble followed the Carthaginian route and attempted to circumnavigate Africa, but after many hardships, gave up when he was stalled by adverse tides.

In the second century B.C. the Greek mariner Eudoxus made another attempt. He left Cadiz in Spain prepared for all eventualities—his crew included carpenters, doctors, and even dancing girls to keep up morale—but was driven aground on the coast of Morocco. Even the skilled Portuguese navigators of the fifteenth century took twenty-five years familiarizing themselves with the west coast of Africa before they managed to sail past the Cape and around the continent.

How then could Necho's Phoenicians have succeeded where so many later explorers failed? The answer lies in the direction of their voyage. The Carthaginians and the Portuguese were attempting to circumnavigate Africa in a counterclockwise direction, against difficult winds and currents. The Phoenician clockwise route is much easier. They would already have been familiar with the coast as far as the horn of Abyssinia (the Egyptians' "land of Punt"), and from there the monsoon winds drive sailing ships on a steady southward course. Once the Cape is rounded, as Carpenter noted, the prevailing currents carry ships northward along the coast, the only really difficult patch being the windless doldrums off the coast of western Africa, which affect traffic coming either way. In fact, once around the Cape the Phoenicians would have had little choice but to carry on northward if they wanted to return home.

This is not to underestimate the achievement of Necho's Phoenician sailors. If we accept, with Rhys Carpenter, that it should be taken as "historical fact," then it rates as the most outstanding feat of ancient exploration of which a record survives.

If the Phoenician sailors were skilled enough to accomplish the circumnavigation of Africa, it is only natural to wonder whether they managed to get to the Americas as well. There is, of course, a crucial difference. When they sailed around Africa they did not need to lose sight of land for more than a day or so. To cross the Atlantic—

although it is a much shorter voyage—is a very different matter. How much fear would have affected Phoenician mariners, had they traveled across the uncharted and empty waters of the Atlantic, is impossible to assess; but it seems unlikely that they would have deliberately sailed in that direction out of pure curiosity. But that does not, of course, rule out accidental voyages. . . .

THE LOST ROMAN ARMY

Though the idea sounds like a gaffe from a badly researched 1960s B movie, there is evidence that a group of Roman soldiers, lost through the exigencies of war, drifted so far to the east that they eventually came into conflict with the armies of Imperial China. The itinerant Roman legionaries may even have been resettled in China, in a town named after them.

This extraordinary contact is thought to have taken place in the time of the Chinese Han Dynasty (200 B.C.–A.D. 200), contemporary with the heyday of the Roman Republic and Empire. The Han rulers turned China into a formidable military power whose arms were carried far beyond the traditional borders. One of its most extraordinary achievements was a westward strike in 36 B.C. into Central Asia, a full thousand miles beyond the official Chinese frontier. Its sheer audacity reminds one of the famous raid on Entebbe in June 1976, when Israeli commandos flew to Africa, stormed a Ugandan airport, and rescued a group of hijacked passengers. In this case, the aim of the Han generals was not to rescue captives but to "take out" a threat to their authority, even though his base was now at the other end of Asia. It was there, it is believed, that the Chinese encountered and captured a lost unit of the Roman army.

A Fishy Story

In Han Dynasty times, the Huns were the main threat to Chinese authority in Central Asia, and their most troublesome leader was a contender for the Hunnic throne known as Jzh-jzh (or Chih-chih). Jzh-jzh had had the effrontery to murder an official Chinese envoy and, to escape the inevitable retaliation, he fled with his band far to the west of Sogdiana, a kingdom to the south of Russia that occupied the territory of modern Uzbekistan. Jzh-jzh was taking up an invitation from the Sogdianian king to help him in repelling some nomadic invaders. Successful in Sogdiana, Jzh-jzh then planned to start his own Central Asian empire, and built himself a new capital on the Talass River. From here he began levying tribute from neighboring tribes, some of whom were officially under Chinese protection. Determined to get rid of this pest once and for all, Chen Tang, the "Associate Protector General of the Chinese Western Frontier," decided in 36 B.C. to march straight to Jzh-jzh's city and kill him.

Chen Tang pulled together a strike force, marched the thousand miles to Jzh-jzh's stronghold, and took it by storm. Jzh-jzh was captured and beheaded. The Chinese frontier army had won, yet Chen Tang had problems. In his eagerness to raise his army, he had taken the desperate shortcut of forging an order from the emperor himself. For a crime of this nature, death was the usual punishment, but Chen Tang hoped that his success would be enough to absolve him of blame. To achieve this he made special efforts to publicize his victory. A series of paintings or maps were made to depict his capture of Jzh-jzh's city and sent back to the court in China. They made a great impression at an imperial banquet, and were even shown off to ladies from the emperor's harem. Chen Tang's gamble paid off and he escaped disgrace and execution.

These illustrations (now lost) served as the main source when the campaign was written up a century later, in a book called the *History of the Former Han Dynasty*. Its compiler gives a blow-by-blow account of the siege, including the disposition of Jzh-jzh's forces in and around the city when the Chinese arrived:

> More than a hundred horsemen had come out and were galloping back and forth below the wall. More than a hundred foot-soldiers, lined up on either side of the gate in a fish-scale formation, were practising military drill. The men on the wall, one after another, challenged the Chinese army, shouting "Come on and fight"!

The reference to a "fish-scale" formation is intriguing. It is difficult to imagine that it could mean anything other than a maneuver involving overlapping shields, which immediately recalls the tactics developed by the Romans. Few armies of the ancient world were drilled well enough for such maneuvers, and only the Romans had the right-shape shields to form anything like a fish-scale formation. The *scuta*, standard shield of the legionaries, was rectangular and semicylindrical in shape, hence perfect for linking in rows to form temporary defensive "walls." Their most famous shield tactic was the *testudo* ("tortoise"),

Siege of German town from the Column of Emperor Marcus Aurelius (in Rome), showing Roman *testudo* ("tortoise") formation.

perfected in the late first century B.C., in which a square of legionaries would link their shields on both the sides and the top, giving them complete cover from enemy fire.

When he noticed the "fish-scale" reference in the 1930s, orientalist Homer Dubs was immediately reminded of the Romans:

A line of Roman *scuta*, exending without a gap along the front rank of a line of foot-soldiers, would look to someone who had never seen such an array before, like a "fish-scale formation," especially because of their rounded surfaces. It would indeed be difficult to describe it otherwise.

A second clue led in the same direction. The *History of the Former Han Dynasty* says that the Chinese army found the city gate defended by a double palisade. This again has a distinctly Roman air—legionaries were past masters at building this kind of defense, consisting of a ditch with lines of sharpened timbers both in front and behind it. Dubs checked with fellow historians and found that no other ancient people used this style of fortification. The nomadic Huns, in particular, were not skilled in any kind of military engineering.

Putting together the clues of the "fish-scale" formation and the double palisade, Dubs suggested that Jzh-jzh's army included a force of a hundred or so Roman legionaries, who had somehow wandered far to the east and entered his employ as mercenaries. The idea is intriguing, yet seems slightly crazy. What would Roman soldiers have been doing so far from home, within reach of the Imperial Chinese army?

The Defeat of Crassus

As it happens, evidence from the Roman side shows that there *would* have been a large number of Roman soldiers in nearly the right place and at exactly the right date.

The greatest threat to Roman power in the east was always the Parthian Empire, based in Iran. Resurrecting the old imperial ambitions of Persia, the Parthians extended their control over Iraq, Syria, and Palestine (see **The Star of Bethlehem** in **Watching the Skies**). In 54 B.C. Crassus, one of Rome's most ambitious (though least competent) generals, set off to break the Parthian stranglehold on the Near East. At first he was successful. His army—seven Roman legions, four thousand cavalry, and as many light-armed troops (totaling about 42,000 men)—marched deep into northern Iraq. Then, in May 53 B.C., it came face-to-face with the enemy at Carrhae (Harran).

Crassus' allies deserted before the battle even began, taking with them most of the cavalry. He was left with a force that, though much larger than the enemy's, was almost entirely composed of foot soldiers. The army that faced them was all mounted, including a highly trained unit of some 9,000 horse archers. The Parthian heavy cavalry quickly took care of the Roman auxiliaries, while the swift-moving archers harassed Crassus' main force. The legionaries formed a defensive square, locking their shields around them, but not to much effect. The Romans had yet to perfect the *testudo* maneuver, so while Crassus' soldiers were protected from the sides they were still vulnerable from above. Shooting high into the air, the Parthians rained arrows down on them. Beaten, the Romans retreated to higher ground to regroup. Crassus was lured away from his troops by promise of a treaty and killed, his head being sent back to Parthia for sport. The Romans were now in complete disarray. Twenty thousand were killed on the spot, and another ten thousand captured. It was one of the worst military disasters Rome ever suffered.

The Romans never forgot the shame of Carrhae. The famous Marc Antony returned to Parthia eighteen years later to avenge Crassus' defeat. This time the Romans had fully developed the art of forming a *testudo*, providing them with complete cover from the Parthian arrows, and Antony's expedition, while not exactly successful, was nowhere near as disastrous as Crassus' campaign had been.

Meanwhile, what happened to the ten thousand legionaries captured at Carrhae? Roman records tell us that the king of Parthia transported them 1,500 miles to the opposite end of his empire.

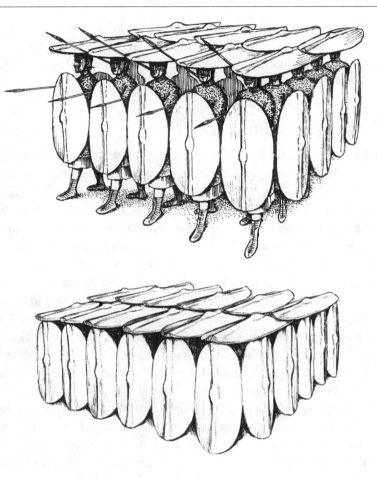

Roman soldiers practice forming the *testudo*.

Many would have died during the long and arduous journey, but those who survived were settled as mercenary troops in the province of Margiana on Parthia's eastern border. The Roman poet Horace surmised that the soldiers, despairing of ever returning home, married local women and settled into their new lives.

So we know that about 50 B.C., several thousand Roman legionaries were actually stationed in central Asia, at a point only another five hundred miles from Jzh-jzh's capital on the Talass River. This, Dubs argued, could explain the apparent presence of Romans in Jzh-jzh's army seventeen years after the battle of Carrhae. Perhaps the king of Parthia sold some of his legionaries to the neighboring king of Sogdiana, Jzh-jzh's patron; or perhaps some of the Romans simply escaped and made their way eastward as soldiers of fortune.

Whatever the case, the evidence from the Roman end about the aftermath of the battle of Carrhae makes it entirely feasible that the soldiers performing the "fish-scale" formation at Jzh-jzh's capital in 36 B.C. were indeed Roman legionaries. So what would have happened to them after the battle with Chen Tang's imperial force? Can we follow their trail any farther?

Romans in China

The Chinese record states that at the end of the battle with Jzh-jzh, 145 of the enemy were captured in battle, while another thousand surrendered. The prisoners were then distributed as slaves among the various allied kings who had provided forces for the expedition. Dubs noted that the figure of 145 battle captives tallies curiously with the number ("over a hundred") of soldiers performing the fish-scale maneuver, and speculated that these may have been the Romans.

In any case, it is reasonable to suppose that the Romans would not have been gratuitously slaughtered; they were a curiosity, and as such a valued commodity. They may have been moved farther east, to serve as slaves or mercenaries, in one of the states of Chinese Turkestan, which supplied troops for Chen Tang's expedition. Concluding his study in 1941, Dubs wondered whether any of them ever reached China, "but such an event seems somewhat unlikely."

A few years later Dubs approached the subject again, with a new piece of evidence suggesting that the legionaries *did*, after all, get to China. As well as supplying the final leg of the journey taken by our accidental Roman voyagers, it seems to provide confirmation of the story as a whole. A census from about A.D. 5 includes among the cities of the Kansu province of northwestern China a place called Li-jien (or Li-kan), which happens to be one of the Chinese terms for the Greco-Roman world. Why should a Chinese city be given such a curious name? The mystery is compounded by a change that happened in A.D. 9, when Emperor Wang Mang decreed that all city names should "correspond with reality." In accordance, Li-jien was changed to Jieh-lu, which can mean "prisoner raised up" or "prisoners [captured] in taking by storm." The literal and only conclusion one can draw is that the city had been settled by people from somewhere in the Roman Empire, who were captured when a city was stormed. Here, it seems, is the final trace of Jzh-jzh's "fish-scale" soldiers, a tiny remnant of Crassus' legions who inadvertently crossed half the world. (If the population of Li-jien has not changed significantly in the last two thousand years, DNA testing could one day provide the last piece of the jigsaw puzzle.)

With this Chinese city, named after Roman captives, the story of the itinerant legionaries ends—but this was not the last contact between the Chinese and Roman worlds. Trade was now beginning to introduce these two distant civilizations. Initially there seems to have been no direct contact; instead the Romans became familiar with the Chinese, whom they knew of as the "Seres," through their products brought by the caravan routes across Central Asia and Parthia to the Mediterranean. Silk, of course, was the thing that intrigued the Romans the most. Apparently unaware of the existence of the silkworm, the poet Virgil (1st century B.C.) wrote in terms of wonder of the "delicate wool that the Seres comb from the leaves of their trees."

Indirect contact continued in this fashion for two or three centuries until, in A.D. 166, a surprising entry appears in the Chinese annals. They record the arrival of an "embassy" from king An-tun of Ta-ch'in, one of the two Chinese names for the Roman Empire. An-tun was evidently the Emperor Marcus Aurelius Antoninus (A.D. 161–80). The "embassy," or rather trade delegation, offered gifts of ivory, rhinoceros horn, and tortoiseshell, but, as the annals note rather snottily, "their tribute contained no jewels whatsoever." The enterprising Romans appear to have arrived by sea, as the annals state that they came from the direction of Vietnam. Presumably they had sailed around India in order to arrive, clearly showing that Roman traders were not put off by distances.

This extraordinary stray scrap of history may be merely the tip of the iceberg in terms of direct Roman-Chinese contacts. On the other hand, the Chinese annals specifically state that the embassy of A.D. 166 was the *beginning* of formal trade relations between Rome and China. The ineptness of the embassy's gifts (ivory, rhinoceros horn, and tortoiseshell) suggests that the Roman traders or ambassadors were indeed inexperienced. What need did the Emperor of China have for eastern products such as ivory, rhinoceros horn, and tortoiseshell? To him the products of the Mediterranean and European world—such as amber from the North Sea, Phoenician glassware from the Lebanon, or even blond wigs made from German hair—would have been far more "exotic" and interesting. Whether later Roman traders learned their lesson and came back again for regular visits is something we may never know.

Medallion of the Emperor Marcus Aurelius.

THE VIKINGS IN AMERICA

The Vikings, the restless adventurers of old Scandinavia, were not just bloodthirsty raiders and conquerors. Their roving bands founded new kingdoms as far afield as Sicily and Russia, explored the coasts and rivers of the whole of northern Europe, and opened up the North Atlantic, discovering Iceland and then Greenland. They were without doubt the greatest explorers of the medieval world.

Yet not all their voyages were so well planned. According to one of the Norse Sagas (medieval works of literature recording the deeds of the great figures of the past), one Bjarni Herjolfsson reached the coast of North America quite by accident. *The Greenlanders' Saga* relates how, in the year A.D. 986, Bjarni set out from Norway to return home to Iceland with a cargo of trade goods. Arriving in Iceland, he received the surprising news that his father Herjolf had joined Eirik the Red in the first settlement of Greenland earlier that summer. Stubbornly, Bjarni pushed on toward Greenland, although he and his crew had only a sketchy idea of where they were heading.

Fog descended after three days at sea, and the wind changed direction, blowing them away from Greenland. Several days later the fog lifted and they sighted land, "covered with forest, with low hills there." Bjarni realized this could not be Greenland, so they worked their way north, two days later reaching "flat country covered with woods," and farther north again to a land that was "high, mountainous and glaciered." Bjarni was unimpressed, declaring "to me this land looks good for nothing," so he set out to sea once more, this time arriving safely in Greenland.

In the Sagas, Bjarni is ridiculed for his timidity in not setting foot on this new land. But when the news of his sighting eventually reached Greenland, it apparently set off a wave of enthusiasm for "discovering new countries." By A.D. 1000 Leif, son of Eirik the Red, had bought Bjarni's boat, hired a crew, and sailed back along Bjarni's route. Leif and his crew first came ashore on the land of mountains and glaciers, which Leif named Helluland ("Slab Land"), then landed at the flat country of woods, dubbed Markland ("Forest Land"), and finally set down on much richer land to the south. Here they built wooden houses and went exploring. Among other things, Tyrkir the German discovered grapes and vines, giving the country its name of Vinland. The following spring, Leif and his men sailed back to Greenland, their expedition of exploration over.

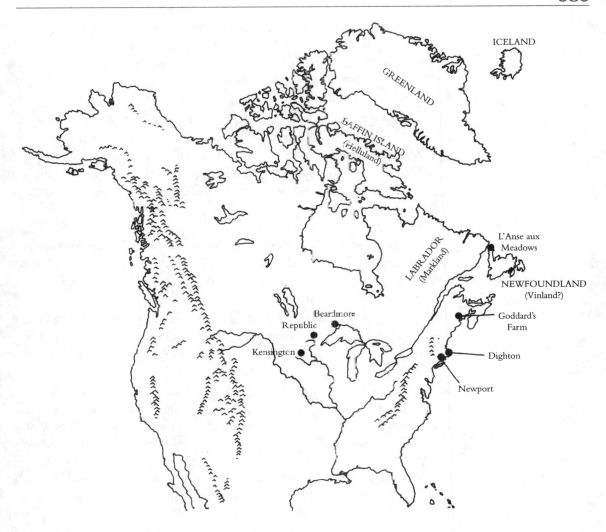

The Viking Atlantic, showing sites of claimed Viking activity and the probable locations of Helluland, Markland, and Vinland.

Much the most ambitious Viking plan for North America was Thorfinn Karlsefni's attempt at settlement around A.D. 1025. He set sail with a mixed group of some sixty-five would-be colonizers, including his wife, Gudrid. They reached Vinland, landing at Leif's old settlement according to one Saga, and stayed for perhaps three years, during which Gudrid gave birth to their son Snorri, the first Scandinavian child born in the Americas. Shortly thereafter, conflict broke out between the settlers and locals, called the Skrælings ("wretches") by the Norse. Despite the Vikings' contempt for them, the natives terrified the invaders by using some kind of catapult against them. Karlsefni decided that the colonists were too few in number to contend with hostile natives. As *Eirik the Red's Saga* puts it:

It now seemed plain to Karlsefni and his men that though the quality of the land was admirable, there would always be fear and strife dogging them there on account of those who already inhabited it. So they made ready to leave, setting their hearts on their own country.

Further trading missions to the new lands followed, but Karlsefni's failed attempt at settlement seems to have marked the high point of Viking interest in Vinland. That need not, of course, mean that private voyages to Markland would have ceased and, indeed, one is recorded in Icelandic documents as late as 1347. Greenlanders had one very good motive for continuing to sail to Markland rather than to Vinland: the drastic shortage of good-quality timber for boat building in Greenland itself. In addition, the furs and narwhal or walrus tusks they could have acquired from the Inuit (Eskimos) were of far greater value in the Viking economy than anything to be had farther south in Vinland.

But even if Vinland was no longer visited, it was not forgotten. The German churchman Adam of Bremen claimed to have been told of Vinland by the Danish king Svein Estridsson (A.D. 1068–1076):

He told me too of yet another island, discovered by many in that ocean, which is called Wineland from the circumstance that vines grow there of their own accord, and produce the most excellent wine. That there is abundance of unsown corn there we have learned not from fabulous conjecture but from the trustworthy report of the Danes. Beyond that island, he said, no habitable land is found in that ocean, but every place beyond it is full of impenetrable ice and intense darkness.

Already Vinland was taking on an air of mystery. While there are later medieval references to Vinland, they add nothing further and appear to become more removed from any possible firsthand knowledge.

But how reliable are the Sagas as historical sources? In the early nineteenth century many commentators began to doubt whether they contained even a grain of truth. Several factors encouraged the doubters: there was a gap of two or three hundred years between the Vinland voyages and their recording; the different accounts disagree at various points, and certain individuals seem to have their roles magnified at the expense of others; the Sagas were, of course, commissioned works of literature, not history, so it would hardly be surprising if they exaggerated the deeds of the forebears of those in power at the time they were composed; and they contain fantastic scenes, traveler's tales, and echoes of earlier fictional voyagers. With all these potential pitfalls it was hardly surprising that archskeptics could happily dismiss the Sagas as evidence of Vikings in America.

The Newport Tower

Still, the doubters would be silenced if only some physical trace of the Vikings in America could be found. After all, if the Norse had reached the New World they should have left *something* behind. In the 1830s, Danish scholar Carl Rafn set off a concerted hunt for signs of Viking settlement by appealing to historical societies across the United States to send him news of anything of possible Viking origin. Reports flooded in of objects, buildings, and possible inscriptions. From this mass Rafn picked out two sites that he found particularly interesting: the Dighton Rock and the Newport Tower.

Puritan settlers were the first to notice and record the strange markings on the Dighton Rock in Massachusetts. Cotton Mather, infamous for his role in instigating the Salem Witch Trials, published a drawing of the carvings in 1690. President George Washington saw a later copy of the markings in 1789 on a visit to Harvard, commenting that the "writing" looked like that made by the Indians of Virginia, which he had seen "in the younger part of his life." For Rafn, however, the Dighton markings were a mixture of Norse runes (a simple system of writing with lines used by Germans and Scandinavians from around A.D. 200, completely unlike modern letters), and Roman numerals. He read it as saying "Thorfinn [Karlsefni] and his 151 companions took possession of this land."

Seen without the benefit of such certainty, the Dighton Rock is covered with a confusing jumble of symbols, some added since Cotton Mather's day, which have been equally convincingly identified as Phoenician, Portuguese, Welsh, Hebrew, and Chinese. Archaeologists have agreed since the 1880s that the most likely carvers of the rock are the local Algonkian Indians.

Rafn's second "Viking site," the Newport Tower (Rhode Island), has been taken much more seriously. The tower today survives, following an explosion in 1780, as the romantic shell of a circular stone building some 25 feet high. The essence of the Viking case is that the architectural style of the building closely resembles fortified medieval churches in Scandinavia. Henry Wadsworth Longfellow was inspired by a recently discovered burial and Rafn's theory concerning the

Supposed Viking tower at
Newport, Rhode Island.

tower to write his romantic ballad *"The Skeleton in Armor"* (1840), about a Viking who builds the tower for his lady love, although the skeleton turned out to be a Native American buried with local copper ornaments.

Later historians proposed a much less exciting identification of the tower as a combination watchtower and storehouse, later converted into a windmill, built around 1650. Benedict Arnold, Governor of Rhode Island, who owned the tower at his death, referred to it in his will as "my stone built wind mill." The "medieval" architectural style and building techniques of the tower are also found in other buildings from colonial New England, so most people accepted that the tower dated to the mid–seventeenth century.

Reviving the Viking claim to the Newport Tower was the work of archaeologist Philip Means, best known for his work in Peru before publishing *Newport Tower* in 1942. After a lengthy review of the evidence, Means argued for a date around A.D. 1120 for the tower, utterly dismissing the colonial theory on the grounds that Governor Arnold was simply reusing a far older building. The most recent defender of Means's work is American meteorologist Rolf Nilsestuen, who chides the inhabitants of Newport for failing to recognize the treasure in their midst:

> Alternative explanations simply don't fit the facts. The Tower is also the first known Christian house of worship built in America. It is time for Americans, including the residents of Newport, to be guided by the force of reason and to recognise that as a medieval church the Tower is a far greater source of national and community pride than an imaginary mill or watchtower, neither of which can stand up to the test of the evidence.

Nilsestuen's "evidence" is a curious beast, as it manages to omit the main points in favor of the colonial theory. Unlike the Dighton Rock, a far less conspicuous monument that was spotted at an early date, the Newport Tower goes strangely unmentioned by settlers until Arnold's time, and only in the nineteenth century is there any suggestion of it being anything other than a perfectly ordinary colonial structure.

Doubts have been thrown on the ability of the tiny Newport community (founded only in 1639) to construct such a monument. Yet a 1632 petition by New England colonists survives that requests a tower, apparently like the one at Newport. Sir Edward Plowden was asked to provide "several commodities . . . so that idle men as souldiers or gent be resident in a rownde stone towre." Strongpoints like this were constructed up and down New England in the early days of English settlement, so there is no reason to think the community at Newport could not have built one.

There is also vital archaeological evidence in favor of a colonial date. Following World War II, the Peabody Museum of Harvard University took up the problem of the tower and formed a committee to find a suitable excavator. Step forward William Godfrey Jr., a graduate student at Harvard and a descendant of Governor Arnold to boot. Who could be a better choice?

Godfrey's excavations at the tower were absolutely definitive. In the foundation trench of the building (into which the stone columns holding it up had been set) he found a series of items that must have dated to the time when the Tower was built. These were without exception of the colonial period—pieces of brick and plaster, pottery, clay pipes, glass, and a gun flint (for striking a spark to fire a musket). Godfrey's conclusion was crystal clear:

> Individually, these items may appear insignificant. Collectively, however, they are conclusive. One find, or two, might be the result of faulty excavating technique. Many finds, documented and carefully observed, excavated under circumstances which in each case preclude error, add up to a positive and unshakeable conclusion. The tower could not have been built before the latter half of the 17th century. The Norse theory can no longer be entertained.

Incredibly, Nilsestuen, in his 1994 study, fails to mention Godfrey's excavations at all.

Fighting Over Weapons

The majority of the reports sent to Rafn of Viking traces in America were of weapons, but Rafn himself paid them little attention, as accurate drawings of them were not available. Interest in possible finds of American Viking weaponry was revived by historian Hjalmar Holand in the first part of this century. In a string of publications he examined a large number of curious weapons—axes, swords, and halberds—that had been found in Minnesota and Wisconsin. In Holand's view their shapes could be matched with examples known from Scandinavian museums. Altogether they make up an impressive body of finds.

However, Birgitta Wallace of the Canadian Parks Service, who has carried out a detailed study of these items and their Scandinavian counterparts, has come to an entirely opposite view. For example, the axe from Republic in Minnesota has an exact counterpart in the Lillehammer Museum in Norway. So far so good for Holand's case, but the Lillehammer Museum is primarily a museum of historical folk craft. Indeed, the Lillehammer curator informed Wallace that their axe had been transferred from the Museum of Antiquities in Oslo because "it does not date from the Middle Ages but from the Historic Period," that is, the last two to three centuries. In fact, Wallace has identified all of Holand's "Viking" axes as "early American lumbering tools."

Holand's swords fare no better. These are far shorter than the very large two-handed medieval swords. According to Wallace, they are most likely to have been produced for pageants and military parades at the beginning of the nineteenth century.

Strangest of all are the miniature halberds, thought by Holand to be ceremonial weapons because they are of soft iron and flimsy construction. Although Holand was unable to trace a single example of a medieval Scandinavian halberd, he was not deterred. Then, in 1946, he triumphantly published a letter from the University Museum of Oslo that he believed vindicated him. However, as Wallace points out, careful reading of the letter shows that the Oslo Museum actually told Holand that the halberds in its collection dated to after A.D. 1500, which would be far too late for the Vikings. Her own researches agree, showing that "Scandinavians did not in fact use halberds until about 1500," so they are hardly likely to have made ceremonial versions before that.

Almost unbelievably, Holand's miniature halberds have been identified by modern historians as late-nineteenth-century tobacco cutters, made as part of an advertising campaign! The American Tobacco Company tried to boost sales of its Battle-Ax brand of plug tobacco by giving away cutters shaped in the form of a halberd attached by a hinge to a chopping board. As they fell out of use as tobacco cutters, many of these unusual and attractive objects were detached from their boards to be kept as ornaments.

The only American weapon finds archaeologists will accept as genuinely Norse are those from Beardmore in Ontario, Canada. In 1931, James Dodd, a railwayman and part-time gold prospector, produced an impressive group of three items—a sword, an axe, and a rattle used as part of horse trappings. In 1936, he brought them in to the Royal Ontario Museum in Toronto, which authenticated all three objects and bought them for $500. They went on display at the museum as the possible burial goods of a Norse explorer from Leif Eiriksson's time.

Although the museum undertook excavations at the find spot—Dodd's mining claim—only a few scraps of iron were recovered. Then doubts set in. As early as 1938, local newspapers suggested that Dodd, rather than having dynamited the objects out of the ground at Beardmore, had found them in the basement of the house where he lived in Port Arthur. J. M. Hansen, owner of the property, stated that he had received some old weapons as security on a loan to an employee, Jens Bloch, who had inherited a collection of armor from his father, a well-known Norwegian artist. Unfortunately, Bloch had died in 1936, but his widow confirmed the story. Claim and counterclaim followed,

Viking sword said to have been found at Beardmore, Ontario.

with various parties, including Dodd's foster son, confessing to the fraud and then withdrawing their statements. Today the Beardmore weapons are "in limbo," as the Royal Ontario Museum puts it, held in a storeroom. Museum authorities regard them as genuinely Norse, but think they probably reached Canada with Jens Bloch in 1923 rather than with a Viking explorer a thousand years before.

Then there are the holes, thought to have been made for mooring boats to rocks, found in large numbers along the east coast of the United States and even inland along midwestern rivers. Many Viking enthusiasts from Holand onward have argued that these are a sure sign of Norse presence. The idea is that Viking ships exploring the coasts would have needed a way of slipping away quickly if hostile Indians appeared: a mooring pin in a hole can be swiftly detached. Nilsestuen, for example, claims that "since the mooring holes are unique to the Scandinavian culture, they are solid evidence that Norsemen were in the American Midwest hundreds of years ago." On the other hand, Wallace points out the impractical nature of going about drilling holes in a situation where the noise would easily betray the boat's presence to an enemy. She dismisses the whole idea:

> Drilling a new hole for each mooring is entirely unknown from the Norse culture area. Mooring bolts are, of course, familiar objects, but they are ring bolts permanently installed in rocks along the shores where people anchor regularly. . . . For quick mooring the Norse simply threw a line around a boulder or tree.

So what are these mysterious mooring holes? One clue is that, as Wallace notes, many of them would have been underwater in Norse times, so they must belong to more recent times. Two different explanations have been put forward for the inland and the coastal examples. For those inland, archaeologists generally agree that most are holes drilled for blasting rock to use in building houses and barns; thousands of rocks were broken apart using this method, and they believe that some boulders simply escaped destruction. Those on the coast have an equally mundane explanation. Admiral Samuel Morison, the well-known naval historian, commented on one mooring hole enthusiast's catalog of examples from Maine:

> These were made by the English natives of New England to receive iron eye-bolts through which to reeve a line to a boat mooring or fish trap. I could have shown him some made for me!

The Kensington Rune Stone

Of all the finds put forward to demonstrate a Norse presence in the United States, by far the best known and most fiercely contested is the Kensington Rune Stone.

In November 1898, a Swedish immigrant farmer, Olof Ohman, was clearing a small knoll near his house of trees, with the help of his young son, Edward. As he pulled out one tree a stone came out of the ground tightly clasped in its roots. Ohman spotted some markings on the stone and took it to the nearby village of Kensington in Minnesota, a community of Scandinavian immigrants, where it was put on display. Soon afterward, one of the villagers apparently realized that the markings were an inscription in runes, the old Nordic alphabet, still taught in Scandinavian schools at the time.

A rough copy of the markings was sent to O. J. Breda, Professor of Scandinavian Languages at the University of Minnesota. Breda was unimpressed, as were other Scandinavian experts, who thought the inscription to be a modern fake. Disheartened, Ohman took the stone back to his farm. There it lay until Hjalmar Holand visited the area in 1907 and saw the stone. He was convinced it was genuine, and spent the next fifty years trying to bring the world around to his opinion. He had a proper translation of the runes produced, which showed the potential importance of the inscription:

8 Goths and 22 Norwegians on exploration journey from Vinland westward. We had camp by 2 rocky islets one day's journey north from this stone. We were out and fished one day. After we came home found 10 men red with blood and dead. AVM save from evil. Have 10 men by the sea to look after our ships 14 days' journey from this island. Year 1362.

Was this concrete evidence of Viking explorers in the Americas at last?

Holand was in good company in championing the authenticity of the stone. In the late 1940s it was prominently displayed by the Smithsonian Institution in Washington, where Dr. Matthew Stirling, Director of the American Bureau of Ethnology, described it as "probably the most important archaeological object yet found in North America." Today it forms the centerpiece of the Rune Stone Museum at Alexandria, the nearest town to Kensington. In Runestone Memorial Park, a giant granite reproduction of the stone sits on a four-ton

ᚠ᛬ᚤᚯᛏᛏᚱ᛬ᚾᛉ᛬ᚠᚠ᛬ᚼᚱᚱᚤᚾ᛬ᛒᛏ᛬
᛬ᛁᚼᛒᚠᚷᚤᛏᛁ�435ᛏᚠᚷᚱᚦ᛬ᚠᚱᛏ᛬
ᚤᛁᛏᚷᛉᛏ᛬ᚠ᛬ᚤᛏ�᛬ᚤᛁ᛬
ᛏᚷᛣᛏ᛬ᛁᚷᚷᛏᚱ᛬ᚤᛏᛒ᛬ᚠ᛬�452ᚷᚱ᛬ᛏᛏ᛬
ᚦᚷᚷᚱ᛬ᚱᛁᛌᛏ᛬ᚼᚱᚱ᛬ᚠᚱᛏ᛬ᚦᛏᛏᛉ᛬ᛌᛏᛉ᛬
ᚤᛁ᛬ᚤᚷᚱ᛬ᛉᛉ᛬ᛌᛣᛌᛏᛁᛁᛏ᛬ᚷᚤᛏᛣᛒᛏᛁᚱ᛬
ᚤᛁ᛬ᛉᛏᚤ᛬ᛉᛏᚤ᛬ᚠᚷᛏ᛬ᚠ᛬ᚤᚷᛏ᛬ᚱᚯᚦᛏ᛬
ᚷᚠ᛬ᛒᛁᛏᛦ᛬ᛉᛇ᛬ᛦᛏ᛬ᚦ᛬ᛡᚢᛦᛊᛚ᛬
ᚠᚷᛣᛏᛁᛌᛏ᛬ᚷᚠ᛬ᛁᛁᛒᚤ᛬

ᚼᚷᚱᚠᛦ᛬ᚤᚷᛏᛌ᛬ᚤᛁ᛬ᛉᚷᚤᛏᛏ᛬ᚷᛏ᛬ᛌᛏᛦ᛬
ᚷ᛬ᛒᛏᛁᚱ᛬ᚤᛏᚱᛏ᛬ᛌᛉᛁᛒ᛬ᚠᚠ᛬ᛏᚷᚤᛏ᛬ᚱᛁᛌᛏ᛬
ᚠᚱᛌᚤ᛬ᚼᛁᛏ᛬ᚦᛏᚷᛦᛏᚱ᛬ᚠᚠᛡ᛬

The Kensington Stone from
Minnesota—with copy of its
runic inscription.

base, near a monstrous concrete Viking on whose shield is embla-
zoned the legend ALEXANDRIA. BIRTHPLACE OF AMERICA.

So, is the Kensington Rune Stone genuine? Unfortunately the circumstances of its discovery were never satisfactorily resolved. Surviving accounts differ on the details, even regarding the tree under which the stone was found. Had anyone at the time thought of preserving the tree stump, counting its growth rings could have at least established a minimum age for the stone's burial. Subsequent estimates of the tree as being some seventy years old—so dating the burial of the stone to a time before modern Scandinavians settled the area—depend entirely on Ohman's suggestion that it was stunted. Skeptics suggest it could have grown in just a dozen years.

What about the inscription itself? Surely we must know enough about runic texts to tell if this is a forgery or not? Many runic experts are wholly confident that we do. Professor Erik Wahlgren of the University of California, Los Angeles, has devoted years of study to the Kensington Rune Stone, which he identifies as a fake on the basis of the vocabulary, grammar, and dating system. Specifically, the inscription includes many unusual forms of words, the apparently English-derived *ded*, and a made-up term *opdagelsesfard*, which would mean "voyage of exploration." The grammar is strange, with word endings that seem out of place in the fourteenth century but were standard in the nineteenth. All of the numbers in the text are in Arabic form, while medieval runic inscriptions were written using Roman numerals.

Defenders of the Kensington Rune Stone, from Holand to Nilsestuen, have assiduously trawled the archives of Scandinavia and all its languages and dialects to find parallels for the words and have come up with a series of matches, although no example of *opdagelsesfard*. They have also been able to demonstrate that Arabic numerals were used in Scandinavia in the fourteenth century. However, that is not the same as using Arabic numerals within a runic inscription, for that involves mixing two entirely different systems of communication. As for the alleged parallels, finding similar words and grammatical uses in the various Scandinavian tongues of the Middle Ages is not enough in itself. While the individual elements of the Kensington Rune Stone might be genuine, runologists argue that the text has to be considered as a whole before it can be authenticated.

Wallace sums up runological opinion with a critical verdict on the language of the text:

> A simple test may be applied to the runes of the inscription of the Kensington Stone. If we eliminate from consideration all its inscribed runes that do not have another uncontested fourteenth-century provenance, then only the simplest forms remain, such as those for

"and" and "we." These forms have remained unchanged from earliest medieval through modern times.

"Possible, but not at all likely" has been the expert verdict on the inscription, ever since Holand took the stone on a tour of Scandinavia in 1911. Attempts to bolster the case for the Rune Stone by bringing into the debate other claimed runic inscriptions from the United States have foundered on the declarations of runologists that all of these are either obvious modern fakes or entirely natural cracks in the rock surface.

A broader historical approach might help to resolve the issue of the Kensington Rune Stone. Is a Scandinavian presence in the United States likely in 1362? Might an expedition have been sent out from there into the Midwest?

Two pieces of Scandinavian evidence have been brought into the equation. One is the Vinland Map, which has been argued to demonstrate early-fifteenth-century Scandinavian knowledge of a successful expedition to America by Bishop Eirik of Greenland in A.D. 1118. Unfortunately, this unique document is as mired in controversy as the Kensington Rune Stone (see **The Vinland Map** in **Hoax?**).

More directly relevant is Holand's attempt to link the date of the Rune Stone (1362) to Scandinavian history. Magnus Eiriksson, king of Sweden and Norway, asked one Powell Knutsson to sail to Greenland in 1354 to "protect" the Christians there. Holand speculated that Knutsson's expedition of Swedes and Norwegians had traveled farther west, ending up in Vinland and then exploring the interior of America. The party met with disaster, as recorded on the Kensington Stone. He wondered if the survivors of the massacre may have become founders of the "White Indian" tribe of the Mandans who lived along the Missouri (see **The Welsh Indians** in this chapter).

Unfortunately, we have no reason to believe that the Knutsson expedition even set out. No Norwegian or Greenlandic records confirm their departure or return. Indeed, it seems as though the whole Knutsson episode may have been a cynical smoke screen.

King Magnus Eiriksson has gone down in history as a man keenly interested in the religious welfare of his subjects. According to Nilsestuen he was a man of "fanatical missionary zeal," who invaded Russia in an attempt to force the inhabitants to convert from Orthodoxy to Catholicism. But historian Kirsten Seaver's more critical analysis produces a very different picture of Magnus. In 1351 the pope had allowed Magnus to tax the clergy to finance his Russian campaign, and matched this projected tax revenue with a loan. However the war fizzled out the same year, and the cash-strapped king diverted the pope's money to fill a hole in his finances. By 1354 things must have been getting sticky with the pope, who wanted his loan back; matters came to a head in 1358, when the pope excommunicated Magnus for his failure to come up with the money. Seaver argues that this is the true context of the Knutsson "expedition":

> It is doubtful that it ever took place and even more doubtful that Magnus had ever intended for it to take place. Most likely, he was putting on a pious performance as a serious Defender of the Faith who deserved whatever money he could lay his hands on.

Of course, the Kensington Rune Stone doesn't actually mention Knutsson, so the expedition it refers to could be some other unrecorded act of exploration. But why Minnesota? Critics of the stone have always found this fertile ground for doubt, as there is no sign of inland journeys in either the Sagas or Greenlandic history. Admiral Morison seized on this point to discredit the stone:

> The Kensington story is preposterous. Norsemen were sea discoverers, not land explorers; what possible object could they have had in sailing into Hudson Bay, or through Lake Superior to the Portage, and striking out into the wilderness.

Nor have the Kensington Stone supporters mapped out a feasible route, along lakes and rivers, for the Vikings to have reached the interior.

Linguistics, history, and archaeology all fail to support the Kensington Rune Stone. But if it is not genuine, then it must be a fake. Is there any reason to suspect this? Certainly the circumstances of the time at which the stone appeared almost guaranteed a receptive audience. The World's Columbian Exposition scheduled to occur in Chicago in 1892, celebrating Columbus's "Discovery of America," had angered many Scandinavian Americans in the Midwest, who felt that their forebears were being ignored. Only three years earlier a pioneering study of the Vinland voyages by historian Gustaf Storm had been reprinted in the main Swedish-language newspaper in America. By the time the Chicago Fair opened a year late in 1893, a replica of the Viking ship found at Gokstad in Norway had been sailed across the Atlantic and was anchored on Lake Michigan. Many Scandinavian Americans were only too pleased to welcome the discovery of a runic

Viking ship excavated at
Gokstad in Norway.

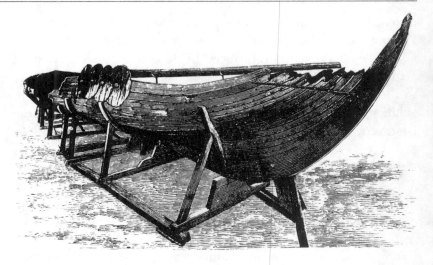

inscription as confirmation of their belief that they were following in the footsteps of their Viking ancestors.

But a fake needs a faker. Suspicion has naturally tended to fall on Olaf Ohman, who would have to have been involved in any hoax. Opinions vary dramatically on his learning and intellectual capacities, but he was probably far from the virtual illiterate painted by Holand. Of course, Ohman need not have created the inscription himself. There were certainly others in the community whose knowledge of runes was greater than his, while the historical background of Powell Knutsson's expedition had been provided by Storm. Suspiciously, it was the serialization of Storm's work that first introduced the crucial term *opdagelsesfard* (for Viking voyages of exploration) to an American audience.

Yet is there any direct evidence of fraud? Two items, seldom commented on by the pro-stone writers, seem to point in that direction.

On New Year's Day, 1899, J. P. Hedberg, a Kensington businessman, sent a supposedly exact copy of the inscription to the editor of a Swedish-language newspaper in Minneapolis, hazarding the guess that it was "in old Greek letters." Later comparison with the stone shows Hedberg's copy to contain several errors. At face value this merely seems to confirm the confusion that reigned when the Kensington Stone was discovered. However, when Hedberg's copy was brought to the attention of the runologist Erik Moltke of the Danish National Museum in Copenhagen, he jumped at it. In his view (seconded by Wahlgren), Hedberg had sent a preliminary draft of the fake inscription to the newspaper, rather than a copy. The grounds for his conclusion are that the mistakes are not the gross errors one would imagine someone making who didn't even know what language he was copying. Instead the mistakes are actually proper runes, not nonsense, and more difficult to write than are those on the stone itself. Certainly, one would imagine a poor copy to simplify the original, or turn it into complete confusion, rather than make it more complex. According to Wahlgren, Hedberg's copy "was made by a person completely familiar with these 'runes,' inasmuch as the confident and purposeful way in which the runes are drawn seems to exclude an uninitiated outsider." One is led to suspect that Hedberg was more involved in the "discovery" of the inscription than he admitted

For the critics, the final blow against the Stone comes in the form of a confession. In 1973, one Walter Cran recorded a tape on his deathbed in which he stated that his father, John, had confessed (while he was dying) to having carved the inscription with Olaf Ohman. Walter had then sought and gained confirmation of this story from John Ohman, Olaf's son, just before he breathed his last. The motive, according to Walter Cran, was to "bluff the people around the country, especially the educated ones, that think you are cumb . . . [giving the hoaxers] the biggest haha they ever had in their life." This sounds pretty conclusive, and many skeptics have concluded that it lays the Kensington Stone to rest, although three deathbed confessions seems a little too good to be true.

L'Anse aux Meadows—Leif's Settlement?

The story of the Vikings in America had been one long story of false hopes, fakes, and lost causes until the Norwegian explorer Helge Ingstad and his archaeologist wife Anne arrived on the island of Newfoundland in 1960. They came in search of Leif Eiriksson and his camp. Traveling around the coast they arrived at L'Anse aux Meadows, on the north side of Newfoundland. It struck Helge Ingstad as a promising spot, with a strong resemblance to Bjarni and Leif's descriptions of Vinland. George Decker, the unofficial leader of the L'Anse aux Meadows settlement, took Ingstad out to Black Duck Brook, a small stream running into Épaves Bay, beside which there were the outlines of several houses beneath the heather. According to Decker, they predated the earliest fishing settlements in the area.

The Ingstads started excavating at L'Anse aux Meadows the following year, and continued for seven summers. Further work was undertaken by the Canadian Parks Service in the 1970s, after the settlement was given the status of a National Historic Site.

The Viking settlement at L'Anse aux Meadows, Newfoundland, with a workshop and hall in the foreground and the bog to the right.

The typically Viking bronze pin from the settlement at L'Anse aux Meadows.

Excavations uncovered seven buildings in three complexes, with a hall and one or two workshops in each group. Maybe slightly less than a hundred people lived there. All the buildings are constructed in the same way, with turf walls and roofs over a wooden framework. This is the typical method of house construction in both Iceland and Greenland in Viking times. The date of the occupation is clear. The building style is matched by Icelandic houses from about A.D. 1000, while over fifty radiocarbon dates point to the same period. The lack of a buildup of rubbish strongly suggests that the site was used for only a few years, an observation confirmed by the fact that the houses show no signs of repair.

Next to the houses was a bog, and just outside one hall a heap of discarded pieces from woodworking was discovered. This heap came mainly from ship repair, judging by the kind of debris found. Among these wooden scraps were pieces of Scots or Red pine, both species foreign to Newfoundland, with Scots pine being found only in Europe.

In one of the other halls there was a smithy, and pieces of iron were found scattered throughout L'Anse aux Meadows, mostly in the form of rivets, as used in Norse shipbuilding. A charcoal kiln and a furnace where the iron was smelted were located a safe distance away on the other side of the bog.

Individual objects also betrayed a Scandinavian presence. A bronze pin for fastening a cloak is a typical Viking type, as are a small whetstone for sharpening metal tools, a spindle whorl for spinning wool, and a bone needle with a hole drilled through it.

Most intriguing of the finds are four local American objects, three butternuts (a kind of walnut), and a piece of butternut wood worked with metal tools. Butternut trees have never grown as far north as Newfoundland, and may point to contacts southward along the coast of New England, as may the Maine Penny, although this is a slightly later find (see **Box: The Maine Penny**).

But was L'Anse aux Meadows Leif Eiriksson's Vinland base? Certainly Birgitta Wallace, now in charge of the site, thinks so. Quite reasonably, she argues that if Helluland was Baffin Island in the Canadian Arctic and Markland was Labrador, points on which nearly all commentators agree, then Newfoundland, as the next landmass that would be sighted heading south, ought to be at least part of the territory called Vinland. L'Anse aux Meadows would have made a good base camp at this time, as it was a convenient staging point on the way from Greenland, and it was free of native population, unlike areas to the south.

The main debate concerning the site has been over the significance of Tyrkir the German's discovery of vines and grapes, which gave Vinland its name. Most archaeologists have concluded from the fact that Newfoundland lies north of the farthest extent of wild grapes that it could not be the same as Vinland. Yet we know from L'Anse aux Meadows that the Vikings were bringing butternuts from the very area where grapes were also growing, so contact with the south was clearly happening. Perhaps Vinland was a much larger region that included Newfoundland.

What impact did the Vikings have? Seemingly almost none. They left no trace in Amerindian traditions, and no spread of metalworking or boat-building technology can be detected, either. Even epidemic diseases, which wiped out whole communities like a tidal wave sweeping ahead of the Spanish conquerors, can't be tied to the Vikings. But one thing is certain—the Vikings did reach the American continent.

THE MAINE PENNY

The only *definite* find of Viking origin in the United States of America is a tiny coin, found a thousand miles south of the Viking settlement at L'Anse aux Meadows on Newfoundland, Canada. In 1957, amateur archaeologists excavated at Goddard's Farm, by the mouth of Penobscot Bay in Maine. Thousands of Native American stone tools and pieces of pottery were discovered, along with one oddity—a coin. This was originally

identified as an English penny of the twelfth century, and for some strange reason was ignored for twenty years, until a coin expert who happened to look at the Goddard's Farm find reidentified it as a Norwegian penny minted by King Olaf Kyrre between A.D. 1067 and 1093.

Excitement mounted—here at last was evidence that Vinland (land of the grapes) was true to its name and lay in New England, where wild vines would have been growing when the Vikings reached the American continent about A.D. 1000. A major excavation was carried out, yet the prospect of a New England Vinland soon faded when no other Viking artifacts were found. But the excavators did uncover clues as to how the penny had arrived in Maine.

The penny itself has a hole drilled through it, by which it could be suspended as a pendant, suggesting that it was not in use as money when it was lost. This is supported by the radiocarbon dates for the Amerindian settlement at Goddard's Farm, which fall in the thirteenth century, a hundred years after the penny was minted. Although the penny was the only Viking find there, many other items had been brought to Goddard's Farm from the north. Throughout the site there were tools made from rocks from Nova Scotia and Labrador, one of them produced by reworking an existing stone tool of a type known to be made only by Inuits (Eskimos), who were at this time occupying parts of Labrador.

An indirect connection between the Amerindians of Maine and the Vikings through the medium of Eskimo traders is by far the most likely explanation of how this Norwegian coin traveled so far. It also acts as a reminder that Vikings continued to visit Markland (as they dubbed Labrador) long after abandoning dreams of permanent settlement in North America.

(Top) The Viking penny from Maine. (Bottom) A mint coin of Olaf Kyrre, King of Norway.

THE WELSH INDIANS

When Welshman John Evans crossed the icy Mississippi to reach St. Louis on Christmas 1794, he was seized and thrown into jail as a British spy. After all, he had a patently invented reason for entering the Spanish territory of Louisiana. Evans claimed that he had come in search of a tribe of white Indians who lived up the Missouri, descendants of a Welsh colony that had landed on the shores of the Gulf of Mexico six centuries earlier, long before Columbus.

The Spanish had good reason to be wary of strangers, no matter how innocent, if crazy, their mission might sound. This was a time of acute political tension in the North American West. The new American Republic, British Canada, and the Spanish empire (trying to hang on to its territories north of Mexico) were all contending for mastery over the Plains—the ultimate prize being to discover and claim a route over the Rocky Mountains to the Pacific Ocean. Many schemes had been hatched and armed groups of traders sent forth, only for native American tribes to block their way. It was one of these powerful tribes that Evans was desperate to contact.

Only when the lieutenant-governor was convinced by Welshmen on the American side of the border that Evans's mission was genuine did he release the would-be explorer. In August 1795, Evans pressed on with his quest, now as a representative of the Spanish government.

Prince Madoc

But why should Evans imagine that he would find his countrymen among the native Americans of the Plains? Strange as it seems, by Evans's time there had been two centuries of sightings of Welsh people in the Americas. The first dramatic encounter was provided by one David Ingram, put ashore at the Gulf of Mexico by the English fleet under Sir John Hawkins in 1568. He claimed to have walked some 2,000 miles through North America before being rescued by a French ship. Finally back in England, he related his extraordinary adventures to a government inquiry that met in 1582 to consider the possibility of setting up colonies in North America. Ingram said he had encountered pillars of gold, elephants, red sheep, and penguins on his march, and been treated kindly by a friendly tribe whose language contained a number of Welsh words. Among these words was *penguin*, supposedly derived from Welsh *pen* (head) and *gwyn* (white).

Unfortunately penguins have black heads and aren't to be seen so far north.

Despite its fantastic elements, Ingram's account struck a chord with his influential audience. In 1580 the brilliant and controversial Welsh scientist, sorcerer, and grand strategist Dr. John Dee had confidentially approached Queen Elizabeth with a map of the Americas. On the back of this document, which survives today, Dee had outlined a series of prior British claims for the Spanish territories in North America. At the top of Dee's list was a medieval Welsh venture: "The Lord Madoc, sonne to Owen Gwynedd, Prince of Northwales, led a Colonie and inhabited in Terra Florida or therabowts." As Owain Gwynedd had died in A.D. 1169, long before Columbus's time, Dee suggested that the queen, rather than the Spanish king, could rightfully lay claim to the whole of the eastern seaboard of North America. Elizabeth chose to forgo her apparent rights, not wishing to risk a final break with Spain.

The first publication of the British claim to the Americas came in 1583, with Sir George Peckham's *True Reporte*. He had been one of Ingram's amazed listeners, and presented Ingram's account as proof of Madoc's voyage. Peckham stated that in A.D. 1170 Madoc had set up a Welsh colony, somewhere in the Americas, then journeyed home. More details emerged the following year, in a history of Wales (the first ever printed) written by Humphrey Llwyd, John Dee, and David Powel. According to their account, which quoted poets and chroniclers as its source, Madoc left Wales while his brothers fought for control of their father's kingdom, spying out a refuge in North America before returning to Wales to recruit colonists. He then set sail, never to see his homeland again.

Peckham's book was followed by a steady trickle of encounters with Welsh-speaking tribes. The Reverend Morgan Jones had been appointed a naval chaplain in 1660, and sent to minister to two ships bound for Port Royal in Carolina to establish a military base. A larger fleet arrived at Port Royal, and the party moved upriver. Six months later they were at the point of starvation, so Reverend Jones set off across the country with five others, looking for help. Entering the territory of the Tuscarora tribe, they were captured, then informed by an interpreter that they would be executed the following morning. Reverend Jones recounted the remarkable escape that followed:

> Whereupon, being something cast-down, and speaking to this effect in the British [i.e., Welsh] tongue, "Have I escaped so many dangers, and must I now be knocked on the head like a dog?" an Indian came to me, who afterwards appeared to be a war-captain . . . and told me in the British tongue I should not die; and thereupon went to the Emperor of the Tuscaroras, and agreed for my ransom and the men that were with me, and paid for it the next day. Afterwards they carried us to their town, and entertained us civilly for four months, and I did converse with them of many things in the British tongue, and did preach to them three days a week in the British tongue.

The Reverend Jones's account eventually reached the British public in 1740. In 1752 they learned, via a letter from Philadelphia, that Welsh Indians had been found beyond the Mississippi. The trickle of sightings quickly turned into a flood. Governor Dinwiddie of Virginia asked for a report to be prepared in the summer of 1753. He was so convinced by the evidence gathered, which spoke of French encounters with Welsh Christians up the Mississippi, that he offered to put up £500 of his own money to finance an expedition. Unfortunately he was recalled to Britain before anyone could set out. A generation later everyone along the frontier was aware of stories of Welsh Indians, who by now were situated along the Missouri. Even President Jefferson, proud of his Welsh forebears, became a believer.

In Wales itself, Madoc fever really broke out in 1791, when Dr. John Williams published his *Enquiry into the Truth of the Tradition concerning the Discovery of America by Prince Madog ab Owen Gwynedd about the year 1170*, bringing the accumulating evidence to the attention of Madoc's land. Welsh excitement was tremendous, for this meant that in a distant land their countrymen lived free from the English yoke. As Baptist minister William Richards wrote to his compatriot, Dr. Samuel Jones, minister of the Pennepek Baptist Church in Philadelphia:

> And if such a nationality [as the Welsh Indians] exists, and there seems now to be no great room to doubt the fact, it will then appear that a branch of the Welsh Nation has preserved its independence even to this day.

Back in Wales, nationalists immediately tried to recruit a trustworthy and self-reliant young man who could seek out the Welsh Indians as a preliminary step toward carving a new Welsh homeland out of the American West.

Enter John Evans. He came from a Methodist family in northwest Wales, and seems not to have left home before late 1791. Still, what Evans lacked in experience he more than made up for in vigor and strength of purpose. With a minimum of preparation he sailed from London in the summer of 1792, arriving in Baltimore that autumn. Outdoing his proposed backers in enthusiasm, he set off alone on his quest with just $1.75 to his name. He reached New Madrid on the Mississippi, and from there headed into the wilderness toward Illinois with just a single companion. The "expedition" was a disaster, and Evans staggered into the American frontier post at Kaskaskia in July 1793. The following Christmas he was well enough to try again, and reached St. Louis, only for the Louisiana Spanish to throw him in jail on suspicion of spying.

Once freed by the lieutenant governor, Evans made new plans to locate the Welsh Indians. By now fully aware of the dangers of the wilderness, he had to find a place on a properly organized expedition. As luck would have it, the Spanish, desperate to secure a northwestern route to the Pacific, were backing a trading party led by Scotsman James McKay. McKay's aim was to search out a newly discovered tribe that matched the Welsh Indian stories remarkably well. Five years earlier the French trader Jacques d'Eglise had penetrated far up the Missouri from St. Louis, becoming the first to reach the area from the south. He encountered the numerous and highly civilized Mandan people, 5,000 of them, who lived in eight great fortified towns, and wore the best of furs, which they obtained through extensive trade networks. Most remarkable of all, d'Eglise reported that they were "white like Europeans." Here, surely, thought Evans, were Madoc's people.

Discovering the Mandans

At the end of August 1795, Evans left St. Louis in McKay's fleet, heading upriver into Indian country. By winter the party had already become bogged down in negotiations with tribes along the way. McKay determined to send Evans ahead with a small group. His task was to reach the Mandan, establish a Spanish government presence there, then hunt out a route across the Rockies to the Pacific—for the Spanish, the real prize.

On September 24, 1796, four years after leaving London, John Evans finally reached the Mandan, some 700 miles up the Missouri from St. Louis. His first act was to run down the British flag on the small

Mandan bull boats, made from stretched buffalo skin on a wooden frame. In the background is a Mandan village on the Missouri River, North Dakota. Sketch made by Karl Bodmer, artist for the expedition of Prince Maximilian, 1832–34.

wooden fort built by Canadian traders and hoist the Spanish ensign. By this time, however, Evans's trade goods were almost exhausted and he now realized that the Pacific lay hundreds of miles away, beyond the giant Rocky Mountains. Eventually admitting defeat, Evans and his party began the long trek south in May 1797. All he had to show for his time among the Indians were a journal and a detailed map of the Missouri, which proved to be of immense value to the famous American explorers Meriwether Lewis and William Clark when they reached the Pacific via Mandan territory eight years later.

One final melancholy task remained to Evans. With a heavy heart he wrote on July 15, 1797, to his supporter Dr. Samuel Jones, the Baptist minister in Philadelphia, concerning the Welsh Indians.

> Thus having explored and charted the Missurie for 1,800 miles and by Communications with the Indians this side of the Pacific Ocean from 35 to 49 Degrees of Latitude, I am able to inform you that there is no such People as the Welsh Indians.

Yet this was not the end of the story as far as the Welsh Indians were concerned. Sightings continued in the West, while Evans himself sank into an alcoholic decline, dying in July 1799. Soon afterward, rumors began to circulate that he had been much more forthcoming on the subject of Welsh Indians with a few drinks inside him. The American Jabez Halliday reported that Evans himself had confessed to being bribed to keep quiet.

A generation later belief in the Welsh Indians received a dramatic boost. A Pennsylvania artist, George Catlin, realized that Native American cultures were fast disappearing, and set out to record their life and customs for future generations. He spent several weeks among the Mandan in 1832 and came away convinced that they *did* indeed have Welsh origins. First he stressed their light complexion— "amongst the women particularly, there are many whose skins are almost white." Mandan crafts also betrayed their Welsh heritage, especially a round boat known as the bull boat, made of hide stretched over a wooden frame, seen by Catlin as exactly like the Welsh coracle. Catlin also saw pottery in use among the Mandan apparently identical to that found in burial mounds far to the southeast, toward the Gulf of Mexico. This would confirm the Madoc story—if he had landed on the coast, then later moved inland. Then there were traces of the Bible in their legend of a flood, which the culture hero called the Lone Man survived in a canoe, to which a dove brought willow leaves, showing that the waters were abating. Catlin compiled a list of a dozen words with similar sounds and meanings in both Mandan and Welsh, including "head"—*pan* in Mandan and *pen* in Welsh. The Mandans, he argued, retained a trace of Madoc in their very name: "the *Mandans* [is] a corruption or abbreviation, perhaps, of '*Madawgwys,*' the name applied by the Welsh to the followers of Madawc."

Unfortunately, there was little time left in which to study the Mandan further, for, as Catlin reported, a smallpox epidemic devastated the population in 1838. He believed that the Mandan had been utterly destroyed, but this seems to have been an exaggeration. The survivors banded together with their neighbors the Hidatsa and the Arikara, themselves much reduced by epidemics.

Thereafter the story of Madoc's colonization of North America, and the identification of the Mandan as the survivors of that enterprise, have had mixed fortunes. In Wales the high point of Madocian feeling was in 1805 with the publication of the epic poem *Madoc* by Robert Southey, the poet laureate. However, once the cold light of historical scholarship was focused on Madoc, belief in his legend began to falter. In 1858, the Llangollen *eistoddfod* (Welsh cultural festival) instituted a prize for the best essay on Madoc's discovery of America. Six efforts were submitted, five of them fully in agreement with the basic truth of the story, the sixth a radical review of the evidence. Its author was Thomas Stephens, a chemist and literary man, who already had the first critical history of Welsh literature to his credit.

The judges were split, one for Stephens; a second agreeing that it was definitely the prize entry, but proposing that Stephens share the honors with the best of the pro-Madoc essays; the third simply resigning. Stephens would have been awarded the prize, but the main eistoddfod committee overruled the judges, and disqualified Stephens's work as "not upon the given subject." When Stephens began to object, the organizers ordered the band to play, hoping to drown him out, but the audience shouted them down and Stephens made a fierce speech attacking the committee for wishing to sweep the truth under the carpet.

Stephens took a straightforward approach to Madoc himself—he could find no trace of a Prince Madoc in the medieval chronicles and biographies that detail the lives and times of the Welsh rulers, including Owain Gwynedd and his sons, and so no such Madoc existed. While this was a strong argument, it was not in itself conclusive, but shame over Stephens's ill treatment meant that pro-Madoc views have rarely been expressed since.

No such dramatic confrontation took place in America, where Madoc's voyage was simply taken as given. Admiral Samuel Morison, the naval historian, recalled the level of belief in a Welsh origin for the Mandans: "it was in my first history textbook, about 1895; and I well remember teacher saying with a smile, 'Oh yes! the Mandan Indians still speak a kind of Welsh.'" The Daughters of the American Revolution set up a plaque to honor Madoc at Fort Morgan, Mobile, Alabama, in 1953, which begins thus: "In memory of Prince Madoc, a Welsh explorer, who landed on the shores of Mobile Bay in 1170 and left behind, with the Indians, the Welsh language." Some doubts seem to have set in recently, as the plaque now languishes in a warehouse.

The Viking Connection

So what evidence is there today in favor of Madoc's voyage? Was Stephens right to dismiss the very existence of a Prince Madoc? We have to grant that any historical event first mentioned four hundred years after it was supposed to have taken place must be treated as doubtful. The sources given by Llywd, Dee, and Powel were Gutyn Owain, a poet active from 1470 to 1500, and the chronicler Caradoc of Llancarfan, a contemporary of Madoc. Unfortunately, it is as true today as in Stephens's time that there is no trace of Madoc in the known writings of either man. Nor do any of the other sources that date from Madoc's supposed time mention him. Gwyn Williams, Professor of History at the University of Cardiff, and author of the main work on Madoc in modern times (1979), praised Stephens as "one of the most formidable critical intelligences in Welsh (or any other) history. His work on Madoc could serve apprentice historians as a very model of totally destructive historical criticism." However, negative evidence of this kind can never be absolutely conclusive, for the fragments of Welsh medieval writing that survive today are only a fraction of what once existed.

By casting his net wider than Stephens's chronicles and biographies, Williams was actually able to trace a seafaring Madoc back some way into the past. The Welsh poet Maredudd ap Rhys, writing around 1440, praises a "Madoc the bold," son of Owain Gwynedd, claiming that "A Madoc am I to my age and to his passion for the seas have I been accustomed." As Williams concludes, there must have been a fifteenth-century tradition of Madoc the seafarer.

Surprisingly, to pursue Madoc farther back in history we have to look outside Wales, in continental Europe. People from Flanders in Holland, known as Flemings, were settled in southern Wales during the twelfth century, and seem to have been the channel through which stories of Madoc reached Europe. Fleming writers produced the first popular literature, most famously the medieval satire *Reynard the Fox*. The author of *Reynard* was one Willem, possibly a priest, who lived early in the thirteenth century. At the beginning of *Reynard* he introduces himself as the author of another work, entitled *Madoc*. No copy of Willem's original survives, so it is impossible to be sure whether this was the same Madoc. However, a French abridgment of Willem's *Madoc* does exist. In this French version of the romance, Madoc is a noble Welshman whose grandfather was "half a Viking" and who becomes a famous sailor. He visits the French court, goes looking for the fountain of youth, uses an island called Ely as a base, and eventually finds an island paradise bathed in sunshine that he colonizes with his followers.

Despite the romantic trappings that the tale contains, Williams notes some intriguing hints, especially the link with the Vikings. We know from the contemporary biography of Grufydd ap Cynan, Owain Gywnedd's father, that he had strong Viking connections, having used them as mercenaries to expel the Normans from the Isle of Anglesey, which became the heart of his kingdom. Ely, Madoc's island stronghold in the romance, provides a further clue. It is an old name for Lundy Island, off the south coast of Wales, the base of an anonymous Welsh pirate who raided up and down the western coast of Britain in the years 1139 to 1148, according to the Norse Sagas. These glimpses of Viking links with the Welsh in the twelfth century do lend a degree of plausibility to the story of Madoc's voyage to the New World, for the Vikings had already reached Newfoundland a century before (see **The Vikings in America** in this chapter).

Since Williams wrote, archaeology has confirmed the Viking connection. One of the royal centers used by Owain Gwynedd, at Rhosyr on Anglesey, has now been uncovered from the sand that had hidden it for centuries. David Longley, the excavator, sees the style of houses at Rhosyr as heavily influenced by the Vikings, which makes good sense if it was founded by Grufydd ap Cynan, who landed nearby with his Viking mercenaries at the beginning of his successful campaign against the Normans.

So what is the verdict on Madoc? We certainly have strong indications of a renowned figure of romance with Viking connections, but is this the Madoc who supposedly colonized America? While there is no contemporary trace of a Madoc son of Owain Gwynedd, there is always the possibility, as Williams concedes, that he was one of the many children known to have been fathered by Owain outside marriage. The Viking links with Anglesey and Madoc's claimed family, and with Lundy and the Madoc of the romances, do provide a plausible background for voyages out into the Atlantic. Through the Vikings, tales of Vinland across the ocean might well have inspired losers in a civil war to seek their fortune far away.

Mandans on the Missouri

The possibility of a Welsh expedition to the Americas just remains open, but what about the Welsh Indians? Of all the candidates presented, by far the most convincing were the Mandans. What light can tradition, history, and archaeology throw on this people?

The Mandans themselves had two competing stories about their origins. In one version they had always lived on the Missouri River; in the other, they originated on the coast at the mouth of the Mississippi, moving upriver later in their history. Madocians like the second account, as it places the Mandans in the right place to be Madoc's colonists.

Then we have the evidence of history. How far can Catlin's account of the Mandan, central to the Madocians' case, be relied upon? It is certainly true that he had a wholly mistaken idea of the Mandans' exposure to the outside world. According to Catlin, the Mandans' "traditions, so far as I have yet learned them, afford us no information of their having had any knowledge of white men before the visit of Lewis and Clark." In fact, the French explorer La Vérendrye met Mandans as early as 1739, and Canadian traders were living among them before Evans's visit. Catlin even failed to note Evans's stay of seven months with the Mandans, so one has to wonder how deep his understanding of Mandan society actually was.

There were other, more skeptical, visitors to the Mandan before their destruction by smallpox in 1838, but their views are seldom considered by enthusiasts for Welsh Indians. James McLaird, the most recent historian to consider the "White Mandan" problem, stresses that several Canadian fur traders, the Welshman David Thompson, explorers Lewis and Clark, politician Henry Brackenridge, and the scientist Maximilian, Prince of Wied, all visited or stayed with the Mandan, yet none of them noticed anything out of the ordinary about them. Prince Maximilian was dismissive of the Welsh Indian theory after visiting the Mandan:

Mandan village, surrounded by a wooden palisade. Sketch by George Catlin (1832). The bull boat on the nearest house would have been placed there to protect the smoke hole during heavy rain.

Some have affirmed that they have found, in North America, Indians who spoke the Gaelic language; this has been said of the Mandans; but it has long been ascertained that this notion is unfounded, as well as the assertion that the Mandans had a fairer complexion than the other Indians.

McLaird backs up Prince Maximilian's views by pointing to several early accounts of other tribes, including the Crow, Cheyenne, and Arikara, which describe them as having unusually fair skin. It seems as though this was simply one way in which explorers of the West tried to make sense of the bewildering number of tribes they encountered. Similarly, the Swiss artist Rudolph Kurz, who met some of the surviving Mandans in 1851, poured scorn on the supposed unique resemblance between the Mandan bull boat and the Welsh coracle: "All Indians who dwell on the prairies make use of skin boats on account of the scarcity of wood."

On the crucial issue of Catlin's word list linking Mandan and

Welsh, linguists have without exception found absolutely no trace of Welsh in Mandan, or indeed any Amerindian language, and place Mandan quite confidently within the Siouan language family.

Do the Welsh Indians fare any better at the hands of archaeology? The most recent survey of early Mandan sites shows that the pottery Catlin saw being made by the Mandans was not the same as that found in much earlier burial mounds along the Missouri to the south. However, the most likely archaeological candidates for Mandan ancestors were Siouan groups living on the Lower Missouri and eastward toward the Mississippi, so Mandan traditions of moving up the Missouri are partly matched by the archaeological record. This, however, still leaves them 800 miles from the coast.

More important, it is clear that the Mandan were far from unique in living in settled village communities. Along the major river valleys running into the Missouri lived groups of Pawnees, Arikaras, Hidatsas, and Mandans, all settled in villages of semisubterranean houses surrounded by a wooden stockade, with fields of maize (corn) growing outside. Proponents of Welsh Indians could argue that Madoc's Mandans had, over the years, persuaded their neighbors to adopt a more settled existence. However, radiocarbon dating puts the movement of the village-dwelling ancestors of at least the Mandans and Hidatsas to the Middle Missouri at the same time, about A.D. 950. This strongly suggests that any influencing of the Hidatsa by the Mandan happened long before Madoc's day.

Even more tricky for the Madocians to explain is that what appear to be the forebears of these early Mandan were living in settled village communities and growing crops, lower down the Missouri, as early as A.D. 850, before moving to their present lands. So the earliest Mandans had a supposedly Welsh-influenced lifestyle at least 300 years before Madoc's supposed arrival in North America. Archaeology is therefore the final nail in the coffin of the Welsh Indians, a tribe that should now be left to rest in peace.

CHAPTER SIX

LEGENDARY HISTORY

INTRODUCTION

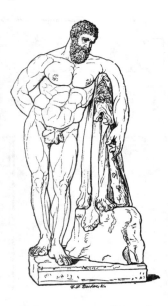

Roman statue of Hercules.

Every age has its heroes and heroines, be they real or fictional. Today we have figures as varied as Princess Diana, Che Guevara, and Superman, and we can be sure that even 50,000 years ago, when our Stone Age ancestors sat around the campfire, they entertained themselves with stories of heroic struggles against the forces of darkness.

Yet few societies seem to have created their heroes from whole cloth. Today we often talk of actors, sportspeople, politicians, and others in the public eye as becoming living legends when the image begins to obscure the real person behind it. The ancient world was no different. It lionized—or demonized—its outstanding figures and through that simple process some of the great legends of the past were born.

Even the most patently fictional characters, by borrowing imagery from earlier heroes and heroines, may ultimately have their roots in historical characters. The creators of Superman, DC Comics, freely admit that they owe much to the classical stories of Hercules—or Heracles, to use his original Greek name. Heracles was thought to be so phenomenally strong that he could hold up the skies on his bare shoulders (having taken on the job temporarily from Atlas the Titan). In turn, the Greeks borrowed much of Heracles' character from the ancient Babylonian hero Gilgamesh, whose story—a ripping yarn of lion slaying and monster killing—circulated throughout the Near East during the second millennium B.C. Behind this legendary Gilgamesh, half-god and half-mortal, there seems to have been a real individual. The legends say that Gilgamesh was king of Uruk in Sumer (southern Iraq), and Sumerian inscriptions indicate that a King Gilgamesh indeed ruled over Uruk around 2600 B.C.

So, strange though it may seem, there exists a long chain of storytelling and story-borrowing that connects Superman with a historical figure who lived over four and half thousand years before Metropolis was invented.

Whether a real hero (or king) called Heracles ever existed (as Gilgamesh seems to have done) is a question that is rarely asked, though it is actually with Heracles that we reach an important watershed in Greek myth. Heracles effectively begins what the classical Greeks saw as a past Age of Heroes, one that preceded the rather mundane Age of

Lion-killing hero on a jasper signet ring from Late Bronze Age Mycenae. The details of the scene reflect Babylonian influence.

Iron in which they lived. Most of what we know as "Greek mythology" is actually legends about this Heroic Age, a time of noble deeds, quests, and wars. The ancient Greeks had quite a clear idea as to when this age was and its relationship to their own, and could point to the very sites where events happened and its heroes were buried.

With the Heroic Age of Greece we enter a quasi-historical reality, where we can sensibly ask: how much is real, how much fiction? The basic clues are given by the Greeks themselves, and the major sources are their earliest epics, namely the *Iliad* and the *Odyssey*, composed by the great poet Homer in the eighth century B.C. The world that Homer described was not the one he lived in. In the *Iliad*, he gives a detailed list of the cities that provided contingents of Greek warriors to fight the great war against Troy. (Their purpose was to recover Helen, queen of Sparta, who had been abducted by the Trojan prince Paris.) Surprisingly, the leading cities are not those that were powerful in Homer's own time, and the list even includes many that no longer existed at all. This very fact shows that the milieu of Homer's tales of the Trojan War has genuine roots in traditions that stretched back into the archaeological Bronze Age of Greece. During the Late Bronze Age (15th to 12th centuries B.C.) the very cities that Homer talks of flourished, chief among them being Mycenae, seat of King Agamemnon, who led the Greeks against Troy. For this reason, archaeologists refer to Late Bronze Age Greek civilization as "Mycenaean." Not only does Homer manage to give a reasonably accurate list of the important Mycenaean cities, but he describes their material culture, from armor and weapons to palaces and drinking vessels. There were no written records available to Homer. Somehow he had inherited oral traditions that had preserved memories of the Mycenaean era in extraordinary detail.

Bust of the great Greek poet Homer, found at Baiae in Italy.

If the archaeological background to Homer's epics is so sound, was there really a Trojan War? The story of Heinrich Schliemann's discovery of Troy, supposedly fulfilling a childhood ambition, is well known (see **Schliemann's Treasure** in **Hoax?**). The city of Troy (in what is now northwestern Turkey) is real enough, and the lingering doubts of other archaeologists that Schliemann had excavated the wrong city have long been dispelled. But the problem is complicated by the fact that the site of Troy is actually a series of cities, each new one being built on the remains of the last, forming something like a giant layer cake. Before we can assess the historicity of the war we need to work out which one of the eight superimposed cities was the one discussed in Homer's *Iliad*.

Schliemann himself was convinced that the walls of the second city (Troy II), which were covered with a thick layer of ash, were those burned by the invading Greeks. He also believed that he had discovered in a tomb at Mycenae the very body of the leader of the Greeks, King Agamemnon, adorned with a golden death mask. Both of Schliemann's bold guesses were wrong. His work was done just before the advent of accurate dating in the Aegean world, and it is now agreed that Troy II was burned about 2300 B.C. (during a widespread natural catastrophe—see **Sodom and Gomorrah** in **Lost Lands and Catastrophes**), while the grave of "Agamemnon" dates to about 1600 B.C. Neither find could have anything remotely to do with the Trojan War—which according to the Greeks took place near the end of the Heroic Age (the archaeological Late Bronze Age) in about the twelfth century B.C. Schliemann eventually recognized the problem himself, though he mentioned it only in private correspondence.

Research since Schliemann's time has focused on two much later cities—VI and VII, both of which fell during the later Mycenaean Age. Most archaeologists agree that Troy VI was destroyed by an earthquake during the late thirteenth or early twelfth century, and that VII was burned by a fire during the twelfth century. Which of these might have been Homer's Troy is a moot point. The "steep walls" harped on by Homer match those of Troy VI best, though most archaeologists agree that this city was destroyed by an earthquake rather than by invaders. Troy VII is less grand, but its systematic burning readily suggests invaders.

The debate over which Troy was Homer's still continues, though the most likely solution is that there was more than one Trojan War. As the pottery styles of cities VI and VII were very similar, the gap between the two destructions can have been only a generation or two, a fact that suggests an interesting tie-in with Greek tradition. According to the Greeks, Heracles himself led an expedition against Troy a couple of generations before the war under Agamemnon. He captured it, killed its king, and placed Prince Priam on the throne. Interestingly enough, the myths say that when Heracles began his attack on Troy it was under siege from a monster created by Poseidon, the Greek god of the sea and of earthquakes. Was the "monster," which was pounding Troy with tidal waves, actually an echo of the earthquake that destroyed Troy VI? If so, then Troy VII was the city sacked by Agamemnon, and we have a perfect match between the two destructions of legend and archaeology.

More direct historical evidence for the Trojan War comes from the

The Trojan horse. Detail from a
Roman sarcophagus.

archives of the Hittite Empire that dominated Anatolia (Turkey) during the Bronze Age (see **The Elusive Amazons** in this chapter). The Hittites extended their power from central Anatolia across to the Aegean seaboard opposite Greece, where there were a number of smaller independent kingdoms (see **Atlantis—Lost and Found?** in **Lost Lands and Catastrophes**). They vied for control of these with another powerful empire that they referred to as "Ahhiyawa." As long ago as the 1920s, some scholars suggested that Ahhiyawa is the same as the Greek word *Achaea*, or land of the "Achaeans," a term used by Homer to describe the Greeks of the Trojan War period. After some seventy years of resistance to the idea, and now that Hittite geography has been considerably clarified by the discovery of new texts, scholars have generally conceded that Ahhiyawa *was* a Mycenaean empire based on mainland Greece. It also seems very likely that a city the Hittites knew as Wilusa was the Greek Ilios, Homer's name for Troy. There is a remarkable Hittite text from the mid–thirteenth century

B.C. that refers—with tantalizing brevity—to a dispute between the Hittite emperor and the king of Ahhiyawa, involving the city of Wilusa. It is tempting to see this as a reference to the Trojan War itself. At the very least it shows that the king of Ahhiyawa may have had designs on Wilusa/Ilios. Other Hittite texts describe the armies of Ahhiyawa landing on the coasts of Anatolia, raiding and pillaging in much the same way that Homer's heroes did during the ten-year siege of Troy. Though we cannot yet point to a specific text from the Hittite archives as contemporary proof of the Trojan War, we may be only a spit away from it.

Archaeological discoveries can also shed light on the wonderful story of Jason and the Argonauts. From Iolkos in Thessaly (northern Greece), another city important in Mycenaean times, Jason was said to have organized a crew of the greatest heroes in Greece (including Heracles, according to some accounts) to man the *Argo* and sail in quest of a mysterious Golden Fleece. This treasure was guarded by the powerful wizard king, Aeetes, who ruled at Aea in Colchis, a kingdom in the present country of Georgia, south of Russia. To reach it the Argonauts would have had to sail past Troy and right across the Black Sea to its farthest end.

Until recently it was easy to scoff at the story, as it was believed that the Greeks began exploring the Black Sea only in the eighth century B.C. No Mycenaean pottery has yet been found on the Turkish coast of the Black Sea, though it is possible that rises in sea level have simply drowned sites dating this early. And, strangely enough, though we know the Hittites had many dealings with the Greeks of the Late Bronze Age, no Mycenaean pottery has been found at the Hittite capitals of central Anatolia—apparently confirming that Mycenaean traders did not penetrate far to the east in this region. However, increasing amounts of Mycenaean pottery, dating to about 1300 B.C., have been identified at a site called Maşat Hüyük, which lies just *beyond* the main Hittite centers and toward the Black Sea coast. During this period Maşat Hüyük was often in the control of the Kashka people, enemies of the Hittite empire. Edmund Bloedlow, a classical archaeologist at the University of Ottawa, has suggested that Mycenaean traders circumvented the Hittite Empire—known to impose trade embargoes on its enemies—by sailing directly through the Black Sea to reach the rich copper deposits of northeastern Turkey and southern Georgia. As the Mycenaean economy consumed vast amounts of metals—mainly for weapons and armor—the picture Bloedlow draws is realistic and provides a feasible historical background for the

Jason and the Argonauts as gold prospectors, as depicted in the *De Re Metallica* of Georgius Agricola (1556). The "Golden Fleece" is a sheepskin suspended in the river to collect gold dust.

story of the Argonauts. Mycenaean traders reaching Maşat Hüyük would be nine-tenths of the way to Colchis.

As for the Golden Fleece itself, there have been many suggestions. The weakest is that the Argonauts were traders seeking the fleeces of yellow sheep, turned that color by a kidney infection. Rather more likely is the idea that the Colchians were using sheepskins to pan for gold dust from rivers, a method known to have been employed by gypsies in Romania in the 1930s. Fine-wooled sheepskins can be suspended in a gold-bearing river, left for a while, and then dried out before combing off the reward. It could have been stories of such gold-covered sheepskins that excited the metal-hungry Mycenaeans to set sail across the unknown waters of the Black Sea.

The idea that Jason and the Argonauts were early metal prospectors may sound rather unromantic, but the story does not simply end there. The magical kingdom of Colchis where they found the Fleece is in itself a completely unsolved riddle. The Greek poet Pindar, writing about 450 B.C., refers to the "dark-faced Colchians," and shortly afterward the historian Herodotus stated as plain fact that the Colchians were black-skinned descendants of an Egyptian army, led there centuries earlier by the legendary Pharaoh Sesostris. As Herodotus stated:

> It is undoubtedly a fact that the Colchians are of Egyptian descent. I noticed this myself before I heard anyone else mention it . . . and found that the Colchians remember the Egyptians more distinctly than the Egyptians remember them. . . . My own idea on the subject was based first on the fact that they have black skins and woolly hair, and secondly, and more especially, on the fact that the Colchians, the Egyptians, and the Ethiopians are the only races which from ancient times have practised circumcision.

The idea that there was a black, possibly Egyptian, colony in Georgia during classical times seems so improbable that most archaeologists simply ignore the whole matter. Yet the testimony of Pindar and Herodotus is confirmed by many other ancient writers. The black inhabitants of Colchis were still so conspicuous in the late fourth century A.D. that early Christian writers referred to Colchis as "a second Ethiopia." As it happens, there *is* a black population living in Abkhazia on the Georgian coast, who have somehow survived the attempts of the U.S.S.R. this century to displace its ethnic minorities from their homelands. Whether all, or any of them, are descendants of the original Colchians is hard to say. The question is confused by a bizarre historical coincidence. The Turkish Empire, which ruled this region in the sixteenth to eighteenth centuries, is known to have imported slaves from Africa into Abkhazia. So whether any of the original black Colchians might survive remains just as much a mystery as how they arrived there in the first place.

Yet the testimony of Herodotus on the Colchians cannot be taken lightly. Another people encountered by Jason and the Argonauts on the farthest shores of the Black Sea were the ferocious warrior-women, the Amazons. Incredible though it may seem, what Herodotus had to say about the location of a real tribe of Amazons, and even partly their customs, has now been dramatically confirmed by archaeological discoveries. Georgian archaeology, which is still in its infancy, may well have some surprises in store when it discovers Aea, seat of the mysterious King Aeetes of Colchis.

Even contemplating the idea that there was some connection between ancient Egypt and Georgia would sound absurd to most archaeologists. Yet the track record of Greek legend, in the broad outlines of the civilizations it describes, is *extremely* good. The confirmations that have come from the archaeology of Troy, Mycenae, and other Greek Bronze Age sites can be matched by the amazing discoveries made on Crete. In classical times Crete, the southernmost and largest of the Aegean islands, was something of a cultural backwater. Yet the traditions of the Greeks told of a glorious past. During the Age of the Heroes in Greece, Crete had been the seat of a powerful empire, ruled by the family of King Minos. The legends told of their palace at Knossos, their wealth and luxury, the importance of bulls in their religious worship, their organized navy, and their technological expertise. All these things have been confirmed by the excavations at Knossos and other Bronze Age palace sites of Crete, and the "Minoans" are now recognized as one of the earliest and most distinctive civilizations of prehistoric Europe.

The traditions, again, had come up trumps. Almost everything that the Greek legends said about Knossos had proved to be true, except perhaps the strangest story of all—that the palace of Knossos held a dark secret in the shape of a bull-headed monster, known as the Minotaur, which the Cretans fed on the flesh of innocent children. Is the Minotaur merely a fanciful detail of the Greek storytellers? Recent archaeological discoveries on Crete suggest, strangely enough, that even the story of the Minotaur has some basis in reality.

With the heroes and villains of Greek myth we are in a privileged position. Greece must be one of the most intensively excavated countries in the world and continues to reveal new evidence that can throw light on the origin of Greek legend. We also have the massive documentation of Near Eastern texts—from Babylonian myth to Hittite diplomatic archives—with which to compare the Greek tales of their Heroic Age.

We are not so lucky when it comes to some of the other great characters of legend. King Arthur, probably the most renowned hero since Heracles, was supposed to have ruled in Britain during the fifth or sixth century A.D., a time from which, unfortunately, there are practically no written records to help us. The political history of

"Dark Age" Britain, when the Romans had left and the country reverted to the control of local Celtic kings, is an almost complete blank. There is, of course, an incredibly rich Celtic literature detailing the legendary history of Arthur and his time, but it was all written down centuries after the time he supposedly existed. It has been very easy, therefore, for skeptics to dismiss the deeply held belief in the existence of King Arthur as mere wishful thinking on the part of the Celtic peoples of Britain. On the other hand, the circumstantial evidence for a real King Arthur is compelling and, if the case of legendary Greece is anything to judge by, archskeptics rarely have the last laugh.

A similar problem—of late sources—arises when we examine Quetzalcoatl, the chief hero of ancient Mexican traditions. The versions of his story, as recorded by the Spanish *conquistadores* in the sixteenth century, talk of Quetzalcoatl as a great culture-bringer who arrived in Mexico from across the sea at some point in the distant past. After teaching the people arts, crafts, and the correct way of life, he then mysteriously disappeared. He was either white-skinned or wore white robes, or both. Through Spanish sources we get much the same impression of Viracocha, the Peruvian/Bolivian version of Quetzalcoatl. The whiteness of Quetzalcoatl/Viracocha has naturally inspired many theories. Maybe he represented the memory of an early explorer from the Old World—a Phoenician, a Viking, or an Irish

Quetzalcoatl (left), the Aztec deity of Venus as the Morning Star.

monk—who sailed to the New World and brought them civilization? (See **Introduction** to **Voyagers and Discoveries**.) Such ideas merely fall into the trap of accepting the late Spanish accounts at face value. Recent analysis has shown that while practically everything else that the *conquistadores* reported about Quetzalcoatl/Viracocha is genuine, there is not a scrap of evidence from pre-Columbian times that Native Americans believed he was white-skinned. The versions recorded in the sixteenth century were clearly tailored by the Indians to suit the vanity and preconceptions of their Spanish masters, including evangelizing monks, who were keen to see themselves as restoring to grace natives who had fallen from teachings already received from an earlier missionary, such as St. Thomas (see **Tiahuanaco** in **Architectural Wonders**).

This still leaves the problem of Quetzalcoatl unsolved. He is a highly complex character who perfectly typifies many of the problems involved with separating the varied strands that went into the creation of an ancient hero figure. He was part teacher, part warrior, and even part planet. Ancient Mexican texts and iconography leave no doubt that his identification with the Morning Star, or Venus, was an integral part of his cult. The story told of his death, his time spent in the underworld, and his resurrection fits a pattern that is very familiar from ancient Near Eastern hero-gods such as Tammuz and Adonis, worshiped in ancient Babylonia and Syria. They too were connected with the Morning Star, so the likelihood is that the parallel stories of these dying and resurrected heroes on both sides of the Atlantic arose from observations of the planet Venus. For a certain number of days each year Venus becomes invisible, reappearing after its apparent "death" as the evening star.

So far so good, but when we touch on the subject of another great hero from the Near East, things begin to become more sticky. According to the New Testament, Jesus compared himself to the Morning Star. This has encouraged some Mormon scholars to see the story of the dying and resurrected teacher Quetzalcoatl as evidence for their belief that Christ visited the Americas after his resurrection. Other Mormon scholars have appreciated that the argument provides a two-edged sword, and a very sharp one at that, as there is evidence that the belief in Quetzalcoatl's resurrection goes back long before the time of Christ. The same problem is faced by Christian theologians dealing with Near Eastern figures like Adonis and Tammuz, stories of whom were circulating hundreds of years before Christ was born. Was the life of Jesus modeled, either by his biographers or by himself, on the old stories of the dying and resurrected hero worshiped throughout the Near East? The similarity of Christ's life pattern to those of ancient Venus deities forms the core of a much wider historical riddle that has never been satisfactorily resolved, though theologians have been aware of it for some two thousand years.

This is not to say that the stories of heroes from Christ to Quetzalcoatl can be reduced to one single explanation, based on the mythology surrounding the planet Venus. Far from it. But the problem serves to show the complexity of the issues involved. In the nineteenth century, German scholars developed highly persuasive theories that all the heroes of ancient times were based on stories about the Sun god. Even William Tell, the medieval archer of Swiss tradition who fought the Austrian oppressors of his homeland, was pressed into the mold of being a "solar hero." (The apple placed on his son's head that he was forced to shoot was, of course, a Sun symbol!) Equally simplistic theories have been concocted about Robin Hood, the English equivalent of the Swiss peasant hero Tell. It has been argued many times that both he and King Arthur were originally gods, who were reduced to being mortals in the retelling of their stories—but the evidence in both cases is unconvincing.

Heracles takes a ride in the golden cup used by the Sun god to sail across the ocean from the sunset to the sunrise. Though Heracles had solar connections, he cannot be "explained" simply as a version of the Sun god.

There are, unfortunately, no simple or universal answers to understanding myth and legend, no one key that unlocks their meanings. Each case has to be judged individually, against the background of historical and archaeological evidence, and generalizations are impossible. While truths often lie behind the legends, they are as varied as the legends themselves.

Sometimes the reasons for the development of a legend are far from being religious and are simply political. Athens became a major Mediterranean power in the fifth century B.C., when the legend of their hero Theseus took off like a rocket, the tales of his adventures rivaling those of Heracles himself. A great city needed a great hero to represent it. The stories of Robin Hood were wildly popular in medieval England among the lower classes, who resented the wealth accrued by their masters. The church in particular was disliked for its materialistic greed, and the richer and fatter the abbot in a story, and the worse humiliation that Robin and his men gave him, the more the people loved it.

The stories of King Arthur, king of the Britons, were most popular on the "Celtic fringe" of Britain and France, where native British populations in Cornwall, Wales, and Brittany had survived the onslaughts of Saxon and Norman invaders of the early Middle Ages.

After the Normans seized the English throne of Britain from the Saxons in A.D. 1066, they skillfully turned the stories of Arthur to their own advantage. Arthur was not a Saxon (like the oppressed serfs of England), but a king of all of Britain, and by the twelfth century the Norman-Angevin kings were associating themselves with the cult of Arthur (see **King Arthur's Grave** in **Hoax?**). That there were stories of Arthur's conquests of Scotland, Ireland, France, and even beyond suited their own imperialistic designs very nicely.

All the same, the political motives for the *growth* of their stories does not mean that characters like Theseus and Robin Hood never existed in the first place. There were political reasons behind the growth of the legends that accrued around the American revolutionary hero George Washington. But neither that fact, nor the unlikelihood that he ever managed to throw a penny right across the River Delaware, would lead us to believe that he was not a real person.

It may sound bizarre to accept that the Amazons actually existed, that there was a monster in the Cretan Labyrinth, that the stories of King Arthur and Robin Hood are based on real-life characters, and even that Dracula was a historical ruler of Transylvania—but, as the old adage runs, truth can indeed often be stranger than fiction.

THESEUS AND THE MINOTAUR

The Minotaur, the Greek mythological monster with a man's body and a bull's head, naturally had a strange origin. When the legendary ruler Minos claimed the throne of Crete, largest of the Aegean islands, he prayed to the sea god Poseidon to send him a sign to confirm his rights. Poseidon made a dazzlingly white bull appear from the sea, which Minos was expected to sacrifice to him. Yet Minos hid the bull among his herds and sacrificed an ordinary bull instead. Poseidon took his revenge. He made Pasiphae, the wife of Minos, fall in love with the bull, with such a burning passion that she asked the help of Daedalus, the famous technician and inventor, to help her consummate it. Daedalus built a hollow wooden cow, covered with cowhide and mounted on wheels concealed in the hooves. It was wheeled into the field where Minos kept the white bull. Pasiphae got inside the contraption, and the bull was tempted to come and mount her inside her disguise. As a result, Pasiphae gave birth to the Minotaur. To hide his wife's shame, Minos confined the monster to a huge maze called the Labyrinth, where it was fed on the flesh of children, sent as tribute

Theseus kills the Minotaur.
From a 5th-century B.C.
Athenian vase.

by the subject city of Athens. Eventually the young hero Theseus, one of the fourteen Athenian boys and girls sent each year as fodder for the Minotaur, slew the monster with his bare hands and escaped from the Labyrinth with the help of Minos' daughter, the princess Ariadne.

So runs the tale of Theseus and the Minotaur, as related by the Greeks from the eighth century B.C. onward. Yet how and why did this bizarre story originate? When, in 1900, British archaeologist Sir Arthur Evans opened up the site of Knossos on Crete, an answer seemed to be immediately forthcoming. Evans had been drawn there by the legends, which said that Knossos was once the capital of King Minos, and what he found exceeded all expectations. The palace of Knossos, which he unearthed, was a virtual wonderland, built some 3,500 years ago. A huge rambling structure on several floors connected by staircases, the palace had lavatories with sophisticated drainage systems, bathrooms, and walls decorated with exquisite frescoes, their scenes evoking images of a highly cultured and leisured society. The Bronze Age civilization that Evans rediscovered was named by him "Minoan," after the legendary king. Images of bulls seemed to be everywhere, from tiny carvings on seal stones and signet rings to dramatic frescoes showing acrobats leaping over the backs of bulls. Evans was naturally reminded of the story of the Minotaur. Maybe, he reasoned, the youths and maidens sent by Athens as tribute to be eaten by the Minotaur were actually trained as acrobats for the bull games, which he assumed were part of some dramatic religious rituals. Few would have survived the dangerous sport of somersaulting over the sharp horns of a massive bull. Could this have given rise to the legend of the manslaying Minotaur?

Likewise, the palace of Knossos, composed of a vast complex of interconnected courtyards and rooms, could have been the prototype for the mythical Labyrinth where the Athenian youngsters were condemned. As for the image of the Minotaur as a man with a bull's head, perhaps the Minoans, like the Egyptians, saw one of their gods as having a partly animal form.

Into the Labyrinth

As a general background to the legends, the finds from Knossos certainly fit the bill. Yet is this enough to explain the origin of the Minotaur? While we cannot expect myths and legends to have a "rational" explanation as such, the traditional view that the story of the Minotaur had its origin in bull-leaping games held in the labyrinthine palace leaves some unsatisfying loose ends.

To begin, the idea that the Labyrinth was the palace at Knossos itself has been overturned by some extraordinary new discoveries made, surprisingly enough, not in Crete but in Egypt. In 1991, the Austrian archaeologists excavating the site of Tel ed-Daba in the Egyptian Delta uncovered a palace complex with a culture that was definitely not Egyptian. The buildings date from the time of the Hyksos, foreign rulers of Egypt during the seventeenth and early sixteenth centuries B.C. In the past the "foreignness" of the Hyksos seemed to be eastern—pottery, metalwork, and other finds from Tel ed-Daba continued to suggest that the Hyksos kings came from Palestine or Syria, and that they were a Semitic people like the Arabs and Israelites. Then, in the center of this Hyksos city, came some breathtaking finds: fragments of plaster frescoes showing scenes with unmistakably Aegean scenes highly reminiscent of those from Crete, though they actually predate those from Knossos. They include

Animal-headed monster on a Bronze Age seal stone from Crete.

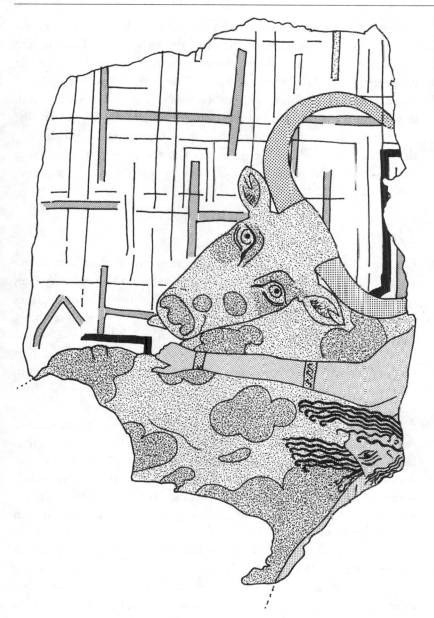

Fragment of Aegean-style fresco from Tel ed-Daba (northern Egypt), showing an acrobat hanging from a bull's neck. A labyrinth pattern forms the background to the scene.

Minoan-style floral scenes, bulls' heads, and even fragments of a fresco showing the Cretan bull-leaping sport. There are also repeated motifs of a labyrinth pattern, surrounding the bulls' heads. The labyrinth motif is a pure abstraction, utterly dissimilar from the ground plans of the palace at Knossos. It is clearly far more related to the archetype of the maze, an almost universal symbol connected with the mysteries of life and death (see **The Glastonbury Spiral** in **Earth Patterns**).

If the Cretan Labyrinth was not the palace at Knossos, but an abstract concept belonging to a religious cult, perhaps the Minotaur, the monster who lurked at its heart, was something other than a simple reflection of the dangerous bull games. The traditions of King Minos, his palace, his navy, and his empire were preserved by the Athenians in the story of Theseus and the Minotaur. Archaeology has shown that there is a solid background to these tales. Could there also be any rhyme or reason behind the ugliest part of the tale—that the tribute of Athenian children sent to Knossos every seven years was meant as food for the Minotaur?

Human Sacrifice?

Evidence has long been available that may completely shatter the image of ancient Minoan civilization derived from the frescoes. Scenes of lilies and lotus flowers rub shoulders with those of elegant ladies gossiping and preening themselves—all in all the picture of a highly sophisticated, cultured society at play, marred only by the scenes of the suicidally dangerous "game" of bull leaping. A much darker shadow is cast by the grisly discoveries made in 1979 by Peter Warren, Professor of Classical Archaeology at Bristol University, in the basement rooms of a large house at Knossos.

The top rooms of the house had collapsed into the basement, where their contents were found—mainly mundane objects such as loom weights for weaving, beads, tools, and pottery. There was also one large storage jar containing burnt earth, the remains of edible snails and shellfish, and three human bones, one of which (a cervical vertebra) had evidence of cut marks. Why were foodstuffs mixed with human remains in this way? The trail of evidence continued in an adjacent room excavated by Warren, which he came to call the "Room of the Children's Bones." Here he found 251 animal bones, belonging to cattle, sheep, pigs, and dogs, alongside 371 human bones and bone fragments. Analysis showed that the remains of at least four individuals were present, all of them children. Overall, 79 of the bones had marks, made by cutting or sawing with a fine blade. In other rooms of the house a further 54 human bones were found, all belonging to children, and 8 with cut marks.

Warren and his team puzzled over the meaning of this evidence. In some ancient cultures bodies were dismembered or defleshed before burial, or even excavated after decomposition and buried a second time. Yet in the case of the children's bones, the signs of cutting were far from the ends, where one would expect marks if the various parts of the body (e.g., upper arm, forearm, hand) were being deliberately separated. This suggested to Warren, and the bone expert Louis Binford, that the cutting had been done not to dismember the skeletons but to remove flesh. But the absence of longitudinal scraping marks showed that the purpose was not to remove every trace of flesh—rather just chunks—so defleshing does not seem to have been the aim. It seems, then, that whatever was done to the bones was not part of a burial ritual. Some other cultic practice was taking place, and Warren was led to the grisly conclusion that it involved the ritual sacrifice of infants, who were then cooked and eaten.

The Minotaur on a classical coin from Knossos, Crete.

Of course, as Warren himself admits, there can be no absolute proof that the children's flesh was consumed after it was removed from the bones. All the same, it seems to be a more likely explanation than other alternatives, such as simple murder or burial preparations. Classicist Dennis Hughes of Iowa University has suggested that the bones were brought to the basement as part of a secondary burial practice, and that they had already been separated and defleshed before they were deposited there. Still, as he admits, there is no evidence of any burial rites. Though secondary burial is known from Bronze Age Crete, there is no known instance of the removal of flesh or the deliberate disarticulation of bodies before reburial. The ugly fact has to be faced that, had the cut marks been found on animal bones, archaeologists would have assumed without a second thought that they were looking at the remains of a meal.

Warren's explanation of ritual consumption remains the best, though it grates heavily against the traditional preconceptions of a "peaceful" Minoan society. The presence of animal bones with similar cut marks, the burnt earth, and the edible snails suggests that the children were slaughtered, cooked, and eaten along with the animals in feasts associated with some ghoulish religious cult. It is also not too hard to imagine that the victims of this cannibal cult were drawn from subject countries—like Athens as in the legend of Theseus. If Warren is right we have a new explanation of how the legend arose of a monster at Knossos that ate children; there *was* a monster at Knossos, without a bull's head, but real enough, and more sinister than the legendary Minotaur itself.

THE ELUSIVE AMAZONS

With the treasure houses of Mexico and Peru nearly exhausted, the Spanish *conquistadores* turned their attention in the mid–sixteenth century to the heart of the South American continent—cut through by vast, seemingly endless rivers, surrounded by impenetrable jungle, and inhabited by unknown tribes. Their interest was piqued by rumors of a hidden civilization in the interior of the continent, an empire rich in gold that was ruled by a race of fearsome warrior-women, known as the Amazons.

By 1500 the Spanish had already begun exploring the river mouths on the coast of Brazil and Venezuela. Yet penetrating the rivers to any great distance was a problem. Many explorers attempted to locate a central channel and sail upstream, but the colossal size of the river estuaries, spilling out in every direction, meant that finding the main branch of a river was like looking for a needle in a haystack. Problems were aggravated by the hostile climate and often aggressive natives. The first sight of the interior came only in 1544, when Francesco de Orellana and his party pulled off a feat of exploration that was as audacious as it was foolhardy. Starting from Peru on the opposite coast of South America, they spent ten months fighting their way through

Dutch engraving of the 17th century showing an Amazon, dressed in classical Greek style, seated upon an armadillo, one of the strange new animals encountered by early explorers of the Americas.

mountain and forest into the interior. They eventually came to the source of a major river, the Marañon, built boats, and spent nine more months sailing down it to the Atlantic coast and safety. Of all the adventures that befell them as they explored the interior of Brazil, their brush with the mysterious Amazons drew the most attention.

According to the expedition's chronicler, as de Orellana's party were sailing down the Marañon River, they rounded a bend in the river and saw "on the shore ahead many villages, and very large ones, which shone white. Here we came suddenly upon the excellent land and dominion of the Amazons." Forewarned of the arrival of the Spanish, natives ran to the shore mocking and threatening them, "that they were there to seize us all and take us to the Amazons." The Spanish opened fire, and when they beached their boats were counterattacked by an army of Indians, led by a dozen or so female "captains," described by the expedition's chronicler as "very white and tall." He continued: "They are very robust, and go naked with their private parts covered, with bows and arrows in their hands, doing as much fighting as ten Indian men." A captive taken during the fighting told them more: these warrior-women, or Amazons, mated with men once a year, kept only the female children that resulted, and seared off their right breast, to make shooting with a bow easier.

After this incident de Orellana renamed the Marañon the "Rio das Amazonas," or Amazon River, and so it remains today.

Stories of the American Amazons arose as soon as Columbus's first voyage of discovery. On his way home, in January 1493, he was told by the Carib people of Hispaniola (now known as Haiti) that a nearby island, called Mantinino, was entirely populated by women: they supposedly imported men at certain times of the year, then sent them away, keeping only the daughters that were born to them. The women were devoted to warfare, wore brass armor, and were accomplished archers. Though he looked for it on subsequent voyages, Columbus never found the mysterious island of women; indeed, to this day Mantinino has never been located. Yet the rumors of the warrior-women continued. Only their supposed location changed, moving progressively westward into increasingly remote areas as the elusive Amazons stubbornly refused to be found.

By de Orellana's time the Amazons had been relocated deep in the Brazilian jungle. It was not mere curiosity about this female tribe that interested the *conquistadores*. In the words of one Spanish writer of the time, "if these are the Amazons made famous by historians, there are treasures shut up in their territory which would enrich the world."

Another claimed that there was so much gold and silver in the realm of the Amazons that even chairs and household utensils were made from them. The only legend that could compete with the South American Amazons was that of El Dorado ("the gilded man"), the king of another hidden empire, who was supposed to have plastered himself with gold dust as if it were talcum powder. Sir Walter Raleigh, the ill-starred English explorer and founder of Virginia, was convinced that both El Dorado and the Amazons were real. He led two expeditions to find them, in 1595 and 1616. Raleigh found neither, and earned himself only public contempt at home.

Likewise the Spanish and Portuguese made repeated attempts to find the Amazons, but were no more successful. As early as 1553 one Spanish chronicler, Francisco López de Gómara, had scoffed:

> I do not believe that any woman burns or cuts off her right breast in order to be able to shoot with a bow: for they shoot very well enough with [both breasts]. . . . No such thing has ever been seen along this river, and never will be seen! Because of this imposture many already write and talk of the "River of the Amazons."

De Gómara's rather testy comments were perfectly fair. None of the *conquistadores* had brought back to Spain any proof of their claims, such as a captive warrior-woman with an amputated breast. South American women undoubtedly fought alongside their menfolk to defend their villages against the marauding Spanish, but that did not make them members of an Amazon race.

Furthermore, when explorers such as Columbus and de Orellana interrogated the natives they had to use interpreters, who often may not have been genuinely acquainted with the languages involved. With the interpreters keen to please their masters, and with the interviewees under threat of torture, it is easy to see how, by one means or another, the Spanish were told not the truth but what they *wanted* to hear: confirmation of their belief that there were fabulous hidden kingdoms ruled by warrior-queens awash with gold. It is clear from their journal entries that they paid little real attention to the actual customs of the tribes whose villages they were ransacking for clues of "lost empires."

So what was the source of these Spanish dreams? Why did they expect to find a lost Amazon empire in Brazil? It was not because of the River Amazon, which was named after the legendary race, rather than the other way around. What the Spanish "heard" from their sources, tortured or otherwise, was simply the rehearsal of a much older legend, drawn from the classical writers of the Old World. Everything the sixteenth-century Spanish said about the warrior-women of Brazil had already been said two thousand years earlier by the ancient Greeks.

How did the Amazons of classical legend come to be relocated in faraway Brazil, a land (as far as we know) completely unknown to the ancient Greeks? The growth of the legend is an extraordinary tale in itself, which takes us halfway across the globe and back again. At the end of the trail there is, amazingly enough, evidence that there *were* real Amazons, though they lived a long way from the Brazilian jungle.

Heroes and Amazons

The legend of the Amazons is as old as Greek literature itself. In the eighth century B.C., Homer referred in his great epic the *Iliad* to "the Amazons, who go to war like men," with whom Priam, the aged king of Troy, had skirmished in his youth. Far from being a western tribe, these Amazons came from east of Troy—Priam fought them in Phrygia, in central Anatolia (Turkey). Homer says little more about them, and it seems he assumed his audience was already well aware of the Amazons.

More detail comes in the works of the later Greek poets and play-wrights, for whom the Amazons were a favorite theme. One story has them joining in the Trojan War, this time working as allies of King Priam. After she had slaughtered large numbers of the Greek army, their beautiful queen Penthesilea was eventually killed in combat by the Greek hero Achilles. Seeing her dead body, he fell passionately in love with her, and according to one version of the story had sex with her corpse on the battlefield.

Many other Greek heroes had adventures with the Amazons. When Heracles (Roman Hercules), most famous of the heroes, was assigned his Twelve Labors by the king of Mycenae, one of the supposedly impossible tasks given him was to win the girdle of Hippolyte, queen of the Amazons. Heracles and his band sailed to the Black Sea (which separates Russia from Turkey), where the Amazons lived, and decided the best way to get the girdle was to court Hippolyte. Attracted by his muscular body, she offered him the girdle. However, the other Amazons assumed that Heracles had come to abduct their queen and crowded around to protect her. Even Heracles panicked at the sight of them. He killed Hippolyte, snatched her girdle, and led his band back, fighting all the way, to the safety of their ships. The Greek heroes captured large numbers of Amazons in the fray and abducted them.

The Amazons took full revenge. Allying with the nomadic Scythian tribe of southern Russia, they invaded Greece and ravaged it. It was only after four months of war that Theseus, king of Athens (see **Theseus and the Minotaur** in this chapter), managed to repel them. While the whole episode is almost certainly fabulous, the Greeks of classical times were able to point to the exact sites where the battles took place, and even identify the tombs where fallen Amazons were buried.

In the same Greek sources we find the original descriptions of Amazon social customs, as repeated by later Spanish writers. The Greeks firmly believed that the custom of removing the right breast of girl children existed and it lies behind the Greek interpretation of the name "Amazons" (from *a*, "without" and *mazos*, "breast"). They were thought to live in communities composed entirely of women. Men were imported from neighboring tribes for mating purposes, then sent away again. Male offspring were either given away or crippled at birth to ensure that they would never be fit enough to fight.

Heracles struggles with the Amazons (note the single breasts). Scene from a Greek vase of the 5th century B.C.

While skilled in all the arts of war, Amazon specialties were archery and horsemanship, or rather horsewomanship.

So ran the legend of the mighty Amazons. The earliest Greek accounts are unanimous in placing the land or lands of the Amazons to the east of Greece. They were supposed to have founded some cities in Asia Minor, such as Ephesus and Smyrna on the Aegean coast of Turkey, having arrived as invaders and colonists from farther east. The homelands of the Amazons were said to lie near the coasts of the Black Sea, a region that was, from the perspective of the early Greeks, populated by mysterious tribes with savage and often bizarre customs.

One Amazon homeland was thought to be in the southeastern corner of the Black Sea, around a river called the Thermodon. It was here that Heracles was said to have encountered Hippolyte. The other homeland was near the ancient "River Amazon," also known to the Greeks as the Tanais, on the north side of the Black Sea. It was seen by the Greeks as the dividing line between Europe and Asia and is better known today as the Russian river Don, or Dnieper.

Accounts varied as to which of these two rivers was the real Amazon motherland, though the geographical details of the legends do not matter too much. The Greeks generally agreed that the Amazons lived on the fringes of the eastern Black Sea, and it is in this region that we encounter an interesting phenomenon. After the fifth century B.C. the Greeks became much better acquainted with the lands surrounding the Black Sea. Yet rather than disappearing, stories of the Amazons continued to circulate, and even became more detailed and concrete. Unlike the Spanish in America two thousand years later, the Greeks did not have to continually move the mythical lands of the Amazons ever farther away because, in southern Russia, they were convinced that they had come into contact with the genuine article.

Real Amazons?

The earliest record of the Amazons approaching believability comes from the Greek historian Herodotus (5th century B.C.). Herodotus often included fantastic material in his *History*, such as stories of flying snakes in Arabia. Yet much of his account of the Amazons, by contrast, seems very matter-of-fact, written in the same way that he describes the customs of the Egyptians or the Babylonians. His description may not be firsthand, but by this time his fellow Athenians were well acquainted with the peoples of southern Russia. Many

Scythians (a generic name used by the Greeks for the tribes of ancient Russia) were now living in Athens, where a corps of Scythian archers, publicly owned slaves, were used by the courts as policemen. (One ancient Greek comedy gives a policeman a funny "Russian" accent.)

According to Herodotus, the tribe known as the Sauromatians (Sauromatae) were descended from intermarriage between the Scythians and the Amazons. He begins with a legend of how the Amazons arrived in southern Russia. When the Greek heroes raided the Thermodon, they were said to have crammed their ships with Amazon captives. Some of the Amazons murdered their captors and seized command of the ships, placing themselves in a quandary; they had never sailed a ship before. At the mercy of wind and wave, they drifted across the Black Sea to its northern shore, where they found horses and began raiding the local Scythians. Realizing that the raiders were women, the Scythians decided to father children on them. Gaining the trust of the Amazons, they paired off with them, and migrated across the Tanais to a new home. The Sauromatians are their descendants. Herodotus continued:

> The women of the Sauromatians have kept to their old ways, riding to the hunt on horseback sometimes with, sometimes without, their menfolk, taking part in war and wearing the same sort of clothes as men. The language of these people is Scythian, but it has always been a corrupt form of it because the Amazons were never able to learn to speak it properly. They have a marriage law which forbids a girl to marry until she has killed an enemy in battle; some of their women, unable to fulfil this condition, grow old and die in spinsterhood.

There is nothing intrinsically incredible about the latter part of his report. And in the centuries that followed, other writers repeatedly confirmed the existence of these contemporary Amazons. There were always, of course, more fanciful rumors in circulation. Some ancient writers reported with caution the claim that Alexander the Great (356–323 B.C.), the young Macedonian conqueror whose empire extended far into central Asia, was visited by the queen of the Amazons in order to discuss a romantic alliance. Many years after Alexander's death, one of the generals who had campaigned with him heard this story and simply remarked: "I wonder where I was that day." Other accounts, particularly those written in Roman times, are less easy to reject out of hand.

Two centuries after Alexander, the brilliant Roman general Pompey, for a while Julius Caesar's greatest rival, was campaigning in the east. War had broken out with Mithridates VI, ruler of Pontus (a powerful kingdom on the southern coast of the Black Sea), who had massacred the Roman colonists of Asia Minor. When Pompey faced him in battle in 65 B.C., Mithridates' vast army included auxiliaries from Scythia and Sarmatia (Sauromatia). Pompey won the day, and the Roman historian Appian reported the aftermath: "There were found among the prisoners and the hostages several women whose wounds were as great and as dangerous as the men. These women were said to be Amazons."

After defeating Mithridates, Pompey conquered neighboring Armenia and then led his armies into areas where no Roman had been before. His legions marched north into the Caucasus Mountains, which lie between the Black Sea and Caspian Sea (the region of the modern state of Georgia), into a land known as Albania (not to be confused with the Balkan state). A Greek writer called Theophanes accompanied Pompey's army and recorded the customs of the Albanians and their neighbors. According to the findings of Theophanes and others, as reported by Strabo, the Amazons lived in the mountains just beyond Albania. When they were not at war, Strabo said,

Classical statue of an Amazon.

> the Amazons occupy their time performing various tasks such as ploughing, planting, pasturing cattle, and particularly training horses, though the bravest engage mostly in hunting on horseback and practising warlike exercises. The right breasts of all are seared when they are infants, so that they can easily use their right arm for every needed purpose, especially that of throwing the javelin. They also use the bow, sagaris [a Scythian axe] and light shield, and make helmets, clothing, and girdles from the skins of wild animals. They have two special months in the spring when they go up into the neighboring mountain which separates them from the Gargarians. The Gargarians, in accordance with an ancient custom, go there to make sacrifices with the Amazons and also to have intercourse with them in order to beget children, doing this in secrecy and darkness, any Gargarian at random with any Amazon. After making them pregnant they send them away. The females that are born are kept by the Amazons themselves, but the males are taken to the Gargarians to be brought up.

Here, in a nutshell, was the core of the Amazon legend. Yet this time it was not being related about an ancient race who fought Heracles and Theseus in the mists of the Greeks' mythological past. This was the information brought back after a Roman expedition to the Caucasus Mountains in 65 B.C. Truth or fiction?

Modern classicists give little serious attention to what the Greek historians accepted as fact. Instead, they produce analyses of the meaning of the Amazon image to the Greeks largely in terms of a parable of the struggle between the sexes. In 1949, the *Oxford Classical Dictionary* stated that the story of the Amazons was

> in all probability nothing more than the common travellers' tale of the distant foreigners who do everything the wrong way about . . . Attempts to find a sociological significance in the legend or other explanations postulating a foundation of fact are mistaken.

More recent research by classicists, which concentrates on the social function of the Amazon stories in Greek and Roman society (i.e., an allegory of the battle between the sexes), has continued to take the same dim view of Amazons as a historical possibility. One of the most recent studies, by William Tyrrell, took this agnostic stance:

> Were there ever Amazons? May we not dismiss them out of hand? . . . There is, in fact, no way historically to deny their existence and no way to prove it. . . . Archaeologists have thus far not uncovered the remains of an Amazon grave or city.

It is a sad reflection on the way modern scholarship can become compartmentalized that a classical scholar could make this statement without first consulting the work of experts in Russian archaeology. For over a hundred years ago, Russian archaeologists claimed that they *had* found Amazon burials.

Amazon Graves

In the late nineteenth century, the Russian scholar Count A. A. Bobrinskoi was investigating the burial mounds near Smela in Ukraine when he made a surprising discovery. The burials he excavated were accompanied by a rich array of weapons, yet Bobrinskoi, one of the first excavators to take a serious interest in skeletal evidence, soon realized that most of the graves in question actually belonged to women.

The first of these "Amazon" graves, as he called them, dates to the

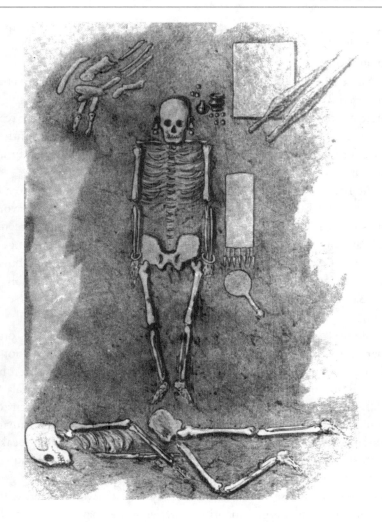

fourth century B.C. and is typical of the group. In a large burial pit, covered by a wooden framework and a mound of earth (kurgan), were two skeletons. The first, clearly the most important person in the grave, was female and had been carefully laid to rest in an east-west direction. Laid at a right angle at her feet was another skeleton, probably male. Almost without exception the rich grave goods were clustered around the female skeleton. She wore large silver earrings, a necklace made of bone and glass beads, and a bronze arm ring. Around her lay domestic possessions, including pottery, a bronze mirror, a clay spindle, offerings of food, and some eating knives. But she also had weapons: two enormous spear blades of iron, one nearly two feet long, stones (maybe slingstones), and the remains of a brightly decorated quiver made of wood and leather, containing two iron knives and forty-seven bronze arrowheads. There were no weapons with the skeleton at her feet. It had, by comparison, an arm ring, two small bronze bells, and two ornamental pipes.

Since Bobrinskoi's time, Russian and Ukrainian archaeologists have discovered dozens more "Amazon" burials. Almost as surprising as their contents is the geographical spread of these graves. They reach from the southern Ukraine right through the steppes of southern Russia to Pokrovka, near the border of Kazakhstan, a thousand miles distant.

At Pokrovka, Jeannine Davis-Kimball, director of the Center for the Study of Eurasian Nomads (Berkeley, California), has been working since 1992 with her Russian colleagues on the excavation of fifty kurgans or burial mounds, ranging in date from about 600 B.C. to the second century A.D. Each kurgan originally contained one burial, and then was continually reused over the centuries—presumably by the same family—until it contained as many as twenty-five extra bodies.

Significantly, the original burial in the Pokrovka kurgans is often that of a woman, placed in a pit at the center. While it is not enough to prove a matriarchal society, this certainly suggests that women had equal standing with men. There were different kinds of burials for both men and women, the grave goods apparently reflecting their role in society. Forty male burials contained weapons and were presumably warriors. Another contained ore samples and an iron crucible caked with slag—it probably belonged to a metalworker. Four other males were buried with a small child on their arm and barely any grave goods—poor house-husbands? Generally women were buried with a wider variety and larger quantity of grave goods than men. One class of women was buried with the kind of artifact traditionally associated with femininity and domesticity—such as mirrors (ritually broken at the funeral), spindle whorls, and glass and stone beads. Another group of women, laid to rest with clay or stone altars, seashells, bronze mirrors, and bone spoons, may, as Davis-Kimball suggests, have been priestesses. The most striking group comprised the seven women who were buried not only with beads and spindle whorls but also with iron swords or daggers, bronze arrowheads, and whetstones for weapon sharpening. The handles of the swords and daggers are noticeably smaller than those in the male warrior graves. Kimball has drawn the perfectly logical conclusion that these women were also warriors, whose weapons were specially made to fit their hand grip. As she rightly points out, no one normally bats an eyelid when it is suggested that a male skeleton accompanied by weapons belonged to a warrior. At Pokrovka, about 14 percent of the burials with weapons belong to women. As Davis-Kimball concludes,

> some Early Iron Age Pokrovka females held a unique position in society. They seem to have controlled much of the wealth, performed rituals for their families and clan, rode horseback, and possibly hunted . . . steppe antelope and other small game. In times of stress, when their territory or possessions were threatened, they took to their saddles, bows and arrows ready, to defend their animals, pastures and clan.

There is no area in the steppes where graves with weapons are exclusively female. Yet significantly, Sauromatia (the lower Volga region), which Herodotus pinpointed as the center of Amazon survival, has the highest percentage of female warrior burials. Twenty percent of the graves containing weapons in Sauromatia belong to women. Arrowheads, quivers, bows, and horse harnesses are the most typical finds in these graves, providing striking confirmation of the classical descriptions of the Amazons as mounted archers. There are also a wide variety of other weapons—lances, spears, swords, daggers, and sling stones—together with metal-plated belts that would protect the loins while riding.

Professor Renate Rolle of Hamburg University has gone some way to reconstruct the life of these Amazon warriors:

> This relatively large and varied arsenal of weapons indicates a mastery of the different martial skills. Riding, so necessary for hunting and fighting, must have been learnt and practised from early youth onwards. . . . Long-distance riding would have been a major part of this training owing to the nomadic way of life in the north Pontic and Caspian steppe region and the great distances involved. Extensive training in the use of various weapons was doubtless also a requirement from childhood onwards.

Some archaeologists have been more reluctant to accept the evidence of these Amazon graves, arguing that the weapons may have a purely ritual or symbolic meaning. The facts do not bear them out. Weapons from "Amazon" burials generally show signs of wear and tear—one way or another, they have been used. The skeleton of a teenage girl from Pokrovka (about thirteen or fourteen years old) included a dagger and a quiver containing dozens of arrowheads. Her bowed leg bones showed that she had spent much of her life on horseback, while an arrowhead found in a pouch around her neck was presumably an amulet to reinforce her prowess in archery. Other graves clearly show that their owners were warriors. Some skulls show signs of wounds, while one skeleton has a bronze arrowhead still embedded in its knee. To try to explain away this evidence, which mirrors perfectly the classical descriptions of the warrior-women of the Russian steppes, is merely to blind oneself to the obvious.

Amazons on the Move

There seems little doubt that the original Amazons have been found. Too many details from the archaeological and classical record match— the general area involved, the economy based on herding, the riding skills, and the choice of bow and arrow as favorite weapon. The society now being uncovered by Davis-Kimball and other archaeologists was not quite the rigidly matriarchal, or "separatist," system that the Greeks imagined, but we can easily imagine how these nomadic women of the steppes may have given the impression, perhaps quite correctly, that they were in charge.

Reading Herodotus again in the light of the archaeological discoveries, it seems that when the early Greeks became acquainted with the women of Sauromatia they assumed the preexistence of an exclusively female warrior tribe, who had intermingled with the Scythians. As women in Greek society generally did not fight in battle, perhaps this kind of story was needed to explain why things were so different in southern Ukraine and Russia. Or it could even be that tales of the "good old days" when the women rode and fought alone, with little need of men at all, were told by the Sauromatian women themselves. In any case, once the legend of the ancient Amazons had started, it continued to grow and was still snowballing in Renaissance times, two thousand years later.

The first step was the growth of a belief in a bygone Amazon empire, reaching through Europe, Asia, and Africa. There were plenty of eastern models for the Greeks to use. The great Hittite Empire that dominated Anatolia and northern Syria during the Late Bronze Age (c. 1600–1200 B.C.) actually had its center just south of the river Thermodon, the legendary Amazon homeland on the south coast of the Black Sea (see **Atlantis—Lost and Found?** in **Lost Lands and Catastrophes**). One name by which the Hittites were known to the Greeks seems to have been *Alizones*, which might easily have been confused with *Amazones*. Such confusion probably started the idea of the Amazon domination of Anatolia. The legends claimed that the

Amazons founded Ephesus and other cities on the Aegean coast of Turkey, which would have been impossible for the Russian Amazons, but not so for the Hittites, who about 1300 B.C. marched to the Aegean and conquered Ephesus (see **Introduction** to **Watching the Skies**).

Once the Amazons were confused with the Hittites, the legend grew uncontrollably, influenced by other "barbarian" empires that the Greeks saw rise and fall. The Scythians, nomadic neighbors of the real Amazons, swept down across the Caucasus Mountains into the Near East in the late seventh century and, with awesome suddenness, conquered or ravaged everything in their path as far south as Egypt. In the following century the Persians of Iran conquered the entire Near East as far as India, as well as swallowing up Egypt, southern Russia, and the Balkans as far as Greece. The Greeks held back the mighty Persian war machine at the battles of Marathon (490 B.C.), Thermopylae, and Salamis (480 B.C.), but the struggle would have left them in no doubt that the hordes of Asia had the potential to conquer the world. If the Scythians and Persians could establish such huge empires, why not the Amazons of old?

Later Greek writers elaborated on the mythical Amazon empire and made it one of truly epic, intercontinental proportions. After taking over Anatolia, the Amazons were thought to have invaded and conquered Libya, the Greek name for North Africa as a whole. One adventurous writer of the second century B.C., Dionysius "Leather-Arm," concocted a war between the Amazons and the highly civilized Atlanteans, whom he borrowed from Plato's writings (see **Atlantis—Lost and Found?** in **Lost Lands and Catastrophes**) and relocated in northwestern Africa, "on the edge of the ocean." The Amazons won this imaginary war and seized control of the Atlantic coast of Africa. Yet they eventually failed in Asia, according to Dionysius, being beaten in pitched battle by an army of Scythians and others. The remainder of the Amazons retreated to Libya, where they were later mopped up by Heracles.

Medieval writers, nevertheless, refused to believe that the mighty Amazons would have been wiped out that easily. Rumors grew of the survival of some Amazon tribes in the Far East, in the unexplored regions of the Asian continent or on a remote island off the coast of China. In the other direction it seemed natural to suppose that the Amazons of northwestern Africa had also controlled the islands of the Atlantic, and that when their empire was destroyed they had used these, and the lands even farther west, as retreats where they could hide their gold and rebuild their power. The idea is not dissimilar to the modern legends of Hitler's aides setting up secret Nazi bases in South America and Antarctica after the destruction of the Third Reich.

So when Columbus first sailed the Atlantic he fully expected to find traces of the mighty Amazons of yesteryear—especially since he imagined that the remote islands of the Atlantic were off the coast of Asia. His successors were merely caught up in the same delusion. The strange legend of the Amazons, having spread from the steppes of southern Russia to the jungles of Brazil, still continues to grow in pulp science fiction and fantasy. Wonder Woman, the all-American Amazon princess of comics and television, has a surprisingly respectable ancestry—not only in classical legend but, ironically enough, in Russian prehistory as well.

KING ARTHUR

Few stories can have been written that are as compelling and romantic as the cycle of legends surrounding King Arthur. In their classic form they are most familiar to us from the writings of the fifteenth-century English knight Sir Thomas Malory. He tells how Arthur, who had been born secretly to King Uther Pendragon, came to the throne of Britain during a period of bitter civil war, proving his claim by drawing the "sword in the stone." Arthur found his second sword, the famous Excalibur, when Merlin the magician led him to a lake: a mysterious hand rose from the waters and presented Arthur with the sword, which through its enchantment ensured his victory in every battle. Merlin tutored him in kingship, and Arthur not only restored order in Britain but also founded an empire taking in Ireland, Scandinavia, and large parts of France. Arthur even crushed in battle Lucius, the emperor of Rome, and freed Britain forever from the threat of Roman invasion.

Despite the loss of Merlin—who met his destiny when an alluring young witch condemned him to eternal sleep in a cave—Arthur succeeded in turning his reign into a golden age of peace and plenty. Young warriors from every neighboring kingdom flocked to become Knights of Arthur's Round Table, an elite club with their own highly evolved code of honor, sworn to the idea of using their might for just causes. Dragons, giants, witches, and black knights were all kept in their place, so that maidens and old folk, nobles and peasants, could live their lives in peace, knowing that the Knights of the Round Table were always there to defend them against aggressors.

King Arthur defeats the Roman Lucius. From a medieval adaptation of Geoffrey of Monmouth's *History of the Kings of Britain*.

Arthur's knights were so pure of heart that many of them came close to the ultimate spiritual quest—finding the Holy Grail used by Christ at the Last Supper. Sir Lancelot, the hardiest and bravest knight of the Round Table, and Arthur's closest personal friend, came close to completing the quest, but for one fault—his secret love affair with Arthur's wife Queen Guinevere. This weakness was exploited by a faction at court that had long held its own dark secrets. In his youth Arthur had inadvertently slept with his sister Morgause, who conceived a son. Knowing that this son would eventually bring about Arthur's downfall, Merlin advised him to order a Herod-like destruction of all the children of noble blood born the following May Day. The son, however, escaped and grew to become Sir Mordred.

Joining the Round Table, Mordred plotted revenge on his father. He skillfully framed Lancelot, exposing his relationship with Guinevere, and compelled Arthur to banish him. With Lancelot away Arthur fell prey to the schemes of Mordred's party. Arthur was forced to lead a military expedition that laid siege to Lancelot's castle in

France, and left Mordred as his regent in Britain. Mordred quickly made his bid for power. He seized Guinevere and tried to force her into marriage, but she escaped to take refuge in the Tower of London. Arthur, meanwhile, learned of Mordred's treachery and rushed home to defend his realm. He met the rebel army in battle, and father and son engaged in mortal combat. Arthur killed Mordred, but was mortally wounded himself. Knowing he was about to die, Arthur ordered his companion Sir Bedevere to throw Excalibur into a nearby lake. Bedevere reluctantly complied and was amazed to see a hand rise from the lake and catch the sword as it fell. A strange barge then sailed into view, bearing three queens clothed in black, who carried Arthur off to the Island of Avalon to heal his wounds. Lancelot arrived with his army too late to save the day. Guinevere joined a nunnery and died there a few years later, ridden with guilt that it was her love for Lancelot that had caused such ruin. When he heard of her death, Lancelot refused food and drink and wasted away.

As for Arthur himself, Malory gives two versions. As he mentions that Lancelot buried Guinevere next to Arthur's body at Glastonbury, one assumes that the king died of his battle wounds. Yet Malory notes a different tradition:

> Some men say in many parts of England that King Arthur is not dead, but had [i.e., went] by the will of our Lord Jesus into another place; and men say that he shall come again, and he shall win the Holy Cross.

All said and done, a wonderful story and one far too good to be true as it stands. It was also supposed to have taken place a thousand years before Malory, who states that Lancelot's son, the pious Sir Galahad, became a member of the Round Table 454 years after the Crucifixion of Christ—that is, about A.D. 483. Given the enormous period of time that elapsed, it seems a fairly slim chance that the cycle of Arthurian stories reflects any historical reality. Did Arthur himself, the central figure, really exist?

There was obviously some debate in Malory's own day. William Caxton, the English pioneer of printing who published Malory's work in A.D. 1485 (as *Le Morte D'Arthur*), was keen to list in his preface the evidence for Arthur's existence. There were accounts of Arthur's life in earlier histories, and relics from Arthur's time could be seen in many parts of the country: at Glastonbury there was the sepulchre over the king's grave (see **King Arthur's Grave** in **Hoax?**), and at Winchester his Round Table. At Westminster Abbey they kept a piece of red wax bearing the imprint of Arthur's royal seal, which described him as the emperor of Britain, Gaul, Germany, and Dacia, while visitors to Dover Castle could see Sir Gawain's skull and Sir Cradok's mantle. Even Lancelot's sword was still in existence. Caxton's "archaeological" evidence seems laughable by today's standards, and there is no doubt that most of it was deliberately forged to attract tourists or was simply misunderstood. Caxton should have known that the famous Round Table at Winchester was actually made by King Henry III (A.D. 1216–1272) or one of his successors, in a token attempt to revive the chivalrous ethos of the Arthurian Golden Age.

The main evidence available in Caxton and Malory's time was the various written accounts of Arthur and his deeds. Malory's main source was slightly earlier French prose writings, and he humbly presented his work as a translation (although he certainly added his own material). Tracing back the works used by these French writers takes

King Arthur's table from Winchester. The paintings date to 1522 (under King Henry VIII), but the table itself was built in the late 13th or early 14th century A.D.

us through a minefield of complexities. One of their major sources was certainly the *History of the Kings of Britain*, written by one Geoffrey of Monmouth about A.D. 1136. Geoffrey's work still survives in many manuscripts. Written in racy Latin, it was the first British bestseller, and also the first work to characterize Arthur as a chivalrous king of international standing. In Geoffrey's *History* we can already see many of the elements familiar from Malory, such as Excalibur, the involvement with Merlin, the European conquests, the treachery of Mordred, and the departure to the Isle of Avalon. However, other key elements are missing, such as Lancelot, the Holy Grail, and the Round Table. We can most likely trace these elements back through continental sources. Here, for example, the cycle of legends surrounding the Holy Grail had been already developing before Geoffrey of Monmouth wrote. Continental Arthurian romances seem to have been current as early as A.D. 1050, when we know of a nobleman from Normandy in northern France by the name of Arthur. Before that date we are lost. Wandering troubadours certainly played a large part in the transmission and growth of the legends, but committed nothing to paper. At home, the Welsh also preserved tales of Arthur, but how much they inspired Geoffrey of Monmouth (who was from Wales) or vice versa is impossible to say, as the earliest written material in Welsh appeared almost simultaneously with the *History*.

A Dark Age King

So we are faced with the problem of a huge gap between the composition of the medieval romances and the time (5th–6th centuries) when King Arthur was supposed to have lived. Before the medieval writings there are a few very brief allusions to Arthur in Welsh poetry, recognizing him as a heroic icon. Though first committed to paper in the twelfth to fourteenth centuries, they are thought to have been originally composed as early as the seventh or eighth century—but because of remaining uncertainty the poems cannot count as firsthand evidence.

Yet within the gulf that lies between, there stand two key testimonies supporting the idea of a historical King Arthur. One comes from the *Welsh Annals*, a chronicle of dated events commissioned by Hywell, king of Wales, in the tenth century. It has two tantalizingly brief entries on Arthur:

517. The battle of Badon, in which Arthur carried the Cross of our Lord Jesus Christ for three days and three nights on his shoulders [i.e., shield?] and the Britons were the victors.

538. The battle of Camlann, in which Arthur and Medraut fell: and there was plague in Britain and Ireland.

The Camlan reference is especially interesting, as it contains the earliest reference to Sir Mordred (Medraut), although there is no hint of the father-son conflict that dominates the climax of the medieval romances. Indeed, the earliest references to Mordred in Welsh poetry refer to him as a paragon of virtue, leading some scholars to argue that at an early date he was thought to have been on the same side as Arthur at the battle of Camlan. What could have brought about Mordred's transformation into an image of Machiavellian evil? Was it simply a misunderstanding of the entry in the *Annals*?

The second key piece of evidence takes us even closer in date to the legendary time of Arthur. About A.D. 830 a monk called Nennius, dismayed by the lack of interest that the original British people had in their own history, produced the first history of his nation. In contrast to the Irish, and the Anglo-Saxon (English) invaders who had conquered most of the island, Nennius complained, the stupidity of the British people had led them to "cast out" most of their history. After investigating every available source, including the records of Roman, Irish, and English writers and also "the tradition of our elders," Nennius apologized that he had "made a heap of all that I have found." It is thanks to the small heap of information culled by the industrious Nennius that any case can be made at all for a historical Arthur.

Nennius's *History* is a ragbag of curiosities, boiled down and condensed, by an almost shorthand style of writing, into a tantalizingly small number of pages—just over thirty of a modern printed book. It begins with a brief description of the British Isles and the fantastic claim that they were first colonized by kings descended from the royal house of Troy, then takes us through British history from the Roman conquest to Nennius's own time and concludes with an account of the "wonders" or mysterious things to be found in Britain. Nennius was keen on chronology and, although he does not give a precise date for Arthur, he places his account of him between the arrival of the Anglo-Saxons (Nennius gives A.D. 428) and the reign of the Saxon king Ida, king of Northumbria (which started about A.D. 547). So we are in much the same era that Malory indicated—the "Dark Age" of Britain that descended when Roman authority was removed from the island (about A.D. 410). As Nennius relates, the British were at a loss how to protect themselves without the Roman legions. Appeals were made for help, but Rome was unable to respond, while Britain was ravaged by "barbarian" raiders from Scotland and Ireland. A local king, Vortigern, assumed control of the island and had to take desperate measures. After nearly four hundred years of Roman rule the native British were unused to military affairs, so, in keeping with the custom of the later Roman emperors, Vortigern employed barbarian mercenaries as a means of defense. He called over a small force of Saxon fighters from Germany, who at first did sterling service against the country's enemies. But step by step Vortigern became reliant on them, first giving them money, and then lands in Kent and near Hadrian's Wall in the north of the island. The Saxons in their turn invited over increasing numbers of their relatives, until the point was reached where they could no longer be controlled. The erstwhile defenders of Britain broke into rebellion and indulged in an orgy of murder, rape, and pillage from coast to coast. A contemporary chronicle written in Gaul relates glumly how Britain, in A.D. 441, had fallen under the control of the Saxons. Vortigern's son tried to rally the native British against the invaders, but he was killed in the attempt. Vortigern himself, according to Nennius, was burned in his castle by fire sent from heaven. He was succeeded as "great king" by one Ambrosius, whose father had been a Roman consul.

Nennius tells us little of Ambrosius's reign, but continues with his account of the English settlement: "at that time the English increased their numbers and grew in Britain." "Then," continues Nennius, "Arthur fought against them in those days, together with the kings of the British; but he was their leader in battle."

So begins Nennius's enigmatic account of Arthur. Interestingly, he does not actually call Arthur a king, but merely "leader" (*dux,* "duke"), though this can be interpreted in a number of ways. It has been argued as meaning that Arthur adopted the Roman military title *dux*, used during the later part of the empire to describe the chief field commander of the Roman army in Britain, and that he was employed as a professional general by the British kings. Others have argued that Arthur, by being a leader of kings, was a virtual emperor. Whatever the case, Nennius goes on to list the sites of Arthur's twelve great battles. Their locations, almost without exception, are utterly obscure. There are only a few scraps of extra information. Nennius tells us that at Badon "nine hundred and sixty men fell in one day, from a single charge of Arthur's, and no one laid them low save he alone." At the battle of Guinnion Castle, Arthur is portrayed as a Christian paragon, contrasting him with his enemies. There he carried an image of the Virgin Mary on his shield, so that "the heathen were put to flight on that day, and there was great slaughter upon them, through the power of Our Lord Jesus Christ and the power of the holy Virgin Mary his mother." After telling us Arthur was victorious in all his campaigns, Nennius moves on to say that the defeated English sought help from Germany, inviting new kings to come over with their armies to bolster their numbers, until the time of Ida of Northumbria, the first Anglo-Saxon king to achieve some kind of dominance over the island.

The only other information that Nennius gives on Arthur comes from two jottings in his list of "wonders" of the island of Britain. In the land of Builth in Wales was a pile of stones, of which the topmost bore the imprint of a dog's paw, made by Arthur's dog Cafal when they were out hunting the mighty boar Troit. If the stone was removed, Nennius reports, it always mysteriously returned to its place by the next morning. The second wonder was the tomb of Arthur's son Amr in Herefordshire (an English county near Wales). Arthur himself was supposed to have killed him and buried him there. Nennius wrote: "Men come to measure the tomb, and it is sometimes six feet long, sometimes nine, sometimes twelve, sometimes fifteen. At whatever measure you measure it on one occasion, you never find it again of the same measure, and I have tried it myself." In both entries Nennius describes Arthur, not as a king, but as "the soldier."

What are we to make of Nennius's curious jottings on Arthur? Was he simply making things up? This seems unlikely in the extreme. The character of Nennius's writings shows him to be a straightforward and uncritical reporter. The passages from the "wonders" about Arthur's dog and son seem like genuine snippets of folklore; it is generally agreed that they show that Arthur, whoever or whatever he may have been, was an established figure in Welsh tradition by the mid–ninth century at the latest. This is consistent with the seventh- to eighth-century date usually attributed to the earliest Welsh verses mentioning Arthur. And the very obscurity of the information given by Nennius is a strong point in its favor. If Nennius—or a source he relied upon—were to concoct a series of battles for an imaginary British hero, surely they would have gone for more recognizable locations, such as London, York, or Canterbury. (None of Arthur's twelve battle sites is included in Nennius's list of Britain's cities.) Most likely Nennius took his battle list from a surviving poem glorifying Arthur's achievements.

Overall it is not unreasonable to believe that Nennius was recording some genuine memories of a historical figure. If we allow that, what more can we tell about him? It is clear from Nennius's account that Arthur organized the local kings of Britain to rally together under his command. Their enemies, in most of their battles, would have been the Anglo-Saxon invaders, plus the Picts and Scots from the north. Following the best identifications for Arthur's battle sites, the scope of his activities seems to have included the whole island of Britain. This has suggested that he led a highly mobile force, able to reach and strike invaders long distances away from his base. As a response to barbarian invaders, who were often mounted on horseback, the later Roman emperors successfully developed heavily armed cavalry forces. Such cavalry are frequently mentioned in the heroic Welsh poetry echoing the Dark Age period, and it has been reasonably argued that the tradition of Arthur's mounted "knights" may reflect real fifth- or sixth-century British practice. That Arthur may have emulated Roman developments is consistent with his role as successor of the Romanized Ambrosius, and the name Arthur itself may derive from the Roman "Artorius."

Using such clues, historians in this century have built up a picture of a hypothetical chief called Arthur, the last champion of Romanized Britain. Using the Roman military title Dux, he organized a successful resistance against the Saxon invaders for many years and may even have subdued them. It has even been hypothesized that he assumed imperial titles, once he had imposed peace on the island—indeed, the earliest Welsh traditions commonly referred to Arthur as "The Emperor."

The Elusive Emperor

Though such a model seems reasonable, the fact must be faced that we have no contemporary evidence, such as an inscription, that would clinch the case. Indeed, skeptical historians simply dismiss the idea of a historical Arthur, arguing that he was a heroic ideal developed by the native British during the Dark Ages. The more positive approach is to assess whether it was *likely* that such a person as Arthur really existed.

There is a slight problem in that we are not sure exactly *where* we should look in history to test the case. The dates given by the medieval accounts are hopelessly inconsistent. Geoffrey of Monmouth, for example, dates the death of Arthur at the battle of Camlan to A.D. 542, yet (as we see later) all the specific indications he gives place the reign of King Arthur in the decades around A.D. 460. Among historians, the dates provided by *The Welsh Annals* are usually preferred: 517 for Arthur's victory at Badon and 538 for his death at the battle of Camlan. Following these pegs for the zenith and the end of Arthur's career, we could place its beginning around A.D. 500.

Some scholars in favor of a historical Arthur have argued that these dates agree with those recorded by the Anglo-Saxon chroniclers (about the same time as *The Welsh Annals*). For example, the *Anglo-Saxon Chronicle* gives many entries between 449 and 488 describing the stages by which Kent was conquered by Hengest, after he was invited in as a mercenary leader by Vortigern. But after 488, when Hengest's son Oisc took the throne, there are no further Kentish entries in the *Chronicle* until A.D. 565. This certainly suggests a recession in the activity of the leading Saxon kingdom during these decades. All that we are told is that Oisc (or Ossa) had a reign of "twenty-four winters," which would mean that he died in 512 A.D. As Welsh tradition says that this king (remembered as Osla "Big-Knife") was the leader defeated by Arthur at the battle of Mount Badon, there seems to be a reasonable convergence between the Welsh and Saxon records—with an acceptable difference of only five years for the date of the battle, in which Arthur presumably killed the king of Kent.

A battle of Mount Badon c. 515 has also been held to suit the archaeological picture of the Saxon invasions. It has been suggested that the evidence of early Saxon graves shows a great influx of invaders around A.D. 450, that this had slowed down by about A.D. 500, and that the expansion of the Saxons took off again only about fifty years later. Somebody, it is argued, must have been organizing a resistance during this period. Were it not for the traditions about Arthur, history might have to hypothesize the existence of a great military leader capable of holding back the Saxon advance for so many years. There are many parallels from the European continent at the time: several *generalissimos* are known (sometimes "barbarian" or semibarbarian themselves), who through a mixture of strategic skill and diplomacy held back the successive waves of "barbarians" invading the Roman Empire. So why not accept the British tradition of Arthur?

The final piece of evidence for the existence of a real Arthur comes from the popularity of this name shortly after the time he was supposed to have lived. In the late fifth and early sixth century, no fewer than six British princes were christened "Arthur." None of them seems to have been important enough in his own right to have given rise to the Arthur legend; so it seems a natural assumption that the popularity of the name comes from the existence of a real, eminent

Arthur in the recent past (in the same way that lots of girls born in the later twentieth century have been christened "Diana").

Camelot

Appealing as the idea of a historical Arthur may seem, it is still only based on circumstantial evidence. Can archaeology help to confirm or deny his existence?

Places connected with King Arthur, with colorful names like "Arthur's Chair" and "Arthur's Round Table," are scattered practically the length and breadth of Britain, and cases have been made for localizing him in Scotland, Wales, Cornwall, and the English Midlands. Yet the best Arthurian sites, from a historical perspective, are those in the West Country of England—in the counties of Cornwall, Devon, and Somerset. We know that this region long held out against the Saxon invaders, while its proximity to the continent makes good sense if Arthur really was a Romanized leader, possibly in touch with the vestiges of the old Empire on the continent.

Here in the West Country there are three sites particularly associated with Arthur: Glastonbury, Tintagel, and Cadbury. The *Life of Saint Gildas* (written before Geoffrey of Monmouth) tells how Guinevere was carried off by Melwas, king of Somerset, and kept prisoner on Glastonbury Tor, a natural fortress because of its steep sides and marshy surroundings. Arthur raised his forces and was about to lay siege when the monks of Glastonbury interceded and negotiated the release of Guinevere. The abbot was richly rewarded by the two kings. Archaeological excavation has shown that there was, as the story said, an important monastic settlement at Glastonbury during the fifth century, perhaps the earliest one of its kind in Britain. Later tradition held that Glastonbury was the "Isle of Avalon," where Arthur went to heal his wounds. The monks of Glastonbury even claimed to have exhumed his body (see **King Arthur's Grave** in **Hoax?**). Monasteries, of course, were the hospitals of the time, and a likely place where a dying king would be taken for safety.

Arthurian tradition also scores a hit at Tintagel. According to Geoffrey of Monmouth, King Arthur was conceived here: King Uther developed a passion for the wife of Gorlois, the Duke of Cornwall, and with the aid of Merlin he sneaked into Gorlois's castle at Tintagel and had his way. The castle that tourists visit at Tintagel is of medieval date, far too late to have any connection with a historical Arthur. On the other hand, archaeologists have long known that there was a Dark

Age settlement at Tintagel, though for many years it was assumed to have belonged to a small monastic community. Recent work, including the discovery of a striking amount of luxury goods imported from the Mediterranean, has changed the picture completely. The present excavators of Tintagel now see it as an important commercial center and a stronghold of the local kings of Cornwall.

But the greatest surprise came from Cadbury, a site in Somerset not far from Glastonbury. Cadbury "Castle" is a steep-sided, freestanding hill converted during the Iron Age into a fortified camp—the Romans stormed and took it about A.D. 43. On the surface there was little sign of later activity, yet the great sixteenth-century antiquarian John Leland claimed that it was nothing less than Camelot, the capital of King Arthur: "Camallate, sumtyme a famose toun or castelle." The name Camelot first occurs in a French Arthurian romance of the twelfth century A.D., and at first glance one would simply have assumed that Leland, inspired by the place-names Queen Camel and West Camel, which lie near Cadbury, was simply hazarding a guess about the location of an entirely mythical place.

The Camelot problem took on an entirely different complexion when the hill of Cadbury Castle was examined by archaeologists in the 1960s and '70s. Excavation showed that the site was a hive of activity during the Arthurian period (5th century A.D.). The hilltop was fortified with a well-built stone-and-timber wall nearly three-quarters of a mile in perimeter, surrounding, among other structures, a large hall, 63 by 34 feet in size, where the inhabitants would have sat to feast. Was Leland right, after all, that this was King Arthur's capital? And if so, was it the result of a lucky guess or did he have access to a genuine local tradition?

A surprising number of times archaeology has confirmed legends, remote and fanciful though they may have seemed. Yet frustratingly with Arthur they have only partially confirmed the story. The archaeological "hits" scored at Glastonbury, Tintagel, and Cadbury, impressive as they seem, can still be dismissed by skeptics as mere coincidence. Yet they do, in a general sense, confirm the background to the legends. At the very least somebody, clearly a British chieftain of great status, fortified Cadbury Castle in the fifth century.

As persistent traditions, backed by circumstantial evidence, suggest that there was a powerful leader called Arthur at this time, no one could reasonably deny the possibility that a real King Arthur fortified Cadbury. This is the position taken by most historians and archaeologists conversant with the evidence. Most of the jigsaw seems to be in

Was this Camelot? Drawing of Cadbury Castle, Somerset, by the antiquarian William Stukeley (1723). The actual castle has fewer ramparts— Stukeley has multiplied the number by including agricultural terraces.

place—except the central, key, piece, which unequivocally proves that a real King Arthur existed.

"A Certain Very Ancient Book"?

Something else may be lacking from the standard interpretation of the evidence. A rounded picture can be drawn of Arthur as a Romanized British leader organizing his countrymen against the Saxon invaders in the fifth century A.D. Yet what about the European conquests of Arthur that are such an integral part of his traditional image? And why was Arthur so well known on the continent, and at such an early date? As Caxton noted in his preface to Malory, Arthur "is more spoken of beyond the sea [and] more books made of his noble acts, than there be in England . . . in Dutch, Italian, Spanish and Greekish as well as French." Indeed, after the rash of "Arthurs" about A.D. 600, the next occurrence of the name comes not from Wales but from Normandy, about 1050. The earliest depiction of Arthur in art comes from a sculpture at Modena Cathedral in Italy, dated between 1099 and 1120, showing the king and his knights rescuing Guinevere from the clutches of some evildoers. Arthur's long-standing popularity on the continent seems inextricably bound up with the legend that his empire extended far beyond Britain.

At first glance the tradition that Arthur campaigned overseas during such troubled times at home seems hopelessly far-fetched. Surely a historical Arthur would have been too busy at home keeping the Saxons at bay. And in the early 500s, when the standard interpretation places Arthur, there is not the slightest hint of a British invasion in the chronicles of France. But is there any value in casting the net somewhat wider? This is the approach taken by Geoffrey Ashe, the grand old man of Arthurian studies. Always a writer prepared to chance his arm, Ashe nonetheless has the respect of most academics working in the Dark Age field—for example, he is co-founder and honorary secretary of the Camelot Research Committee, which excavated Cadbury Castle. Ashe has probably also done more than any other writer to establish Arthur as a likely historical figure within the standard framework. Yet the feeling that something was missing prompted him to reexamine his own arguments—published over many years in several books—and throw open a startling new resolution to the Arthurian question.

Ashe began again with the Geoffrey of Monmouth problem. Geoffrey's key addition to the Arthurian tradition was his lengthy account of a continental campaign, which occupies more than half of his account of Arthur's reign. Geoffrey claimed to have a special source for his *History*. He says that his friend Walter, the archdeacon of Oxford, "a man well-informed about the history of foreign countries," had presented him with "a certain very ancient book written in the British language." The mysterious book supposedly contained the forgotten history of the British kings, from the earliest times to the Dark Ages. That such a book really existed seems highly unlikely. For one thing, for large parts of the *History* we can detect Geoffrey's sources, which included known works like Nennius. At best the "book" may have been a compilation of sources. Significantly, the only place in the whole of the *History* where Geoffrey specifically invokes the "book" is for the story of Mordred's treachery while Arthur was campaigning on the continent.

Scholars either tend to reject Geoffrey's "book" claim entirely, or assume that if he had such a source at his disposal, it would have been in Welsh, the language of the surviving British natives. Yet an alternative has long been known. The word *British* also applied to the British who colonized the peninsula of Brittany (or "Little Britain") during the Dark Ages—today they are known as the Bretons and still have their own language, which is very close to Welsh. The Bretons played a crucial role in the development of the Arthurian legend, transmitting oral tradition from Wales and Cornwall to Europe. Did information also flow in the opposite direction? Ashe notes, as many scholars have done before, how much Breton interest there is in the *History*—for example, Arthur's main allies are from Brittany. Did Geoffrey work from a Breton source highlighting connections between Britain and the continent during the Dark Ages?

At this point, Ashe pulls his ace rabbit out of the hat. There *was* a powerful British king who campaigned on the continent during the Dark Ages. We know about him from various snippets of information written in continental chroniclers, which refer to him as "Riothamus, King of the Britons." In the middle of the fifth century, Gaul (modern France) was still nominally under the control of the Western Roman Empire, but had already been invaded by several barbarian groups. Some were pacified by being given lands and became controllable. Others, like the Goths, were more difficult to manage. The whole concept of an emperor ruling from Rome was in itself beginning to crumble, and a series of puppet rulers were put in place by barbarian generals. Eventually the emperor of the Eastern Roman Empire, Leo, made a last-ditch attempt to stabilize the Western Empire. He sent a relative of his, Anthemius, accompanied by a large army, to Rome to be crowned as the new Augustus of the West. Gaul could be controlled from Rome only by juggling various alliances with the barbarian settlers or by seeking outside help. This Anthemius did—in order to smash the power of the Goths and restore imperial control he invited in Riothamus, king of the Britons, who arrived with a force of 12,000 soldiers. The size of this army is noteworthy in itself. Many of the Dark Age battles in Britain were fought between tiny forces involving only tens or hundreds of soldiers.

The name Riothamus, as Ashe recognizes, can hardly have given rise to that of Arthur. Yet what is in a name? Ashe points out that Riothamus, in the Celtic language of Britain, means something like "supremely royal," which sounds more like a title than a name. Was the warrior who was recognized on the continent as "his supreme majesty" or the like known at home by his personal name of Arthur?

The Real King Arthur?

Whoever he was, Riothamus was a major force on the Dark Age political scene. The previous understanding of earlier historians—that he was a local ruler in Brittany—has, as Ashe notes, been scuppered; the Gothic chronicle that describes his arrival clearly says that this king of the Britons arrived in France in a fleet of ships, which means that he came overseas from Britain proper. This is only the first in a series of remarkable coincidences with the campaign of King Arthur as described by Geoffrey of Monmouth. The Eastern Roman Emperor when the Riothamus episode took place was Leo I (A.D. 457–474), and Geoffrey of Monmouth specifically states that the emperor at the time of Arthur's continental campaign was called Leo. Geoffrey also names the Pope at the time as being Sulpicius, which seems a reasonable scribal error for the name of Simplicius, whose reign as Pontiff (A.D. 468–483) overlaps the period in question.

Ashe has also traced the route of Riothamus's army from the available contemporary sources. Riothamus presumably landed in Brittany and marched from there to Berry in central France, where he was defeated by the Goths before he could join forces with the imperial Roman allies. The battle took place in A.D. 470. The British retreated eastward, and were beaten again at Bourges. If they retreated farther in the same direction, Ashe calculates, they would have had to enter northern Burgundy. And then, all trace of them vanishes. Could the disappearance of Riothamus and his army in western France have given rise to the legend of Arthur, the king whose death was never witnessed and whose return home was always awaited? Strikingly enough, there is a town in Burgundy, along the line of Riothamus's retreat as Ashe has reconstructed it, called "Avallon."

There are, of course, some obvious differences between the legend of Arthur's continental campaign and the activities of the historical Riothamus. Arthur fought the Romans, whereas Riothamus was their ally against the Goths. Arthur "won," whereas Riothamus failed. Still, these are understandable differences that may have come about in the retelling of the story, which would have passed through the hands of many different chroniclers before the composition of the "book" that Geoffrey of Monmouth read and embellished. Ashe has made a powerful case, and in various articles continues to add extra circumstantial detail. Perhaps the most compelling is that his scenario might also explain the theme of Arthur's betrayal (by Mordred) that is so central to the whole legend. The Prefect of Gaul, under the Emperor Anthemius, was one Arvandus. In A.D. 469 he was taken to trial in Rome for conspiring to bring about the events that eventually led to the destruction of Riothamus's army. Arvandus had written to the Goths encouraging them to attack the British troops in Gaul (now the mainstay of the emperor) and divide the country up with the Burgundians. He was executed for high treason, but it seems that the harm he intended was already done—the Goths took his tip and pounced on Riothamus's army. Could the story of Mordred's treachery have arisen from the stab in the back that Riothamus received from Arvandus?

"Arvandus" is an extremely rare name, and it is surely beyond coincidence that the betrayer of King Arthur in one medieval chronicle is called "Morvandus," which looks like an attempt to blend "Arvandus" with "Mordred." Ashe mentions it in support of his identification of Riothamus and Arthur. In one sense it does, but in another, it signals where the problems for his thesis begin. The medieval writer who composed the name "Morvandus" must himself have been aware of a theory that Riothamus and Arthur were the same. If he was, has Ashe merely rediscovered a medieval theory, one that Geoffrey of Monmouth himself followed? There is the ugly possibility that Geoffrey, or the author of the Breton book he followed, was simply following a hunch in making Arthur the defender of Britain and Riothamus the continental adventurer the same.

Ashe has faced this problem and admitted that we are still effectively dealing with two historical prototypes for the legendary King Arthur: one British, the other apparently Breton. The final step, to assume that a single historical figure lay behind both traditions, is one that Ashe himself is tentative in suggesting. Yet, as he points out, someone like Riothamus must surely have been powerful enough to achieve such feats as the subjugation of the Saxons and the construction of the unique fortifications at Cadbury. Are we looking at the real King Arthur here? A man who, swelled with his successes at home, felt confident enough to draw off the bulk of his troops in a madcap scheme to restore the Roman Empire in western Europe against the barbarians?

As Ashe puts it, Riothamus "is the only 'King of the Britons' anywhere near the time assigned to Arthur; he is the only firmly attested person whose career is, to any significant extent, Arthurian." Ashe's case certainly wins on this underlying appeal. If he is right, Arthur at last springs into history as a real person. We would even possess a letter written to him (as Riothamus) by the Roman bishop Sidonius, who pleaded with him about the case of runaway slaves in an area of northern France under his control.

Ashe's theory about "Riothamus, King of the Britons" has opened up the most promising line of Arthurian investigation in decades. Final proof is still lacking, while a number of loose ends await explanation. Many historians believe that Riothamus was not a mighty conqueror, but a minor British king who led a large party of Britons, fleeing from the Saxons, to take refuge in Brittany—and that he is remembered in Breton genealogies as "John Reith," a nobleman and not a king of Arthurian status. Back home, none of the native Welsh traditions refers to Arthur as Riothamus, while they give scant mention to continental adventures. Is it likely that Arthur's British subjects preserved themselves no better record of their savior's disappearance on an overseas venture? Ashe has found an Avallon in Burgundy, France, where conceivably the "King of the Britons" was last reported. Yet what about the claims made by Glastonbury in England to be Avalon, and the last resting place of the "once and future king"? (See **King Arthur's Grave** in **Hoax?**) Or did Riothamus, about whose fate the continental sources are extremely vague, actually return to Britain, like the conquering Arthur of legend, and die in his own land?

Arthur, despite centuries of the most intensive research, still determinedly remains the greatest enigma of early British history.

ROBIN HOOD

Robin Hood has the unique distinction of being the only person in English history to have had an entry in the *Dictionary of National Biography* whose purpose was to argue that he was entirely imaginary. The entry on Robin Hood was written in 1891 by the biographer and historian Sir Sidney Lee, in an attempt to lay the ghost of the English outlaw to rest once and for all. Despite Lee's eloquence, a century later most people still believe Robin Hood to be a real figure, but what historical basis is there for the legend as portrayed by Douglas Fairbanks, Errol Flynn, and Kevin Costner?

"The Rhymes of Robin Hood"

Robin Hood, as everyone knows, is a character from medieval England. Yet the adventures of Robin and his Merry Men, in the versions most familiar to us today, took shape in the sixteenth century, when stories and plays about them were immensely popular. To look for the historical Robin—if there ever was one—we naturally have to search out the oldest accounts of his deeds.

The first written references to our hero are tantalizingly brief. The very earliest comes in the poem *Piers Plowman*, written in 1377 by the London cleric William Langland. One of his characters, an idle priest, says in passing, "I know the rhymes of Robin Hood," but that is all. Unfortunately, like so much popular verse from the Middle Ages, the rhymes heard by Langland have not survived. One verse may be preserved in a scrap of manuscript from Lincoln Cathedral of about 1410, which gives the words "Robin Hood in Sherwood stood."

Robin Hood as an outlaw makes his first definite appearance in 1420, when Andrew de Wyntoun dates him to the years 1283–85 in his verse *Chronicle of Scotland*:

Then Little John and Robin Hood
As forest outlaws were well renowned,
In Inglewood and Barnsdale
All this time they plied their trade.

The Robin Hood statue at
Nottingham Castle.

Some twenty years later another Scottish chronicler, Walter Bower,
sets Robin in the year 1266:

Then arose the famous murderer, Robert Hood, as well as Little John,
together with their accomplices from among the dispossessed, whom

the foolish populace are so inordinately fond of celebrating both in tragedy and comedy.

Bower adds that "certain praiseworthy things" were recorded of this "murderer," including his devotion to mass. On one occasion Hood was hearing mass in Barnsdale forest when the authorities came to arrest him. He refused to interrupt his devotions and flee, and tackled his enemies only when the service had finished. He defeated them and won a rich ransom for his captives.

These all too brief accounts from Scottish sources agree in placing the famous outlaw in the north of England. Inglewood Forest is in Cumberland, just below the Scottish border and Barnsdale Forest a hundred miles away in south Yorkshire. Robin's best-known hideout, Sherwood Forest, is about twenty miles south of Barnsdale. As for the outlaw's first name, while Langland and Wyntoun call him Robin, Bower calls him Robert; the inconsistency is, however, only apparent— Robin is a French diminutive of Robert, both names becoming extremely popular after the Norman invasion (A.D. 1066).

By the time Bower was writing, Robin Hood was already a familiar enough figure to be cited in legal settings. In 1429 we have the first use in a lawsuit of the phrase "Robin Hood in Barnsdale stood" (echoing the rhyme from Lincoln), as a proverb describing something that is undeniably true. In 1439 a gentleman from Derbyshire was accused in court of having "gathered and assembled with him many misdoers . . . and as in an insurrection had gone into the woods of that area as if they had been Robyn Hode and his men.' Clearly by this time Robin Hood was an inspiration to men setting themselves against the law and a revolutionary image feared by those who wished to maintain the status quo.

Apart from the curious tale related by Bower, our earliest sources tell none of the familiar adventures of Robin Hood, Little John, Maid Marion, Friar Tuck, and the rest of the merry band in the green-wood, as they thwarted their sworn enemies, the Sheriff of Nottingham and Sir Guy of Gisborne. The oldest surviving substantial account of Robin Hood in his wider setting was printed around 1510, and is called *A Geste of Robin Hood*, the word *Geste* probably meaning a tale of heroic exploits. Although it was published in 1510, the language has features such as the word endings *e* and *es* which are usually thought to date its composition to about 1400.

In this tale Robin Hood, Little John, Will Scarlet, and Much the Miller's Son are outlaws in the forest of Barnsdale. They meet a

Frontispiece of *A Geste of Robin Hood*, A.D. 1510.

knight down on his luck and lend him the money to repay his debts to the greedy abbot of St. Mary's in York. Then a monk of St. Mary's falls into the outlaws' hands, and they relieve him of twice the money lent to the poor knight. In response to this outrage, the Sheriff of Nottingham stages an archery contest with the plan of trapping Robin's band. Robin wins the prize and the outlaws escape the Sheriff's trap, though Little John is wounded, so they take refuge in the castle of Sir Richard at the Lee (usually thought to be the same person as the poor knight from the beginning of the tale). In their next encounter, Robin kills the Sheriff. This brings down the wrath of King Edward on the outlaws. The king arrives in Sherwood while investigating the state of his royal forests in Lancashire and Yorkshire, and dons a disguise to hunt Robin down. When the outlaws meet the king, Robin shows his allegiance and is pardoned. He then enters Edward's service at court, but after a year or more becomes homesick and returns to the forest, where he lives an outlaw's life for another twenty-two years. Eventually, he is betrayed by his cousin, the prioress of Kirkless Abbey, whom he visits when ill to be bled (a common medieval cure). With her secret lover, Robin's enemy Sir Roger of Doncaster, she allows him to bleed to death.

So by about 1440 many of the familiar elements of the Robin Hood legend were already in place. King Richard the Lionheart and his troublesome brother Prince John, stock-in-trade characters of the film versions, are conspicuously missing. So are Maid Marion and Friar Tuck, who do not appear in the tale of Robin Hood until later.

A True Tale of ROBIN HOOD.

Or, A Brief Touch of the Life and Death of that renowned Outlaw *Robert* Earl of *Huntington*, vulgarly called *Robin Hood*, who lived and dyed in A. D. 1198. being the 9th. year of the Reign of King *Richard* the First, commonly called *Richard Cœur de Lyon.*

Carefully collected out of the truest Writers of our English Chronicles : And published for the satisfaction of those who desire truth from falshood.

By *Martin Parker.*

Printed for *J. Clark*, *W. Thackeray*, and near *West-Smithfield*. 1687.

Robin Hood identified as the Earl of Huntingdon in a book of 1687.

They are therefore generally regarded as additions to the basic story, and can probably be discounted when searching the historical record for the real Robin Hood.

A Rebel Earl?

The first historian to try to track down the origin of Robin Hood was the famous antiquarian William Stukeley (1687–1765). He was an early investigator of Stonehenge and a great believer in Druids (see **Stonehenge** in **Architectural Wonders**), but also took an interest in genealogy. Stukeley's starting point was the plays of Anthony Munday written in 1598, which portrayed Robin Hood as a nobleman—Robert, earl of Huntingdon, who died in the year 1247. Stukeley perused William Dugdale's Baronage of 1675 for the Huntingdon noble line, publishing the results of his researches in 1746. He concluded that the man behind the legend was "Robert Fitz Ooth, commonly called Robin Hood, pretended earl of Huntingdon," who died in 1274, tracing back his descent to Judith, the niece of the Norman William the Conqueror on the one side and Waltheof, earl of Northumberland and Huntingdon, a survivor from the Saxon nobility, on the other.

Unfortunately, Stukeley's researches among the noble pedigrees had carried him only so far, and he was forced to fill in the gaps with some leaps of imagination. Professor Sir James Holt of Cambridge University, in his major study of Robin Hood published in 1982, provides a devastating summary of the shortcomings of Stukeley's work:

> He concocted a marriage between Gilbert de Gant and Rohaise, daughter of Richard Fitz Gilbert, both great lords of the Norman settlement, which only occurred between their descendants, of the same name, two generations later. Among the children of this misplaced, misdated marriage he added a daughter, Maud, who was entirely fictitious. He then married the fictitious Maud to a fictitious husband, Ralph fitz Ooth, after which not surprisingly, it was easy to discover a fictitious family of fitz Ooth with Robert fitz Ooth . . . in the third generation. Stukeley could not even get the spurious date of Robin's death correct; he converted 1247 into 1274. He also made the fitz Ooths lords of Kime in Lincolnshire. This too was fictitious; the pedigree of the lords of Kime is well established and leaves no room for such intrusion. "Fitz Ooth" itself seems redolent of antiquity. It is a strange name, otherwise unknown.

Given these creative additions, it is not surprising that modern scholars have largely set aside Stukeley's theories.

In 1995, however, the self-styled "historical detectives" Graham Phillips and Martin Keatman revived Stukeley's fitz Ooth, suggesting that he had somehow confused him with the similarly named Sir Robert fitz Odo, a knight known from the reign of King Richard "the Lionheart" (A.D. 1189–1199), whose estates lay at Loxley in Warwickshire. They argue that Robin Hood is often said to come from Loxley (Locksley), which they suggest could be the Warwickshire Loxley rather than the usual identification with a Loxley in Yorkshire. This Robert fitz Odo may have been stripped of his knighthood in 1196, as a Sir Robert is not mentioned after this date, although there is a Robert fitz Odo in nearby Hanbury in 1203. Finally, as the element "fitz" in Sir Robert's name indicated illegitimacy, he could have chosen to drop this, leaving himself as Robert Odo, a name very close to "Robin Hood."

There is little of real substance here. First, the Loxley connection with Robin Hood can be traced back only to about 1600. Second, there is no compelling reason to assume the Warwickshire Loxley is the one referred to, especially as it is so far away from Robin's traditional haunts in Yorkshire and Nottinghamshire. Indeed, the earliest mention of Loxley says only that it was Robin's birthplace (with no mention of owning estates there) and plumps for the Yorkshire location. Third, we can't be sure that Sir Robert fitz Odo didn't simply die in 1196. Finally, there is not a scrap of evidence that he became an outlaw.

Robyn Hode, the King's Servant?

The first serious contender for the title of the original Robin Hood was put forward by Joseph Hunter, who was appointed assistant keeper of the newly created Public Record Office in London in 1838. Hunter came from Sheffield in Yorkshire, and not surprisingly took an interest in this hero of northern English culture. First he argued that the *Geste* showed that the earliest location for Robin Hood's career was the forest of Barnsdale in Yorkshire, rather than the more famous Sherwood, a day's ride to the south. Second, he argued that "Edwarde our comely kinge" mentioned in the *Geste* must be Edward II (A.D. 1307–1327), who made a royal progress through the area late in the year 1323, during which he investigated the poaching of deer from the royal forests, finally reaching Nottingham in November.

Effigy of King Richard the Lionheart (1157-1199) from his tomb.

Effigy of King Edward II
(1284–1327) from his tomb.

However, Hunter went further than this, revolutionizing the study of Robin Hood by searching diligently in the official records for any trace of a Robin Hood at the right place and time.

Amazingly, Hunter managed to come up with just that. As he put it himself, hardly able to control his excitement:

> Now it will scarcely be believed, but it is nevertheless the plain and simple truth that in documents preserved in the Exchequer containing accounts of expenses in the king's household we find the name of "Robyn Hode" not once but several times occurring, receiving, with about eight and twenty others, the pay of 3d [pence] a day, as one of the "valetz, porteurs de la chambre" of the king.

This Robyn was shown to be a member of the king's household from March to November 1324, thus fitting in extremely well with the story in the *Geste* of Robin being pardoned by a King Edward (in Nottingham to investigate the shooting of deer in his forests) and entering royal service for a year. Robyn Hode was paid off by Edward II on November 22, 1324—to return to his beloved greenwood, if Hunter is right.

Hunter went on to try to trace Robin in his earlier days, and found a possible candidate in a Robert Hood, with a wife called Matilda, who was recorded at Wakefield, only ten miles from Barnsdale, in 1316–17. So far so good, but there was no direct evidence that this Robert Hood was an outlaw. To provide a motive Hunter turned to a national crisis, the revolt of Thomas, earl of Lancaster, against Edward II in March 1322. The earl planned to join forces with Robert the Bruce of Scotland, but his army was intercepted only some thirty miles north of Barnsdale. Lancaster's troops were cut down by a hail of arrows and scattered in defeat. The earl himself was condemned to death in a speedy trial and beheaded outside his castle at Pontefract, on the edge of Barnsdale. Many of his supporters were outlawed and fled into the forests, where they evaded capture. In 1323, Edward II was facing the possibility of a civil war with other rebellious barons, and traveled north in April to try to raise support. One of his tactics was to pardon the remaining Lancastrians, so what would be more natural than to contact the outlaw Robin Hood at large in Barnsdale and bring him onto the royal side? We do indeed know that when Edward II arrived at Nottingham in November 1323 from Lancashire after his long tour, he was accompanied by many pardoned rebels.

Later historians have tried to flesh out the background to Hunter's case by investigating possible candidates for the other characters in the *Geste* who were active in the 1320s. This has yielded some possible identifications, such as a Richard de la Lee who was parson of Arksey near Doncaster, and a Roger of Doncaster, an adulterous chaplain, although neither was a knight. While these are interesting discoveries, they do not really add much to Hunter's original theory. The Sheriff of Nottingham is unfortunately not named in the *Geste*, so he can be of no help here.

In 1989 Professor Holt, Stukeley's critic, reviewed the documentary evidence available today and found nothing to strengthen Hunter's argument. First, he points out that no Hoods appear in the list of sixty tenants in the manor of Wakefield who had their lands confiscated because they had supported Lancaster's rebellion. Some of these were very minor characters, to judge by the value of their land, so either Robert Hood of Wakefield was an even less important person, or he didn't join the rebels, or he was for some unknown reason left off the list. In any case there is nothing here to support the theory that he became an outlaw.

Second, a fragment of an earlier account book for the royal household, so faint it can be read only under ultraviolet light, shows Robyn Hode being paid on June 27, 1323, for service earlier that month. He was therefore in royal service before the king arrived at Nottingham Castle in November from Lancashire at the end of his northern tour to gather support. The idea of an earlier encounter between Robin and the king is not impossible, however, for Edward had actually visited Nottingham briefly back in March, so the *Geste* could still be right about this. However, an earlier meeting does undermine the close resemblance between the story in the *Geste* of Robin and a King Edward meeting in Sherwood after the king had been looking into accounts of poaching and Edward II's known investigation of deer poaching in the royal forests of Lancashire in the autumn of 1323.

Finally, there is the issue of Robyn Hode's reasons for leaving the king's service in November 1324. The court records apparently show that he was in some way incapacitated: "To Robyn Hod, formerly one of the porters, because he can no longer work, five shillings as a gift, by command." If we follow the most obvious reading of this passage, it seems that Robyn Hod(e) was physically unable to continue in his duties and therefore discharged. This hardly sounds like the vigorous outlaw of the *Geste*, who left the king's side because he was bored, to spend another twenty-two years in the forest before he was betrayed. On the other hand, the *Geste* describes Robin as growing lonely and homesick at court and feigning sleeplessness and a loss of appetite in order to escape back to the greenwood.

The crucial weakness of Hunter's case, which still remains after another century of detective work on Robyn Hode the king's servant and Robert Hood of Wakefield, is that there need be no connection between them at all. Hood is not that unusual a name, another of Edward II's servants being a Simon Hode, and there is no direct evidence that Robert of Wakefield became an outlaw or that Robyn the valet had been one, either.

Robin the Forest-Elf?

The difficulties in Hunter's solution were always apparent, which gave heart to those attempting a completely different approach to Robin Hood. Sir Sidney Lee came to the view in his entry on Robin Hood in the *Dictionary of National Biography* that "the arguments in favour of Robin Hood's historical existence, although very voluminous, will not bear scholarly examination." Convinced that Robin was not a real character, he sought out a mythical origin:

> There can be little doubt, however, that, as in the somewhat similar case of Rory o' the Hills in Ireland, the name originally belonged to a mythical forest-elf, who filled a large space in English, and apparently in Scottish, folk-lore, and that it was afterwards applied by English ballad-writers . . . to any robber-leader who made his home in forests or moors, excelled in archery, defied the oppressive forest laws, and thus attracted popular sympathy.

He goes on to suggest that "in its origin the name was probably a variant of 'Hodekin,' the title of a sprite or elf in Teutonic folk-lore." Historians are generally agreed, however, that the primary meaning of "Hood" was always simply hood (meaning head covering), and that it is simply unnecessary to bring in German folklore to explain the origin of a perfectly ordinary English word. They are also unable to trace Lee's forest elf in English mythology, and argue that the link between Robin Hood and folklore came about through his incorporation into the pageants for May Day festivals in the sixteenth century.

Egyptologist Margaret Murray went even further in her interpretation of Robin Hood. She argued in her extremely influential volume *The God of the Witches*, published in 1931, that Robin Hood was "the god of the old religion." Her evidence was that Robin and his band of

Robin Hood standing alone in Sherwood Forest (engraving of 1795).

twelve merry men were like "a Grand Master and his coven," that they wore "the fairies' colour" green and were anti-church, and that Robin was a common term for the Devil. Unfortunately, none of this really stands up: the early sources talk of seven-score outlaws with Robin, and medieval witch trials do not call the Devil Robin or refer to people dressed in green.

Robert Hod the Outlaw?

The dominant historian of Robin Hood in modern times is undoubtedly Sir James Holt, who has searched the published archives of medieval England diligently for traces of Robin Hood. As we have seen, he remains unconvinced by Hunter's theory of Robyn Hode the king's servant and Robert Hood of Wakefield, which places Robin Hood in the 1320s. Instead he sees the original Robin Hood as belonging to the thirteenth century. The *Geste* therefore for Holt is not such a primary source, and may include later additions brought about by cross-fertilization with other heroic tales. In particular, he has to set aside the identification of the king in the story as an Edward, for none of them reigned early enough to suit Holt's theory.

Stephen Knight, Professor of English at the University of Wales, has provided a degree of support for Holt's caution regarding the *Geste*. He has reexamined the language of the *Geste*, concluding that the traditional date is too early, and that a better date would be around A.D. 1450. In this case the King Edward could even be a contemporary intrusion, as King Edward IV (reigned 1461–83) was both handsome ("comely") and spent much time in the north of England.

In putting forward his own Robin candidate, Holt first argues that although our earliest historical sources don't agree on a precise dating for Robin Hood—de Wyntoun placing him in the years 1283–85 and Bower in 1266—they are agreed on the thirteenth century. De Wyntoun, indeed, wrote within a hundred years of Robyn Hode the valet's career (1323–24), yet he clearly saw Robin Hood as a figure of an earlier generation. Second, careful searching by Holt and others of the surviving records from the thirteenth century has uncovered several people bearing the surname Robynhod, Robynhoud, Robehod, or Rabunhod. Some of these seem simply to have been named after their fathers, such as Katherine Robynhod, daughter of Robert Hood of London, but it is still unusual for an English surname to be formed from a combination of first and last names. The majority of these people are known because they were in some trouble with the law,

Medieval archery contest.

from which Holt concludes that "Robinhood" was a nickname given to criminals.

The most interesting of these cases from Holt's perspective is the earliest, that of a man called "William son of Robert le Fevre" (Fevre = Smith), who came from Enborne in Berkshire near the River Thames. William was accused of being part of a criminal gang responsible for a spate of robberies. William and the others had fled the jurisdiction of the court and were therefore outlawed in the year 1261, by order of the local court at Reading. At Easter 1262 he is again mentioned, this time in a royal document concerning the seizing of his land, but now he is referred to as "William Robehod, fugitive." Holt's interpretation is that one of the clerks responsible had altered William's name, giving him this nickname:

> What led him to do so was that William son of Robert had Robert in his name and was a member of an outlaw gang indicted for robbery. So he became William Robehod. It follows that the man who changed the name knew of the legend. The earliest reference to Robin Hood must now therefore be taken to be not 1377 but 1261–2. In all senses this is an enormous advance.

Holt goes on to propose an original Robin Hood. This was a Yorkshireman called Robert Hod, recorded at the assize court in York in 1225–27 as a fugitive from justice and therefore an outlaw. In the 1226 records he is given the nickname "Hobbehod"; unfortunately the meaning of this is unknown. We know nothing more of this Robert Hod, but as Holt stressed, "He was an outlaw. He is the only possible original of Robin Hood, so far discovered, who is known to have been an outlaw."

Holt's Robin Hood would therefore be slightly earlier than the oldest historical sources suggest, but that is surely a more likely possibility than that he would be later in date. Not surprisingly there have been critics of Holt's theory, most notably Professor Knight, who takes a decidedly skeptical line toward these attempts to tie Robin down. His view of William "Robehod" is that it could be just a misunderstanding of his name and that of his father—"William Robert would be a common way of recording this man's name at the time." This suggestion seems a little implausible, but a clerical error (of Robehod for Robert) certainly can't be ruled out. Knight also regards Robert Hod, the Yorkshire outlaw of 1225, as a rather flimsy candidate, given the fact that all we know about him is that he was an outlaw.

So what is the final verdict on Robin Hood? The approach that sees him as entirely a figure of folklore seems highly unconvincing, for mythical elements such as giant killing and magical encounters are conspicuously missing from the early tales. Hunter's identification of Robyn Hode the valet with Robert Hood of Wakefield is possible, but hardly compelling, and in any case there is no trace of the outlaw about either of them. Holt's suggestion of a thirteenth-century setting does seem more likely given the dates proposed by the earliest chroniclers. While William Robehod might be a case of acquiring a nickname, this is open to question.

There is also the possibility, unexplored by Holt, that the Robinhoods he has found in the later thirteenth century may be using this as a surname, for surnames were appearing at this date. They may have started as Hoods, but became Robinhoods in an attempt to claim kinship with the famous outlaw. Such adoptions of better-known surnames are common during medieval times, before surnames became

Robin Hood fights off the Sheriff of Nottingham's men in Sherwood Forest (engraving of 1795).

more strictly fixed. This avoids the need to demonstrate criminal activity on the part of all those named "Robinhood" or variants on that. The clear weakness in Holt's theory is that several of the people bearing this name (including Katherine Robynhod of London) have no criminal connections at all. Rather, we have the intriguing possibility that there were a number of families in the late thirteenth century who, rightly or wrongly, claimed to be descendants or relatives of Robin Hood!

This would only strengthen Holt's case for dating an original Robin Hood before 1262, when William Robehod is recorded. However, Holt's candidate, Robert Hod or Hobbehod of Yorkshire, certainly doesn't leap off the page as a Robin Hood figure; so little is known about him that he simply can't be judged.

This is highly unlikely to be the end of the story, however, for there are still thousands of medieval documents in the record houses of England, which could yet produce a definitive reference to Robin Hood, while it is certainly not impossible that a copy of the "rhymes of Robin Hood" known by Langland's lazy priest may yet be discovered.

DRACULA

Almost everyone is familiar with the movie image of Dracula, the smooth but sinister Transylvanian count, elegantly dressed in evening clothes and a cape, who throws his disguise aside to reveal fearsome fangs that strike for the neck of his innocent victim. The vampire Count Dracula is the supreme creation of Irish writer Bram Stoker, now a century old yet showing no signs of losing his popularity. But Stoker did not dream up his Dracula entirely from nothing, for historians have fixed on a plausible and horrific original for Dracula himself, while there are many well-attested accounts of vampirism in modern and ancient times.

The best recorded mass outbreak of vampirism happened in Poland and Russia during 1693. According to the contemporary French newspaper *Mercure galant*, this was a quite horrific ordeal for those affected:

They appear from midday to midnight and come to suck the blood of living people and animals in such great abundance that sometimes it comes out of their noses, and especially their ears, and that sometimes the body swims in its blood which has spilled out into its coffin. They say the vampire has a kind of hunger that causes him to eat the cloth he finds around him. This revenant [ghost] or vampire, or a demon in his form, comes out of his tomb and goes about at night violently embracing and seizing his friends and relatives and sucking their blood until they are weakened and exhausted and finally causes their death. This persecution does not stop . . . unless one interrupts its course by chopping off the head or cutting open the body of the vampire. Then one should find the body, in its coffin, limp, pliable, bloated and ruddy, even though he may have been dead for a long time. A great quantity of blood pours from his body.

Vampires are certainly not a product of the seventeenth century, as belief in the undead preying on the living has been extremely widespread, both in time and geography. Their chronological extent is impressive, with modern, medieval, classical Greek and Roman, Babylonian, and Jewish records of vampirism. The ancient Babylonian bloodsuckers were known as *Ekimmu*, and apparently represented individuals who, having died a bad death, returned to devour the flesh and suck the veins of the living. According to Jewish tradition, the first woman on earth actually became a vampire. Adam's original wife (before the creation of Eve) was Lilith, who proved to be too independent-minded for Adam. Following an argument about their sex life, Lilith flew off to the Red Sea and took up with a gang of demons. Despite the intervention of a deputation of angels, Lilith never returned, and became a demon preying on children and seducing men while they slept, then biting at them, eating their flesh and sucking their blood.

The most famous of the early records of vampires comes from the Greek writer Philostratus in his *Life of Apollonius of Tyana*, the philosopher. One of Apollonius' poor but worthy pupils, the handsome youth Menippus, was entranced by a rich and beautiful lady who wished to marry him. Suspicious, Apollonius turned up on the wedding day and unmasked her as a vampire, forcing her to admit that she "was fattening up Menippus with pleasures before devouring his body, for it was her habit to feed upon young and beautiful bodies, because their blood is pure and strong."

Vampires are also known in folklore and legends from Africa, East Asia, Australasia, the Near East, the Americas, and of course Europe, where they seem to be most common in Greece and the Balkans. In India the batlike *baital* were feared as a spirit that possessed and reanimated the dead. The *vrykolakas* of rural Greece was still a menace in this century, showing itself almost immediately after its death in a

An Indian vampire takes flight from two soldiers.

wave of attacks on villagers leading to panics of terror and revulsion. In Romania, according to folk tradition, "there was once a time when vampires were as common as blades of grass, or berries in a pail, and they never kept still, but wandered round at night among the people."

The strength of the evidence is such that we have to accept that if any belief is firmly established and well-nigh universal, it is that in vampires.

Why were people believed to turn into vampires? A whole variety of reasons are given in folklore and historical records, ranging from incomplete burial and sudden death through those who died cursed, unbaptized or excommunicated, to those whose bodies were walked over by a cat while they were awaiting burial.

Naturally, much thought was given to ways of stopping vampires. The best method was to bury potential troublemakers in such a way as to keep them in the grave. They were buried in swamps or, if on a high place, then under a stone cairn, or upside down, or pinned to the coffin or to the ground in the grave, or weighted down with heavy objects. Stones, potsherds, or coins were put in their mouths to give them something harmless to suck on, or their mouth might be tied shut.

If they were already walking at night and menacing the living, then vampires could be stilled by driving a stake through the body, cutting off the head, or burning the heart or even the whole body. A dead witch haunting Germany in 1345 proved to be a particularly tough customer. She had wandered about at night in the form of a small animal, which was caught and thrown into a ditch. This only made matters worse, for the angry witch created even more havoc in the shape of a huge filthy beast. The next step was to exhume her body, which the fearful villagers thought bore clear signs of her being a vampire. They hammered a stake through her chest and reburied her, relieved that her reign of terror was over. But even this did no good, and the witch-vampire resumed her nightly wanderings, this time using the stake as a weapon against her victims. So she had to be dug up again, and this time her body was thoroughly burned—at last this did the trick and she was never seen again.

Explaining Vampirism

We can safely set aside the idea that vampires really were the undead, back from the grave to feast on the blood of the living.

Instead folklorists and historians have proposed a wide variety of theories in an attempt to come up with a satisfying rational explanation. One of the oldest is that vampires were people who had been buried alive. Premature burials undoubtedly did happen, and digging up someone who had tried to escape from his or her coffin by scratching a way out would certainly have made a permanent impression on the witnesses. However, most vampires were dug up long after their interment, and none of the signs by which they were detected relate to attempts to claw their way from the grave. This theory probably has more to do with eighteenth- and nineteenth-century romantic novelists' fears of being buried alive than folk beliefs.

Others have suggested that vampirism is actually a disease. The most popular candidate is porphyria, sufferers from which have great sensitivity to light and are treated today with blood extracts. This theory is without any medical foundation, and in the 1970s irresponsible broadcasting of this notion (by doctors!) caused great concern to those with the disease, frightened they would be abused as a result of these wild speculations.

Much the most sensible theory is that proposed by cultural historian Paul Barber in his book *Vampires, Burial and Death* (1988). Drawing on the findings of pathologists, he shows that many of the signs used to detect a vampire, such as bodies being red in the face and bloated with blood, the lack of rigor mortis and the apparent growing of hair and nails after death, can be explained by completely natural changes that occur to the body after death. (Blood turns a darker color after death as the oxygen within it is used up, the internal organs decompose, producing gases that swell the body, rigor wears off quite quickly, and the appearance of hair and nails growing actually results from the skin contracting.) Before training in pathology existed, Barber argues, the most obvious way to interpret these developments was that the individual was in some way still alive.

Although much of what Barber says helps to explain how belief in vampires became so widespread, it does not really deal with the question of why particular individuals were identified as vampires. He notes that murder victims, suicides, and the victims of plague were the main types of people thought to be likely to become vampires. Barber's explanation is that all three groups were buried inadequately, and that their corpses were then revealed by dogs or other scavengers, leading to their identification as vampires. While this seems plausible for plague victims, those who are murdered or kill themselves are often buried in just as deep a grave as those whose death was expected (although suicides would not be interred on consecrated ground in Christian communities). There seems no good reason to think that their burials would be particularly prone to disturbance.

Here we need to return to beliefs in the supernatural. Individuals who had suffered a "bad" death—other bad ends apart from plague, murder, and suicide being death in childbirth or far from home, or as the victims of witchcraft—were precisely those most likely not to lie still in their graves, perhaps returning as vampires. They were therefore singled out for special treatment. For example, suicides were commonly buried at crossroads in Britain from the fifteenth century A.D. onward, until an Act of Parliament in 1823. A common contemporary interpretation of burials at crossroads was that the sign of the cross would deter the devil. A more likely explanation, given that such burials were known outside the Christian world (for example, one is mentioned in the great Greek philosopher Plato's *Laws*), is that crossroads were where boundaries met and so the suicides could be said to be buried in no-man's-land. They would also be confused by the alternative routes offered if they did come back from the dead and try to vampirize their old community.

The suicide's body was also frequently staked or weighted down, which has little to do with official Christian belief, and fits much better with a more supernatural interpretation—that people had a very real fear of the dead coming back, perhaps as vampires, to confront them. Barber's rationalistic view cannot be a complete explanation.

Vlad the Impaler

Vampires are real enough, at least in terms of ancient communities' beliefs, but what about Dracula himself? Remarkably, there are good grounds for believing that Bram Stoker based him on a real character, Vlad the Impaler, the ruler of Wallachia in modern Romania in the mid–fifteenth century A.D.

Vlad bore a family Christian name, his father also being a Vlad, while "the Impaler" was a nickname he earned from his horrific behavior. He was born in Transylvania in 1431, becoming the heir to the neighboring princedom of Wallachia in 1437 after his father expelled the previous ruler. But a giant shadow loomed over the Balkans

The only surviving painting of Vlad the Impaler. From the "freaks" collection at Castle Ambrus, near Innsbruck, Austria. The collection was formed by Frederick II, Count of Tyrol, who owned Castle Ambrus during the 16th century.

in the form of the Ottoman Empire established by the Islamic Turks, which had conquered Serbia and Bulgaria and was completing its takeover of Greece. Wallachia became a strategic border state, between the Ottomans and the major Christian power of Hungary to the north. To be sure of Wallachian loyalty, the Turkish sultan took as hostages the young Vlad and his brother Radu in 1442. Nevertheless, the Wallachians undertook a series of campaigns against the Turks, with some success, until the older Vlad was put to death after falling out with his allies, the Hungarians.

Woodcut of Vlad enjoying an impalement. From a 1499 pamphlet. The accompanying text read: "Here begins a very cruel and frightening story about a wild and bloodthirsty man, Dracula the *voevod* [prince]. How he impaled people and roasted them and with their heads boiled them in a kettle, and how he skinned people and hacked them into pieces like a cabbage-head. He also roasted the children of mothers and made them eat their own children. And many other horrible things . . ."

Escaping from captivity, Vlad embarked on a long campaign to regain his father's throne, now occupied by a distant relative. His efforts finally bore fruit in 1456 with the assassination of his rival, and he became prince of Wallachia. Vlad's subjects were soon to find out that their new ruler intended to crush any lingering opposition. Calling a meeting of nobles, Vlad reportedly asked them how many princes' reigns they had lived through. The mocking nobles called out the number in turn, with thirty being the highest estimate. It was only too obvious how little they thought of their ever-changing princes. Vlad made his intentions abundantly clear. His armed guards entered the room and seized the five hundred nobles, leading them outside, where they were impaled on sharpened stakes, along with their wives and servants, and left to rot.

Vlad's cruelty became famous, as he turned against Transylvania, land of his birth, because of its economic control of Wallachia. Believing that the German merchants who dominated Transylvania had been engaged in unfair trade, he led a series of raids on the major towns from 1457 to 1460, massacring vast numbers of men, women, and children, with torture being followed up by slow impaling. Moreover, Vlad showed every sign of enjoying these horrors. According to a German pamphlet printed in 1499, he was perfectly at home sitting down to watch the death throes of his victims at the town of Brasov:

> All those whom he had taken captive, men and women, young and old, children, he had impaled on the hill by the chapel, and all around the hill, and under them he proceeded to eat at table and enjoyed himself in that way.

These German accounts of the terrors of Vlad the Impaler's reign began during his reign and continued after his death, and gained him his later reputation as a bloodthirsty tyrant. They gave a boost to the printing industry, just beginning in Europe, as pamphlets detailing Vlad's horrors became the earliest best-sellers.

Romanians have often preferred to remember Vlad the patriot, fighting the Turks, although here too one of his main weapons was terror. By 1461, it was clear that war between Wallachia and the Ottoman Empire was brewing, and Vlad seems to have encouraged this. His reception of the Turkish ambassadors at his new palace in the capital, Tirgoviste, is famous. Vlad demanded that they remove their turbans in his presence. This can hardly have been in ignorance of Turkish dress code, given his time as a hostage. They answered quite reasonably that "This is the custom of our country, my lord." Vlad countered with the sarcastic suggestion "I too wish to strengthen your law," and he ordered the ambassadors' turbans to be fixed to their heads with iron nails. He then allowed them to leave, with a message for the sultan: "Go and tell your master that while he is accustomed to endure such shame, we are not. Let him not impose his customs on other rulers who do not wish them, but let him keep them in his land."

A reply from the sultan was inevitable. It came in the form of a plot to assassinate Vlad, which the prince discovered. He no doubt gained considerable pleasure from the subsequent treatment of the captured conspirators. Vlad attacked the Turks, invading Bulgaria, where he massacred tens of thousands of civilians as well as taking vast numbers of captives. In the summer of 1462, the Turks entered Wallachia. Greatly outnumbered, Vlad retreated before the invaders, laying waste the countryside ahead of them to deny them supplies and mounting a guerrilla campaign. The key battle was a ferocious night attack, which almost stopped the Turks, but also inflicted heavy casualties on the Wallachians. The Turks pressed on to Tirgoviste, which had been stripped and burned before they reached it. Passing by the city, the Turkish army entered a narrow gorge, where they were confronted by a horrific sight—a forest of impaled rotting bodies, some 20,000 in all. They were the captives taken by Vlad the previous year. On the tallest stake were the bodies of the two would-be assassins. Even the battle-hardened Turks were deeply affected by this dreadful spectacle; the sultan turned around and began the long march home.

However, this triumph marked the end of Vlad's successes. The re-treating sultan left behind Radu, Vlad's brother and rival for the throne. Radu soon gained support among the aristocracy, who could not forgive Vlad's massacres of their fellow nobles, while Vlad's army faded away once the unifying threat from the Turks had been lifted. Vlad escaped to Hungary, where he was captured and imprisoned on false charges, based on forged letters, of allying himself with the Turks. Twelve years of confinement followed, until Radu's death, when Vlad agreed to subject himself to Hungarian control, convert-ing to Catholicism from Orthodoxy and marrying a Hungarian prin-cess. Supported by the Hungarians and his cousin, Prince Stephen of Moldavia, Vlad regained his throne in 1476, but he was in grave dan-ger as soon as the foreign armies withdrew. In a final battle against an army of Wallachian nobles supported by the Turks, Vlad was himself impaled by a lance. The Turks cut off his head and delivered it to the sultan, where it was put on display as proof that their deadly foe was finally vanquished.

But appalling though the deeds of Vlad the Impaler undoubtedly were, where does the Dracula connection come in? Vlad was the son of Vlad Dracul. The Dracul part was a nickname with a double meaning—"dragon" and "devil." The official version was probably "dragon," as the elder Vlad had been invested with the Order of the Dragon in 1431, making him a member of a secret organization dedicated to driving back the Turks. Thereafter Vlad Dracul minted coins with a dragon symbol and flew a flag bearing a dragon. The alternative meaning of his name, "devil," was, we can be sure, not unwelcome, for his rule was based on fear.

Dracula means "son of Dracul," and Vlad the Impaler actually signed himself "Dracula" on official documents. Perhaps he relished the idea of being known as the son of the devil—certainly the Turkish ambassadors would have agreed with the description. It may well have been this understanding of Vlad's name that was uppermost in the mind of the court poet Michel Beheim in 1463, when he composed an epic entitled *Story of a Bloodthirsty Madman Called Dracula of Wallachia*. It seems to have been to the taste of Beheim's master, the Holy Roman Emperor Frederick III, for it was read to distinguished guests on several occasions. Historians Raymond McNally and Radu Florescu, who have done more than anyone else to strengthen the claims of the Vlad-Dracula equation, also note that technically he *was* a vampire, for he reportedly dipped his bread in the blood of his victims at his macabre feasts of the dying.

Vlad Dracula's image in modern Romania has been rather mixed. He was greatly admired by Nicolae Ceaușescu, dictator of Romania until his execution following the 1989 overthrow of his regime. In 1976, the five hundredth anniversary of Vlad Dracula's death was marked by a film, paintings, novels, favorable historical accounts, and even a commemorative postage stamp. In the last few years a Dracula tourist industry has rapidly grown up, although not all Romanians welcome this bizarre development. In 1993 someone who claimed to be Vlad Dracula's last descendant took out a libel suit against Columbia Pictures over their portrayal of his supposed ancestor in Francis Ford Coppola's *Bram Stoker's Dracula*. The Californian court was no doubt relieved that it never had to judge on the question of Vlad Dracula's reputation, as the case was withdrawn.

Vampires definitely existed in the strongly held beliefs of past people concerning the dead. Dracula was not a vampire in the folklore tradition, but he was certainly bloodthirsty in more ways than one.

Contemporary woodcut portrait of Vlad.

CHAPTER SEVEN

HOAX?

INTRODUCTION

Archaeologists have the dubious honor of being the victims of the greatest scientific hoax ever perpetrated: Piltdown Man. In the early 1900s, somebody—as yet still unidentified—put together an unusually thick human skull with an ape's jawbone, stained them to give them an air of great antiquity, and cleverly planted the finds, along with the remains of prehistoric animals, in the gravel beds at Piltdown in Sussex, southern England. Between 1908 and 1912, local archaeologist Charles Dawson, alerted by workmen, began searching through the gravel beds and found pieces of the skull. Systematic excavation at Piltdown began in February 1912, Dawson being joined by Arthur Smith Woodward, keeper of geology at the Natural History Museum (London), and Pierre Teilhard de Chardin, a bright young Jesuit scientist and fossil hunter. Almost immediately the jawbone was discovered and found to fit perfectly with the human skull. The fossil animal remains from the gravel beds suggested that Piltdown Man was some half a million years old.

The Piltdown team announced that they had made a sensational discovery—nothing less than the long-sought "missing link" between ape and man. Darwin had been finally vindicated. The Piltdown finds immediately became world famous, and were presented as one of the main pieces of evidence in the defense of John Scopes, a high school teacher who was tried in Dayton, Tennessee, in 1925 for teaching the theory of evolution.

Dawson's discovery rapidly entered textbooks as the most important human fossil ever found and dominated understanding of human origins for some forty years. Piltdown Man—with its combination of a fully developed cranium and an extremely primitive jaw—was believed to show that increase in brain size was the determining factor in human evolution. Genuine human fossils from Africa with small brains were dismissed as belonging to irrelevant dead ends of hominid evolution.

By 1950, however, with no other fossils having been discovered that were remotely like those from Piltdown, the Natural History Museum began to wonder whether it was Piltdown that was the odd man out in evolutionary terms. Then, in 1953, the finds were reexamined and the ghastly truth was revealed. To their horror, the museum experts discovered that the teeth in the jawbone had been filed down

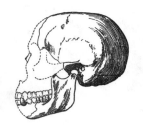

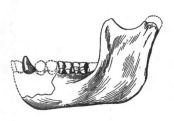

The notorious Piltdown skull and jaw. (The skull was human, the jaw from an ape.)

to conceal their identity. Scientific tests showed that Piltdown was no-where near as old as everyone had been led to believe, nor could it have lain in the gravel beds for any great length of time. (Further work has established that the jaw is that of an orangutan, and that both jaw and skull are no more than 600 years old.)

Doubts should surely have set in earlier, however. Finds continued to turn up until 1915, including a flat piece of elephant bone shaped like a cricket bat. The hoaxer, whoever he was. seemed to have slipped this in as a joking reminder that things at Piltdown were not quite as they seemed.

The identity of the Piltdown hoaxer has exercised the ingenuity of researchers since it was first exposed. No one can yet say for sure who was responsible, but the three most obvious suspects were those involved in the excavation: Dawson, Woodward, and Teilhard de Chardin. Most of the scientists who have examined the case tend to feel that Dawson, as an amateur, lacked the technical expertise to pro-duce such a plausible fake. Woodward is almost universally regarded as an innocent dupe. The fact that he devoted his retirement in the 1930s to carrying out further excavations at Piltdown at his own ex-pense rules him out as a candidate. That leaves the Jesuit Teilhard de Chardin, whose training in chemistry has made him, for many, a prime suspect. Despite his lifelong quest to reconcile evolutionary theory with Christianity, he wrote remarkably little about Piltdown, which has been interpreted as almost a silent confession. On the other hand, this might equally mean that he was merely suspicious of the finds.

With no actual proof against the three main suspects, the net has been cast ever wider, taking in a huge cast of characters who had some connection with Piltdown. The most surprising candidate is Sir Arthur Conan Doyle, the British writer famed for his creation of Sherlock Holmes. Doyle lived very near the Piltdown site and took a great interest in the excavations, driving down occasionally to moni-tor their progress. He could have salted the dig, certainly had the scientific knowledge necessary (he was a medical doctor), was a tal-ented cricketer, and had a special motive for making scientists look foolish. Doyle's passionate interest in the paranormal (see **The Curse of Tutankhamun** in **Archaeology and the Supernatural**) had led him to be taken in by some of the more dubious psychic claims of the day, and he was deservedly lambasted by scientists for being so gullible. By forging Piltdown Man, the theory goes, Conan Doyle could have had the last laugh—at the expense of the scientific establishment.

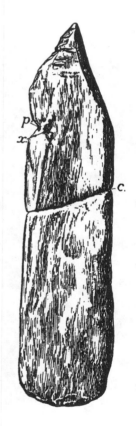

The prehistoric "cricket bat" from Piltdown.

The idea that Doyle, the greatest detective writer ever, should also have left the world its greatest scientific "whodunit" is extremely attractive. It has even been argued that he left clues in his writings. In Doyle's *The Lost World* (the real prototype of the film *Jurassic Park*), hero Professor Challenger sets off with a small team of experts to penetrate the secrets of a mysterious plateau hidden in the South American jungle. They encounter rampaging dinosaurs, but also grunting ape-men. The novel contains a map of the Lost World—described by Challenger as "an area, as large perhaps as Sussex"—which has been argued to represent the very area where Piltdown Man was found. Another character baldly states at one point: "If you are clever and know your business you can fake a bone as easily as you can fake a photograph." Most strikingly, these tantalizing scraps of information were written and published during the very time that Piltdown Man was being found—1911–1912.

Yet elegant as the Doyle theory is, it lacks any hard evidence, and to perpetrate such an elaborate hoax, involving discoveries made on at least fifteen separate occasions, Doyle would have to have practically haunted the site, or at least have had an accomplice who was there constantly. The key to Piltdown is surely the nature of the discoveries themselves. Whoever the hoaxer was, he must have been intimately associated with finding them. Simply salting sites around Piltdown with material in the hope that someone would one day find them would not have worked. Woodward, for example, dug for many years in the area and found absolutely nothing. The conclusion has to be that the hoaxer was on the spot to ensure that the fakes were recovered. Only one person was present throughout—and that was Charles Dawson, who picked up most of the important "evidence" with his own hands. It can hardly be a coincidence that after the death of Dawson in 1916 no more finds were made at Piltdown.

Of all the suspects, Dawson had the most to gain. As an amateur he sought academic recognition, and discovery of the "missing link" itself was surely a good way to boost his status. Woodward indeed immortalized Dawson by naming Piltdown Man *Eoanthropus dawsoni* ("Dawson's Dawn Man"). And surprisingly overlooked by most scientists who have investigated the case is Dawson's appalling track record. He seems to have had a remarkable knack for discovering "unique" finds that decades later proved to be dubious or forged: a Roman statuette, supposedly the earliest example of iron casting from Britain, but actually modern; Roman tiles from about A.D. 400, commemorating the rebuilding of the port of Pevensey in Sussex, which

The Piltdown excavation. (Left) laborer Venus Hargreaves, (center) Arthur Smith Woodward, (right) Charles Dawson, and "Chipper" the goose.

have been scientifically dated to about 1900; a ceremonial mace, supposedly from medieval Hastings, now shown to have been manufactured in the nineteenth century; and so on and so on. The catalog of Dawson's hoaxes seems to be endless.

This pattern of behavior clearly shows that Dawson was capable of the hoax. He was also around at all the right times, and the only argument that can be made in his defense—that he lacked the scientific skills necessary to create the Piltdown finds—seems merely to stem from the reluctance of scientists to believe that they could be taken in by an amateur. Dawson was in fact a master hoaxer, perhaps the most successful in this century. He needed no accomplices, and the suspicions thrown on Teilhard and Doyle are unnecessary. In the case of Doyle, the apparent hints of skulduggery at Piltdown contained in his writings may suggest that the master detective writer, rather than being implicated in the fraud, was, in the absence of proof, subtly airing his suspicions.

Charles Dawson was heir to a long tradition of faking archaeological remains, which may stretch back even to the ancient Egyptians. In 1992, Turkish archaeologists announced a strange discovery that had just come to light in the basement of the Topkapi Museum in Istanbul. This was an ancient Egyptian mummy in a wooden coffin. There was nothing particularly unusual in that, for the Sultans of the Ottoman Empire had removed many curiosities from Egypt during their centuries of rule over the country. However, when they unwrapped the mummy from its bandages the archaeologists were amazed to find that the upper half was a young boy while the lower parts came from a crocodile.

No definitive explanation has yet emerged for this extraordinary find. Some archaeologists have wondered whether the young boy had been partly eaten by the crocodile and, in order to ensure that the child could reach the afterlife, his family had killed the offending animal and replaced their son's missing limbs with crocodile parts. This seems highly unlikely, especially as we know that the Egyptians sometimes provided false limbs for those whose original bodies had been mutilated. It hardly seems plausible that the boy would want to enter the next world with a crocodile's legs and tail.

Instead, the boy-crocodile could well be an ancient fraud. Most likely, given the careful burial, it was a religiously inspired hoax, perhaps related to the worship of the crocodile-headed god Sebek, the ancient Egyptian guardian of waterways. Or it might even have been created for public exhibition as a curiosity, just like those made by joining together a monkey and an alligator that were until recently a feature of American carnivals.

There were also ancient literary hoaxes. In the first century A.D. two unknown Greek writers decided that the story of the Trojan War would have been much better told through eyewitness accounts. Basing themselves on Homer's poetry (see **Introduction** to **Legendary History**), they created "Dares of Phrygia" on the Trojan side, and "Dictys of Crete" for the Greeks. This hoax became established across Europe when the adventures of Dares and Dictys were translated into Latin and convincing detail provided by letters explaining how the manuscripts had been found—Dares' by a famous Roman historian and Dictys' in his tomb on Crete. In the medieval period the fake accounts of the Trojan War were actually far better known than that of Homer, and only in the Renaissance did critics reject them.

Yet why have people produced fakes and perpetrated hoaxes about the past? The most obvious motive, of course, was to make money. Faking antiquities from Roman statues to Chinese vases is a familiar enough way to relieve museums and collectors of their money. Less well known and unlikely as a source of financial gain has been the production of fake chastity belts, once thought to be a popular way of ensuring wifely fidelity in medieval Europe. The value of such belts shot up this century as they were collected by a number of eccentric but extremely wealthy individuals. The greatest collector, and perhaps also the most trusting, was American millionaire Ned Green. Not only was he fascinated by chastity belts, he also announced that he would buy only examples that were encrusted with diamonds. It was no great surprise, when Green's collection was sold off after his death, that none of his belts proved to be genuine. Although we do know from written sources that chastity belts were invented in Italy around 1400, it seems that their use has been greatly exaggerated and the market overwhelmingly dominated by fakes. Even the Cluny Museum in Paris, famous for its collection, admitted in 1950 that they were all fakes, and took all but one off display.

Literary frauds could also be extremely lucrative at least until this century when scientific advances made them easier to detect. The most prolific of all literary forgers was Denis Vrain-Lucas, a French clerk. Vrain-Lucas was talented and ambitious but lacked the formal education necessary to climb the social ladder in nineteenth-century France. The only work he was able to obtain was as a copyist to a dealer in rare manuscripts. On the dealer's death, Vrain-Lucas seems to have discovered that he could sell the same documents several times over by the simple expedient of copying them.

Vrain-Lucas's career as a forger really took off in 1861, when he was put in contact with Professor Michel Chasles, newly appointed librarian to the Paris Academy. Chasles was determined to build up the library, in particular its French collections. Vrain-Lucas offered a unique chance of doing just that, claiming that he had access to a major collection of manuscripts belonging to a nobleman down on his luck. Over the following years he sold a stream of thousands of documents to Chasles for a total of 170,000 francs. The documents covered a remarkable range, including some quite extraordinary ancient letters. Among these were one from the Holy Roman Emperor Charlemagne; several written by Attila the Hun to a chief of the Franks; another sent by a French doctor to Jesus; one from Lazarus to Saint Peter; a note from Mary Magdalene to the king of the Burgundians (early rulers of France) enclosing Jesus' last communication to her; a letter written by the national hero Vercingetorix, who fought against the Romans under Julius Caesar; and a note to the great philosopher Aristotle from Alexander the Great allowing him to visit France in order to learn druidic wisdom (see **Box: The Druids** in **Architectural Wonders**).

All these incredible finds seem to have been accepted as genuine by Professor Chasles. It was only the more recent letters that eventually led to Vrain-Lucas's exposure. Suspicions were aroused by correspondence apparently showing that Sir Isaac Newton had learned the theory of gravity from the French mathematician Blaise Pascal, and that William Shakespeare had borrowed his plots from French writers. British scholars naturally challenged the letters, while the Paris Academy vigorously defended them. When the matter came to court in February 1870, Vrain-Lucas insisted that he was merely a middleman, and that he was the faker's victim as much as Chasles. However, no trace of the supposed nobleman could be found, while comparisons between Vrain-Lucas's handwriting and that of the letters convinced the court that he was their real author. Vrain-Lucas received a two-year prison sentence. Professor Chasles was not charged with anything by the courts, but found guilty by the public of incredible gullibility. In particular, the revelation that the librarian of the Paris Academy could believe that Mary Magdalene, Alexander the Great, Attila the Hun, and Lazarus had written in medieval or modern French on paper (not used in France before the 14th century A.D.) turned Chasles into a laughingstock.

Such scandals involving forged documents—and the fear of being made to look like complete fools—encouraged scholars to adopt a dogmatically skeptical stance toward any unfamiliar material. Ironically, this fear may well have contributed to the haste with which the parchment scrolls offered for sale by Moses Shapira in 1883 were rejected by the experts. Shapira believed that his parchments were the earliest biblical texts yet discovered. Indeed, many scholars now wonder if these were actually the first Dead Sea Scrolls, and if priceless texts were spurned by those whose first thought was of fraud.

Making money out of hoaxes is often the strongest motive, but even where financial gain is involved that need not preclude other more complex motives. This certainly appears to be the case with the Cardiff Giant. In October 1869, one Stub Newell hired some men to dig a well on his farm at Cardiff, New York. About 3 feet down they hit something solid, so they widened their pit, eventually revealing a quite amazing discovery—the giant figure of a man over 10 feet tall who had apparently turned to stone.

Word of this remarkable fossil man spread through the neighborhood and by the following day a crowd of onlookers had arrived. Newell moved swiftly into action. In just two days he obtained a license to exhibit the Cardiff Giant and erected a tent over the pit, charging a fifty-cent entrance fee to the thousands of visitors who flooded in. His distant cousin George Hull provided food and drink for the crowd. Businessmen in the nearby town of Syracuse saw an economic boom ahead and made Newell an offer he could not refuse, buying a three-quarters share in the giant for the enormous sum of $30,000. This proved to be a sound investment, for in the next two weeks over 30,000 visitors came to see the Cardiff Giant.

The giant consortium decided that Newell's farm was too out of the way, and they moved their star attraction to a specially built exhibition hall in Syracuse. So great was the excitement caused by the Cardiff Giant that the famous showman P. T. Barnum offered $60,000 to take him on a three-month tour.

The bubble was bound to burst, but began by slowly deflating. Local newspapers reported that a large wagon bearing a heavy load had been seen heading out to Cardiff the previous year. This, of course, could be dismissed as the gossip of jealous neighbors. More difficult to brush off were the negative comments from scientists who examined the giant. One of the first on the scene was geologist Dr. J. F. Boynton of the University of Pennsylvania, who saw the giant while it was still at Newell's farm. He was absolute in his condemnation:

> It is positively absurd to consider this a fossil man It has none of the indications that would demonstrate it as such, when examined by a practical chemist, geologist, or naturalist.

The most heavyweight critic was fossil expert Professor Otheniel Marsh. He declared the giant to be "very remarkable," but when asked by one of the owners if they might quote his opinion he replied: "No. You may quote me on this though: a very remarkable fake!" Marsh's firm opinion that the giant was carved from gypsum had some effect and New York newspapers now became more critical.

Any doubts as to the nature of the giant were laid to rest in December, when George Hull confessed that the whole thing was a fake. In 1866, Hull, a convinced atheist, had had a violent disagreement over the literal truth of the Bible with a Methodist minister. He decided to test the faith of the public in giants by making a modern-day Goliath. Hull hired Chicago sculptors to form a huge block of gypsum into the figure of a gigantic man, then pierced the surface with knitting needles and rubbed acid into the "skin" to hide the tool marks. With Newell in on the joke, Hull transported the finished statue to Cardiff and buried it in November 1868.

The businessmen of Syracuse at first tried to talk down Hull, but when the Chicago sculptors came forward the game was up. Despite this, they sent the giant on tour around the state, while Barnum had his own copy made (a fake of a fake!) and exhibited it in New York. Many people still preferred to believe that the Cardiff Giant was confirmation of the existence of biblical giants. Eventually the public tired of the giant and today he lies at rest in the Cooperstown Farmers' Museum in New York State.

Fame, of course, has certainly been a spur to those tempted into hoaxing, Charles Dawson being a prime example. Controversy has raged for over a century about the extent to which founder of archaeology Heinrich Schliemann may have misled his colleagues and the public over the circumstances surrounding his discovery of Priam's Treasure at Troy. He was either a cunning fraudster, with a history of deceit, or a vain and self-promoting man who made careless mistakes in his hurried excavations. Either way, Schliemann and Troy will always be remembered in the same breath.

Worldwide fame briefly touched Liani Souvaltzi a few years ago, when she claimed to have made an equally momentous discovery: the tomb of Alexander the Great. When Alexander died in 323 B.C. in Babylon, his body was embalmed and brought to Egypt, where he had been regarded as a god since the Oracle of Ammon at the oasis of Siwa declared him to be the son of the resident deity. Ancient accounts say that he was buried at Alexandria, the city he founded, and it is generally assumed that his tomb lies beneath the bustling streets of the present city.

However, in February 1995 world news media broke the story of a dramatic discovery at Siwa Oasis. Liani Souvaltzi of the Athens-based Institute of Hellenistic Studies announced that she had uncovered the true burial place of Alexander after six years of excavating. She had unearthed not only a massive building with an eight-pointed star (symbol of the Macedonian royal family) marked on the wall but also three Greek inscriptions that she argued had been written by Ptolemy I, Alexander's successor in Egypt. These appeared to show that Alexander had been poisoned in Babylon and that Ptolemy had brought the body secretly to Siwa for burial.

Archaeologists were rather more wary of this exciting development, probably because they had heard something suspiciously like it before. Back in 1991, Souvaltzi had announced the discovery of Alexander's tomb at Siwa, only for it to turn out to be a well-known Roman temple. Greek government archaeologists went to Siwa to investigate her new claims but found nothing to reassure them. They identified the new building as the Temple of the Oracle, saw no sign of Macedonian stars, and produced completely different translations of the inscriptions, which they dated to several hundred years after Alexander's death.

Disbelief turned to incredulity when the *New York Times* reported that Souvaltzi had "received mystical guidance in her search, in part from snakes." Souvaltzi insisted that she had been misunderstood, and that her source of inspiration was actually "saints." (Though neither group seems a very likely source of information on Alexander.) One of these saints appears to be a mysterious figure known as Aristander, who has prophesied that whoever controls the body of Alexander will rule over a stable and wealthy realm. While Souvaltzi does not aim to become a queen, she does belong to a nationalist group that believes passionately that ancient Macedonia belongs within the borders of modern Greece, and possessing Alexander's body would somehow ensure that. The Egyptian authorities became perturbed by this intrusion of twentieth-century politics into their archaeology and at the end of 1996 they revoked Souvaltzi's permit to excavate at Siwa.

The Bible, of all religious texts, has been at the center of the most heated debates concerning claimed archaeological discoveries (see **Sodom and Gomorrah** in **Lost Lands and Catastrophes**). The hunt for the remains of Noah's ark has been on since early Christian times. This great ship, which enabled all of creation to survive the Flood, would be one of the most spectacular finds in the history of archaeology and a powerful weapon in support of the literal truth of the Bible and indeed the Koran. The Book of Genesis (8:4) states that Noah came aground on the "mountains of Ararat," agreed by most ancient commentators to be Mount Ararat itself, the highest peak in the range, though alternative candidates are obviously possible.

The first modern claim to have seen the ark on Ararat was apparently made by a Russian pilot in 1917, but the earliest reports of this sighting come from a 1940s ark hunter trying to raise money for an expedition, and have therefore been dismissed by later writers. By far the best known of the Ararat claims is that made by French junk dealer Fernand Navarra in 1955. He had climbed to a height of nearly 17,000 feet above sea level, reaching a glacier in which were locked large pieces of wood. After a struggle Navarra managed to remove a substantial beam, which he brought back down the mountain.

Various scientific tests apparently showed that the wood was oak and some five thousand years old, but the methods used—assessing the density and color of the wood—are hardly infallible guides to age, for they depend entirely on environmental conditions. Although pieces of Navarra's wood were submitted for radiocarbon dating at different laboratories, it took the radiocarbon scientists themselves to gather together the results and publish them. These consistently showed that the wood was actually from the sixth to seventh centuries A.D. Their conclusion was that it probably came from a monument built by Armenian or Byzantine Greek Christians. Further work on Mount Ararat has been hampered by its location on the politically sensitive border between Turkey and Russia, now Armenia.

The alternative candidate to Mount Ararat first came to public notice in 1960, when an aerial photograph taken by a Turkish Air Force pilot of an area some 6,300 feet high in the Akyayla mountain region showed up a large boat-shaped formation. An expedition to the site, about twenty miles from Mount Ararat, was mounted in 1960, but no convincing evidence was recovered that this was anything but a geological feature, of a kind known elsewhere in Turkey and around the globe.

Nevertheless, in 1977 ark hunter Ron Wyatt visited the site and began a campaign to have this recognized as the true ark. He followed this up in a 1985 expedition with adventurer David Fasold and, crucially, scientist Dr. John Baumgardner of the Los Alamos National Laboratory at the University of California. Among the claims made for this expedition, and a later one with biblical historian Allen Roberts, are that standard scientific methods of looking for buried structures revealed the outline of a ship with lines of iron showing its internal structure; iron rivets, brackets and washers have been discovered; masses of petrified wood were found; and the Akyayla region contains large numbers of stone anchors marked with crosses left behind as the ark drifted.

None of these claims has passed muster, and, indeed, Roberts was taken to court in his native Australia by geologist Professor Ian Plimer of the University of Melbourne for misleading the public. The judges eventually ruled that Roberts is not subject to the laws of trade, although they did note that Roberts had made "misleading statements" in lectures. Wyatt's anchor stones are interpreted by Armenian archaeologists as pagan monuments reused in the Christian period that occurred across ancient Armenia. The deck timber removed from the ark has never been confirmed as wood. Metal objects collected from the site appear to be naturally occurring lumps of iron oxide. These may also account for the claimed lines of iron that a metal detector picked up in 1985; in any case, a metal detector would locate iron only in the top foot of a deposit, not if it was deeply buried.

The other scientific device that confirmed the metal detector findings seems to have been the cause of some falling out with Baumgardner. It is described as a "molecular frequency generator/discriminator," but is actually a fancy dowsing device composed of brass rods connected to batteries. Like all archaeological devices involving dowsing, this electrical version is not accepted by the vast majority of scientists (see **Introduction** to **Archaeology and the Supernatural**). Whatever Wyatt and Fasold may have thought of it, it seems a strange choice on a project where standards of evidence would have to be of the highest, given the extraordinary nature of the claims put forward. In fact, when the appropriate technology (ground-penetrating radar) was used at the Akyayla site it showed no sign of anything other than natural geological features.

This doesn't necessarily mean the "arkeologists" went to Turkey with the intention of pulling off a massive hoax. But once there, the power of belief seems to have convinced them that whatever they came across was what they were seeking—and no amount of scientific evidence to the contrary could convince them otherwise. The eye of faith can easily fill in the gaps inconveniently left by history. When the medieval monks of Glastonbury in England claimed to have excavated the grave of King Arthur himself, it is possible that they had indeed come across an ancient burial. But how much of the circumstantial detail they provided was simply restored from what they "knew" that they should find?

Unfortunately we can assess the claim of the Glastonbury monks only on the basis of probability, as most of the crucial evidence—including the "bones of King Arthur"—has long since disappeared, leaving nothing that can be scientifically tested. The greatest change in archaeology since the Piltdown hoax is, of course, the heavy reliance on new methods that can unmask forgers or, by the same token, affirm the genuine status of discoveries accused of being fakes. The iceman found in the Italian Alps in 1991 has been claimed to be a mummy brought from Egypt or even South America, but analyses of his DNA show him to be of European stock. This cleared up at least one aspect of the mystery surrounding the iceman.

Still, archaeologists and historians do need to be reminded from time to time that science is not foolproof. The Vinland Map, bought by Yale University in 1957, was announced to the world in 1965 as ultimate proof that the Vikings had colonized North America. Doubts set in because of the lack of a firm history for the map, leading to the decision to submit it to scientific tests that would settle the authenticity question. Yet subsequent disagreements between different laboratory teams about which is the definitive method to apply mean that the argument still rages.

Sometimes scientists and archaeologists simply cannot agree. The

Dr. Albert Morlet examines one of the curious inscribed tablets from Glozel.

site of Glozel, sometimes called the French Piltdown, was an archaeological conundrum in the 1920s and again from the 1970s onward. In March 1924, a cow fell down a hole on the farm belonging to the Fradin family. Seventeen-year-old Emile Fradin, helped by his grandfather, opened up the hole and found an oval brick paving about 8 feet long with stones set around the edge; on the pavement were glass and bricks with a glassy surface, one with some strange marks on it. A visiting archaeologist soon afterward told the Fradins that they had uncovered a Roman or medieval glass kiln, but a far more exciting alternative had caught their imagination. Local teachers suggested that it was a cremation grave and that more might be found. One of the teachers, taking the bright but unschooled Emile under his wing, lent him some archaeology books so that he might know what to look out for.

Thus far, Glozel was simply another enthusiastic amateur investigation, but early in 1925 it acquired its champion. Albert Morlet, a doctor from the nearby spa town of Vichy, with an interest in Roman France, arrived on the scene. He told the Fradins that they had an important archaeological site on their hands, which should be fenced off and could well produce valuable finds.

Morlet acquired sole rights to excavate and publish the results, and Emile and he began digging. Their discoveries are at the heart of the controversy. A vast number of finds were recovered from the shallow soil of the hillside they dubbed "The Field of the Dead," incredible in its range. There were carved bones like those from the Old Stone Age caves of France, with pictures of deer and horses, sometimes with letters and even whole inscriptions. They also uncovered grotesque little faces of the Glozel people, about an inch high. Then there was material of a later date, including polished stone axes and crude pots with faces and similar inscriptions to those carved on the bones. Some of the pottery is bizarre: phallic figures and hand impressions three times life size. The most enigmatic of the Glozel finds were the dozens of inscribed bricks, which resemble the baked-clay writing tablets of the Near East, but were written in no known language. In all some 5,000 objects were recovered and placed on display in the little museum created by the Fradins.

Putting together this extraordinary collection, Morlet argued that the Glozel culture must have flourished just after the end of the last Ice Age, around 8000 B.C., when Old Stone Age and later developments might have been mixed. The unique character of the Glozel finds led many French archaeologists to give them only a cautious welcome, but strong support was provided by Salomon Reinach, director of the National Museum of Antiquities at Saint-Germain. He

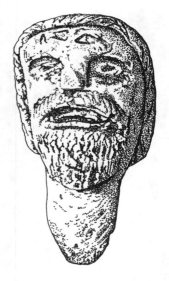

Carved head from the Glozel site.

stressed the early date of both the pottery and the inscriptions, pro-claiming France to be the center of ancient civilization. Glozel be-came famous, with a steady stream of visitors arriving to visit the Fradins' museum and the café they set up with the takings.

However, the anti-Glozelians were also gathering strength. To many the circumstances of the discovery seemed highly suspicious. The finds were a complete jumble, mixing material from completely separate periods. They all came from a thin layer of soil without any sign of strata belonging to the different periods represented. There were no pits or floors in which finds could have been preserved, yet most of the pots were found complete, the exact opposite of a normal excavation. Then there were the mysterious untranslatable tablets, un-like anything known from France. Examination of some of the carved bones and stone axes seemed to show that they had been worked using steel tools. Worse still, the curator of a nearby museum announced that he had taken shelter from a storm in the stable at the Fradins' farm and seen some inscribed but unfired tablets.

To settle this embarrassing debate, the 1927 International Anthro-pological Congress sent a commission of archaeologists to examine the site. Selecting spots at random, they started digging, finding noth-ing on the first day. On the second day they began to uncover typical Glozelian material, which they suspected had been planted—especially an inscribed tablet that was found at the bottom of a pocket of loose brown soil quite different from the gray soil around it. In an attempt to guard against finds being introduced overnight, the commission powdered their trench with plaster. While checking the plaster the next morning, the young English archaeologist Dorothy Garrod was seen by Morlet, who accused her of attempting to plant finds to dis-credit him. Relations were never the same again, and the pro-Glozelians were certain that the commission was biased against them. They were therefore not surprised at its conclusion: "Relying on our unanimous observations and discussions, we have decided that everything we were able to study at Glozel was of no very great age."

Incensed, Reinach and Morlet set up their own commission the following year, which not surprisingly came up with a favorable ver-dict on the site. In the meantime, however, the police had raided the Fradins' farm, and taken away finds from the farm and museum. Their tests showed that the pottery was soft and dissolved in water, that mosses and cotton were found in the clay making up some of the pots, so it could not have been fired, and that many of the bone and stone items had indeed been created using steel tools.

The French prehistory society took legal proceedings for fraud against an "unknown person," which the court upheld. But when Emile Fradin was directly accused of fraud he sued for damages and won. He was, however, awarded only one franc, so it was hardly a resounding triumph. By the 1950s Glozel was generally agreed to have been largely a fraud, encouraged by overeager and uncritical archaeologists, and was quietly set to one side.

Then, in 1974, Glozel suddenly emerged from the shadows. A number of objects from the site had been dated using the relatively new method of thermoluminescence (TL), which measures the build-up of radioactivity in heated materials since they were last fired. The Glozel finds came out at around 600 B.C. to A.D. 200. This would be far later than the dates canvassed by Morlet and Reinach, but certainly not modern either. The dating was carried out at several laboratories, so a simple error seems unlikely. Would the archaeologists accept that they had been wrong?

There was no possibility of that, for the Glozel finds seemed even less plausible after half a century of further research. No examples of inscribed tablets or pottery like those at Glozel had been found anywhere else in France, so they stood out as more anomalous. Moreover, the new dates made less sense than the old ones. The archaeology of Celtic or Roman Gaul (modern France) is extremely well known, and the Glozel objects do not belong there. Neither is there any trace of the normal finds of this date at Glozel. Olwyn Brogan, a leading authority on the archaeology of the period, confirmed this from her examination of the Glozel collection:

> What I can't understand is that, if we are to believe the TL dates, we should find Celtic and/or Gallo-Roman potsherds or other objects from the site. But in that Museum I could see no single Gallo-Roman or indeed Celtic object.

Other samples then produced medieval dates, but these may have come from the original glass kiln. Despite further French investigation of the problem, no resolution of the clash between science and archaeology has yet been achieved. After seventy years of controversy, the "French Piltdown" still remains a complete mystery.

Whatever the motives behind an individual case, hoaxes have been successful only when people have been prepared to believe in them— because of their faith, national pride, or conviction that the scientific models of the day must be right. Unfortunately these very same reasons mean that genuine archaeological and historical finds can sometimes be rejected by those afraid of making a mistake.

THE MAN FROM THE ICE

Not every couple on vacation comes across a dead body, let alone a deep-frozen one. But this is precisely what happened to Helmut and Erika Simon while walking through the Tyrolean Alps in 1991. On Thursday, September 19, they were some ten thousand feet above sea level, and had just crossed the Hauslabjoch Pass, which would bring them down to Italy, when they noticed a body protruding from the ice. Hikers sometimes get caught by Alpine storms—six bodies were found in 1991—so the Simons naturally assumed they had found a recent casualty. Reporting their find to the nearest mountain center, they proceeded on their trip, little knowing what would follow.

Markus Pirpamer, the manager of the center, was unsure which side of the border the body had been found on, so he informed both the Italian and the Austrian police, as well as the mountain rescue chief for the area. The following day the Austrian police arrived at the Hauslabjoch Pass and began chiseling out the body, which lay in a natural hollow covered by the remains of a glacier. The first suggestion, that it was the body of an Italian music professor who went missing in 1941, was rapidly scotched by the collection of ancient-looking objects that came up with the body, including skin clothing and an axe, apparently with an iron blade.

On Saturday afternoon, the well-known Tyrolean mountaineers Reinhold Messner and Hans Kammerlander (with local guide Kurt Fritz) arrived in the area on a well-publicized tour of the South Tyrol peaks. The axe was now safely locked away in the nearest police station, but Pirpamer drew a sketch of it from memory and showed it to

The iceman's body laid out for examination.

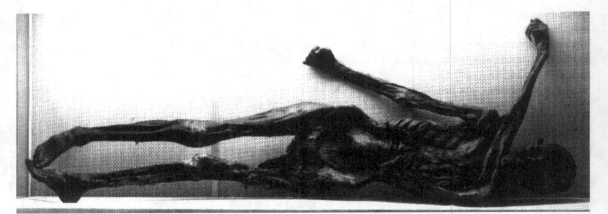

Messner, who was familiar with local archaeology. Messner suggested on the basis of its shape that the axe must be over five hundred years old—and perhaps even as old as three thousand years. Messner's group, together with Hans and Gerlinde Haid, two experts on local folk-culture, then went up to view the body. By now the police had largely freed the body from the ice, and the group were able to see the clothing on the lower part of its body and even look into its face.

Frozen in Time

Every night during his Tyrolean tour Messner made statements to the press, and that evening he presented his views on the body's date. Finding the idea that it was potentially thousands of years old rather incredible, the press preferred to adopt the lower, 500-year estimate offered by Messner and came up with the idea that the "iceman" may have been a mercenary in the army of Frederick Empty-Purse, a fifteenth-century count of Tyrol who had campaigned in the Ötz Valley below the find spot of the body. Marks on the body looked like the result of whipping and burning, while the skull was said to be broken. The theory was floated that the iceman, caught by the enemy while retreating, had been tortured and left for dead.

On September 23, the body was finally released from the ice and delivered by helicopter to the Institute of Forensic Medicine in Innsbruck, Austria. Routine checks ruled out foul play and the body was pronounced to be of historical rather than criminological interest. The corpse turned out to be that of a man over forty who had apparently died of exposure. Earlier reports that the skull had been battered were untrue, while the whip marks turned out to be tattoos. The following morning Konrad Spindler, Professor of Archaeology at Innsbruck, arrived to view the body after being alerted by press reports. On seeing the finds, particularly the axe, which he thought had a bronze rather than an iron blade, he announced that the body was at least 4,000 years old. Initial radiocarbon dating tests performed on grass samples found with the Iceman confirmed Spindler's judgment, though they suggested an even earlier date—somewhere between 2,600 and 2,900 B.C. Proper archaeological excavations at the site were begun and gradually revealed the amazing repertoire of equipment carried by a prehistoric man going about his business: a pair of grass-lined leather shoes; a fur hood; a patchwork jacket made of deer fur; fur leggings; a leather apron; a woven-grass cloak; a thong with a stone pendant; a goat-fur rucksack; a net; a beaker made of birch bark; a bow; a copper axe with wooden handle; a fur quiver stuffed with twelve wooden arrow shafts, two arrows complete with flint arrowheads and an arrow repair kit; flint and bone tools; and a calf's-leather pouch containing a fire-making kit. It soon became clear that the iceman, dubbed "Ötzi" by the press, was one of the greatest archaeological finds of the century.

Though the first radiocarbon tests were widely reported in the press in December 1991, some people were still not convinced. A woman from Zurich claimed that the body was that of her father, who had vanished in the 1970s while climbing mountains near the Ötz Valley. She explained that he was a very resourceful character and assumed that, had he been trapped in the mountains by bad weather, he could have survived for some time by making primitive weapons and clothing before being overcome by the cold. Her claim was not actually that crazy: even some of the archaeologists involved in the project acknowledged that pictures of her father bore "a remarkable likeness" to the iceman, although, given the radiocarbon evidence and the complete absence of modern finds on the body, they had to dismiss it as "a curious coincidence."

Whose Iceman?

In the meantime, an undignified row regarding the ownership of the iceman's body had developed between Italy and Austria. Once the archaeological importance of the find had been appreciated, the press on both sides of the Alps trumpeted a battle of words over the frozen corpse. A five-hundred-year-old mercenary was not so special; but the world's oldest preserved body of a prehistoric hunter, complete with all his equipment, was a precious commodity that had to be part of somebody's national heritage. But whose? It is difficult to determine border lines through the snowy terrain of the Alps, but it is now agreed, after a new survey specially commissioned to solve the problem, that the body was found just within the Italian side of the border. Yet Ötzi and his belongings had come into the hands of the Austrian authorities and were being worked on by archaeologists and scientists in Austria and Germany—all of whom were naturally reluctant to let go of such precious finds. The war of words became more bitter when Italian officials accused the Austrians of badly conserving the body; soon after his removal to Innsbruck, Ötzi's skin had begun to sprout with fungus. Eventually the authorities of the North Tyrol (Austrian) and South Tyrol (Italian) came to an agreement that the iceman could remain in Innsbruck until the scientific studies were completed; Italian archaeologists were also invited to inspect the body to satisfy themselves that it was now being conserved correctly. In February 1998, Ötzi was returned to Italy, although now the Austrians objected to the Italian plan to place him on display.

A very different kind of political group was also laying claim to Ötzi. A Viennese gay magazine started a rumor that the radiocarbon tests had been performed on semen discovered in Ötzi's anus. This find, the magazine suggested, identified him as the world's oldest known passive homosexual, while his skin clothing surely revealed him to be a "leather queen." The story was repeated by the world's gay press but was undoubtedly a hoax. Aside from the sheer impossibility of finding enough traces of semen to radiocarbon date—which would be extremely hard to do on contemporary samples—the claim is easy enough to disprove. As it happens the corpse's bottom had been destroyed during the police's clumsy attempts to free the body with a pneumatic chisel.

More difficult to dispute was the ecstatic cult theory, which began with the claim that Ötzi's penis was missing. It was even suggested, though few believed it, that Professor Spindler had stolen it as a macabre souvenir. Several explanations were offered in all seriousness to explain the missing penis, ranging from the archaeologists' favorite—that it simply hadn't survived—to the notion that the iceman must have belonged to an ecstatic religion whose members would castrate themselves in a frenzy of fervor. While such sects undoubtedly existed in the ancient world—and are well documented from the Mediterranean and Near East—why one of these devotees should choose to drag himself up into the Alps after mutilating himself is difficult to imagine. In any event, when Ötzi's genitals were examined in April 1993, his penis proved to be there after all, shrunk to about 5 centimeters—quite a creditable length after five thousand years of deep-freezing

Will the Real Iceman Please Stand Up?

One thing is now quite clear about the iceman, and that is his age. Radiocarbon dating done by three laboratories (the safest way to do such tests) has confirmed beyond any reasonable doubt that the body (and the associated objects) is about 5,200 years old. Still, this hasn't stopped the amazing flood of speculations about the nature of the find.

The body, after all, may be old, but did the man really die in the Alps? This is the question raised by Dr. Michael Heim, a producer for

Bavarian state television, and Werner Nosko, an Austrian photographer, who put their heads together to produce a book entitled *The Ötzal Fraud*, published in 1993. It refers scathingly to the "trio" of Professor Spindler, Professor Werner Platzer (the anatomist at Innsbruck University in charge of analyzing the body), and Dr. Hans Moser (Director of the Research Institute for Alpine Prehistory), raises doubts about their competence, and goes on to imply that they are dupes taken in by an audacious hoax.

Heim and Nosko insist that no glacier was present at the site and that therefore the corpse could not have been preserved in a frozen state for thousands of years. As evidence they point to photographs in which the gully where Ötzi was found appears quite clear of ice. They also raise a number of questions about the official account of the iceman's discovery. For example, why had the fragile objects with him survived the slow movement of tons of glacial ice over thousands of years? And why were the cell membranes in the eyes not damaged by freezing as one would expect? Putting these doubts together, they argue that the body was never deep-frozen as claimed. Instead they believe that the "iceman" is a mummy brought in from abroad—perhaps from Egypt, South America, or even Tibet—planted in the snow with carefully selected archaeological "finds" to add authenticity.

While they do not directly name the hoaxer in their book, elsewhere they pointed a finger at Messner, a successful self-publicist who had previously claimed to have spotted the Yeti on an expedition to the Himalayas. Interviewed by the *Sunday Times* in August 1992, Heim stated: "I don't have any answers, but perhaps Mr. Messner does." Heim also claims that Messner was able to describe Ötzi's footwear before the body was fully pried from the ice.

The archaeologists involved in the project have been indignant in dismissing claims that the iceman is anything less than 100 percent genuine. Indeed, it is not difficult to show that Heim and Nosko's doubts about the official account, though apparently based on common sense, can be easily answered. DNA evidence shows that Ötzi was of European stock. The iceman's equipment was not crushed and swept away by the glacier simply because it lay together with the body in a hollow. As for the cell membranes in his eyes, nobody would deny that the preservation of the body is miraculous; Spindler himself had admitted that the survival of the body intact for so long under glacial conditions is extraordinary. But here we simply have to accept that freak conditions will produce freak results. That the body was deeply embedded in the remnant of a glacier is demonstrated by a wealth of video and photographic evidence, as well as the testimony of dozens of witnesses, from the police to archaeologists, who excavated the site. So Heim and Nosko's central claim is undermined. In fact, the photographs they use as "evidence" to the contrary simply show the body after archaeologists had cleared the gully of ice during their excavation of Ötzi's equipment. The fraud interpretation is based on such a weak case that it seems almost fraudulent itself. Ötzi is genuine, beyond any shadow of a doubt.

These stories are no doubt only the small beginnings of a popular publishing industry on the iceman that will come to rival that on Tutankhamun. Still, the speculations of academics themselves have sometimes lacked restraint. One of the most bizarre interpretations was suggested by Professor Heinrich Tilly, an expert on mythology at Innsbruck, who describes himself as an "outlaw" because he was not invited to join the group organized to study the body. He has ridiculed the official idea that Ötzi was caught by bad weather, arguing that "if he had died alone he would have been eaten by animals and birds of prey in five minutes." It is a reasonable enough criticism in itself, but Tilly then goes on to develop an extraordinarily elaborate version of the religious cult theory to explain how and why the Iceman was buried in the Alps. Ötzi, it seems, was one of a tribe of star worshipers from Mesopotamia who had climbed the Alps to propitiate the Moon god. Without pausing to wonder why there is not a single Mesopotamian object at the site, Tilly convinced himself of a fantastic scenario. "I have no doubt he was the youngest of a group of priests who went up into the high mountains to be near the stars," Tilly explained in an interview with the *Sunday Times*.

> This young man would have been a willing sacrifice in a ritual including days of dancing before he was placed alive in a special vertical grave. At the end of the ceremonies he would have stood in it and then taken poison before the others buried him to appease the moon.

With this kind of speculation coming from the academic world, it may be only a matter of time before a book is published claiming that Ötzi was an alien who landed on the Alps in a spaceship.

SCHLIEMANN'S TREASURE

Heinrich Schliemann, the discoverer of Troy and excavator of Mycenae, is surely the most famous and romantic figure of archaeology. His search for the truth behind Homer's immortal epic of the siege of Troy by the Greeks under Agamemnon has itself become the stuff of legend. Driven by his boyhood dream in rural Germany of proving Homer right, Schliemann set about amassing a fortune through trade, turning to archaeology in 1868 once his finances were secure. In a series of impressive excavation campaigns in 1870–73, 1878–79, and 1889–90, he demonstrated beyond doubt that the mound at Hissarlik in Turkey was the site of Homer's Troy. In 1876 he also set to work at Mycenae, Agamemnon's capital, uncovering the fabulously rich Shaft Grave burials, which Schliemann was certain were the mortal remains of Agamemnon and the other rulers of Mycenae. In a few short years he was single-handedly responsible for transforming the legendary world of the Greek heroes into archaeological reality.

At Troy, Schliemann's most spectacular discovery was made late in the 1873 season. He had earlier revealed the Scaean Gate, the main en-

Engraving of Schliemann's excavations, looking west from the Scaean Gate. The place where the Treasure was found is marked with a tiny letter *a*.

Hellespont.
Plain of Troy.
Scamander.

Greek Tower
(where the
man stands).

a. Place where
the largest
Treasure
was found.

Wall of Troy,
Gate, and
Paved Road to
the Plain.

trance to Troy and scene of crucial events in Homer's *Iliad*, including the fatal acceptance of the wooden horse full of Greek warriors (see **Introduction** to **Legendary History**). By the end of April he was busy excavating to the north of the gate, where he found a major structure that he was sure must have been the palace of King Priam. Schliemann continued to work in this general area through May, uncovering more of the city wall to the west of the gate, and on May 31 made one of the most famous discoveries in archaeological history. In *Troy and its Remains*, published in Germany in 1874 and translated into English the following year, Schliemann describes the find in dramatic terms:

> I came upon a large copper article of the most remarkable form, which attracted my attention all the more as I thought I saw gold behind it. On the top of this copper article lay a stratum of red and calcined ruins, from 4¾ to 5¼ feet thick, as hard as stone, and above this again lay the . . . wall of fortification. . . . In order to withdraw the treasure from the greed of my workmen, and save it for archaeology, I had to be most expeditious, and although it was not yet time for breakfast, I immediately had *"païdos"* [break time] called. . . . While the men were eating and resting, I cut out the Treasure with a large knife, which it was impossible to do without the very greatest exertion and the most fearful risk to my life, for the great fortification-wall, beneath which I had to dig, threatened every moment to fall down upon me. But the sight of so many objects, every one of which is of inestimable value to archaeology, made me foolhardy, and I never thought of any danger. It would, however, have been impossible for me to have removed the Treasure without the help of my dear wife, who stood by me ready to pack the things which I cut out in her shawl.

He was even able to reconstruct the events leading up to the loss of the treasure:

> As I found all the above objects packed together on the great divine wall, it seems certain that they lay in a wooden chest, such as those which are mentioned in the *Iliad* (xxiv. 228) as being in Priam's palace. This seems all the more certain as I found directly next to the objects a large copper key. . . . Presumably, some member of Priam's family packed the treasure in the chest in great haste, carried it outside without having the time to remove the key, was overcome on the wall by the hand of the enemy or by the fire and had to abandon the chest, which was immediately buried 6 ft deep in the red ashes and debris of the nearby palace.

Gold sauceboat from the Trojan Treasure (about four inches high).

The Trojan Treasure, as
displayed by Heinrich
Schliemann.

Priam's treasure, as Schliemann dubbed it, did indeed merit the
name: it included 2 diadems, a headband, a bottle, cup, and "sauceboat," 60 earrings, and 8,750 small ornaments, all of gold; a cup made
of electrum (alloy of gold and silver); 9 cups or jugs, 6 ingots, and 6
bracelets of silver; and numerous weapons, tools, and containers of
copper and bronze. All were of the highest quality, the most extraordinary item being a splendid gold diadem made up of over 16,000
tiny gold leaves threaded on 90 gold chains joined by small gold bars.

One of the main conditions Turkish authorities placed on Schliemann's excavation was that the finds should be shared equally between

himself and the National Museum. Schliemann, however, seems to have had no intention of sticking to this bargain. He packed up the treasure and sent it off to a friend's farm while the government representative searched Schliemann's quarters in vain. On June 6, he sent two trusted workmen to collect the treasure and load it onto a ship and take it back to Athens. The first account of the discovery of the treasure, penned by Schliemann himself, who was a phenomenally prolific writer, appeared in the German newspaper *Augsburg Allgemeine Zeitung* on August 5. His glowing account of Priam's treasure did much to convince the doubters that Hissarlik was indeed Troy. Turkish outrage was no doubt complete when they saw the photograph later published of Sophia, Schliemann's wife, decked out in the finest jewelry from the treasure like Helen of Troy—at least in Schliemann's imagination. To Schliemann's western audience it seemed a fitting reward for her sterling efforts in aiding her husband's rapid and risky recovery of the treasure.

Schliemann's Enemies

Such was the official account of the discovery of one of the archaeological finds of the century. Yet almost as soon as Schliemann had penned his inspiring account doubters and critics arose, and not merely among those who had dismissed him as a rank amateur in the newly emerging science. He had proposed to the British Museum that it purchase his entire Trojan collection for the sum of £50,000 (roughly $5 million in today's terms), and Charles Newton, keeper of Greek and Roman antiquities at the museum, came to Athens in December 1873 to inspect the collection for himself. He was amazed to be told that Sophia Schliemann had, in fact, been in Athens when the treasure was discovered, her father having died in early May. Schliemann wrote Newton a letter at the end of December, trying to explain the discrepancy:

> On account of her father's sudden death Mrs. Schliemann left me in the beginning of May. The treasure was found end of May; but, since I am endeavouring to make an archaeologist of her, I wrote in my book that she had been present and assisted me in taking out the treasure. I merely did so to stimulate and encourage her for she has great capacities.

Newton seems to have been satisfied with this explanation, for he continued to deal with Schliemann perfectly amicably in later years,

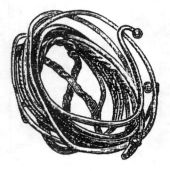

A gold ring from the treasure.

although he was unable to persuade the British government to part with the money. The result was that the collection eventually came to rest in Berlin.

Those who had wildly complained that the treasure was some sort of fraud, made up of modern pieces commissioned by Schliemann or items purchased on the antiquities market, were silenced in January 1874 when the news broke that a separate group of gold jewelry had been discovered and smuggled out of the Troy excavations by two of Schliemann's workmen in March 1873. Some of it was melted down to be turned into jewelry for the fiancée of one of the men, but the thieves were betrayed to the authorities in December, and the remaining jewelry was taken to the National Museum in Constantinople. Clearly, Schliemann's Troy did produce treasures.

More subtle archaeological criticism was to come from the noted English antiquarian William Borlase, who was given a tour of Hissarlik in 1875 by Schliemann's personal servant, Nikolaos Yannakis, who had been in charge of paying the workforce. Yannakis told Borlase that Sophia had not been there when the treasure was discovered, that it had not been found "on" but close to the outside of the wall in an area defined by stones, and that the key, central to Schliemann's argument, had actually been found some 200 yards away. Borlase expressed his shock in an article published in *Fraser's Magazine* in February 1878. Schliemann, as he always did, defended himself with the utmost vigor, denying that Yannakis was a trustworthy witness.

These early debates were eventually eclipsed as Schliemann steadily convinced his critics that his identification of Hissarlik with Troy was correct. Further excavations by his German architect assistant Wilhelm Dörpfeld in 1893–94 and by the American Carl Blegen in 1932–38 only strengthened the Hissarlik–Troy identification, although they did show conclusively that Schliemann's Scaean Gate, Priam's Palace, and Priam's treasure were all far older than the Late Bronze Age date (around 1200–1100 B.C.) in which Homer's Troy is set. Schliemann's discoveries instead date to around 2500 B.C., in the Early Bronze Age.

Unfortunately for archaeology, Schliemann's treasure went on to acquire an unwelcome role as the spoils of war. During World War II, Nazi officials systematically looted occupied countries of their artworks, destroying what they could not take with them when they were forced to retreat. Consequently, when Russian troops reached Berlin, they were accompanied by special squads whose role was to strip the capital of its artworks by way of recompense. The most im-

portant pieces from the Berlin museums had been stored in a large
concrete antiaircraft battery tower on the grounds of the Berlin Zoo.
Of these, perhaps the most valuable was the Trojan goldwork. This
was packed up in crates for protection, which made it all too easy for
the victorious Russians to ship it off to Russia in 1945, where it vanished from sight.

Treasure and Deceit

Despite Priam's treasure being lost to sight, perhaps even destroyed altogether, its importance remained. Furthermore, the treasure became
a central issue for those modern critics who returned to the question
of Schliemann's reliability. What has made their attacks more damaging than those of nineteenth-century skeptics is that they have used
Schliemann's own diaries as evidence against him. This searching investigation has led to widespread doubts about *anything* Schliemann
said. The most persistent critic of Schliemann is American classical
scholar Professor David Traill of the University of California at Davis,
while his main defender has been English archaeologist Dr. Donald
Easton. The debate has raged since 1972, with both sides having
claimed to settle the question on more than one occasion.

What are the major elements of dispute over the treasure? First
comes the question of its location: where exactly was it found? An account written by Schliemann for his German publishers, Brockhaus of
Leipzig, on the day of the discovery (May 31, 1873) places it in one of
the rooms of Priam's Palace, while his version published in *Troy and Its
Remains* in 1874 locates it on top of the city wall enclosing the palace.
Neither of these find spots, however, matches the plan given in *Troy
and Its Remains*, which shows the treasure lying outside the wall. This
third location is also that described by Yannakis in his account to Borlase. Easton has argued that Schliemann was simply inaccurate, in that
the treasure could have been found in debris accumulated outside the
wall but still above its base, for this massive defense work was not vertical, but built to slope inward toward the top.

Traill places a more sinister interpretation on the discrepancies,
suggesting that Schliemann was forced to abandon his earlier account
when he realized that Adolphe Laurent, the French engineer he had
employed to draw up plans of Hissarlik, had already marked the find
spot of the treasure outside the wall. Schliemann had to develop an
unconvincing compromise version in which the treasure was located
on the wall. Certainly, it is difficult for Schliemann's defenders to

Laurent's plan of the area around the Scaean Gate *(d)*, as published in *Troy and Its Remains*—scale 1:750. The letters *h* mark rooms in the so-called Priam's Palace, the city wall is *f*, and the findspot of the Treasure is at *g*.

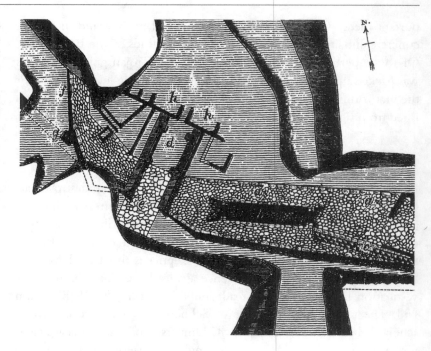

justify his earliest version of events in which the treasure turned up inside the palace itself.

Another striking discrepancy between the May 31 account and that later written up in Athens concerns the vast hoard of jewelry found inside the copper vessel. For there is no mention of any jewelry whatsoever in the May 31 letter. How did Schliemann manage to miss over 10,000 earrings, beads, sequins, and studs? His own account, accepted by his defenders, is that it was all contained within some solidly packed soil in the bottom of one of the large silver jugs, so that it was only when he cleaned this out that the additional treasure trove came to light. Against this is the fact that Schliemann himself in *Troy and Its Remains* says that he spotted a gold cup inside the silver jug before he had even removed the finds from the ground. Traill suggests that the amateurish Schliemann would normally have cleaned out such a find on the spot. In Schliemann's defense, we have to remember that he was intent on cheating the Turks out of their share of the finds, and therefore his priority was to remove the treasure as quickly as possible before the Turkish officials heard of its existence.

Yet there is also the strange question of the caption in the 1874 excavation report. The page of drawings of jewelry from the excavations, produced for this report, was originally labeled with a brief handwritten caption by Schliemann stating simply that these were earrings and other items of jewelry. Only at the last minute before publication did Schliemann add to the page a hastily written heading (which doesn't even line up with the drawings), stating that the finds came from Priam's treasure, while the caption had further details of the location of the material hurriedly scribbled at the end. This is either grounds for suspicion that a decision had been taken to incorporate this magnificent jewelry into the treasure (as Traill argues) or evidence of careless editing (as Easton would have it).

Finally, there are some peculiarities regarding the contents of the treasure. Traill has noted that a number of pieces later cataloged by the Berlin Museum as belonging to the treasure seem to appear on photographs and drawings made by Schliemann before the 1873 excavation season began. Easton sees this as an innocent misunderstanding, brought about by the photographs of the treasure being taken in a hurry and so including a couple of items found at an earlier date; and later by confusion between similar-looking objects on the part of the Berlin Museum staff. Again, we have to balance claims of deception against quite extraordinary carelessness.

If there was a deliberate deception on Schliemann's part, how did he manage it and what was the purpose? Traill once argued that he bought finds with the intention of claiming to have found them himself (a theory still maintained by other critics), but has now decided that Schliemann developed a practice of storing up major finds in order to make a spectacular discovery. Here the aim would have been to convince any doubters that he had truly discovered Priam's Palace by uncovering an extraordinary treasure inside it. Unfortunately he had to abandon his original story (because of the map drawn up by Laurent), which would have tied the treasure directly to the palace. Still, with characteristic panache, Schliemann went one better and concocted the romantic but implausible notion of Priam's treasure being carried out of the palace as it was set to the torch by the victorious Greeks.

Could Schliemann possibly have been such a practiced liar as to invent or dramatically improve his discovery, then shift its location so as to support his claims? Here we must take a wider view of Schliemann the man and the archaeologist. Indeed, it was some oddities in Schliemann's diary accounts of his visit to America on business in 1851, long before his archaeological activities began, that first led to the modern reassessment of his reputation. He states that on February 21 he visited President Millard Fillmore at the White House, spending an hour and a half in private conversation with him before an eight-hundred-guest soirée began, at which Schliemann met other leading politicians. However, skeptics have found it difficult to believe that the harassed Fillmore would have chosen to prepare for a major political occasion by passing the time with an unknown German businessman. Moreover, there is no trace of this distinguished reception in the newspapers of the time.

More extraordinary is the detailed account given by Schliemann in his diary of the San Francisco fire on the night of June 3. This is a remarkable event, for the fire actually took place a month earlier, when Schliemann was in Sacramento. This is no mere dating mistake, for the account follows the May diary entries. The best that Schliemann's defenders have been able to manage here is the theory that this was an unacknowledged English exercise in which Schliemann rewrote a newspaper report! While Schliemann must have honed his English skills, it is hardly common practice to do so in one's diary. Schliemann later opened an office in Sacramento, buying gold dust from miners and shipping it to a San Francisco bank, leaving California in April 1852 after his partner accused him of cheating by providing underweight gold shipments.

Schliemann the Archaeologist

Did Schliemann turn over a new leaf on leaving the cutthroat world of business to enter the sedate world of archaeology in order to fulfill his boyhood dream? It seems not, for there are even problems with Schliemann's account of how he was inspired to become an archaeologist in the first place. In the autobiographical introduction to *Ilios*, published in 1880, Schliemann states that when he was only seven his father had given him as a Christmas present a book with an engraving depicting the Trojans fleeing their burning city. There and then the determined young boy, who refused to believe that the once-great city had disappeared without trace, declared that he would someday uncover its remains. Sadly, there is actually no trace of Schliemann recording this desire until after he had excavated Troy. Indeed, in his book *Ithaque, le Péloponnèse et Troie*, published in 1869, after trips to the main Homeric sites, he gives a completely different childhood anecdote in which he wrote an essay in Latin on the Trojan War, and says that his lifetime's ambition had been satisfied by visiting the sites of Homer's epic.

Worse still, Schliemann's frequently published claim to have discovered the site of Troy is completely fraudulent. To take the credit he had to suppress the contribution made by its real discoverer, Englishman Frank Calvert. A pioneer of archaeology in Turkey, Calvert was the first excavator of Hissarlik, uncovering the temple of Athena in 1865 and playing a key part in persuading Schliemann to dig there in 1868–69. Indeed, it seems as though Schliemann was at first entirely unaware of Hissarlik's claim to be Troy, spending most of his efforts in fruitless excavations at Bunarbashi, the more popular candidate, considering Hissarlik only after Calvert had drawn his attention to it. To Schliemann's credit, he took up Calvert's suggestion with enthusiasm. At the time this seemed to be the ideal solution, for although Calvert owned half the land on which the massive Hissarlik mound stood, he was unable to fund further excavations himself.

The aged Anchises being carried from burning Troy on the shoulders of his son Aeneas. Schliemann claimed that his boyhood memory of this picture inspired him to search for the remains of Troy.

However, Schliemann was later unwilling to share "his" discovery, and proceeded to systematically deny Calvert any credit, going so far as to claim in *Troy and Its Remains* that he, instead of Calvert, had found the temple of Athena, and that Calvert had dug only two small trenches, rather than four, thus minimizing Calvert's earlier efforts. These claims were clearly untrue, as Calvert had published an account of his work in 1865, and Schliemann's own plans showed all Calvert's trenches. Schliemann went on to break the agreement they had over the division of finds from Calvert's land, deliberately misleading him about the value of the sculptures discovered. Indeed, Calvert's heirs are now pursuing a claim on the treasure itself.

Still, Schliemann would not be the last archaeologist trying to grab all the glory that comes with a famous discovery. What were his standards when it came to more humble finds? Revealing instances have been brought to light of Schliemann's falsifying evidence to suit himself. In 1888, he had extensive work carried out on one of the houses he owned in Athens, in the course of which a dozen inscribed tombstones from a classical cemetery were discovered. Schliemann, prompt as ever in publishing his findings, dashed off a brief note for the prestigious journal of the German Archaeological Institute in Athens. So far, so good. In 1974, however, Dr. George Korres of the University of Athens made the unsettling discovery that four of these supposedly new inscriptions had already been in private collections before 1888, and even published. The source of the inscriptions seems to have been the previous owner of the house, who had at least three in his collection. Once again Schliemann can be seen magnifying his own role and importance, even though by this time he was world famous.

Returning to Troy, can we see at the scene of Schliemann's greatest triumph any sign of deceit? In one minor instance we certainly can. A role played by Schliemann overlooked by both his defenders and his attackers is that of seeker after the Aryan race. In his excavations at Hissarlik, Schliemann found hundreds of examples of pottery and other items adorned with the swastika, which enabled him to pronounce with confidence that the Trojans had been Aryans. The majority of these items had a rather everyday appearance given their stamping with such a supposedly sacred symbol. There was, fortunately, one major exception, a figurine of a goddess made from lead, found in an early level of the site, described by Schliemann as having a figure of a swastika on the pubic area, and illustrated in *Ilios* His collaborator A. H. Sayce, the English archaeologist, interpreted the figurine as a fertility symbol. However, in the 1902 catalog of the

Schliemann addresses the
Society of Antiquaries,
London, March 1877.

Schliemann collection produced by the Berlin Museum, Hubert Schmidt, who had dug with Dörpfeld at Troy, noted that the swastika shown in the illustration and discussed by Schliemann and Sayce did not exist. Sayce, it seems, not surprisingly just took Schliemann's word that the engraving was there.

What of the Trojan gold, then? In one respect it is clear that Schliemann, in public at least, continued to mislead. He had admitted privately to Newton back in 1873 not only that his wife Sophia had no part in the discovery but also that it was "the labourers and servant [Yannakis] who struck the treasure and assisted me to get it off [to Athens]." However, when William Borlase's account of his interview with Nikolaos Yannakis appeared in 1878, Schliemann wrote to Professor Max Müller, a renowned expert on languages, asking him to reply to Borlase on his behalf, assuring him that:

Nikolaos never came into the trenches and never saw the treasure or the key of copper which was found with it. I swear on the bones of my father that the key was found together with the treasure precisely so as I described it in my book. Mrs. Schliemann of course was present and assisted me; she never left me.

If Schliemann could deceive his friends so completely, what are the chances of his setting out to mislead the world?

If the story of the finding of the treasure is largely fictional, can even the existence of the treasure be relied upon? Could the whole discovery be a fraud? Did Schliemann buy up valuable pieces from elsewhere, or collect together all the best objects from his season at Troy, in order to create a spectacular discovery to convince the world that he had truly found Priam's Palace?

There is a better chance of being able to answer these questions now than at any time in the previous half-century, for one of the consequences of the end of Soviet communism was the reappearance of Priam's treasure. It had been stored in the Pushkin Museum, Moscow, and the Hermitage Museum, St. Petersburg, and appears to be none the worse for its travels. Various archaeological experts, including Donald Easton, have examined the objects and come to the conclusion that the finds are all genuine items and all of the same date.

Heinrich Schliemann. From a contemporary newspaper.

This definitively rules out the idea that Schliemann bought up valuables through dealers in order to make up a treasure. He had only the vaguest of notions about archaeological dating in 1873, so it seems highly unlikely that he would have put together such a well-matched collection of items, all with good parallels from the Early Bronze Age of northwestern Turkey.

More credible is David Traill's theory that Schliemann's treasure included material found at an earlier date, but held back to make sure the season ended on a high note. It is clear from Schliemann's behavior that a major find was made on May 31, as Easton has stressed and Traill now concedes. This was probably from a burial, as Yannakis's account of the find spot surrounded by stones sounds like a grave. So the bulk of Schliemann's treasure was found in one place, but it seems highly likely that Schliemann added other items to this core. It was certainly fortunate that these additions matched the rest of the treasure so well, but then Schliemann was on any account both indomitable and lucky. We need not assume that a stock of valuables was built up painstakingly piece by piece, but instead follow Traill's persuasive theory that most of the extra items came from a hoard of jewelry found in March 1873 (the items stolen by the workmen forming a small part of this find). Schliemann then set the remainder of this hoard aside until he could find a far more spectacular location—the claimed palace of Priam, king of Troy. Unfortunately for Schliemann, Laurent's plan, showing the true find spot of the treasure, spoiled his scheme, forcing him to concoct a fudge in which the treasure was supposedly dropped on the city wall.

The items making up Schliemann's treasure are real enough. The fraud, ironically, was the man who discovered them.

THE FIRST DEAD SEA SCROLLS?

In July 1883, Moses Shapira, a Christianized Jew who worked as an antiquities dealer in Jerusalem, arrived in London with quite a remarkable find. Shapira was carrying fifteen narrow strips of parchment—covered with Hebrew writing—that he said had been discovered by Arab shepherds in a cave in the Palestinian hills. The text on the parchments contained versions of passages from the biblical book of Deuteronomy, including the Ten Commandments, while the style of the Hebrew script dated it to the sixth century B.C. or even earlier. The find, if genuine, predated the earliest known manuscripts of the Old Testament (9th century A.D.) by an almost incredible one and half thousand years. No wonder Shapira was asking one million pounds for them.

However, Shapira had a bad name in the antiquities world. Ten years earlier he had been involved in a scandal involving bogus finds from Dhiban in Jordan. The inscription on a large slab of basalt found there in 1868 was the most spectacular single discovery in biblical archaeology yet made. The Hebrew text on the stone related the story of the conflict between Mesha, King of Moab, and the Israelites around 850 B.C., and provided striking confirmation of the Bible's accuracy. (The biblical version of the story is in II Kings 3.) The fame of the Mesha Stone, as it is known, led to a search for other finds in the same area. Some pots inscribed with similar writing to the Mesha Stone were "discovered" by

Arabs near Dhiban and bought by Shapira, who sold them to the German government. With the money from the sale he paid his Arab contacts to excavate more pots. They were, however, fakes, the deception continuing until it was exposed by Charles Clermont-Ganneau, author of the first academic publication about the Mesha Stone. Even if Shapira had himself been an innocent victim, his reputation had been irreparably damaged.

It was therefore no real surprise that when Shapira approached a German authority in 1878 with his parchments, he was swiftly rebuffed. He set the scrolls aside for a while, but his interest was rekindled a few years later when he read about recent advances in biblical scholarship. A new analytical approach (now known as the "higher criticism") argued that the work of different authors could be detected in the writing of the Old Testament. For example, some passages used the name Yahweh (Jehovah) for God, while others used Elohim. Using such clues, German scholars claimed that they could separate the sources used by the compilers into different strands. When he took another look at his parchments, Shapira was excited to find that they used only the name Elohim. Shapira now convinced himself that he was holding nothing less than one of the sources for the Bible. In financial terms, such a discovery would have meant more than a life of luxury. Shapira's daughter later recorded the naive dreams that his family indulged in: not just of living in a palace but also of building a beautiful garden sanctuary for lepers, even of buying the whole of Palestine.

By 1883, Shapira had completed a new translation of the parchments and, encouraged by Professor Schröder, the German consul in Beirut, he took his finds to Berlin to be examined by a committee of experts. After only one and a half hours of deliberation they declared the manuscripts to be a "clever and impudent forgery." The affair of the Moabite pottery had not been forgotten.

Fate and Fortune

Shapira, already the subject of considerable press interest, now moved on rapidly to London, where his precious manuscripts were better received—at least initially. The British Museum deputized its expert on Palestine, Christian Ginsburg, to examine the texts and produce a transcript; his translations were serialized in *The Times* that August. Two of the parchments had already been put on display in the museum, where they became a center of attention and controversy among both the public and scholars. Prime Minister William Gladstone, himself an erudite student of the ancient world, broke his busy schedule to visit the museum and engaged in a lengthy discussion with Shapira about the style of the script on the parchments. Rumor had it that the Treasury had already agreed to bankroll their purchase by the British Museum. Meanwhile, Shapira's family in Jerusalem had embarked on a reckless spending spree.

Yet the debate was beginning to turn against Shapira. Several scholars, including the Director of the British Museum, proclaimed that no parchment could possibly have survived in the rainy climate of Palestine for over 2,000 years. Then Shapira's nemesis Clermont-Ganneau arrived to announce, after a cursory inspection of the parchments through their glass case, that they were forgeries. He produced plausible arguments to show that they had been cut from the bottom of relatively modern manuscripts and aged by chemical means. Not wishing to be shown up by his French colleague, Ginsburg suddenly changed tack and completed his series in *The Times* with an article denouncing Shapira's "finds" as fakes. He improved on Clermont-Ganneau's theory by claiming that he could detect the hand of several scribes, masterminded by a learned Hebrew of Polish, Russian, and German extraction. The style of the script, he argued, had simply been copied from the Mesha Stone.

No doubt appeared to remain—the manuscripts were forgeries and Shapira was therefore either a crook or a fool. On August 23, he wrote a letter to Ginsburg from his London hotel, castigating him for his extraordinary turnabout: "You have made a fool out of me by publishing and exhibiting things which you believe to be false. I do not think I will be able to survive this shame." Shapira meant every word. In March 1884, he committed suicide in a Rotterdam hotel. His family, who had run up considerable debts while anticipating the sale of the manuscripts, sold everything they owned in Jerusalem and moved to Germany.

The parchments, meanwhile, were auctioned by Sotheby's of the Strand for the princely sum of ten pounds and five shillings to a bookseller. The last trace of them comes from the bookseller's 1887 catalog, priced at £25 and listed with an estimated date of 1500 B.C. to A.D. 1800! No one knows where they are today.

The story would have ended there, as yet another triumph of scholarship over the forger, had it not been for a discovery made in 1947—when a Bedouin shepherd, exploring a cave high in the cliffs near the Dead Sea at Qumran, chanced upon the world-famous Dead

Grossly anti–Semitic cartoon from the satirical magazine *Punch* (September 8, 1883), showing the hapless Shapira being arrested by British museum expert Ginsburg.

PUNCH'S FANCY PORTRAITS.—NO. 152.

MR. SHARP-EYE-RA.

SHOWING, IN VERY FANCIFUL PORTRAITURE, HOW DETECTIVE GINSBURG ACTUALLY DID MR. SHARP-EYE-RA OUT OF HIS SKIN.

Sea Scrolls. The shape and appearance of these undoubtedly genuine manuscripts was remarkably similar to those possessed by Shapira; they mostly date to the first century B.C., but were written in a deliberately archaic style of the Hebrew alphabet, using letter forms that had fallen out of general use hundreds of years earlier. Unfortunately, we cannot subject Shapira's manuscripts to the same intense scrutiny and battery of scientific testing, so there is no real comparison possible.

So were the Shapira manuscripts genuine after all, and was Shapira a victim of narrow academic certainty? This is the opinion of John Allegro, an acknowledged authority on the Dead Sea Scrolls, and one of several scholars to reopen the Shapira case. With hindsight we can see that Shapira's own assessment of the manuscripts was far better than those of the "experts" who denounced him. He was cautious of the obvious conclusion that the manuscripts were as old as the Mesha Stone, and allowed that they may have been made in the last centuries before Christ, by an unorthodox Jewish sect living near the Dead Sea—a remarkably accurate prediction of the Qumran community we now associate with the Dead Sea Scrolls. Allegro pleaded that:

> we should learn from [past] mistakes and keep our minds open to possibilities and ideas that our present imperfect understanding cannot encompass. This is particularly so in the archaeological field, where almost every season brings fresh discoveries that demand a reassessment of outmoded theories and presumptions.

Wise words, but for the hapless Shapira and his family they come a century too late. So does the acknowledgment by the British Museum, in the catalog for a 1990 exhibition on fakes, that the Shapira case is a classic example of where the experts may have got it wrong. As for the manuscripts, they were quite possibly everything that Shapira believed—the oldest fragments of the Old Testament yet found. But until they are rediscovered—perhaps moldering away in someone's attic—the mystery will not be solved.

KING ARTHUR'S GRAVE

"A mystery to the world a grave for Arthur." So runs a line in a medieval Welsh poem describing the burial places of the great warriors of Britain's past. The wording is enigmatic, and has been variously translated as "unthinkable a grave for Arthur" or "not wise the thought, a grave for Arthur" *(Anoeth bid bet y Arthur)*. The meaning, however, is clear: no one knows where, if anywhere, the famous King Arthur of old was buried, and it is best not to even think about it.

The reason behind this curious idea is that the medieval Welsh and their cousins—the Cornish of southwestern Britain and the Bretons of northwestern France—refused to believe that their national hero King Arthur had ever really died. Though some records stated that he fell at the battle of Camlann (around A.D. 540), many people believed that he had not died on the battlefield, but had been taken to the Isle of Avalon to be healed by fairy queens (see **King Arthur** in **Legendary History**). Six centuries later, in the Middle Ages, the idea was widespread that Arthur was merely sleeping, either on the paradisical isle of

Avalon or in some hidden cave, restoring his strength until the day that his country needed him again. If a dire national emergency arose he was on hand to step in and rescue the people of Britain from destruction. Hence Arthur's title of "The Once and Future King" (in Latin *Rex Quondam Rexque Futurus*).

The belief in Arthur's immortality was held passionately. In A.D.

King Arthur. Detail from the Round Table in Winchester.

1113, some French priests carrying the sacred relics of Our Lady of Laon visited Bodmin in Cornwall, where the locals gathered at the church to see the relics and be healed of their illnesses. Trouble started when an old Cornish man with a withered arm turned up and happened to mention to the priests that King Arthur was not really dead. One of the Frenchmen laughed and a fight actually broke out inside the church. (The man's arm, hardly surprising, was not healed.)

Death of a Hero

The belief in Arthur's immortality seemed to be completely shattered when, in A.D. 1190 (or 1191), the monks of Glastonbury in southwestern England claimed to have discovered nothing less than the grave of King Arthur and Queen Guinevere, complete with bodies and an inscription identifying them. It must have been the archaeological sensation of the Middle Ages.

There are several descriptions of this amazing discovery, but the earliest, possibly even an eyewitness account, comes from the churchman and writer Gerald of Wales. He appreciated the impact that the discovery would have on popular belief:

> In our own lifetime Arthur's body was discovered at Glastonbury, although the legends had always encouraged us to believe that there was something otherworldly about his ending, that he had resisted death and had been spirited away to some far-distant spot.

Gerald explained how the monks were inspired to search for Arthur's grave at Glastonbury after some of them had had dreams and visions. Further, King Henry II himself (A.D. 1133–1189) let them in on a centuries-old secret he had gleaned from an ancient British bard learned in history: Arthur's body would be found at Glastonbury in an oak coffin, 16 feet underground. The monks' attention was drawn by two stone markers, shaped like tall pyramids, in the churchyard of St. Dunstan. They were covered with inscriptions, so worn that they were barely readable, suggesting that they marked something of great antiquity. The monks dug down between the pyramids to a depth of 16 feet, where they discovered a huge coffin made from a hollowed-out oak tree. Inside were the bones of a gigantic man, which Gerald was able to examine personally:

> The Abbot showed me one of the shin bones. He held it upright on the ground against the foot of the tallest man he could find, and it

King Henry II—supposedly told by an ancient bard where to find King Arthur's grave. (Effigy from Henry's tomb.)

stretched a good three inches above the man's knee. The skull was so large and capacious that it seemed a veritable prodigy of nature, for the space between the eyebrows and the eye-sockets was as broad as the palm of a man's hand. Ten or more wounds could clearly be seen, but they had all mended but one. This was larger than the others and it had made an immense gash. Apparently it was this wound which had caused Arthur's death.

Two-thirds of the coffin was occupied by these gigantic bones, while the lower third contained those of a woman, buried at the man's feet. Gerald's conviction about the identity of the burials came from the other evidence that he was shown. Beneath the oak coffin, the monks said, they found a large stone slab, underneath which they found an inscribed cross made of lead:

I have seen this cross myself and I have traced the lettering which was cut into it on the side which was turned towards the stone. . . . The inscription read as follows:

HERE IN THE ISLE OF AVALON
LIES BURIED THE RENOWNED KING ARTHUR,
WITH GUINEVERE, HIS SECOND WIFE.

The discovery of Guinevere's burial gave rise to a ridiculous incident that Gerald used as a cautionary tale on the sins of the flesh:

In the same grave there was found a tress of woman's hair, blond and lovely to look at, plaited and coiled with consummate skill, and belonging no doubt to Arthur's wife, who was buried there with her husband. The moment that he saw this lock of hair, one of the monks, who was standing there in the crowd, jumped down into the deep grave in an attempt to snatch hold of it before any of the others. It was [a] pretty shameless thing to do and it showed little reverence for the dead. This monk . . . a silly, rash, impudent fellow . . . dropped down into the hole, which was a sort of symbol of the Abyss from which none of us can escape.

So what *did* the monks actually find in St. Dunstan's churchyard? In medieval England it was blithely accepted that the monks had discovered precisely what they claimed to have. It was not done to challenge the authority of the Glastonbury monks, particularly when they said that they had been working on the advice of the king himself. In

Wales, Cornwall, and Brittany, however, the announcement was greeted with a stunned silence. Perhaps it was assumed in these areas to be an English trick.

There was, after all, great political significance to the matter. The Norman rulers of England were now largely accepted by their Saxon subjects, but not so in the Celtic fringes. In Wales the legend of King Arthur became a rallying point against the Norman invaders: around 1150 a French writer noted that the Welsh were threatening the Normans that they would win back their lands with the help of King Arthur. The Norman monarchs of England needed to neutralize such dangerous nostalgia. Like most of the medieval kings, Henry II was embroiled in a lengthy struggle to subdue the rebellious Welsh, and the discovery of King Arthur's grave at Glastonbury would certainly have suited his political aims.

That Henry and his dynasty were interested in the discovery there can be no doubt. Gerald tells us that the king advised the monks to reinter the bones of Arthur and Guinevere in a new marble tomb in the abbey. It must have been very soon after the discovery that Henry's son Richard "the Lionheart," on his way to the Third Crusade (March 1191), presented to Tancred of Sicily a sword claimed to be the real Excalibur, supposedly excavated from Glastonbury Abbey.

The supposed bones of King Arthur and Queen Guinevere were reburied here in 1278—in front of the high altar in the church at Glastonbury Abbey.

In 1278, King Edward I commanded that the marble tomb containing Arthur's and Guinevere's bones be moved to a new position of prominence in front of the high altar. While King Edward reinterred the bones of Arthur in a new casket, sealing it with the royal seal, Queen Eleanor did the same honor for the bones of Guinevere. By doing so Edward was effectively associating his kingship with the mystique of Arthur, the greatest emperor of Britain's legendary past. He was also making sure that he would have less trouble from the (still-rebellious) Welsh with their crazy notion that Arthur could somehow restore their independence.

A Dark Age Burial?

There was one Welshman who *did* believe the Glastonbury claims: Gerald the churchman. With about one-quarter Welsh blood and three-quarters Norman, Gerald aimed to preserve the cultural identity of Wales under the umbrella of Norman-English kingship. As a devout Christian he must also have had problems with the folklore concerning Arthur's immortality.

Gerald was also a fairly critical writer. Yet he was completely convinced by the evidence that the Glastonbury monks showed him. He was particularly impressed by the way the inscription naming the grave as Arthur's was found only *after* the skeletal remains and the stone slab were removed. Gerald praised the cleverness of the builders, who, in the troubled times of Arthur's death, had the foresight to place the grave at such a great depth and conceal the identity of its occupants by hiding the inscribed side of the lead cross under a huge stone slab. The grave therefore escaped the ravages of Arthur's Saxon enemies and held its secret until the time and circumstances were right for it to be revealed.

For all its fanciful details—such as the visions of the monks and the ridiculous episode concerning Guinevere's golden hair—is it possible that the monks really did uncover an ancient grave? In favor of their claim it has been pointed out that the ancient British did indeed bury some of their dead in hollowed-out tree trunks, just like the coffin they held to be Arthur's. Surely if their discovery was a complete forgery, it has been argued, they would have claimed to have found something rather more grand—such as a stone sarcophagus—to increase the importance of their discovery. Or did they indeed, by one means or another, stumble upon a real Dark Age burial, possibly even that of Arthur himself?

Unfortunately most of the original evidence has now gone astray. Arthur's bones may have been destroyed or simply thrown away during Henry VIII's dissolution of the monasteries in 1539, when Glastonbury Abbey was pillaged by the king's officers. The lead cross went into the possession of the Hughes family of Wells (a nearby town) and was last reported in the seventeenth or early eighteenth century, although in 1980 there was a claim that the cross had been rediscovered. One Derek Mahoney of North London spotted the place-name "Camelot" on an old map of the Enfield area and managed to persuade a local archaeological team to dredge a nearby pond. They found nothing, but Mahoney claimed, in a letter to the British Museum, that he had sifted through the dredgings and discovered a lead cross bearing an inscription concerning Arthur's burial. He showed the cross to the museum staff but refused to leave it with them for further study. In the meantime Mahoney was charged by Enfield Council (the owners of anything found in the pond) and when he failed to obey a court order to hand over the cross, he was sent to prison for a year. The whole dubious case is made even more suspicious by the fact that Mahoney is known to be an expert at casting metals.

Fortunately the inscription on the *original* cross was copied and transmitted through the Middle Ages, and we are fortunate in possessing a detailed drawing of it published by the great British antiquarian William Camden in A.D. 1607. (Mahoney's cross was apparently identical to this illustration and was most likely copied from it.) Camden's text is slightly different from that given by Gerald—"Here lies Arthur, the famous king, in the island of Avalon"—and the extra phrase about Guinevere is conspicuously missing. However, Camden was a meticulous reporter and there is no reason to doubt that his illustration is an accurate copy of the lead cross displayed at Glastonbury (at least in the 16th century).

Amazingly enough the shapes of the Latin letters on the cross are *not* those of the sixteenth century, and may even be earlier than the twelfth. Leslie Alcock, a leading Dark Age archaeologist, would place them in the tenth century A.D. Kenneth Jackson, Professor of Celtic languages at Edinburgh University, has gone even further: *if* Camden's drawing of the letters is reliable (Jackson stresses the "if"), then "the late 6th century would be perfectly acceptable." If by "late" Jackson means "the second half" of the sixth century (A.D. 550 onward), then we are only a spit away from the traditional dates for King Arthur's death, A.D. 537 and A.D. 542. So if the cross was a forgery, it was at least a very good one.

Drawing of King Arthur's burial cross, as published in William Camden's *Britannia* (1607).

On the green in the foreground lies the spot where medieval monks claimed to have excavated King Arthur's burial. (In the background is the nave of Glastonbury Abbey church.)

There is further circumstantial evidence in favor of the monks' claims. Ralegh Radford, director of archaeological research at Glastonbury Abbey for many years, located the area where the grave was said to have lain and excavated it. At the spot where the monks claim to have dug he found an area of disturbed earth, the remains of a deep pit. Reexcavating this ancient excavation, Radford was able to determine from the finds that it had been dug sometime in the 1180s or 1190s. Radford was unfortunately very lax in publishing full details of this important find, yet in his opinion he was certain that this was the hole dug in order to recover the burial of King Arthur.

Since the monks do seem to have excavated at Glastonbury around 1190, and since the lettering on the cross could very well be as early as the sixth century, it is not surprising that many archaeologists, including Radford and Alcock, have toyed with the idea that this really may have been the burial of King Arthur. The identification of Glastonbury with the mysterious "Isle of Avalon," where he was taken when mortally wounded, also seems reasonable. Glastonbury was founded on a group of hilltops, which in prehistoric, Roman, and even medieval times was largely surrounded by water (marshes and the River Brue). Moreover, stories and legends from before A.D. 1190 show that Glastonbury was thought of as a special site, linked with beliefs in the afterlife and the spirit world. Like the mythical Avalon, it may have been seen as a portal to the underworld (see **The Glastonbury Spiral** in **Earth Patterns**).

The archaeological arguments, together with the testimony of Gerald and others, provide a case that is deliciously tempting. After all, if the lead cross were genuine, we would finally have the elusive piece of hard evidence that proves the historicity of King Arthur.

A School of Forgery?

Doubt sets in when we consider the other circumstances behind the "discovery." In 1184, the church and monastic building at Glastonbury were reduced to ashes in a raging fire, and the cost of rebuilding was immense. One of the main ways monasteries raised money in the Middle Ages was through the prestige of their relics. The more and better relics, the more famous the saint whose bones were preserved, then the greater the status of the monastery. This would give the abbot more clout at church councils, and a lever with which to increase the privileges and property of the abbey. Pilgrims would flock to see the relics of a great saint, leaving offerings and spending money on food and drink in the same way that tourists do today. Tourism was a major source of revenue for the monasteries.

Glastonbury's problem was that it lacked a major saint. Saint Dunstan (c. A.D. 910–988) had once been abbot there, but he moved on to Canterbury, where his bones were buried with full honors. Arthur was not a saint, but as he ranked as the greatest hero and emperor in the whole of British history, he was something even better. It seems too much of a coincidence that it was only just after the disastrous fire of 1184 that the monks made the miraculous discovery of his bones. The involvement of King Henry only adds to the suspicion; as we have seen, the Norman kings had their own political motives for proving Arthur dead. Needing royal support, the monks could have entered into a mutually beneficial arrangement.

The monks of Glastonbury also had a bad track record with regard to forgery. Shortly after the fire they announced that they had the bones of Saint Patrick, thought to have visited the abbey in its early days. As everyone knew that Saint Patrick was buried in Ireland, few, least of all the Irish, were impressed by Glastonbury's claim. At the same time the monks tried to reclaim Saint Dunstan from Canterbury. The explanation they gave as to how Saint Dunstan supposedly came to be *re*buried in Glastonbury was incredibly convoluted, and like the case of King Arthur's bones, was fleshed out with a mass of detailed "evidence." Supposedly Saint Dunstan's bones were moved from Canterbury to Glastonbury for safekeeping, their new burial place being known to only two monks who passed the secret down the generations. Shortly after the disastrous fire the secret location was revealed, and sure enough two stone coffers, inscribed respectively with the letters "S" and "D" (for "Saint Dunstan"!), were unearthed in front of witnesses. The story shares conspicuous similarities with the King Arthur case—the secret information, the revelation, the inscribed evidence, and the public excavation. It was dismissed, quite rightly, by the authorities at Canterbury, who were satisfied that the bones of Saint Dunstan had never left their cathedral.

It is difficult to avoid the impression that, after the failure of the Saint Patrick and Saint Dunstan claims, the monks were merely putting on another performance, this time slightly better stage-managed. A further damning detail about the discovery comes from Adam of Domerham, a Glastonbury monk writing about a century later than Gerald of Wales. Adam wrote that the abbot, intent on recovering Arthur's bones, "one day surrounded the place with curtains and ordered that digging should be carried out." Why the need for curtains if there was nothing untoward going on? On the other hand, they would have provided perfect cover for all manner of skulduggery, such as the introduction of bones, the inscribed cross, blond hair, and other props.

As to the cross itself, a key point seems to have eluded those scholars impressed by the forms of the lettering. The lettering comes from the early-seventeenth-century work of Camden. Yet the text he gives differs from that given by Gerald of Wales, who claims to have actually handled the cross. Camden's drawing omits, and certainly allows no room for, the extra information given by Gerald about the burial of "Guinevere, Arthur's second wife." Thus two star witnesses disagree. Gerald's is the earliest, yet Camden's version is supported by two thirteenth-century texts that also omit Guinevere. It seems more likely that Gerald was shown one cross, and that another was substituted later, perhaps when the monks realized that the claim of having found Queen Guinevere as well as King Arthur was stretching people's credulity. This would mean that the Camden version is of little value in authenticating the inscription. Anyway, even if the letters are Dark Age in style this proves little, as the crafty monks may have copied them from an old inscription.

Both versions of the inscription, however, agree in including the words "in the island of Avalon," which is quite damning in itself. Grave markers do not normally include a location. It is superfluous for a burial in Westminster Abbey or Canterbury Cathedral to give a place name. The only purpose for the extra wording in the Glastonbury inscription can have been to "prove" that it was the original "Isle of Avalon." It was an identification of immense, almost infinite value. Avalon was the last resting place of Arthur, but more besides. A French Burgundian writer had already fingered "Avaron" (most likely Avallon in Burgundy) as the western destination of the guardians of the Holy Grail, led by the family of Joseph of Arimathea (see **The Company of Avalon** in **Archaeology and the Supernatural**). Saint Joseph, according to the New Testament, actually buried Jesus before his resurrection. It was only a matter of time before Glastonbury was to draw these traditions into its orbit as well.

By the mid–thirteenth century the monks were using the Avalon link to develop a new story, of how Joseph of Arimathea and other assorted apostles had arrived at Glastonbury to found the first church in the whole of the West. In 1345, the monks tried, unsuccessfully this time, to exhume the bones of Saint Joseph. The effect has continued to snowball ever since. Even after the dissolution of Glastonbury Abbey in 1547 the traditions continued to grow. A century later tourists were being shown a thorn tree that blossoms around Christmas, said to have been grown from a fragment of the crown of thorns that Christ wore at his crucifixion, which Saint Joseph planted. By the eighteenth century, local churchmen had taken the ultimate step; they were arguing that Christ himself, as a child, had visited Glastonbury in the company of Saint Joseph, who had sailed from the Eastern Mediterranean to buy British tin.

The final, most telling point is that some years before the disastrous fire and the "discovery" of the grave, the monks of Glastonbury commissioned an outsider, William of Malmesbury, to write a history of their abbey in order to raise its profile. William utilized all the records and folklore of the abbey in the book he wrote. Yet it does not contain a single reference to a tradition that Arthur was buried at Glastonbury. This is particularly strange, as William was well aware of Arthurian legends, which he discussed in his other writings. There he clearly stated that the grave of Arthur was unknown: "the tomb of Arthur is nowhere beheld, whence the ancient ditties fable that he is yet to come."

It does not take an Hercule Poirot to conclude that the "discovery" of King Arthur's burial by medieval monks was an exceedingly clever and timely forgery, designed to kill two birds with one stone: raise desperately needed funds for the monastery and ingratiate themselves with the dynasty of King Henry II, by producing evidence for his political ambitions and crediting him with a hand in the discovery. All in all, a stroke of genius on the part of the monks who conceived it . . . but one not quite clever enough.

THE VINLAND MAP

It seemed to be the final nail in Christopher Columbus's coffin. Not only had the Vikings beaten him to America, it now appeared as though they had left behind a document mapping their exploits. On the eve of Columbus Day, October 12, 1965, Yale University revealed to the public the existence of a hitherto unknown map, dating some fifty years before the great discoverer set off across the Atlantic, which showed the location of Vinland, the Norse territory on the eastern coast of North America (see **The Vikings in America** in **Voyagers and Discoveries**). The Vinland Map was hailed by Yale as "the most exciting cartographic discovery of the century." Taking a more political view, the *Chicago Tribune* headlined their story "The Map that Spoiled Columbus Day."

The document that made such a stir is a pen-and-ink drawing of the world, 11 inches by 16, on a thin sheet of parchment. It shows the world familiar to the medieval European geographer—Europe, Asia, the northern part of Africa, and the Atlantic. In the northern Atlantic are drawn Iceland and Greenland, and beyond them "Vinland Island discovered by the companions Bjarni and Leif." Above Vinland is a longer inscription recording the Norse discovery of America and a later voyage:

> God willed that after a long journey from Greenland to the farthest remaining parts of the western ocean sea the companions Bjarni and Leif Ericsson, sailing south through the ice discovered a new land, which was very rich and which even had vines; they called it Vinland Island. Eric, bishop of Greenland and the neighbouring regions and

legate of the apostolic see in this truly vasty and rich land, arrived in the name of the Almighty God in the last year of the reign of Pope Pascal. Eric stayed some time in summer and in winter before returning to Greenland and later proceeding southward in obedience to God's will.

This caption relates to the discovery of Vinland by Bjarni Herjolfsson and Leif Eiriksson around A.D. 1000 (see **The Vikings in America** in **Voyagers and Discoveries**), and an event otherwise known from an entry in the *Icelandic Annals* for A.D. 1121 when "Bishop Eirik of Greenland set out in search of Vinland," matching pretty well the last year of Pope Pascal (A.D. 1118).

The Vinland Map is bound together in a volume with a manuscript called the Tartar Relation—this is an otherwise unknown record (made by Friar Benedict the Pole) of the Franciscan mission to the Mongols in A.D. 1245–1247, led by Friar John de Plano Carpini, whose own *History of the Mongols* has long been famous. The Vinland Map seems to have been produced to illustrate the Tartar Relation, as

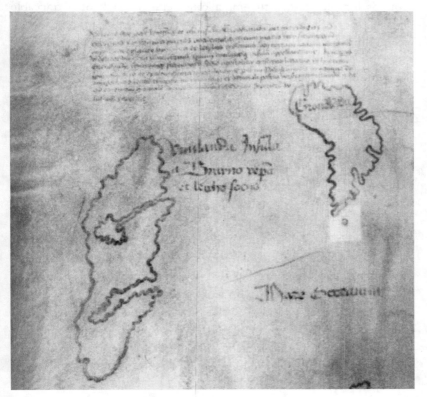

Detail from Vinland map showing Vinland and Greenland. The caption at the top describes the Norse discovery of Vinland and a visit paid there by Eric the Bishop of Greenland in A.D. 1118.

many of the brief notes scattered across the Asian section concern missionary activity. Puzzlingly, the wormholes in the map and the text did not match, but this was resolved when a third manuscript (part of the fifteenth-century work *Speculum Historiale*) was found that had once been bound between the map and the Tartar Relation.

So when and why had the Vinland Map been drawn up? The style of handwriting on both the map and the Tartar Relation pointed to a time in the early fifteenth century and a location in Central Europe, as did the watermarked paper on which they were written. Given the missionary interest of both the main documents, one event presented itself as an obvious occasion for such a record being made—this was the major church council held at Basle in Switzerland from A.D. 1431 to 1439. So not only was the Vinland Map firm evidence that the Norse really did reach North America, it also opened up the possibility that Columbus was well aware of their achievement.

As Dr. Raleigh Skelton, keeper of maps at the British Museum, wrote at the time, it was "of so arresting a character as to prompt scepticism, if not incredulity." The very fact of its existence clearly made the map difficult for some to swallow. And there were other grounds for skepticism, the main one being its lack of a traceable history.

Yale University had paid an undisclosed sum, perhaps hundreds of thousands of dollars, for the map, thanks to the generosity of an anonymous benefactor. They had bought it from the American rare books dealer Laurence Witten. He had purchased the Vinland Map and the Tartar Relation from Enzo Ferrajoli (a small-scale supplier of medieval books and manuscripts) back in 1957, and assumed that they came from a library down on its luck in postwar Europe. Thousands of manuscripts were certainly sold off, often under the counter, by hard-pressed institutions at this time. As a result of one such transaction Ferrajoli was convicted of stealing books from the Cathedral Library in Zaragossa, although letters from the cathedral authorities existed asking him to arrange the sale of their manuscripts. Witten was well aware that this incident would be used by doubters of the authenticity of the Vinland Map against it, but despite repeated questioning, Ferrajoli never told him where it had come from. Left out on a limb, at a conference held at the Smithsonian Institution in 1968 Witten claimed to know the library from which the map originated. Shortly afterward, Ferrajoli died, and with him went the last hope of tracing the ownership of the map any further.

The Verdict of Science

Given the continuing uncertainty over the Vinland Map on scientific grounds, which the Smithsonian meeting did nothing to resolve, Yale University decided to commission tests that could settle the issue one way or the other. They invited in a team from Walter McCrone Associates of Chicago to analyze the chemical makeup of the ink, using a battery of newly developed methods.

The McCrone report, issued in 1974, was utterly damning. Having examined the ink using both X-ray bombardment and an electron microscope, the McCrone team showed that the ink used to draw the Vinland Map was *not* the same as that in which the Tartar Relation and the *Speculum Historiale* were written. Further, the Vinland Map ink had an unusual composition. In many of the twenty-nine samples there were extremely high concentrations of the chemical compound titanium dioxide, in a form known as anatase. This had given the ink its yellow-brown color. Anatase can be found as a mineral compound in the natural world, although rarely, but the McCrone results demonstrated that "the anatase in the Vinland Map was a refined product, chemically quite pure."

Anatase in this pure form, made up of uniform grains, has been manufactured only since 1920. The McCrone team ruled out the possibility that medieval monks could have created the anatase. They argued that its production would have required heating to a higher temperature than they could achieve and involved the use of concentrated acids not available at this date. In their view the Vinland Map was a deliberate "fraud made to deceive the beholder into believing it to be a genuine fifteenth century product."

Reaction on the part of Yale University was swift. On January 26, 1974, it sent out a press release to break the bad news:

> Yale University Library reported today that its researches suggest that the famous Vinland Map may be a forgery. This conclusion is based on exhaustive studies initiated by the Yale Library taking advantage of techniques of chemical analysis only recently developed by scientists.

Although fifteen years had passed since he sold the map, Laurence Witten was summoned to a meeting at Yale by Rutherford Rogers, the chief librarian, who demanded the return of the purchase price. Witten had to break the bad news that most of it had already gone to the tax man as well as to Ferrajoli, and that the original source of the map was actually unknown, and volunteered to write to the anonymous donor to explain. The patron generously accepted that the transaction had contained an inevitable element of risk and refused to press for the return of his money.

Despite Yale's about-face, the original authors of the monograph hailing the Vinland Map remained undaunted. The immediate reaction of George Painter, Assistant Keeper of Printed Books at the British Library, shows how offended he was by the suggestion that he could have been fooled by a forged map:

The complete Vinland Map.

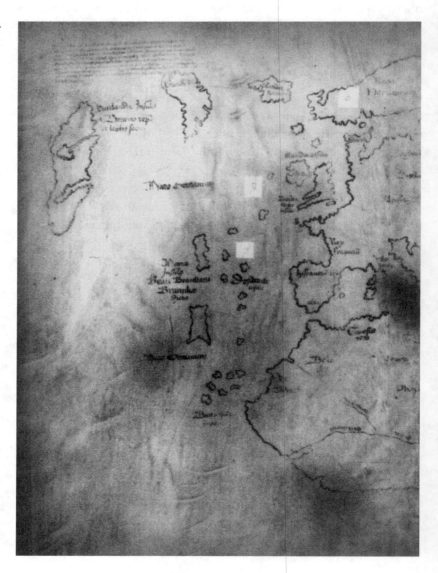

I do not dispute Mr. McCrone's results; but it is paradoxical that the Vinland Map is so far the only medieval map to have its ink investigated by this method. I think scientific method demands that all the others should be micro-analysed. . . . Perhaps it will turn out that they were all fakes; or perhaps it will turn out that the Vinland Map is genuine.

Painter certainly had a point. The lack of comparative tests was a serious weakness in the McCrone analysis. Perhaps they had been in too much of a hurry, under pressure to come up with a definitive

judgment. The continued support of influential voices and the nagging doubt over the conclusiveness of the McCrone results eventually led Yale to subject the map to further scientific scrutiny.

In 1985, a team under the direction of Dr. Thomas Cahill of the University of California at Davis undertook nondestructive X-ray analyses of the Vinland Map, the Tartar Relation, and the *Speculum Historiale*. The results of their 160 tests could hardly have been more different from those of the McCrone investigation. While they did agree that the Vinland Map differed from the other two manuscripts in containing titanium, they did not see this as a cause for suspicion. Cahill's group argued that the titanium was present only in minuscule amounts; that it was found in the parchment as well as the ink; that levels of titanium in the parchments were no higher than in other, indisputably genuine manuscripts they had examined; and that in some inked lines they could detect no titanium at all, even though these were the same yellow-brown color attributed by the McCrone team to the use of anatase. Altogether, it seemed as though the importance of titanium had been greatly exaggerated, perhaps by a factor of thousands, although they did not speculate as to how this could have come about. However, while the Cahill study undermined the value of the earlier scientific judgment, it could not be used as a positive argument that the Vinland map is genuine, as its authors frankly admitted:

> In conclusion, we must stress that, while our work argues strongly against the specific McCrone Associates proof that the Map is fraudulent, we do not claim therefore that the map is authentic. Such a judgment must be based on all available evidence, cartographic and historical as well as compositional.

A reply from Walter McCrone was not long in coming, and it was firm in rejecting Cahill's analysis. He argued that the discrepancy between the results obtained by the two methods came about because they were analyzing different things. While McCrone's work had examined only the ink itself, by virtue of removing scrapings from the map, Cahill's team could not examine such a small area as just the line of ink itself—and so inevitably obtained readings for the parchment both below and around the ink as well. This, he concluded, would have artificially lowered the values for titanium in their analyses.

McCrone had to concede one point, however. Jacqueline Olin of the Smithsonian Institution had succeeded in producing anatase using medieval methods. Even so, he found this unconvincing, as the shape and size of the particles Olin had made did not match those on the Vinland Map. The only way this could be achieved was to subject her anatase to a further step, heating to a temperature of 800–1000 degrees Celsius, which he felt was "inconceivable as a 15th century process." In any case, why should they bother? There were perfectly good yellow pigments available to the medieval scribe that needed none of this complicated production process. Accordingly, McCrone was even stronger in his opinion of the impossibility of producing anatase in medieval times to match that on the Vinland Map:

> The pigment is identical in composition, crystal structure, size and shape with commercial titanium white available only since 1917. The materials needed and the processing steps required for its preparation are a convincing argument against its availability before 1917.

McCrone felt "fully justified" in sticking to his view that "the Vinland map is a post–1920 forgery."

Dr. Kenneth Towe of the Smithsonian Institution entered the fray in support of McCrone, with further arguments against Olin's theory of medieval anatase production. Not only would a heating stage be required, but the resulting substance would then have to be milled or ground to produce anatase like that seen by McCrone Associates.

This was not, of course, the end of the scientific debate, which resumed in 1995 when Yale University Press published a second edition of *The Vinland Map and the Tartar Relation*. Cahill replied vigorously to his critics with strongly expressed doubts concerning the McCrone team's expertise in dealing with medieval manuscripts. As he stressed, their normal area of work was the detection of air pollutants, in which the particles for analysis are collected on a completely clean background. Cahill himself had observed that the surface of the Vinland Map was, by contrast, liberally coated with stray particles. He had undertaken no examination of these because they probably represented modern contamination, but the likelihood was that they would contain anatase:

> After all, almost all modern paints are anatase-based. Millions of tons of the material is made annually, and spread (in fine crystalline form) on virtually every wall and ceiling in the developed world. Presence of such particles would be expected from the extensive handling that any rare document receives.

Turning the hoax theory on its head, Cahill wondered why a "forger would choose a 1920s paint designed for houses in order to imitate a medieval ink, when a small amount of linseed oil, and an hour in the oven, delivers a much more convincing 'aged' line." He also makes much of his group's observation "that about ⅓ of the brownish-yellow lines had no titanium at all," which is difficult to understand if it was a consistently high component of the ink used. Unlike the McCrone team, Cahill's group has analyzed many other historical manuscripts, finding titanium present in many of them, often at higher levels than for the Vinland Map, which supports the accidental anatase theory.

George Painter of the British Museum, longtime supporter of the map, backed Cahill to the hilt, attacking the reaction of McCrone and Towe to Olin's medieval anatase theory. He rejected scornfully their arguments that heating and milling or grinding were unlikely stages in the production of a medieval ink:

> In fact calcination (by crucible in a bellows-operated charcoal-burning furnace) and pestle-and-mortar milling were standard methods for the conversion of ingredients to powder in medieval ink and pigment formulas, and the necessary instruments and procedures are shown in innumerable contemporary illustrations of working laboratories. The required temperatures . . . are assumed by [McCrone and Towe] to be "inconceivable as a 15th-century process." In the real world such metallurgical temperatures were not only familiar to medieval chemists and alchemists but have also been evident ever since the prehistoric bronze-smiths of 3000 B.C.

Cahill may be exaggerating when he claims that the McCrone forgery theory is now "in shreds," but it is certainly badly compromised. Science had failed to establish the genuineness or fraudulence of the Vinland Map. Once again the map had to be judged primarily on its cartographic plausibility.

The Map Itself

Doubts were expressed by a minority of cartographers concerning the Vinland Map right from the beginning, although this swiftly turned into a majority as the McCrone verdict became known.

An initial problem is that, as Kirsten Seaver, the historian of Scandinavian seafaring in the Atlantic, puts it: "the medieval Norse did not use cartographical representations to convey their sailing lore." It is certainly true that the earliest Scandinavian maps are well over a century later in date than the Vinland Map is purported to be. While there could have been earlier maps that don't survive, none are mentioned in any of the Norse Sagas, in which sailing directions are always committed to memory, rather than being written down. However, this is not an insurmountable problem, as navigation might have been changing by the fifteenth century, when maps became much more commonly used in Europe.

As for the contents of the map, the outstanding bone of contention is that Greenland, drawn with a fair degree of accuracy, is shown as an island. From the beginning this has been seen as a fatal mistake. Professor Eva Taylor of the University of London argued that no one had known Greenland to be an island until the polar explorer Robert Peary mapped

Map of the northern Atlantic drawn by Icelander Sigardur Stefansson (late 16th century).

its northern coastline in 1892; the map could therefore be branded a crude fake. However, the real point at issue is not what people in the fifteenth century could prove, but what they believed. Here again, opinion was strongly against the map, with Admiral Samuel Morison, the naval historian, arguing that Greenland was never depicted as an island "on any map prior to 1650, but as a peninsula of Asia."

On this point Morison is undoubtedly wrong. As Painter has recently pointed out, there are several maps from A.D. 1500 and later that show Greenland as an island. Moreover, he has collected a number of medieval references, from the eleventh century onward, that refer to the island of Greenland. One possible source of this knowledge has been suggested by Max Vinner of the Viking Ship Museum at Roskilde in Denmark. Back in 1949, the polar explorer Eigil Knuth found a large Inuit (Eskimo) skin boat on the shore of Pearyland at the northern tip of Greenland. The boat is of a type used by the Inuit in the medieval period. So news of Greenland's island status could have reached the Viking settlers of southern Greenland and been transmitted by them to other Europeans.

Although it is somewhat surprising to see Greenland depicted as an island, it is definitely not enough in itself to condemn the Vinland Map as a fake. Neither is the apparent accuracy of the Greenland and Vinland coastlines, although these are, along with Iceland, much closer to reality than Scandinavia, which would at first sight appear to be the wrong way around. As with the scientific evidence, it seems that anti-map cartographers were too quick to condemn it.

What about the inscription on the American part of the map? Does this strengthen or weaken its plausibility? The focus of discussion here has been the idea of Bjarni Herjolfsson and Leif Eiriksson as "companions," when all the medieval Norse sources clearly state that they reached Vinland in two entirely separate voyages. It is certainly difficult to understand how a Norse mapmaker sufficiently knowledgeable of Iceland, Greenland, and the Americas to produce the Vinland Map could possibly be so ignorant of the Sagas to have thought that Leif and Bjarni were partners.

For Seaver this slip provides a vital clue not only to the status of the Vinland Map but also to the identity of its creator. As she announced triumphantly in 1995:

> I have found literary evidence that the map is a fake—it cannot possibly have been made before 1765, the publication year of the only source putting Leif Eiriksson and any sort of Bjarni aboard one ship.

The 1765 error was made by the German scholar David Crantz, who wrote a *History of Greenland* despite the disadvantage of having to rely on secondary non-Scandinavian sources, which he misunderstood. Despite this, Cranz's history became well known, being translated into English and French.

Seaver goes on to finger the German geographer Father Josef Fischer as the culprit behind the forgery. Not only was Fischer an expert in fifteenth-century maps, but he also wrote a book in 1902 on the Norse in America and early maps. Significant for Seaver's case, Fischer was unable to read the original Norse sources on the discovery of Vinland, and concluded that it was impossible to tell whether Bjarni or Leif got there first.

Fischer was still actively studying early maps, the Norse, and the role of the church in exploration when Hitler and the Nazi party came to power in 1933. As a Jesuit priest, Fischer was suspect under the new regime, and he dropped his interest in the Norse and the Catholic Church. After the Jesuit College where he had taught was forced to close, he retired to Castle Wolfegg, where, Seaver surmises, he came across the Tartar Relation, and determined to produce an accompanying map that would embarrass future Nazi scholars by its record of the global spread of Rome's missionaries. Fischer died in 1944, at which point his worldly goods were returned to the Jesuits, and Seaver argues that his map then found its way to Ferrajoli, who removed any telltale signs of its previous owner.

While Seaver has undoubtedly put forward a plausible faker with a real motive, there is no absolute proof here. No hidden message reveals Father Fischer's hand, while the Bjarni and Leif confusion is highly suspicious but not completely impossible to imagine. The role of the Tartar Relation is also not clear. Why should its discovery by Fischer lead to the production of a fake map of the Americas, since it contains no reference to Vinland?

The most recent theory presented concerning the Vinland Map does attempt to deal with this question. Scandinavian historian Lars Lönnroth notes that in a conference held at Yale in 1996, to follow up the republication of the Vinland Map and Tartar Relation, some intriguing new information was revealed. Dr. Garmon Harbottle, of the Brookhaven National Laboratory, had carried out a statistical test of the ink analyses that seemed to show that the ink used to draw the Vinland part of the map was different from the ink on the rest. He pondered the significance of his results, wondering if "maybe someone came along a few years later and added Vinland to a map that already existed. The island does seem to be stuck out on the edge."

Lönnroth sees Harbottle's findings as far more significant than the scientist himself realized. Without the North Atlantic islands of Iceland, Greenland, and Vinland, and the accompanying texts, the map would all fall within an oval outline, typical of the medieval view of the world. If someone had added Vinland and the other North Atlantic territories to an existing map, this completely undermines theories that the Vinland Map was drawn up on a specific occasion. And if these were tacked onto an older map, why should this not have happened a few hundred years later?

Lönnroth's persuasive interpretation is that the text of the Tartar Relation was accompanied by a map. This original fifteenth-century map (dated by the paper it was drawn on) contained an extremely crude representation of Scandinavia, which manages to place Sweden south of the Baltic. Still, the Nordic countries were hardly central to the location of the Tartars. Then, perhaps much later, an unknown hand added a far more accurate Iceland and Greenland and a controversial Vinland, trying to match their ink as closely as possible to that used originally. Only the specific composition of the ink gives them away. After a battery of tests and thirty years of dispute, perhaps science has at last pointed to a solution in the case of the Vinland Map. Columbus may have known of Viking voyages to North America, but his source was not, it seems, a "Vinland Map."

CHAPTER EIGHT

ARCHAEOLOGY AND THE SUPERNATURAL

INTRODUCTION

On a Saturday evening in March 1892, Hermann Hilprecht, Professor of Assyriology at the University of Pennsylvania, was working late checking the publisher's proofs of a catalog of inscriptions. He had before him copies of the texts from the ancient Babylonian city of Nippur (southern Iraq). Most of the inscriptions were damaged or in fragments, and though he had done his best to make sense of them, many still defied interpretation. By midnight he was exhausted and went to bed, falling into a deep sleep. He then had "a remarkable dream."

It started with the appearance of a tall, thin priest dressed in Babylonian robes, who led Hilprecht to the treasure chamber of the temple of the god Bel in Nippur. The priest took him into a room, where scraps of agate and lapis lazuli lay scattered on the floor, and announced to Hilprecht the following:

> The two fragments which you have published separately on pages 22 and 26, belong together. They are not finger-rings. Their history is as follows: King Kurigalzu once sent to the temple of Bel, among other articles of agate and lapis lazuli an inscribed votive cylinder of agate.
>
> Then we priests suddenly received the command to make a pair of earrings of agate for the statue of the god Ninib. We were in great dismay, since there was no agate as raw material at hand. In order to carry out the king's command there was nothing for us to do but cut the votive cylinder into three parts, thus making three rings, each of which contained a portion of the original inscription. The first two rings served as earrings for the god; the two fragments which have given you so much trouble are portions of them.
>
> If you will put the two together you will have confirmation of my words. But the third ring you have not yet found during your excavations, and you will never find it.

With these words the priest disappeared and the dream ended. Hilprecht immediately told his wife, and the following morning reexamined his copies of the Nippur inscriptions. He found that the texts on two ring-shaped objects of agate fitted together perfectly:

> to my astonishment [I] found all the details of the dream precisely verified in so far as the means of verification were in my hands. The

original inscription on the votive cylinder read: *To the god Ninib, son of Bel, his lord, has Kurigalzu, pontifex of Bel, presented this.*

Yet when Hilprecht excitedly told a colleague about the insight he had received in the dream, the matter took a different turn. His colleague drew his attention to the notes of the excavator, Dr. Peters, which stated that the agate rings, by now in a museum at Istanbul, were actually of different color. As he had not yet handled the original objects, Hilprecht made a point of seeking them out on his next visit to Istanbul:

> I found one fragment in one case, and another in a case far away from it. When I put them together the truth of my dream was demonstrated *ad oculos* [before my eyes]. They had in fact once belonged to one and the same votive cylinder!
>
> As it originally had been of finely veined agate, the stone-cutter's saw had accidentally divided the object in such a way that the whitish vein of the stone appeared only upon one fragment and the larger grey surface upon the other. Thus I was able to explain Dr. Peters' discordant description of the two fragments!

Somehow Hilprecht's "remarkable dream" had enabled him to piece together two objects hundreds of miles away that he had never personally seen. Was his revelation simply a result of his subconscious working overtime, after many hours of puzzling over the inscriptions? Or did he really, as the dream itself suggested, receive an insight from ancient Babylonia by some very different means?

Many psychics believe that objects can transmit "impressions" of the time when they were made, and that places as well can carry similar imprints—of the events that took place there and the people who once inhabited them. Under the right circumstances—or with a receptive mind on the right "wavelength"—there may be ways to retrieve valuable information from the past.

The most extreme cases are when such imprints are believed to control events in the present, against the will of bystanders, receptive or otherwise. The widely believed story of the "curse of Tutankhamun," if true, would mean that the ancient Egyptians had a far more advanced knowledge of the supernatural than our own, and that they were able to deliberately "program" his tomb by some unknown means to punish anyone who intruded on the Pharaoh's resting place. Could this really be possible, or is there a more rational explanation of the famous curse?

A much more typical example of a place carrying an "imprint" of the past concerns the strange experience undergone by one Miss E. F. Smith in 1950. On a rainy January night she was driving home, to the village of Letham in Scotland, when her car skidded into a ditch. She had no choice but to walk the remaining eight miles home along the farmroads, accompanied by her dog. Half a mile from her goal, at 2:00 A.M., she saw a crowd of mysterious figures, dressed in what looked like tights and tunics. They were clearly lit by the long flaming torches they carried in their hands, and appeared to be examining dead bodies that lay scattered in the fields.

Miss Smith was glad to pass the spot, and only fully realized the strangeness of the weird spectacle she had seen when she awoke in the morning. Her story was later carefully examined by psychic researcher Dr. James McHarg, who, satisfied that it was not a simple hoax, concluded that she may have somehow witnessed the aftermath of a battle that had taken place on that very spot in A.D. 685, between the English Northumbrians and the Picts from Scotland. The battle was fought by a loch called Nechtansmere, which has subsequently disappeared, and it was only a careful historical study that had been able to locate it in the fields near Letham.

The only problem is that this study was published in the British archaeological journal *Antiquity* two years previously. Miss Smith insisted that she had no knowledge of such an article, but the suspicion always remains that she *may* have heard of it—say, through a report in the local news—and that it was this that triggered her imagination during her lonely walk through the countryside. Miss Smith's experience remains a good ghost story, but as with so many similar cases, we are always left short of real proof that anything genuinely paranormal was involved.

However, with fields of study like archaeology and ancient history, it should be possible to check claims that information from the past can reach us by supernatural means because new information can always be brought to light that can prove or disprove these claims. Many believe that Bligh Bond, the excavator of Glastonbury Abbey in southwestern England, provided such proof earlier this century. Unknown to his employers, Bond had allowed his excavations to be subtly directed by messages from a group of ghosts known as "the company of Avalon," and Bond claimed that his archaeological discoveries demonstrated that spirit voices could indeed be trusted. Unfortunately the case is nowhere near as clear-cut as his supporters argue.

Bligh Bond was a pioneer in the field of psychic archaeology, which burgeoned and grew alongside professional archaeology during the 1960s, when a wave of dissatisfaction with the materialism of the western world was accompanied by an explosion of interest in the paranormal generally. The adventurous began to experiment with a whole gamut of alternative approaches to studying the past, and every conceivable technique was tried, from hypnotic regression into past lives to psychometry, a method used by mediums to "read" impressions from the past by feeling or concentrating on ancient objects.

The favorite subject of New Age psychometrists is a group of mysterious skulls beautifully carved from rock crystal. There are at least a dozen in existence and, like the one in the Musée de l'Homme in

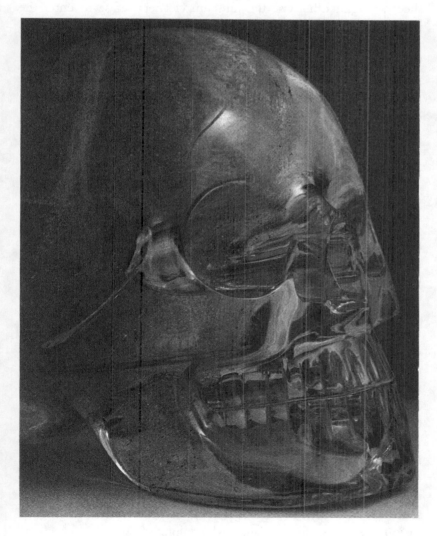

The crystal skull from the Museum of Mankind, London (now part of the British Museum). Many psychics believe that it contains "impressions" of the remote past, which can be retrieved by gazing into it.

Paris thought to be from pre-Columbian Mexico, nearly all are much smaller than a real skull. They have been claimed to be powerful and potentially dangerous objects for focusing psychic energies. Held by some psychics to be 12,000 years old and to be remnants of the lost civilization of Atlantis (see **Atlantis—Lost and Found?** in **Lost Lands and Catastrophes**), the crystal skulls have acquired an awesome reputation as the most extraordinary objects surviving from the ancient world. As pieces of art, these bizarre transparent skulls are certainly evocative. Yet are they really that strange, or for that matter, even ancient?

Of the two life-size examples known, one is housed in the Museum of Mankind, London. The skull is said to be covered with a sheet at night, otherwise the museum cleaners refuse to enter the room where it is displayed. It is presented to the public with only the sketchiest of details. The display states merely that the skull is "possibly of Aztec origin," although it goes on to say that at the earliest it dates to a time after the Spanish conquest of Mexico (A.D. 1520). This lack of knowledge is explained by the fact that the museum bought it in 1898, for £120, from the New York jewelers Tiffany's, who seem to have kept no note of its provenance.

The other skull is far more mysterious, or at least is said to be. This was supposedly found by Anna Mitchell-Hedges in 1927 while excavating with her father, explorer Mike Mitchell-Hedges, at the Mayan city of Lubantuum in Belize. She spotted the crystal skull below an ancient altar, then three months later found the jaw nearby. Her father gave the skull to the local Maya but, before the expedition left, the grateful Maya returned the skull as a parting gift, informing the Mitchell-Hedgeses that it was "their god used for healing or to will death."

Of all the crystal skulls, the Mitchell-Hedgeses' example has provoked the most repeated claims of supernatural phenomena. On one occasion, Frank Dorland, Canadian art conservation expert, was studying the Mitchell-Hedges skull when he had to keep it in his house overnight, as he was too late to return it to its usual location in a bank vault. That night he was the victim of intensive poltergeist activity, which he naturally connected with the presence of the skull. Anna Mitchell-Hedges had the skull examined by her local psychical research group. Mediums gazed deep into its interior (like a gypsy's crystal ball) and reported seeing a whole series of images, including the skull suspended high above an altar. Other psychics handling the skull reported receiving messages from its past owners, ranging, in various "readings," from Atlanteans to dolphins.

The supposed Atlantis connection receives support from Mitchell-Hedges himself, who was searching for traces of Atlantean civilization when he was excavating at Lubantuum. Mitchell-Hedges also confirmed the view that the skull is a vessel of psychic energies:

> It is at least 3,600 years old and according to legend was used by the high priest of the Maya when performing esoteric rites. It is said that when he willed death with the help of the skull, death invariably followed. It has been described as the embodiment of evil.

However, the antiquity of both the Museum of Mankind and the Mitchell-Hedges skulls has recently been questioned. In 1995, a detailed reexamination, using a high-powered microscope, of the Museum of Mankind example revealed several minuscule cut marks on the teeth inside the skull that appear to have been made by a steel tool, probably a jeweler's wheel. This would mean that the Museum of Mankind skull was almost certainly a nineteenth-century creation.

Equally, the Mitchell-Hedges skull has been surrounded by controversy ever since it was discovered. Strangely for such a self-publicist, Mike Mitchell-Hedges said almost nothing about the skull in his autobiography *Danger My Ally* (1954), stating that "how it came into my possession I have reason for not revealing." He also said nothing about it to friends for the next sixteen years; neither did he mention it in his public lectures on returning from the expedition; nor did contemporary newspapers mention the skull; nor do any photographs of Anna with her spectacular find appear to have been taken for the expedition records. Suspicion is also aroused by the date when Anna supposedly found it, on her seventeenth birthday (in 1927).

Oddly, when it was first scientifically examined, in 1936, the skull was in the hands of London art dealer Sydney Burney. Burney kept the skull until 1943, when it was placed for auction at Sotheby's. According to notes made by the Museum of Mankind, who unsuccessfully tried to buy the skull at the sale, Burney then *sold it privately* to Mitchell-Hedges for £400. Although Anna explains this as the result of her father's having deposited the skull with Burney as security for a loan, then redeeming it when Burney pressured him by putting it up for auction, the overall effect is to place the circumstances surrounding its discovery in severe doubt. Coincidentally, it is only after 1943 that any connection between the Mitchell-Hedgeses and the skull can be documented. If the Mitchell-Hedges skull, like the one in the Museum of Mankind, is actually a modern piece, then the information derived from it by psychics must be equally dubious. Of what value are visions of fabled Atlantis when they are derived from staring into an object made in the nineteenth century?

Perhaps to be taken more seriously are the claims that people can access information from the past through reincarnation. The famous American psychic Edgar Cayce had a trance technique that he believed enabled him to tap into the previous incarnations of others. He recorded literally hundreds of "past lives," many of them supposedly from ancient Egypt or Atlantis. Other people have had no need of a therapist to help them remember living before. Sometimes such memories crop up in dreams, or quite spontaneously impinge on one's daytime thoughts. According to the account of Omm Seti, a wonderfully eccentric Anglo-Irish woman who believed she was a reincarnated Egyptian, it was a near-fatal accident when she was a child that jolted her into remembering her past life. Her sincerity and her knowledge of ancient Egypt were impressive enough that even Egyptologists did not dismiss her as a fraud.

The study of reincarnation is, naturally, a vastly complex matter. Part of the difficulties spring from different cultural approaches to the problem. While many people in the western world may have a gut feeling that we "come back" again after death, this is not the Judeo-Christian (or indeed Islamic) teaching, and belief in reincarnation has never been sanctioned by orthodox western religion. In other parts of the world, notably the Hindu and Buddhist countries of Asia (including India, Tibet, and China), reincarnation is simply taken for granted. Serious research therefore tends to be carried out in the East.

For many years Dr. Ian Stevenson, Carlson Professor of Psychiatry at the University of Virginia Medical School, has been researching possible examples of reincarnation among children, particularly in India. Many of the case studies are striking. Children, sometimes as soon as they can speak, begin to give details and opinions that sound like those of a fully grown person, including facts about jobs, relationships, and even the names of relatives from "another" family. In a surprising number of instances Stevenson and his team have been able to match these utterances with the lives of real people, who had sometimes lived in villages hundreds of miles away, but who had very often died a violent or tragic death.

Interestingly enough, of the convincing cases examined by Stevenson, none involve "reincarnation" going back more than two or three generations at the most. Indeed, some might argue from this that we are not dealing with reincarnation as such, but perhaps some form of telepathy, with information being transferred from the relatives of the deceased to newborn children. In some cases, the spirit of the deceased is said to have entered its new host after they were born—a phenomenon more like spirit possession than reincarnation. Whether the lack of cases going back more than a couple of generations is telling us something about the mechanics of reincarnation, or simply something about the nature of the evidence itself, has yet to be clarified.

All the same, the mass of evidence accumulated by Stevenson strongly argues that reincarnation is certainly worthy of serious study. Excepting the cases that are patently hokey—like the oft-repeated claims of having been Cleopatra, Napoleon, or Elizabeth I—we should treat with an open mind the claims that people can remember past lives from historical times.

A frequently cited case of historical reincarnation concerns psychiatrist Arthur Guirdham. He was working in the spa town of Bath in Somerset in 1961 when a "Mrs. Smith" came to see him suffering from nightmares. Indeed, she had been tormented by dreams of murder and massacre since she was a small child. Guirdham at first thought she was merely neurotic, but changed his view when Mrs. Smith showed him some stories she had written as a schoolgirl some twenty years before. In these often-horrific accounts she described her life as a member of the Cathar sect of southern France. The Cathars, who believed in reincarnation, had been wiped out in a bloody crusade in the thirteenth century. Smith herself remembered being burned at the stake. Told that he himself featured in the story, as her lover, Guirdham became intrigued and in 1967 visited the Cathar area to check Smith's recall of events against documents and with local historians. These all confirmed her stories as a highly accurate account of Cathar life and death. Yet Mrs. Smith denied ever having studied the Cathars in any way.

Further conversations with Smith revealed that many of her friends and neighbors had also played a part in her earlier life. Many of them confirmed it, making this an apparent case of group reincarnation.

Unfortunately, it is difficult to investigate the case further, for Mrs. Smith remains anonymous, while only one person has come forward claiming to be a member of the Cathar group and that individual's story has not been confirmed. Could this be a case of people interpreting their dreams in the light of strong influences from others, especially when a psychiatrist makes it scientifically respectable? And is it really believable that Mrs. Smith would *never* have tried to make sense of her vivid dreams by reading about the Cathars?

In cases of hypnotic regression, this problem is often thought not to apply, as it is argued that hypnotism can reveal long-buried and genuine memories. Arnall Bloxham was an experienced hypnotherapist who tried to use past-life regression as a way of curing patients of anxiety problems. In the 1970s he released a series of tapes he had made of subjects reliving former incarnations while under hypnosis. Of these, the most compelling were those recorded with "Jane Evans," pseudonym for a Welsh housewife who described in convincing detail seven previous lives—including that of the Roman matron Livonia, married to the tutor of the future Emperor Constantine (late 3rd century A.D.), and most famously, a Jewess called Rebecca who lived in the twelfth century in York in northern England.

St. Mary's Church, Castlegate, near the Coppergate road in York. The discovery of its crypt has been held to provide proof of reincarnation.

The Bloxham tapes made with Evans record Rebecca's life in great detail, up to the dramatic developments that led to her death. She dated the last years of her life quite precisely, mentioning the accession of King Richard (A.D. 1189–1199) and the specific year 1189, according to the Christian era. According to "Rebecca," the Jewish community in York was suffering from savage persecution. In fear of her life, Rebecca took refuge with one of her children in a small church "near a big copper gate." From the roof of the church she watched fires spreading all around. The end in sight, Rebecca and her child hid in the crypt beneath the church, but they were discovered and brutally murdered.

Historians investigating the case checked out the facts, and agreed that Rebecca's story fit well into the context of the historical anti-Semitic riots that took place in York in A.D. 1189. They were even able to identify the church where she had hidden as St. Mary's Church near Coppergate in York. The only problem was that the church had no crypt, as described in the tapes. But in 1975, during building work, a crypt *was* discovered in St. Mary's, thus confirming Evans's story. With this apparent proof to back it up, the case of Rebecca and the crypt became world famous as proof of reincarnation.

Yet there is another possible explanation of the extraordinary Bloxham tapes. Bloxham himself admitted that people were highly suggestible under hypnosis and that they could elaborate on information they had acquired by normal means but somehow forgotten. Detective work by psychic researcher Melvin Harris has shown how Evans's memories might be of a rather more mundane kind. The Roman matron Livonia strikingly resembles a character in a historical novel called *The Living Wood* by Louis de Wohl. Harris identified convincing sources for two more of Jane Evans's "seven lives." In each case comparison revealed that idiosyncrasies and fictional elements particular to the novels appear in the Bloxham tapes. One can only conclude that Jane Evans, one way or another, knew of these books.

No one novel has yet been fingered as the possible source of Rebecca's life, but there are certainly strong echoes of Sir Walter Scott's *Ivanhoe* (written in 1820). In this famous novel, set in Yorkshire, one of the two heroines is a Jewess called Rebecca, daughter of Isaac of York. (In the Bloxham tapes, "Rebecca" mentions an old Jew called Isaac also living in York.) *Ivanhoe* is set in exactly the same time period, the early reign of Richard I, whose lengthy Crusade in the Holy Land was partly financed by Jewish moneylenders. No sooner had the king set off than the populace in many towns turned on the Jews savagely, massacring them in crowds. Scott's novel, like the tape recordings, stresses how the wealth and rich clothing of Rebecca's family had bred jealousy and resentment among the English. A dramatic high point of *Ivanhoe* comes when a castle in which Rebecca is imprisoned is ravaged by fire, though Rebecca narrowly escapes with her life. It is not hard to see how many elements of Walter Scott's extremely well known novel were rearranged kaleidoscopically in Jane Evans's unconscious into a slightly different version.

Yet what of the apparent confirmation of Rebecca's story—the discovery of the crypt of St. Mary's? It should be noted that the claimed crypt spotted by a builder had to be hurriedly covered over again for safety reasons before any archaeological investigation could take place, so we merely have the workman's word that it was a crypt rather than a hole in the ground. Yet even assuming that St. Mary's genuinely does have a crypt, its existence hardly confirms a paranormal revelation. Crypts are one of the most common features of medieval churches. Against the apparent success of Rebecca in predicting the discovery of the crypt, there also stands a conspicuous error. Rebecca said the church in which she took refuge was near a "big copper gate." There is a "Coppergate" in York, but in medieval times (as now) it was the name of a road, not a gate. Nor did it have anything to do with copper. As Norse expert Magnus Magnusson, who took an interest in the Bloxham tapes, pointed out, the "copper" part of the name actually derives from an old Scandinavian word for "carpenters."

Unfortunately the historical accuracy of Jane Evans's "memories" probably reflects the meticulous way in which historical novelists research their subjects, rather than a paranormal phenomenon. The most famous of the Bloxham tapes seems to be a case of long-buried memories (gleaned from reading, or even listening to radio plays) innocently "replayed" when the subject, Jane Evans, was under hypnosis.

Indeed, one of the earliest investigations of past lives, at the beginning of this century, produced evidence of precisely this effect. The British Society for Psychical Research was examining a woman who claimed to take on the persona of a fourteenth-century lady called Blanche Poynings. Details of her contemporaries were exact and convincing, and the investigators marveled at this new source of information about the past. Until, that is, chief investigator G. Lowes Dickinson had the idea of asking how they might confirm the truth of the story:

"How can we confirm what you are telling us?"

"Read his will."

"Whose will?"

COUNTESS MAUD;

OR,

The Changes of the World.

A TALE OF THE FOURTEENTH CENTURY.

BY

EMILY SARAH HOLT,

AUTHOR OF
"MISTRESS MARGERY," "THE WHITE ROSE OF LANGLEY," ETC.

" With mercy and with judgment
My web of time He wove,
And aye the dews of sorrow
Were lustred with His love :
I'll bless the hand that guided,
I'll bless the heart that planned,
When throned where glory dwelleth,
In Immanuel's Land."
—MRS. COUSINS.

LONDON :
JOHN F. SHAW AND CO.
48 PATERNOSTER ROW.

[All rights reserved.]

Frontispiece and title page from *Countess Maud*, a novel by Emily Holt.

"Wilshere's."

"Where is it?"

"Museum. On a parchment."

"How can we get at it?"

"Ask E. Holt."

"Where is he?"

"Dead. There is a book. Mrs. Holt."

"Do you know where she lives?"

"No. Wrote a book. *Countess Maud* by Emily Holt."

When Dickinson tracked down Emily Holt's *Countess Maud*, he "discovered within it every person and every fact (with one or two trifling exceptions) which had been referred to in the supposed life of Blanche Poynings!" It is amazing that Bloxham and his supporters paid apparently no attention to this devastatingly cautionary tale.

Professor Stevenson, undoubtedly the world's leading researcher into reincarnation, is highly dismissive of hypnotic regression into past lives: "nearly all such hypnotically evoked 'previous personalities' are entirely imaginary." That is why he avoids this technique and usually works with children, the younger the better, so as to reduce the chance that they may have picked up information through reading or similar means. It is only to be regretted that careful researchers like Stevenson and his team were not to hand earlier this century, when little Dorothy Eady (Omm Seti) began recalling her life as an ancient Egyptian.

Of all the methods tried of psychically probing the past, the most down to earth, in more senses than one, is dowsing. Dowsing—also known as water divining or water witching—may have been used since time immemorial as a method of finding water, though the first certain records of the practice associate it with metal mining. A Viennese manuscript written by a surveyor about A.D. 1420 refers to the use of a divining rod to detect "metallic exhalations" from the earth, and by the sixteenth century dowsing for metal had become an established geological method in Germany.

The method used to dowse for water and metals is much the same. A dowser holds in his hands a "dowsing rod," a device that can be as simple as a forked twig, but balanced in such a way that it can move easily. When the dowser passes over water, the rod will twitch. It is generally assumed that it is not the rod itself that is "picking up" information from beneath the ground but that a sixth sense informs the dowser, with subconscious muscular reactions causing the rod to react.

The vast majority of attempts to scientifically test dowsing have involved the detection of water. None of these has demonstrated that the success rate of the dowsers tested was statistically above chance. But the great problem with the results of mass dowsing experiments is that those taking part could include both talented and untalented dowsers. Taking a statistical measure of the overall success rate at detecting water flowing through pipes or concealed water bottles may therefore show only how variable the abilities of dowsers are, rather than debunking the whole idea of dowsing. Dowsing seems to be one of those intuitive skills that does not lend itself readily to laboratory testing and can vary considerably according to the circumstances.

The fact remains that dowsing is accepted as a method of finding water by highly practical people such as farmers, who don't lightly throw away their hard-earned money on parapsychological experiments. In Britain, both farmers and the water authorities employ professional dowsers to help them find water. (Skeptics might argue,

Sixteenth-century dowsers prospect for metals. From the *De Re Metallica* of Georgius Agricola (1556).

however, that a well drilled almost anywhere will come across water.) And surprisingly enough, dowsing has been used extensively by archaeologists during this century. This has usually been on a casual basis, with dowsing thrown in as an "extra" technique that, as it involves no financial outlay, means the excavators have nothing to lose by trying it. Nothing to lose, that is, except their scientific credibility, which is why dowsing is rarely mentioned in archaeological site reports.

Because of dowsing's fringe reputation, archaeologists have been reluctant to organize rigorous tests. (Doing so would eat into the already limited budgets for excavation, so archaeologists happily pass the buck to parapsychologists.) The results of one early experiment, carried out in 1958, were also rather off-putting. The abilities of a single dowser, who offered himself for testing, compared unfavorably with those of a magnetometer, a device for measuring local variations in the earth's magnetic field. The dowser failed to locate a reburied Roman pottery kiln, while the magnetometer had no problem finding it.

A much broader range of tests was carried out during the 1980s by two experts on medieval church archaeology, Richard Bailey of the

Dowser Denis Briggs at work.

University of Newcastle and Eric Cambridge from Durham University. They were contacted by Denis Briggs, a retired engineer who had begun dowsing a number of churches in the north of England and felt that he could detect traces of vanished structures that would be of interest to archaeologists. Bailey and Cambridge decided to test his claims, sometimes confirmed by other dowsers, with excavation wherever possible. By 1988 they had been able to assess his dowsing results at thirteen churches and published the results as a book.

Excitingly, Bailey and Cambridge were able to confirm the features located by Briggs at eight of the sites. (The other five tests were less successful.) In the cases where the excavations matched the dowsing predictions there was often a remarkable level of accuracy, with buried walls being uncovered within inches of the lines drawn by the dowsers.

Even where there were no archaeological remains to match Briggs's dowsing responses, in one case the intriguing possibility emerged that he was picking up some trace of temporary features. At St. Mary's Church in Ponteland, Briggs and half a dozen other dowsers had detected traces of a division running across the church and a rectangular area at its eastern end. Although no sign of these

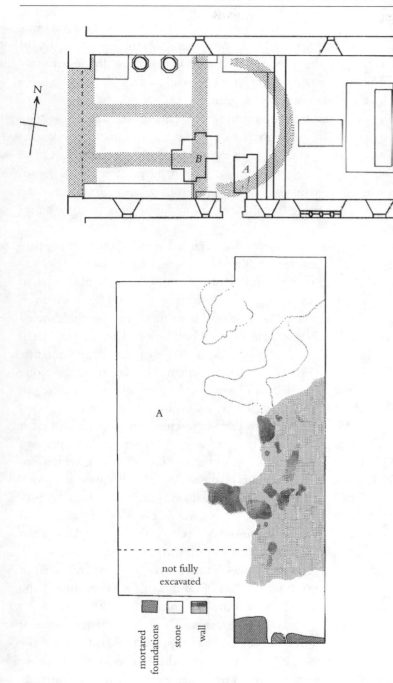

(Top) Plan of the chancel of St. Mary's Church, Woodhorn, northern England. The shaded areas indicate features that Denis Briggs claimed to have detected by dowsing. *A* and *B* are the archaeological trenches dug to test his findings. (Below) The results from trench *A* compare very well with Briggs's dowsing results. Trench *B*, however, revealed nothing to match Briggs's plan. As in the case of St. Mary's Church in Ponteland, the excavators suggested that Briggs may somehow have detected the pattern of 19th-century wooden seats and steps long since removed.

not fully
excavated

mortared
foundations

stone

wall

features emerged during the excavation, an architect's plan from 1972, consulted after the dowsing, showed that a wooden step and a plinth for an altar had been set on the floor here between 1885 and 1972. So had the dowsers somehow detected an imprint of this church furniture even though it had left no physical trace? This possibility would undermine any theory that the dowsers were picking up traces, say, of magnetism from the ground, and means that supposedly negative results from other sites may also have been cases where features invisible today have left some kind of imprint.

Bailey was cautiously optimistic in his conclusion, acknowledging that "archaeologists are rightly on their guard against the extravagant claims flooding in on them from the wilder shores of the occult," but warning them at the same time of the dangers of a closed mind: "Nevertheless, it would be equally dangerous if, through fear of scorn from their fellow professionals, they ignored what appears to be a tool of great value."

His pro-dowsing pleas have not been answered, despite this apparent passing of a rigorous test. This is, perhaps, because of the very nature of the experiment. While churches are obviously ideal sites in that they are likely to produce hidden features that can be dowsed for, they are also built on quite standard plans. In every case the dowsed walls fit with the plan of the existing building and might have been predicted by someone with a good knowledge of church architecture. Even the Ponteland steps and altar are in entirely logical places. None of Briggs's work revealed an earlier building on an entirely different plan from the current church or utterly unsuspected rooms.

The verdict on the church dowsing experiment has to be that it was a valiant but flawed attempt, and until a dowser produces plans of a completely unknown building in the middle of a field, which can then be confirmed by excavation, archaeologists will not be abandoning their high-tech equipment for the dowsing rod.

The same applies, of course, to the use of every other paranormal technique that has been suggested as having value for exploring the past. In each case—from reincarnation, through conversations with spirits and "angels" to psychometry and dowsing—the verdict has to be a resounding "not proven." But of course this is the nature of the supernatural world itself. When the day comes that a given paranormal phenomenon is proven—in terms of modern science—then it will probably no longer be regarded as supernatural. And while the human race's boundless fascination with the "unknown" may have led to many false—even sometimes bizarre—trails, it is an intrinsically healthy one. However far science progresses, there will always be more unknowns. The day we stop searching for answers to the great mysteries of life and death will be the day we cease to be truly human.

THE CURSE OF TUTANKHAMUN

Almost as well known as the discovery of Tutankhamun's tomb itself is the belief that it was protected by a powerful curse. When Egyptologist Howard Carter and his wealthy patron Lord Carnarvon opened the tomb on November 26, 1922, they, and the world with them, marveled at the spectacular discovery. The long-lost tomb of the boy Pharaoh Tutankhamun, who had died at age eighteen about the year 1320 B.C., was the most amazing treasure house of Egyptian antiquities ever discovered, crammed with furniture, statues, clothing, ornaments, weapons, and a whole host of other objects to enable him to lead a comfortable existence in the afterlife. Yet was there something else in the tomb? Starting with a mysterious illness that struck down Lord Carnarvon, a series of inexplicable disasters blighted the lives of those associated with the discovery—even visitors. Had the excavators, by desecrating the tomb, unwittingly unleashed some malignant force?

"Wonderful things . . ." These treasures heaped up in the antechamber were the first objects glimpsed by Carter and Carnarvon when they pierced a hole in the outer door of Tutankhamun's tomb.

Lord Carnarvon (left) and Howard Carter begin removing the stones that sealed the door to the inner chamber (sepulchre) of Tutankhamun's tomb.

Work on the tomb had begun smoothly enough. On November 5, Carter had uncovered a doorway marked with Tutankhamun's name, and immediately sent a coded telegram to Carnarvon, who was on his family estate at Highclere Castle in England:

> AT LAST HAVE MADE WONDERFUL DISCOVERY IN VALLEY STOP A MAGNIFICENT TOMB WITH SEALS INTACT STOP RE-COVERED SAME FOR YOUR ARRIVAL STOP CONGRATULATIONS ENDS

On November 23, Carnarvon and his daughter Lady Evelyn Herbert arrived at Luxor, and Carter could resume work. After three days of heavy labor the workmen had cleared the 30-foot length of passage leading down into the tomb. Tension was high as the moment of truth neared. In Carter's book *The Tomb of Tutankhamen*, written the following year with Arthur Mace of the Metropolitan Museum of Art (New York), there is no mistaking the drama of the occasion:

> The decisive moment had arrived. With trembling hands I made a tiny breach in the upper left-hand corner . . . candle tests were applied as a precaution against possible foul gases, and then, widening the hole a little, I inserted the candle and peered in. Lord Carnarvon, Lady Evelyn and Callender [an old friend of Carter's] standing anxiously beside me to hear the verdict. At first I could see nothing, the hot air escaping from the chamber causing the candle flames to flicker, but presently, as my eyes grew accustomed to the light, details of the room within emerged slowly from the mist, strange animals, statues and gold—everywhere the glint of gold. For the moment—an eternity it must have seemed to the others standing by—I was struck dumb with amazement, and when Lord Carnarvon, unable to stand the suspense any longer, inquired anxiously, "Can you see anything?", it was all I could do to get out the words, "Yes, wonderful things."

That day Carter came face-to-face with history and ensured himself a place in it.

The official opening of the tomb took place on November 29, in the presence of both British and Egyptian officials, and Arthur Merton of the London *Times*, whose report, printed the next day, set the whole world talking.

For the time being the excavation slowed down, as Carter tried to figure out how to deal with this momentous discovery. During December he put together a team of experts with help from the Metropolitan Museum of Art. Meanwhile, a herd of newspaper reporters had descended on the site, demanding access and stories to satisfy their news-hungry readers. Carnarvon's response was to sign an exclusive agreement with the *Times*; this was to prove a major source of resentment in later years.

After a Christmas break, the time-consuming task of cataloging the thousands of finds and supervising their safe removal commenced. Carter naively imagined this would take a few weeks. In fact, he was there until 1930, and the paperwork produced in recording the objects now fills a large room at the Griffith Institute in Oxford University.

Death of an Earl

Yet a tragedy was soon to strike that would overshadow the whole enterprise. Around March 6, Carnarvon was bitten on the cheek by a mosquito. While shaving he cut the bite and it became inflamed. After treating the cut with iodine and taking to his bed for a couple of days, Carnarvon felt well enough to travel to Cairo, where his daughter hoped he would recover completely under medical supervision. A week later he was running a fever and the blood poisoning caused by the cut had turned into pneumonia. Carter rushed to the bedside, as did Carnarvon's wife from England and son from India. The press found out and Lady Carnarvon's dramatic flight made front-page news.

With Carnarvon's life in the balance, the romantic novelist Marie Corelli contacted the *New York World* with the startling news that she had written to him, warning of the dangers presented by disturbing Tutankhamun's peace. She spelled out the reason for her concern:

> I cannot but think some risks are run by breaking into the last rest of a king of Egypt whose tomb is specially and solemnly guarded, and robbing him of his possessions. According to a rare book I possess . . . entitled *The Egyptian History of the Pyramids* . . . the most dire punishment follows any rash intruder into a sealed tomb. The book . . . names "diverse secret poisons enclosed in boxes in such wise that those who touch them shall not know how they come to suffer." That is

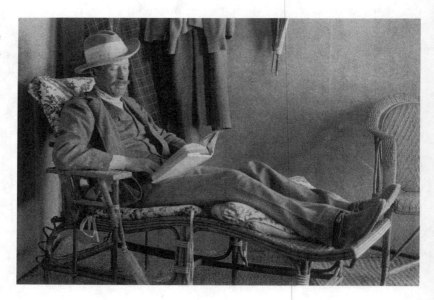

The calm before the storm. Lord Carnarvon relaxes on the veranda of Carter's Egyptian house.

why I ask, was it a mosquito bite that has so seriously affected Lord Carnarvon?

The worries expressed by Corelli increased as Carnarvon's condition deteriorated, with letters filling the correspondence columns of the newspapers. Many writers speculated on the possibility that the Pharaoh's resting place might be protected by unknown forces, either physical or mental. These fears reached a crescendo when Carnarvon passed away during the night of April 5.

The following day reporters besieged Sir Arthur Conan Doyle, creator of Sherlock Holmes, author of two of the great mummy horror stories, and now a leader of the spiritualist movement. He stepped down the gangplank of the SS *Olympic* onto American soil to be quizzed on his reaction to Carnarvon's death. According to the London *Morning Post*:

> He was inclined to support to some extent the opinion that it was dangerous for Lord Carnarvon to enter Tutankhamun's tomb, owing to occult and other spiritual influences. He said, 'An evil elemental may have caused Lord Carnarvon's fatal illness. One does not know what elementals existed in those days, nor what their form might be. The Egyptians knew a great deal more about these things than we do.'

Doyle's remarks are the official beginning of the theory of a curse on the tomb.

The following day, Doyle explained to the London *Daily Express* why he was so certain that occult powers had been at work in Carnarvon's death. This was not the first case he had seen of Egyptian black magic masquerading as illness. His good friend, the *Daily Express* reporter Fletcher Robinson (who had helped in the preparation and writing of Sherlock Holmes's greatest adventure, *The Hound of the Baskervilles*), had lost his life in a similar fashion several years previously.

Robinson had been investigating claims that a priestess's mummy held by the British Museum in London "had an evil influence." Doyle had warned his friend against pursuing the story, but he had carried on regardless and met an untimely death. As with Carnarvon, Robinson's demise apparently arose as a result of a straightforward illness, but again Doyle detected darker forces at work:

> The immediate cause of death was typhoid fever, but that is the way in which the elementals guarding the mummy might act. They could

have guided Mr. Robinson into a series of such circumstances as would lead him to contract the disease, and thus cause his death—just as in Lord Carnarvon's case, human illness was the *primary* cause of death.

At first the newspapers mostly ignored occult suggestions, instead pursuing Corelli's theory of poisonous traps, with the London *Daily Mail* suggesting that the deadly mosquito "may have previously settled on embalming fluids found buried with Tutankhamun." But Professor Percy Newberry, one of Carter's team cataloging the tomb's contents, swiftly disposed of that idea. He stated categorically that the Valley of the Kings itself was free of mosquitoes, so Carnarvon must have been bitten by one at Luxor on the Nile, where he was staying during the excavations.

But as time went on, further particulars came to light that made Carnarvon's death seem more mysterious. Highly significant was the report in the *Daily Express* that at the moment of Carnarvon's death a power failure had occurred:

> Suddenly all the electric lights in the Cairo Hospital went out, leaving them all in complete darkness. After a lapse of a few minutes the lights came on again, only to go out abruptly. This curious occurrence was interpreted by those anxiously awaiting news as an omen of evil.

Over the following weeks, more details emerged. Apparently, the entire electricity grid of Cairo had failed for five minutes at the moment of Carnarvon's death. British officials were said to have launched an urgent inquiry, which could come up with no technical explanation.

Then from the newly ennobled sixth Earl of Carnarvon came another piece of strange news. He reported that at exactly two in the morning on the night of April 5, Susie, his father's beloved pet dog, had howled and dropped dead.

Psychic Warnings

All this appeared to point in the direction of the occult: strange powers beyond the knowledge of ordinary people were at work. Two individuals sensitive to dark forces later revealed that they had, in fact, warned Carnarvon against meddling with a Pharaoh's final rest. The palmist Velma wrote that Carnarvon had consulted him shortly before

After removing two outer coffins of gilded wood, Carter was amazed to find inside yet another "made of solid gold!" Just over 6 feet long, this third coffin of Tutankhamun was "as much as eight strong men could lift."

leaving for Luxor in November 1922. Velma was concerned by a large spot on the lifeline of Carnarvon's hand and tried to alert him to the danger it foretold.

The clairvoyant Cheiro later provided an equally extraordinary revelation in his memoirs. While under the control of the spirit of Princess Makitaton, seventh daughter of Pharaoh Akhnaton, he wrote an urgent warning to Carnarvon from the other side:

> It was to the effect that on his arrival at the tomb of Tut-Ankh-Amen he was not to allow any of the relics found in it to be removed or taken away. The ending of the message was "that if he disobeyed the warning he would suffer an injury while in the Tomb—a sickness from which he would never recover, and that death would claim him in Egypt."

In the aftermath of Carnarvon's untimely death, the popular newspapers began to carry revelations that suggested that the danger had been known not only to Carnarvon himself but also to the whole excavation team. Nevertheless, their lust for fame had led them to press on without regard to their own safety, concealing the warnings they had been given.

Many stories circulated concerning an inscription found over the entrance to the tomb, buried by the excavators lest their workmen become frightened by it. A concerned Egyptologist had translated it and anonymously leaked it to the press—"Death shall come on swift wings to whoever toucheth the tomb of Pharaoh." In one highly imaginative account Carnarvon had had the nerve to replace the ancient curse with a tablet bearing his coat of arms, adding a touch of "pride before a fall" to the story.

Understandably, most Egyptologists tried to play down any idea of occult powers reaching out from beyond the grave to threaten them. Even here, however, there were a few brave souls who stood out against their colleagues to admit that they had seen things that could not be explained. Foremost among these apparently more open-minded Egyptologists was Arthur Weigall, ex–Chief Inspector of Antiquities for the Luxor region, who had acted as a special correspondent for the *Daily Mail* during the exploration of the tomb. In the summer of 1923 he brought out a book of reminiscences that included a chapter on "The Malevolence of Ancient Egyptian Spirits," with a mixed bag of anecdotal evidence: the Priestess's mummy case (which, despite Conan Doyle, didn't actually contain a mummy) connected with the Robinson death; other "unlucky" Egyptian objects; a possible spirit photograph; and the dramatic consequences of a light-hearted attempt to contact the spirit of Akhnaton.

Weigall told one story specifically related to Tutankhamun—the tale of Carter's canary. This fine songbird was eaten by a cobra, which somehow got into its cage on the very day that the entrance to Tutankhamun's tomb was uncovered:

> Those who believed in omens, therefore, interpreted this incident as meaning that the spirit of the newfound Pharaoh, in its correct form of a royal cobra, had killed the excavators' happiness symbolised by this song-bird so typical of the peace of an English home.

Weigall ended his discussion of the darker side of Egyptology by stressing his willingness to consider this controversial topic:

> I have heard the most absurd nonsense talked in Egypt by those who believe in the malevolence of the dead; but at the same time, I try to keep an open mind on the subject.

In April 1926, the press reported that Dr. Douglas Derry of the Cairo Medical School had discovered something strange during the examination of Tutankhamun's mummy. On the Pharaoh's face was a blemish in exactly the same place as Carnarvon's fatal mosquito bite. Weigall commented to the *Morning Post* on this striking "coincidence":

> While I cannot exactly say that I subscribe in believing the efficacy of such curses, I must admit that some very strange things—call them co-incidences if you will—have happened in connection with the Luxor excavations.

With even Egyptologists themselves accepting that there might be some evil power at work, it was only to be expected that the British Museum began to be inundated with packages sent by anxious collec-tors of Egyptian antiquities who feared themselves to be under a simi-lar curse.

The Curse Spreads

After Carnarvon's death there followed a string of tragedies that could be linked to Tutankhamun. Only a few months later Carnarvon's half brother, Colonel Aubrey Herbert, died of septicemia after a minor operation. Then Dr. Evelyn White, an Egyptologist at Leeds University, England, killed himself in a taxicab in September 1924. According to the *New York Times*, he had removed fragments of ancient books from a monastery in Egypt and feared the consequences. He left a note giving his reasons for his appalling decision: "I know there is a curse on me, although I had leave to take those manuscripts to Cairo. The monks told me the curse would work all the same. Now it has done."

The toll of victims attributed to the perils of disturbing the Egyptian dead mounted rapidly. George Jay Gould, the millionaire American collector of antiquities and friend of Carnarvon, died of a sudden fever just twenty-four hours after persuading Carter to show him the tomb. The doctors declared him to be a victim of plague, but not everyone was satisfied with this verdict.

On March 26, 1926, the *New York Times* reported yet another tragedy under the headline "Sixth Tomb Hunter Succumbs in Egypt—Dr. Mardrus Advances Theory of Strange Force." The new victim was Professor Georges Bénédite, Director of Egyptian Antiquities at the Louvre Museum, Paris, who had fallen while visiting the tomb and then contracted pneumonia. Dr. J. C. Mardrus, translator of the *Arabian Nights*, asked by the newspaper to comment, was not afraid to voice his fears of an occult involvement:

> This is no childish superstition which can be dismissed with a shrug of the shoulder. . . . We must remember that the Egyptians, during a period of 7,000 years, in order to assure the calm of subterranean existence which was supposed to delight their mummies and prevent all attempts to disturb their rest, practised magical rites the power of which held no doubts for them. I am absolutely convinced they knew how to concentrate upon and around a mummy certain dynamic powers of which we possess very incomplete notions.

By 1934, Herbert Winlock, the Director of the Metropolitan Museum of Art, was able to compile an impressive list of "Victims of the Curse, According to the Newspaper Reporters." To the deaths of Lord Carnarvon and his two half brothers (Mervyn Herbert died suddenly at the age of 41 in 1930), along with Evelyn White and Georges Bénédite, Winlock was able to add several more fatalities: Dr. Archibald Reed, an X-ray specialist, of exhaustion, after examining Tutankhamun's mummy; Arthur Mace, Carter's assistant, of pleurisy;

Carnarvon's secretary, Richard Bethell, of a heart attack; Bethell's grief-stricken father, Lord Westbury, by suicide; an eight-year-old child knocked down by Lord Westbury's hearse; Prince Ali Kamal Fahmy Bey of Egypt, who had entered the tomb, murdered in London; an attendant in the British Museum who had dropped dead while labeling objects from the tomb; and, ironically, given his own writings on the subject, Arthur Weigall, of a fever.

Even long after the participants in the violation of Tutankhamun's rest were themselves all dead and buried, the curse continued to reach out. In 1972, Egypt's Director General of Antiquities, Dr. Gamal Mokhtar, died as Tutankhamun's treasures were moved to England for an exhibition. In 1978, the London *News of the World* revealed the misfortunes of the crew of the airplane that had flown the Tutankhamun relics over to England—a catalog of heart attacks, injuries, and personal disasters.

Even today, it seems, those who inquire too deeply into such matters are putting themselves at risk. In 1992, the historian Christopher Frayling wrote and presented a series for the BBC on the impact of the boy Pharaoh's discovery on the western world, including an investigation of the curse. He recounts a whole series of incidents, several of which could easily have ended in tragedy:

> The lights abruptly going out when I first mentioned the curse while standing over Tutankhamun's glass-topped sarcophagus deep within the tomb itself; the sound packing up, for no apparent reason, when I started my commentary next to the gold portrait mask of the pharaoh, in the Egyptian Museum in Cairo; the director suffering a sudden trouble with the gallstones (the illness that Howard Carter himself suffered in the early 1920s) midway through the shoot; the snapping of the main cable holding up the elevator in the Cairo hotel where we were staying, and its dramatic fall for twenty-one floors with the director and the presenter still in the elevator; a very nasty respiratory attack . . . virtually the entire crew getting conjunctivitis after we had filmed a night-time sequence in the Valley of the Queens about [Weigall's attempt] to raise the ghost of Akhenaton.

Statuette of the boy-pharaoh Tutankhamun.

The Curse of the Curse

From the time the curse stories began appearing in the newspapers there have been vigorous attempts to find alternative explanations for the apparent catalog of fatalities associated with Tutankhamun.

The most prosaic theory—that the curse was invented to keep thieves at bay—was touted in an interview with apparently the last survivor of Carter's expedition, published in the *Daily Mail* in August 1980. Richard Adamson's story was remarkable. A military policeman in Egypt, he had been seconded to assist Carter in packing up and moving out at the end of the work, but on November 4, just as they were about to abandon the search for Tutankhamun's tomb, the entrance was found.

Clearly some drastic action was needed to prevent the ever-present grave robbers from ransacking the tomb. Adamson himself was in charge of the guards, but they could be bribed or overwhelmed. Together with Carter he came up with a cunning ruse:

> Quite suddenly, we thought about a curse. Inscriptions laying curses on intruders had been found on the walls of tombs nearer Cairo and it so happened that a reporter had been hanging around asking about curses there. We saw no such inscriptions laying curses in Tut's tomb but, let's say, we didn't encourage him from thinking there was. With a wink and a nod from us he was quite happy to make up the tale of a curse over King Tut's tomb.

Adamson himself carried on guarding the tomb for seven years, sleeping in it on many occasions, without a single ghostly incident.

Naturally, skeptics have seized on Sergeant Adamson's recollections as the obvious explanation, but there is a whiff of unreality about his account. As Frayling notes, no photographs show him at the tomb and none of the many published works or private diaries mention his presence at all. Adamson is certainly wrong on one significant point. He claims that Carter was ready to give up and leave on the morning of November 4, yet Carter had only begun that season's excavation three days earlier! Neither does the chronology match the newspaper stories, which really only featured the curse after Carnarvon fell ill. In any case, it is hard to imagine that Carter would really have believed that reports of a curse in English newspapers would have any impact on the activities of Egyptian thieves.

The most frequent attempt at a rational explanation has been that the tombs present health problems. One suggestion that appeared promising was the idea that mummies could pass on viruses. In 1962 a viral infection that spread through the Egyptian Antiquities Service was traced back to a mummy, but it was later discovered that the virus had been left on it by handling from a person already affected.

More frequent are suggestions that some deaths at least were brought about by a condition related to histoplasmosis, which often attacks cave explorers. This unpleasant disease is caused by a fungus that thrives in bat droppings, and can be inhaled in the dust created as the droppings dry out. It produces pneumonia-like symptoms, which was the diagnosis for several of the dead. R. G. Harrison, Professor of Anatomy at Liverpool University, followed up the theory while in Egypt examining Tutankhamun's mummy. He found out from local villagers that during the first few months bats would enter the passage to spend the night inside, and that Carter would ask them to shoo the bats out in the morning. From accounts of Carnarvon's illness, Harrison concluded that histoplasmosis was a likely candidate:

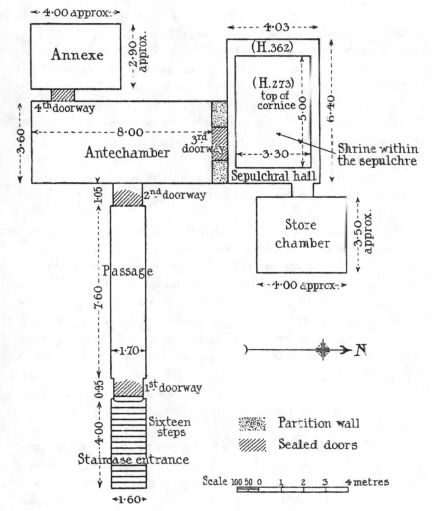

Howard Carter's plan of the tomb.

We may never know for certain, but the evidence strongly suggests that Lord Carnarvon's death was due to inhalation of dust containing the fungus histoplasma from dried bat-droppings in the passage leading to King Tutankhamun's tomb.

The main problem with this attractive theory is that there is no contemporary record of the bats. Perhaps they were just such a common problem that no one thought to remark on their presence. It is also difficult to imagine that bats would have carried on living in the passage for any length of time in the circumstances described by Harrison. They are timid creatures, and if repeatedly disturbed while roosting, they will simply leave and find a quieter spot elsewhere.

Whatever the merits of the histoplasmosis theory, there is little doubt that Egypt was a very unhealthy place to spend any time in. Breathing in dust, whether contaminated or not, day in day out, would hardly have done much good for Carnarvon's respiratory difficulties. As Frayling puts it, "I simply can't fathom why Victorian and Edwardian Britons went to Egypt *for the healthy climate*."

So what is the real story behind the curse of Tutankhamun? Unfortunately, much of the accumulated evidence seems to be a matter of exaggeration and downright lies. In the case of Carnarvon, we know that he was in poor health, that he was susceptible to insect bites, and that even after he took ill he continued to ignore his doctors' advice. His death may have been tragic, but it was hardly mysterious.

Winlock compiled his list precisely to show the kind of misrepresentations that the newspapers were peddling. For example, neither Evelyn White nor Carnarvon's half brothers had anything to do with Tutankhamun; Bethell's involvement was minor, and his father's death and that of the child stemmed from Bethell's early demise; Mace was already a sick man before the expedition started; Prince Ali may well never have visited the tomb, and was in any case shot by his jealous wife, as a consequence of years of philandering; no items from Tutankhamun's tomb went to the British Museum, so no attendants could have suffered as a consequence; and Weigall, although an Egyptologist, was not part of the expedition and as a reporter was able to enter only along with tourists.

Weigall himself was responsible for fanning the belief in the curse, giving it some academic respectability by virtue of his Egyptological standing. It seems as though he was bitterly resentful of the monopoly given to the *Times* by Carnarvon. In January, Weigall had appealed against his exclusion to his ex-colleague Carter, and indeed he was a special case as the only Egyptologist acting as a correspondent. However, Carter and he had never seen eye-to-eye and Carter was not about to show him any special favors. For Weigall, playing up the curse was a way of guaranteeing good newspaper coverage for himself and boosting sales of his book. Nor was he above bending the evidence. Whereas Weigall reported the dramatic story of Carter's canary and the cobra as taking place on the very day of the tomb's opening (November 4), other witnesses recorded the event as happening in mid-December.

Other events seemed peculiar only because they fit in with the curse. Carnarvon's dog presumably died because she was pining for her absent master, and the coincidence of their deaths—if really true—could be simply that. The lights going out at the time of Carnarvon's death and during the making of Frayling's program are hardly surprising when the average condition of Egyptian electrical grids and wiring is considered. Frayling himself saw no occult influences behind this or any of the other disasters that plagued his filming trip.

But what about the curse above the door? Here we enter the realms of pure invention. No curse was found here or indeed anywhere in the tomb, although there was a protective spell on a reed torch next to a statue of the dog-headed god Anubis, guardian of the tomb. This is concerned with holding back the desert sand rather than archaeologists. Indeed, curses are fairly rare in Egyptian tombs, nearly always occur on private tombs (not those of the Pharaohs), and are unknown from Tutankhamun's time. In any case, what the ancient Egyptians were afraid of was damage to the mummy or the tomb that would render the dead individual unidentifiable. As Weigall himself admitted, this made Egyptologists unlikely victims:

> The mummy and the tomb were the earthly home of the disembodied spirit, and to wreck either was to render the spirit homeless and nameless. On the other hand, to enter a tomb for the purpose of renewing the dead man's memory was always considered by the Egyptians to be a most praiseworthy proceeding. . . . Thus the scientific modern excavators, whose object is to rescue the dead from that oblivion which the years have produced, might be expected to be blessed rather than cursed for what they do. Only the robber would come under the scope of the curse.

Weigall's views are borne out by the longevity of many of the people who were first to enter the tomb and of the main investigators on

Carter's team. Carter himself died of a heart attack at the age of sixty-six in 1939, his friend Callender dying (also over sixty) about the same time, while Lady Herbert was alive until 1980. As three of the four people to enter the tomb first, their lives were surely at risk from any curse, while Carter should have been its prime target. Nearly all of Carter's experts were over seventy at the time of their deaths, many going on to successful careers in Egyptology. Dr. Derry, who unwrapped Tutankhamun's mummy, and therefore ought to have felt the wrath of the Pharaoh, lived for another forty-six years, to the age of eighty-seven. One might conclude, therefore, that the curse of Tutankhamun was a beneficial one for those most closely involved.

THE CASE OF OMM SETI

When Mr. and Mrs. Eady took their four-year-old daughter to the British Museum one day in 1908, they got more than they had bargained for. They were dreading the prospect of dragging a bored and fractious child around the museum. For the most part, little Dorothy was just that—until they reached the Egyptian galleries, where she suddenly sprang into action, exhibiting the most peculiar behavior. She ran around crazily, kissing the feet of the statues, eventually settling down by a mummy in a glass case and refusing to move. Her family wandered off and returned half an hour later to find her still rooted to the spot. Mrs. Eady bent down to pick her up, but Dorothy clung to the glass case and in a rasping, unrecognizable voice she barked: "Leave me here, *these* are my people."

Dorothy's odd behavior had begun a year earlier, with an incident that she was never to forget:

> When I was three years old, I fell down a long flight of stairs and was knocked unconscious. The doctor was called; he examined me thoroughly and pronounced me dead. About one hour later he returned with my death certificate and a nurse to "lay out the body," but to his astonishment, the "body" was completely conscious, playing about, and showing no signs of anything amiss!

After the fall Dorothy began to have a recurring dream of a large building with columns and a garden with trees, fruits, and flowers. She also entered a depressive stage, frequently bursting into tears for no apparent reason and explaining to her parents that she wanted to go home. Reassured that she was at home, she denied it, but could not say where she believed her real home was. The first glimmering of her lifelong conviction that she belonged in Egypt came only during the fateful visit to the British Museum.

Dorothy's obsession was confirmed a few months after the museum incident, when her father brought home part of a children's encyclopedia. It contained some photographs and drawings of ancient Egypt, which completely mesmerized her. Dorothy was particularly intrigued by a photograph of the famous Rosetta Stone (a trilingual text that had enabled the decipherment of hieroglyphics) and pored over it for hours with a magnifying glass. To the amazement of her mother, she declared that she knew the language it was written in but had merely forgotten it.

When Dorothy was seven the recurring dream of the large, columned building began to make sense to her. The catalyst was a magazine, which happened to include a photograph bearing the caption "The Temple of Seti the First at Abydos." She was utterly transfixed by the photograph. "*This* is my home! *This* is where I used to live!" she shouted gleefully to her father, followed by a wistful note— "But why is it all broken? And where is the garden?" Her father told her not to talk such nonsense—Dorothy could not possibly have seen that building, which was far away and built thousands of years ago; besides, they don't have gardens in the desert.

Forty-five years later, Dorothy Eady, now an employee of the Egyptian Antiquities Department, went to work at Abydos, taking up residence in a small house not far from the Temple of Seti. As far as she was concerned, she was "home" and she stayed in her beloved Abydos from 1956 until her death in April 1981. By then she had come to be known to all and sundry as Omm Seti, meaning "Mother of Seti," the name of her half-Egyptian son.

As for the garden that haunted her, sure enough, archaeologists eventually discovered it just where she claimed it would be, on the southern side of the temple.

The Lure of Egypt

Dorothy Eady was certainly one of the most extraordinary characters of the twentieth century. No one who met her could fail to be charmed by her personality; she was artistic, feisty, funny, fearlessly single-minded, and perfectly eccentric. Whatever one makes of her claims to be a reincarnated ancient Egyptian, her life was so colorful and romantic that few can match it.

In her early teens Dorothy Eady began her studies of Egyptology in earnest. Sir Ernest Wallis Budge, Keeper of Egyptian Antiquities at the British Museum and a pioneer in the field, took her under his wing and coached her in hieroglyphics during the hours she stole from school. Meanwhile, the strange dreams, as well as bouts of sleep-walking, continued.

Dorothy spent her late teens and early twenties with her family in Plymouth, on the south coast of England, where her father opened a cinema. She continued her avid reading of anything Egyptological, studied drawing at the local art school, and attended meetings of a local group interested in reincarnation, her first opportunity to pursue openly her conviction that she had once been an ancient Egyptian. But she found the meetings unsatisfying. When one member suggested that she may have had several incarnations, including Joan of Arc, her reaction was simply "Why the hell should I have been Joan of Arc!" She tried a local spiritualist group, which suggested that, rather than being a reincarnation, she *had* actually died when she tumbled down the stairs, and that her body had been possessed by a discarnate ancient spirit. Again, she does not seem to have been satisfied with this explanation.

Eady's first real step toward approaching her own reality came at the age of twenty-seven, when, against her parents' wishes, she went to London to take a job with an Egyptian public-relations magazine. She drew political cartoons and wrote articles in support of Egyptian independence from Britain. At the House of Commons she bumped into a handsome young Egyptian, Imam Abdel Maguid, and fell in love with him. Two years later she accepted his offer of marriage. Shortly afterward, in 1933, she packed her bags and sailed off to Egypt—much to the consternation of her parents—and almost immediately on arrival became Mrs. Abdel Maguid.

The Mother of Seti

Soon after the wedding day it became clear that Dorothy had merely replaced her long-suffering parents with a long-suffering husband. Imam was devoted to the modernization of Egypt—he worked in Egyptian education—whereas Dorothy cared only about its ancient past. They rapidly fell out over a choice of accommodation, Imam wanting to live in the center of modern Cairo, Dorothy in the suburbs so that she could gaze out over the Pyramids.

Despite their problems, Mr. and Mrs. Maguid soon had a child. It was a boy, whom Dorothy insisted, against her husband's wishes, on calling Seti, after the famous warrior Pharaoh who ruled at the beginning of the Nineteenth Dynasty (about 1300 B.C. on the generally accepted dating). It was after that, following the polite Egyptian custom of not referring to women by their first name, that Dorothy Eady came to be known as "Omm Seti."

Still, the appearance of little Seti did little to improve things. Unfortunately Dorothy was preoccupied with questions far beyond her family. In the second year of their marriage, Imam was frequently woken at night by his wife leaving the bed, sitting at a desk by the window, and scratching hieroglyphics on paper by the light of the moon. Omm Seti later described her state on those nights as "rather unconscious, as though I was under a strange spell, neither asleep nor awake"—as she heard a voice in her head slowly dictating Egyptian words to her. (The phenomenon is known to mediums as "automatic writing.") Omm Seti's midnight writing sessions lasted for almost a year, in which time she had filled about seventy pages with hieroglyphics that she pieced together and deciphered. The words, which she said were dictated to her by a spirit called Hor-Ra, described her earlier life in Egypt.

The mysterious writings, which Omm Seti felt were "true because of things I remember," said that in her earlier life she had been an Egyptian girl called Bentreshyt. Born of humble parents, she was sent to the Temple at Kom El Sultan (just north of the Temple of Seti, which was then being built), to be brought up as a priestess. At the age of twelve she had been asked by the high priest Antef whether she wanted to go out into the world and marry or remain in the temple. Unaware of the outside world, Bentreshyt elected to remain in the temple, where she took a vow to remain a virgin. She then underwent arduous training to play a part in the dramatized rituals of the temple, in which the death and resurrection of the great Osiris were reenacted.

Omm Seti kept the end of the story, in which Bentreshyt met Pharaoh Seti himself in the garden of his new temple, secret for many years—especially from her husband. In fact, she told him nothing about the significance of her nocturnal scribblings, which greatly disturbed him. Strange events continued to put a strain on their relationship. Imam's father came to stay with the couple, and ran out of the house screaming one night, exclaiming that he had seen "a pharaoh" sitting on Omm Seti's bed. After three years of marriage, Imam left to take up a teaching post in Iraq. As soon as her husband had left for

Pharaoh Seti I (c. 1300 B.C.). From a wall painting in his tomb.

Iraq, Omm Seti resettled, with her son, near the Great Pyramids of Giza (at first in a tent), and got a job as a draftsman with the Egyptian Department of Antiquities, becoming its first female employee.

For the next twenty years she assisted two leading Egyptologists, Selim Hassan and Ahmed Fakhry, in their work recording and excavating the pyramids of the Giza plateau and Dashur. Having trained at art school, Omm Seti was a skilled draftsman, and she was also invaluable as an editorial assistant, correcting or rewriting their English as Hassan and Fakhry prepared articles and site reports on their discoveries. Her contribution to Egyptology over these years was considerable, as was her knowledge. Dr. William Kelly Simpson, Professor of Egyptology at Yale University, was impressed by her grasp of the subject: "Some people know the Egyptian language backwards and forwards, but don't have a sense of Egyptian art; others know Egyptian art but not the language. Dorothy Eady knew them both."

Abydos

Though she was now in the land she loved, it is rather puzzling that Omm Seti did not make straight for Abydos, but waited nineteen years before making her first visit. "I had only one aim in life," she said, "and that was to go to Abydos, to live in Abydos, and to be buried in Abydos. [Yet] something outside my power had stopped me from even *visiting* Abydos."

When she did eventually go there for a short trip in 1952, she dropped her suitcase at the rest house of the Antiquities Department and marched straight to the Temple of Seti, where she spent all night lighting incense and praying to the gods. She returned again in 1954 for two weeks, then spent months badgering her employers to find her a position in Abydos. They were very reluctant; Abydos was then a tiny backwater village of mud-brick houses with no plumbing or electricity, where no one spoke a word of English. Not surprisingly, the Antiquities Department did not think it a fit place to send a single woman, especially a foreigner. In 1956, when Fakhry's project at Dashur finished, the department conceded and gave her a job at Abydos—recording the temple reliefs at two dollars a day. As young Seti had now moved to live with his father in Kuwait, she was free to go. Apart from a few short visits to nearby places, she remained in Abydos for the rest of her life. Shortly after her arrival she was involved in the archaeological work that discovered the remains of a garden at the Temple of Seti—the garden she had dreamed about all her life.

Pharaoh Seti approaches the goddess Sekhmet. A relief sculpture from his great temple at Abydos.

She lived in a small peasant house, with a succession of animals—cats, a goose, a donkey (called Idi Amin), and even the occasional snake. In the nearby temple she regularly made her devotions, openly worshiping the ancient Egyptian gods to the amazement of locals and visitors alike. The initial reaction of the villagers was to treat her with utmost caution, almost as a dangerous witch. But when they realized that nothing could intimidate her, their feelings changed to admiration and then warmth.

As the resident expert on ancient Abydos, Omm Seti became a tourist attraction in her own right. Everyone going there would try to meet her for a chat, and if they were lucky enough (or showed enough sincere interest), enjoy a personal guided tour of the temple, always peppered with examples of her irreverent, and sometimes ribald, sense of humor.

She never tried to proselytize on behalf of ancient Egyptian religion or force her views on anyone. Dr. Harry James, former Keeper of Egyptian Antiquities at the British Museum, stated: "She was in her devotion matter-of-fact and quite free from occult irrationalism." This was true, but only up to a point. The ancient Egyptian belief system, like most religions, was far from being "rational" in the sense that modern western science would understand the word. Omm Seti was, in fact, a great believer in the efficacy of ancient Egyptian magic. She demonstrated an extraordinary rapport with animals, with whom she felt she could communicate, and spoke of her experiences in charming snakes, even cobras—she was, at least, never bitten. Omm Seti also believed that the power of the Egyptian gods was still working through their sacred places, noting with evident pride that local Egyptian women, who were nominally Moslems, would come to touch the feet of a carving of the goddess Isis at the temple if they were worried they might be infertile.

She also made no secret of the conviction that was the driving force in her life. Without a shadow of a doubt, Omm Seti believed that she was a reincarnation of an Egyptian temple girl of humble origins, who had lived and worked in the Temple of Abydos during the reign of Pharaoh Seti. Whether this fit in with Egyptian thinking is hard to say; there is no written evidence that the ancient Egyptians believed in reincarnation as such.

No one who met her ever doubted her sincerity or the depth of her conviction. She was known to hundreds of Egyptologists, and worked closely with some of the best in the field. None had a bad word to say about her, and none dismissed her as a mere crank. Egyptology is a notoriously stuffy discipline, yet Omm Seti was calmly tolerated and accepted almost as one of its own, albeit a rather strange one.

Lover of Seti

But Omm Seti kept the most outrageous of her claims relatively secret, as they were of a deeply personal nature. She committed them to her diary and told only one friend about them in detail, her trusted colleague Dr. Hanny El Zeini.

A research chemist, industrialist, and dedicated amateur Egyptologist, Dr. El Zeini met Omm Seti at the Temple of Abydos, about nine months after she had set up home there. They eventually became firm friends and then colleagues. Together they spent twelve years researching and writing a number of publications, including *Abydos: Holy City of Ancient Egypt*, for which El Zeini took the photographs.

Early on in their relationship, El Zeini decided to check Omm Seti's claim to have predicted the location of the temple garden. He interviewed the foreman in charge of the excavators from the local village, who immediately showed El Zeini where the garden had been found. The irrigation channels were still visible. The tree stumps had been covered over again by sand, so the foreman quickly cleaned off two of them for El Zeini's benefit. A few months later El Zeini met the Antiquities Inspector responsible for the Seti Temple, and asked him about Omm Seti's role in discovering the garden. The Inspector replied:

> She was directly responsible for the discovery of those tree roots, and she was instrumental in the discovery of the tunnel running underneath the northernmost part of the temple. . . . She's not just a good "draftsman," but she seems to have an uncanny sixth sense about the terrain on which she walks, and she really stunned me with her very deep knowledge of the temple and its surroundings. . . . I would almost venture to say that she would be indispensable for any archaeological mission attempting any serious work in the Abydos area.

From then onward, El Zeini never doubted Omm Seti again. A mutual trust established, El Zeini came to learn the most incredible part of her story.

According to Omm Seti, the Pharaoh Seti fell in love with Bentreshyt, at the age of fourteen, when he met her in the temple gardens. Their liaison was dangerous, as the temple laws required her to remain a virgin. She became pregnant, and the temple authorities forced her to confess that she had a lover, threatening her with death for her crime. Fearing that she might implicate Seti if she were tried, Bentreshyt killed herself to protect her lover's name. When Seti returned to find her he was heartbroken, and vowed never to forget her.

Here the story becomes really incredible. Omm Seti says that when she was fourteen Pharaoh Seti kept his promise and actually "returned" to see her. As she explained to El Zeini about fifty years later, she was roused from her sleep one night by the sensation that something was pressing down on her chest. As she awoke she saw the mummified face of Seti staring down at her, with his hands resting near her shoulders: "I was astonished and shocked, and yet I was overjoyed. . . . It was the feeling of something you have waited for that has come at last. . . . And then he tore open my nightdress from neck to rim."

The next visitation came when Omm Seti moved to Cairo. Seti appeared to her again, this time not as a mummy but as a handsome man in his late fifties. The visits continued, and Omm Seti and her astral lover would spend night after night together. As if these claims were not bizarre enough in themselves, Omm Seti explained that the timing and extent of Seti's visits were all controlled by a strict moral code. Seti could return from the afterlife only because he had special permission from the Council of Amentet, the Egyptian Underworld, and under their scrutiny the lovers had to follow strict rules. Thus when Seti visited her as a married woman the meetings were strictly platonic. After she was divorced that was no longer the case, and Seti let her know that he planned to marry her himself when she joined him in Amentet.

The head of Pharaoh Seti's mummy. It was in this form that he made his first nocturnal "appearance" to Omm Seti.

It was this love affair with a ghostly pharaoh, Omm Seti explained to El Zeini, that was the real reason for the long delay in her "returning" to Abydos. For once at Abydos she would take on the role of a priestess again and have to remain a virgin. And this time Omm Seti was determined to follow the rules. That way, when she died, her previous crime would be forgiven and she and Seti could be properly united for all eternity.

During the last years of her life Omm Seti kept a record of her romantic encounters with a Pharaoh in a secret diary, begun at El Zeini's request.

Supernatural Knowledge?

On the face of it Omm Seti's claims, while romantic, touching, and extremely racy, are so far-fetched as to be ridiculous beyond belief. Yet their very audacity gives pause for thought. Would a woman of her intelligence and reputation have concocted such an elaborate yarn, replete with details spanning an entire lifetime? Omm Seti seems to have been utterly trustworthy, and certainly no one has ever accused her of lying about anything.

Then was she simply mad? Omm Seti herself considered this possibility, allowing that her fall down the stairs at an early age may have simply "knocked a screw loose." Yet in all other respects, including such frank statements as this, her personality showed every sign of being well balanced. Journalist Jonathan Cott, who has written the only biography of Omm Seti, discussed her mental state with a number of experts. A psychiatrist specializing in young people suggested that if a particular area of her brain had been damaged during the fall, it would have resulted in "long-term characterological discomfiture"—in other words she would have been left with a lasting feeling that she was not at home with her environment. The obsession with Egypt would have been a secondary effect.

Yet the simple conclusion of brain damage hardly explains Omm Seti's story. She exhibited no "problems" as such, even her obsessional desire to live in Egypt. That merely led her to her Egyptological career, which was successful in its own right, especially considering that she was a foreign woman working alone in an Islamic country. Dr. Michael Gruber, a prominent New York psychologist, asked by Cott to assess Omm Seti's story, concluded that while she lived in a parallel reality of her own, it did nothing to impair her ability to work within everyday reality. To the contrary, it merely enriched her normal life. In short, she was in no need of therapy or psychiatric help of any kind.

Someone once remarked about the British visionary poet and artist William Blake (1757–1827) that though he was a little "cracked," it was the crack that enabled the light to come through. By the same token, there is no point dwelling on whether Omm Seti was insane; it is surely better to evaluate her vision and experience on their own merits.

After all, is it merely our own—or rather, western—prejudice about reincarnation that makes her story seem so outrageous? Her case history matches very well with the best-evidenced cases produced by researchers into reincarnation, in which children, typically between the ages of two and four, begin experiencing "memories" that are not theirs (see **Introduction** to this chapter). Dorothy Eady was three when she had the accident that began her own experiences. If reincarnation as such was not involved in her case, was Omm Seti receiving information from the past by some other means? Were the most incredible parts of her experiences, involving the love affair with Seti, perhaps lucid and informative dreams that she had no other way of interpreting or explaining? Maybe she had an experience similar to that of the archaeologist Bligh Bond, who said that the "voices" of friendly "ghosts" helped him in his excavations at Glastonbury (see **The Company of Avalon** in this chapter).

However she learned about them, what are we to make of the things that Omm Seti claimed to "know" about ancient Egypt? No one has ever made a formal list and checked off those that have been subsequently proved or disproved. Her best-known claim, regarding the existence of a garden at the Temple of Abydos, loses its punch when we realize that practically *all* Egyptian temples had gardens. Still, a four-year-old child in 1908—when Egyptology itself was still in its infancy—could hardly be expected to know that. Further, we have it on the authority of Dr. El Zeini, who interviewed the workmen and antiquities inspectors involved in the discovery of the garden at Abydos, that she not only pinpointed its location but also led them to the site of a tunnel underneath the northern part of the temple. Indeed, her "sixth sense" about the site seems to have been universally acknowledged. She also repeatedly made another claim about the temple—that underneath it there lies a secret vault containing a library of historical and religious records. If discovered, it would be an archaeological sensation that would make Tutankhamun's tomb seem like small-fry. Unfortunately no one yet seems to have followed up her lead by searching for it.

Unlike her predictions about the location of the garden and tunnel—which came from her "own" memories, as it were—her claim about the hidden library chamber seems to have come mainly from these conversations with Pharaoh Seti. Extracts from these conversations, recorded in her secret diary, are published in Cott's biography and, fantasy or not, they make riveting reading. We are introduced to Seti's views on a wide range of subjects from sexual morality to the possibility of space flight, which Seti apparently deems "evil." (By an ironic coincidence the scientific program for searching for extraterrestrial life is called, in acronym, SETI.)

Among Seti's more specific archaeological claims, he told Omm Seti that he did *not* build the Osirion at Abydos and that it dates to long before his time. Seti also stated that the Sphinx was built for the god Horus and was much older than the reign of Pharaoh Chephren (c. 2500 B.C.), who is usually thought to have built it. Some early Egyptologists shared both these positions, which have been revived in

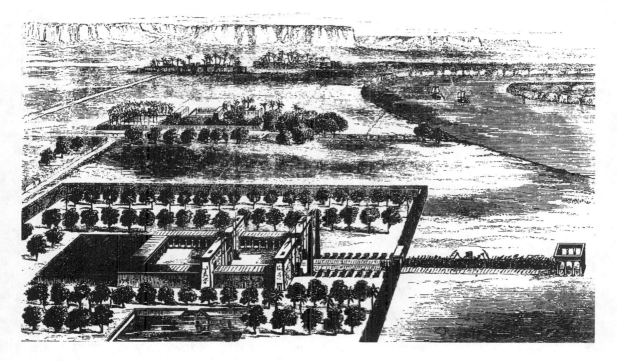

Reconstruction of a typical Egyptian temple with well-tended garden.

a number of nonacademic books. Many modern Egyptologists might agree that the Sphinx was not a likeness of Chephren (as once believed), preferring to describe it as a statue of Horus in his role as Sun god. Yet the rider, that the Sphinx may have been built *before* the time of Chephren, is presently a hotly debated issue (see **The Riddle of the Sphinx** in **Architectural Wonders**).

So, intriguing as they are, many of Omm Seti's substantial claims about Egyptian history still remain generally unconfirmed, and until her private diaries are published in full, it is impossible to produce a realistic "score sheet" of which claims might be right or wrong. A full analysis would make an interesting thesis, perhaps for a student majoring in both psychology and history, and would finally give us a better picture of Omm Seti's Egyptological ideas. Until then, unfortunately, we are left with a number of small insights she made about Egyptian customs and the reading of texts, and the apparent confirmation of her predictions about the Abydos garden and tunnel.

It is a matter of regret that someone as interesting as Omm Seti was never formally tested by parapsychologists. All we have is the anecdotal evidence of informal challenges. Omm Seti told the story of how, on one of her earliest visits to Abydos, she was tested on her knowledge of the temple by the Chief Inspector from the Antiquities

Department and two of his colleagues. It was nighttime, she related, and while the archaeologists had torches, she had none. Whichever part of the enormous complex they specified—and the temple was still uncataloged and unpublished at the time—she said she could run to it in the dark without taking a wrong turn or falling down a hole.

Yet unfortunately we have no real independent testimony of this test—no one ever interviewed the archaeologists in question, and the incident, as described, is known only from Omm Seti's memory of it. And from her own accounts, it is clear that Omm Seti must have been to the temple at least once already. On the very night she arrived in Abydos she went straight to the temple by herself. How much did she learn, or could she have learned, about the temple's layout during that first nocturnal visit?

False Memories?

Many people have "discovered" that they had lived in Egypt in a previous existence, either through dreams, conscious memories, or regression under hypnosis. But none of them has made a case as powerful or persuasive as Omm Seti. The strength of her claim lies partly in her undoubted and enormous devotion to the belief that she "belonged" in Egypt. It also rests on the narrative of the strange events of her childhood and the many anecdotes of her later life, which can make a considerable, cumulative impact—for example, when read as they are presented in the biography written by Jonathan Cott.

Yet it has to be said that the only evidence that we have about her crucial childhood experiences comes from Omm Seti herself. It is now far too late to interview anyone who knew her during those years. What of the doctor and nurse who she said "pronounced her dead" at the age of four? No doctor's report can be cited. What of relatives, and neighbors, who would have presumably known about the apparent tragedy, or witnessed or heard from her parents about her odd behavior at the British Museum, or at home? None of them, unfortunately, left any records, in diaries or interviews, giving their impressions of events. The same applies to her experiences in Egypt, including the trancelike states in which she received automatic hieroglyphic writing telling her of her past life, or even the story of her father-in-law running from the house because he had seen the ghost of "a pharaoh." In the end we really have only Omm Seti's word for any of these incidents.

Skeptics are free to wonder just where her memories of "death" and the British Museum incident came from. She never made clear whether they were her own memories or if she was remembering things that her parents told her. In any case, memories can be faulty, as is manifestly obvious and as recent research into the "false memory syndrome" has dramatically underscored. It is now well documented that people can sincerely "remember" things, ranging from being abused as children to being abducted by aliens, that never actually happened.

This is not to say that Omm Seti imagined all the experiences she described. Nor is it to deny the validity of her knowledge about ancient Egypt. One way or another, she provided numerous insights into ancient Egyptian life, literature, and archaeology. Yet nothing can be proved about the way in which she received her information. There are more ways than one to arrive at insights into the past. No modern person, western or Egyptian, has ever been so intimately acquainted with ancient Abydos as Omm Seti was, and it is doubtful whether anyone could ever be again.

While he admired her, Kenneth Kitchen, Professor of Egyptology at Liverpool University and an expert on Pharaoh Seti's family (the 19th Dynasty), drew attention to this obvious problem:

> Omm Seti came to all sorts of perfectly sensible conclusions about the actual, objective material of the Seti Temple—which may have *also* coincided with things that she felt she knew some other way—because she had time on the site that ninety-nine percent of us don't have . . . and that paid dividends. So even in a minimal interpretation, she had the opportunity to make many quiet little observations. Never mind the last life . . . *this* one was quite enough!

Other Egyptologists who met her were more moved, or rather confused, by her story. Dr. James P. Allen, former head of the American Research Center in Egypt, reminisced as follows:

> She was absolutely not a con artist. . . . Omm Seti really believed in all the craziness—she *really* did. She believed it enough to make it spooky, and it made you doubt your own sense of reality sometimes.

Maybe, one day, future archaeological discoveries will provide further vindication of Omm Seti's claims about ancient Egypt. If a magnificent library of records were ever discovered underneath the Temple of Seti there would certainly be cause to look at her claims in a completely new light. Yet even then, we would still have no way of determining where her insights came from. Were they simply based on her intimate knowledge of Abydos, as Kitchen suggests, or did her intuitions genuinely involve a paranormal element? Was this reincarnation, as she imagined, or was she receiving impressions from the past by some means she could not understand, and interpreting them in the only way she could? Or was it all, literally, a dream?

Alas, the chance of answering these questions in any satisfactory way disappeared the day Dorothy Eady died. Omm Seti will always remain an enigma. One suspects that, wherever she is now—hopefully, as planned, in Amentet (the Egyptian afterworld)—she would accept this situation with a knowing smile.

EDGAR CAYCE ON ATLANTIS

Edgar Cayce (1877–1945) has sometimes been hailed as the most successful psychic of the twentieth century. His most spectacular prediction concerned the rediscovery of the lost continent of Atlantis, confirmation of which apparently came more than twenty years after his death. Cayce foretold that part of Atlantis would "rise again" in 1968 or 1969 in the region of Bimini near the Bahamas. Sure enough, during those very years, mysterious underwater structures were discovered just where he predicted.

On what did Cayce base his extraordinary claim? Cayce committed to paper screeds of psychic "readings" about Atlantis, based on a curious method whereby he would "recall" the past lives of people who had come to consult him about their psychological problems. Believing that many people's deep-seated fears are the result of traumas in previous incarnations, Cayce would place himself in a trance and allow himself to be possessed by "entities" from their earlier lives. His utterings would be jotted down by an amanuensis and then interpreted. Clients must have felt that this was helping them in some way, as they kept coming, though one doubts whether Cayce's visionary counsel was always particularly useful. He calmly informed one couple that their son, whom they had brought along for treatment, had been Alexander the Great and Thomas Jefferson in previous lives, which may have led his parents to expect a little too much from him when he grew up.

No fewer than 2,500 of Cayce's "life readings" are on file, drawn from about 1,600 individuals. Of these about 700 involve Atlantean incarnations.

Atlantis Self-destructs

Cayce's "life readings" are littered with the most staggering claims about our prehistory. The human race, apparently, existed on Earth as long as 10 million years ago. Cayce's supporters have claimed this as another successful prediction, as fossils of our remote ancestors *australopithecus* date back a good 5 million years, and even earlier hominids to about 15 million years. The match is rather spoiled, however, by Cayce's belief that the earliest human beings existed only as ethereal, bisexual, "thought forms"—something rather difficult to trace in the fossil record.

At some unspecified date, the readings continue, these spiritual beings began to become more tangible and divided into five races—white, black, yellow, brown, and red. The red race developed a flourishing civilization on Atlantis, but at the expense of becoming more materialistic and tied to the gross matter of their bodies. The human race became completely physical, and Atlantis saw the first separation of the human race into two sexes.

The peace of Atlantis, however, was threatened by monstrous animals, "those of the beast form that overran the earth in many places." It has been suggested that Cayce meant dinosaurs, though they are generally thought (despite the films) to have become extinct about 63 million years ago. Explosives were developed to deal with the beasts, but drunk with the power of these new destructive forces, Atlanteans became monsters themselves. They turned to the forces of evil, even beginning the practice of human sacrifice. While spiritually depraved, they became technologically advanced, to a degree even greater than our own. The Atlanteans, according to Cayce, had gas balloons, airplanes, submarines, elevators, X-ray devices, "photographing at a distance," tape recorders, antigravity machines and, yes . . . television! Cayce's son later proclaimed it as a brilliant insight that Cayce had implied that television was "commonplace in Atlantis" and that "this reading was given before television was commercially profitable in the United States."

Cayce revealed that the most corrupted Atlanteans, known as the "Sons of Belial," developed a machine made of crystals that harnessed the rays of the Sun. The device overloaded, and in the resulting explosion, around 50,000 B.C., Atlantis split into five islands. Continued misuse of such powers brought about further destruction of Atlantis, in 28,000 and 10,000 B.C. The last was the final cataclysm (the one described by the Greek philosopher Plato—see **Atlantis—Lost and**

Found? in **Lost Lands and Catastrophes**), though many Atlanteans managed to escape to found colonies elsewhere in the world.

For the last days of Atlantis, it seems that Cayce had personal
knowledge, as he believed that he had once been a priest called Ra Ta,
who ruled in the Caucasus Mountains (southern Russia and Georgia)
about 10,500 B.C. Sensing the breakup of Atlantis, Ra Ta instructed
part of his people to go to Egypt, where they built the Sphinx and the
Great Pyramid. Near the Sphinx they constructed an underground
"Hall of Records," to house a library preserving the wisdom of Atlantis. A secret passage leads from one of the Sphinx's paws to this hidden treasure.

It was in the refugee areas—Egypt, Morocco, the Pyrenees, British
Honduras, Yucatán, and the Americas generally—that Cayce predicted direct "evidence of this lost [Atlantean] civilization are to be
found." This was claimed in 1932 (Reading No. 364-3), when he also
noted that the Bahamas were a portion of the lost continent "that
may be seen in the present." In the following year he stated that inscriptions recording how to construct the deadly "firestone" device of
Atlantis still survive in three places: Egypt, Yucatán, and "in the
sunken portion of Atlantis, or Poseidia, where a portion of the temple may yet be discovered under the slime of ages of sea water—near
what is known as Bimini, off the coast of Florida" (Reading 440-5).

It is not clear when Cayce felt that the inscriptions themselves
would be found, but in 1940 he specified the date when the Atlantean
fragment that sank near Bimini would be seen again: "Poseidia will be
among the first portions of Atlantis to rise again—expect it in '68 and
'69—not so far away" (Reading 958-3, 1940).

Beneath "The Slime of Ages"

Bizarre as Cayce's predictions may seem, striking confirmation
seemed to come in 1967 when pilots Robert Brush and Trigg Adams
spotted and photographed from the air a rectangular structure off the
coast of Andros, largest of the Bahamas. The published photographs
certainly suggest a submerged building. More was to follow, in " '68
and '69," just as Cayce had foretold. Brush and Adams showed their
photographs to Dmitri Rebikoff, an acknowledged expert on underwater photography. With zoologist Dr. Manson Valentine, who had
been exploring the Bahamas for many years in search of lost civilizations, Rebikoff examined the Andros site in 1968 and found a
building, some 100 by 75 feet, overgrown with seaweed. Valentine,
who had previously been involved in archaeological work in the

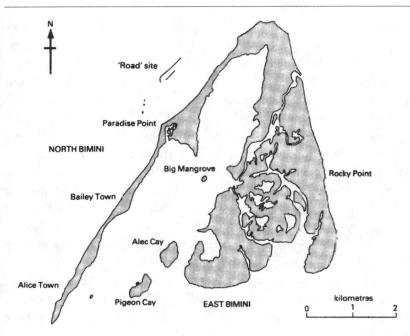

N

'Road' site

Paradise Point

NORTH BIMINI

Big Mangrove

Rocky Point

Bailey Town

Alec Cay

Alice Town

Pigeon Cay

EAST BIMINI

kilometres
0   1   2

Map of Bimini, a tiny island in the Bahamas near the coast of Florida. The *J*-shaped formation of stones claimed to be a megalithic road lies off the northern coast at Paradise Point.

Yucatán, compared its plan to that of the Classic Mayan temple at Uxmal, and, using the rather unusual method of judging its age from its depth underwater (about 6 feet), he concluded that the structure was pre-Columbian.

The very same year, Valentine's attention was drawn by a local fishing guide to an unusual J-shaped configuration of stones lying about 20 feet underwater off the coast of North Bimini. In the *News* of the Museum of Science in Miami (of which he is an Honorary Curator), Valentine reported:

> An extensive pavement of regular and polygonal flat stones, obviously shaped and accurately aligned to form a convincingly artefactual pattern. These stones had evidently lain submerged over a long span of time, for the edges of the biggest ones had become rounded off, giving the blocks the domed appearance of large loaves of bread or pillows of stone.

In an interview published in 1984, Valentine made it clear that he saw the finds as confirmation of Cayce's prediction of Atlantis "rising." The claim has been repeated in literally dozens of books and magazine articles. Meanwhile, diving for further traces of Atlantis has continued apace since the first discoveries and there has been an almost continuous stream of incredible claims. Some divers have "seen," but never managed to successfully photograph, temples, pillars throbbing with energy, and even pyramids, some capped with glowing crystals. (The safest explanation of these may be that the divers involved were suffering from a severe case of the "bends.") At the same time, many other psychics have picked up where Cayce left off and elaborated his case. After Valentine, the leading proponent of the Bimini-Atlantis link became Dr. David Zink, an English literature professor and accomplished diver whose expeditions regularly included psychics to perform readings on the spot. His main clairvoyant, Carol Huffstickler, revealed that the Bimini Road was actually part of a labyrinth, built by advanced beings from the Pleiades star cluster "on a kind of galactic missionary service." They constructed the labyrinth at Bimini as a sacred site that could utilize the Earth's magnetic field, "to raise consciousness and heal." Zink published these readings in all seriousness in his book *The Stones of Atlantis* (1978).

On a more down-to-earth level, the "Bimini Road" and the original structure found near Andros do have the virtue of being tangible objects that have been photographed and studied many times. So how do they stand as proof of Cayce's method of psychic archaeology?

The End of the Road

The Bimini Road became the subject of a protracted controversy soon after its discovery. In 1971, a professional geologist pronounced it to be naturally formed limestone "beachrock," fractured and eroded to give the appearance of large, rounded building blocks. Undismayed, Atlantis enthusiasts insisted that the joints between the stones were far too straight to be the result of natural cracking, and that no beach rock formations are known that are as regular or as elegant as the J shape of the "Bimini Road."

The dispute promised to run for perpetuity until, in 1980, Eugene Shinn of the U.S. Geological Survey published a summary of conclusive evidence he had collected from the stones. If the "Road" had been man-made we would not expect the grains and microstructure within the stones to be consistent from one "block" to another. Yet they proved to be so, in every conceivable test that Shinn applied, showing that they must have been laid by natural means. Further, radiocarbon tests on shells included in the stones gave dates that show the "Road" was formed between only about two to three thousand years ago—hardly the 10,000 years required by Cayce (or the 28,000 by Huffstickler). Finally, the much-vaunted hairpin curve in the "Road" was shown to be the result of its having formed off a section of coast that swung around sharply—the modern beachline parallels this curve today (see map).

The "Bimini Road" was clearly formed in the shallows of an old coastline only a couple of thousand years ago. As for the underwater "temple" near Andros that started the whole thing, Atlantologist David Zink correctly identified it as a sponge storage area built in the 1930s. (Valentine's assumption that its depth showed it was of great age was merely naive.) On the more positive side, Zink's team did find a fragment of worked stone with tongue-and-groove jointing near the "Road." They also found an amorphous lump of marble that, to the eye of the faithful, may be an eroded carving of a jaguar's head. Two swallows, however, do not make up for a bad summer. Without other finds to give them context, the objects might merely be pieces of discarded ship ballast. Some drum-shaped stones found nearby proved to be just that. Though the Atlantologists held them to be column fragments, chemical analysis showed that they were made of nineteenth-century cement. Had the Bimini region been a prominent center of Atlantis, as Cayce and his followers believe, we would surely expect something more convincing than the ambiguous scraps of evidence so far collected. One might have expected the Atlanteans to at least have left some pottery (if not the odd TV antenna).

The truth is that the whole saga of the Bimini "Atlantis" finds is a classic case of a self-fulfilling prophecy. Brush and Adams, the pilots who spotted the Andros structure in 1967, were flying over the area *because* they expected to find traces of Atlantis that year. They were both members of Edgar Cayce's Association for Research and Enlightenment—a fact often glossed over in reports of the "confirmed" Cayce prediction—and obviously wanted to get in early on what they expected to be the archaeological discovery of the century. They then involved Rebikoff, who in turn involved Valentine. Though Valentine says he had already been looking for prehistoric remains in the Bahamas for fifteen years before discovering the "Bimini Road," it is clear enough that his search intensified after the initial Andros discovery. Then Zink and all the others followed. Were it not for Cayce's predictions, it is doubtful that anyone would have associated the Bahama Banks findings with Atlantis in the first place. The shallow waters of the world's coastlines abound with curiosities, from geological features to sunken forests and towns. Perhaps the real surprise is that, despite all the intensive diving that has been done in the Bimini region over the last thirty years, no evidence at all seems to have turned up of pre-Columbian activity.

Now that the "slime of ages" has settled again on the remains of "Poseidia," it can be seen that the Bimini finds—even if they were genuine—match Cayce's prediction only extremely obliquely. Seen in the context of his other readings, it is clear that his prophecy concerned the actual *rise* of a portion of Atlantis in the region of Bimini as part of a massive series of geological upheavals. These would transform Europe "in the twinkling of an eye," tip most of Japan into the sea, break up western America, and raise sunken land in the Pacific as well as the At-lantic. The process would begin in 1958, and after massive disasters in 1976, would be tied in with the Second Coming of Christ by 1998. The fact that you are reading this shows that Cayce was plain wrong.

Perhaps the real marvel of Edgar Cayce is the number of people who have placed any faith at all in his strange utterances. What can one make of a man who claimed to have spent a previous life as a Libyan called Lucius, nephew of the New Testament physician Luke and the real au-thor of the Gospel erroneously credited to his uncle? Or who said he had been with "Mr. and Mrs. Lot" on the very day that Sodom and Gomorrah were struck by fire from heaven (see **Sodom and Gomor-rah** in **Lost Lands and Catastrophes**)? It speaks volumes about the judgment of authors like Graham Hancock, writing in the 1990s, that he can cite in all seriousness Cayce's dating of the Sphinx to "Atlantean times" or his fantasy about an Atlantean "Hall of Records" hidden under the Giza plateau (see **The Sphinx** in **Architectural Wonders**). If Cayce were right, Hancock and the other writers who have recently rediscovered him would probably not be alive.

THE COMPANY OF AVALON

If the ghosts of the past can make themselves heard anywhere, it will be at Glastonbury. Steeped in history, Glastonbury Abbey in Somerset is without doubt one of the greatest monuments of Christianity. It has even been said to be the oldest church in Europe.

King Ina, one of the earliest rulers of the Anglo-Saxon kingdom of Wessex, built a church here in the early eighth century A.D., yet Glas-tonbury was already hallowed ground. Before Ina's time there was the small wooden "Old Church," a gathering place for Christians for un-counted years that survived until a fire in A.D. 1184. Tradition held that this first church had a miraculous origin, in the earliest days of Christianity. According to a *Life of Dunstan*, the tenth-century saint who revived the Abbey after a long period of neglect:

In that place at God's command the first neophytes of the catholic law discovered an ancient church, built by no human skill . . . consecrated to Christ and the holy Mary.

The western end of Glastonbury Abbey church, constructed on the site of the "Old Church."

Writing early in the twelfth century, the chronicler William of Malmesbury, who saw the Old Church, added in the detail that it was supposedly built by Christ's disciples, but obviously felt that there was good reason for caution, ending his discussion with the statement that "I will leave such disputable matters and stick to solid facts."

In later medieval times the Old Church became linked in local tradition with the figure of Joseph of Arimathea. He was said to be Christ's uncle, a tin merchant who had visited Britain, and returned there as the leader of a group of missionaries in A.D. 63, bringing with him sacred relics. Abbot Bere, at the beginning of the sixteenth century, promoted Saint Joseph as Britain's apostle and miracle worker, and Glastonbury as the "holiest earth in England." Under the next abbot, Richard Whiting, disaster struck Glastonbury with the Dissolution of the Monasteries under King Henry VIII in 1539, when England became a Protestant country and the monastic orders were suppressed and their treasures taken to finance Henry's grand ambitions. Abbot Whiting was tried for robbery in the belief that he had secreted the Abbey's treasures, including the Grail, to keep them from the king's commissioners sent to strip Glastonbury of its riches. Following a swift trial with a foregone verdict, Whiting was hanged on a gallows set up on Glastonbury Tor, looking down on the Abbey. After he was dead, Whiting's body was cut into quarters and taken away for display in nearby towns, while his head was set over the gateway into the Abbey.

The commissioners had been right to suspect Whiting. Subsequent searches of the walls and cellars of the Abbey produced nearly five hundred items, including a gold chalice—but no Grail. The estate went to the Duke of Somerset, who cashed in by selling off the fine stonework.

But the Abbey was not forgotten, and from the seventeenth century on visitors came to view the romantic ruins, among which there now grew an offshoot of the "Holy Thorn" tree, which flowers at Christmastime and was said to have been brought from the Holy Land by Saint Joseph himself. Puritans had cut down the original tree as a relic of superstition.

Given this wealth of memories and legends and the leading role played by the Abbey in the history of British Christianity, as the home of more saints than any other single place, it is hardly surprising that the Church of England was keen to buy it when it came up for sale in

The "Holy Thorn" tree at Glastonbury.

1907. As soon as the ownership of the site was secured, the Diocese of Bath and Wells established a Board of Trustees that decided to sponsor excavations of the now sadly dilapidated site under the control of a special Committee of the Somerset Archaeological and Natural History Society, in the hope of recovering traces of its past glories. Glastonbury's ghosts were about to be disturbed.

Frederick Bligh Bond

Who should take charge of this important operation? The obvious candidate was the church architect Frederick Bligh Bond, then in his forties, running a small practice in Bristol. He was an expert on the restoration of old churches and keen to be an archaeologist. In May 1908, he was awarded a license to begin excavating within the Abbey grounds.

From 1908 onward, Bond led a series of campaigns in which one significant discovery followed another. Although he uncovered no remains of the Old Church, probably because it had been destroyed in Abbot Bere's extensive building activities, he did locate two important lost medieval structures, the Edgar and Our Lady of Loretto Chapels. His final, and most extraordinary, find was traces of a ring of twelve circular hermits' cells that had been built around Joseph of Arimathea's original chapel. Incredibly, this was seen as even older than the Old Church, which Bond dated to the second century A.D. This round chapel would be the oldest Christian building anywhere in the world, providing dramatic confirmation of the Glastonbury traditions about Joseph, and forcing the history of the early Church to be completely rewritten.

How did Bond achieve these remarkable discoveries and why is he not hailed as one of the world's great archaeologists?

From the outset of the excavations there were troubling issues concerned with Bond's work. One was his tendency to overstep his position; his was an unpaid post with no real power, but right from the beginning, as he threw himself into the work, Bond imagined it to be something far grander, and therefore proved reluctant to accept advice from others.

Almost immediately, Bond came into conflict with the better-known church architect William Caroe, appointed by the trustees to take charge of renovating what remained of the buildings. Bond was intensely concerned with establishing the precise length of the medieval Abbey, an obsession that Caroe did not share.

The importance of this apparently minor point of detail for Bond was that he firmly believed the Abbey had been laid out on the basis of a system of geometrical measures. He thought that this was a kind of sacred geometry, used especially for churches, expressing eternal and universal mathematical principles. Bond tried to explain the basis of his theory in an article in the *Journal of the Royal Institute of British Architects* of June 1916:

> As to the motive which led the ancients to their preference for geometric truth—that is another question. For the moment we are on safe ground in accepting it as an axiom of their system that they did work where possible on geometric lines, and that from very early times a peculiar respect—even a sanctity—attaches to those proportions which most clearly accorded with the mathematical principles known to Master Masons [builders].

Bond also argued that the Abbey was planned using a unit of 74 feet, or 888 inches. The significance of this figure is that by converting the letters in the Greek version of Jesus (Iesous) into numbers and adding them up one also arrives at a result of 888.

In order to prove his theory, Bond undertook excavations on the site of the Edgar Chapel, which had lain at the eastern end of the

Bligh Bond's 1909 plan of the Edgar Chapel, with the supposed traces of his claimed apse to the right.

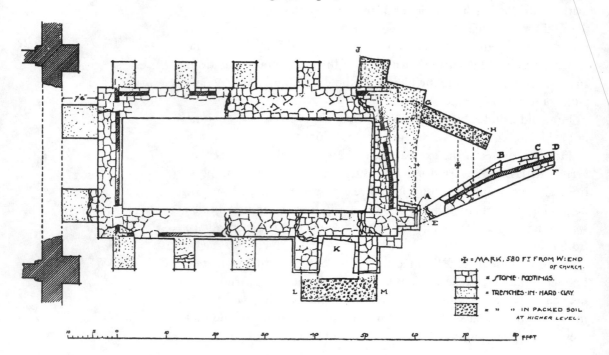

main Abbey church, in 1908–1909. The rectangular plan of the main part of the chapel was easily established, but Bond also located fainter, badly disturbed, remains that he interpreted as the walling and foundations of a triangular extension, or apse. Through this work he established to his own satisfaction that the total length of the Abbey, including the chapel, had been exactly 592 feet. At 592 feet the length of the Abbey would have been precisely eight of Bond's units.

Caroe was concerned when he discovered that Bond was in the process of fixing the stone walls of his supposed apse in cement, contacting Bond to express his fears. Caroe apparently wrote, "I hope you will not allow your enthusiasm to create imaginary records," sending a copy of his letter to the Bishop. The Bishop acted promptly, preventing Bond from completing his restoration. A lasting enmity between the two architects was the result of this clash.

But Caroe did not have the last word. Bond received strong support from the Abbey Excavation Committee in the row over the Edgar Chapel. In May 1910, they signed a note supporting the existence of the extension to the chapel, although the Bishop did not relent and Bond was never able to complete his concreting.

In 1913 money ran short, and nearly all the available funds had to go to remove piles of earth left behind by Bond's workmen, but vast heaps still remained on the site even twelve months later, as the Excavation Committee's annual report recorded rather plaintively. The outbreak of the First World War inevitably led to a slowing down of the excavations, and Bond seems to have taken a backseat. He limited himself to the public expression of his theories on geometrical perfection underlying church architecture and writing a book on the use of the Bible as a means of prophesying the future—all rather unorthodox stuff.

But Bond carried on guiding operations from a distance. His friend Captain John Bartlett was detailed by Bond to undertake a series of small tasks at the Abbey, but without the knowledge of the Excavation Committee, which protested strongly on discovering his unauthorized activities.

The Company of Avalon Speak

Who was Captain Bartlett, and what was his connection with Bond? Unbeknownst to either the Excavation Committee or the trustees, Bond had actually been guided since the very beginning of his excavation by a secret source of information. Interested in the notion of

Spirit drawing of Glastonbury Abbey church. The lines of the eastern extension (Edgar Chapel) are, as Bligh Bond noted, "drawn three times over, as though to emphasize this feature." Across the middle of the Abbey is a signature in Latin: *Gulielmus Monachus* ("William the Monk").

psychic powers from childhood, Bond had been put in touch with Bartlett through the Society for Psychical Research, of which they were members. Bartlett, ex–navy man, songwriter, and keen amateur student of history and legend, had contacted the Society after discovering, quite by accident, that he was able to produce "automatic" writing. This had become the most popular means of spirit communication by the end of the nineteenth century. The writer held a pencil above a sheet of paper and then waited for the words to flow. Essential to the process was the assumption that the medium had no conscious control over, or awareness of, the messages being produced.

Bond soon realized the potential of Bartlett's gift. If Bartlett could receive communications from the past, then they would be able to open a new chapter in both psychical research and archaeological method. The spiritual center of Glastonbury, where Bond was about to start work, was surely the ideal test case.

Bartlett and Bond began their first "sitting" at 4:30 in the afternoon on November 7, 1907, in Bond's Bristol office. Bartlett poised the pencil above a blank sheet of paper, while Bond laid the fingers of his right hand loosely on the back of Bartlett's writing hand. Their first question came directly to the point: "Can you tell us anything about Glastonbury?"

Incredibly, an answer came back out of the ether. As the men strained to keep from looking at the spidery pencil script (aided by Bond reading from a novel to distract their conscious thoughts), a series of replies emerged. The rather vague message "All knowledge is eternal and is available to mental sympathy" was succeeded by something far more specific—"I was not in sympathy with monks—I cannot find a monk yet."

Directly following this was a communication from a Glastonbury Abbey monk himself. A sketch of the layout of the Abbey appeared, with a rectangular addition to the known plan of the eastern end of the Abbey drawn three times until it was a thick line. Down the center of the drawing ran a signature: Gulielmus Monachus (William the Monk). Bartlett and Bond were astounded that their "psychological experiment" had been such a success, and they determined to press on. Pausing to read the answer each time the pencil stopped, they fired off a series of ever more precise questions into the void that eventually produced exact measurements and accurate sketches of the as yet unexcavated Edgar Chapel, named after King Edgar. Their correspondent ended the evening by signing off in the name of Johannes Bryant.

The information provided was a tonic to Bond, no matter what its source, for it confirmed his view that the present Abbey, shorter than his geometrical theories would suggest, was not complete. Bartlett and he continued the sessions of automatic writing throughout the controversial excavations at the Edgar Chapel, receiving constant feedback on Bond's progress in both English and Latin. The monastic correspondents were firm on the question of the reality of the apse, which was to result in the fateful conflict with Caroe.

In the years that followed further remarkable communications emerged, with a variety of individuals providing detailed information on both the Abbey ruins and their lives and times. They even allowed Bond to identify a skeleton he had uncovered as the remains of the unfortunate Abbot Whiting. He then passed the bones on to some Benedictines founding a monastery on Caldey Island off the coast of Wales, who reverently accepted them as holy relics. What the Board of Trustees or the Excavation Committee thought of this unorthodox arrangement is unknown.

Bond's ethereal informants appeared to belong to a group that termed itself "The Watchers" or "The Company of Avalon." Their most consistent correspondent was the monk and stonemason Johannes, a vivid character who had served under Abbots Bere and Whiting, but would rather have played truant and escaped into his beloved countryside.

Naturally, the source of these communications came to be a major concern to their recipients. Bond himself did not believe that a conventional interpretation—in terms of communications from the spirits of the dead—could explain the specific content of all the messages. The standard spiritualistic view was that the medium holding the pencil and posing the questions was simply a channel through which the departed could impart their messages to the world. But even in the case of the characterful Johannes, Bond wondered if contact had really been made with a past individual:

Is this a piece of actual experience transmitted by a real personality, or are we in contact with a larger field of memory, a cosmic record latent, yet living, and able to find expression in human terms related to the subject before us, by the aid of a certain power of mental sympathy which allows such records to be sensed and articulated?

Bond thought that both he and Bartlett were vital to the process of communication, with the words somehow being drawn out of their subconscious minds.

Others concluded that telepathy lay at the root of the messages. The Reverend F. T. Fryer of Bath was asked by the Society for Psychical Research to report on this important research:

It is not thought that any ideas in Mr. Bond's mind were orally communicated by him to [Bartlett]. . . . Judging from our present knowledge and most probable theories of telepathy, I have concluded all through that the originating mind is Bond's, [Bartlett] being his emanuensis.

The Society does not seem to have arrived at an official interpretation of Bond's work.

Bond rejected this more straightforward paranormal explanation. He did not believe that it could account for the messages received from the Company of Avalon, which he saw as ultimately emanating from a group of spirits, residing in Paradise, who still wished to communicate with those of like mind on earth:

So it is, we are told, with the Company of Avalon, a group of souls who are impregnated with the devotional ideal which was translated into architectural symbol by the Benedictine brethren of old time. These, the "Elect of Avalon," combine as a united spiritual force in an effort which is really one of response to those of us who, of our own volition, have attuned ourselves to their "vibrations." But being themselves for the most part so removed in condition from modes of physical expression of the truths they would seek to convey, they choose as spokesmen some who, though liberated in spirit, and of their Company, have retained such sympathy with earth and the dwellers on earth that they are able through this mutual sympathy to creep to us across the "bridge of love" and, entering our atmosphere and conditions of consciousness, speak to us through the mediumship of one or other whose organism is attuned to a psychical responsiveness.

Even if Bond himself wasn't too clear on the source of his information, local churchmen were. In the summer of 1918, when Bond finally brought his experiments into the public eye with the publication of his book *The Gate of Remembrance*, they had no doubts as to what he was dabbling in. This was spiritualism, which had grown into an enormous movement following the slaughter of the First World War. For many in the Church it was a dangerous threat to orthodox belief.

Spirit drawing interpreted by Bligh Bond as a sketch of the Loretto Chapel.

A forceful reaction was inevitable, although at first people were perhaps simply baffled. A friendly but unconvinced notice of the book appeared in the *Proceedings of the Somerset Archaeological and Natural History Society*. Then the storm broke. An anonymous review in a church newspaper, *The Challenge,* although not directly attacking the spirit communications, attempted to undermine Bond's credibility by accusing him of unjustifiably assuming the title "Director of Excavations" and of "reconstructing" the Edgar Chapel apse. Bond's lawyers forced the paper to publish a full apology, but the damage was done. He tried to uncover the author of the review in the belief that Caroe was behind this attack, but he was unsuccessful.

It seemed as though Bond had weathered the storm, for in August 1919 excavations resumed at the Abbey, with him again in charge. Evidently the Excavations Committee was not so hidebound. From December 1916 onward the Company of Avalon had sent a stream of detailed communications regarding the location of the lost chapel of Our Lady of Loretto built by Abbot Bere, in the form of both written measurements and sketch plans. Bond lost little time in following this up with an excavation, which did indeed yield the remains of a building.

This time Bond seems to have been more open about his sources, for the Reverend Fryer visited the excavations in September to see how accurate the "Company" had been. Discrepancies between their messages and the remains being uncovered by Bond left him unimpressed:

On Tuesday last I went to see the excavations made on the supposed site of the Lorretto Chapel. Mr. FBB has been at work there for some days and so far has discovered what he believes to be the western wall foundations of the chapel. But this wall is 10 ft. or so nearer the transept, that is eastward of the chapel, than he thought it should be. . . . So far as I could see there is nothing yet found to substantiate any of the statements of the script beyond the measurements of the walls.

Nineteen twenty-one spirit communication from "Patraic" the monk, showing Joseph of Arimathea's original settlement at Glastonbury as a circle of round huts.

No mention of automatic writing appeared in Bond's report on his work published by the Somerset Archaeological and Natural History Society, although a new edition of *The Gate of Remembrance* contained a full discussion.

Later in 1919 Bond produced another book of communications. *The Hill of Vision* was also based on the automatic writing of Captain Bartlett. This time, however, rather than harking back to the past, he had produced a work of prophecy related to the Great War. It was, apparently, the war to end all wars, inaugurating an era of world peace and enlightenment. Bond lived to see the Second World War— whether he thought *The Hill of Vision* had been a cruel trick we do not know.

Certainly its publication brought him no peace. Both the Board of Trustees and the Excavation Committee seem to have had enough. In 1921 Bond was informed that Dr. Sebastian Evans, Secretary of the Committee and a Holy Grail scholar, had been appointed codirector of excavations. This was to become Bond's final season. He had relocated the site of an ancient stone pillar or pyramid said to mark the edge of the sacred area around St. Joseph's Chapel, finding beneath it a round stone platform. Bond had long held that the very earliest Glastonbury occupation had been by Saint Joseph and eleven disciples, who would have lived in separate round huts arranged in a circle—he was certain that the platform was a base for one of these huts. Opening up a new area on the other side of the circle in hot pursuit of his theory, Bond was abruptly halted:

On removing the top soil there appeared the remains of a heavy stone monument of rectangular form, and beneath this again, traces of what looked like a circular foundation similar to that found under St. David's pillar. Alas! that the knowledge of these things—found too easily and without the usual preliminary of cutting trenches—should have proved so unwelcome to the authorities concerned. Unfortunately in this case, official repugnance to the method of discovery—which was based upon a recall of the latent memories of the past—now speedily put an end to the research. Without warning, and before any measurements could be taken, the excavation was filled up on the order of an executive official.

Bond's activities for the rest of the year were limited to sorting out the finds from his excavations in the Abbot's Kitchen.

Martyrdom of a Psychic Archaeologist

The following January Bond suffered another blow, when one of his architectural clients, the Reverend H. J. Wilkins, brought out a pamphlet attacking his use of automatic writing and his claims concerning the Edgar Chapel apse and the true length of the Abbey. Bond was able to force Wilkins to withdraw this, as it was libelous, but a revised version repeated the same damaging arguments. Bond challenged Wilkins to come and see the remains for himself, but he declined.

This seems to have been the final straw for the Excavation Committee, whose members must have resented being dragged into controversy yet again. They dissolved themselves, bringing to an abrupt end Bond's role as Director of Excavations. The Society of Antiquaries of London was placed in charge, and they had no thought of using Bond's services.

In what at first sight seems a petty and vindictive move, the Abbey trustees informed Bond in April 1924 that he must return his key to the Abbey grounds and would have to enter in future as an ordinary member of the public. However, it is clear that Bond had already been secretly preparing the ground for further excavations based on automatic writing. He had employed several dowsers (see **Introduction** to this chapter) to locate treasures hidden by Abbot Whiting at the time of the Dissolution, whose existence had been revealed to him by the Company of Avalon. The trustees may have feared the Abbey's turning into a paranormal circus, for Bond had just been appointed the editor of *Psychic Science*.

Bond appealed to the highest authority of the church, the Archbishop of Canterbury, in the hope that he would overrule the trustees and allow the excavations to proceed. As far as Bond was concerned, he was the victim of a conspiracy designed to destroy his achievements:

> There is urgent need for a full enquiry if treasures of antiquity are to be saved from the hands of those who would if they could obliterate the record of all that has resulted from my work over the years. Much is already spoiled, much is not available for public view, and there has been mishandling, waste and confusion.

Not surprisingly, the Archbishop refused to intervene.

The Society for Psychical Research was no more successful in its requests to the Society of Antiquaries. Matters certainly can't have been helped by Bond's publishing more revelations from Glastonbury spirits in a volume titled *The Company of Avalon*, this time concerning the Loretto Chapel. His new amanuensis was a lady named "S," whose automatic writings revealed to Bond that he was the reincarnation of Robert, the Abbot of Glastonbury 1171–1178.

Rejected by the Abbey, Bond turned full-time to matters psychic. He left for America in 1925, taking up an editorial position with

The Edgar Chapel as marked on the ground today, without Bligh Bond's eastern extension.

the American Society for Psychical Research. But he eventually fell out with the leading lights there too, over a fraudulent medium whose misdeeds he insisted on publicizing. Bond had meanwhile apparently become a priest in the tiny sect calling itself the Old Catholic Church.

In 1936 Bond returned to Britain, full of hopeless dreams that he would be allowed to excavate at Glastonbury once more, with financial backing from America. He had received further communications on the buried treasures, Saint Joseph's original church and hermits' huts, and the location of the Holy Grail. No permission was forthcoming the moment Bond's involvement came to light. On visiting the Abbey he was appalled to see that the concrete marking he laid down on the line of the disputed apse walls had been removed. Further frenetic letter writing had no effect. Neither did an appeal to a meeting of the Somerset Archaeological and Natural History Society, where no decision was taken. A bitterly disappointed man, Bond retired to North Wales, dying there in 1945.

In accounts of Bond's work written from a stance favorable to the paranormal he is presented almost as a martyr to psychic archaeology, living in constant poverty, continually having to be bailed out by supporters, hounded out of archaeology by prejudice and ignorance, and dying neglected and alone. Oddly, Bond seems to have been reasonably well-off when he died, owning a house and shares in several companies. The idea of his being so dedicated to his work that he neglected himself entirely is something of an exaggeration.

So, too, is the idea that all his archaeological disappointments stemmed from an unreasoning rejection of his psychic methods. For one, the idea that someone entirely self-trained in archaeological methods should be allowed to excavate such an important site as Glastonbury Abbey was no longer acceptable in the 1930s.

Nevertheless, the real questions concern Bond's earlier work, and the degree to which messages from beyond were confirmed by the results of excavation. How accurate were the Company of Avalon in their predictions? In the case of the Edgar Chapel they were correct, with the possible exception of the apse; with the Loretto Chapel they were far less impressive, as the Reverend Fryer noted at the time, and Bond himself admitted in a later edition of *The Gate of Remembrance*.

But whose voices were they? Little attention has been given to the scripts themselves, which are available only in part, introducing the issue of selectivity. Bond's sympathetic biographer, William Kenawell, gives an insight into this process:

The script was of uneven quality; the best relating to the abbey and excavations was culled by Bond and Bartlett from bales of nonsense, private communications, and many on a great number of matters ancient and modern.

In particular, the problem of inauthentic language occurs both in the original Bond and Bartlett transcripts, and even more strikingly in later communications, all of which Bond accepted uncritically. As Dr. Marshall McKusick of the University of Iowa put it in his review of the transcripts:

> Every . . . ghost also speaks modern English larded with anachronisms and archaic words as were fashionable among 19th-century poets—vocabulary such as: asunder, betwixt, ye, seaxe, and olde among others.

Specific anachronisms he points to are the sixth-century B.C. Greek "Phocis the Mariner," who somehow communicates in old-fashioned English, and the common use of *Y* for *TH* (as in *Ye* for *The*); although this looks archaic to us, it actually happened only after the invention of printing.

So, as ghosts, the Company of Avalon are not all that convincing. Perhaps Bond was right to suggest instead that some sort of group mind was operating. But was there anything in the messages that could not have been predicted, and did the automatic writing experiments improve Bond's archaeology? Bond's early work has been praised

Second spirit drawing of the Edgar Chapel, captioned in automatic writing—*Capella St. Edgar, Abbas Beere fecit hanc capellam* ("Chapel of Saint Edgar, Abbot Beere built this chapel").

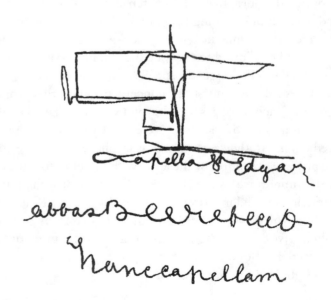

by later excavators of Glastonbury, particularly his standard practice of drawing every stone in a wall so that its method of construction could be determined. Such an interest in building techniques is perhaps only to be expected from an architect. Where they do not find him a reliable guide is when there were no walls to follow. This is the case with the disputed apse of the Edgar Chapel. Bond's published account is not convincing. His side "walls" were interpreted by other archaeologists at the time as drains (an alternative theory he never acknowledged), and he explains away the absence of an end wall as the result of earlier digging, although there is no archaeological evidence to support this. The doubts expressed at the time by Caroe certainly appear to be justified.

Equally, the closing down of Bond's 1921 excavations in search of Saint Joseph's original Glastonbury chapel and hermits' huts seems quite reasonable from an archaeological perspective. From his own account, Bond was clearly digging very small areas, rather than trenches, giving himself much too restricted a view to see what he was finding. By this time the original idea of a psychological experiment had been completely abandoned, and Bond was excavating where he "knew" he would find something. After all, if he had good reason to believe that early remains would be found in the area, then there was nothing to stop Bond from opening up proper trenches of a decent size to test his theory. Later work in the same area has located the bases of more pyramids or pillars, but these are not arranged in a circle, and no sign of earlier round huts has been uncovered. As with the Edgar Chapel, Bond seems to have convinced himself that he was right and that no alternative interpretations were worth considering.

Even if Bond could be unreasonable on specific points, he still had an overall record of success. Yet did this require paranormal input? Archaeologists considering his work at Glastonbury have not been persuaded. As Dr. Stephen Williams argues, nothing out of the ordinary was required:

Why does psychic archaeology claim that Bond could not have found the Edgar Chapel without the medium's help? It truly passes understanding. We know that Bond was a well-trained architect with a specialty in ecclesiastical structures; all he had to do was turn to almost any nearby structure such as Salisbury Cathedral, less than fifty miles to the east, and see its Trinity Chapel behind the main altar and guess that Glastonbury would have one too. It would be a very likely and testable hypothesis, not something that one needs to go to ghostly writings for. In fact, it is even admitted by the most stalwart Bond supporters that such a chapel had been posited before Bond's work at Glastonbury. Much ado about nothing it seems to me.

In the case of the Loretto Chapel, existing descriptions and earlier work indicated that it lay on the north side of the Abbey, and there were few remaining uninvestigated locations large enough to contain it by the time any messages reached Bond. The drawings published by Bond are hardly precise enough to be a real aid, while the written messages proved to be inaccurate. In any case, Bond uncovered only the foundations of a building—there were no traces of the elaborate Italian-style decoration for which the chapel was famous, so we cannot be sure that Bond did actually relocate it.

All in all, there is nothing in Bond's work that requires supernatural forces, and no discovery that could not have emanated from his or Captain Bartlett's subconscious. In retrospect, there were several actions Bond could have taken that might have strengthened his claims. It would have been wiser to keep Bartlett at arm's length from the Glastonbury excavations, to eliminate the possibility that the messages merely came from his imagination. More important is the issue of impartiality and selectivity, as Kenawell stressed:

> It would have been to Bond's advantage to have published the scripts and drawings at the time they were received. In both the Edgar and Loretto Chapels the scripts were revealed only after the excavations had been completed. Such a procedure would leave anyone open to all sorts of charges and suspicions. Bond later repented his reluctance to publish the scripts. Indeed, most of his life's agony could have been avoided.

The skeptic would argue that what was being avoided was any chance for external scrutiny until the correspondence could be tidied up and its agreement with the archaeological evidence ensured.

Bond seems to have learned by the time of the Loretto investigations not to play his cards too close to his chest, for Reverend Fryer of the Society for Psychical Research was clearly aware of the general line taken by the scripts, but even here there was no prior publication. While that might be seen as too elaborate, there was surely nothing to prevent copies of the texts and drawings being made to be placed with trustworthy third parties.

Neither were there any outside checks on Bond's excavations. He was not concerned, in all his wrangles with the Abbey authorities, with preserving the traces of the Edgar Chapel for posterity. The arguments were over his hasty attempt to concrete a permanent mark of his interpretation of the remains. Once this was done it was impossible for anyone else to examine the archaeology and come to his or her own view. Bond's challenge to his critic Reverend Wilkins to come and look at the evidence himself was a meaningless offer, for he had already destroyed it by concreting it over.

Whatever the merits of the communications Bartlett and Bond received from the Company of Avalon, these were never in practice treated as part of a parapsychological experiment. Bond's insistence on carrying out both the automatic writing and the archaeological tests of his predictions himself virtually guaranteed disbelief when he succeeded in confirming his own theories. Unfortunately, archaeological excavation is an unrepeatable experiment—perhaps a great opportunity was lost forever.

The spirit guide Johannes, from a communication of 1934. When the portrait appeared through automatic writing, the medium Mrs. Jessie Stevens wrote: "Question/is this like you?" The response came: "I am as in a glass. Yes, I impelled the stylus. I be not as Apollus—but I be I—what matter? Thus I saw mine own in clear pool o'mere. Johan."

W e have followed here the referencing system developed for *Ancient Inventions*. To give full references for every source consulted while preparing this book might require another volume, so we have listed here only the most important source given for each section within the chapters and arranged, as far as possible, in the order in which they have been used or directly quoted. When several sources were used on a given topic, we have listed the most accessible. Asterisks denote books and articles frequently referred to, full details of which can be found in the Bibliography, which follows the Sources.

INTRODUCTION

K. L. Feder: "Irrationality and Popular Archaeology," *American Antiquity* 49 (1984), pp. 525–541 [statistics]
*Feder 1996
F. B. Harrold & R. A. Eve: *Cult Archaeology and Creationism* (University of Iowa Press, 1995)
S. Williams: *Fantastic Archaeology: The Wild Side of American Prehistory* (University of Pennsylvania Press, 1991)

CHAPTER 1: LOST LANDS AND CATASTROPHES

INTRODUCTION

D. Steel: *Rogue Asteroids and Doomsday Comets* (New York: John Wiley & Sons, 1995), pp. 247–259 [Shoemaker-Levy], 56–57, 105 [Chicxulub]
D. King-Hele: "Truth and Heresy Over Earth and Sky," *The Observatory* 95, No. 1004 (1975), pp. 1–12 [Halley]
J. E. Force: *William Whiston: Honest Newtonian* (Cambridge University Press, 1985)
R. Huggett: *Catastrophism: Systems of Earth History* (London: E. Arnold, 1990) [history of catastrophism]
T. Palmer: *Catastrophism, Neocatastrophism and Evolution* (Society for Interdisciplinary Studies/Nottingham Trent University, 1994) [history of catastrophism, extinctions/geological upheavals]
*James 1995, pp. 120–137, 159–169 [Plato and Aristotle]
L. Sprague de Camp: *Lost Continents: The Atlantis Theme in History, Science, and Literature* (New York: Dover, rev. ed., 1970), pp. 47–75 [Lemuria]
D. V. Ager, *The Nature of the Stratigraphical Record* (London, 1973), p. 100
Anon: "What Really Killed the Dinosaurs?" *New Scientist* (16 August 1997), pp. 23–27
*Clube & Napier 1982 [cometary catastrophism; Proto-Encke]
V. Clube & W. Napier: *The Cosmic Winter* (Oxford: Basil Blackwell, 1990), pp. 263–273 [Ice Ages]
W. K. Stevens: "If Climate Changes, It May Change Quickly," *New York Times*, Science Section, January 27, 1998
C. Schaeffer: *Stratigraphie comparée et chronologie de l'Asie occidentale (IIIe et IIe millénaires)* (Oxford University Press, 1948)
B. J. Peiser: "Comets and Disaster in the Bronze Age," *British Archaeology* 30 (Dec. 1997), pp. 6–7
H. Lhote. *Search for the Tassili Frescoes* (New York: Dutton, 1959)
A. Nur: "The End of the Bronze Age by Large Earthquakes?" in M. E. Bailey, T. Palmer, & B. J. Peiser (eds.): *Natural Catastrophes During Bronze Age Civilizations. Archaeological, Geological and Cultural Perspectives*—Proceedings of the 2nd SIS Cambridge Conference, July 1997 (Oxford: British Archaeological Reports, 1998)
N. Petite-Maire, L. Beufort, & N. Page: "Holocene Climate Change and Man in the Present Day Sahara Desert," in H. N. Dalfes, G. Kukla, & H. Weiss (eds): *Third Millennium B.C. Climate Change and Old World Social Collapse*, NATO ASI Series I: Global Environmental Change, Vol. 49 (Berlin: Springer, 1997), pp. 297–308
M. E. L. Mallowan: "Noah's Flood Reconsidered," *Iraq* 26 (1964), pp. 62–82
J. Bright: "Has Archaeology Found Evidence of the Flood?" *Biblical Archaeologist* 4 (Dec. 1942), pp. 55–62
R. Mestel: "Noah's Flood," *New Scientist* (4 October 1997), pp. 24–27

ATLANTIS—LOST AND FOUND?

L. Sprague de Camp: *Lost Continents: The Atlantis Theme in History, Science, and Literature* (New York: Dover, rev. ed., 1970)
Plato: *Timaeus & Critias*
Strabo: *Geography* II:iii,6 [Aristotle's view]
I. Donnelly: *Atlantis: The Antediluvian World* (New York: Harper, 1882)
*James 1995, pp. 21–31, 40–45 [Donnelly, plate tectonics], 57–86 [Thera], 171–186 [Egypt], 187–280 [Atlas, Tantalus, Tantalis]
E. S. Ramage (ed.): *Atlantis: Fact or Fiction?* (Indiana University Press, 1978) [geology, Thera]
A. Galanopoulos & E. Bacon: *Atlantis: The Truth Behind the Legend* (London: Nelson, 1969) [Thera]
J. V. Luce: *The End of Atlantis* (London: Thames & Hudson, 1969) [Thera]

SODOM AND GOMORRAH

K. D. Politis: "Understanding the Story of Lot," *Inter-Faith Quarterly* 2:3 (26 September 1996), pp. 17–20 [skeptical view]
T. H. Gaster: *Myth, Legend and Custom in the Old Testament* (New York: Harper & Row, 1969) Vol. 1, pp. 156–162 [folklore]
Ovid: *Metamorphoses* VIII:611–724
Strabo: *Geography* 16:2,44
Tacitus: *The Histories* 5:7
Josephus: *The Jewish War* 4:451,476; *Jewish Antiquities* 1:202
W. Whiston (trans.): *The Works of Flavius Josephus* (London, 1737), note to *Antiquities* I:xi,4
G. A. Smith: *The Historical Geography of the Holy Land* (London: Hodder & Stoughton, 1894, rev. ed. 1931), pp. 324–328
T. K. Cheyne: "Sodom and Gomorrah," in T. K. Cheyne & J. S. Black (eds): *Encyclopaedia Biblica* (London: Adam & Charles Black, 1903), Vol. IV, pp. 4677–4678
J. P. Harland: "Sodom and Gomorrah, Part I: The Location of the Cities of the Plain," *Biblical Archaeologist* V:2 (May 1942), pp. 17–32
J. P. Harland: "Sodom and Gomorrah, Part II: The Destruction of the Cities of the Plain," *Biblical Archaeologist* VI:3 (Sept 1943), pp. 41–52
H. Shanks: "Have Sodom and Gomorrah Been Found?" *British Archaeological Review* (Sept/Oct 1980), pp. 27–36 [subsequent correspondence in *British Archaeological Review* (Jan/Feb 1981), pp. 18–20]
D. Vitaliano: *Legends of the Earth* (Indiana University Press, 1973), pp. 89–91 [geological theories]
D. Neev & K. O. Emery: *The Destruction of Sodom and Gomorrah* (Oxford University Press, 1995)
A. Nissenbaum: "Sodom, Gomorrah and the Other Lost Cities of the Plain: A Climatic Perspective," *Climate Change* 26:4 (1994), pp. 435–446
M. Mandelkehr: "An Integrated Model for an Earthwide Event at 2300 B.C. Part I: The Archaeological Evidence," *Society for Interdisciplinary Studies Review* V:3, pp. 77–95
H. Weiss et al.: "The Genesis and Collapse of Third Millennium North Mesopotamian Civilization," *Science* 261 (20 Aug 1993), pp. 995–1004
H. N. Dalfes, G. Kukla, & H. Weiss (eds): *Third Millennium B.C. Climate Change and Old World Social Collapse,* NATO AS1 Series I: Global Environmental Change, Vol. 49 (Berlin: Springer, 1997)
K. Wright: "Empires in the Dust," *Discover* 19:3 (March 1998), pp. 94–99
M. G. L. Baillie: "Dendrochronology and the Chronology of the Irish Bronze Age," in J. Waddell & E. Shee-Twohig (eds): *Ireland in the Bronze Age* (Dublin: Stationery Office, 1995), pp. 30–37

BOX ON THE SIN OF SODOM

V. L. Bullough: *Sexual Variance in Society and History* (University of Chicago Press, 1976), pp. 82–85, 181–182

POLESHIFT

*Hancock 1995, p. 452 [West quote]
C. H. Hapgood: *Maps of the Ancient Sea Kings* (Philadelphia: Chilton Books, 1966)
C. H. Hapgood: *Earth's Shifting Crust* (London: Museum Press, 1959)
C. H. Hapgood: *The Path of the Pole* (Philadelphia: Chilton, 1970)
R. & R. Flem-Ath: *When the Sky Fell* (London: Weidenfeld & Nicolson, 1995), p. 134 [quote]
W. B. Emery: *Archaic Egypt* (Harmondsworth: Penguin, 1961), p. 38
*James 1995, pp. 46–51 [rise of Egyptian civilization]
T. B. Kellogg, R. S. Truesdale, & L. E. Osterman: "Late Quaternary Extent of the West Antarctic Ice Sheet: New Evidence from Ross Sea Cores," *Geology* 7 (1979), pp. 249–253

W. E. LeMasier & D. C. Rex: "The Marie Byrd Land Volcanic Province and Its Relation to Cainozoic West Antarctic Rift System," in R. J. Tingey (ed.): *The Geology of Antarctica* (Oxford: Clarendon Press, 1991), pp. 249–256

G. H. Denton, M. L. Prentice, & L. H. Burkle: "Cainozoic History of the Antarctic Ice Sheet," in R. J. Tingey (ed.): *The Geology of Antarctica* (Oxford: Clarendon Press, 1991) pp. 365–433

Further discussion of the Orontaeus Finaeus map and the theories of Hapgood and Hancock can be found on the extremely useful Internet pages written by geologist Paul Heinrich, http://www.talkorigins.org/faqs/mom/oronteus.html [last updated June 6, 1996] and http://www.talkorigins.org/faqs/mom/atiarts.html [last updated June 3, 1996]

THE RISE AND FALL OF MAYA CIVILIZATION

B. Fagan: *Elusive Treasure* (London: Macdonald and Jane's, 1977). chaps. 8–10 [Stephens and Catherwood]

R. J. Sharer: *The Ancient Maya* (Stanford University Press, 5th ed., 1994), pp. 79–84 [earliest centers], 341–342 [inhospitable environment], 343 [earthquakes and hurricanes], 343–344 [epidemics], 349–353 [Seibal foreigners], 344 [skeletal studies quote], 347 [Dos Pilas], 339–340 [Copán abandonment]

M. D. Coe: *The Maya* (London: Thames & Hudson, 5th ed., 1993), pp. 47 [pre-Classic developments], 66–67 [El Mirador], 7 [quote on changing thinking], 71 [Classic quote], 104–108 [Bonampak], 184–190 [astronomy and mathematics], 98–99 [Copán and Quiriguá], 128 [apocalypse quote]

J. E. S. Thompson: *The Rise and Fall of Maya Civilization* (University of Oklahoma Press, 1966), pp. 302 [theocracy quote], 100–108 [peasant revolt]

H. Stierlin: *The Maya* (New York: Taschen, 1997), pp. 42–56 [Tikal]. 128–151 [Uxmal]

C. Cortez: "The Tomb of Pacal at Palenque," in P. G. Bahn (ed.), *Tombs, Graves and Mummies* (London: Weidenfeld & Nicolson, 1996), pp. 126–129

M. D. Coe: *Breaking the Maya Code* (London: Thames & Hudson, 1992) [decipherment of Mayan]

*Von Däniken 1969, pp. 123–124 [quotes]

T. P. Culbert: "The Collapse of Classic Maya Civilization," in N. Yoffee & G. L. Cowgill (eds.): *The Collapse of Ancient States and Civilization* (University of Arizona Press, 1988), pp. 69–101 [fall of Maya civilization; trade and overpopulation theories]

J. A. Tainter: *The Collapse of Complex Societies* (Cambridge University Press) 1988, pp. 52 [maize mosaic virus], 61–62 [invasion]

L. E. Wright & C. D. White: "Human Biology in the Classic Maya Collapse: Evidence from Paleopathology and Paleodiet," *Journal of World Prehistory* 10 (1996), pp. 147–198 [quote, p. 166]

D. Collison: "The Lost World of the Maya," in R. Sutcliffe (ed.): *Chronicle* (London: BBC, 1978), pp. 95–111 [Thompson quote, p. 108]

BOX ON THE MAYA CALENDAR

M. D. Coe: *The Maya* (London: Thames & Hudson, 5th ed., 1993), pp. 48–52 [calendars], 48 [quote], 155–158 [Itzá and Tayasal]

J. E. S. Thompson: *The Rise and Fall of Maya Civilization* (University of Oklahoma Press, 1966), pp. 39, 166–167 [Tayasal], 87 [Tikal]

R. J. Sharer: *The Ancient Maya* (Stanford University Press, 5th ed.. 1994), p. 346 [katun endings]

CHAPTER 2: WATCHING THE SKIES

INTRODUCTION

S. N. Kramer: *The Sumerians: Their History, Culture and Character* (University of Chicago Press, 1963), pp. 302–305 [earliest writing of "god"]

Aristotle: *Metaphysics* 12:8, 19

J. Britton & C. Walker: "Astronomy and Astrology in Mesopotamia," in *Walker 1996, pp. 42–67

A. F. Aveni: "Astronomy in the Americas," in *Walker 1996, pp. 269–303

Hesiod: *Works and Days* 609–611

*James & Thorpe 1994, pp. 484–487 [Stone Age calendars]

Plato: *Epinomis* 978 C–E

W. J. Phythian-Adams: "A Meteorite of the Fourteenth Century B.C.," *Palestine Excavation Quarterly* 1946, pp. 116–124 [Ephesus]

G. A. Wainwright: "Letopolis," *Journal of Egyptian Archaeology* 18 (1932), pp. 159–172 [Amun]

R. Burton: *A Personal Narrative of a Pilgrimage to Al-Medinah and Meccah* (London: Longman, 1856)

D. Cardona: "The Kabba," *Kronos* XII:3 (Spring 1988), pp. 14–27

Seneca: *Natural Questions* VII,17,2 [Julius & Nero comets]; VII,21,3–4 [Claudius & Nero comets]; VII,3,1; VII, 4,1 [comets return]

Suetonius: *Julius Caesar* 88, *Claudius* 46; *Nero* 36

Tacitus: *Annals* 14:22 [Nero comet]

D. K. Yeomans & T. Kiang: "Long Term Motion of Comet Halley," *Monthly Notices of the Royal Astronomical Society* 197, pp. 633–646

D. King-Hele: "Truth and Heresy Over Earth and Sky," *The Observatory* 95, No. 1004 (1975), pp. 1–12 [history of meteorite studies/Jefferson]

*James 1995, pp. 127–129 [Aristotle], pp. 118–119 [Plato's astronomical knowledge]

A. Koestler: *The Sleepwalkers: A History of Man's Changing Vision of the Universe* (Harmondsworth: Pelican, 1968), pp. 45–83 [Greek astronomical knowledge]

J.-P. Hallet: *Pygmy Kitabu* (New York: Random House, 1974), p. 385

E. Best: *The Astronomical Knowledge of the Maori* (Wellington, New Zealand: Dominion Museum Monograph No. 3, 1922), p. 35

Robert Temple: *The Sirius Mystery* (London: Sidgwick & Jackson, 1976; 2nd ed., London: Century, 1998), pp. 71–73 [Saturn and Jupiter]

Ze-zong, Xi: "The Sighting of Jupiter's Satellite by Gan Dej 2000 Years Before Galileo," *Chinese Journal of Astrophysics* 5 (1981), pp. 242–251

K. Frazier: "Pre-Galileo Sighting of Jovian Moon," *Science News* 23 Jan 1982, p. 59

H. Havelin Adams: "New Light on the Dogon and Sirius," in I. Van Sertima: *Blacks in Science: Ancient and Modern* (New Brunswick & London: Transaction Books, 1985), pp. 47–49 [naked eye observations]

W. E. A. Van Beek: "Dogon Restudied" [with responses], *Current Anthropology* 32 (1991), pp. 139–167

B. R. Ortiz de Montellano: "The Dogon People Revisited," *Skeptical Enquirer* Nov/Dec 1996, pp. 39–42

*Feder 1996, chap. 9 [Martian face]

R. Richard: "Facing Up to Mars," *Fortean Times* 112 (July 1996), p. 30

E. K. Gibson et al.: "The Case for Relic Life on Mars," *Scientific American* 277:6 (Dec 1997), pp. 36–41

MEGALITHIC ASTRONOMERS

E. MacKie: "Wise Men in Antiquity," in C. Ruggles & A. W. R. Whittle (eds): *Astronomy and Society in Britain During the Period 4000–1500 B.C.* (Oxford: British Archaeological Reports, 1981), pp. 111–152 [quote, p. 113]

E. Hadingham: *Early Man and the Cosmos* (London: Heinemann, 1983), pp. 26 [Lockyer quote], 80–81 [quote], 75 [O'Kelly quote]

D. C. Heggie: *Megalithic Science* (London: Thames & Hudson, 1981), pp. 84 [quote on Lockyer], 58 [Megalithic Yard quote], 178 [lunar quote]

G. S. Hawkins: *Stonehenge Decoded* (New York: Doubleday, 1965), p. 15

A. Thom: *Megalithic Sites in Britain* (Oxford: Clarendon Press, 1967), pp. 43 [Megalithic Yard quote], 164 [geometry quote]

A. Thom & A. S. Thom: *Megalithic Remains in Britain and Brittany* (Oxford University Press, 1978), p. 182 [scientists quote]

E. MacKie: *Science and Society in Prehistoric Britain* (London: Elek, 1977), p. 210 [temples quote]

J. Patrick: "A Reassessment of the Solstitial Observatories at Kintraw and Ballochroy," in C. Ruggles & A. W. R. Whittle (eds): *Astronomy and Society in Britain During the Period 4000–1500 B.C.* (Oxford: British Archaeological Reports, 1981), pp. 211–219

A. Burl: *Prehistoric Astronomy and Ritual* (Princes Risborough: Shire, 1983), chap. 2 [Ballochroy]

C. Ruggles: "Archaeoastronomy in Europe," in *Walker 1996, pp. 15–27 [quote, p. 23]

THE ORION MYSTERY

R. Bauval & A. Gilbert: *The Orion Mystery: Unlocking the Secrets of the Pyramids* (New York: Crown Publishers, 1994), pp. 2, 4 [quotes]

R. Bauval & G. Hancock: *Keeper of Genesis* (London: William Heinemann, 1996)

I. E. S. Edwards: *The Pyramids of Egypt* (Harmondsworth: Penguin, rev. ed., 1993), pp. 284–285 [stellar alignments]

R. Chadwick: "The So-called 'Orion Mystery,'" *KMT* 7:3 (Fall 1996), pp. 74–83

C. Ronan, in *Walker 1996, p. 254 [Chinese Orion]

THE DAY THE SUN STOOD STILL?

T. H. Gaster: *Myth, Legend and Custom in the Old Testament* (New York: Harper & Row, 1969), Vol. 2, pp. 414–415 [Fuller, early theories]

J. S. Holladay: "The Day(s) the Moon Stood Still," *Journal of Biblical Literature* 87 (1968), pp. 166–178

J. F. A. Sawyer: "Joshua 10:12–14 and the Solar Eclipse of 30 September 1131 B.C.," *Palestine Excavation Quarterly* July–Dec 1972, pp. 139–146

A. Ben-Menahem: "Cross-dating of Biblical History via Singular Astronomical and Geophysical Events Over the Ancient Near East," *Quarterly Journal of the Royal Astronomical Society* 33 (1992), pp. 175–190

J. Gribbin & S. Plagemann: "Discontinuous Change in Earth's Spin Rate Following Great Solar Storm of August, 1972," *Nature* 243 (1973), pp. 26–27

T. Michelson: "Mechanics Bear Witness," *Pensée: Immanuel Velikovsky Reconsidered* VII, pp. 15–21 [Earth deceleration, Laplace]

I. Velikovsky: *Worlds in Collision* (New York: Doubleday, 1950), pp. 51–58, 63–64

A. de Grazia (ed.): *The Velikovsky Affair* (London: Abacus/Sphere, rev. ed., 1978), pp. 32–32 [Edmondson quote, from Indianapolis *Star* 9 April 1950]

C. Sagan: "An Analysis of Worlds in Collision," in D. Goldsmith (ed.): *Scientists Confront Velikovsky* (Ithaca & London: Cornell University Press, 1977), pp. 41–104 [esp. pp. 63–66, 99–100]

P. Warlow: "Geomagnetic Reversals?" *Journal of Physics* A 10 (1978), pp. 2107–2130

P. Warlow: *The Reversing Earth* (London: Dent, 1982), pp. 69–71

V. J. Slabinski: "A Dynamical Objection to the Inversion of the Earth on its Spin Axis," *Journal of Physics* A #14 (1981), pp. 2503–2507

M. J. Aitken, A. L. Allsop, G. D. Bussell, & M. B. Winter: "Geomagnetic Intensity in Egypt and Western Asia During the Second Millennium B.C.," *Nature* 310 (1984), pp. 305–306

A. Roy: "The Stability of the Solar System," *Ages in Chaos?*, Proceedings of the S.I.S. Conference, Glasgow, 7–9 April 1978, Society for Interdisciplinary Studies Review VI:1–3, 1982, pp. 66–68

★Clube & Napier 1982, pp. 140–144 [Tunguska]

R. Stone: "The Last Great Impact on Earth," *Discovery* 17:9 (Sept. 1996), pp. 60–71 [Tunguska]

D. Steel: *Rogue Asteroids and Doomsday Comets* (New York: John Wiley, 1995), pp. 173–183 [Tunguska "long day"; composition and trajectory of object]

W. J. Phythian-Adams, "A Meteorite of the Fourteenth Century B.C.," *Palestine Excavation Quarterly* 1946, pp. 116–124

BOX ON THE "MISSING DAY"

C. J. Ransom: *The Age of Velikovsky* (Glassboro, N.J.: Kronos Press, 1976), pp. 262–263

R. W. Loftin: "Origin of the Myth About a Missing Day in Time," *Skeptical Enquirer* 15:4 (Summer 1991), 350–351

THE STAR OF BETHLEHEM

M. Grant: *The Search for the Historical Jesus: An Historian's Review of the Gospels* (London: Heinemann, 1977)

A. T. Olmstead: *History of the Persian Empire* (University of Chicago Press, 1948), pp. 28–29, 477–479 [Magi]

N. Kokkinos: *The Herodian Dynasty* (Sheffield Academic Press, 1998), pp. 100, 158–160 [Herod and Parthia]

D. Hughes: *The Star of Bethlehem Mystery* (London: Dent, 1979), pp. 129 [quote], 129–133 [Sinnot], 139–163 [comets & novae]

Josephus: *Jewish War*, 289

J. K. Fotheringham: "The New Star of Hipparchus," *Monthly Notes of the Royal Astronomical Society* 79:3 (Jan 1919), pp. 162–167 [Mithridates]

W. Keller: *The Bible as History* (London: Hodder & Stoughton, 1956), pp. 328–336

A. J. Sachs & C. B. F. Walker: "Kepler's View of the Star of Bethlehem and the Babylonian Almanac for 7/6 B.C.," *Iraq* 46 (1984), pp. 43–55

R. C. Fleck: "The Comet of Bethlehem: An Early Thirteenth-century Representation by Nicholas of Verdun," *Journal of the History of Astronomy* 22 (1992), pp. 137–140

N. Kokkinos: "Crucifixion in A.D. 36: The Keystone for Dating the Birth of Jesus," in J. Vardaman & E. M. Yamauchi (eds): *Chronos, Kairos, Christos* (Winona Lake, Ind.: Eisenbrauns, 1989), pp. 133–163

F. R. Stephenson & C. B. F. Walker: *Halley's Comet in History* (London: British Museum, 1985)

Dio Cassius: *History* 54:29.8 [Agrippa's death-comet]

CHAPTER 3: ARCHITECTURAL WONDERS

INTRODUCTION

Pausanias: *Guide to Greece* II:xvi,4; II:25,7 [Cyclopes]

Saxo Grammaticus: *Gesta Danorum*, Preface 9

Geoffrey of Monmouth: *History of the Kings of Britain* VIII:12

A. von Hagen: "The Incas," in M. Barnes et al. *Secrets of Lost Empires* (London: BBC 1996), pp. 180–221, [Garcilaso de la Vega quote, pp. 183–185], [Ivan Watkins, p. 194], [Cieza de León quote, p. 185]

R. Story: *The Space-Gods Revealed* (London: New English Library, 1976), chap. 1 [von Däniken book sales]

*Feder 1996, chap. 9 [von Däniken]

G. Daniel: *The Idea of Prehistory* (Harmondsworth: Pelican, 1964), pp. 88–107 [hyperdiffusionism]

C. Renfrew: *Before Civilization: The Radiocarbon Revolution and Prehistoric Europe* (London: Jonathan Cape, 1973)

I. J. Thorpe: *The Origins of Agriculture in Europe* (London: Routledge, 1996), pp. 56–62 [earliest megaliths]

L. & C. C. Sprague de Camp: *Citadels of Mystery* (London: Souvenir Press, 1965), pp. 111–138 [Zimbabwe and King Solomon's Mines]

W. Ndoro: "Great Zimbabwe," *Scientific American*, Nov 1997, pp. 62–67

J. Michell: *Eccentric Lives and Peculiar Notions* (London: Thames & Hudson, 1984), pp. 84–88 [Leedskalnin]

R. Apfel: "A Lift for Material Science," *New Scientist* 13 (Dec 1979), pp. 857–859 [acoustic levitation]

J-P. Mohen: *The World of Megaliths* (New York: Facts on File, 1989), pp. 158–159 [colossi, Baalbek, St. Petersburg]

A. Bonnano et al.: "Monuments in an Island Society: The Maltese Context," *World Archaeology* 22 (1990), pp. 190–205

J. Evans: "What Went on in a Maltese Megalithic 'Temple'?" in A. Pace (ed.), *Maltese Prehistoric Art 5000–2500 B.C.* (Valletta: Patrimonju, 1996), pp. 39–44 [quote, p. 44]

STONEHENGE

C. Chippindale: *Stonehenge Complete* (London: Thames & Hudson, 2nd ed., 1994), pp. 20 [Henry of Huntingdon quote], 24–25 [Geoffrey of Monmouth], 47 [Aubrey quote], 72 [Stukeley quote], 117 [Cunnington quote], 123 [Colt Hoare quote], 137 [Petrie quote], 182–183 [Hawley quotes]

R. J. C. Atkinson: *Stonehenge* (London: Pelican, 1979), p. 185 [Geoffrey of Monmouth]

R. M. J. Cleal, K. E. Walker, & R. Montague: *Stonehenge in its Landscape* (London: English Heritage, 1995)

R. Castleden: *The Making of Stonehenge* (London: Routledge, 1993), pp. 10 [Jones/Webb quotes], 18 [Constable quote], 101 [Geoffrey of Monmouth Merlin quote]

D. Souden: *Stonehenge* (London: Collins & Brown, 1997) p. 83 [Steep Holm bluestone]

C. Page: "Stonehenge," in M. Barnes et al.: *Secrets of Lost Empires* (London: BBC, 1996), pp. 8–45 [quote, p. 30]

R. J. C. Atkinson: "The Date of Stonehenge," *Proceedings of the Prehistoric Society* 18 (1952), pp. 236–237

A. Burl: "The Sarsen Horseshoe Inside Stonehenge: a Rider," *Wiltshire Archaeological and Natural History Magazine* 90 (1997), pp. 1–12 [quote, p. 8]

C. Scarre: "Misleading Images: Stonehenge and Brittany," *Antiquity* 71 (1997), pp. 1016–1020

G. S. Hawkins: *Stonehenge Decoded* (New York: Doubleday, 1965)

R. J. C. Atkinson: "Moonshine on Stonehenge," *Antiquity* 40 (1966), pp. 212–216

BOX ON THE DRUIDS

Caesar: *Gallic Wars* VI:13–14

M. Green: *Exploring the World of the Druids* (London: Thames & Hudson, 1997)

S. Piggott: *The Druids* (London: Thames & Hudson, 1968)

R. M. J. Cleal, K. E. Walker & R. Montague: *Stonehenge in its Landscape* (London: English Heritage, 1995), chap. 8

Tacitus: *Annals* XIV:30

R. Jones: "Sylwadau cynfrodor ar Gôr y Cewri; or a British aboriginal's land claim to Stonehenge," in C. Chippindale et al.: *Who Owns Stonehenge?* (London: Batsford, 1990), pp. 62–87 [*Morning Chronicle* quote, p. 80]

HOW WERE THE PYRAMIDS BUILT?

G. Andreu: *Egypt in the Age of the Pyramids* (London: John Murray, 1997)

*Von Däniken 1969, pp. 96–102

I. E. S. Edwards: *The Pyramids of Egypt* (Harmondsworth: Penguin, rev. ed., 1993), pp. 19–97 [pyramid evolution], 195 [quote], 104 [shafts/Dixon], 151 [Gantenbrink]

M. Lehner: *The Complete Pyramids* (London: Thames & Hudson, 1997), pp. 72–105 [pyramid evolution], 208–223 [building experiment; quote, 209], 67, 114 [Gantenbrink]

R. Porter: "An Easy Way to Build a Pyramid," *Göttinger Miszellen* 138 (1994), pp. 903–904

J. B. Pritchard (ed.): *Ancient Near Eastern Texts Relating to the Old Testament*, 3rd ed. (Princeton University Press, 1969) pp. 441–444 [Ipuwer]

C. P. Smyth: *Our Inheritance in the Great Pyramid* (London: W. Isbister, 1880), pp. 427–431 [Dixon]

THE RIDDLE OF THE SPHINX

R. Bauval & G. Hancock: *Keeper of Genesis* (London: Heinemann, 1996), pp. 8–10 [Domingo], 15–22

J. A. West: *Serpent in the Sky* (Wheaton, Ill: Quest Books 1993), pp. 221–230 [Sphinx and geology], 230–232 [Domingo]

M. Lehner: "Computer Rebuilds the Ancient Sphinx," *National Geographic* 179:4 (April 1991), pp. 32–39

M. Lehner: "Reconstructing the Sphinx," *Cambridge Archaeological Journal* 2:1 (1992), pp. 3–26

E. A. Wallis Budge: *The Mummy: Chapters on Egyptian Funerary Archaeology* (Cambridge University Press, 2nd ed., 1894), pp. 14–15

J. B. Pritchard (ed.): *Ancient Near Eastern Texts Relating to the Old Testament* (Princeton University Press, 3rd ed., 1969), pp. 448–449 [Sphinx Stela]

R. M. Schoch: "Redating the Great Sphinx," *KMT* 3:2 (1992), pp. 53–70

J. A. Harrell: "The Sphinx Controversy: Another Look at the Geological Evidence," *KMT* 5:2 (1994), pp. 70–74

T. L. Dobecki & R. M. Schoch: "Seismic Investigations in the Vicinity of the Great Sphinx of Giza, Egypt," *Geoarchaeology* 7, 1992, pp. 527–544

R. M. Schoch: "The Great Sphinx Controversy," *Fortean Times* 79, 1995, pp. 35–39

R. M. Schoch: "Sphinx Links" (letter), *Archaeology* 48 (Jan/Feb 1995), pp. 10–12

Anon: "Sphinx Riddle Put to Rest?" *Science* 255 (14 Feb 1992), p. 793

K. Gauri, J. J. Sanai, & J. K. Bandyopadhyay: "Geologic Weathering and Its Implications on the Age of the Sphinx," *Geoarchaeology* 10, 1995, pp. 119–133

M. Lehner: "Notes and Photographs on the West-Schoch Sphinx Hypothesis," *KMT* 5:3 (1994), pp. 40–48

Z. Hawass & M. Lehner: "The Sphinx: Who Built It, and Why?" *Archaeology* 47:3 (Sept/Oct 1994), pp. 30–47

A. Gardiner: *Egypt of the Pharaohs* (Oxford University Press, 1961), p. 82 [origin of word "Sphinx"]

TIAHUANACO

A. Kolata: *The Tiwanaku* (Oxford: Blackwell, 1993), pp. 1–4 [Cieza de León], 12 [de Castelnau], 27–28 [Squier quote], 96 [alignment quote], 97 [Akapana quote], 12 [Chalon quote], 15–16 [quote on Posnansky's appeal], 283 [natural catastrophe quote]

A. Posnansky: *Tihuanacu: The Cradle of American Man* (New York: J. J. Augustin, 1945) Vol. II, p. 156 [pier quote], I, 55 [catastrophe quote], II, 4 [Gateway of Sun quote], I, 33 [Altiplano races quote]

★Hancock 1995, chaps. 8, 10–12 [quote, p. 89]

E. Hadingham: *Lines to the Mountain Gods* (London: Harrap, 1987), p. 35

N. Davies: *Voyagers to the New World* (London: Macmillan, 1979), chap. 6 [Viracochas]

N. Davies: *The Ancient Kingdom of Peru* (London: Penguin, 1997), p. 60 [Aymara lungs]

B. Fagan: *The Time Detectives* (London: Simon & Schuster, 1995), chap. 11 [raised fields]

THE MYSTERY OF EASTER ISLAND

C. & M. Orliac: *The Silent Gods: Mysteries of Easter Island* (London: Thames & Hudson, 1995), pp. 98–99 [Roggeveen], 100–103 [La Pérouse]

T. Heyerdahl: *Easter Island: The Mystery Solved* (London: Souvenir Press, 1989), pp. 18–27 [Roggeveen], 27–35 [Spanish in 1770], 35–48 [Cook], 48–55 [La Pérouse], 202–207 [carving statues], 207–208, 223–227, 240–242 [moving statues (quote p. 240)], 173 [slaves quote], 233 [fishermen quote], 229 [Gill's work quote], 45 [Cook quote]

P. Bahn & J. Flenley: *Easter Island, Earth Island* (London: Thames & Hudson, 1992), pp. 13 [Roggeveen], 13–16 [Cook], 14–16 [La Pérouse], 124–133 [carving statues], 134–146 [moving statues], 38–68 [Heyerdahl's theories], 55 [Mulloy quote]

J. A. Van Tilburg: *Easter Island: Archaeology, Ecology and Culture* (London: British Museum Press, 1994), pp. 22–23 [statue statistics], 154 [quote on Heyerdahl experiment], 125–129 [purpose of statues], 73–76 [Polynesian statues and platforms]

★Von Däniken 1969, pp. 113–115

J. R. Flenley: "The Palaeoecology of Easter Island, and Its Ecological Disaster," in S. R. Fischer (ed.): *Easter Island Studies* (Oxford: Oxbow Monograph 32, 1993), pp. 27–45 [ancient landscape]

J. A. Van Tilburg: "Moving the Moai," *Archaeology* 48 (Jan/Feb 1995), pp. 34–43

T. Heyerdahl: *The Kon-Tiki Expedition* (London: Allen & Unwin, 1950)

P. Bellwood: *The Polynesians* (London: Thames & Hudson, 2nd ed., 1987), pp. 16–21 & 111–130 [Heyerdahl's theories], 129 [Vinapu quote]

J. R. Flenley: "The Present Flora of Easter Island and Its Origins," in S. R. Fischer (ed.): *Easter Island Studies* (Oxford: Oxbow Monograph 32, 1993), pp. 7–15

C. Lee: "The Rock Art of Rapanui," in S. R. Fischer (ed.): *Easter Island Studies* (Oxford: Oxbow Monograph 32, 1993), pp. 112–121

G. W. Gill & D. W. Ousley: "Human Osteology of Rapanui," in S. R. Fischer (ed.): *Easter Island Studies* (Oxford: Oxbow Monograph 32, 1993), pp. 56–62

F. Hagelberg et al.: "DNA from Ancient Easter Islanders," *Nature* 369 (5 May 1994), pp. 25–26

BOX ON RONGORONGO

S. R. Fischer: *Rongorongo: the Easter Island Script* (Oxford: Clarendon Press, 1997), chap. 3 [Eyraud], p. 12 [Eyraud quote], chap. 32 [dating of rongorongo], chaps. 9–10 [Jaussen and Croft], chap. 12 [Ure Va'e Iko]

T. Heyerdahl: *Easter Island: The Mystery Solved* (London: Souvenir Press, 1989), pp. 80–86

S. R. Fischer: "Preliminary Evidence for Cosmogonic Texts in Rapanui's *Rongorongo* Inscriptions," *Journal of the Polynesian Society* 104, pp. 303–321

P. G. Bahn: "Making Sense of *rongorongo*," *Nature* 379 (18 Jan 1996), pp. 204–205

M. Coe: "Phallus and Fallacy," *Times Higher Education Supplement* 1325 (27 March 1998), pp. 24–25

CHAPTER 4: EARTH PATTERNS

INTRODUCTION

A. Whittle: *Sacred Mound, Holy Rings* (Oxford: Oxbow, 1997) [Silbury Hill]

R. J. C. Atkinson: "Silbury Hill," in R. Sutcliffe (ed.): *Chronicle* (London: BBC, 1978), pp. 159–173

G. R. Willey & J. A. Sabloff: *A History of American Archaeology* (New York: W. W. Freeman, 2nd ed., 1980), chap. 2 [moundbuilders; Jefferson quote, p. 28]

B. Fagan: *Elusive Treasure* (London: Macdonald & Jane's, 1977), chaps. 3, 5–6, 11, 14 [moundbuilders]

J. Saunders et al.: "A Mound Complex in Louisiana at 5400–5000 Years Before the Present," *Science* 277 (19 Sept 1997), pp. 1796–1799 [Watson Brake]

H. Pringle: "Oldest Mound Complex Found at Louisiana Site," *Science* 277 (19 Sept 1997), pp. 1761–1762 [Saunders quote]

P. Newman: *Lost Gods of Albion* (Stroud: Sutton, 1997), chap. 1 [Uffington], chap. 5 [Cerne], chap. 8 [Wilmington]

D. Miles & S. Palmer: "White Horse Hill," *Current Archaeology* 142 (March 1995), pp. 372–378

R. Castleden: *The Cerne Giant* (Wincanton: Dorset, 1996)

S. Plog: *Ancient Peoples of the American Southwest* (London: Thames & Hudson, 1997), chaps. 5–6 [Anasazi]

A. Sofaer, M. P. Marshall, & R. M. Sinclair: "The Great North Road: A Cosmographic Expression of the Chaco Culture of New Mexico," in A. F. Aveni (ed.): *World Archaeoastronomy* (Cambridge University Press, 1989), pp. 365–376

S. H. Lekson: "Rewriting Southwestern Prehistory," *Archaeology* 50 (Jan 1997), pp. 52–55

G. Underwood: *The Pattern of the Past* (London: Museum Press, 1969) [underground springs and megaliths]

F. Hitching: *Earth Magic* (New York: William Morrow, 1977), pp. 186–188, 211–213 [dowsing experiment]

P. Devereux: *Places of Power* (London: Dent, 1990), p. 141 [Taylor]

P. Devereux: *The New Ley Hunter's Guide* (Glastonbury: Gothic Image, 1994), p. 75 [Tom Graves]

THE GLASTONBURY SPIRAL

Geoffrey Ashe: *Avalonian Quest* (London: Methuen, 1983)

G. N. Russell: "The Secret of the Grail," in M. Williams (ed.): *Glastonbury and Britain: A Study in Patterns* (Orpington, Kent: Research into Lost Knowledge Organisation, 1990; originally published 1969/1971), pp. 27–30

D. Fortune: *Avalon of the Heart* (London: The Aquarian Press, 1934), pp. 57, 97

G. Ashe: *The Glastonbury Tor Maze* (Glastonbury: Gothic Image, 1979), booklet reprinted in Ashe 1983 [see above], pp. 256–265

N. R. Mann: *Glastonbury Tor: A Guide to the History and Legends* (Butleigh, Somerset: Triskele Publications, 1993), pp. 32–33, 40–43, 60–63

P. Rahtz: *Glastonbury* (London: Batsford, 1993), pp. 51–75

P. Rahtz: "Excavations on Glastonbury Tor, Somerset, 1964–6," *Archaeological Journal* 127 (1970), pp. 1–81, 2–5, 11, 43–45 [prehistoric finds]; 6 [geological explanation]

T. Williamson & L. Bellamy: *Ley Lines in Question* (Tadworth, Surrey: World's Work), pp. 82, 148–149

R. Hutton: *The Pagan Religions of the Ancient British Isles* (Oxford: Blackwell, 1991), pp. 107 [labyrinth], 323 [date of life of Saint Collen]

J. Rhys: *Arthurian Legend* (London: Dent, 1891), 338ff [Saint Collen]

R. S. Loomis: " 'The Spoils of Annwm': An Early Welsh Poem," in *Wales and the Arthurian Legend* (Cardiff: University of Wales, 1956), pp. 162–178

Diodorus Siculus: *Library of History* II:47,1–6

F. Hitching: *Earth Magic* (New York: William Morrow, 1977), pp. 243–249

R. S. Loomis: *Celtic Myth and Arthurian Romance* (Columbia University Press, 1926), pp. 190, 212–214 [Melwas], 80 [May Day festivals]

THE SOMERSET ZODIAC

P. Benham: *The Avalonians* (Glastonbury: Gothic Image, 1993), pp. 265–273

I. Burrow: "Star-spangled Avalon," *Popular Archaeology* 4, 8 (1983), pp. 28–31

M. Caine: "The Glastonbury Giants or Zodiac," in A. Roberts (ed.): *Glastonbury: Ancient Avalon, New Jerusalem* (London: Rider, 1978), pp. 43–72

K. Maltwood: *A Guide to Glastonbury's Temple of the Stars* (London: James Clarke, 1929)

T. Williamson & L. Bellamy: *Ley Lines in Question* (Kingswood, Surrey: World's Work, 1983), pp. 162–170, 176

J. Coles: "Prehistory in the Somerset Levels 4000–100 B.C.," in M. Aston & I. Burrow (eds): *The Archaeology of Somerset* (Taunton: Somerset County Council, 1982), pp. 29–41 [ancient landscape of Glastonbury area]

LEY LINES

A. Watkins: *The Old Straight Track* (London: Methuen, 1925)

Bede: *A History of the English Church and People* I:30 [Pope Gregory]

G. Daniel: *Megaliths in History* (London: Dent, 1972), p. 36

T. Williamson & L. Bellamy: *Ley Lines in Question* (Kingswood, Surrey: World's Work, 1983)

P. Devereux & R. Forrest: "Straight Lines on an Ancient Landscape," *New Scientist* (23/30 December 1982), pp. 822–826

P. Devereux: *The New Ley Hunter's Guide* (Glastonbury: Gothic Image Publications, 1994)

P. Devereux: "Leys—No Question [review of Williamson & Bellamy 1983]," *The Ley Hunter* 97 (1985), pp. 11–24

R. Forrest & M. Behrend: "The Coldrum Ley: Chance or Design?" (Privately published: Bob Forrest, Manchester, 1985) [status of Saintbury & Craigern leys]

R. Forrest, in P. Devereux (ed.): "Archaeologists vs. Ley Hunters," *The Ley Hunter* 90 (1981), pp. 21–32, 26 [prehistoric ability]

D. Sullivan: "Ley Lines: Dead and Buried. A Reappraisal of the Straight Line Enigma," *3rd Stone* 27 (Autumn 1997), pp. 13–17

THE NAZCA LINES

T. Morrison: *The Mystery of the Nasca Lines* (Woodbridge, Suffolk: Nonesuch, 1987), chap. 1 [discovery], chaps. 2–5 [Reiche], p. 82 [Reiche astronomy quote], 131 [Reiche geometry quote]

E. Hadingham: *Lines to the Mountain Gods* (London: Harrap, 1987) chap. 4 [Kosok & Reiche], p. 159 [La Estaqueria], 85 [Kosok priests quote], 241 [Métraux quote], 244–247 [Reinhard]

*Von Däniken 1969, pp. 31–33

P. B. Clarkson: "The Archaeology of the Nazca Pampa," in *Aveni 1990, pp. 115–171

H. Silverman: "The Early Nasca Pilgrimage Center of Cahuachi and the Nazca Lines," in *Aveni 1990, pp. 208–244

P. Millson (ed.): *Flightpaths to the Gods* (London: Broadcasting Support Services, 1997), pp. 22 [Silverman quotes], 20 [Browne quote]

P. Kosok & M. Reiche: "The Mysterious Markings of Nazca," *Natural History* 56 (1947), pp. 200–207, 237–238 [Kosok discovery quote, p. 203]

G. Hawkins: *Beyond Stonehenge* (New York: Harper & Row, 1973), p. 117 [quote]

A. Aveni: "An Assessment of Previous Studies of the Nazca Geoglyphs," in *Aveni 1990, pp. 1–40 [astronomy theory, pp. 15–19, walking quote, p. 29]

A. Aveni: "Order in the Nazca Lines," in *Aveni 1990, pp. 41–113, [astronomy theory, pp. 88–98; processions, pp. 107–113; water and lines, pp. 82–87]

CHAPTER 5: VOYAGERS AND DISCOVERIES

INTRODUCTION

P. Bellwood: "Ancient Seafarers," *Archaeology* 50 (March/April 1997), pp. 20–22

A. Gibbons: "Ancient Island Tools Suggest Homo Erectus Was a Seafarer," *Science* 279 (13 March 1998), pp. 1635–1637

T. Severin: *The Brendan Voyage* (London: Hutchinson, 1978)

G. Ashe: "Analysis of the Legends," in G. Ashe (ed.): *Quest for America* (New York: Praeger, 1971), pp. 15–52 [Saint Brendan]

*Morison 1971, chap. 2 [Saint Brendan], pp. 206–209 [Bristol]

J. Needham: *Science and Civilization in China* IV:3 (Cambridge University Press, 1971), pp. 536–540 [Australia]

F. Parsche, S. Balabanova, & W. Pirsig: "Drugs in Ancient Populations," *The Lancet* (20 Feb. 1993), p. 503

* James & Thorpe 1994, pp. 340–351 [ancient coca, hashish and tobacco use, Rameses II]

B. Ortiz de Montellano et al.: "They Were NOT Here before Columbus: Afrocentric Hyperdiffusionism in the 1990s," *Ethnohistory* 44 (1997), pp. 199–234

G. Haslip-Viera et al.: "Robbing Native American Cultures: Van Setima's Afrocentricity and the Olmecs," *Current Anthropology* 38 (1997), pp. 419–441

S. Balabanova et al.: "Nicotine and Cotinine in Prehistoric and Recent Bones from Africa and Europe and the Origin of these Alkaloids," *Homo* 48 (1997), pp. 72–77

I. Whitaker: "The Scottish Kayaks and the 'Finn-men,' " *Antiquity* 28 (1954), pp. 99–104

D. B. Quinn: "Columbus and the North: England, Iceland, and Ireland," *The William and Mary Quarterly* (49) 1992, pp. 278–297 [Inuits, Bristol]

*Seaver 1996, chap. 8 [Bristol]

THE FIRST AMERICANS

B. Fagan: *The Great Journey* (London: Thames & Hudson, 1987), pp. 52–54 [Clovis], chap. 7 [ice corridor], chap. 9 [Martin], pp. 80–92 [Siberian sites]

J. Alsoszatai-Petheo: "An Alternative Paradigm for the Study of Early Man in the New World," in A. L. Bryan (ed.): *New Evidence for the Pleistocene Peopling of the Americas* (Orono, Me.: Center for the Study of Early Man, 1986), pp. 15–26 [quote, p. 18]

V. Deloria: *Red Earth, White Lies* (New York: Scribner, 1995) [Amerindian reactions]

J. F. Hoffecker, W. R. Powers, & T. Goebel: "The Colonization of Beringia and the Peopling of the New World," *Science* 259 (1 Jan. 1993), pp. 46–53

S. Elias et al.: "Life and Times of the Bering Land Bridge," *Nature* 382 (4 July 1996), pp. 60–63

D. Meltzer: "Clocking the First Americans," *Annual Review of Anthropology* 24 (1995), pp. 21–45 [Old Crow River]

M. D. Coe: *Mexico* (London: Thames & Hudson, 1994), p. 24 [Tepexpan Man]

J. Adovasio, J. Donahue, & R. Stuckenrath: "The Meadowcroft Rockshelter Radiocarbon Chronology 1975–1990," *American Antiquity* 55 (1990), pp. 348–354

J. Adovasio, J. Donahue, & R. Stuckenrath: "Never Say Never Again," *American Antiquity* 57 (1992), pp. 327–331

D. Chisman et al.: "Late Pleistocene Human Friction Prints from Pendejo Cave, New Mexico," *American Antiquity* 61 (1996), pp. 357–376

D. F. Dincauze: "Regarding Pendejo Cave," *American Antiquity* 62 (1997), pp. 554–555

D. Chisman et al.: "Reply to Dincauze," *American Antiquity* 62 (1997), pp. 556–558

T. Dillehay (ed.): *Monte Verde: A Late Pleistocene Settlement in Chile* (Washington, D.C.: Smithsonian Institution Press, 1997)

A. Gibbons: "Monte Verde: Blessed But Not Confirmed," *Science* 275 (28 Feb 1997), pp. 1256–1257

D. Meltzer: "Monte Verde and the Pleistocene Peopling of the Americas," *Science* 276, (2 May 1997), pp. 754–755 [quote, p. 755]

A. Roosevelt et al.: "Paleoindian Cave Dwellers in the Amazon: The Peopling of the Americas," *Science* 272, (19 April 1996), pp. 373–384 [quote, p. 381]

C. V. Haynes: "Dating a Paleoindian Site in the Amazon in Comparison with Clovis Culture," *Science* 275 (28 March 1997), p. 1948

D. J. Meltzer, J. M. Adovasio, & T. D. Dillehay: "On a Pleistocene Occupation at Pedra Furada, Brazil," *Antiquity* 68 (1994), pp. 695–714 [charcoal quote, p. 702]

D. Meltzer: "Stones of Contention," *New Scientist* (24 June 1995), pp. 31–35 [pseudo-artifact production calculations]

N. Guidon et al.: "Nature and Age of the Deposits in Pedra Furada, Brazil: Reply to Meltzer, Adovasio and Dillehay," *Antiquity* 70 (1996), pp. 408–421 [ridiculous quote, p. 414]

R. Dennell & L. Hurcombe: "Comment on Pedra Furada," *Antiquity* 69 (1995), p. 604 [quartzite artifacts]

M. R. Waters, S. L. Forman, & J. M. Pierson: "Diring Yuriakh: A Lower Paleolithic Site in Central Siberia," *Science* 275 (28 Feb 1997), pp. 1281–1284

C. Holden: "Tooling Around: Dates Show Early Siberian Settlement," *Science* 275 (28 Feb 1997), p. 1268 [Waters quote]

J. Greenberg, C. G. Turner, & S. L. Zegura: "The Settlement of the Americas: A Comparison of the Linguistic, Dental and Genetic Evidence," *Current Anthropology* 27 (1986), pp. 477–497

T. Powledge & M. Rose: "The Great DNA Hunt, Part II: Colonizing the Americas," *Archaeology* 49 (Nov/Dec 1996), pp. 58–68

A. Slayman: "A Battle over Bones," *Archaeology* 50 (Jan/Feb 1997), pp. 16–23 [Kennewick Man]

L. Asher: "Oldest North American Mummy," *Archaeology* 49 (Sept/Oct 1996), p. 32 [Spirit Cave Man]

V. Morell: "First Floridians Found Near Biscayne Bay," *Science* 275 (28 Feb 1997), pp. 1259–1260 [Cutler Ridge and San Miguel Island]

H. Josenhans et al.: "Early Humans and Rapidly Changing Holocene Sea Levels in the Queen Charlotte Islands-Hecate Strait, British Columbia, Canada," *Science* 277 (4 July 1997), pp. 71–74 [Prince of Wales Island]

PHOENICIANS AROUND AFRICA

Herodotus II:158–159; IV:41–43

A. Lloyd: "Necho and the Red Sea: Some Considerations," *Journal of Egyptian Archaeology* 63 (1977), pp. 142–155

R. Carpenter: *Beyond the Pillars of Heracles: The Classical World Seen Through the Eyes of Its Discoverers* (Delacorte Press, 1966), pp. 72–77 [quote, p. 74]

G. Sarton: *A History of Science I: Ancient Science Through the Golden Age of Greece* (New York: Norton Library, 1952), Vol. I, p. 183

*James & Thorpe 1994, p. 91 [ancient Suez canal]

S. Lancel: *Carthage: A History* (Oxford: Blackwell, 1995), pp. 102–109 [Hanno]

Strabo: *Geography* II:98–102

P. T. Keyser: "From Myth to Map: The Blessed Isles in the First Century B.C.," *The Ancient World* 24:2 (1993), pp. 149–167

THE LOST ROMAN ARMY

H. H. Dubs: "An Ancient Military Contact Between Romans and Chinese," *American Journal of Philology* 62 (1941), pp. 322–330

H. H. Dubs: "A Roman Influence Upon Chinese Painting," *Classical Philology* 38 (1943), pp. 13–19

Plutarch: *Crassus*

W. W. Tarn: "Parthia," in S. A. Cook et al. (eds): *The Cambridge Ancient History* (Cambridge University Press, 1st ed., 1951), pp. 574–613 [Crassus, Carrhae]

J. Needham: *Science and Civilization in China*, Vol. 1 (Cambridge University Press, 1954), pp. 236–237; Vol. 3 (Cambridge University Press, 1959), pp. 536–537

N. Sitwell: *The World the Romans Knew* (London: Hamish Hamilton, 1984), pp. 187–188 [lost army], 101–103 [Carrhae], 147–150 [Antun embassy]

THE VIKINGS IN AMERICA

G. Jones: *The Norse Atlantic Saga* (Oxford University Press, 2nd ed., 1986) [The Greenlanders' Saga; Eirik the Red's Saga]

*Morison 1971, pp. 51 [Adam of Bremen quote], 74 [Newport tower], 75 [mooring holes quote], 76 [Kensington Rune Stone quote]

E. Wahlgren: *The Vikings and America* (London: Thames & Hudson, 1986), pp. 106 [Rafn], 100–101 [Kensington Rune Stone displayed], 102–103 [Kensington Rune Stone language and numerals]

S. Williams: *Fantastic Archaeology* (University of Pennsylvania Press, 1991), pp. 213–217 [Dighton Rock], 212–213 [Beardmore], 194 [Kensington Rune Stone background]

R. M. Nilsestuen: *The Kensington Runestone Vindicated* (Lanham, Md.: University Press of America, 1994), pp. 200 [Newport Tower quote], 31 [mooring holes quote], 2 [Magnus Eiriksson quote]

B. Wallace: "Viking Hoaxes," in E. Guralnick (ed): *Vikings in the West* (Chicago: Archaeological Institute of America, 1982), pp. 53–76 [Newport Tower], 64 [axe quotes], 65 [halberd quote], 67 [mooring holes quote], 60 [Kensington Rune Stone quote]

W. S. Godfrey: "The Archaeology of the Old Stone Mill in Newport, Rhode Island," *American Antiquity* 17 (1951), pp. 120–129 [quote, p. 128]

H. Holand: *A Pre-Columbian Crusade to America* (New York: Twayne, 1962) [Kensington Rune Stone]

E. Wahlgren: *The Kensington Stone, a Mystery Solved* (University of Wisconsin Press, 1958), p. 146 [Hedberg quote]

*Seaver 1996, pp. 110–111 [Knutsson expedition]

M. W. Hughey & M. G. Michlovic: " 'Making' History: The Vikings in the American Heartland," in *Politics, Culture, and Society* 2 (1989), pp. 338–360 [Kensington Rune Stone]

E. Moltke: "The Kensington Stone," *Antiquity* 25 (1951), pp. 87–93

G. Daniel: "Editorial," in *Antiquity* 48 (1974), pp. 82–83 [Kensington Rune Stone confession]

H. Ingstad: *Westward to Vinland* (London: Jonathan Cape, 1969), chap. 10 [discovery of L'Anse aux Meadows]

B. Wallace: "Appendix VII—The L'Anse aux Meadows Site," in G. Jones: *The Norse Atlantic Saga* (Oxford University Press, 2nd ed., 1986), pp. 285–304

B. Wallace: "L'Anse aux Meadows, the western outpost," in B. Clausen (ed.): *Viking Voyages to North America* (Roskilde, Denmark: The Viking Ship Museum, 1993), pp. 30–42

BOX ON THE MAINE PENNY

R. McGhee: "Contact Between Native North Americans and the Medieval Norse," *American Antiquity* 49 (1984), pp. 4–26

THE WELSH INDIANS

G. A. Williams: *Madoc: The Making of a Myth* (London: Eyre Methuen, 1979), pp. 30 [John Evans arrives], 40–43 [Ingram], 34–41 [Dee], 41–47 [Peckham & Llwyd], 76 [Reverend Jones quote], 89 [Reverend Richards quote], 7–8 [d'Eglise], chaps. 9 & 10 [Evans & Mandan], 199–201 [Stephens], 49–52 [Maredudd ap Rhys & Willem]

G. Catlin: *Illustrations of the Manners, Customs and Condition of the North American Indians* (London: Henry Bohn, 1855), Letter 13 [complexion quote], Appendix [Welsh & Mandans], Letter 13 [tradition quote]

*Morison 1971, p. 85 [quote]

D. Longley: "Rhosyr," *Current Archaeology* 150 (1996), pp. 204–208

R. P. Winham & E. J. Lueck: "Cultures of the Middle Missouri," in K. H. Schlesier (ed.): *Plains Indians, A.D. 500–1500* (Norman: University of Oklahoma Press, 1994), pp. 149–175 [traditions and archaeology of Mandans]

J. D. McLaird: "The Welsh, the Vikings, and the Lost Tribes of Israel in the Northern Plains: The Legend of the White Mandan," *South Dakota History* 18 (1988), pp. 245–273 [Maximilian quote, p. 258; Kurz quote, p. 264]

CHAPTER 6: LEGENDARY HISTORY

INTRODUCTION

*Gantz 1993, pp. 374–466 [Heracles], 557–717 [Trojan War], 340–373 [Argonauts]

S. N. Kramer: *The Sumerians: Their History, Culture and Character* (University of Chicago Press, 1963), pp. 45–50 [historical Gilgamesh]

J. V. Luce: *Homer and the Heroic Age* (London: Thames & Hudson, 1975)

S. Hood: "The Bronze Age Context of Homer," in J. B. Carter & S. Morris (eds): *The Ages of Homer: A Tribute to Emily Townsend Vermeule* (University of Texas Press, 1995), pp. 25–32

M. Wood: *In Search of the Trojan War* (London: Guild Publishing, 1985)

*James 1995, pp. 222, 258–259 [Ahhiyawa]

D. W. Smit: "KUB XIV 3 and Hittite History," *Talanta* XXII-XXIII (1990–91), pp. 79–111 [Wilusa war]

M. L. Ryder: "The Last Word on the Golden Fleece Legend?" *Oxford Journal of Archaeology* 10:1 (1991), pp. 57–60

G. J. Smith & A. J. Smith: "Jason's Golden Fleece," *Oxford Journal of Archaeology* 11:1 (1992), pp. 119–120

E. F. Bloedlow: "The Trojan War and Late Helladic IIIC," *Prähistorische Zeitschrift* 63 (1988), pp. 23–52

Pindar: *Pythian Ode IV,* 212

Herodotus: *History* II:104

M. Bernal: *Black Athena,* Vol. II (London: Free Association Books, 1991), pp. 249–250 [black Abkhazians], 253 [Saint Jerome]

D. A. Mackenzie: *Myths of Pre-Columbian America* (London: Gresham, 1923), pp. 254–270 [white Quetzalcoatl]

L. Séjourné: *Burning Water: Thought and Religion in Ancient Mexico* (New York: Vanguard Press, 1956) [Quetzalcoatl]

J. G. Frazer: *Adonis, Attis, Osiris* (London: Macmillan, 1907)

THESEUS AND THE MINOTAUR

*Gantz 1993, pp. 260–270 [earliest Greek versions]

L. Cotterell: *The Bull of Minos* (London: Pan, 1995) [Evans's discoveries]

*James & Thorpe 1994, pp. 549–551 [bull games]

M. Bietak: "Minoan Wall Paintings Unearthed at Ancient Avaris," *Egyptian Archaeology: The Bulletin of the Egypt Exploration Society* 2 (1992), pp. 26–28

D. D. Hughes: *Human Sacrifice in Ancient Greece* (London: Routledge, 1991), pp. 13–26 [Cretan archaeological evidence]

THE ELUSIVE AMAZONS

G. C. Rothery: *The Amazons* (London: Francis Griffiths, 1910; reprinted Senate, London, 1995), pp. 139–163 [American Amazons], 23–61 [classical Amazons]

J. H. Parry: *The Discovery of South America* (London: Paul Elek, 1979), pp. 261–274 [de Orellana]

J. Hemming: *The Search for El Dorado* (London: Michael Joseph, 1978), pp. 90–91, 119, 122 [de Gómara], 133, 152

Homer: *The Illiad* III:185, VI:185

R. Graves: *The Greek Myths* (Harmondsworth: Penguin, 1955), Vol. I, pp. 352–355; Vol. II, pp. 124–132, 313

Herodotus: *History* IV:110–117; IX:27

Arrian: *The Campaigns of Alexander* VII:13

Plutarch: *Life of Alexander,* 46

Diodorus Siculus: *Library of History* XVII:77, 1–2 [Alexander]

Strabo: *The Geography* XI:5, 1–2; XII:3,21

W. B. Tyrell: *Amazons: A Study in Athenian Mythmaking* (John Hopkins University Press, 1984), p. 23 [quote]

R. Rolle: *The World of the Scythians* (London: Batsford, 1989), pp. 86–91

J. Davis-Kimball: "Warrior Women of the Eurasian Steppes," *Archaeology* 50:1 (Jan/Feb 1997), pp. 44–51

C. Watkins: "The Language of the Trojans," in M. J. Mellink (ed.): *Troy and the Trojan War* (Bryn Mawr College, Pa., 1986), pp. 45–62 [Amazons and Hittites, pp. 52–55]

*James 1995, pp. 274–278 [Amazons in Libya]

KING ARTHUR

E. Vinaver (ed.): *Malory: Works* (London: Oxford University Press, 1954)

Thomas Malory: *Works: Book XIII: The Quest of the Holy Grail,* p. 2 [date for Galahad]

J. Morris (ed. and trans.): *Nennius: British History and the Welsh Annals* (Arthurian Period Sources 8, London & Chichester: Phillimore, 1980)

R. S. Loomis (ed.): *Arthurian Literature in the Middle Ages* (Oxford: Clarendon Press, 1959), pp. 7 [Nennius's source], 12–19 [early Welsh poetry], 52–63 [Breton role in oral diffusion], 60–61 [Modena]

J. Morris: *The Age of Arthur: A History of the British Isles from 350 to 650* (London: Weidenfeld & Nicolson, 1973), pp. 111–115 [Arthur's battles], 116, 558–559 [rash of Arthurs c. A.D. 600]

L. Alcock: *Arthur's Britain: History and Archaeology A.D. 367–634* (Harmondsworth: Allen Lane, 1971), pp. 55–71 [Arthur's battles], 220–227 [Cadbury]

T. Charles-Edwards: "The Arthur of History," in R. Bromwich, A. O. H. Jarman, & B. F. Roberts (eds): *The Arthur of the Welsh* (University of Wales Press, 1991), pp. 15–32

P. Rahtz: *English Heritage: Glastonbury* (London: Batsford, 1993)

C. Thomas: *English Heritage Book of Tintagel: Arthur and Archaeology* (London: Batsford, 1995)

L. Alcock: *Cadbury Castle Somerset: The Early Medieval Archaeology* (Cardiff: University of Wales, 1995)

G. Ashe: " 'A Certain Very Ancient Book'—Traces of an Arthurian Source in Geoffrey of Monmouth's History," *Speculum* 56:2 (1981), pp. 301–323 [Riothamus]

G. Ashe: "The Origins of the Arthurian Legend," *Arthuriana* 5:3 (Fall 1995), 1–24 [Riothamus]

ROBIN HOOD

S. Lee: "Hood, Robin," in *Dictionary of National Biography* (London: Smith, Elder & Co., 1891) Vol. 26, pp. 258–291

J. C. Holt: *Robin Hood* (London: Thames & Hudson, 2nd ed., 1989), pp. 40 [de Wyntoun and Bower], 17–25 [*A Geste of Robin Hood*], 42–43 [Stukeley], 45–50 [Hunter], 51–54, 187–193 [Robert Hod: quote, p. 189]

S. Knight: *Robin Hood: A Complete Study of the English Outlaw* (Oxford: Blackwell, 1994), pp. 25 [Derbyshire outlaw], 12 [Murray], 47–48 [date of Geste], 24–26 [Robert Hod]

G. Phillips and M. Keatman: *Robin Hood: The Man Behind the Myth* (London: Michael O'Mara, 1995), pp. 133–144

J. Bellamy: *Robin Hood: An Historical Enquiry* (London: Croom Helm, 1985), pp. 7–13 [Hunter], 117 [Robin feigns illness to escape the court]

M. Murray: *The God of the Witches* (London: Faber, 1931), pp. 35–36

P. H. Reaney: *The Origin of English Surnames* (London: Routledge & Kegan Paul, 1967), chap. 16

DRACULA

P. Barber: "Forensic Pathology and the European Vampire," *Journal of Folklore Research* 24 (1987), pp. 1–32 [Mercure galant quote, p. 1]

A. Masters: *The Natural History of the Vampire* (London: Rupert Hart-Davis, 1972), pp. 169–170 [Ekimmu], 167–169 [Apollonius of Tyana], 124 [German witch]

T. H. Gaster: *Myth, Legend, and Custom in the Old Testament* (New York: Harper and Row, 1969), pp. 22–23, 578–580 [Lilith]

J. du Boulay: "The Greek Vampire: A Study of Cyclic Symbolism in Marriage and Death," *Man 17* (1982), pp. 219–238

P. Barber: *Vampires, Burial and Death* (New Haven: Yale University Press, 1988), pp. 98–99 [live burial theory], chap. 12 [body changes theory], p. 78 [Plato's Laws]

M. G. Winkler & K. Anderson: "Vampires, Porphyria, and the Media: Medicalization of a Myth," *Perspectives in Biology and Medicine* 33 (1990), pp. 598–611

R. T. McNally and R. Florescu: *In Search of Dracula* (London: Robson, 2nd ed., 1995), chaps. 1–8 [Vlad the Impaler and Dracula], pp. 86 [Brasov quote], 39 [ambassadors quote], x [bloody bread]

R. Tannahill: *Flesh and Blood* (London: Abacus, 1996), p. 225 [court case]

CHAPTER 7: HOAX?

INTRODUCTION

F. Spencer (ed.): *The Piltdown Papers* (London: Natural History Museum, 1990)

F. Spencer: *Piltdown: A Scientific Forgery* (London: Natural History Museum, 1990)

J. E. Walsh: *Unravelling Piltdown* (New York: Random House, 1996)

K. P. N. Shuker: *The Unexplained* (London: Carlton, 1997), p. 97 [human-crocodile mummy]

M. Jones (ed.): *Fake? The Art of Deception* (London: British Museum, 1990), p. 61 [Dares & Dictys]

C. Sifakis: *Hoaxes and Scams* (London: Michael O'Mara, 1994), p. 53 [chastity belts]

K. Newnham: *The Guinness Book of Fakes, Frauds and Forgeries* (London: Guinness, 1991), pp. 111–117 [Vrain-Lucas]

*Feder 1996, chap. 3 [Cardiff Giant]; p. 41 [Boynton quote]; p. 42 [Marsh quote]

S. Piggott: *William Stukeley* (London: Thames & Hudson, 2nd ed., 1985), chap. 6

R. S. Bianchi: "Alexander's Tomb . . . Not!" *Archeology* 48, Part 3 (May 1995), pp. 58–60

R. E. Taylor & R. Berger: "The Date of 'Noah's Ark,'" *Antiquity* 54 (1980), pp. 34–36

P. Pockley: "Geologist Fails to Overturn Creationist Judgement," *Nature* 390 (11/12/97), p. 542

A. Snelling: "Amazing Ark Exposé," *Creation Magazine* 14, Part 4 (September 1992), pp. 26–38

A. Reith: *Archaeological Fakes* (London: Barrie & Jenkins), pp. 92–107 [Glozel]

P. Jordan: "Glozel," in R. Sutcliffe (ed.): *Chronicle* (London: BBC 1978), pp. 67–81

THE MAN FROM THE ICE

K. Spindler: *The Man in the Ice* (London: Weidenfeld & Nicolson, 1994)

L. Barfield: "The Iceman Reviewed," *Antiquity* 68 (1994), pp. 10–26

T. Taylor: *The Prehistory of Sex* (London: Fourth Estate, 1996), pp. 14–15 [homosexual theory]

SCHLIEMANN'S TREASURE

H. Schliemann: *Troy and Its Remains* (London: John Murray, 1875)

H. Schliemann: *Ilios* (London: John Murray, 1881), p. 17

H. Duchéne: *The Golden Treasures of Troy* (London: Thames & Hudson, 1996)

D. A. Traill: *Schliemann of Troy: Treasure and Deceit* (London: John Murray, 1995), pp. 111–114 [discovery and interpretation of treasure quotes], 116–118 [Schliemann letter to Newton], 179 [Schliemann letter to Müller]

D. Easton: "The Troy Treasures in Russia," *Antiquity* 69 (1995), pp. 11–14

W. C. Borlase: "A Visit to Dr. Schliemann's Troy," *Fraser's Magazine* 17 (Feb 1878), pp. 228–239

D. A. Traill: "Schliemann's Discovery of 'Priam's Treasure,'" *Antiquity* 57 (1983), pp. 181–186

D. Easton: "Schliemann's Mendacity—A False Trail?" *Antiquity* 58 (1984), pp. 197–204

D. Easton: "Priam's Gold: The Full Story." *Anatolian Studies* 44 (1994), pp. 221–243

M. Robinson: "Pioneer, Scholar and Victim: An Appreciation of Frank Calvert (1828–1908)," *Anatolian Studies* 44 (1994), pp. 153–168

M. Quinn: *The Swastika: Constructing the Symbol* (London: Routledge, 1994), pp. 37, 146 [Troy goddess]

THE FIRST DEAD SEA SCROLLS?

J. M. Allegro: *The Shapira Affair* (London: W. H. Allen, 1965), pp. 118–119 [quote]

K. Newnham: *The Guinness Book of Fakes, Frauds and Forgeries* (London: Guinness, 1991), pp. 117–121

KING ARTHUR'S GRAVE

R. S. Loomis (ed.): *Arthurian Literature in the Middle Ages* (Oxford: Clarendon Press, 1959), pp. 53–54, 64–71 [Arthur's immortality]

Gerald of Wales: *De principis instructione* 1:20; *Speculum Ecclesiae* 11:8–10; trans. L. Thorpe: *Gerald of Wales. The Journey Through Wales and the Description of Wales* (Harmondsworth: Penguin, 1978), pp. 280–288

G. Ashe: *King Arthur's Avalon: The Story of Glastonbury* (London: Collins, 1957), pp. 173–184

A. Gransden: "The Growth of the Glastonbury Traditions and Legends in the Twelfth Century," *Journal of Ecclesiastical History* 27:4 (1976), pp. 337–358

C. A. R. Radford: "Glastonbury Abbey," in G. Ashe (ed.): *The Quest for Arthur's Britain* (London: Pall Mall Press, 1968), pp. 97–110

K. Jackson, review of Alcock 1971, *Antiquity* 47 (March 1973), pp. 80–81

P. Rahtz: *Glastonbury* (London: Batsford, 1993), pp. 42–46

THE VINLAND MAP

F. D. Logan: *The Vikings in History* (New York: Routledge, 2nd ed., 1991), pp. 105–111 [announcement]

H. Wallis: "The Strange Case of the Vinland Map: Introduction," *The Geographical Journal* 140 (1974), pp. 183–187 [Chicago Tribune quote & Skelton quote]

R. A. Skelton, T. E. Marston, & G. D. Painter: *The Vinland Map and the Tartar Relation* (Yale University Press, 1965)

L. C. Witten II: "Vinland's Saga Recalled." in ★Skelton et al., 1995, pp. xli–lviii

W. C. McCrone & L. B. McCrone: "The Vinland Map Ink," *The Geographical Journal* 140 (1974), pp. 212–214

G. D. Painter: "The Matter of Authenticity," *The Geographical Journal* 140 (1974), pp. 191–194

T. A. Cahill et al.: "The Vinland Map, Revisited: New Compositional Evidence on Its Inks and Parchment," *Analytical Chemistry* 59 (1987), pp. 829–833

W. C. McCrone: "The Vinland Map," *Analytical Chemistry* 60 (1988), pp. 1009–1018 [inconceivable quote, p. 1016, pigment quote, p. 1014]

K. Towe: "The Vinland Map: Still a Forgery," *Accounts of Chemical Research* 23 (1990), pp, 84–87

T. A. Cahill & B. H. Kusko: "Compositional and Structural Studies of the Vinland Map and the Tartar Relation," in ★Skelton et al., 1995, pp. xxix–xxxix [anatase quote, p. xxx; forger quote, p. xxxvi]

G. D. Painter: "Introduction to the New Edition," in ★Skelton et al., 1995, pp. ix–xix [quote, p. xii]

★Seaver 1996, 164–167 [Norse maps]

★Morison 1971, p. 69 [quote]

M. Vinner: "The Mysterious Vinland Map (The Map that Spoiled Columbus Day)," in B. Clausen (ed.): *Viking Voyages to North America* (Roskilde, Denmark: The Viking Ship Museum, 1993), pp. 77–82

K. A. Seaver: "The 'Vinland Map': Who Made It, and Why? New Light on an Old Controversy," *The Map Collector* 70 (1995), pp. 32–40 [quote, p. 32]

L. Lonnroth: Review of ★Skelton, et al., 1995, *Alvismal* 7 (1997), pp. 115–120

CHAPTER 8: ARCHAEOLOGY AND THE SUPERNATURAL

INTRODUCTION

A. E. Roy: *A Sense of Something Strange* (Glasgow: Dog & Bone), pp. 196–197 [Hilprecht], 161–164 [Nechtansmere]

C. Morton & C. L. Thomas: *The Mystery of the Crystal Skulls* (London: Thorsons, 1997)

S. Welfare & J. Fairley: *Arthur C. Clarke's Mysterious World* (London: Collins, 1980), p. 78 [Mitchell-Hedges quote]

J. M. Walsh: "Crystal Skulls and Other Problems or 'Don't look it in the eye,' " in A. Henderson & A. L. Kaeppler (eds): *Exhibiting Dilemmas: Issues of Representation at the Smithsonian* (Washington, D.C.: Smithsonian Institution Press, 1997), pp. 116–139 [scientific tests]

H. TenDam: *Exploring Reincarnation* (Harmondsworth: Penguin/Arkana, 1990)

A. Guirdham: *The Cathars and Reincarnation* (London: Neville Spearman, 1970)

M. Aitken: "Test for Corelation Between Dowsing Response and Magnetic Disturbance," *Archaeometry* 2 (1959), pp. 58–59 [1958 test]

R. Bailey, E. Cambridge, & H. D. Briggs: *Dowsing and Church Archaeology* (Wimborne: Intercept, 1988)

R. Bailey: "Dowsing for Medieval Churches," *Popular Archaeology* 4, no. 8 (Feb 1983), pp. 33–37 [quote, p. 37]

THE CURSE OF TUTANKHAMUN

H. Carter & A. Mace: *The Tomb of Tutankhamen* (London: Cassell, 1923), Vol I, pp. 95–96 [quote]

C. Frayling: *The Face of Tutankhamun* (London: Faber & Faber, 1992), pp. 1–37 [discovery and reactions], 43 [Marie Corelli], 37–38 [death of Carnarvon], 46–47 [Conan Doyle quotes], 51 [*Daily Mail* quote, lights and dog stories], 243–245 [Velma], 245–254 [Cheiro], 49–50 [entrance curse], 53–56, 232–242 [Weigall], 54 [Weigall occult quotes], 58 [White quote], 57 [Mardrus quote], 52 [Winlock's list], xiii [filming problems], 141–142 [Adamson], xiii [healthy climate quote], 232–233 [Weigall tomb curse quote]

D. Silverman: "The Curse of the Curse of the Pharaohs," *Expedition* 29 (1987), pp. 56–63 [Mokhtar & tomb curses]

C. El Mahdy: *Mummies, Myth and Magic in Ancient Egypt* (London: Thames & Hudson, 1989), p. 173 [*News of the World* story]

A. P. Leca: *The Cult of the Immortal* (London: Souvenir Press, 1980), pp. 262–263 [medical explanations]

R. Harrison: "The Tutankhamun Post-Mortem," in R. Sutcliffe (ed.): *Chronicle* (London: BBC, 1978), pp. 41–52 [histoplasmosis theory; quote, p. 51]

THE CASE OF OMM SETI

H. James: Obituary of Omm Seti, *The Times* (London) 29 April 1981, reprinted *Antiquity* 55 (1981), p. 170

D. L. Eady: *Omm Sety's Abydos* (Benben Publications: Society for the Study of Egyptian Antiquities, Studies No. 3, 1982), pp. 1–4 [brief autobiography]

Omm Sety & H. El Zeini: *Abydos: Holy City of Ancient Egypt* (Los Angeles: L. L. Company, 1981), pp. i–viii [biographical information]

J. Cott (in collaboration with H. El Zeini): *The Search for Omm Seti: A Story of Eternal Love* (London: Rider, 1987), pp. 50, 63 [Sphinx, Osirion], 79 ["test" at Abydos temple], 113–114 [Kitchen quote], 230–231 [Allen quote]

BBC documentary (Chronicle series): "Omm Seti and Her Egypt" (May 1981)

E. F. Loftus: "Creating False Memories," *Scientific American*, September 1997, pp. 51–55

EDGAR CAYCE ON ATLANTIS

H. H. Bro: *Edgar Cayce: A Seer out of Season* (London: Aquarian, 1990) [Cayce as therapist; his past lives]

E. E. Cayce, G. Cayce Schwartzer, & D. Richards: *Mysteries of Atlantis Revisited* (New York: St. Martin's Press, 2nd ed., 1997)

M. Ebon: *Atlantis: The New Evidence* (New York: New American Library, 1977), pp. 102–118 [Bimini finds]

F. Hitching: *The World Atlas of Mysteries* (London: Collins/Pan, 1978), pp. 141–143 [Bimini finds]

D. Zink: *The Stones of Atlantis* (New York: Prentice Hall, 1978) [Bimini finds]

M. McKusick & E. A. Shinn: "Bahamian Atlantis Reconsidered," *Nature* 287 (1980), pp. 11–12

M. McKusick: "Psychic Archaeology: Theory, Method and Mythology," *Journal of Field Archaeology* 9 (1982), pp. 99–118

D. G. Richards: "Archaeological Anomalies in Bahamas," *Journal of Scientific Exploration* 2:2 (1988), pp. 181–201

THE COMPANY OF AVALON

P. Rahtz: *English Heritage Book of Glastonbury* (London: English Heritage, 1993), chaps. 5, 7 [Abbey], p. 47 [Dunstan and Malmesbury quotes]

W. W. Kenawell: *The Quest at Glastonbury* (New York: Helix, 1965) [Bligh Bond]; pp. 12 [Bond geometry quote], 57–58 [Caroe quote], 122 [selection problem quote], 144 [publication quote]

P. Benham: *The Avalonians* (Glastonbury: Gothic Image, 1993), chaps. 13–14 [Bligh Bond], pp. 195–197 [quotes from automatic writing], 201 [actual experience quote], 205 [Reverend Fryer telepathy quote], 206 [Company of Avalon quote], 220–221 [Reverend Fryer Loretto Chapel quote], 222 [Bond letter to Archbishop]

F. B. Bond: "The Mystery of Glastonbury," in K. Matthews (ed.): *A Glastonbury Reader* (London: Aquarian, 1991), pp. 198–209 [closing down excavations quote, p. 200]

M. McKusick: "Psychic Archaeology: Theory, Method and Mythology," *Journal of Field Archaeology* 9 (1982), pp. 99–118 [quote, p. 102]

S. Williams: *Fantastic Archaeology* (University of Pennsylvania Press, 1991), p. 288 [quote]

G. Saunders: "Obituary: Frederick Bligh Bond," *Proceedings of the Somerset Archaeological and Natural History Society* 91 (1945), pp. 114–115 [apse "walls"]

Aveni, A. (ed.). *The Lines of Nazca*. Philadelphia: American Philosophical Society, 1990.

Clube, V., & W. Napier. *The Cosmic Serpent*. London: Faber & Faber, 1982.

Feder, K. *Frauds, Myths and Mysteries: Science and Pseudoscience in Archaeology,* 2nd ed. Mountain View, Calif.: Mayfield, 1996.

Gantz, T. *Early Greek Myth: A Guide to Literary and Artistic Sources*. Baltimore: Johns Hopkins University Press, 1993.

Hancock, G. *Fingerprints of the Gods*. London: Heinemann, 1995.

James, P. *The Sunken Kingdom*. London: Jonathan Cape, 1995.

James, P., & N. Thorpe. *Ancient Inventions*. New York: Ballantine, 1994.

Morison, S. E. *The European Discovery of America*. New York: Oxford University Press, 1971.

Von Däniken, E. *Chariots of the Gods?* London: Souvenir Press, 1969.

Seaver, K. A. *The Frozen Echo*. Palo Alto: Stanford University Press, 1996.

Skelton, R. A., T. E. Marston, and G. D. Painter (eds). *The Vinland Map and the Tartar Relation,* 2nd ed.: New Haven: Yale University Press, 1995.

Walker, C. (ed.). *Astronomy Before the Telescope*. London: British Museum Press, 1996.

INDEX

Page numbers in italics indicate illustrations

PICTURE CREDITS

The authors gratefully acknowledge permission to use illustrations (listed by page number) by the following individuals and institutions.

CHAPTER 1: LOST LANDS AND CATASTROPHES
12 © Jean Dominique Lajoux
18 © Nikos Kokkinos
20 © Francis Hitching
43 Courtesy, Konstantinos D. Politis, Director, Deir 'Ain 'Abata Project (Jordan)
47 Courtesy, Konstantinos D. Politis, Director, Deir 'Ain 'Abata Project (Jordan)
49 Courtesy, Konstantinos D. Politis, Director, Deir 'Ain 'Abata Project (Jordan)
53 Courtesy, Konstantinos D. Politis, Director, Deir 'Ain 'Abata Project (Jordan)
57 Courtesy, Konstantinos D. Politis, Director, Deir 'Ain 'Abata Project (Jordan)
67 © Francis Hitching
72 © Topkapi Museum, Istanbul
74 © Francis Hitching
83 © Barry Kass/Anthro-Photo (Cambridge, MA)
85 © Instituto Nacional de Antropología e Historia, Mexico

CHAPTER 2: WATCHING THE SKIES
108 © Robert Temple
113 Courtesy, Malin Space Science Systems/NASA
119 Crown Copyright: Royal Commission on the Ancient and Historical Monuments of Scotland (Professor A Thom Collection)
125 © Office of Public Works, Department of Arts, Heritage, Gaeltacht and the Islands, Eire
126 © Francis Hitching
159 © Musei e Biblioteche, Commune di Padova

CHAPTER 3: ARCHITECTURAL WONDERS
168 © Nikos Kokkinos
175 © Zimbabwe Tourism Authority
196 Reprinted by permission from *Nature* (vol. 200, no. 4904, October 26, 1963), p. 307; Macmillan Magazines Ltd.
201 © Corbis/Bettmann
212 © Rudolf Gantenbrink
214 © Corbis/Bettmann
219 © Frank Domingo
242 © Corbis/Bettmann
247 © Corbis/Bettmann
250 © Charles Love
251 © The Kon–Tiki Museum, Oslo, Norway
253 © The Kon–Tiki Museum, Oslo, Norway

CHAPTER 4: EARTH PATTERNS
281 © The Executors of Guy Underwood/courtesy, Pearson Education
286 © Geoffrey Ashe
301 © Estate of Anthony Roberts, by kind permission of Jan Roberts
304 © Estate of Alfred Watkins, by kind permission of Rev. Felix Watkins
305 © Estate of Alfred Watkins, by kind permission of Rev. Felix Watkins
318 © Richard Muir
321 © Estate of Alfred Watkins, by kind permission of Rev. Felix Watkins
330 © Clive Ruggles
334 © Clive Ruggles

CHAPTER 5: VOYAGERS AND DISCOVERIES
338 © Francis Hitching
358 Courtesy, Tom Dillehay
358 Courtesy, Tom Dillehay
362 © Paul Bahn
366 © James C. Chatters
367 John Sibbick, © *Fortean Times*
385 Courtesy, Ken Feder
392 © Minnesota Historical Society
398 Photo by B. Schönbäck; courtesy, Birgitta Wallace, Canadian Parks Service
405 Courtesy, Department of Library Services, American Museum of Natural History
411 Courtesy, Department of Library Services, American Museum of Natural History

CHAPTER 6: LEGENDARY HISTORY
418 © Ashmolean Museum, Oxford
427 © Ashmolean Museum, Oxford
432 Courtesy, New York Historical Society
436 © Ashmolean Museum, Oxford
447 © Trustees of the British Library
481 Courtesy, Kunsthistorisches Museum, Vienna

CHAPTER 7: HOAX?
491 © Natural History Museum, London
504 © Institut für Anatomie, Innsbruck
539 Courtesy, Beinecke Rare Book and Manuscript Library, Yale University
542-543 Courtesy, Beinecke Rare Book and Manuscript Library, Yale University

CHAPTER 8: ARCHAEOLOGY AND THE SUPERNATURAL
555 © Trustees of the British Museum, London
566 © Richard Bailey
569 © Griffith Institute, Ashmolean Museum, Oxford
570 © Griffith Institute, Ashmolean Museum, Oxford
572 © Griffith Institute, Ashmolean Museum, Oxford
575 © Griffith Institute, Ashmolean Museum, Oxford
601 © Francis Hitching

ABOUT THE AUTHORS

PETER JAMES is a professional writer on ancient history and archaeology. He studied at Birmingham and London Universities and describes himself as a "generalist" in the ancient Near East and Mediterranean. He has published numerous articles on ancient technology, chronology, and the history of science. He is the principal author of *Centuries of Darkness* (1991), coauthor of *Ancient Inventions* (1994), and author of *The Sunken Kingdom* (1995).

DR. NICK THORPE, an archaeologist specializing in prehistory, studied at Reading and London Universities, and is presently Lecturer in Archaeology at King Alfred's College, Winchester. A director of research projects in Britain and Denmark, he has contributed articles on early agriculture, archaeological methods, prehistoric astronomy, burial, metalworking, and society to numerous books and journals. He is coauthor of *Centuries of Darkness* (1991) and *Ancient Inventions* (1994) and the author of *The Origins of Agriculture in Europe* (1996).

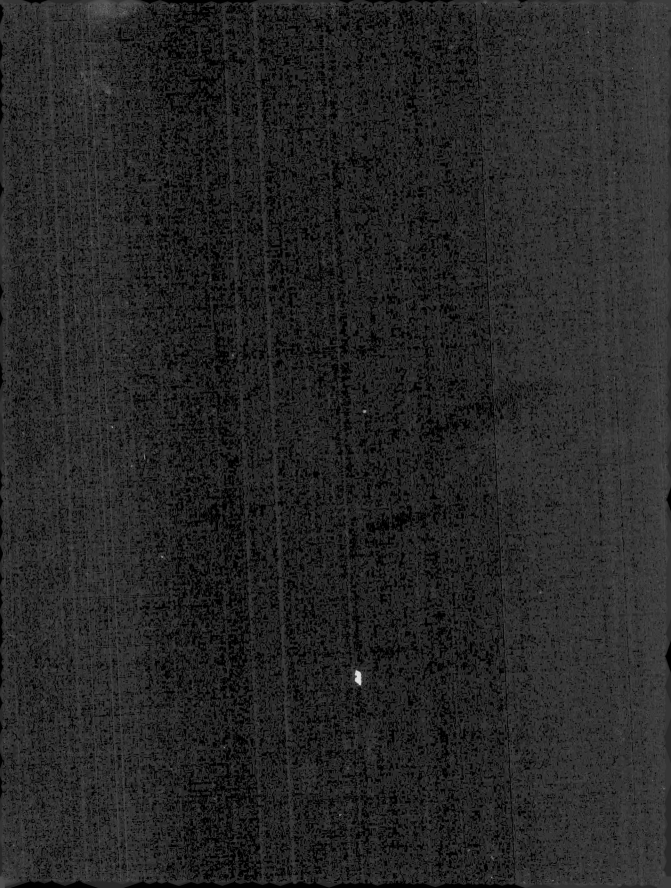